The mirror neuron system: New frontiers

Christian Keysers
University of Groningen, and University Medical Center, Groningen, The Netherlands

Luciano Fadiga
University of Ferrara, Ferrara, Italy, and Italian Institute of Technology, Genoa, Italy

Routledge
Taylor & Francis Group
LONDON AND NEW YORK

First published 2008 by Psychology Press

Published 2017 by Routledge
2 Park Square, Milton Park, Abingdon, Oxfordshire OX14 4RN
711 Third Avenue, New York, NY 10017

First issued in paperback 2017

Routledge is an imprint of the Taylor and Francis Group, an informa business

ISBN 13: 978-1-138-87781-8 (pbk)
ISBN 13: 978-1-84169-866-3 (hbk)

SOCIAL NEUROSCIENCE, 2008, 3 (3–4), 193–198

Psychology Press
Taylor & Francis Group

The mirror neuron system: New frontiers

Christian Keysers
University of Groningen, and University Medical Center, Groningen, The Netherlands

Luciano Fadiga
University of Ferrara, Ferrara, Italy, and Italian Institute of Technology, Genoa, Italy

Since the discovery of mirror neurons, much effort has been invested into studying their location and properties in the human brain. Here we review these original findings and introduce the main topics of this special issue of *Social Neuroscience*. What does the mirror system code? How is the mirror system embedded into the mosaic of circuits that compose our brain? How does the mirror system contribute to communication, language and social interaction? Can the principle of mirror neurons be extended to emotions, sensations and thoughts? Papers using a wide range of methods, including single cell recordings, fMRI, TMS, EEG and psychophysics, collected in this special issue, start to give us some impressive answers.

INTRODUCTION

The discovery of mirror neurons in the premotor cortex of the monkey has been considered one of the most exciting recent breakthroughs in neuroscience. These neurons have been so named because they "mirror" actions of other individuals by re-enacting them on the observer's motor repertoire. Indeed, mirror neurons respond both when a monkey performs an action and when it observes (di Pellegrino, Fadiga, Fogassi, Gallese, & Rizzolatti, 1992; Gallese, Fadiga, Fogassi, & Rizzolatti, 1996; Rizzolatti, Fadiga, Gallese, & Fogassi, 1996), knows that (Umiltà et al., 2001) or hears (Keysers et al., 2003; Kohler et al., 2002) someone else performing a similar action. What has made these neurons so popular is that they opened a window into the neural clockwork that allows us to understand other individuals—a capacity that had fascinated philosophers and psychologists for centuries. With mirror neurons, it became clear that the brain could understand other people's actions by a process of "motor embodiment" or, in other words, by feeling what one would feel during the execution of a similar action.

Two techniques have been critical in studying this system in humans. On one hand, transcranial magnetic stimulation (TMS) has provided the first neurophysiological evidence that motor programs are facilitated by observing other people's actions (Fadiga, Fogassi, Pavesi, & Rizzolatti, 1995). Over the past decade, much effort has been expended in characterizing this observation-induced motor resonance (Borroni, Montagna, Cerri, & Baldissera, 2005; Gangitano, Mottaghy, & Pascual-Leone, 2004; Montagna, Cerri, Borroni, & Baldissera, 2005; Patuzzo, Fiaschi, & Manganotti, 2003; Romani, Cesari, Urgesi, Facchini, & Aglioti, 2005; Strafella & Paus, 2000; Urgesi, Candidi, Fabbro, Romani, & Aglioti, 2006), leading to the observation that human motor facilitation is evoked also by

Correspondence should be addressed to: Christian Keysers, School of Behavioral and Cognitive Neurosciences NeuroImaging Centre, University Medical Centre Groningen, Groningen 9713 AW, The Netherlands. E-mail: c.m.keysers@rug.nl
CK is supported by a Marie Curie Excellence Grant of the European Commission, and a VIDI grant of the Dutch National Science Foundation, NWO.

www.psypress.com/socialneuroscience DOI:10.1080/17470910802408513

intransitive hand gestures. This might explain the capability of our species to imitate also new (never seen/never executed) actions. Neuroimaging techniques, and fMRI in particular (Avenanti, Bolognini, Maravita, & Aglioti, 2007; Buccino et al., 2001; Buccino, Lui et al., 2004a, 2004b; Calvo-Merino, Glaser, Grèzes, Passingham, & Haggard, 2005; Calvo-Merino, Grèzes, Glaser, Passingham, & Haggard, 2006; Cross, Hamilton, & Grafton, 2006; Gazzola, Aziz-Zadeh, & Keysers, 2006; Gazzola, Rizzolatti, Wicker, & Keysers, 2007a; Gazzola et al., 2007b; Grafton, Arbib, Fadiga, & Rizzolatti, 1996; Grèzes, Armony, Rowe, & Passingham, 2003; Hamilton & Grafton, 2006; Iacoboni & Dapretto, 2006; Iacoboni et al., 1999, 2001, 2005; Lamm, Fischer, & Decety, 2007; Molnar-Szakacs, Iacoboni, Koski, & Mazziotta, 2005; Molnar-Szakacs, Kaplan, Greenfield, & Iacoboni, 2006; Nelissen, Luppino, Vanduffel, Rizzolatti, & Orban, 2005), have allowed us to pinpoint the regions in which mirror neurons could be in humans. Experiments in which the same participants were scanned while they executed actions and while they viewed or heard other individuals perform similar actions have shown that voxels in the dorsal and ventral premotor, supplementary motor, posterior parietal, temporal and sometimes somatosensory cortices are indeed activated during both action execution and action perception, pinpointing the most likely location for the human mirror system (Buccino et al., 2004b; Gazzola et al., 2006; Gazzola et al., 2007a, 2007b). Interestingly, such activations are somatotopical: Dorsal premotor regions are more active both during the perception and the execution of hand actions as compared to mouth actions, while ventral regions are more active during the perception and the execution of mouth actions as compared to hand actions (Gazzola et al., 2006).

One additional area, almost constantly active during action observation and the sound of actions in particular (Gazzola et al., 2006) is Broca's region (BA44–BA45). The fact that Broca's region is classically considered the frontal area for speech suggests a possible evolutionary link between the implicit communication provided by the action-understanding mechanism based on monkey auditory and visual mirror neurons (Keysers et al., 2003; Kohler et al., 2002) and the explicit, verbal communication characterizing the human language (Fadiga et al., 2006; Fadiga, Roy, Fazio, & Craighero, 2007; Rizzolatti & Arbib, 1998). Recently, Roy Mukamel and his colleagues at UCLA have recorded the first single cells with motor mirror property in the supplementary motor cortex of humans, but these findings are still unpublished.

The confidence with which we can now claim that both monkeys and humans have a mirror system sets a solid foundation for investigating a much more complex set of questions: What does the mirror system code? How is the mirror system embedded into the mosaic of brain circuits that compose our brain? How does the mirror system contribute to communication, language and social interaction? Can the principle of mirror neurons be extended to emotions, sensations and thoughts? This special issue will try to tackle some of these questions.

WHAT DOES THE MIRROR SYSTEM CODE?

Although everyone seems to agree that mirror neurons transform the sight or sound of an action into a corresponding motor representation, what people mean by "corresponding" is often less clear: an action involving the same muscles or one with the same goal? Mirror neurons in the monkey vary in selectivity. Strictly congruent mirror neurons require the observed action to be extremely similar to the effective executed action for the neuron to respond. For these neurons—about 30% of mirror neurons—"corresponding" seems to mean an action that achieves a similar goal and that involves the same motor details. Broadly congruent mirror neurons, making up about 60% of all mirror neurons, however, are less picky about the details of the observed action: It needs to achieve a similar goal (e.g., grasping an object) but can often involve another effector (e.g., grasping with the mouth or with the hand). For such neurons, "corresponding" thus means "having the same goal." Together, strictly and broadly congruent mirror neurons could therefore represent both *what* another individual did, and *how* he did it (Thioux, Gazzola, & Keysers, 2008).

But what about the human mirror system? A number of TMS studies have shown how precise the matching of observed and executed action seems to be in humans as well (Borroni et al., 2005; Fadiga, Craighero, Buccino, & Rizzolatti, 2002; Gangitano et al., 2004; Montagna et al., 2005; Urgesi et al., 2006). A number of fMRI studies, on the other hand, evidence a combination of "what" and "how" similar to that found at the level of single cells in monkeys. Repetition suppression experiments show that certain parts of the mirror system are sensitive to the precise kinematics of observed movements, while others seem to represent the goal of an action (Hamilton & Grafton, 2006). Other fMRI experiments show an important consequence of goal matching: The human mirror system can resonate with actions even if the observer lacks the body parts that would directly match those with which the agent performed the action (Gazzola et al., 2007a, 2007b). In this issue, these questions are addressed further. Is the mirror system, for instance, involved in the representation of biologically impossible or intransitive gestures (Borroni & Baldissera, 2008 this issue; Candidi, Urgesi, Ionta, & Aglioti, 2008 this issue; Lui et al., 2008 this issue)? Does the mirror system resonate for actions different from hand or mouth ones (Saarela & Hari, 2008 this issue)? How quickly does the mirror-neuron system respond (van Schie et al., 2008 this issue)? Does it respond to non-biological stimuli (Engel et al., 2008 this issue)? What do these properties tell us about what the mirror system represents (de Vignemont & Haggard, 2008 this issue)? When, during ontogenesis, do mirror neurons start responding to others' actions (Nyström, 2008 this issue)?

EMBEDDING THE MIRROR SYSTEM

The more we understand the mirror neuron system, the more we have to ask ourselves how this circuitry interacts with other brain systems. How, for instance, can regions involved in spatial attention interact with the mirror neuron system to help us distinguish our own actions from those we observe while they are performed by other people? What brain circuits are responsible for inhibiting motor output while we observe the actions of others? Gangitano, Mottaghy, and Pascual-Leone (2008 this issue) and Jeannerod and Anquetil (2008 this issue) provide new insights into these important questions.

THE MIRROR SYSTEM AND COMMUNICATION

The capacity of the mirror system to activate action representations in the observer links it to communication, an issue that Gallese (2008 this issue) explores in detail. The mirror system has shown us how social cognition is at least partially based on our own bodily representations. Aziz-Zadeh (2008 this issue) and her coworkers show us that the understanding of words that refer to bodyparts may also be embodied. Oberman and Ramachandran (2008 this issue) give data that suggests that linking vocal sounds to shapes is abnormal in autism, and interpret these results within the framework of mirror neurons, and Pratt and Kelly (2008 this issue) show that our own emotional state colors our processing of emotional words.

THE MIRROR SYSTEM AND SOCIAL INTERACTIONS

By influencing the observer's actions, the mirror neuron system creates a bond between the behaviors of social partners. This bond is reciprocal: During most social interactions there is not a single agent and a single observer: both partners are both observer and agent, both the source and the target of the social contagion the mirror neuron system conveys. It is therefore essential to start exploring the reciprocal nature of social influences within the framework of the mirror system. Fujii and his team (2008 this issue) pave the way to such investigations. They record the brain activity simultaneously from two interacting monkeys, and show how this allows novel analysis methods to capture how mirror neurons participate in such unconstrained social interactions. Whenever humans collaborate to achieve a goal together (e.g., sending a rocket onto the moon), an important element of the social interaction goes beyond the actions themselves: Both partners need to keep the goals and rules of the interaction in mind. Atmaca and colleagues show that this process of goal-sharing is a strong and spontaneous property of the human mind. Finally, Paus et al. (2008 this issue) investigate the functioning of the mirror-neuron system in adolescents with different degrees of resistance to peer influence.

GOING BEYOND ACTIONS

One of the most fundamental breakthroughs in the study of the mirror neuron system has been the observation that the concept of mirror neurons extends beyond actions: Not only does the sight of an action activate regions involved in motor execution, but the sight of touch also activates somatosensory regions (Blakemore, Bristow, Bird, Frith, & Ward, 2005; Keysers et al., 2004) and the perception of other people's emotions such as pain, happiness and disgust activates regions involved in experiencing similar emotions (Jabbi, Swart, & Keysers, 2007; Singer et al., 2004; Wicker et al., 2003) and producing similar facial expressions (van der Gaag, Minderaa, & Keysers, 2007). We will see that the sight of emotional body movements leads to similar activations (Pichon, de Gelder, & Grèzes, 2008 this issue). Most recently, Michael Platt and colleagues have possibly extended the concept of mirror neurons to eye movements: Certain neurons in the lateral intraparietal region, thought to control eye movements, respond to the sight of another monkey's eye movements as if they were mirror neurons for gaze (Shepherd, Deaner, Klein, & Platt, 2007). This discovery may help elucidate the neural basis of gaze-following, and Ferrari and coworkers (2008 this issue) explore the development of gaze-following in the macaque.

CONCLUSION

Now that we know that both humans and monkeys have a mirror neuron system, we need to focus on understanding the architecture and the functional properties of this system. It is hoped that this special issue will inspire this research.

REFERENCES

Atmaca, S., Sebanz, N., Prinz, W., & Knoblich, G.N. (2008). Action co-representation: The joint SNARC effect. *Social Neuroscience*, *3*(3–4), 410–420.

Avenanti, A., Bolognini, N., Maravita, A., & Aglioti, S.M. (2007). Somatic and motor components of action simulation. *Current Biology*, *17*(24), 2129–2135.

Aziz-Zadeh, L., Fiebach, C.J., Naranayan, S., Feldman, J., Dodge, E., & Ivry, R.B. (2008). Modulation of the FFA and PPA by language related to faces and places. *Social Neuroscience*, *3*(3–4), 229–238.

Blakemore, S.J., Bristow, D., Bird, G., Frith, C., & Ward, J. (2005). Somatosensory activations during the observation of touch and a case of vision–touch synaesthesia. *Brain*, *128*(7), 1571–1583.

Borroni, P., & Baldissera, F. (2008). Activation of motor pathways during observation and execution of hand movements. *Social Neuroscience*, *3*(3–4), 276–288.

Borroni, P., Montagna, M., Cerri, G., & Baldissera, F. (2005). Cyclic time course of motor excitability modulation during the observation of a cyclic hand movement. *Brain Research*, *1065*(1–2), 115–124.

Buccino, G., Binkofski, F., Fink, G.R., Fadiga, L., Fogassi, L., Gallese, V., et al. (2001). Action observation activates premotor and parietal areas in a somatotopic manner: An fMRI study. *European Journal of Neuroscience*, *13*(2), 400–404.

Buccino, G., Lui, F., Canessa, N., Patteri, I., Lagravinese, G., Benuzzi, F., et al. (2004a). Neural circuits involved in the recognition of actions performed by nonconspecifics: An FMRI study. *Journal of Cognitive Neuroscience*, *16*(1), 114–126.

Buccino, G., Vogt, S., Ritzl, A., Fink, G.R., Zilles, K., Freund, H.J., et al. (2004b). Neural circuits underlying imitation learning of hand actions: An event-related fMRI study. *Neuron*, *42*(2), 323–334.

Calvo-Merino, B., Glaser, D.E., Grèzes, J., Passingham, R.E., & Haggard, P. (2005). Action observation and acquired motor skills: An FMRI study with expert dancers. *Cerebral Cortex*, *15*(8), 1243–1249.

Calvo-Merino, B., Grèzes, J., Glaser, D.E., Passingham, R.E., & Haggard, P. (2006). Seeing or doing? Influence of visual and motor familiarity in action observation. *Current Biology*, *16*(19), 1905–1910.

Candidi, M., Urgesi, C., Ionta, S., & Aglioti, S.M. (2008). Virtual lesion of ventral premotor cortex impairs visual perception of biomechanically possible but not impossible actions. *Social Neuroscience*, *3*(3–4), 388–400.

Cross, E.S., Hamilton, A.F., & Grafton, S.T. (2006). Building a motor simulation de novo: Observation of dance by dancers. *NeuroImage*, *31*(3), 1257–1267.

de Vignemont, F., & Haggard, P. (2008). Action observation and execution: What is shared? *Social Neuroscience*, *3*(3–4), 421–433.

di Pellegrino, G., Fadiga, L., Fogassi, L., Gallese, V., & Rizzolatti, G. (1992). Understanding motor events: A neurophysiological study. *Experimental Brain Research*, *91*(1), 176–180.

Engel, A., Burke, M., Fiehler, K., Bien, S., & Rösler, F. (2008). How moving objects become animated: The human mirror neuron system assimilates non-biological movement patterns. *Social Neuroscience*, *3*(3–4), 368–387.

Fadiga, L., Craighero, L., Buccino, G., & Rizzolatti, G. (2002). Speech listening specifically modulates the excitability of tongue muscles: A TMS study. *European Journal of Neuroscience*, *15*(2), 399–402.

Fadiga, L., Craighero, L., Destro, M.F., Finos, L., Cotillon-Williams, N., Smith, A. T., et al. (2006). Language in shadow. *Social Neuroscience*, *1*(2), 77–89.

Fadiga, L., Fogassi, L., Pavesi, G., & Rizzolatti, G. (1995). Motor facilitation during action observation: A magnetic stimulation study. *Journal of Neurophysiology*, *73*(6), 2608–2611.

Fadiga, L., Roy, A.C., Fazio, P., & Craighero, L. (2007). From hand actions to speech: Evidence and speculations. In P. Haggard, Y. Rossetti, & M. Kawato (Eds.), *Sensorimotor foundations of higher cognition: Attention and performance*. Oxford: Oxford University Press.

Ferrari, P. F., Coudé, G., Gallese, V., & Fogassi, L. (2008). Having access to others' mind through gaze: The role of ontogenetic and learning processes in gaze-following behavior of macaques. *Social Neuroscience*, *3*(3–4), 239–249.

Fujii, N., Hihara, S., & Iriki, A. (2008). Social cognition in premotor and parietal cortex. *Social Neuroscience*, *3*(3–4), 250–260.

Gallese, V. (2008). Mirror neurons and the social nature of language: The neural exploitation hypothesis. *Social Neuroscience*, *3*(3–4), 317–333.

Gallese, V., Fadiga, L., Fogassi, L., & Rizzolatti, G. (1996). Action recognition in the premotor cortex. *Brain*, *119*(2), 593–609.

Gangitano, M., Mottaghy, F.M., & Pascual-Leone, A. (2004). Modulation of premotor mirror neuron activity during observation of unpredictable grasping movements. *European Journal of Neuroscience*, *20*(8), 2193–2202.

Gangitano, M., Mottaghy, F.M., & Pascual-Leone, A. (2008). Release of premotor activity after repetitive transcranial magnetic stimulation of prefrontal cortex. *Social Neuroscience*, *3*(3–4), 289–302.

Gazzola, V., Aziz-Zadeh, L., & Keysers, C. (2006). Empathy and the somatotopic auditory mirror system in humans. *Current Biology*, *16*(18), 1824–1829.

Gazzola, V., Rizzolatti, G., Wicker, B., & Keysers, C. (2007a). The anthropomorphic brain: The mirror neuron system responds to human and robotic actions. *Neuroimage*, *35*(4), 1674–1684.

Gazzola, V., van der Worp, H., Mulder, T., Wicker, B., Rizzolatti, G., & Keysers, C. (2007b). Aplasics born without hands mirror the goal of hand actions with their feet. *Current Biology*, *17*(14), 1235–1240.

Grafton, S.T., Arbib, M.A., Fadiga, L., & Rizzolatti, G. (1996). Localization of grasp representations in humans by positron emission tomography. 2. Observation compared with imagination. *Experimental Brain Research*, *112*(1), 103–111.

Grèzes, J., Armony, J.L., Rowe, J., & Passingham, R.E. (2003). Activations related to "mirror" and "canonical" neurones in the human brain: An fMRI study. *NeuroImage*, *18*(4), 928–937.

Hamilton, A.F., & Grafton, S.T. (2006). Goal representation in human anterior intraparietal sulcus. *Journal of Neuroscience*, *26*(4), 1133–1137.

Iacoboni, M., & Dapretto, M. (2006). The mirror neuron system and the consequences of its dysfunction. *Nature Reviews Neuroscience*, *7*(12), 942–951.

Iacoboni, M., Koski, L.M., Brass, M., Bekkering, H., Woods, R.P., Dubeau, M.C., et al. (2001). Reafferent copies of imitated actions in the right superior temporal cortex. *Proceedings of the National Academy of Sciences of the United States of America*, *98*(24), 13995–13999.

Iacoboni, M., Molnar-Szakacs, I., Gallese, V., Buccino, G., Mazziotta, J.C., & Rizzolatti, G. (2005). Grasping the intentions of others with one's own mirror neuron system. *PLoS Biology*, *3*(3), e79.

Iacoboni, M., Woods, R.P., Brass, M., Bekkering, H., Mazziotta, J.C., & Rizzolatti, G. (1999). Cortical mechanisms of human imitation. *Science*, *286*(5449), 2526–2528.

Jabbi, M., Swart, M., & Keysers, C. (2007). Empathy for positive and negative emotions in the gustatory cortex. *NeuroImage*, *34*(4), 1744–1753.

Jeannerod, M., & Anquetil, T. (2008). Putting oneself in the perspective of the other: A framework for self–other differentiation. *Social Neuroscience*, *3*(3–4), 356–367.

Keysers, C., Kohler, E., Umiltà, M.A., Nanetti, L., Fogassi, L., & Gallese, V. (2003). Audiovisual mirror neurons and action recognition. *Experimental Brain Research*, *153*(4), 628–636.

Keysers, C., Wicker, B., Gazzola, V., Anton, J.L., Fogassi, L., & Gallese, V. (2004). A touching sight: SII/PV activation during the observation and experience of touch. *Neuron*, *42*(2), 335–346.

Kohler, E., Keysers, C., Umiltà, M.A., Fogassi, L., Gallese, V., & Rizzolatti, G. (2002). Hearing sounds, understanding actions: Action representation in mirror neurons. *Science*, *297*(5582), 846–848.

Lamm, C., Fischer, M.H., & Decety, J. (2007). Predicting the actions of others taps into one's own somatosensory representations—A functional MRI study. *Neuropsychologia*, *45*(11), 2480–2491.

Lui, F., Buccino, G., Duzzi, D., Benuzzi, F., Crisi, G., Baraldi, P., et al. (2008). Neural substrates for observing and imagining non-object-directed actions. *Social Neuroscience*, *3*(3–4), 261–275.

Molnar-Szakacs, I., Iacoboni, M., Koski, L., & Mazziotta, J.C. (2005). Functional segregation within pars opercularis of the inferior frontal gyrus: Evidence from fMRI studies of imitation and action observation. *Cerebral Cortex*, *15*(7), 986–994.

Molnar-Szakacs, I., Kaplan, J., Greenfield, P.M., & Iacoboni, M. (2006). Observing complex action sequences: The role of the fronto-parietal mirror neuron system. *NeuroImage*, *33*(3), 923–935.

Montagna, M., Cerri, G., Borroni, P., & Baldissera, F. (2005). Excitability changes in human corticospinal projections to muscles moving hand and fingers while viewing a reaching and grasping action. *European Journal of Neuroscience*, *22*(6), 1513–1520.

Nelissen, K., Luppino, G., Vanduffel, W., Rizzolatti, G., & Orban, G.A. (2005). Observing others: Multiple action representation in the frontal lobe. *Science*, *310*(5746), 332–336.

Nyström, P. (2008). The infant mirror neuron system studied with high density EEG. *Social Neuroscience*, *3*(3–4), 334–347.

Oberman, L.M., & Ramachandran, V.S. (2008). Preliminary evidence for deficits in multisensory integration in autism spectrum disorders: The mirror neuron hypothesis. *Social Neuroscience*, *3*(3–4), 348–355.

Patuzzo, S., Fiaschi, A., & Manganotti, P. (2003). Modulation of motor cortex excitability in the left hemisphere during action observation: A single- and paired-pulse transcranial magnetic stimulation study of self- and non-self-action observation. *Neuropsychologia*, *41*(9), 1272–1278.

Paus, T., Toro, R., Leonard, G., Lerner, J.V., Lerner, R.M., Perron, M., et al. (2008). Morphological properties of the action-observation cortical network in adolescents with low and high resistance to peer influence. *Social Neuroscience*, *3*(3–4), 303–316.

Pichon, S., de Gelder, B., & Grèzes, J. (2008). Emotional modulation of visual and motor areas by dynamic body expressions of anger. *Social Neuroscience*, *3*(3–4), 199–212.

Pratt, N.L., & Kelly, S.D. (2008). Emotional states influence the neural processing of affective language. *Social Neuroscience*, *3*(3–4), 434–442.

Rizzolatti, G., & Arbib, M.A. (1998). Language within our grasp. *Trends in Neuroscience*, *21*(5), 188–194.

Rizzolatti, G., Fadiga, L., Gallese, V., & Fogassi, L. (1996). Premotor cortex and the recognition of motor actions. *Brain Research: Cognitive Brain Research*, *3*(2), 131–141.

Romani, M., Cesari, P., Urgesi, C., Facchini, S., & Aglioti, S.M. (2005). Motor facilitation of the human cortico-spinal system during observation of biomechanically impossible movements. *NeuroImage*, *26*(3), 755–763.

Saarela, M.V., & Hari, R. (2008). Listening to humans walking together activates the social brain circuitry. *Social Neuroscience*, *3*(3–4), 401–409.

Shepherd, S.V., Deaner, R.O., Klein, J.T., & Platt, M.L. (2007). *Latency of social-cued attention signals in macaque area LIP.* Paper presented at Neuroscience 2007, the 37th annual meeting of the Society for Neuroscience, San Diego, CA.

Singer, T., Seymour, B., O'Doherty, J., Kaube, H., Dolan, R. J., & Frith, C. D. (2004). Empathy for pain involves the affective but not sensory components of pain. *Science*, *303*(5661), 1157–1162.

Strafella, A.P., & Paus, T. (2000). Modulation of cortical excitability during action observation: A transcranial magnetic stimulation study. *NeuroReport*, *11*(10), 2289–2292.

Thioux, M., Gazzola, V., & Keysers, C. (2008). Action understanding: How, what and why. *Current Biology*, *18*, R431–R434.

Umiltà, M.A., Kohler, E., Gallese, V., Fogassi, L., Fadiga, L., Keysers, C., et al. (2001). "I know what you are doing": A neurophysiological study. *Neuron*, *31*(1), 155–165.

Urgesi, C., Candidi, M., Fabbro, F., Romani, M., & Aglioti, S.M. (2006). Motor facilitation during action observation: Topographic mapping of the target muscle and influence of the onlooker's posture. *European Journal of Neuroscience*, *23*(9), 2522–2530.

van der Gaag, C., Minderaa, R., & Keysers, C. (2007). Facial expressions: What the mirror neuron system can and cannot tell us. *Social Neuroscience*, *2*, 179–222.

van Schie, H.T., Koelewijn, T., Jensen, O., Oostenveld, R., Maris, E., & Bekkering, H. (2008). Evidence for fast, low-level motor resonance to action observation: An MEG study. *Social Neuroscience*, *3*(3–4), 213–228.

Wicker, B., Keysers, C., Plailly, J., Royet, J.P., Gallese, V., & Rizzolatti, G. (2003). Both of us disgusted in My insula: The common neural basis of seeing and feeling disgust. *Neuron*, *40*(3), 655–664.

SOCIAL NEUROSCIENCE, 2008, 3 (3–4), 199–212

Psychology Press
Taylor & Francis Group

Emotional modulation of visual and motor areas by dynamic body expressions of anger

Swann Pichon
LPPA, CNRS – Collège de France, Paris, France

Beatrice de Gelder
Donders Laboratory, Tilburg, and F. C. Donders Centre, Nijmegen, The Netherlands, and Massachusetts General Hospital and Harvard Medical School, Charlestown, Massachusetts, USA

Julie Grèzes
LPPA, CNRS – Collège de France, Paris, France

The ability to detect emotional meaning in others' behavior constitutes a central component of social competence. Expressions of anger in particular present salient signals that play a major role in the regulation of social interactions. Investigations of human anger signals have to date used still pictures of facial expressions but so far the neurobiological basis of bodily communication of anger remains largely unknown. Using functional magnetic resonance imaging, the present study investigated the neural bases involved in perceiving anger signals emanating from the whole body. Our study also investigates what the presence of dynamic information adds to the perception of body expressions of anger. Participants were scanned while viewing stimuli (stills or videos) of angry and neutral whole-body expressions. Whole-body expressions of anger elicit activity in regions including the amygdala and the lateral orbitofrontal cortex, which play a role in the affective evaluation of the stimuli. Importantly, the perception of dynamic body expressions of anger additionally engages the hypothalamus, the ventromedial prefrontal cortex, the temporal pole and the premotor cortex, brain regions that are coupled with autonomic reactions and motor responses related to defensive behaviors.

INTRODUCTION

The ability to detect nonverbal signals in others' actions and emotional expressions constitutes a central component of social competence. Expressions of anger in particular present salient signals that play a major role in the regulation of social interactions. Angry expressions signal a potential physical and/or symbolic attack (Schupp et al., 2004), are perceived as threatening (Dimberg, 1986; Strauss et al., 2005) and trigger adaptive action in the observers (Frijda, 1986). To date, the neural basis of anger perception has been investigated mainly by presenting pictures of angry facial expressions (see Hennenlotter & Schroeder, 2006, for a review; also overview in Table 1). The lateral orbitofrontal cortex (OFC), amygdala, superior frontal gyrus, premotor cortex

Correspondence should be addressed to: Julie Grèzes, Laboratoire de Physiologie de la Perception et de l'Action (LPPA), CNRS – Collège de France, 11 Place Marcelin Berthelot, F-75005 Paris, France. E-mail: julie.grezes@college-de-france.fr

SP, BdG and JG were partly supported by Human Frontier Science Program HFSP—RGP0054/2004-C and by EC-contract number FP6-NEST-2005-Path-IMP-043403. BdG was also supported by a grant from NWO (Netherlands Organisation for Scientific Research).

We are grateful to D. A. Hopkins for comments on the manuscript, to W. van de Riet for recruiting the subjects, P. Gaalman and F. Maloumian for technical assistance.

www.psypress.com/socialneuroscience DOI:10.1080/17470910701394368

TABLE 1
Overview of brain regions detected in previous neuroimaging studies during the presentation of facial expressions of anger

		Brain regions								
References	*Modality*	*Lat OFC*	*AMG*	*mSFG*	*PM*	*FF*	*ACC*	*PCC*	*TP*	*IFG*
Blair, Morris, Frith, Perrett, & Dolan (1999)[b]	Still	X					X			
Esslen, Pascual-Marqui, Hell, Kochi, & Lehmann (2004)[c]	Still	X		X						
Fitzgerald, Angstadt, Jelsone, Nathan, & Phan (2006)[a*]	Still	X	X	X						
Grosbras & Paus (2006)[a*]	Dynamic		X		X	X				
Kesler-West et al. (2001)[a]	Still	X		X	X	X				
Kilts et al. (2003)[b]	Dynamic			X						X
Sprengelmeyer, Rausch, Eysel, & Przuntek (1998)[a]	Still	X						X		
Whalen et al. (2001)[a]	Still		X		X					
Williams et al. (2004)[a]	Still		X			X	X		X	

Notes: Inclusion criteria were an explicit (vs. subliminal) presentation of facial expressions of anger without aversive conditioning, and the presentation of results contrasting anger versus neutral (or baseline*) conditions. Note that the hypothalamus and the ventromedial prefrontal cortex were not detected in previous studies. Superscripts indicate the imaging method used ([a]fMRI, [b]PET and [c]EEG, respectively). Lat OFC: lateral orbitofrontal cortex (BA 47); AMG: amygdala; mSFG: medial superior frontal gyrus (BA 8, BA 9); PM: premotor cortex; FF: fusiform gyrus; ACC/PCC: anterior/posterior cingulate cortex; TP: temporal pole; IFG: inferior frontal gyrus (BA 45—pars triangularis).

and fusiform gyrus are often involved but there is considerable variability among the results obtained by different investigators, with the exception of lateral OFC, which is consistently identified across almost all studies (Murphy, Nimmo-Smith, & Lawrence, 2003).

Facial expressions of anger are an integral part of angry behavior that involves the whole body (de Gelder, 2006). Bodily expressions of anger are of prime importance in regulating social interactions and in negotiating aggressive confrontations in primates (Emery & Amaral, 2000) and in humans (Argyle, 1988). Once the scope of anger investigations is extended beyond individual facial expressions to whole-body behaviors, attention is drawn to two novel dimensions of anger signals. One is that whole-body expressions of emotion often do not simply consist of purely emotional expressions but show a person in the course of performing an action with an emotional overtone. Bodily expressions of emotion not only inform the observer about the state of mind but also show the actions being undertaken by the angry person, which may consist of a direct threat towards the observer. For example, a simple action of throwing a ball, when done in anger, may be perceived as an attack. Also, the more anger colors the action the more it may be perceived as a threat and elicit a defensive reaction in the observer. Neurophysiological findings indicate that when an animal is confronted with signals of danger, characteristic defensive responses like fight, flight or freezing are elicited allowing the animal to shield from the source of threat (Blanchard & Blanchard, 1988; McNaughton & Corr, 2004). The amygdala is hypothesized to play a critical role in a network of brain structures mediating fear responses and triggering threat-related behaviors (Amaral, 2003; Blanchard & Blanchard, 1972; LeDoux, 2000) via its connections with other structures such as the medial prefrontal cortex and the hypothalamus (Ongur & Price, 2000).

Another dimension that comes to the foreground when we broaden the scope of emotion research and include the whole body concerns the contribution to emotion and action understanding from movement. So far the importance of movement has only been recently investigated for facial expressions of emotions using neuroimaging (Decety & Chaminade, 2003; Kilts, Egan, Gideon, Ely, & Hoffman, 2003; LaBar, Crupain, Voyvodic, & McCarthy, 2003; Sato, Kochiyama, Yoshikawa, Naito, & Matsumura, 2004; Simon, Craig, Miltner, & Rainville, 2006). Better recognition rates for movies than for still images have also been reported for body stimuli (Atkinson, Dittrich, Gemmell, & Young, 2004; de Meijer, 1989). To our knowledge only three functional brain imaging studies have explored the perception of dynamic expressions of anger using either facial expressions (Kilts et al., 2003; LaBar et al., 2003) or hand actions (Grosbras & Paus, 2006).

Here our goal was to investigate the brain regions involved in perceiving anger signals emanating from the whole body. Using event-related fMRI, we scanned participants while they viewed short movies and still images of neutral and angry whole-body actions. We predicted: (1) that whole-body actions expressing anger would be perceived as threat signals and would consequently enhance the level of activation in amygdala and in high-level visual cortices; (2) furthermore, that they would elicit activity in frontal regions, particularly in the lateral OFC (see Table 1); and, finally, (3) that there would be a significant interaction between emotional and motor processes during the perception of dynamic whole-body expressions of anger.

METHODS

Participants

Sixteen right-handed subjects (7 females and 9 males, ranging from 18 to 26 years of age) with no neurological or psychiatric history participated in the imaging study. All provided written informed consent according to institutional guidelines of the local ethics committee (CMO region Arnhem–Nijmegen, The Netherlands).

Materials

Construction of materials started with the recording of video films. In order to account for variability in acting style, a large group of actors was hired (6 males and 6 females). All actors were graduates from professional acting schools and they performed different scenarios familiar from daily life under professional direction. For the scenario used in the present experiment the actors were instructed to open the door in front of them, react to a specified encounter and close the door again. The anger version of this scenario required the actors to open the door and react to something or someone that made them angry. The performance was repeated till deemed satisfactory by the director. Recordings were made with a video camera positioned directly in front of the door viewed from the outside. The video films were then computer edited and a continuous fragment of 3 s (25 frames per second) was selected from initial materials which had an average length of 5 s. Subsequently the faces were blurred using the After-effect software (Adobe®), such that only information from the body was available.

From these edited materials a subset was used for stimuli in the present experiment. Selection of the stimuli was based on the results of a pilot study ($n = 12$) using the edited video clips. A total of 141 video clips (fear, anger and neutral door-opening scenarios) were presented individually to participants on a PC screen with a 2 s interval. Participants were instructed to categorize each stimulus in a forced-choice procedure by pressing one of the three response buttons corresponding to each type of scenario. Average recognition rate for anger and neutral scenarios was 76% ($SD = 28$) and 97% ($SD = 5$), respectively. The 48 highest-ranked videos, average recognition of anger 89% ($SD = 15$) and of neutral 97% ($SD = 5$), were chosen for use in the present study (12 actors $\times$ 2 anger scenarios + 12 actors $\times$ 2 neutral scenarios). To check whether there were quantitative differences in movement between anger and neutral movies, we estimated the amount of movement per video clip by quantifying the variation of light intensity (luminance) between pairs of frames for each pixel. For each frame ($n = 75$–1), these differences were averaged across pixels that scored (on a scale reaching a maximum of 255) higher than 10, a value which corresponds to the noise level of the camera. These estimations were then averaged for each movie and the resulting scores were used to test the hypothesis of a difference in movement between neutral and anger movies. No significant difference was detected (Student's two-tailed t-test, $p = .64$).

A total of 116 still images was obtained from the selected anger, fear and neutral video clips by sampling in each video one or two frames judged to be at the apex of the expression. Selection of the stimuli was then based on the results of a pilot study ($n = 14$). Participants were shown the 116 images of bodies expressing fear or anger as well as the neutral actions. Each picture was presented for 3 s on a PC screen with a 3 s interval. Participants were instructed to categorize each stimulus in a forced-choice procedure by pressing one of the three response buttons corresponding to the three situations. The 24 highest-ranked anger pictures (average recognition rate 68%, $SD = 30$) and the 24 highest-ranked neutral pictures (average recognition rate 78%, $SD = 16$) were selected for use in the present study.

Finally, 24 scrambled video clips and 24 scrambled static images were derived from the videos and still images to serve as control conditions. This was done with After-effect software

(Adobe®) and consisted in applying a mosaic effect on each video clip and image. This creates a low-resolution effect by filling a layer with solid rectangles colored with the average color of the corresponding region in the unaffected layer.

Experimental design

During the scanning session, a total of 462 stimuli were presented, consisting of 24 stimuli for each of the 6 conditions: anger dynamic (Ad), anger static (As), neutral dynamic (Nd), neutral static (Ns), scrambled neutral dynamic (Sd) and scrambled neutral static (Ss), as well as 15 oddball stimuli (upside-down neutral video clips) and 72 null events (black screens). The stimuli were presented twice and the experiment was split in two contiguous sessions with the event order fully randomized between subjects. Each stimulus lasted 3 s followed by a 960 ms black interval. Visual stimuli were back projected on a screen located behind the subject's head and were viewed inside the head coil using a mirror. The vertical and horizontal size of the stimuli was about 18 and 12 degrees. Participants were asked to press a button each time an oddball stimulus appeared such that trials of interest were uncontaminated by motor response (Figure 1). Following the scanning session, subjects were asked to explicitly categorize the stimuli as neutral or angry body expressions (see behavioral results).

Data analysis

Gradient-echo T2*-weighted transverse echo-planar images (EPI) with blood oxygenation level-dependent (BOLD) contrast were acquired with a 1.5 T Siemens SONATA scanner (Siemens, Erlangen, Germany). Each volume contained 43 axial slices, repetition time (TR) = 3790 ms, echo time (TE) = 40 ms, 2.5 mm thickness with 0.5 mm gap, flip angle = 90°, field of view (FOV) = 320 mm, acquired sequentially in an ascending direction. An automatic shimming procedure was performed before each scanning session. A total of 496 functional volumes were collected for each subject as well as high-resolution T1-weighted anatomical images (TE = 3.68 ms, TR = 2250 ms, slice thickness = 1 mm, 176 sagittal slices, FOV = 256 mm).

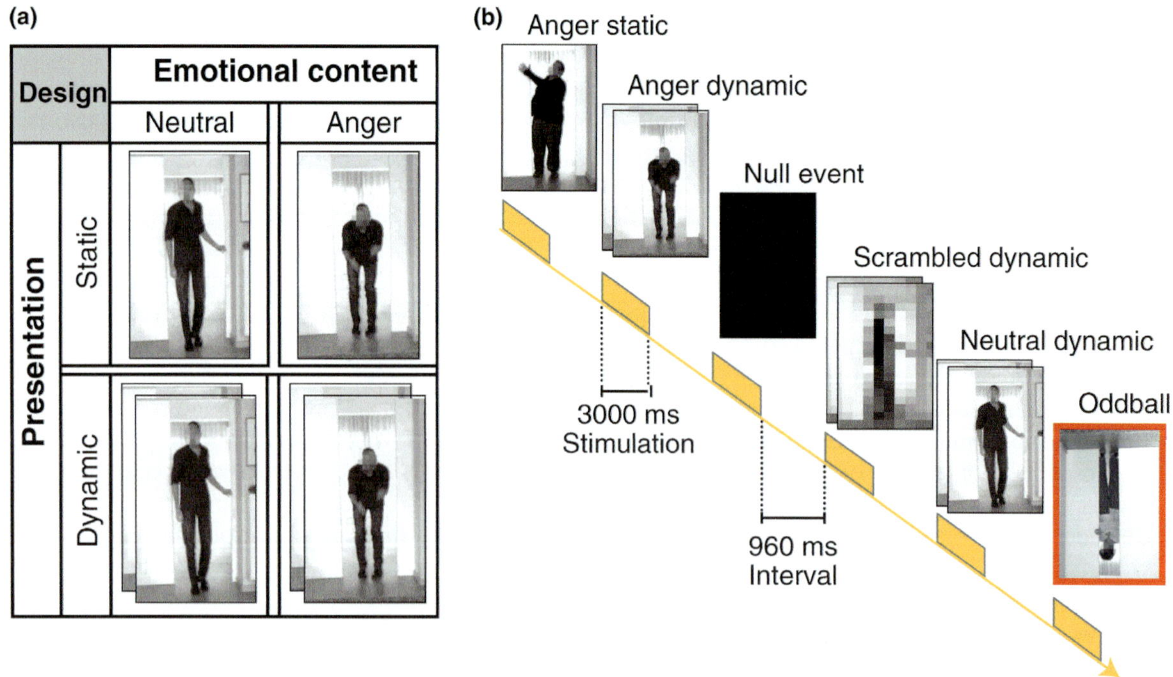

Figure 1. Experimental design and example of stimuli. (a) 2 × 2 factorial design. Trials were either movies or still pictures of whole-body expressions of actors opening a door in a neutral mode or angry mode. (b) Example of a run and timing. Participants were instructed to press a button when they saw an upside-down video clip among a run of body expressions (41% of the trials), scrambled (21%) and null (31%) stimuli. Targets were oddball (7%) trials. Stimuli were presented for 3 s, followed by a 960 ms long black screen.

fMRI data computation

Functional images were processed using the SPM2 software package (http://www.fil.ion.ucl.ac.uk/spm). The first five volumes of each functional run were discarded to allow for T1 equilibration effects. The remaining 491 functional images were reoriented to the AC–PC line, spatially realigned to the first volume by rigid body transformation and slice-time corrected to the middle slice. These images were normalized to the standard Montreal Neurological Institute (MNI) reference brain and subsampled at an isotropic voxel size of 2 mm. The normalized images were spatially smoothed by a 6 mm full width at half maximum (FWHM) isotropic Gaussian kernel.

Statistical analysis was carried out using the general linear model framework (Friston et al., 1995) implemented in the SPM2 software (SPM2; Wellcome Department of Imaging Neuroscience, London, UK). At the subject level, 7 effects of interest were modeled as follows: two represented the trials where subjects perceived body expressions of anger in a static (As) or dynamic way (Ad), two represented the trials where subjects perceived neutral body expressions in a static (Ns) or dynamic way (Nd). Finally, two represented the trials where subjects perceived scrambled static (Ss) or dynamic stimuli (Sd), and one represented the oddball stimuli. Null events were implicitly modeled. The BOLD response to the stimulus onset for each event type was convolved with the canonical hemodynamic response function of 3 s (0.79 TR). Also included for each subject's session were six covariates in order to capture residual movement-related artifacts (the 3 rigid-body translations and the 3 rotations determined from initial spatial registration), and a single covariate representing the mean (constant) over scans. To remove low frequency drifts from the data, we applied a high-pass filter using a cut-off frequency of 1/128 Hz.

To implement a random effect analysis in SPM2, we first smoothed the images of parameter estimates of our 6 *t*-test contrasts of interest (As, Ad, Ns, Nd, Ss, Sd) using a 6 mm FWHM isotropic Gaussian kernel. Those images were then entered into a second-level analysis using within-subjects ANOVA with 6 hemodynamic response functions comprising a factor. A non-sphericity correction was applied for variance differences between conditions and/or subjects. The following contrasts were calculated for the group:

- Main effect of bodies versus scrambled stimuli, (As + Ad + Ns + Nd) – 2(Ss + Sd).
- Main effect of anger versus neutral bodies, (As + Ad) – (Ns + Nd).
- Simple effect of anger dynamic versus anger static bodies, (Ad–As).
- Simple effect of neutral dynamic versus neutral static bodies, (Nd–Ns).
- Simple effect of anger dynamic versus neutral dynamic bodies, (Ad–Nd).
- Interaction between anger and dynamic bodies, (Ad–As) – (Nd–Ns).

All statistical parametric maps were thresholded at $p < .001$ (uncorrected for multiple comparisons), and activation foci with a minimum cluster extent of 10 voxels are reported here. Coordinates that survive False Discovery Rate (FDR) correction at $p < .05$ are indicated in tables by an asterisk. The maps were then overlaid on the MNI reference brain and labeled using the atlas of Duvernoy (1999). The reported coordinates in tables 2–5 represent peak activations of significant clusters except when their extent was important, in which case we also report subpeak coordinates corresponding to a different brain area from the maximum peak. For areas activated in both hemispheres, we report the coordinates of the strongest peak activation and provide both Z-values.

BEHAVIORAL RESULTS

After the scanning session, the participants performed a behavioral experiment. They viewed all 96 stimuli (24 static anger, 24 dynamic anger, 24 static neutral, 24 dynamic neutral) and were instructed to categorize each stimulus in a forced-choice procedure by pressing one of the two response buttons corresponding to the two emotional situations (anger or neutral). The average recognition rates for pictures and movies showing anger were respectively 80% ($SD = 16$) and 95% ($SD = 10$). The average recognition rates for neutral pictures and movies were respectively 90% ($SD = 9$) and 98% ($SD = 4$).

RESULTS

Effects of viewing body expressions irrespective of movement and emotion

The main effect of perceiving body expressions, irrespective of the movement properties and of the emotional content of the stimuli, (As + Ad + Ns + Nd) – 2(Ss + Sd) revealed significant increased activity in the amygdala, the fusiform gyrus, the middle occipital gyrus and the occipital pole in both hemispheres. In the right hemisphere, we observed activity in the pars orbitalis of the inferior frontal gyrus (BA 45) and the hippocampus. The full list of activations is presented in Table 2.

Effects of observing anger expressions irrespective of movement

The second analysis determined the activations specific to the presentation of anger expressions irrespective of the presence of movement in the stimuli by calculating the main effect of perceiving anger versus neutral body expressions: (As + Ad) – (Ns + Nd). This contrast revealed significant bilateral activations in the superior temporal sulcus (STS), the temporoparietal junction, the fusiform gyrus and the premotor cortex. In addition, in the right hemisphere there were significant activations in the amygdala, the thalamus, the medial part of the superior frontal gyrus (BA 9) and the pars triangularis of the inferior frontal gyrus (IFG, BA 45) extending onto the lateral OFC (BA 47). Loci in the left hemisphere also included the lateral OFC (BA 47), the IFG (BA 45/BA 44) and the posterior cingulate sulcus. The full list of activations is presented in Table 3 (see Figure 2).

Effects of observing dynamic expressions

Data were then analyzed according to whether the images were dynamic or static by calculating the simple main effect of viewing dynamic versus static body expressions for anger (Ad–As) and for neutral (Nd–Ns) conditions separately. Neutral dynamic expressions elicited activity mainly located in the dorsal pathway whereas anger expressions recruited brain regions mainly located in the ventral pathway (see Figure 3a). Observing neutral dynamic expressions (Nd–Ns) is associated with bilateral activations in the MT/V5 complex, the posterior STS, the superior parietal lobe and the precuneus. In the right hemisphere, loci of activation were also detected in the fusiform gyrus and the premotor cortex. Observing angry dynamic expressions (Ad–As) elicited bilateral activations in the MT/V5 complex, the posterior STS, the fusiform gyrus, the temporal pole and the lateral OFC (see Figure 3a). Furthermore, in the right hemisphere, clusters of activity were detected along the STS extending to its anterior part as well as in the premotor cortex. In the left hemisphere, activations were elicited in the hypothalamus and the cerebellum. The full list of activations is presented in Table 4.

TABLE 2
Effects of observing body expressions versus scrambled stimuli (As + Ad + Ns + Nd) – 2(Ss + Sd)

		MNI coordinates				
Hemisphere	*Anatomical region*	*x*	*y*	*z*	*Z-value*	*Cluster size*
R	Inferior frontal gyrus-pars triangularis (BA 45)	56	30	−8	3.38*	10
L	Amygdala	−34	2	−24	3.64*	10
R	Amygdala	20	−2	−14	3.35*	38
R	Hippocampus	24	−24	−6	3.35*	65†
R	Hippocampus	12	−32	−4	3.7*	65
R	Fusiform gyrus	42	−52	−20	Inf*	676
L	Fusiform gyrus	−40	−42	−22	5.26*	2988†
R	Middle occipital gyrus	50	−76	0	Inf*	3410
L & R	Middle occipital gyrus	±44	−86	0	Inf*/7.73*	2988/3410†
L & R	Occipital pole	±26	−100	−4	6.96*/7.28*	2988†/3410†

Notes: $p < .001$ uncorrected, *$p < .05$ FDR correction, minimum cluster extent = 10 voxels. Inf: Infinite. †for subpeaks.

TABLE 3
Main effect of anger versus neutral expressions (As+Ad)-(Ns+Nd)

		MNI coordinates				
Hemisphere	*Anatomical region*	*x*	*y*	*z*	*Z-value*	*Cluster size*
R	Superior frontal gyrus (BA 9)	10	60	40	4.54*	97
R	Inferior frontal gyrus (BA 45)/lateral orbitofrontal cortex (BA 47)	60	32	0	3.64*	93
L	Lateral orbitofrontal cortex (BA 47)	−42	30	−8	3.85*	26
L	Inferior frontal gyrus/sulcus (BA 45/BA 44)	−54	22	32	3.34*	12
L	Premotor cortex	−46	10	54	3.95*	27
R	Premotor cortex	42	2	44	4.30*	95
R	Amygdala	28	0	−26	3.84*	46
R	Thalamus	10	−12	6	3.53*	17
L	Posterior cingulate sulcus	−12	−6	42	3.57*	11
R	Superior temporal sulcus: middle part	54	−18	−14	3.78*	46
R	Temporoparietal junction–supramarginal gyrus	66	−34	36	3.61*	12
L & R	Temporoparietal junction-superior temporal gyrus	±66	−40	20	3.57*/4.92*	17/1343†
L & R	Superior temporal sulcus: posterior part	±56	−42	4	5.55*/5.83*	1045/1343
L & R	Fusiform gyrus	±44	−44	−18	4.08*/4.68*	113/66
L & R	Middle occipital gyrus	±46	−74	0	5.27*/4.03*	1045†/55
L & R	Occipital pole	±12	−102	2	5.30*/4.14*	540/79

Notes: $p < .001$ non-corrected. *$p < .05$ FDR correction, minimum cluster extent = 10 voxels. †for subpeaks.

Effects of observing dynamic expressions of anger

To identify brain activations specific to the perception of dynamic body expressions of anger, we calculated the interaction between the Presentation Mode (dynamic vs. static) and the factor Emotion (anger vs. neutral); (Ad–As)-(Nd–Ns). This contrast revealed significant bilateral activations in the lateral part of the temporal pole. In addition, in the right hemisphere, activations were detected all along the STS from its posterior ($y = -42$) to its anterior part ($y = -6$), in the anterior part of the ventromedial prefrontal cortex (gyrus rectus), in the dorsal premotor cortex and the superior frontal gyrus (BA 9). In the left hemisphere, significant hemodynamic responses were detected in the hypothalamus and in the medial part of the temporal pole. The full list of activations is given in Table 5 (see also Figure 4).

DISCUSSION

We investigated how the brain processes still images and short movies of actions involving the whole body and performed in a neutral or an angry fashion, and we show the condition-specific brain regions when participants view these stimuli. Perceiving body expressions of anger, whether static or dynamic, revealed activations in the amygdala, the fusiform gyrus, the lateral OFC and the inferior frontal gyrus (BA 45). Additionally, perceiving anger movies specifically enhances activity in the hypothalamus, the temporal pole as well as the premotor and the ventromedial prefrontal cortex (vmPFC). Our discussion first addresses how seeing body expressions of anger influences activity in amygdala and within temporal cortices. We then consider whether these brain areas, in association with the lateral OFC, reflect an evaluation of emotional content. Finally, we highlight the possible involvement of the regions specifically recruited by the perception of movies of anger expressions in the modulation of autonomic reactions and motor responses known to be associated with defensive behavior.

Seeing anger stimuli activates the amygdala and fusiform gyrus

As predicted, the amygdala and the fusiform gyrus play a significant role in processing whole-body expressions of anger. To our knowledge this is the first report of amygdala activation triggered by the perception of whole-body expressions of anger. This new result extends previous findings that have already established the role of the amygdala in perceiving anger expressed in facial (see Table 1) and vocal expressions (Scott et al., 1997) as well as in actions involving body parts (Grosbras & Paus, 2006). The middle part of the

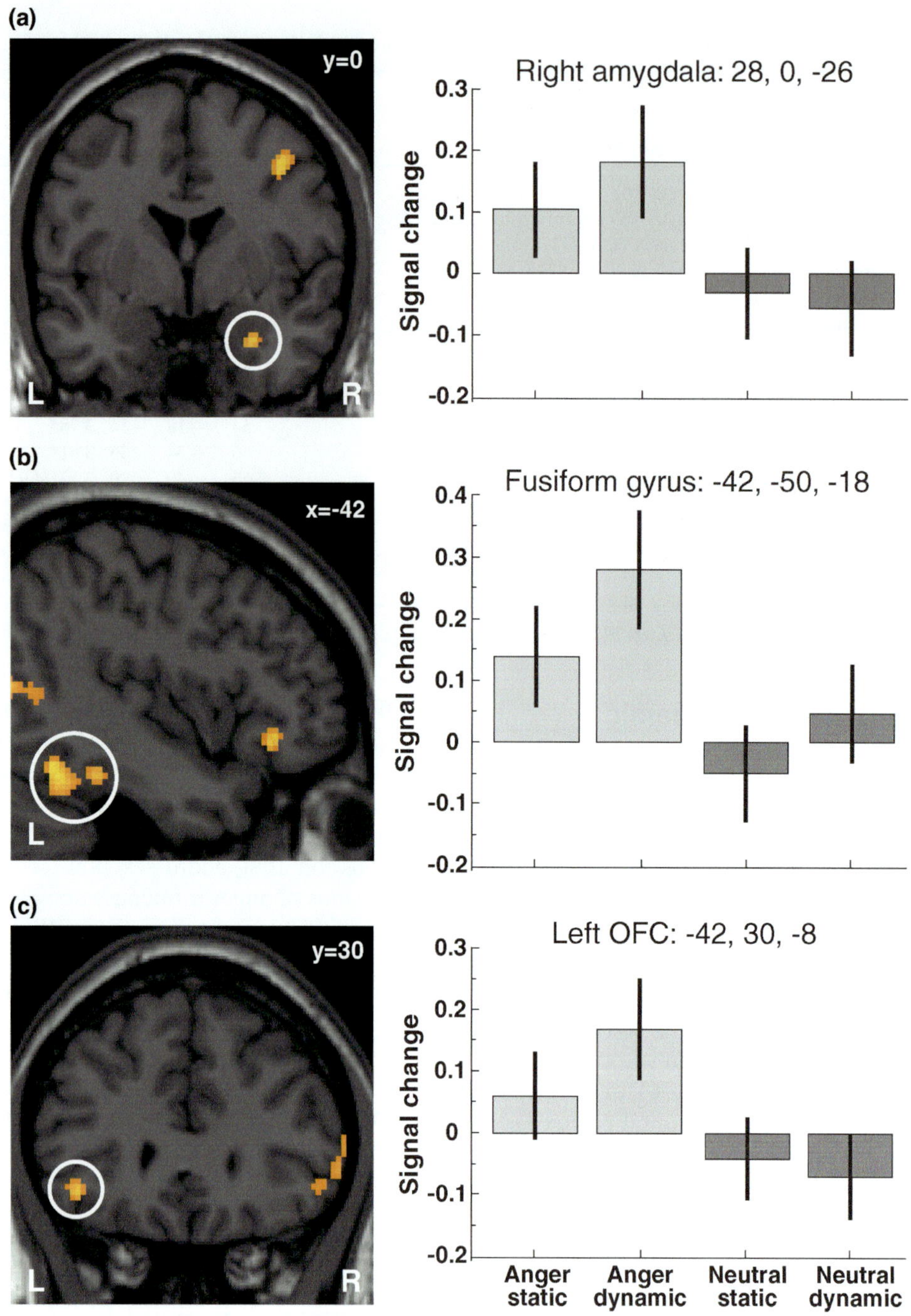

Figure 2. Regions showing amplitude difference when subjects observed static and dynamic expressions of anger. Localization of significant BOLD signal changes and parameter estimates (arbitrary units, mean centered) of the (a) right amygdala (b) left fusiform gyrus and (c) left OFC. Results superimposed on SPM standard single subject T1-weighted coronal and lateral sections, results listed in Table 3.

fusiform gyrus is associated with face perception but has also been associated with the processing of dynamic and static whole body movements and postures (Bonda, Petrides, Ostry, & Evans, 1996; Grossman & Blake, 2002; Kanwisher, Stanley, & Harris, 1999; Peelen & Downing, 2005; Vaina, Solomon, Chowdhury, Sinha, & Belliveau, 2001).

The observed involvement of amygdala and fusiform gyrus is also consistent with previous studies on body expressions of emotion using still images (de Gelder, Snyder, Greve, Gerard, & Hadjikhani, 2004; Grèzes, Pichon, & de Gelder, 2007; Hadjikhani & de Gelder, 2003). Recent fMRI studies using neutral faces and bodies have

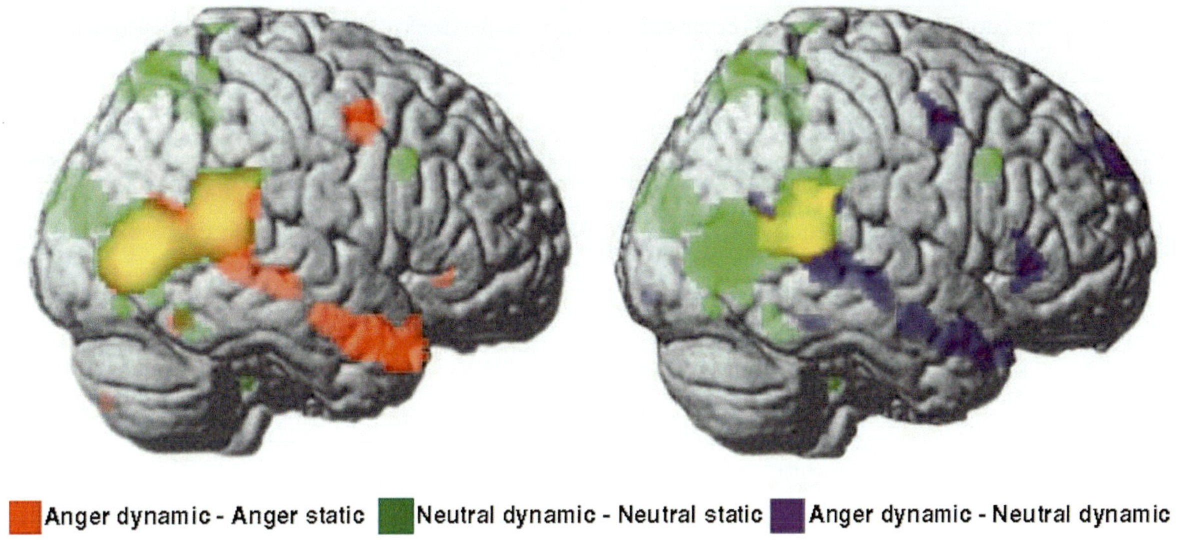

Figure 3. Cortical activations elicited by anger and neutral dynamic expressions. Statistical parametric maps ($p < .001$ uncorrected, minimum cluster extent of 10 voxels) of brain activation in response to the observation of (a) dynamic versus static anger expressions (red) and dynamic versus static neutral expressions (green) as well as (b) anger versus neutral dynamic expressions (purple). Common activations in both contrasts in yellow. Results listed in Table 4.

argued for a fine spatial segregation between the so-called body and face areas in the fusiform gyrus (Schwarzlose, Baker, & Kanwisher, 2005) but also show a substantial overlap between them (Peelen, Wiggett, & Downing, 2006; van de Riet, Grèzes, & de Gelder, 2007).

TABLE 4

Brain regions involved during the observation of dynamic expressions (Ad–As)/(Nd–Ns)

		MNI coordinates				
Hemi-sphere	*Anatomical region*	*x*	*y*	*z*	*Z-value*	*Cluster size*
Dynamic vs. static anger expressions (Ad–As)						
L & R	Lateral orbitofrontal cortex (BA 47)	±38	30	0	3.56*/3.35*	10/11
L & R	Temporal pole: medial part	±28	12	−30	3.50*/3.70*	13/33
R	Middle temporal gyrus: anterior part	54	8	−22	4.75*	562†
L	Hypothalamus	−6	0	−14	3.45*	12
R	Premotor cortex	50	2	48	4.35*	130
R	Superior temporal sulcus: anterior part (aSTS)	54	−2	−24	5.02*	562
R	Temporoparietal junction (TPJ)	68	−38	22	5.51*	2972†
L & R	Fusiform gyrus	±42	−42	−20	3.88*/3.60*	52/17
L & R	Superior temporal sulcus: posterior part	±54	−44	12	5.88*/7.65*	1343†/2972†
L & R	Middle occipital gyrus (MT/V5)	±48	−68	4	7.68*/Inf*	1343/2972
L	Cerebellum	−12	−80	−46	3.5*	15
Dynamic vs. static neutral expressions (Nd–Ns)						
R	Inferior frontal gyrus (BA 44)	52	16	32	3.61*	56
L & R	Intraparietal/postcentral sulcus	±42	−46	62	3.56*/3.54*	15/33
L & R	Superior temporal sulcus: posterior part	±62	−44	16	4.68*/6.71*	1488†/2790†
L & R	Precuneus	±8	−74	56	3.51*/3.24*	21/14
R	Precuneus	8	−50	50	4.69*	115
L	Superior parietal lobule/intraparietal sulcus	−34	−62	52	4.34*	254
R	Superior parietal lobule	26	−66	66	4.22*	225
R	Fusiform gyrus	42	−56	−18	3.86*	36
L & R	Middle occipital gyrus (MT/V5)	±48	−70	2	Inf*/Inf*	1488/2790
L & R	Superior occipital gyrus	±24	−94	24	4.77*/3.97*	348/163
L & R	Occipital gyrus	±46	−76	−14	3.37*/3.65*	14/2790†

Notes: $p < .001$ non-corrected. *$p < .05$ FDR correction, minimum cluster extent = 10 voxels, Inf: Infinite, †for subpeaks.

TABLE 5
Brain regions specifically involved during the observation of dynamic expressions of anger revealed by the interaction (Ad–As)-(Nd–Ns)

		MNI coordinates				
Hemisphere	*Anatomical region*	*x*	*y*	*z*	*Z-value*	*Cluster size*
R	Superior frontal gyrus (BA 9)	6	56	48	3.35	10
R	Ventromedial prefrontal cortex/gyrus rectus	2	48	−26	3.53	25
R	Premotor cortex (PM): dorsal part	56	−4	52	3.62	22
L	Hypothalamus	−6	0	−12	4.24	53
R	Superior temporal sulcus: posterior part	48	−42	8	3.49	37
R	Superior temporal sulcus: middle part	54	−22	−6	3.84	31
R	Superior temporal sulcus: anterior part	54	−6	−20	3.87	80
L & R	Temporal pole: lateral part	±54	14	−26	3.98/3.83	29/72
L	Temporal pole: medial part	−32	12	−30	3.85	25

Notes: $p < .001$ uncorrected, minimum cluster extent = 10 voxels.

Our results provide support for the hypothesis that the amygdala plays a major role in detecting threat and add to the significant literature on the contribution of the amygdala to the perception of fear and the brain's response to threat (Anderson & Phelps, 2000; LeDoux, 2000). The combined activation of the amygdala and fusiform gyrus triggered by anger in body actions is also consistent with functional data from healthy subjects (Morris et al., 1998), findings with brain-injured patients (Vuilleumier, Richardson, Armony, Driver, & Dolan, 2004) and tracing studies in animals showing massive projections from the amygdala to all levels of the ventral visual pathway (Amaral, Behniea, & Kelly, 2003), which suggests that the amygdala can influence sensory processing in the fusiform gyrus. It also extends the previously observed activations in the amygdala and fusiform for fear body actions (de Gelder et al., 2004; Hadjikhani & de Gelder, 2003; Grèzes et al., 2007) by showing that the amygdala's reaction to threat in anger stimuli is combined with activity in the fusiform gyrus.

Anger-related activations and the lateral OFC

In addition to the amygdala and fusiform gyrus, we observed activation in the inferior frontal gyrus and lateral OFC in response to anger expressions. Previous neuroimaging findings that have used facial expressions of anger have frequently reported enhanced activity in the lateral OFC (see Table 1). Besides anger, this region was also detected during the perception of an emotional tone of voice (Wildgruber et al., 2004, 2005) and facial expressions (Nakamura et al., 1999). In keeping with this, patients with OFC lesions are impaired at recognizing that actions leading to social violation are inappropriate (Hornak, Rolls, & Wade, 1996). Interestingly, the lateral OFC is also active in healthy subjects judging scenarios describing transgressions of social norms (Berthoz, Armony, Blair, & Dolan, 2002). When combining these results it seems that the brain areas activated in the main effect of body expressions of anger may be linked to the integration of emotion-related information and processes assigning affective meaning to the stimuli.

Perception of dynamic body expressions of anger and neural substrate

In addition to brain areas responding to body images of anger irrespective of whether the information is provided by videos or still images, the interaction revealed regions specifically activated in response to dynamic expressions of anger. These include the temporal pole, which is the site of convergence of sensory and limbic inputs (Moran, Mufson, & Mesulam, 1987) and has an important role in affective processes (Adolphs, Tranel, & Damasio, 2001; Anderson & Phelps, 2000). Our analysis also reveals the hypothalamus, the vmPFC and the premotor cortex (see Figure 4). The hypothalamus is known to play a key role in regulating autonomic systems as well as in sustaining complex behavioral responses. Electrical stimulation of the hypothalamus induces typical defensive reactions in

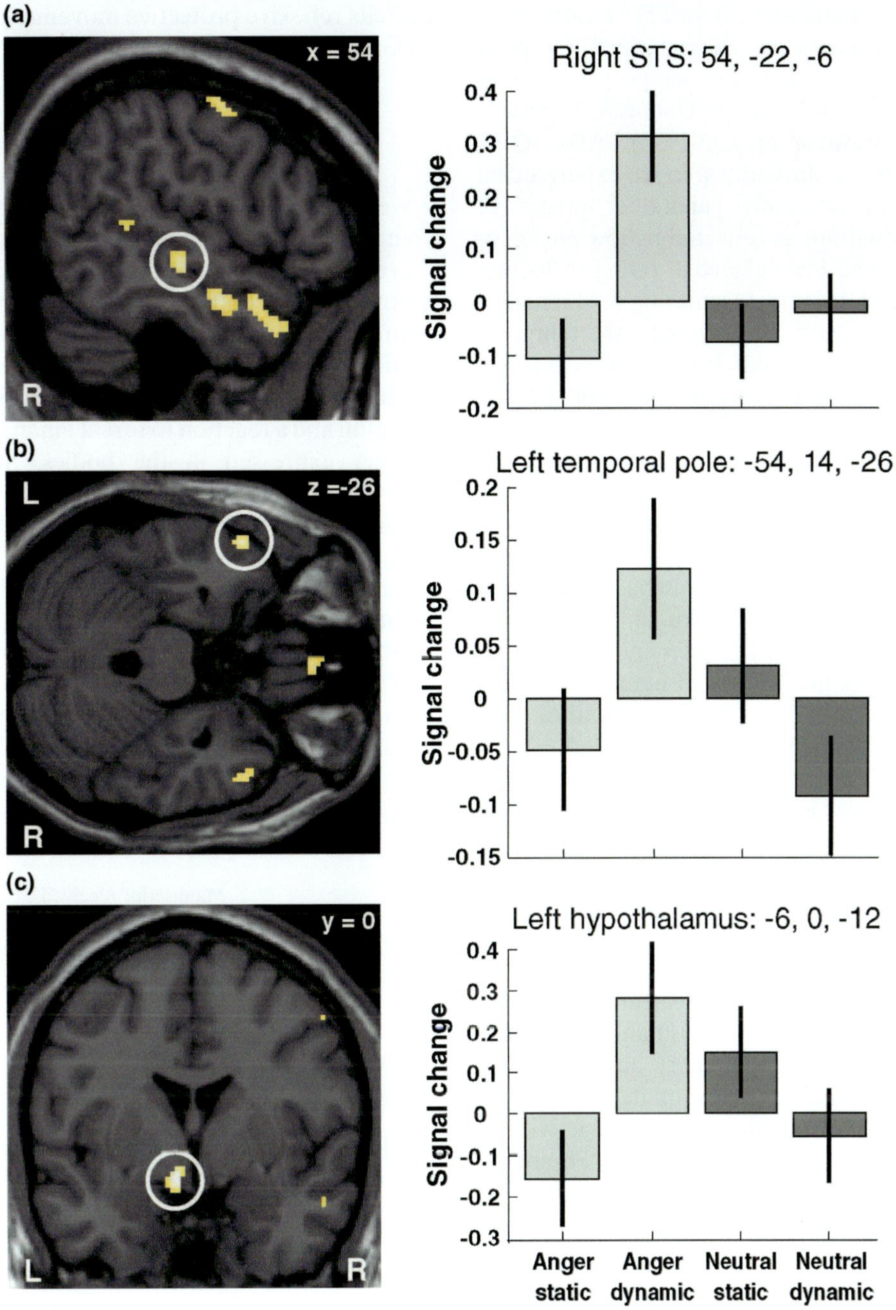

Figure 4. Regions showing amplitude difference when subjects observed dynamic expressions of anger revealed by the interaction. Localization of significant BOLD signal changes and parameter estimates (arbitrary units, mean centered) of the (a) right STS (b) left temporal pole and (c) left hypothalamus. Results superimposed on SPM standard single subject T1-weighted sagittal, axial and coronal sections, results listed in Table 5.

animals (Hess & Akert, 1955) ranging from stereotypical flight to attack (Brown, Hunsperger, & Rosvold, 1969), and aggressive reactions in humans (Bejjani et al., 2002), suggesting that the hypothalamus plays a role in emotional processes by preparing the body for action. Moreover, it was also shown to be elicited during the recall of autobiographic emotional memories (Damasio et al., 2000).

The vmPFC has massive direct excitatory projections onto the hypothalamus (Ongur, An, & Price, 1998) and was suggested to be involved in the regulation of social and aggressive behaviors (Blair, 2004; Damasio, 1994; Davidson, Putnam, &

Larson, 2000). Patients with vmPFC lesions have behavioral impairments characterized by poor personal decision making and inappropriate social behavior (Bechara, Damasio, Damasio, & Anderson, 1994; Grafman et al., 1996). Also, OFC lesions result in difficulties in re-experiencing emotion from internally generated images of emotional situations as reflected by low physiological activity and low subjective rating of feeling the emotion (Bechara, Damasio, & Damasio, 2003). Together with the amygdala, the temporal pole and the hypothalamus, the vmPFC is part of a tightly connected anatomical network in the rhesus monkey (Barbas, Saha, Rempel-Clower, & Ghashghaei, 2003; Ongur & Price, 2000) that appears preferentially linked with the expression of emotional responses by exerting a direct control on autonomic activity in response to threatening stimuli. Against this background, an explanation for the recruitment of this network may be that responding to dynamic signals of anger modulates the activity of neural structures that are involved in the elaboration of autonomic and defensive responses.

Finally, the perception of dynamic body expressions of anger is also associated with specific increased hemodynamic activity in the dorsal premotor cortex. This activation may reflect preparation for action. This interpretation is supported by significant differences in premotor activity when the perception of anger is contrasted to the perception of fearful static facial expressions (Whalen et al., 2001) and by the fact that, in the present study, angry actions clearly involve the precentral gyrus in its dorsal part ($z = 52$), whereas neutral actions elicit activity in the dorsal part of Broca area 44 (see Figure 3). The dorsal premotor cortex is known to be implicated in motor preparation and environmentally triggered actions (Hoshi & Tanji, 2004; Passingham, 1993). Finally, the possibility that activity in the premotor cortex may reflect preparation for action is also supported by the presence of activity in subcortical nuclei, e.g., hypothalamus and amygdala, in response to anger expressions. Subcortical structures such as the periaqueductal grey, hypothalamus and amygdala play an important role in organizing defensive reactions (Panksepp, 1998) and there is evidence of direct projections from the hypothalamus to the amygdala's basal nucleus (Barbas et al., 2003) that projects to the premotor cortex (Avendano, Price, & Amaral, 1983). Interestingly, stimulation of a polysensory zone in the precentral gyrus elicits reflexive protective movements in monkeys (Graziano & Cooke, 2006).

CONCLUSION

We show that viewing whole-body expressions of anger elicits activity in amygdala and fusiform gynes indicating detection and associated modulation of visual cortical areas. Furthermore, taking into account equally strong activation in the lateral OFC, we submit that the activity in these areas may reflect the evaluation of emotionally laden stimuli and a reaction to threat emanating from the anger expressed in the bodies. Strikingly, we observed that anger movies additionally activate viscero-motor areas such as the hypothalamus, the premotor cortex, and the ventromedial prefrontal cortex, which are involved in the elaboration of autonomic and defensive reactions. Our results provide novel insights into the neural substrates of emotion and adaptive action in the face of social threat. They also underscore the importance of using stimuli consisting of emotional expressions by the entire body including biological movement in future neuroimaging investigations of emotional processes.

Manuscript received 31 December 2006
Manuscript accepted 30 March 2007
First published online 25 May 2007

REFERENCES

Adolphs, R., Tranel, D., & Damasio, H. (2001). Emotion recognition from faces and prosody following temporal lobectomy. *Neuropsychology*, *15*, 396–404.

Amaral, D. G. (2003). The amygdala, social behavior, and danger detection. *Annals of the New York Academy of Sciences*, *1000*, 337–347.

Amaral, D. G., Behniea, H., & Kelly, J. L. (2003). Topographic organization of projections from the amygdala to the visual cortex in the macaque monkey. *Neuroscience*, *118*, 1099–1120.

Anderson, A. K., & Phelps, E. A. (2000). Expression without recognition: Contributions of the human amygdala to emotional communication. *Psychological Science*, *11*, 106–111.

Argyle, M. (1988). *Bodily communication* (2nd ed.). New York: Methuen.

Atkinson, A. P., Dittrich, W. H., Gemmell, A. J., & Young, A. W. (2004). Emotion perception from dynamic and static body expressions in point-light and full-light displays. *Perception*, *33*, 717–746.

Avendano, C., Price, J. L., & Amaral, D. G. (1983). Evidence for an amygdaloid projection to premotor

cortex but not to motor cortex in the monkey. *Brain Research, 264*, 111–117.
Barbas, H., Saha, S., Rempel-Clower, N., & Ghashghaei, H. T. (2003). Serial pathways from primate prefrontal cortex to autonomic areas may influence emotional expression. *BMC. Neuroscience, 4*, 25.
Bechara, A., Damasio, A. R., Damasio, H., & Anderson, S. W. (1994). Insensitivity to future consequences following damage to human prefrontal cortex. *Cognition, 50*, 7–15.
Bechara, A., Damasio, H., & Damasio, A. R. (2003). Role of the amygdala in decision-making. *Annals of the New York Academy of Sciences, 985*, 356–369.
Bejjani, B. P., Houeto, J. L., Hariz, M., Yelnik, J., Mesnage, V., Bonnet, A. M., et al. (2002). Aggressive behavior induced by intraoperative stimulation in the triangle of Sano. *Neurology, 59*, 1425–1427.
Berthoz, S., Armony, J. L., Blair, R. J., & Dolan, R. J. (2002). An fMRI study of intentional and unintentional (embarrassing) violations of social norms. *Brain, 125*, 1696–1708.
Blair, R. J. R. (2004). The roles of orbital frontal cortex in the modulation of antisocial behavior. *Brain and Cognition, 55*, 198–208.
Blair, R. J. R., Morris, J. S., Frith, C. D., Perrett, D. I., & Dolan, R. J. (1999). Dissociable neural responses to facial expressions of sadness and anger. *Brain, 122*, 883–893.
Blanchard, D. C., & Blanchard, R. J. (1972). Innate and conditioned reactions to threat in rats with amygdaloid lesions. *Journal of Comparative and Physiological Psychology, 81*, 281–190.
Blanchard, D. C., & Blanchard, R. J. (1988). Ethoexperimental approaches to the biology of emotion. *Annual Review of Psychology, 39*, 43–68.
Bonda, E., Petrides, M., Ostry, D., & Evans, A. (1996). Specific involvement of human parietal systems and the amygdala in the perception of biological motion. *Journal of Neuroscience, 16*, 3737–3744.
Brown, J. L., Hunsperger, R. W., & Rosvold, H. E. (1969). Defence, attack, and flight elicited by electrical stimulation of the hypothalamus of the cat. *Experimental Brain Research, 8*, 113–129.
Damasio, A. R. (1994). *Descartes' error: Emotion, rationality and the human brain*. New York: Grosset/Putnam.
Damasio, A. R., Grabowski, T. J., Bechara, A., Damasio, H., Ponto, L. L., Parvizi, J., et al. (2000). Subcortical and cortical brain activity during the feeling of self-generated emotions. *Nature Neuroscience, 3*, 1049–1056.
Davidson, R. J., Putnam, K. M., & Larson, C. L. (2000). Dysfunction in the neural circuitry of emotion regulation—a possible prelude to violence. *Science, 289*, 591–594.
de Gelder, B. (2006). Towards the neurobiology of emotional body language. *Nature Reviews Neuroscience, 7*, 242–249.
de Gelder, B., Snyder, J., Greve, D., Gerard, G., & Hadjikhani, N. (2004). Fear fosters flight: A mechanism for fear contagion when perceiving emotion expressed by a whole body. *Proceedings of the National Academy of Sciences of the USA, 101*, 16701–16706.
de Meijer, M. (1989). The contribution of general features of body movement to the attribution of emotions. *Journal of Nonverbal Behavior, 13*, 247–268.
Decety, J., & Chaminade, T. (2003). Neural correlates of feeling sympathy. *Neuropsychologia, 41*, 127–138.
Dimberg, U. (1986). Facial expressions as excitatory and inhibitory stimuli for conditioned autonomic responses. *Biological Psychology, 22*, 37–57.
Duvernoy, H. M. (1999). *The human brain: Surface, three-dimensional sectional anatomy with MRI, and blood supply*. Vienna: Springer-Verlag.
Emery, N. J., & Amaral, D. G. (2000). The role of the amygdala in primate social cognition. In R.D. Lane & L. Nadel (Eds.) *Congnitive neuroscience of emotion* (pp. 156–191). New York University Press.
Esslen, M., Pascual-Marqui, R. D., Hell, D., Kochi, K., & Lehmann, D. (2004). Brain areas and time course of emotional processing. *NeuroImage, 21*, 1189–1203.
Fitzgerald, D. A., Angstadt, M., Jelsone, L. M., Nathan, P. J., & Phan, K. L. (2006). Beyond threat: amygdala reactivity across multiple expressions of facial affect. *NeuroImage, 30*, 1441–1448.
Frijda, N. H. (1986). *The emotions*. Cambridge, UK: Cambridge University Press.
Friston, K. J., Holmes, A. P., Worsley, K. J., Poline, J. B., Frith, C. D., & Frackowiak, R. S. J. (1995). Statistical parametric maps in functional imaging: a general linear approach. *Human Brain Mapping, 2*, 189–210.
Grafman, J., Schwab, K., Warden, D., Pridgen, A., Brown, H. R., & Salazar, A. M. (1996). Frontal lobe injuries, violence, and aggression: a report of the Vietnam Head Injury Study. *Neurology, 46*, 1231–1238.
Graziano, M. S., & Cooke, D. F. (2006). Parieto-frontal interactions, personal space, and defensive behavior. *Neuropsychologia, 44*, 845–859.
Grèzes, J., Pichon, S., & de Gelder, B. (2007). Perceiving fear in dynamic body expressions. *NeuroImage 35*, 959–967.
Grosbras, M. H., & Paus, T. (2006). Brain networks involved in viewing angry hands or faces. *Cerebral Cortex, 16*, 1087–1096.
Grossman, E., & Blake, R. (2002). Brain areas active during visual perception of biological motion. *Neuron, 35*, 1167–1175.
Hadjikhani, N., & de Gelder, B. (2003). Seeing fearful body expressions activates the fusiform cortex and amygdala. *Current Biology, 13*, 2201–2205.
Hennenlotter, A., & Schroeder, U. (2006). Partly dissociable neural substrates for recognizing basic emotions: a critical review. *Progress in Brain Research, 156*, 433–456.
Hess, W. R., & Akert, K. (1955). Experimental data on role of hypothalamus in mechanism of emotional behavior. *AMA Archives of Neurology and Psychiatry, 73*, 127–129.
Hornak, J., Rolls, E. T., & Wade, D. (1996). Face and voice expression identification in patients with emotional and behavioural changes following ventral frontal lobe damage. *Neuropsychologia, 34*, 247–261.

Hoshi, E., & Tanji, J. (2004). Functional specialization in dorsal and ventral premotor areas. *Progress in Brain Research, 143*, 507–11.

Kanwisher, N., Stanley, D., & Harris, A. (1999). The fusiform face area is selective for faces not animals. *Neuroreport, 10*, 183–187.

Kesler-West, M. L., Andersen, A. H., Smith, C. D., Avison, M. J., Davis, C. E., Kryscio, R. J., et al. (2001). Neural substrates of facial emotion processing using fMRI. *Brain Research Cognitive Brain Research, 11*, 213–226.

Kilts, C. D., Egan, G., Gideon, D. A., Ely, T. D., & Hoffman, J. M. (2003). Dissociable neural pathways are involved in the recognition of emotion in static and dynamic facial expressions. *NeuroImage, 18*, 156–168.

LaBar, K. S., Crupain, M. J., Voyvodic, J. T., & McCarthy, G. (2003). Dynamic perception of facial affect and identity in the human brain. *Cerebral Cortex, 13*, 1023–1033.

LeDoux, J. E. (2000). Emotion circuits in the brain. *Annual Review of Neuroscience, 23*, 155–184.

McNaughton, N., & Corr, P. J. (2004). A two-dimensional neuropsychology of defense: fear/anxiety and defensive distance. *Neuroscience and Biobehavioral Reviews, 28*, 285–305.

Moran, M. A., Mufson, E. J., & Mesulam, M. M. (1987). Neural inputs into the temporopolar cortex of the rhesus monkey. *Journal of Comparative Neurology, 256*, 88–103.

Morris, J. S., Friston, K. J., Buchel, C., Frith, C. D., Young, A. W., Calder, A. J., et al. (1998). A neuromodulatory role for the human amygdala in processing emotional facial expressions. *Brain, 121*, 47–57.

Murphy, F. C., Nimmo-Smith, I., & Lawrence, A. D. (2003). Functional neuroanatomy of emotions: a meta-analysis. *Cognitive, Affective & Behavioral Neuroscience, 3*, 207–233.

Nakamura, K., Kawashima, R., Ito, K., Sugiura, M., Kato, T., Nakamura, A., et al. (1999). Activation of the right inferior frontal cortex during assessment of facial emotion. *Journal of Neurophysiology, 82*, 1610–1614.

Ongur, D., An, X., & Price, J. L. (1998). Prefrontal cortical projections to the hypothalamus in macaque monkeys. *Journal of Comparative Neurology, 401*, 480–505.

Ongur, D., & Price, J. L. (2000). The organization of networks within the orbital and medial prefrontal cortex of rats, monkeys and humans. *Cerebral Cortex, 10*, 206–219.

Panksepp, J. (1998). *Affective neuroscience: The foundation of human and animal emotions*. New York: Oxford University Press.

Passingham, R. E. (1993). *The frontal lobes and voluntary action*. Oxford: Oxford University Press.

Peelen, M. V., & Downing, P. E. (2005). Selectivity for the human body in the fusiform gyrus. *Journal of Neurophysiology, 93*, 603–608.

Peelen, M. V., Wiggett, A. J., & Downing, P. E. (2006). Patterns of fMRI activity dissociate overlapping functional brain areas that respond to biological motion. *Neuron, 49*, 815–822.

Sato, W., Kochiyama, T., Yoshikawa, S., Naito, E., & Matsumura, M. (2004). Enhanced neural activity in response to dynamic facial expressions of emotion: an fMRI study. *Brain Research Cognitive Brain Research, 20*, 81–91.

Schupp, H. T., Ohman, A., Junghofer, M., Weike, A. I., Stockburger, J., & Hamm, A. O. (2004). The facilitated processing of threatening faces: an ERP analysis. *Emotion, 4*, 189–200.

Schwarzlose, R. F., Baker, C. I., & Kanwisher, N. (2005). Separate face and body selectivity on the fusiform gyrus. *Journal of Neuroscience, 25*, 11055–11059.

Scott, S. K., Young, A. W., Calder, A. J., Hellawell, D. J., Aggleton, J. P., & Johnson, M. (1997). Impaired auditory recognition of fear and anger following bilateral amygdala lesions. *Nature, 385*, 254–257.

Simon, D., Craig, K. D., Miltner, W. H. R., & Rainville, P. (2006). Brain responses to dynamic facial expressions of pain. *Pain, 126*, 309–318.

Sprengelmeyer, R., Rausch, M., Eysel, U. T., & Przuntek, H. (1998). Neural structures associated with recognition of facial expressions of basic emotions. *Proceedings: Biological Sciences, 265*, 1927–1931.

Strauss, M. M., Makris, N., Aharon, I., Vangel, M. G., Goodman, J., Kennedy, D. N., et al. (2005). fMRI of sensitization to angry faces. *NeuroImage, 26*, 389–413.

Vaina, L. M., Solomon, J., Chowdhury, S., Sinha, P., & Belliveau, J. W. (2001). Functional neuroanatomy of biological motion perception in humans. *Proceedings of the National Academy of Sciences of the USA, 98*, 11656–11661.

van de Riet, W. A., Grèzes, J., & de Gelder, B. (2007). Neural correlates of perceiving the facial and the bodily expression simultaneously. *Human Brain Mapping,* Abstract.

Vuilleumier, P., Richardson, M. P., Armony, J. L., Driver, J., & Dolan, R. J. (2004). Distant influences of amygdala lesion on visual cortical activation during emotional face processing. *Nature Neuroscience, 7*, 1271–1278.

Whalen, P. J., Shin, L. M., McInerney, S. C., Fischer, H., Wright, C. I., & Rauch, S. L. (2001). A functional MRI study of human amygdala responses to facial expressions of fear versus anger. *Emotion, 1*, 70–83.

Wildgruber, D., Hertrich, I., Riecker, A., Erb, M., Anders, S., Grodd, W., et al. (2004). Distinct frontal regions subserve evaluation of linguistic and emotional aspects of speech intonation. *Cerebral Cortex, 14*, 1384–1389.

Wildgruber, D., Riecker, A., Hertrich, I., Erb, M., Grodd, W., Ethofer, T., et al. (2005). Identification of emotional intonation evaluated by fMRI. *NeuroImage, 24*, 1233–1241.

Williams, L. M., Brown, K. J., Das, P., Boucsein, W., Sokolov, E. N., Brammer, M. J., et al. (2004). The dynamics of cortico-amygdala and autonomic activity over the experimental time course of fear perception. *Cognitive Brain Research, 21*, 114–123.

SOCIAL NEUROSCIENCE, 2008, 3 (3–4), 213–228

Psychology Press
Taylor & Francis Group

Evidence for fast, low-level motor resonance to action observation: An MEG study

Hein T. van Schie
Radboud University Nijmegen, Nijmegen, The Netherlands

Thomas Koelewijn
Vrije Universiteit, Amsterdam, The Netherlands

Ole Jensen and Robert Oostenveld
F. C. Donders Centre for Cognitive Neuroimaging, Nijmegen, The Netherlands

Eric Maris and Harold Bekkering
Radboud University Nijmegen and F. C. Donders Centre for Cognitive Neuroimaging, Nijmegen, The Netherlands

Lateralized magnetic fields were recorded from 12 subjects using a 151 channel magnetoencephalograpy (MEG) system to investigate temporal and functional properties of motor activation to the observation of goal-directed hand movements by a virtual actor. Observation of left and right hand movements generated a neuromagnetic lateralized readiness field (LRF) over contralateral motor cortex. The early onset of the LRF and the fact that the evoked component was insensitive to the correctness of the observed action suggest the operation of a fast and automatic form of motor resonance that may precede higher levels of action understanding.

INTRODUCTION

During many of our daily activities we observe and interpret the movements, goals and intentions of other people's actions. The exact mechanisms or functional processes that provide the basis for our action-understanding abilities are the subject of increasing scientific study. Central within most contemporary ideas on action understanding is that action recognition is facilitated by motor representations that become activated with perception of the action during observation. Although the idea of using motor representations to facilitate perception is certainly not new (Gibson, 1979), many recent studies have been inspired by the finding of Rizzolatti and colleagues (di Pellegrino, Fadiga, Fogassi, Gallese, & Rizzolatti, 1992; Gallese, Fadiga, Fogassi, & Rizzolatti, 1996; Rizzolatti, Fadiga, Gallese, & Fogassi, 1996a) who found motor neurons in monkey premotor area F5 activated during execution and during the observation of goal-directed actions by another individual. Following the discovery of this particular class of visuo-motor neurons called "mirror neurons", several neuroimaging studies have provided evidence for the existence of a

Correspondence should be addressed to: Hein T. van Schie, Nijmegen Institute for Cognition and Information (NICI), University of Nijmegen, PO Box 9104, NL-6500 HE, Nijmegen, The Netherlands. E-mail: h.vanschie@nici.ru.nl

The present study was supported by the EU-Project "Joint Action Science and Technology" (IST-FP6-003747).
We would also like to thank Ali Mazaheri for assisting source analysis.

www.psypress.com/socialneuroscience DOI:10.1080/17470910701414364

mirror neuron system (MNS) in humans (Buccino et al., 2001; Grafton, Arbib, Fadiga, & Rizzolatti, 1996; Iacoboni et al., 1999; Rizzolatti et al., 1996b) involving Broca's area (the human homologue of monkey area F5) and the intraparietal sulcus (IPS) that are innervated via the superior parietal sulcus (STS) during action observation. Furthermore, neurophysiological studies using TMS (transcranial magnetic stimulation), MEG (magnetoencephalography) and EEG (electroencephalography) have shown activation of the primary motor cortex during action observation (Babiloni et al., 2002; Fadiga, Fogassi, Pavesi, & Rizzolatti, 1995; Hari et al., 1998; Nishitani & Hari, 2000, 2002; Strafella & Paus, 2000; van Schie, Mars, Coles, & Bekkering, 2004), which suggests that motor resonance may actually work its way up through the entire visuo-motor system, from visual input to motor output.

Although the above studies provided consistent evidence for the involvement of motor structures during action observation, still little is known about the functional properties or the nature of the representations contained with in the MNS. Theoretical reviews on the MNS (Gallese, Keysers, & Rizzolatti, 2004; Rizzolatti, Fogassi, & Gallese, 2001) stress both low-level processes such as motor resonance and direct matching, together with high-level functionality of the MNS in terms of action understanding and social cognition. In many of the experiments that have been done, however, it is difficult to determine precisely what type of process (automatic visuo-motor resonance, or higher levels of action understanding) actually caused the effects that were found. The aim of the present study was to investigate the nature of motor representations that become activated with action observation. In particular, we intended to determine if motor resonance to observed actions is sensitive to the correctness of observed behavior, or indifferent.

The ability to classify the outcome of other peoples' actions as correct or incorrect may support social functions such as imitation learning (Heyes, 2001), joint action (Sebanz, Bekkering, & Knoblich, 2006), and nonverbal communication in general. Important for the present study, furthermore, is that sensitivity of motor areas to the correctness of observed behavior could be taken to reflect the involvement of the MNS in higher forms of action understanding. Insensitivity to action correctness on the other hand could reflect the operation of low-level resonance that matches between visual and motor representations without involvement of higher forms of action understanding (Rizzolatti, 2005).

Previous research that compared action observation of correct and incorrect behaviors is both scarce and inconclusive. A recent fMRI study by Manthey et al. (Manthey, Schubotz, & von Cramon, 2003) found that left and right Broca's area and IPS were activated differentially during the observation of object manipulation movies in which objects were either manipulated correctly, with movement errors, or with object errors. These findings suggest that correct and incorrect actions may be processed differentially by the MNS, but conclusions were limited by the fact that movies were not matched well between conditions. Another fMRI study by Pelphrey et al. (Pelphrey, Morris, & McCarthy, 2004) found less activity in posterior STS when subjects passively viewed an animated character making reaching-to-grasp movements toward a blinking dial (correct action), as compared to movements away from the dial (incorrect action). However, differences in STS may have been caused by the "goal-directedness" of grasping actions instead of the "correctness" of the actions, which were confounded in the design.

For the present study we have chosen MEG to study the time-course of motor activation to understand the role of the motor system in distinguishing correct from incorrect behaviors in action observation. MEG captures the magnetic fields produced by electrical activity in the brain on a millisecond by millisecond basis (the same goes for EEG), which may complement neuroimaging techniques such as PET and fMRI that have excellent localization properties, but are limited in the temporal domain. Here, we use MEG to measure the onset latency or speed of motor activation in action observation—motor resonance—and distinguish that from any activation preceding the response—motor anticipation (Kilner, Vargas, Duval, Blakemore, & Sirigu, 2004; van Schie et al., 2004). The speed at which visual information is transited to motor cortex may provide important information on the type of process (automatic or controlled) that underlies motor resonance in action observation. Additionally, sensitivity to the correctness of observed behavior (e.g., reflected in the amplitude or latency of induced motor activation) could help to disambiguate the functional nature (low-level motor resonance or high-level action understanding) of motor activation during action observation.

METHOD

Participants

Twelve healthy participants with no known neurological impairments and normal or corrected-to-normal vision (3 female, 9 male, 6 left-handed, 6 right-handed, age between 22 and 33) participated in the experiment. All participants received 6 euros per hour and provided written consent according to institutional guidelines of the local ethics committee (CMO region Arnhem–Nijmegen, Netherlands). All subjects were treated according to the principles expressed in the Declaration of Helsinki.

Apparatus

Subjects were seated in a 151-channel axial-gradiometer whole-head MEG system (VSM Medtech, Coquitlam, British Columbia, Canada) in a magnetically shielded room. Three marker coils placed at anatomical landmarks (left and right ear canal and nasion) were used to measure subjects' head position before and after the experiment by measuring the magnetic signals produced by currents passed through the coils. Together with MEG, electroencephalograms (EEG) were recorded from the locations C3 and C4 over the left and right motor cortices, respectively, and FCz over medial frontal cortex. Vertical and horizontal electrooculograms (EOG) were recorded bipolarly from electrodes located at the supraorbital and infraorbital ridge of the left eye and lateral to the outer canthus of each eye, respectively. Electromyograms (EMG) were recorded bipolarly on both forearms with electrodes placed in parallel over the muscles controlling flexion (Flexor Digitorum Profundus) and extension (Extensor Digitorum) of the index fingers. EEG, EOG, and EMG signals were all recorded using Ag/AgCl electrodes. Electrode impedances were kept below 5 kOhm. All (MEG, EEG, EOG, and EMG) channels were recorded in parallel with acquisition software on a Linux computer at a sampling rate of 600 samples per second following 150 Hz low-pass filtering.

Two LUMITouch (Photon Control Inc., Baxter, Canada) optical button boxes (one for each hand) were used for recording and monitoring subjects' responses. The two button boxes were placed next to each other in front of the subject (see Figure 1). The position of the boxes was

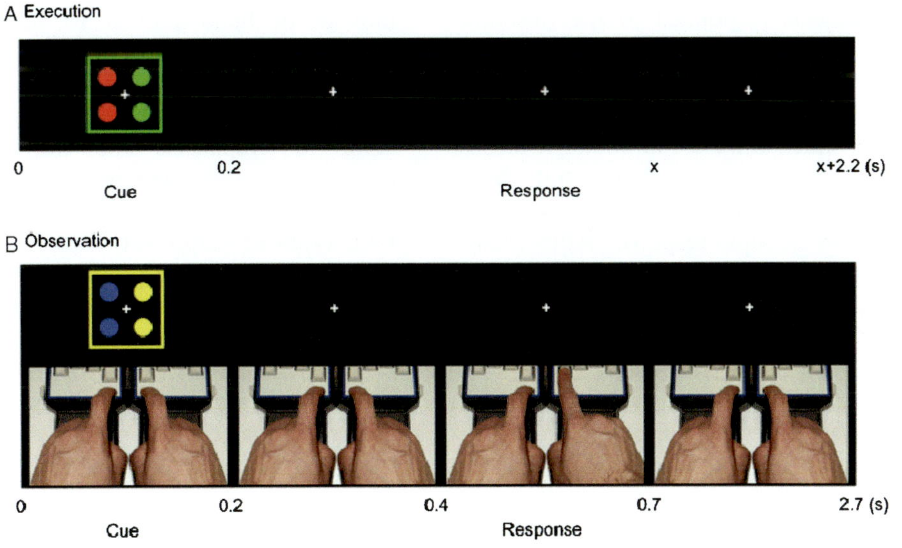

Figure 1. Experimental procedure. (A) Stimuli and timing of events in the execution task. Participants responded to the onset of a cue stimulus that provided instructions on which finger to move to and which action goal. The relevant finger (left/right) and action goal (left/right) were indicated by the two dots that had the same color (green or red) as the surrounding square (green or red). (B) Stimuli and timing of events in the observation task. Subjects were presented with a cue stimulus of which the square color was kept constant during the observation block. In the lower part of the screen two virtual hands were shown continuously in a starting posture. Virtual apparent responses were created by replacing the photograph of the starting posture with a photo showing an end posture in which one of the hands had moved to press a button. Subjects' task during observation was to detect and count occasional errors. Errors could be hand errors (10%), goal errors (10%), or a combination of a hand and goal error (10%). In correct trials (70%) the virtual action was in agreement with the cue instruction.

adjusted so that the subjects had their arms in a comfortable position. The subjects' elbows were supported by cushions to minimize movement of the upper arms. Index fingers of the subjects' left and right hand were placed in a bent posture in front of the buttons to minimize hand movements.

Visual stimuli were projected on a semi-transparent screen (42 × 32 cm) 70 cm in front of the subject via an LCD projector placed outside the room. Stimuli were of two types: cue stimuli (112 × 112 pixels) subtending 4.7 visual degrees and action stimuli (300 × 174 pixels) measuring 12.6 by 7.3 visual degrees in width and height, respectively.

Procedure

The experiment consisted of 11 execution and 11 observation blocks containing 80 trials each. The blocks were presented in an alternating fashion, and the starting order was counterbalanced over the subjects. The first two blocks were used for practice and were not recorded. The duration of the experiment was approximately 75 minutes.

In the execution task the participants were asked to respond both fast and accurately to cue stimuli and to try and avoid correcting errors. During this task, which is represented in Figure 1A, subjects responded to the onset of cue stimuli (200 ms duration) by making ipsi- or contralateral finger movements with their left or right hand to target buttons immediately in front of their index fingers (additional buttons were present on the button boxes but these were irrelevant for the task and not active). See Figure 1B for an example response. After pressing the button subjects returned their index finger to the starting position. Following the button-release a 2000 ms inter-trial interval was presented before start of the next trial.

The cue stimulus consisted of a square with four dots embedded (see Figure 1A) that provided information on the response hand (left/right) and goal location (left/right). Participants were informed that the two dots in the bottom half of the square represented the starting positions of the two index fingers, and that the two dots in the upper half indicated the two target buttons. The color of the square, which could be either red or green, indicated whether to attend to the red or green dots, and to execute the movement in line with the spatial layout of those dots. For example, in Figure 1A the green square emphasizes the green dots, which provide instructions to make an ipsilateral movement with the right index finger to the right target button. The color of the square was randomly varied between trials in execution blocks to enforce execution errors under time pressure. During all blocks a fixation cross was presented continuously aligned to the centre of the cue stimulus.

In the observation task the order of events was chosen to be similar to the execution blocks. Participants were first presented with a 200 ms cue stimulus (see Figure 1). In the lower part of the screen two virtual hands were shown continuously in a starting posture shown from an egocentric perspective. The starting posture of the hands was replaced by a different photo 400 ms after the onset of the cue stimulus. This showed an end posture in which of one of the index fingers pressed one of the buttons, resulting in the apparent motion of a hand moving to press the ipsi- or contralateral button. This action stimulus stayed on for 300 ms after which the starting posture was presented again resulting in the percept of the hand returning to its starting position. The next trial was presented 2000 ms later.

To make sure that subjects kept their attention on the screen and observed responses of the virtual actor, the subject's task was to detect and count occasional errors (e.g., wrong hand moved, or hand moved to the wrong target button, or both). To make the task of the observer as unambiguous as possible the color of the square was kept constant. We chose a yellow color to emphasize the difference between observation and execution blocks. Dots were colored yellow (relevant) and blue (irrelevant). Four types of responses were shown: in 70% of the trials a correct response was shown in which the correct index finger went to the correct target ("hand correct, goal correct"); in 10% of the trials a hand error was shown in which the wrong index finger went to the correct target ("hand incorrect, goal correct"); in 10% of the trials a target error was shown in which the correct index finger went to the wrong target ("hand correct, goal incorrect"); and in 10% of the trials both index finger and target were wrong ("hand incorrect, goal incorrect"). Each observation block started with 8 correct trials, after which the remaining 72 trials were presented in a random order. Subjects were asked to report the number of observed errors at the end of each block. The number of errors was the same in each block. The reports show small deviations in counted errors for each block, which suggests that the subjects were not aware that the number of errors was fixed.

During both execution and observation tasks subjects were asked to keep their eyes on the fixation cross and to minimize blinking. After each block subjects received feedback about their blinking behavior if this was necessary. Subjects rested between blocks. During tasks and during pauses subjects were asked to maintain their head position within the MEG helmet.

Data analysis

Behavioral data were analyzed for reaction times and accuracy. Reaction times reflect the time between the onset of the cue stimulus and the subsequent button press. Analysis of the EMG data was used to determine which hand was moved in each trial. This was done by calculating the average absolute power for each EMG signal in a time window of 500 ms prior to the button press. The strongest signal corresponded to the responding hand. The signal of the moving hand had to be at least twice the power of the stationary hand, otherwise the trial was marked as ambiguous and discarded during preprocessing. The end position of the finger movement was determined by the button that was pressed. Four types of responses were classified based on the correctness of the chosen index finger (correct/incorrect hand) and the correctness of the button press (correct/incorrect goal). Reaction times and accuracy were analyzed separately with repeated measures ANOVAs, using Greenhouse–Geisser corrections where necessary.

MEG data analysis was done using the FieldTrip toolbox that was developed at the F. C. Donders Centre for Cognitive Neuroimaging (http://www.ru.nl/fcdonders/fieldtrip) using Matlab 7.0 (MathWorks, Natick, MA). Due to excessive noise in the EEG signals of 5 subjects EEG data were not further analyzed. MEG data from the execution task and observation task were analyzed separately. Trials containing eye artifacts, movement artifacts, and jump artifacts in the SQUIDs were discarded using semi-automatic artifact rejection routines and remaining trials were low-pass filtered at 30 Hz. For the execution task MEG data were averaged in alignment with the event generated by the button press and in the observation task data were aligned to the presentation of the finger movement. In both cases, the averaging interval ranged from -500 ms ~ 500 ms relative to the action event, with a baseline from -500 ms ~ -400 ms.

As a preprocessing step to calculate asymmetry between left and right motor activation, first an approximation of the planar gradient at each sensor was ascertained by using the MEG signals from the neighboring sensors (Bastiaansen & Knosche, 2000). Typically each sensor has six neighbors (except those in the rim). The contribution to the gradient for a given sensor and a neighboring sensor was calculated by subtracting the difference of the measured fields divided by the distance (~ 4 cm) projected to the horizontal and vertical plane. The horizontal and vertical components of the planar gradients approximate the signal measured by MEG systems with planar gradiometers in which maximal signal power is located above the source (Hämäläinen, Hari, Ilmoniemi, Knuutila, & Lounasmaa, 1993). It should be noted that in comparison to physical planar gradiometers, the noise from the planar gradient approximation used here will be higher. Conversion to planar gradient makes MEG signals suitable for calculating asymmetries in motor activation over the left and right motor cortices comparable to calculating the lateralized readiness potential (LRP) on the basis of ERP data. For the MEG data we will refer to lateralized readiness field (LRF).

The asymmetry between left and right motor activation was estimated separately for trials in which left hand movements were correct and trials in which right hand movements were correct according to the following formula: LRF = [left hand (right hemisphere activation − left hemisphere activation) + right hand (left hemisphere activation − right hemisphere activation)]/2. LRFs were calculated for 71 pairs of bilateral gradiometers to allow a topographical representation of lateralized motor activation, including 142 out of the total of 151 gradiometers. In agreement with existing LRP standards, negative values of the LRF are presented to indicate relative activation of the hemisphere contralateral to the response hand whereas positive values indicate relative activation of the ipsilateral response hand. It should be noted that since we apply the combined planar gradient it is the magnitude of the magnetic fields that are used in the LFR calculations. Thus the actual polarity of the dipolar fields are no longer relevant.

During data analysis we consciously took into account the number of trials per condition.

Because of insufficient trials in two conditions of the execution task, LRFs were calculated pooled over conditions with correct hand movements (93.75% + 0.46%) and conditions with incorrect hand movements (4.48% + 1.16%) to have enough trials per average. (Note that pooling was not required for the observation condition where number of trials per condition were controlled experimentally). The distribution of errors over conditions was found comparable between participants. For the hand incorrect condition a minimum of 10 errors and a maximum of 52 errors were detected with an average of 27 errors per subject (SD=13) that were included in the average. Although with small amounts of trials per average there is always a chance of noise surviving the averaging procedure, the similarity between the incorrect hand average and the correct hand average (the latter being calculated on the basis of 445 trials per subject) in Figure 2A suggests that this was not the case.

Statistical analysis of the difference between LRFs to correct and incorrect hand movements was done using a nonparametric randomization test (Maris, 2004; Nichols & Holmes, 2002) to handle the multiple comparisons problem that arises when performing statistics on a high-dimensional dataset (151 channels; 600 Hz sampling). Below is a brief description of this method. In a first step, the method identified all (sensor, time point-) pairs whose *t*-statistics for the LRF-difference between correct and incorrect exceeded a statistical threshold ($p < .05$, two-sided). The selected (sensor, time point-) pairs were then grouped into a number of clusters in such a way that, within every cluster, the (sensor, time point-) pairs form a set that is connected spatially and/or temporally. Each cluster was assigned a cluster-level test statistic whose value equaled the sum of the (sensor, time point-) specific test statistics. Thus, the cluster-level test statistic depends on both the extent of the cluster and the size (sensor, time-) specific *t*-statistics that belong to this cluster. The Type-I error rate for the complete spatiotemporal data matrix was controlled by evaluating the cluster-level test statistic under the randomization null distribution of the maximum cluster-level test statistic. This randomization null distribution was obtained by randomizing the order of the correct and the incorrect data within every participant. By creating a reference distribution from 500 random draws, the *p*-value was estimated as the proportion from this randomization null distribution in which the maximum cluster-level test statistic exceeded the observed maximum cluster-level test statistic. (This proportion is called a Monte Carlo *p*-value in the statistics literature.) With this number of 500 random draws, our Monte Carlo *p*-value is an accurate estimate of the true *p*-value.

For the statistical analysis of EMG data the absolute power of EMG in the segmentation epoch was pooled across hands and divided into 10 consecutive 100 ms intervals. EMG activation in each interval was tested against the activation in the baseline interval (−500 ms ~ −400 ms before the action event), resulting in nine separate randomization tests for both execution and observation tasks.

Based on the outcome of the statistical analyses of LRFs in the execution and observation tasks a topographical analysis was conducted to compare the distribution of LRFs between the two respective tasks. To test the hypothesis that LRFs found during execution and observation of finger movements have a common neural basis, the overlap in distribution of LRFs in both tasks was investigated with a series of correlation analyses comparing the relative activation per sensor over tasks. *Z*-transformed LRFs were first compared across the entire set of bilateral gradiometers using the average activation per sensor, calculated from the interval in which LRFs were found significant, as entries to calculate a Pearson's correlation. In a second correlation, entries were restricted to contain only the sensors of the cluster that were significant in the randomization analyses. A third analysis further restricted entries to include only significant sensors that exceeded a threshold of 1 *SD* from the average time contributed to the cluster. The eight gradiometers that were found to fulfill this criterion in both tasks were selected and used for displaying the time course of LRF activation. In addition to the above correlation analysis a standard analysis of topography was conducted to compare the distribution of the LRF in both tasks across a 3 by 5 sensor-grid located over sensory-motor cortex where the LRF amplitude was found to be maximal. Normalized LFR data from both tasks averaged over the interval where randomization tests found the LRF to be significant were exported and tested for significance with SPSS 13.0 for windows (SPSS Inc., Chicago, IL) using an ANOVA repeated measures design with Huynh–Feldt correction for sphericity for within-subjects factors Task (Execution, Observation), SensRow (five levels) and SensCol (three levels).

Motor activation accompanying the execution of finger movements was localized in two individual subjects using BESA 5.1.6 (Brain Electrical Source Analysis, MEGIS Software, Germany). BESA uses a spherical head model (Sarvas, 1987) fitted through marker coils at specific anatomical landmarks of the head to determine the sources of magnetic fields (axial, not planar transformed) in Talairach space. Subjects were selected for localization by visual inspection of readiness fields recorded to left and right hand finger movements in the execution and observation conditions. For both conditions readiness fields corresponded with the usual distribution of readiness fields shown in previous studies (e.g., Mayville, Fuchs, & Kelso, 2005). Source localization windows were selected to contain an interval around the response event where readiness fields were continuously identifiable. Magnetic fields accompanying finger movements were localized using a symmetrical source pair in accordance with the known contribution of bilateral motor cortices to unimanual tasks (Kristeva, Cheyne, & Deecke, 1991). One or two additional sources were included in the source model of both subjects to control the influence of signals unrelated to motor activation and optimize the localization of the symmetric sources. Coordinates of source pairs were exported to Brain Voyager QX (Brain Innovation B. V., Maastricht, The Netherlands) to identify the anatomical location of sources in each subject's Talairach transformed structural MRI.

In order to test if motor sources found for the execution condition could also underlie the motor activation in the observation condition, the goodness of the source model's fit in BESA was compared between the execution and the observation conditions. For the observation condition the data intervals for modeling were selected to occur after response presentation from an interval during which readiness fields could be continuously identifiable, comparable with the procedure taken for the execution condition.

RESULTS

Execution condition

The analysis of behavioral data showed that participants generated correct responses in 93.75% of the trials and incorrect responses in 6.25% of all trials. Response times between correct (757 ms) and incorrect responses (833 ms) were not significantly different, $F(1,11) = 3.27$; $p = .098$. Incorrect responses were most often of the "hand incorrect, goal incorrect" type (4.48%, 840 ms), as compared to errors of the other types: "hand incorrect, goal correct" (1.16%, 775 ms) and "hand correct, goal incorrect" (0.46%, 886 ms), $F(1.48,16.29) = 50.86$, $p < .001$. Response time differences between error types were not statistically different, $F(1.67, 11.69) = 0.90$, $p = .414$.

For the analysis of lateralized motor activation in association with left and right hand responses, MEG data were used to calculate LRFs (see materials and methods) and compared between trials in which participants responded with their correct index finger ("hand correct, goal correct" and "hand correct, goal incorrect") and trials in which the incorrect hand was used ("hand incorrect, goal correct" and "hand incorrect, goal incorrect"). For both correct hand and incorrect hand responses LRFs showed stronger activation over motor areas contralateral to the response hand used in the action (see Figure 2A). Randomization tests showed the contrast between correct and incorrect hand actions as a significant cluster over central gradiometers (see Figure 2B) in the interval from -206 ms ~ 47 ms relative to response offset ($p < .002$). The time-course of the LRF is presented in Figure 2C in which lines reflect lateralized motor activation to correct and incorrect hand actions over time, averaged over eight significant channels that contributed maximally to the LRF clusters of both tasks (see "LRF topography" below). In Figure 2C, the LRF to correct hand actions is plotted as a negativity in agreement with the negative polarity of the LRP. Negative values of the LRF reflect stronger activation over the hemisphere that is contralateral to the correct response side. Positive LRF values indicate stronger activation of the hemisphere ipsilateral to the correct response side, e.g., when the index finger of the wrong hand is used.

Randomization tests of the EMG signal (see Figure 2C) recorded during task execution was found statistically different from baseline in the -343 ms ~ 355 ms interval relative to subjects pressing the button on the response box ($p < .02$).

Observation condition

For the analysis of lateralized motor activation in association with the observation of finger

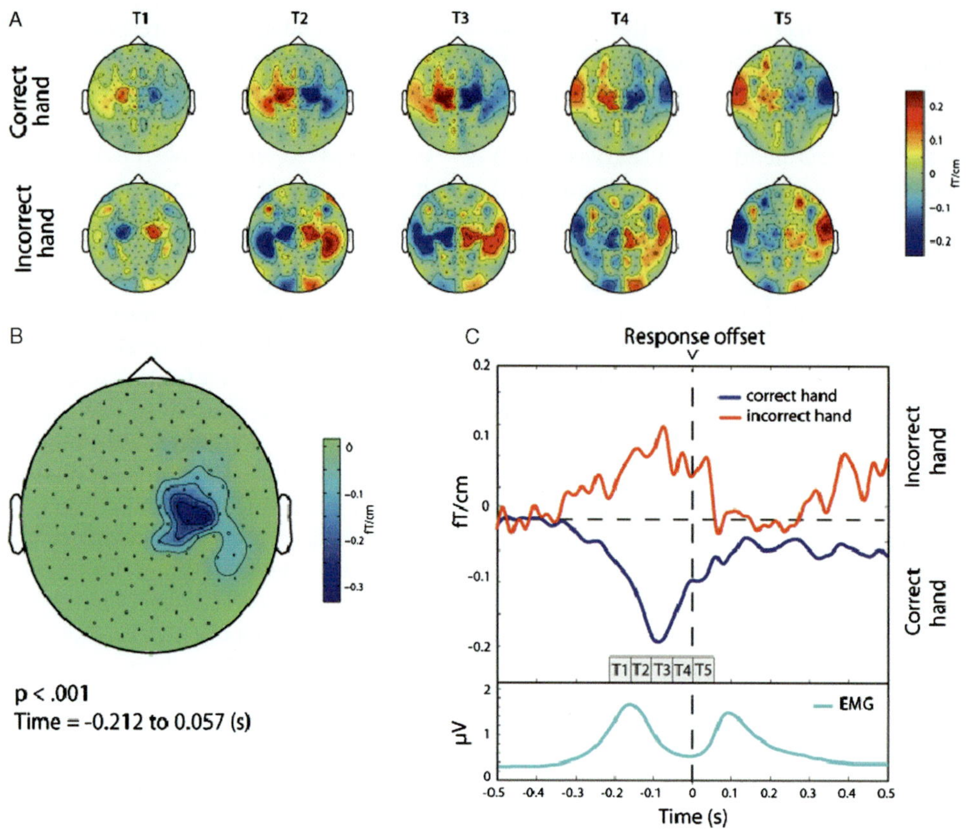

Figure 2. Execution condition. (A) LRF topography in five consecutive windows T1–T5 during which the LRF was found significant. (B) Main statistical cluster reflecting the contrast between LRFs to "hand correct" and "hand incorrect" conditions. (C) LRF time-course for "hand correct" and "hand incorrect" conditions averaged over eight maximally significant channels. In the bottom panel average EMG activation over time is displayed.

movements, LRFs were calculated separately for each of the four response conditions that were presented to the subjects. Randomization test revealed a main effect of Hand (correct hand vs. incorrect hand), significant from 83 ms ~ 498 ms after presentation of the movement ($p < .002$), reflecting stronger activation over motor areas contralateral to the hand that was used in the response. No effects of Goal (correct goal vs. incorrect goal) were found, neither as a main effect ($p > .5$), nor in the individual comparisons between conditions: "hand correct, goal correct" vs. "hand correct, goal incorrect" ($p > .998$) and "hand incorrect, goal correct" vs. "hand incorrect, goal incorrect" ($p > .088$). The latter effect that approached significance was found not over lateral motor areas but over the anterior prefrontal cortex. In Figure 3A the LRFs of the four action observation conditions are presented for five consecutive intervals (T1–T5) during which the main effect of Hand was found significant. The cluster showing the statistical contrast between correct and incorrect hand conditions is plotted in Figure 3B and the LRF time-course of the four action observation LRFs is presented in Figure 3C. In order to be sure that the early onset of the LRF indeed reflected activation over lateral motor areas and not some other region that happened to be included in the statistical cluster, a separate plot was created to reveal the topography of the LRF within the first 17 ms of significance (see Figure 3D).

In order to test for anticipation effects occurring during the cue–response interval, activation in each of the four response conditions was tested against a 100 ms pre-cue baseline period. None of the response conditions showed any significant cluster during the 400 ms cue–response interval (separate test for four consecutive 100 ms cueing intervals) that were tested against baseline.

EMG activation recorded during the observation task (see Figure 2C) was not significantly different from the EMG recorded during the

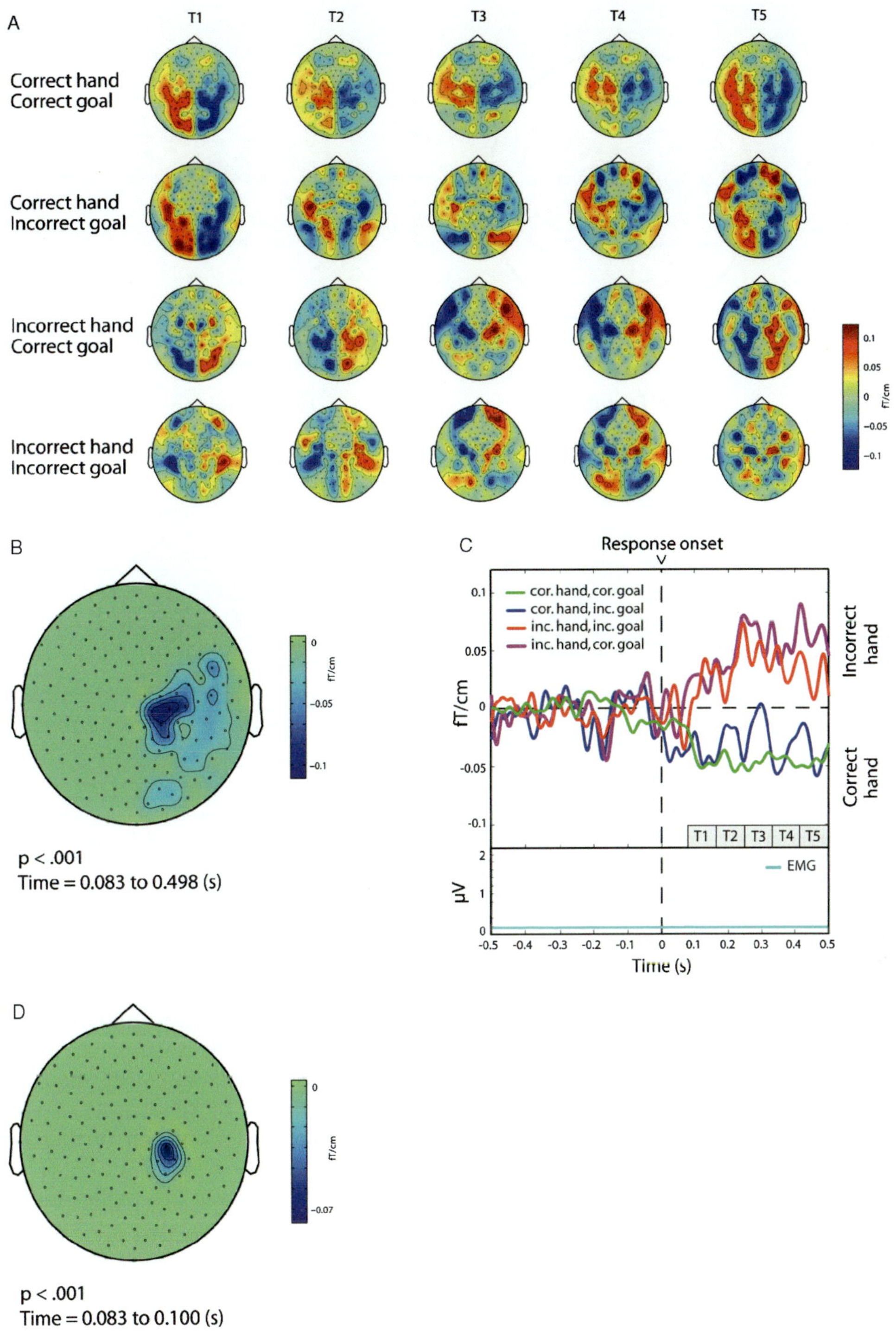

Figure 3. Observation condition. (A) LRF topography in four action observation conditions over a period in which the main effect of "hand correct" versus "hand incorrect" was found significant. (B) Main statistical cluster showing the contrast between "hand correct" and "hand incorrect" conditions. (C) LRF time-course for the four action observation conditions. Traces contain the average of eight channels that maximally contributed to the LRF over time. In the bottom panel average EMG activation is displayed. (D) Topography of the LRF cluster ("hand correct" vs. "hand incorrect" actions) from 83 ms until 100 ms.

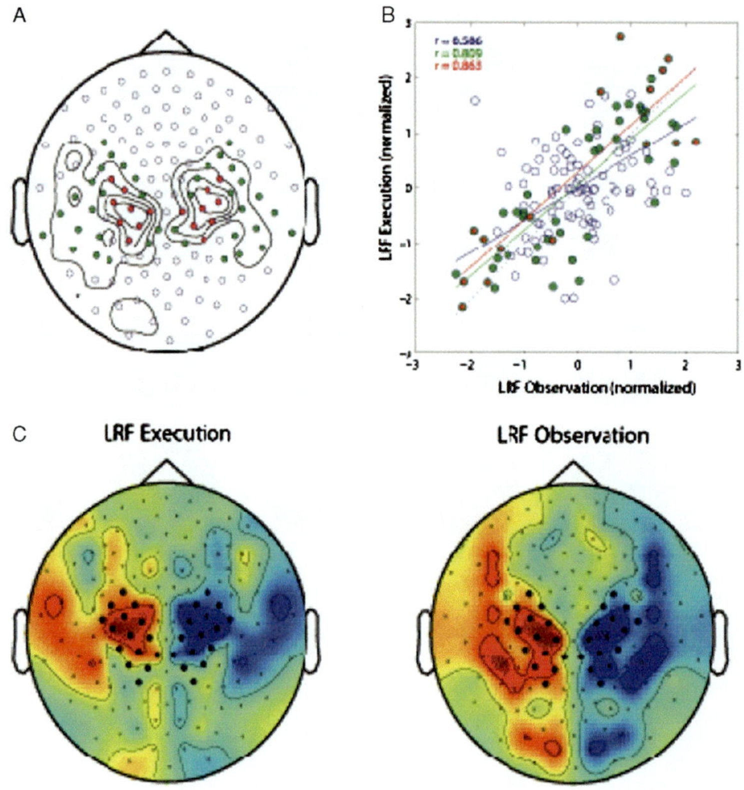

Figure 4. LRF topography. (A) Gradiometer layout showing 27 bilateral sensor pairs (green and red dots) out of 71 bilateral channels that were found in the LRF statistical cluster analysis in both tasks. Red dots represent a set of eight sensors that contributed most consistently over time to LRF clusters in both tasks. Isometric lines show the topography of the LRF statistical contrasts found in the observation task (left) and the execution task (right). (B) Pearson's correlation between normalized LRF topographies in execution and observation tasks, for all bilateral sensors (blue, green, and red), sensors overlapping in the statistical clusters of both tasks (green and red) and a set of eight sensors that contributed most consistently over time in both tasks (red). See Figure 4A for the spatial location of (green and red) sensors. (C) Topography of the LRF in the execution condition (left) and the observation condition (right), with the 3 by 5 sensor grid (black dots) that was used to test for differences in LRF topography between the two tasks.

100 ms pre-cue baseline interval (activation against baseline was tested with nine consecutive 100 ms randomization tests).

LRF topography

In order to test for the overlap between the distribution of the LRF in execution and observation tasks a series of correlation analyses was conducted (Figure 4A and 4B). A first analysis using all 142 lateral sensors indicated a reliable correlation (Pearson's r) between the distribution of the LRF in execution and observation tasks, $r = .586$, $p < .001$ (Figure 4A and 4B, all dots). In a subsequent analysis Pearson's correlation was calculated for a subset of sensors contained by the LRF clusters of both tasks, resulting in a correlation of $r = .809$, $p < .001$ (Figure 4A and 4B, collection of green and red dots). A final correlation analysis was restricted to sensors that contributed maximally over time (expressed as the percentage of time a sensor was activated within the cluster), which further increased the correlation to $r = .863$, $p < .001$ (Figure 4A and 4B, red dots only). The eight gradiometers that were selected on the latter criterion were used for displaying the time course of average LRF activation in Figure 2C and 3C.

In addition to the above correlation analysis an analysis of topography was conducted to compare the distribution of the LRF in both tasks across a 3 by 5 sensor-grid located over sensorimotor cortex, including the set of eight gradiometers identified earlier. Statistics indicated main effects of SensCol, $F(2.83, 11) = 5.84$, $p < .003$, and SensRow, $F(1.31, 11) = 6.28$, $p < .019$, but no interaction with Task was found ($ps > .1$). Figure 4C

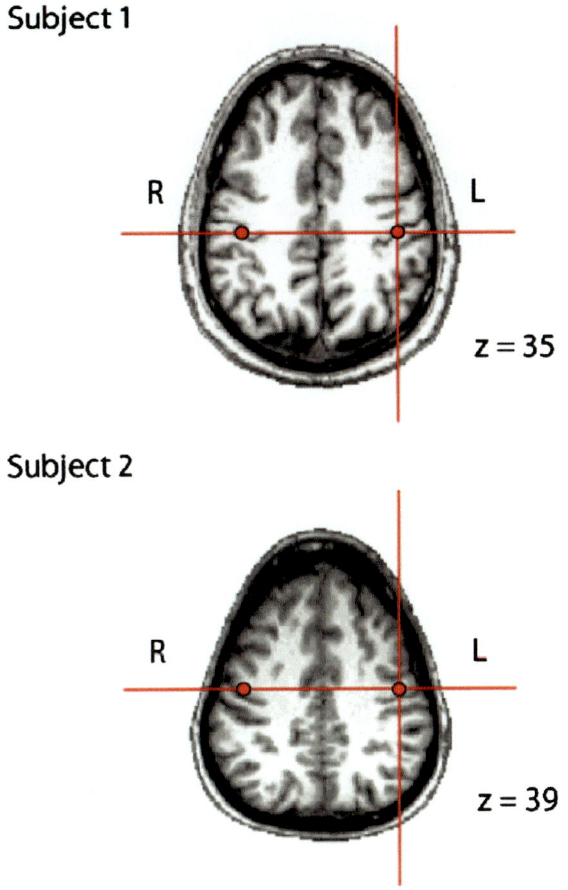

Figure 5. Source localizations of magnetic readiness fields in two subjects fitted on their individual structural MRIs. Sources were localized using BESA (brain electric source analysis). In subject 1 a symmetric pair of regional sources was localized to the subject's left and right central sulci (Talairach coordinates: $x = \pm 43$, $y = -22$, $z = 35$). In subject 2, regional sources were localized to the precentral gyrus (Talairach coordinates: $x = \pm 42$, $y = -18$, $z = 39$). Source models for the execution task also provided a good fit for motor activation evoked in the observation condition (see results section).

shows the average LRF topography for the interval in which the main effect of response hand (correct vs. incorrect) was found significant in the execution (left plot) and observation task (right plot).

Source-localization of readiness fields recorded during execution of finger movements revealed bilateral sources in and anterior to the central sulcus in two respective subjects that were selected for source-analysis (see Figure 5), supporting the generation of readiness fields in left and right primary motor cortex. The source model for the execution condition (goodness of fit: 82% and 83%, respectively) was also found to provide a good fit for the magnetic fields evoked in the observation condition (goodness of fit: 78% and 85%), suggesting similar neural generators in primary motor areas to underlie the readiness fields in both conditions.

DISCUSSION

The aim of our study was to investigate the nature of motor resonance resulting from action observation and to determine if lateral motor activation is in any way sensitive to the correctness of the observed behavior. Results showed LRFs during execution and observation of finger movements, strongest over the sensorimotor areas contralateral to the response hand. During observation, LRFs were found significant already after 83 ms but no statistical difference was found between actions with correct and incorrect action goals. These results are consistent with the existence of a low level form of motor resonance that generates a fast and literal copy for any action that is displayed, irrespective of whether the observed action is correct or erroneous.

LRF methodology and planar gradient

Lateralized measures of motor activation have often been used by electrophysiological (EEG) studies to investigate pre-response selection and covert activation of the motor system. In particular the LRP has been a valuable research tool for many years (Leuthold, Sommer, & Ulrich, 2004) allowing measures of motor activation to reflect, e.g., the temporal organization of response preparation (Osman, Moore, & Ulrich, 2003), motor imagery (Carrillo-de-la-Pena, Lastra-Barreira, & Galdo-Alvarez, 2006), or action observation (van Schie et al., 2004). Whereas EEG studies frequently use the LRP subtraction method, MEG studies typically focus on unlateralized motor activation without applying subtraction. A reason for this is that readiness fields associated with left and right hand movements are not mirror symmetric over the left and right hemispheres (Kristeva et al., 1991) and distribution varies considerably between subjects (Praamstra, Schmitz, Freund, & Schnitzler, 1999) such that cross-hemisphere subtraction, and averaging would result in cancellation of the lateralized field effect.

In the present study we have attempted application of the LRP methodology after transformation of readiness fields to planar gradient

(Bastiaansen & Knosche, 2000). The planar gradient method provides a measure of the steepness of the gradient between the ingoing and outgoing flux around a tangential dipole. The effect of this transformation is that horizontal and vertical components of the planar gradients approximate the signal of MEG systems with planar gradiometers where maximal signal power is measured directly above the source (Hämäläinen et al., 1993). As a result, between hemisphere subtractions can be performed more reliably without chance of cancellation, and averaging over subjects is less sensitive to differences in dipole location and orientation. Planar gradient transformation of axial gradiometer data thus provides a useful method for calculating LRFs as a measure of the balance between ipsi- and contralateral activation of the primary motor cortices.

Source localization and LRF topography

The results of the present study support the general view that similar neural sources are activated during the observation as during the execution of actions. Similar clusters were found to be activated over central motor areas in both conditions. The similarity between the two conditions was supported by (1) a grid analysis that indicated no significant difference to exist between the spatial properties of the LRF distributions of both conditions and (2) a correlation analyses that indicated significant overlap between the spatial distributions of the LRF in both conditions. A subsequent source localization was conducted (1) to confirm the similarity between execution and observation conditions in two single subjects and (2) to replicate earlier MEG studies that localized readiness fields (or Bereitschaftspotentiaal) to primary sensory and motor cortex (Cheyne & Weinberg, 1989; Deecke, Weinberg, & Brickett, 1982; Kristeva et al., 1991). Source localization of readiness fields resulted in bilateral dipole pairs in and just anterior to the left and right central sulcus, in two different subjects that were analyzed. These findings corroborate the results of Praamstra et al. (Praamstra et al., 1999) who showed that individual subjects' source locations of the LRF showed no systematic deviation from the sources to readiness fields, supporting a generation in primary motor cortex. Furthermore, the same sources that accounted for the execution of movements provided a good fit for readiness fields that accompanied the observation of movements in both subjects, supporting a common neural origin in primary motor cortex. These findings are consistent with previous studies that found activation in or attributed activation to primary motor cortex during action observation (Babiloni et al., 2002; Fadiga et al., 1995; Hari et al., 1998; Nishitani & Hari, 2000, 2002; Strafella & Paus, 2000; van Schie et al., 2004).

Absence of motor anticipation

Kilner and colleagues (Kilner et al., 2004) have recently shown that knowledge of an upcoming response may generate a readiness potential in the observer, suggesting that subjects may represent upcoming actions of others in the form of covert motor preparation. Van Schie et al. (2004) in addition found lateralized activation of the motor system in anticipation of left and right hand actions of another person. In the present study, however, no significant motor lateralization was found following the cue (see Figure 3C). The earliest activation that was found was after presentation of the virtual movement. It is important to note that this activation was caused by the observed movement and not by subjects' anticipation of the upcoming movement. Motor activation was found lateralized as a function of the side of the observed response hand (i.e., stronger activation over the left motor cortex to the observation of a right-hand action), irrespective of whether the cue had indicated a right- or a left-hand action.

Several reasons may be considered for the absence of motor anticipation in the present study. One particular difference between the current study and the previous study of van Schie et al. (2004) is that the latter study used an arrow cue to indicate the side of the upcoming correct response. According to Eimer (1995), arrow cues, but not non-spatial forms of cueing (e.g., color cueing), may automatically trigger response activation, resulting in an LRP effect, when cues share a spatial property with a subsequent response. The strength of the automatic response activation relies on the amount of overlap between (spatial) properties of the stimulus and the response (Hommel & Prinz, 1997; Kornblum, Hasbroucq, & Osman, 1990) and the nature of the stimulus involved. That is, response activation is usually strongest if the spatial information carried by a cue is largely overlearned, as is the case with arrows and directional words, but not when stimuli are only arbitrarily or symbolically associated with a specific response, e.g., when color or individual letters are used (Wascher, Reinhard, Wauschkuhn, & Verleger, 1999). Furthermore, Hommel (1994) showed that the spatial S–R compatibility effect disappears when more complex stimuli were used that required a longer identification process. These findings suggest that the absence of lateralized motor anticipation in the present study could be an immediate consequence of the (less direct and the more complex) type of cueing that was used. The 400 ms cue-response interval used in the present design was probably too short to reveal any (non-automatic) motor anticipation in the direction of the correct response. Further study is necessary to determine if more controlled forms of directional motor anticipation may develop under less-stringent temporal constraints.

Automaticity and speed of evoked motor activation

Speed of motor activation to action observation may reveal important clues on the automaticity or controlled nature of motor resonance in primary motor cortex. Evoked magnetic fields recorded in response to left and right virtual finger movements showed a fast contralateral activation over the observers' motor cortex in the form of an LRF. The effect was found significant after 83 ms, consistent with the operation of an automatic process linking the observed hand movement to the contralateral motor cortex. Previous ERP and MEG studies have used lateralized motor activation to investigate automatic response activation evoked by different types of (non-biological) directional stimuli. Studies that used arrows for directional cueing typically found lateralized motor activation to onset between 200 and 250 ms following the presentation of the arrow (Eimer, 1995; Masaki, Takasawa, & Yamazaki, 2000; Praamstra et al., 1999; Rodriguez-Fornells, Kurzbuch, & Munte, 2002; van Schie et al., 2004; Wascher et al., 1999; Willemssen, Hoormann, Hohnsbein, & Falkenstein, 2004), and studies that used peripheral stimuli to investigate spatial congruency between stimuli and responses have found lateralized motor activation to onset as early as 150 ms after stimulus onset (De Jong, Liang, & Lauber, 1994; Kato, Endo, Kizuka, & Asami, 2006; Sturmer, Leuthold, Soetens, Schroter, & Sommer, 2002).

The even earlier latency of the LRF in the present study may be contingent on the biological nature of the stimulus that was used, as compared to the more symbolic types of cueing (e.g., arrow cueing) that are usually employed. Consistent with the special case of biological information, cueing experiments have shown reflexive shifts of attention to changes in gaze direction (Friesen, Ristic, & Kingstone, 2004), and body shadow (Galfano & Pavani, 2005) revealing facilitative effects as early as 50 ms after presentation of the cue. These results are typically interpreted to reflect the operation of specialized neural mechanisms for perception of biological motion in the superior temporal sulcus (STS; Allison, Puce, & McCarthy, 2000; Kingstone, Tipper, Ristic, & Ngan, 2004). Not surprisingly, STS is considered a major input for mirror neuron areas in inferior parietal and ventral premotor cortex (Keysers & Perrett, 2004), creating a pathway for the processing of visual and motor features of observed actions.

Nishitani and Hari investigated cortical activation evoked by different types of biological stimuli using MEG. In a recent study they showed peak activation to photos of lip forms to proceed in a serial manner from occipital visual areas to primary motor cortex via subsequent activation of STS, inferior parietal cortex, and Broca's region in the inferior frontal lobe, revealing sequential activation within the respective parts of the mirror neuron system (Nishitani & Hari, 2002). The entire sequence of activation took between 220 and 250 ms to proceed from occipital to primary motor cortex. Comparable, but slightly slower transmission times (approximately 250 ms from occipital to primary motor cortex) were found in another study by Nishitani and Hari (2000) investigating action observation and imitation of a live experimenter pinching a manipulandum. Interestingly, although it is difficult to compare directly between the present study and the results of Nishitani and Hari, the onset of motor activation in present study appears to be much faster than the peak latencies reported by Nishitani and Hari, suggesting that these studies tap into different functional processes. As a speculative explanation for the temporal differences in activation we suggest the possibility that the experiments of Nishitani and Hari may have yielded a measure of controlled (perhaps higher level) activation within the MNS, whereas the present approach provided a registration of automatic (lower level) resonance of the MNS.

High-level and low-level resonance mechanisms

Consistent with the above classification of the LRF as an automatic form of motor resonance, lateralized motor activation was found to be insensitive to the correctness of the observed response. LRFs remained sensitive to the response side of the observed hand movements (correct and incorrect hands activating motor areas in opposite hemispheres), but no difference was found between LRFs evoked by movements towards correct and incorrect action goals. Although these results support the hypothesis that early motor activation in the primary motor cortex is insensitive to the correctness of the behavior that is observed, this cannot be taken to reflect that the MNS as a whole would be insensitive to the correctness of observed behavior. The present results only inform us about early activation originating from the primary motor area. Any non-lateralized activation was removed by the cross-hemisphere subtraction procedure used for calculating the LRF. Interestingly, a time-frequency analysis, using data of the present study (Koelewijn et al., submitted), revealed differences between correct and incorrect actions in beta power as reflected in the amplitude of ERS/ERD (event-related synchronization and de-synchronization) responses over premotor and primary motor areas during action observation. Importantly, effects of action correctness were found at a latency that exceeded the present effects with several hundred milliseconds. These findings suggest the operation of two separate processes: one fast and automatic process that provides a literal copy of the observed action, irrespective of the correctness of the behavior that is observed, followed by a higher level cognitive process that includes an evaluative component operating at a slower pace.

In accordance with the existence of two separate processes for action observation, theoretical accounts have distinguished between low-level and high-level forms of resonance (Rizzolatti, Fadiga, Fogassi, & Gallese, 2002). Low-level motor resonance may be considered a basic mechanism of direct matching between perception and action without the need for action understanding. In shore birds, e.g., the observation of wing flapping by one individual may trigger the entire flock to fly off (Thorpe, 1963). In humans, a comparable innate mechanism may support the capacity of newborns to imitate facial gestures (Meltzoff & Moore, 1977), or contagious yawning (Schurmann et al., 2005). Furthermore, nonconscious mimicry of gestures, postures, and mannerisms in social conditions is believed to occur because of automatic perception–action matching between individuals (Chartrand & Bargh, 1999).

Whereas low-level matching between perception and action may operate entirely on the basis of peripheral sensorimotor coupling (Fuster, 2004), more complex forms of action understanding probably require resonance at higher functional levels of description. In particular, the capacity to recognize the goal of an action (and not just its means), could reflect action understanding at a higher cognitive level (Hurley, 2005). In accordance with this suggestion, two different classes of mirror neurons have been identified. One class of mirror neurons shows a strict congruence between action observation and action execution at the level of the motor act (e.g., the neuron will only respond to observation or execution of a precision grip with the hand). For other neurons, however, congruence is much broader and is confined to the goal of the action (e.g., broadly congruent mirror neurons may become activated to observation of precision and whole-hand grasping, or even to seeing a grasping action with an entirely different effector, i.e., the mouth; see Fogassi & Gallese, 2002, for a review). These findings in monkeys are consistent with the existence of two different levels of motor resonance: one strictly matching the action means, the other matching higher cognitive aspects of the observed action (Rizzolatti, 2005).

Conclusion

In sum, the present results provided evidence for the existence of a fast and automatic form of motor resonance in primary motor cortex that is insensitive to the correctness of observed behavior. This low-level form of motor resonance may be distinguished from higher-level action understanding within the MNS operating at a slower pace.

Manuscript received 6 December 2006
Manuscript accepted 22 March 2007
First published online 14 May 2007

REFERENCES

Allison, T., Puce, A., & McCarthy, G. (2000). Social perception from visual cues: role of the STS region. *Trends in Cognitive Science*, *4*(7), 267–278.

Babiloni, C., Babiloni, F., Carducci, F., Cincotti, F., Cocozza, G., Del Percio, C., et al. (2002). Human cortical electroencephalography (EEG) rhythms during the observation of simple aimless movements: a high-resolution EEG study. *NeuroImage*, *17*(2), 559–572.

Bastiaansen, M. C., & Knosche, T. R. (2000). Tangential derivative mapping of axial MEG applied to event-related desynchronization research. *Clinical Neurophysiology*, *111*(7), 1300–1305.

Buccino, G., Binkofski, F., Fink, G. R., Fadiga, L., Fogassi, L., Gallese, V., et al. (2001). Action observation activates premotor and parietal areas in a somatotopic manner: an fMRI study. *European Journal of Neuroscience*, *13*(2), 400–404.

Carrillo-de-la-Pena, M. T., Lastra-Barreira, C., & Galdo-Alvarez, S. (2006). Limb (hand vs. foot) and response conflict have similar effects on event-related potentials (ERPs) recorded during motor imagery and overt execution. *European Journal of Neuroscience*, *24*(2), 635–643.

Chartrand, T. L., & Bargh, J. A. (1999). The chameleon effect: the perception–behavior link and social interaction. *Journal of Personality and Social Psychology*, *76*(6), 893–910.

Cheyne, D., & Weinberg, H. (1989). Neuromagnetic fields accompanying unilateral finger movements: pre-movement and movement-evoked fields. *Experimental Brain Research*, *78*(3), 604–612.

De Jong, R., Liang, C. C., & Lauber, E. (1994). Conditional and unconditional automaticity: a dual-process model of effects of spatial stimulus–response correspondence. *Journal of Experimental Psychology: Human Perception and Performance*, *20*(4), 731–750.

Deecke, L., Weinberg, H., & Brickett, P. (1982). Magnetic fields of the human brain accompanying voluntary movement: Bereitschaftsmagnetfeld. *Experimental Brain Research*, *48*(1), 144–148.

di Pellegrino, G., Fadiga, L., Fogassi, L., Gallese, V., & Rizzolatti, G. (1992). Understanding motor events: a neurophysiological study. *Experimental Brain Research*, *91*(1), 176–180.

Eimer, M. (1995). Stimulus–response compatibility and automatic response activation: evidence from psychophysiological studies. *Journal of Experimental Psychology: Human Perception and Performance*, *21*(4), 837–854.

Fadiga, L., Fogassi, L., Pavesi, G., & Rizzolatti, G. (1995). Motor facilitation during action observation: a magnetic stimulation study. *Journal of Neurophysiology*, *73*(6), 2608–2611.

Fogassi, L., & Gallese, V. (2002). The neural correlates of action understanding in non-human primates. In M. I. Stamenov & V. Gallese (Eds.), *Mirror neurons and the evolution of brain and language* (pp. 13–36). Philadelphia: John Benjamins.

Friesen, C. K., Ristic, J., & Kingstone, A. (2004). Attentional effects of counterpredictive gaze and arrow cues. *Journal of Experimental Psychology: Human Perception and Performance*, *30*(2), 319–329.

Fuster, J. M. (2004). Upper processing stages of the perception–action cycle. *Trends in Cognitive Science*, *8*(4), 143–145.

Galfano, G., & Pavani, F. (2005). Long-lasting capture of tactile attention by body shadows. *Experimental Brain Research*, *166*(3–4), 518–527.

Gallese, V., Fadiga, L., Fogassi, L., & Rizzolatti, G. (1996). Action recognition in the premotor cortex. *Brain*, *119*(2), 593–609.

Gallese, V., Keysers, C., & Rizzolatti, G. (2004). A unifying view of the basis of social cognition. *Trends in Cognitive Science*, *8*(9), 396–403.

Gibson, J. J. (1979). *The ecological approach to visual perception*. Boston: Houghton Mifflin.

Grafton, S. T., Arbib, M. A., Fadiga, L., & Rizzolatti, G. (1996). Localization of grasp representations in humans by positron emission tomography. 2. Observation compared with imagination. *Experimental Brain Research*, *112*(1), 103–111.

Hämäläinen, M. S., Hari, R., Ilmoniemi, R. J., Knuutila, J., & Lounasmaa, O. V. (1993). Magnetoencephalography—Theory, instrumentation, and applications to non-invasive studies of the working human brain. *Reviews of Modern Physics*, *65*, 413–497.

Hari, R., Forss, N., Avikainen, S., Kirveskari, E., Salenius, S., & Rizzolatti, G. (1998). Activation of human primary motor cortex during action observation: a neuromagnetic study. *Proceedings of the National Academy of Science of the USA*, *95*(25), 15061–15065.

Heyes, C. (2001). Causes and consequences of imitation. *Trends in Cognitive Science*, *5*(6), 253–261.

Hommel, B. (1994). Effects of irrelevant spatial S R compatibility depend on stimulus complexity. *Psychological Research*, *56*(3), 179–184.

Hommel, B., & Prinz, W. (1997). *Theoretical issues in stimulus–response compatibility*. Amsterdam: North-Holland.

Hurley, S. (2005). The shared circuits hypothesis: A unified functional architecture for control, imitation, and simulation. In S. Hurley & N. Chater (Eds.), *Perspectives on imitation: From neuroscience to social science* (Vol. 1, pp. 177–194). Cambridge, MA: MIT Press.

Iacoboni, M., Woods, R. P., Brass, M., Bekkering, H., Mazziotta, J. C., & Rizzolatti, G. (1999). Cortical mechanisms of human imitation. *Science*, *286*(5449), 2526–2528.

Kato, Y., Endo, H., Kizuka, T., & Asami, T. (2006). Automatic and imperative motor activations in stimulus–response compatibility: magnetoencephalographic analysis of upper and lower limbs. *Experimental Brain Research*, *168*(1–2), 51–61.

Keysers, C., & Perrett, D. I. (2004). Demystifying social cognition: a Hebbian perspective. *Trends in Cognitive Science*, *8*(11), 501–507.

Kilner, J. M., Vargas, C., Duval, S., Blakemore, S. J., & Sirigu, A. (2004). Motor activation prior to observation of a predicted movement. *Nature Neuroscience*, *7*(12), 1299–1301.

Kingstone, A., Tipper, C., Ristic, J., & Ngan, E. (2004). The eyes have it!: an fMRI investigation. *Brain Cognition*, *55*(2), 269–271.

Kornblum, S., Hasbroucq, T., & Osman, A. (1990). Dimensional overlap: Cognitive basis for stimulus–response compatibility: A model and taxonomy. *Psychological Review*, *97*(2), 253–270.

Kristeva, R., Cheyne, D., & Deecke, L. (1991). Neuromagnetic fields accompanying unilateral and bilateral voluntary movements: Topography and analysis of cortical sources. *Electroencephalography and Clinical Neurophysiology*, *81*(4), 284–298.

Leuthold, H., Sommer, W., & Ulrich, R. (2004). Preparing for action: inferences from CNV and LRP. *Journal of Psychophysiology*, *18*, 77–88.

Manthey, S., Schubotz, R. I., & von Cramon, D. Y. (2003). Premotor cortex in observing erroneous action: an fMRI study. *Brain Research Cognitive Brain Research*, *15*(3), 296–307.

Maris, E. (2004). Randomization tests for ERP topographies and whole spatiotemporal data matrices. *Psychophysiology*, *41*(1), 142–151.

Masaki, H., Takasawa, N., & Yamazaki, K. (2000). An electrophysiological study of the locus of the interference effect in a stimulus–response compatibility paradigm. *Psychophysiology*, *37*(4), 464–472.

Mayville, J. M., Fuchs, A., & Kelso, J. A. (2005). Neuromagnetic motor fields accompanying self-paced rhythmic finger movement at different rates. *Experimental Brain Research*, *166*(2), 190–199.

Meltzoff, A. N., & Moore, M. K. (1977). Imitation of facial and manual gestures by human neonates. *Science*, *198*(4312), 74–78.

Nichols, T. E., & Holmes, A. P. (2002). Nonparametric permutation tests for functional neuroimaging: a primer with examples. *Human Brain Mapping*, *15*(1), 1–25.

Nishitani, N., & Hari, R. (2000). Temporal dynamics of cortical representation for action. *Proceedings of the National Academy of Sciences of the USA*, *97*(2), 913–918.

Nishitani, N., & Hari, R. (2002). Viewing lip forms: cortical dynamics. *Neuron*, *36*(6), 1211–1220.

Osman, A., Moore, C. M., & Ulrich, R. (2003). Temporal organization of covert motor processes during response selection and preparation. *Biological Psychology*, *64*(1–2), 47–75.

Pelphrey, K. A., Morris, J. P., & McCarthy, G. (2004). Grasping the intentions of others: the perceived intentionality of an action influences activity in the superior temporal sulcus during social perception. *Journal of Cognitive Neuroscience*, *16*(10), 1706–1716.

Praamstra, P., Schmitz, F., Freund, H. J., & Schnitzler, A. (1999). Magneto-encephalographic correlates of the lateralized readiness potential. *Brain Research Cognitive Brain Research*, *8*(2), 77–85.

Rizzolatti, G. (2005). The mirror-neuron system and imitation. In S. Hurley & N. Chater (Eds.), *Perspectives on imitation: From neuroscience to social science* (Vol. 1, pp. 55–76). Cambridge, MA: MIT Press.

Rizzolatti, G., Fadiga, L., Fogassi, L., & Gallese, V. (2002). From mirror neurons to imitation, facts, and speculations. In A. N. Meltzoff & W. Prinz (Eds.), *The imitative mind: development, evolution, and brain bases* (pp. 247–266). Cambridge, UK: Cambridge University Press.

Rizzolatti, G., Fadiga, L., Gallese, V., & Fogassi, L. (1996a). Premotor cortex and the recognition of motor actions. *Brain Research Cognitive Brain Research*, *3*(2), 131–141.

Rizzolatti, G., Fadiga, L., Matelli, M., Bettinardi, V., Paulesu, E., Perani, D., et al. (1996b). Localization of grasp representations in humans by PET: 1. Observation versus execution. *Experimental Brain Research*, *111*(2), 246–252.

Rizzolatti, G., Fogassi, L., & Gallese, V. (2001). Neurophysiological mechanisms underlying the understanding and imitation of action. *Nature Reviews Neuroscience*, *2*(9), 661–670.

Rodriguez-Fornells, A., Kurzbuch, A. R., & Munte, T. F. (2002). Time course of error detection and correction in humans: neurophysiological evidence. *Journal of Neuroscience*, *22*(22), 9990–9996.

Sarvas, J. (1987). Basic mathematical and electromagnetic concepts of the biomagnetic inverse problem. *Physics in Medicine and Biology*, *32*(1), 11–22.

Schurmann, M., Hesse, M. D., Stephan, K. E., Saarela, M., Zilles, K., Hari, R., et al. (2005). Yearning to yawn: the neural basis of contagious yawning. *NeuroImage*, *24*(4), 1260–1264.

Sebanz, N., Bekkering, H., & Knoblich, G. (2006). Joint action: bodies and minds moving together. *Trends in Cognitive Science*, *10*(2), 70–76.

Strafella, A. P., & Paus, T. (2000). Modulation of cortical excitability during action observation: a transcranial magnetic stimulation study. *Neuroreport*, *11*(10), 2289–2292.

Sturmer, B., Leuthold, H., Soetens, E., Schroter, H., & Sommer, W. (2002). Control over location-based response activation in the Simon task: behavioral and electrophysiological evidence. *Journal of Experimental Psychology: Human Perception and Performance*, *28*(6), 1345–1363.

Thorpe, W. H. (1963). *Learning and instinct in animals* (2nd ed.). London: Methuen.

van Schie, H. T., Mars, R. B., Coles, M. G., & Bekkering, H. (2004). Modulation of activity in medial frontal and motor cortices during error observation. *Nature Neuroscience*, *7*(5), 549–554.

Wascher, E., Reinhard, M., Wauschkuhn, B., & Verleger, R. (1999). Spatial S–R compatibility with centrally presented stimuli. An event-related asymmetry study on dimensional overlap. *Journal of Cognitive Neuroscience*, *11*(2), 214–229.

Willemssen, R., Hoormann, J., Hohnsbein, J., & Falkenstein, M. (2004). Central and parietal event-related lateralizations in a flanker task. *Psychophysiology*, *41*(5), 762–771.

SOCIAL NEUROSCIENCE, 2008, 3 (3–4), 229–238

Psychology Press
Taylor & Francis Group

Modulation of the FFA and PPA by language related to faces and places

Lisa Aziz-Zadeh

University of California and International Computer Science Institute, Berkeley, and University of Southern California, Los Angeles, California, USA

Christian J. Fiebach

University of California, Berkeley, California, USA, and University of Heidelberg, Heidelberg, Germany

Srini Naranayan, Jerome Feldman, and Ellen Dodge

University of California, and USA International Computer Science Institute, Berkeley, California, USA

Richard B. Ivry

University of California, Berkeley, California, USA

Does sentence comprehension related to faces modulate activity in the fusiform face area (FFA) and does sentence comprehension related to places modulate activity in the parahippocampal place area (PPA)? We investigated this question in an fMRI experiment. Participants listened to sentences describing faces, places, or objects, with the latter serving as a control condition. In a separate run, we localized the FFA and PPA in each participant using a perceptual task. We observed a significant interaction between the region of interest (FFA vs. PPA) and sentence type (face vs. place). Activity in the left FFA was modulated by face sentences and in the left PPA was modulated by place sentences. Surprisingly, activation in each region of interest was *reduced* when listening to sentences requiring semantic analysis related to that region's domain specificity. No modulation was found in the corresponding right hemisphere ROIs. We conclude that processing sentences may involve inhibition of some visual processing areas in a content-specific manner. Furthermore, our data indicate that this semantic-based modulation is restricted to the left hemisphere. We discuss how these results may constrain neural models of embodied semantics.

INTRODUCTION

The theory of embodied semantics states that conceptual representations accessed during linguistic processing include sensory and/or motor representations related to the concept in question (Barsalou, 1999; Feldman & Narayanan, 2004; Gallese & Lakoff, 2005; Glenberg, 1997; Glenberg

Correspondence should be addressed to: Lisa Aziz-Zadeh, University of Southern California, 3641 Watt Way, Ste. B20, Los Angeles, CA 90089–2520, USA. E-mail: lisa.azizzadeh@usc.edu

This study was supported by a NIH grant (P01 NS40813) and the Klaus Tschira Foundation. CJF was supported by an Emmy-Noether grant from the German Research Foundation (DFG).

We thank Stephen M. Wilson and Miriam R. L. Petruck for their assistance with this study and members of Mark D'Esposito's laboratory at UC Berkeley for providing stimuli for the localizer task.

www.psypress.com/socialneuroscience DOI:10.1080/17470910701414604

& Kaschak, 2002; Lakoff & Johnson, 1999). This idea has been supported by studies showing activation in motor areas during the comprehension of action phrases (Aziz-Zadeh, Wilson, Rizzolatti, & Iacoboni, 2006; Hauk, Johnsrude, & Pulvermuller, 2004; Hauk & Pulvermuller, 2004; Tettamanti et al., 2005). Moreover, the activation in premotor cortex is, to some degree, somatotopic. For example, phrases such as "grasping" activate premotor areas responsive to hand actions while phrases such as "kicking" activate premotor areas responsive to foot actions. Thus, premotor areas engaged during action production also respond during action observation (Buccino et al., 2001; Wheaton, Thompson, Syngeniotis, Abbott, & Puce, 2004) and during language-based action comprehension (Aziz-Zadeh et al., 2006; Hauk et al., 2004; Tettamanti et al., 2005) in an effector-specific manner. The effects of action-related modulation during language comprehension appear to be limited to the left hemisphere.

While premotor areas show increased activity during action observation, listening to action sounds (Aziz-Zadeh, Iacoboni, Zaidel, Wilson, & Mazziotta, 2004; Gazzola, Aziz-Zadeh, & Keysers, 2006), or semantic comprehension, primary motor areas appear to be inhibited during semantic comprehension (Buccino et al., 2005).[1] This is in contrast to action observation, which activates both premotor and primary motor areas in a somatotopic fashion (Aziz-Zadeh, Maeda, Zaidel, Mazziotta, & Iacoboni, 2002; Buccino et al., 2001). Thus, the direction of modulation appears to depend on the level or role of a particular area within a distributed network.

Various hypotheses, overlapping to some degree, have been suggested to account for the dissociation between the engagement of primary and secondary motor areas during language comprehension. First, it has been proposed that conceptual knowledge requires multimodal representations (Geschwind, 1964). Premotor areas are activated by execution, observation, and sounds of actions, suggesting relatively abstract, multimodal representations of actions. Activation in primary motor areas is more closely linked to planned or executed actions. Thus the primary motor cortex might be unfit for providing a "convergence zone" for abstract semantic representation, though it might participate in a network for conceptual representation at a different level (Damasio, 1989; Damasio, Tranel, Grabowski, Adolphs, & Damasio, 2004).

Second, inhibition of primary motor cortex during linguistic comprehension of action phrases may relate to the fact that language requires more general, abstract representations than those engaged during motor execution. Consider the concept "grasp". In the primary motor cortex, the motor repertoire for grasping may engage a specific configuration of the hand, with associated recruitment of a specific set of muscles, forces, and other parameters related to a particular instance of grasping. The general concept "grasp," however, may not code these specific representations. Thus it is possible that gesture-specific representations in primary motor cortex might need to be inhibited for a more generalized conceptual representation (Buccino et al., 2005).

Third, inhibition of primary motor cortex may be needed to prevent the movement of the limb during language comprehension given the recruitment of conceptual representations that include premotor areas. In a theoretical review on the link between language and motor representations, Gallese and Lakoff (2005) argued that primary sensorimotor areas, in contrast with secondary areas, should be inhibited to minimize cross-talk between the general representation of a given concept and its actualization.

While embodied semantics potentially applies to many kinds of concepts, less attention has been given to the engagement of areas outside of the motor system. Considering concepts beyond

[1] In addition to the study by Buccino et al. (2005), which shows inhibition, a study by Pulvermuller's group may also indicate inhibition. Pulvermuller et al. had participants perform a vocal lexical decision task while TMS was applied to different regions of motor cortex (Pulvermuller, Hauk, Nikulin, & Ilmoniemi, 2005). RTs were facilitated in an effector-specific manner; e.g., judgments of hand-related words were faster when TMS was applied over the hand area compared to the foot area. They interpreted these results as consistent with the notion that activation of motor cortex supports effector-specific lexical retrieval. However, if the TMS pulses are considered to add noise, then one could argue that the effector-specific improvements in RT might be due to the transient disruption of potentially competing signals from motor cortex. For example, judging that the letters "POKE" spell a hand-action word might be faster if a representation of the current posture of the hand is disrupted. Three points suggest that this alternative interpretation is more parsimonious. First, the effects of single-pulse TMS are usually viewed as disruptive to normal processing, rather than facilitatory. Second, a main effect on RT was associated with hand area TMS, a result attributed to the spread of interference effects to the mouth area. Third, this interpretation is consistent with the more direct assay provided by Buccino et al. (2005).

action representation, embodied semantics might predict that concepts regarding visual movement (i.e., a phrase like "flew past me") would modulate activity in MT, concepts regarding "hearing" would modulate temporal auditory cortex, and so forth. However, to our knowledge, only one neuroimaging study has directly evaluated how functionally localized perceptual areas are modulated by linguistic tasks related to that perceptual domain; Chao and Martin (1999) reported that overlapping voxels in the lingual gyrus and the inferior temporal cortex were active for both color perception and color naming.

Here we consider conceptual representation of faces and places. There is now considerable evidence that the visual processing of faces and places activates differential brain areas: the fusiform face area (FFA) and the parahippocampal place area (PPA), respectively (Epstein, Harris, Stanley, & Kanwisher, 1999; Kanwisher, 2001; O'Craven & Kanwisher, 2000). We examined whether language related to faces would modulate activity in the FFA and language related to places would modulate activity in the PPA. In order to circumvent the notorious issues of intersubject variability (Mazziotta et al., 2001), we looked for a congruence between observation of faces/places and language related to faces/places at a subject by subject level. We predicted that sentence comprehension would lead to domain-specific modulation of activation in these regions of interest, and that this modulation would be especially pronounced in the left hemisphere. We did not have strong a priori predictions concerning the direction of this modulation. If activity in FFA and PPA is related to multimodal abstract representations of faces and places, respectively, then we might expect to see a domain-specific increase in activation during sentence comprehension, akin to what has been observed in premotor cortex during action comprehension. Alternatively, if FFA and PPA are more analogous to motor cortex, serving as "primary" processors for face and place perception, then we might expect the modulation to be one of inhibition.

METHODS

Participants

Fourteen healthy right-handed volunteers participated in the study. Three subjects were not included in the analyses due to excessive noise and/or movement in their functional data. Thus 11 subjects contributed to the analyses (7 men, 4 women; mean age = 22.5; range = 18–39). All participants gave informed consent and the study was approved by University of California, Berkeley, Committee for the Protection of Human Subjects. All participants had normal or corrected-to-normal vision. Prior to scanning, participants completed a screening questionnaire to exclude participants who were on prohibited medications or had a history of neurological or psychiatric disorders, substance abuse and other proscribed medical conditions.

Stimuli

The stimulus set consisted of a total of 240 auditory digitized sentences. All sentences were recorded using the voice of a native Californian female speaker and were grouped into five semantic categories. For two of the categories, the sentences focused on facial features, either related to a famous face (e.g., "George Bush has wrinkles around his eyes") or a generic face (e.g., "The farmer has freckles on his cheeks"). Similarly, two of the categories involved sentences pertaining to places, either related to a famous place (e.g., "The Taj Majal faces a long thin reflecting pool") or a generic place (e.g., "The house has a couch near the fireplace"). The fifth category was of control sentences. These referred to generic objects (e.g., "The television has a long antenna"). Our aim was to describe a person's face or a specific scene without directly mentioning the word "face" or "place." For each face and place category, 36 sentences were constructed in which the semantics constituted an accurate or reasonable statement. In addition, there were 4 other sentences in which the semantics constituted an inaccurate or unreasonable statement (e.g., "Marilyn Monroe has a large square jaw"). We constructed 80 control sentences describing objects, 72 of which entailed reasonable declarative statements and 8 of which entailed unreasonable statements (e.g., "The cell phone has signal from other planets"). Half of these were used in the face run and the other half were used in the place run (see below). The five categories were matched in terms of word length and number of syllables (average syllable length per condition = 11). We also did extensive pretesting in an attempt to match the sentences for understandability and difficulty. During pretesting, subjects were accurate on over 95% of the trials and reaction times were similar across the different conditions (average 3 seconds from trial onset).

Procedures

Each participant completed three functional runs in the scanner. In the first run, subjects listened to sentences pertaining to generic faces, generic places, and control objects. In the second run, subjects listened to sentences pertaining to famous faces, famous places, and a different set of control objects. Forty sentences of each type were presented in each run for a total of 120 sentences. Each sentence was presented on average for 2.88 s. Sentences were presented over headphones using an MR confon (Magdeburg, Germany) audio system. The total duration of these 2 language runs was 18 minutes and 20 s. Each run began with 20 s (10 TRs) of dummy scans, which were excluded from the analyses. We used a jittered intertrial interval (6, 8, or 10 s) and BOLD responses during these intertrial intervals constituted the resting baseline. A cross-hair was visually present at the center of the screen during all trials and participants were asked to maintain fixation at this location.

Participants were instructed to listen to each sentence and press a button whenever the sentence described an inaccurate or improbable fact. By including only a few of these "catch" trials, we sought to ensure that participants would pay close attention to the meaning of the sentences while introducing minimal response-related activation in the primary data set of interest. The catch trials were modeled separately in the analysis. Catch trials were detected by all participants without problems, independent of sentence condition. All participants completed 10 practice trials prior to scanning to familiarize them to the task.

In the third run, subjects performed a functional localizer task that allowed us to functionally define ROIs on an individual basis. The functional localizer consisted of seven 16 s blocks of grayscale faces, grayscale scenes, or a fixation cross. In order to insure that subjects were attentive during the localizer task they were instructed to make simultaneous right and left button presses with the thumbs whenever an image repeated. This localizer task has previously been shown to reliably activate parahippocampal (PPA) and fusiform (FFA) regions of inferior temporal cortex for places and faces, respectively (Gazzaley, Rissman, & Desposito, 2004).

The order of the three runs was maintained across subjects in order to minimize motor imagery. We assumed that reading the generic phrases would evoke less imagery than the famous phrases and thus placed the generic task first. Note that each run (i.e., generic and famous) contained a control condition, so that no direct comparisons were made between runs. The localizer task was placed at the end of the session since we expected it might promote imagery given that it included actual faces and places.

fMRI acquisition

Functional MRI scanning was performed on a 4T Varian INOVA scanner using a T2*-weighted BOLD sensitive gradient echo echo-planar imaging sequence (TE = 28 ms, FOV = 22.4 × 22.4 cm, 64 × 64 matrix, resulting in-plane resolution 3.5 × 3.5 mm). Using a two-shot interleaved sequence, half of K-space was acquired in 1 s (i.e., total TR 2 s). A phase map correction was applied to remove Nyquist ghosts. 18 oblique axial slices of 5 mm thickness (1 mm gap) were acquired, providing coverage of the full extent of the frontal and temporal lobes. The dorsal-most aspect of the parietal lobe was not within the field of view in some participants. Each run was preceded by 10 s of dummy gradient RF pulses to achieve steady-state tissue magnetization. A T1-weighted, three-dimensional high resolution MP (magnetization-prepared)-Flash scan was obtained after the functional scans.

Data processing and statistical analysis

The fMRI data were preprocessed using tools from FSL (FMRIB's Software Library, www.fmrib.ox.ac.uk/fsl). Skull stripping was performed with BET (Smith, 2002). Motion correction was carried out with MCFLIRT (Jenkinson, Bannister, Brady, & Smith, 2002; Jenkinson & Smith, 2001). The data were smoothed with a Gaussian kernel (8 mm FWHM) and mean signal intensity was normalized across subjects using the program IP.

Registration was performed with the FSL tool FLIRT (Jenkinson & Smith, 2001; Jenkinson et al., 2002). For each subject, functional images were aligned to high-resolution coplanar images using an affine transformation with 3 degrees of freedom. High-resolution coplanar images were in turn aligned to MPFlash images, with an affine transformation with 6 degrees of freedom. Finally, MPFlash images were aligned to the standard MNI average of 152 brains using an affine transformation with 12 degrees of freedom.

Statistical analysis was carried out using FEAT (FMRI Expert Analysis Tool) Version 5.4, part of FSL (FMRIB's Software Library, www.fmrib.ox.-ac.uk/fsl). There was a separate explanatory variable for each of the 4 (runs 1 and 2; face sentences, place sentences, control sentences, false sentences) or 2 (run 3; face photos, scene photos) conditions. A slice-timing correction using Fourier-space time-series phase-shifting was applied as well as high pass temporal filtering (Gaussian-weighted LSF straight line fitting, with sigma = 37.5 s). Time-series statistical analysis was carried out using FILM with local autocorrelation correction (Woolrich, Ripley, Brady, & Smith, 2001). Z (Gaussianized T/F) statistic images were thresholded using clusters determined by $Z > 2.3$ and a (corrected) cluster significance threshold of $p = .05$ (Worsley, Evans, Marrett, & Neelin, 1992).

Group analysis. Group analysis was performed with FMRISTAT with a mixed effects (i.e., random effects) linear model. Standard deviations from individual subject analyses were passed up to the group level. The resulting t-statistic images were thresholded at $t > 3.106$ ($df = 11$, $p < .005$, uncorrected) at the voxel level, with a minimum cluster size applied so that only clusters significant at $p < .05$ (corrected based on Gaussian random field theory) are reported.

Individual subject analysis. Regions of interest (ROIs) were chosen to test for differences in modulation of visual areas in each subject individually. A scene-selective ROI was defined with the localizer task GLM using a scene minus face contrast to obtain regions responsive to scene perception. The inferior temporal voxel with the highest t-value plus a 16 mm radius Gaussian centered upon the voxel constituted the PPA ROI in each hemisphere. Using the Gaussian radius, voxels further from the peak were weighted less strongly than voxels in the center of the sphere. The FFA ROI was chosen similarly, using the face minus place contrast. Even at minimal thresholds, 3 subjects did not exhibit a left hemisphere FFA (similar to that reported in previous studies, e.g., Wojciulik, Kanwisher, & Driver, 1998). Hence, for the left FFA ROI analysis, all analyses included 8 subjects. Two-way repeated-measures ANOVAs, Sentence Type (face, place) × ROI (FFA, PPA), were used to compare responses to linguistic phrases in these voxels to the control condition to determine whether signal change was dependent on sentence type. Four ANOVAs were run (famous sentences–left hemisphere; famous sentences–right hemisphere; generic sentences–left hemisphere; generic sentences–right hemisphere).

RESULTS

Group analyses

We first compared areas activated during language comprehension relative to rest in order to make sure that the expected language areas were activated. For this analysis, we averaged across the sentence types within a run, but performed the contrast separately for the generic and famous sentence runs. The results are summarized in Figure 1. As expected, compared to rest, language tasks significantly activated areas in the superior temporal gyrus bilaterally (MNI coordinate peak for generic sentences: Left hemisphere $x = -44$, $y = -20$, $z = -8$; Right Hemisphere $x = 58$, $y = -18$, $z = -8$; peak for famous sentences: Left hemisphere $x = -50$, $y = -18$, $z = -8$; Right hemisphere $x = 58$, $y = -20$, $z = -4$), and in the vicinity of Broca's area in the left hemisphere (generic sentences: $x = -46$, $y = 18$, $z = -2$). The generic sentences tended to produce greater activation than the famous sentences. While this may indicate processing differences between the sentence types, this difference may also reflect the fact that the generic sentences were always tested prior to the famous sentences. From our experience, initial runs generally show greater activity than subsequent runs.

Individual subject analysis

The main goal of this study was to assess modulation within FFA and PPA when people performed a comprehension task involving sentences describing faces or places. To account for inter-subject variability (Mazziotta et al.,

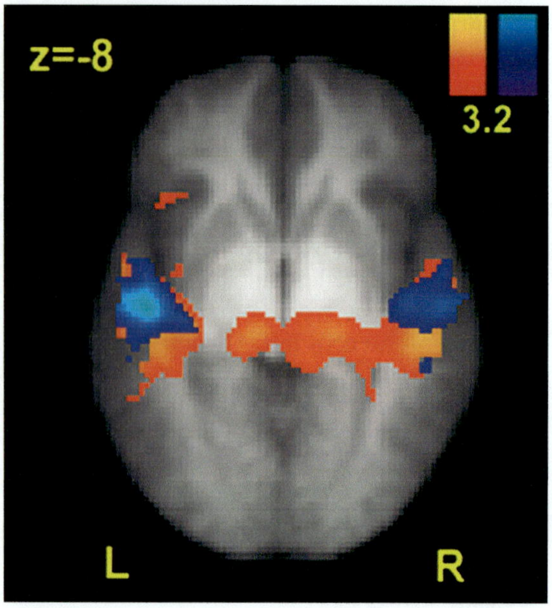

Figure 1. All language trials compared to rest. In red, listening to generic sentences (Run 1); and in blue, listening to famous sentences (Run 2). The temporal auditory areas are significantly active as are the posterior language areas. Broca's area is significantly active for Run 1. All statistic images were thresholded using clusters determined by $Z > 2.3$ and a (corrected) cluster significance threshold of $p = .05$ (Worsley, 1996).

2001), the primary analyses were conducted on individually defined functional ROIs (Friston, Rotshtein, Geng, Sterzer, & Henson, 2006; Saxe, Brett, & Kanwisher, 2006). For each subject, we identified the inferior temporal voxels that were most active during the localizer run in which participants performed a perceptual task involving faces or scenes. This procedure was applied in both the left and right hemispheres (Figure 2). Given that the localizer runs were used to identify the ROIs for the main experiment, we do not make any direct comparisons between the language runs and observation runs.

The top row of Figure 3 shows the percent signal change in the left and right hemisphere ROIs during the localizer run. Not surprisingly, given our method of identification, activation in the ROIs was most responsive when viewing stimuli of the ROI's related domain (e.g., viewing of faces for FFA ROI). The ROI × Picture Type interaction was significant in the left, $F(1, 7) = 80.39$, $p = .0021$, and right, $F(1, 12) = 15.14$, $p < .0001$, hemispheres. Activation in the PPA ROIs showed minimal response during the face perception task. In contrast, activation in the FFA ROIs was also observed during scene perception task. The average MNI coordinates were: left FFA (66, 36, 25), right FFA (23, 36, 25), left PPA (59, 41, 28), right PPA (31, 39, 28) with the corresponding standard errors: (0.7, 1.8, 1.1), (0.5, 2.1, 0.9), (0.3, 0.8, 0.6), and (0.4, 1.3, 1.2). These are within the vicinity of those reported by Kanwisher's group (O'Craven & Kanwisher, 2000): left FFA (63, 43, 28) right FFA (26, 45, 28), left PPA (59, 43, 34) and right PPA (29, 43, 33).

We then examined the response in these voxels during the sentence comprehension task. The percent signal change in these ROIs is shown for the comprehension run with famous sentences (middle row of Figure 3) and generic sentences (bottom row). For the left hemisphere, there was a significant Sentence Type × ROI interaction during the run with sentences involving famous faces or places, $F(1, 7) = 14.35$, $p = .0068$. The left PPA was significantly less active to place sentences compared to face sentences, $F(1, 12) = 5.36$, $p = .039$. A similar trend was observed in left FFA, although this reduction was not significant, $F(1, 7) = 1.78$, $p = .22$. The interaction

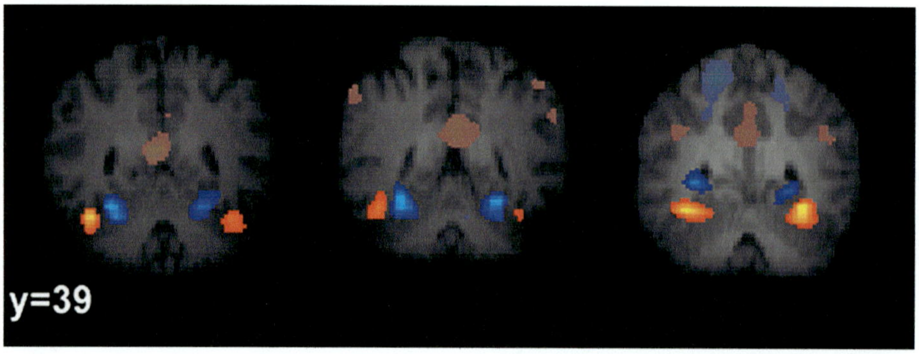

Figure 2. ROIs in three sample subjects: Observation of faces as compared to scenes activates the fusiform face area (FFA; red to yellow) and observation of scenes as compared to faces activates the parahippocampal place area (PPA; blue to light blue). In most participants, activations were bilateral. However in three participants a left hemisphere FFA was not observed. For each subject, the ROIs in each area consisted of the peak voxel with a surrounding 16 mm Gaussian.

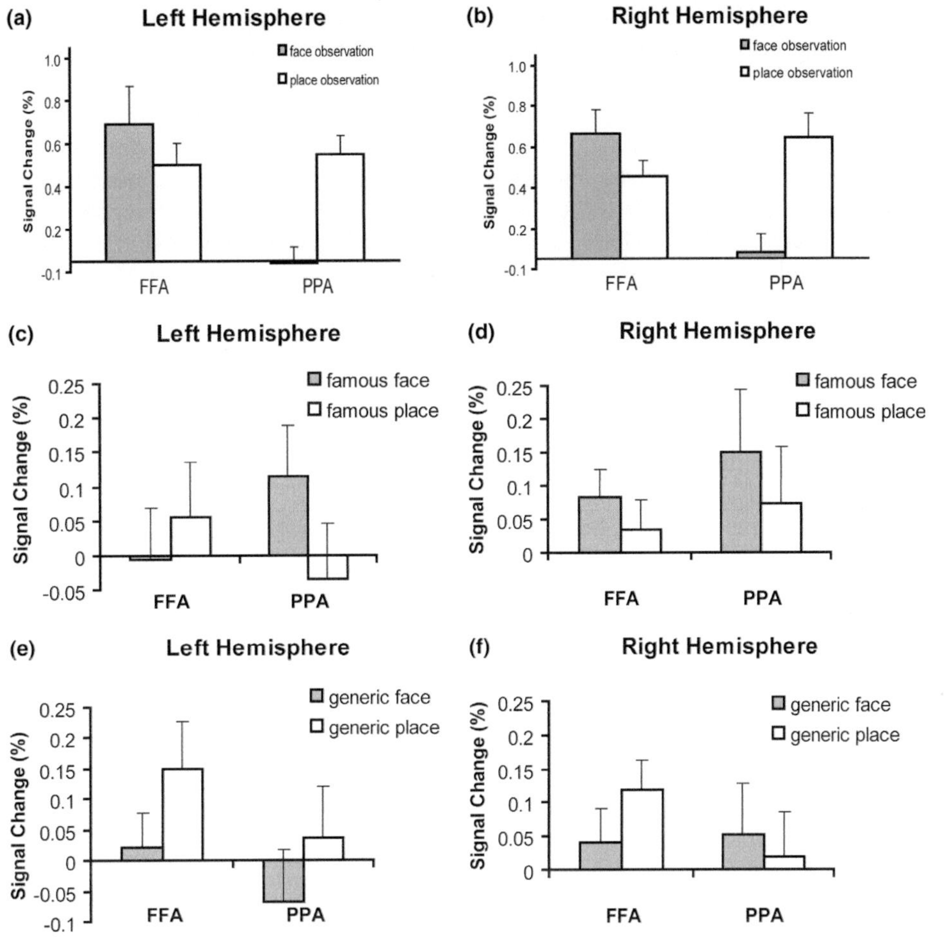

Figure 3. (a) Signal change in the FFA and PPA for observation of faces (gray) and places (white), in peak voxels for the FFA and PPA defined individually for each subject, compared to resting baseline. (b) Right hemisphere response in functionally defined FFA and PPA. Note that it is common to see that the FFA is also activated by observing scenes, and thus activations above 0 are expected for this condition (Ewbank et al., 2005). (c–f) Signal change in the FFA and PPA ROIs during language comprehension for sentences describing faces or places as compared to control sentences (objects). The middle panels are for the run with famous sentences (c–d) and bottom panels are for the run with generic sentences (e–f). The interaction is significant for the famous sentences in the left hemisphere, with activation lower for domain-related sentences.

was not significant during the run with sentences involving generic faces or places, $F(1, 7) = 0.08$, $p = .78$. For these sentences, the mean response in both left FFA and left PPA was lower when listening to face sentences as compared to place sentences.

Interestingly, the signal change in FFA and PPA of the right hemisphere during the sentence comprehension runs was similar in magnitude to that observed in the left hemisphere. However, for both the famous and generic runs, we did not observe a ROI × Sentence Type interaction in the right hemisphere, famous: $F(1, 12) = 0.52$, $p = .49$; generic: $F(1, 12) = 3.6$, $p = .82$. Thus, the modulation of activation in FFA and PPA during a sentence comprehension task was limited to the left hemisphere. Indeed, we found a significant three-way interaction for hemisphere, ROI, and stimulus type, indicating that the deactivation was limited to the left hemisphere for the famous set of stimuli, $F(1, 7) = 21.47$, $p = .0024$.

DISCUSSION

Our results reveal that activity in perceptually identified neural regions is modulated during a sentence comprehension task. Moreover, at least for FFA and PPA, the modulation is manifest as a reduction in activity for sentences that are content related. This effect was limited to the left hemisphere and only obtained in the run with famous faces and places. The modulation of PPA was stronger than the modulation of the FFA.

This may be due to the fact that the FFA is less reliably localized in the left hemisphere (Ishai, Schmidt, & Boesiger, 2005), thus lowering our statistical power for the left FFA. In addition, activity in FFA is observed to non-face stimuli (Grill-Spector, Sayres, & Ress, 2006), including the places used in our localizer task (Figure 3a). In an fMRI-habituation study, habituation to visually presented objects was observed in the FFA and the PPA (Ewbank, Schluppeck, & Andrews, 2005), which may explain why our control object sentences (the baseline in Figure 3) did not significantly differ from our experimental stimuli. We also conducted analyses comparing signal change in the ROIs to a resting baseline and also found the same patterns of results with the interaction reported here to be significant. This indicates that the differences between the two experimental conditions are significant, regardless of the baseline used.

In designing this study, we realized that finding content-specific increases in activation might reflect the use of mental imagery during sentence comprehension. For this reason, we opted to include both generic and famous face/place sentences, and complete the generic run prior to the famous run, based on the assumption that the sentences describing well-known faces or places would entail more imagery. The fact that the modulation was a content-specific reduction in activation rather than increase in activation argues against an imagery hypothesis as mental imagery of faces or places would predict increased rather than decreased activity in the FFA or PPA (O'Craven & Kanwisher, 2000).

Previous studies have shown that the FFA and/or PPA are modulated by expertise (Gauthier, Skudlarski, Gore, & Anderson, 2000; Gauthier, Tarr, Anderson, Skudlarski, & Gore, 1999; O'Craven & Kanwisher, 2000), attention (O'Craven, Downing, & Kanwisher, 1999; Wojciulik et al., 1998), visual imagery (Ishai, Haxby, & Ungerleider, 2002; Ishai, Ungerleider, & Haxby, 2000; O'Craven & Kanwisher, 2000), and emotion (Vuilleumier, Armony, Driver, & Dolan, 2001). Our findings indicate that language also modulates these perceptual processing areas. However, unlike in previous studies, the language effects on FFA and PPA activity observed here are inhibitory.

Modulation in a sensory processing area can show as either an increase in activity (as with premotor areas) or a decrease (as with primary motor cortex or here with the FFA and PPA). Decreases in activity can be explained with three partially overlapping hypotheses. First, during language processing, visual processing areas for the concept in question may need to be inhibited in order to prevent interference between current sensory inputs and the conceptual representations needed for linguistic comprehension (Gallese & Lakoff, 2005). For example, if a dark-haired speaker asks if Marilyn Monroe had blond hair, perception related to the speakers face and hair color could interfere with the retrieval of information required to respond to the linguistic query.

Second, language requires more abstract representation than visual observation. Hearing a phrase like "Marilyn Monroe has blond hair" or "The farmer's chin has a mole" prompts a more generalized representation than perceiving Marilyn Monroe's face with blond hair, her specific expression, tan, make-up, and hairstyle, etc., of the moment. Thus, in order to represent an abstract representation of Marilyn Monroe, it may be that specific visual representations of Marilyn Monroe need to be inhibited.

Third, multimodal processing might be an essential prerequisite for conceptual abstract representation. Areas such as the FFA, PPA, and primary motor cortex—that are not of multimodal nature—may therefore be unfit for providing a "convergence zone" for abstract processing. These results are in line with findings that the primary motor cortex, which codes specific motor representations, is inhibited during processing of language related to actions (Buccino et al., 2005) while premotor multimodal areas are facilitated (Aziz-Zadeh et al., 2006). Similarly, it is possible that multimodal areas functionally connected to the PPA or FFA (i.e., the temporal poles), are facilitated by face and place sentence processing and that these multimodal areas selectively inhibit the FFA and PPA during language processing. In a post hoc group analysis, however, we did not find any brain areas that were more active for face versus place sentences or vice versa. Further research is needed to yield a more complete model of the network of areas that process face and place sentence processing in the brain and their pattern of activations.

The content-specific decreases in activation were only found for famous sentences. This effect was not reliable for generic face and place sentences, although a similar pattern was found bilaterally for the FFA and in the right hemisphere for the PPA. It may be that the mechanisms leading to the decrease in activation may be related to the degree to which the sentences engage more concrete representations. The face of a generic farmer is a more abstract generalization than the face of Marilyn Monroe. Content-specific inhibition of perceptual areas such as FFA or PPA may be greatest for sentences that produce the greatest degree of imagery. This hypothesis is, of course, speculative and a question for future investigation.

Manuscript received 26 September 2006
Manuscript accepted 7 February 2007
First published online 31 May 2007

REFERENCES

Aziz-Zadeh, L., Iacoboni, M., Zaidel, E., Wilson, S., & Mazziotta, J. (2004). Left hemisphere motor facilitation in response to manual action sounds. *European Journal of Neuroscience*, *19*, 2609–2612.

Aziz-Zadeh, L., Maeda, F., Zaidel, E., Mazziotta, J., & Iacoboni, M. (2002). Lateralization in motor facilitation during action observation: a TMS study. *Experimental Brain Research*, *144*, 127–131.

Aziz-Zadeh, L., Wilson, S., Rizzolatti, G., & Iacoboni, M. (2006). Congruent embodied representations for visually presented actions and linguistic phrases describing actions. *Current Biology*, *16*(18), 1818–1823.

Barsalou, L. W. (1999). Perceptual symbol systems. *Behavioral and Brain Sciences*, *22*, 577–609 [discussion 610–560].

Buccino, G., Binkofski, F., Fink, G. R., Fadiga, L., Fogassi, L., Gallese, V., et al. (2001). Action observation activates premotor and parietal areas in a somatotopic manner: an fMRI study. *European Journal of Neuroscience*, *13*, 400–404.

Buccino, G., Riggio, L., Melli, G., Binkofski, F., Gallese, V., & Rizzolatti, G. (2005). Listening to action-related sentences modulates the activity of the motor system: a combined TMS and behavioral study. *Brain Research Cognitive Brain Research*, *24*, 355–363.

Chao, L. L., & Martin, A. (1999). Cortical regions associated with perceiving, naming, and knowing about colors. *Journal of Cognitive Neuroscience*, *11*, 25–35.

Damasio, A. R. (1989). Time-locked multiregional retroactivation: a systems-level proposal for the neural substrates of recall and recognition. *Cognition*, *33*, 25–62.

Damasio, H., Tranel, D., Grabowski, T., Adolphs, R., & Damasio, A. (2004). Neural systems behind word and concept retrieval. *Cognition*, *92*, 179–229.

Epstein, R., Harris, A., Stanley, D., & Kanwisher, N. (1999). The parahippocampal place area: recognition, navigation, or encoding? *Neuron*, *23*, 115–125.

Ewbank, M. P., Schluppeck, D., & Andrews, T. J. (2005). fMR-adaptation reveals a distributed representation of inanimate objects and places in human visual cortex. *NeuroImage*, *28*, 268–279.

Feldman, J., & Narayanan, S. (2004). Embodied meaning in a neural theory of language. *Brain and Language*, *89*, 385–392.

Friston, K. J., Rotshtein, P., Geng, J. J., Sterzer, P., & Henson, R. N. (2006). A critique of functional localisers. *NeuroImage*, *30*, 1077–1087.

Gallese, V., & Lakoff, G. (2005). The brains concepts: The role of the sensorimotor system in reason and language. *Cognitive Neuropsychology*, *22*, 455–479.

Gauthier, I., Skudlarski, P., Gore, J. C., & Anderson, A. W. (2000). Expertise for cars and birds recruits brain areas involved in face recognition. *Nature Neuroscience*, *3*, 191–197.

Gauthier, I., Tarr, M. J., Anderson, A. W., Skudlarski, P., & Gore, J. C. (1999). Activation of the middle fusiform "face area" increases with expertise in recognizing novel objects. *Nature Neuroscience*, *2*, 568–573.

Gazzaley, A., Rissman, J., & Desposito, M. (2004). Functional connectivity during working memory maintenance. *Cognitive and Affective Behavioral Neuroscience*, *4*, 580–599.

Gazzola, V., Aziz-Zadeh, L., & Keysers, C. (2006). I hear what you are doing—An fMRI study of the auditory mirror system in humans. *Current Biology*, *16*(18), 1824–1829.

Geschwind, N. (1964). The development of the brain and the evolution of language. *Monograph Series in Language and Linguistics*, *1*, 186–187.

Glenberg, A. M. (1997). What memory is for. *Behavioral and Brain Sciences*, *20*, 1–19 [discussion 19–55].

Glenberg, A. M., & Kaschak, M. P. (2002). Grounding language in action. *Psychonomic Bulletin Review*, *9*, 558–565.

Hauk, O., Johnsrude, I., & Pulvermuller, F. (2004). Somatotopic representation of action words in human motor and premotor cortex. *Neuron*, *41*, 301–307.

Hauk, O., & Pulvermuller, F. (2004). Neurophysiological distinction of action words in the fronto-central cortex. *Human Brain Mapping*, *21*, 191–201.

Ishai, A., Haxby, J. V., & Ungerleider, L. G. (2002). Visual imagery of famous faces: effects of memory and attention revealed by fMRI. *NeuroImage*, *17*, 1729–1741.

Ishai, A., Schmidt, C. F., & Boesiger, P. (2005). Face perception is mediated by a distributed cortical network. *Brain Research Bulletin*, *67*, 87–93.

Ishai, A., Ungerleider, L. G., & Haxby, J. V. (2000). Distributed neural systems for the generation of visual images. *Neuron*, *28*, 979–990.

Jenkinson, M., Bannister, P., Brady, M., & Smith, S. (2002). Improved optimisation for the robust and accurate linear registration and motion correction of brain images. *NeuroImage*, *17*, 825–841.

Jenkinson, M., & Smith, S. (2001). A global optimisation method for robust affine registration of brain images. *Medical Image Analysis*, *5*, 143–156.

Kanwisher, N. (2001). Faces and places: of central (and peripheral) interest. *Nature Neuroscience*, *4*, 455–456.

Lakoff, G., & Johnson, M. (1999). *Philosophy in the flesh: The embodied mind and its challenge to western thought*. New York: Basic Books.

Mazziotta, J., Toga, A., Evans, A., Fox, P., Lancaster, J., Zilles, K., et al. (2001). A probabilistic atlas and reference system for the human brain: International Consortium for Brain Mapping (ICBM). Philosophical Transactions of the Royal Society of London. *Series B: Biological Sciences*, *356*, 1293–1322.

O'Craven, K. M., Downing, P. E., & Kanwisher, N. (1999). fMRI evidence for objects as the units of attentional selection. *Nature*, *401*, 584–587.

O'Craven, K. M., & Kanwisher, N. (2000). Mental imagery of faces and places activates corresponding stimulus-specific brain regions. *Journal of Cognitive Neuroscience*, *12*, 1013–1023.

Pulvermuller, F., Hauk, O., Nikulin, V. V., & Ilmoniemi, R. J. (2005). Functional links between motor and language systems. *European Journal of Neuroscience*, *21*, 793–797.

Saxe, R., Brett, M., & Kanwisher, N. (2006). Divide and conquer: a defense of functional localizers. *NeuroImage*, *30*, 1088–1096 [discussion 1097–1089].

Smith, S. (2002). Fast robust automated brain extraction. *Human Brain Mapping*, *17*, 143–155.

Tettamanti, M., Buccino, G., Saccuman, M. C., Gallese, V., Danna, M., Scifo, P., et al. (2005). Listening to action-related sentences activates fronto-parietal motor circuits. *Journal of Cognitive Neuroscience*, *17*, 273–281.

Vuilleumier, P., Armony, J. L., Driver, J., & Dolan, R. J. (2001). Effects of attention and emotion on face processing in the human brain: an event-related fMRI study. *Neuron*, *30*, 829–841.

Wheaton, K. J., Thompson, J. C., Syngeniotis, A., Abbott, D. F., & Puce, A. (2004). Viewing the motion of human body parts activates different regions of premotor, temporal, and parietal cortex. *NeuroImage*, *22*, 277–288.

Wojciulik, E., Kanwisher, N., & Driver, J. (1998). Covert visual attention modulates face-specific activity in the human fusiform gyrus: fMRI study. *Journal of Neurophysiology*, *79*, 1574–1578.

Woolrich, M. W., Ripley, B. D., Brady, M., & Smith, S. M. (2001). Temporal autocorrelation in univariate linear modeling of fMRI data. *NeuroImage*, *14*, 1370–1386.

Worsley, K. J. (1996). A unified statistical approach for determining significant signals in images of cerebral activation. *Human Brain Mapping*, *4*, 58–73.

Worsley, K. J., Evans, A. C., Marrett, S., & Neelin, P. (1992). A three-dimensional statistical analysis for CBF activation studies in human brain. *Journal of Cerebral Blood Flow Metabolism*, *12*, 900–918.

SOCIAL NEUROSCIENCE, 2008, 3 (3–4), 239–249

Psychology Press
Taylor & Francis Group

Having access to others' mind through gaze: The role of ontogenetic and learning processes in gaze-following behavior of macaques

Pier F. Ferrari, Gino Coudé, Vittorio Gallese, and Leonardo Fogassi
University of Parma, Parma, Italy

In primates the gaze conveys important information about what others attend to and about their intentions. The ability to follow the gaze direction of conspecifics has been established for several primate species. It has been proposed to be a precursor for more complex cognitive skills related to mind reading. Studies in humans and other primates have shown that this behavior develops during the period between infancy and adulthood; however, the mechanisms responsible for its emergence are still unknown. In a series of experiments we investigated such mechanisms in macaques (*Macaca nemestrina*). Results show that juvenile macaques improve their ability to follow the gaze of a human experimenter and that adults' ability to follow gaze is more accurate than that of juveniles. Our data also show that this behavior can emerge as the result of learning processes. The discrepancy between the relatively long period of time needed for the full establishment of the gaze-following behavior and its high sensitivity to conditioning procedures may suggest that social experience and integration of this behavior with other social-cognitive skills are required for its development.

INTRODUCTION

Social interactions in humans are strongly driven by intentions. For intention we define any purpose guiding behavior. Most researchers would agree that apes, monkeys and other animals possess the capacity to produce behaviors that are goal directed. More questionable is the issue of whether nonhuman primates also understand the behavior of other individuals as purposeful. The pioneering studies by Premack and Woodruff (1978) attempted to answer this conundrum. These authors proposed that some nonhuman primates, at least chimpanzees, interpret other individuals' behavior as intentional. This capacity is considered to be an important evolutionary cognitive achievement because it allows attributing mental states to others (Theory of Mind; ToM) from the observation of their behavior. However, further investigations in nonhuman primates did not reach a conclusive consensus on this issue (Heyes, 1998; Tomasello, Call, & Hare, 2003).

At the ontogenetic level, there is a temporal discrepancy between the capacity of human infants to produce intentional behavior and that of understanding the behavior of other individuals as intentionally driven. In fact, it is known that infants already start to show a series of intentional behaviors in the first year of life (e.g., grasping objects under visual guidance), although they do not establish a full-blown ToM until the age of 3 to 4 years. More recently, however, it has been proposed that 15-month-old infants may show a rudimentary form of ToM, based on a modification of the false-belief task (Onishi &

Correspondence should be addressed to: Pier Francesco Ferrari, Dipartimento di Neuroscienze, Università di Parma, via Volturno 39, I-43100, Parma, Italy. E-mail: ferrari@biol.unipr.it

This study was supported by a MIUR grant.
We thank G. Braghiroli and M. Scalera for the excellent work in drawing the illustrations of Figures 1 and 2, respectively.

www.psypress.com/socialneuroscience DOI:10.1080/17470910701429065

Baillargeon, 2005). Overall, these studies indicate that intention-reading capacity builds up during human infant development and open the issue of whether something similar can occur also in nonhuman primates, provided that they manifest, in adulthood, some form of intention reading.

Understanding intention is very unlikely an all-or-nothing phenomenon. It would rather arise through several steps differing in cognitive complexity. This view fits a multi-layered model of mind-reading development (Baron-Cohen, 1994, 1995). In this model, one of the building blocks for the construction of ToM is the perception of eye gaze and the capacity to follow it. In fact, observation of another individual's gaze directed to a specific location in space is a strong stimulus eliciting a response of the observer's head and eyes in the same direction. Although this response could be considered a stereotyped and automatic reaction, it can be crucial for dyadic interactions in which an object of interest is shared with another individual. By doing so, the observer extracts important elements from visual information to infer what is the intention of the observed agent.

In humans, gaze-following behavior emerges between the ages of 3 to 18 months in response to head movements made toward a specific space location (Butterworth & Cochran, 1980; Butterworth & Jarrett, 1991; Corkum & Moore, 1995; Scaife & Bruner, 1975), and by the age of 14 to 18 months it is triggered by oriented eye movements alone. However, it is only by the age of 18 to 24 months that infants are able to understand the referential aspect of the visual attention of others.

This behavior has been investigated in several primate species (Anderson & Mitchell, 1999; Itakura, 1996; Tomasello, Call, & Hare, 1998; see also Emery, 2000, for a review). The results of these studies showed that apes (chimpanzees and orangutans) and other Old-World monkeys are able to follow the gaze direction of conspecifics (Tomasello et al., 1998) or humans (Ferrari, Kohler, Fogassi, & Gallese, 2000; Itakura, 1996; Paukner, Anderson, Fogassi, & Ferrari, in press; Povinelli & Eddy, 1996) using a combination of head and eye stimuli. Chimpanzees and macaques are also able to follow the gaze direction of a human experimenter observing the eye direction alone, independently of head movement (Ferrari et al., 2000; Lorincz, Baker, & Perrett, 1999; Povinelli & Eddy, 1996; Tomasello, Hare, & Agnetta, 1999). The use of gaze in nonhuman primates has been suggested to be important for conveying information about intentions. It has been reported that in baboons and vervet monkeys it is often displayed in social interactions to solicit help from group members against a third party (Kummer, 1967; Packer, 1977; Walters & Seyfarth, 1987). This type of behavior would inform the potential helper about the intention to challenge another individual and the need to be supported in this action. Other accounts in nonhuman primates, although not conclusive, support the view that gaze-following response (GFR) could be part of a set of behaviors used in communication for intentional purposes (see Emery, 2000, for a review).

Considering the importance of GFR in relation to human development, in recent years there has been an increasing interest in its ontogeny in nonhuman primate species. We have recently shown that juvenile monkeys show marked difference in GFR compared to adults (Ferrari et al., 2000). In fact, similarly to humans, this behavior dramatically improves with age. Independently, Tomasello, Hare, and Fogleman (2001) showed very similar results in captive rhesus monkeys and chimpanzees using similar methodologies. Although there are some differences in the results obtained by the two groups, it is interesting to note a convergence in the interpretation of the findings. It has been proposed that the transition to adulthood is a crucial period in the development of gaze-following behavior in primates. During this period, individuals acquire a series of cognitive and social skills that are integrated into their knowledge of the physical and social world.

The studies of the ontogeny of GFR in nonhuman primates do not show how individual experience influences and shapes this ability. In this respect, Tomasello et al. (2001) have shown that adult rhesus monkeys and chimpanzees, when exposed repeatedly to a human experimenter looking at the same location, learn to ignore the looks and do not follow the experimenter's gaze. Thus, it seems that gaze-following ability can be subjected to modification following individual experience.

In the series of experiments we present here, we aimed to test how the gaze-following behavior changes in the course of the life span of young and adult pigtailed macaques (*Macaca nemestrina*) and whether learning processes may be partly responsible for the improvement of this ability during ontogeny. In Experiment 1 we conducted a two-year follow-up study of gaze-following behavior on six individuals of different ages. In Experiments 2 and 3 we verified whether the increased GFR with age could be due to learning processes. In order to test this, we attempted to improve the performance of macaques by repeated test exposure (Experiment 2) and reinforcement of behavioral response (Experiment 3).

TABLE 1
Age and sex of the subjects included in Experiment 1

Subject	*Sex*	*Age*
Fiona	Female	3
Cesar	Male	4
Ciro	Male	5
Mama	Female	13
Peppo	Male	15
Alcatraz	Male	14

METHODS

Animals and housing. All macaques were captive-born. They lived at the Primate Section of the Department of Neuroscience of the University of Parma. They were housed in indoor enclosures in a connected-cage system (each cage measures: 100 × 160 × 100 cm), which allowed daily periods of interactions between two or more individuals. Environment in the cage is enriched with toys and foraging boards. All monkeys were used to the presence of and the interaction with the experimenters. During testing monkeys were not food deprived. In addition to primate pellets, their diet was enriched daily with ripe fruits, vegetables, seeds, eggs and living coleopteran larva. All experiments complied with the ASAB guidelines and the European law on the humane care and use of laboratory animals.

Experiment 1: Two-year time interval between Test 1 and Test 2

In this experiment we tested the hypothesis that gaze-following behavior improves with age. Therefore, we tracked in the same individual the ability to follow the gaze of other individuals at two different life stages with a two-year interval between the two stages. Subjects were six pigtailed macaques (*Macaca nemestrina*), which were captive-born. The monkeys were subdivided into two groups: juvenile/adolescent and adult monkeys. All monkeys were tested twice with Test 2, employed 2 years after Test 1. The monkeys of the first group (Juveniles, $n = 3$) had an age between 2 and 5 years at the time of the first test (Test 1, see Table 1). The monkeys of the second group (Adults, $n = 3$) had an age > 12 years. The distinction between juveniles and adults was made considering a series of morphological, developmental and behavioral factors typical of macaque species (Fa & Lindburg, 1996; Swindler, 1998; Walters, 1987).

Experiment 2: Two-week time interval between Test 1 and Test 2

In this experiment we tested the hypothesis that the increased ability to follow the gaze of a human experimenter can be attributed to previous exposure to the same experience (i.e., the experimental test). To this purpose we tested the ability of six monkeys to follow gaze on two different sessions (Test 1 and Test 2) separated by a two-week interval.

Subjects were six pigtailed macaques (*Macaca nemestrina*), which were captive-born. The monkeys were subdivided into two groups: juveniles/adolescents monkeys and adult monkeys. All monkeys were tested twice, with Test 2 being employed 2 weeks after Test 1. The monkeys of the first group (Juveniles, $n = 3$) had an age between 3 and 5 years. The monkeys of the second group (Adults, $n = 3$) had an average age of 13.3 years.

Procedures of Experiments 1 and 2. During the test session the monkey was separated from other individuals and restricted in a single cage. The experimenter was seated at 1.5 m distance in front of the cage (see Figure 1). A curtain positioned behind the experimenter prevented the monkey from interacting with other individuals or objects while being tested. In order to determine which stimulus features could elicit a gaze-following response we administered two experimental conditions named "Head/Eyes" and "Eye". In the Head/Eyes condition the experimenter turned the head 70 degrees up, down, left or right, with the eyes always aligned with the head (Figure 1a); in the Eye condition

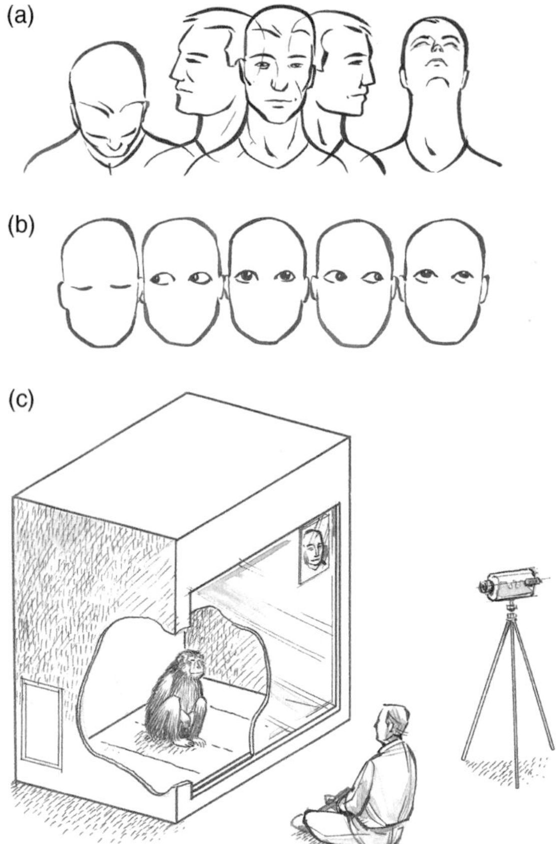

Figure 1. Schematic illustrations of the experimental conditions and setting. (a) Head/Eyes condition. The experimenter turned the head together with eyes about 70 degrees up, down, left or right. (b) Eye condition. The experimenter oriented the eyes up, down, left or right. The experimenter turned the trunk to the left or to the right. (c) The experimenter was sitting in front of the monkey at 1.5 m distance facing it. A video camera placed behind the experimenter videotaped each session. A mirror placed on the front of the cage and facing the experimenter allowed recording of the experimenter's gaze.

the experimenter oriented the eyes up, down, left or right to the extreme position of the orbit (Figure 1b). For each stimulus direction a total of 12 trials were administered (total trials $n = 96$). Each trial started when the stimulus began to move and the final position was kept for 3 s. The trial was considered concluded at the end of the 3 s. Conditions and trials were randomly administered. Each monkey was submitted to one, 20-minute-long, session. The experiment was videotaped by a Panasonic VHS video camera, which was positioned behind the experimenter. A mirror placed to one side of the monkey's head and facing the experimenter allowed recording of the experimenter's gaze. Each monkey was tested only once.

Experiment 3: Learning processes in gaze-following behavior

Subjects were two female pigtailed macaques (*Macaca nemestrina*), which were captive born. Monkey 1 was aged 6 years and Monkey 2 was 5 years old. Both monkeys were trained to sit on a primate chair and were used to the presence of the experimenters and to interacting with them.

Procedures of Experiment 3. During the experimental session the monkey was seated on a primate chair and transferred into a room where no other monkeys were present. The monkey was partially restrained because of the impossibility of videotaping and checking online its head and eye orientation when it was free to move in its cage. Figure 2 illustrates the experimental setting. The monkey was left undisturbed in this room for about 15 minutes. After this period of familiarization with the environment the experiment started. It consisted of two periods: a first period (baseline), followed by a second (training). During the baseline period one experimenter (demonstrator) sat in front of the monkey and turned the head 70 degrees up, down, left or right, with the eyes always aligned with the head. For each stimulus direction a total of 10 trials were administered. Each trial started when the demonstrator began to move the head. The final position was kept for a 3 s period after which the trial was considered concluded. Trials were randomly administered. After every 5–6 trials, the experimenter gave a piece of food to the monkey, independent of its performance. The experiment was videotaped by a Panasonic VHS video camera, which was positioned behind the experimenter. A mirror placed at one side of the monkey's head and facing the experimenter allowed the recording of the experimenter's gaze. The video camera was connected to a monitor. A second experimenter, out of the monkey's sight, watched the experiment online on the monitor. At the end of the baseline period the experiment was interrupted for five minutes followed by the training period. During the training period the experimenter, seated in front of the monkey, turned the head 70 degrees up, down, left or right, with the eyes always aligned with his head, as during the baseline period. The second experimenter watched the experiment online on a screen. The second experimenter was not visible to the monkey and during the

Figure 2. Schematic illustration of the experimental setting of Experiment 3.

training phase judged the gaze-following response of the animal. The judgment was promptly suggested to the demonstrator who, when monkey gazed in the same direction as the demonstrator gazed, stopped the trial and rewarded the monkey with a raisin. If the monkey did not follow the gaze, no food was given. For each stimulus direction a total of 10 trials were administered.

During the baseline and training periods a minimum of 40 and a maximum of 60 trials/period were presented to the monkey. This experiment was performed once a week (one session per week) for three weeks. Each session lasted about 20–30 minutes.

Behavioral analysis. Two experimenters analyzed the videotapes independently. In order to judge the monkey's response to the movements of the experimenter, the direction of the monkey's gaze was subdivided into four classes labeled: up, down, left or right. A trial was considered valid if the monkey engaged its gaze with the stimulus at the beginning of the trial. If this criterion was met, the direction of the first gaze movement after stimulus visual engagement was recorded. If the monkey did not look at the stimulus during the trial, the subject's response was considered invalid and not included in the statistical analysis. Gaze-following response (GFR) was scored if the subject directed its gaze toward the sector corresponding to the stimulus direction. No gaze-following response (NGFR) was scored if the subject directed its gaze toward a sector different from that of the stimulus direction or if the monkey did not move its gaze.

A third scorer was included to determine the inter-observer reliability that was calculated for a sample of 117 trials. The average reliability of the three resulting pairwise comparisons was 92.4% (range = 91.3–94.8%).

In order to check whether the vision of the experimenter showing the stimulus could bias the scorer, two naive scorers analyzed a sample of 103 trials in which the vision of the experimenter on the screen was prevented. We then compared the number of discrepancies between blind scoring and what the actual scorers judged when scoring the 103 trials. The percentage of agreements in the two different types of methodological scoring was close to 100% (scorer 1: 94.1%; scorer 2: 95.1%).

Statistical analysis. The number of GFR divided by the total number of valid trials was recorded for each monkey for Tests 1 and 2 and then they were compared using the binomial test (number of GFR divided by the total number of valid trials of Test 1 was used as the parameter for the expected probability). Data were further analyzed by plotting together results from juveniles and adults within each test and comparing the number of GFR divided by the total number of valid trials with that expected by chance using the binomial test (expected probability of .25). Within each test we also compared juveniles and adults GFR responses using the binomial test (number of GFR divided by the total number of valid trials of juveniles was used as the parameter for the expected probability).

In Experiment 3 during each phase the number of GFR divided by the total of valid trials was compared with that expected by chance using the binomial test (expected probability of .25). The number of GFR divided by the total of valid trials for each training phase was compared to the baseline by a binomial test (number of GFR divided by the total number of valid trials during the baseline was used as the parameter for the expected probability). In order to verify whether there was any improvement in the GFR performance during the three weeks of training, we compared number of GFR divided by the total of valid trials of day 3 with that of days 1 and 2 for both the baseline and the training phase using the binomial test.

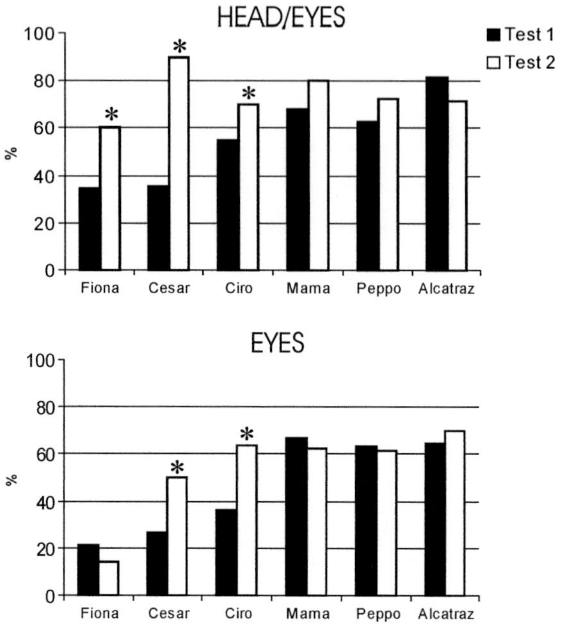

Figure 3. Percent of GFR in six pigtailed macaques tested at two different ages (Experiment 1). Time interval between Test 1 and Test 2 is two years. Top: Head/Eyes condition (see method section). Bottom: eyes condition. Asterisks indicate a significant difference between Test 1 and Test 2 in the same animal ($p < .05$).

RESULTS

The valid trials were equally distributed in the four spatial directions. Considering each spatial direction in the two conditions the percentage of valid trials ranged from 19.4% to 34% (*ns*, McNemar test).

Experiment 1

Head/Eyes condition. Statistical analysis showed a significant increase in the GFR performance in the three juvenile subjects when tested two years after the first test ($p < .05$) but not in the three adult monkeys (Figure 3, top). This result is also confirmed by the marked higher level of GFR of adults compared to juveniles only in Test 1 ($p < .001$) but not in Test 2 (Figure 3, top). Juveniles increase the percent of GFR with age ($p < .001$), while adults do not.

Eyes condition. Similarly to the Head/Eyes condition, we found a significant increase with age in the levels of GFR in two juvenile monkeys ($p < .05$) but not in the adult monkeys (Figure 3, bottom). This trend was also demonstrated when results of the three monkeys were plotted together (Figure 4, bottom). Here the statistical analysis showed that juveniles improve their GFR performance with age ($p < .0001$) while adults do not. Furthermore, adults showed higher levels of GFR compared to juveniles in both Test 1 ($p < .001$) and Test 2 ($p < .05$).

Experiment 2

We did not find any statistical difference between Tests 1 and 2 in juvenile and adult monkeys in either the Head/Eyes or the Eyes condition (see Figure 5). It is worth noting that the levels of GFR of monkeys are very similar to those of Test 1 in Experiment 1. In both the Head/Eyes and Eyes conditions, adults showed higher levels of GFR compared to juveniles in both Test 1 (Head/Eyes, $p < .05$; Eyes, $p < .005$) and Test 2 (Head/Eyes, $p < .05$; Eyes, $p < .005$).

Experiment 3

Figure 6 illustrates the results of the experiment. The binomial test revealed that in both monkeys the levels of GFR during the baseline (Monkey 1: $p < .05$ on day 1; $p < .0001$ on days 2 and 3; Monkey 2: $p < .05$ on days 1 and 2; $p < .005$ on day 3) and the training phase are higher than chance

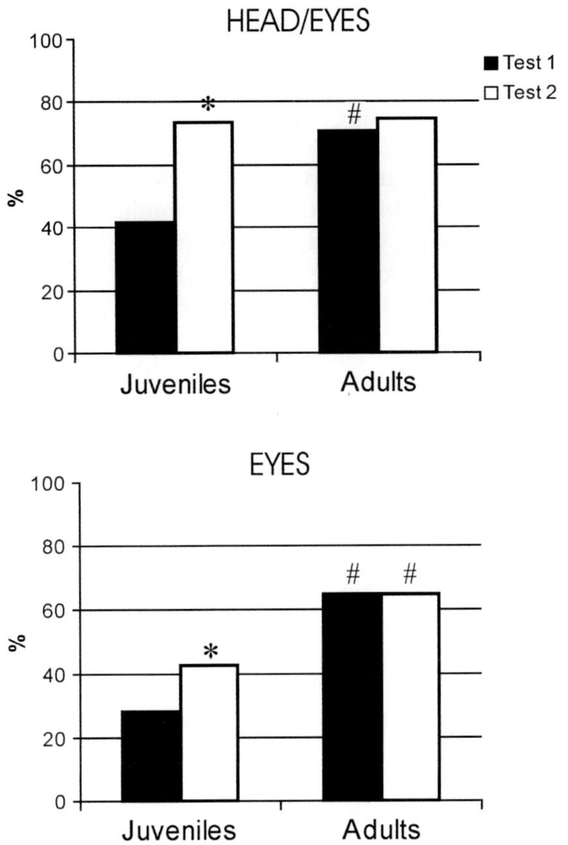

Figure 4. Percent of GFR in juvenile and adult monkeys (Experiment 1). Time interval between Test 1 and Test 2 is two years. The data recorded for the juvenile and adult monkeys are averaged and plotted together. * indicates the significance of the comparison between Test 1 and Test 2 ($p < .05$). # indicates the significance of the comparison between juveniles and adults in Test 1 and Test 2. Top: Head/Eyes condition (see method section). Bottom: eyes condition.

($p < .00001$ for both monkeys on each testing day). In both monkeys during the training phase the levels of GFR are significantly higher than those of the baseline phase on each testing day (levels of significance ranging between $p < .005$ and $p < .000001$). In Monkey 1 the performance of the animal during the baseline improved from day 1 to day 3 (day 1 vs. day 3, $p < .005$; day 2 vs. day 3, $p < .09$). However, this trend just missed statistical significance in monkey 2 (day 1 vs. day 3, $p < .09$).

DISCUSSION

In the follow-up study (Experiment 1) we confirmed previous investigations on the development of gaze-following behavior in macaques (Ferrari et al., 2000; Tomasello et al., 2001). In fact, when compared to juveniles, adult macaques showed a higher percentage of GFR based on the head and eyes as orienting cues. In addition, our data demonstrate an improvement with age of GFR in individuals observed after a two-year gap. This improvement did not occur in adult monkeys tested after the same time lapse. This latter result could be explained by a ceiling effect, in that adult pigtailed macaques' performance can reach a maximum level of 60–80% of correct GFR. Such levels of GFR in our previous study have been showed to be relatively high in adults when compared to controls (Ferrari et al., 2000). Thus, it is unlikely that, under these experimental conditions, adult macaques can further improve their GFR.

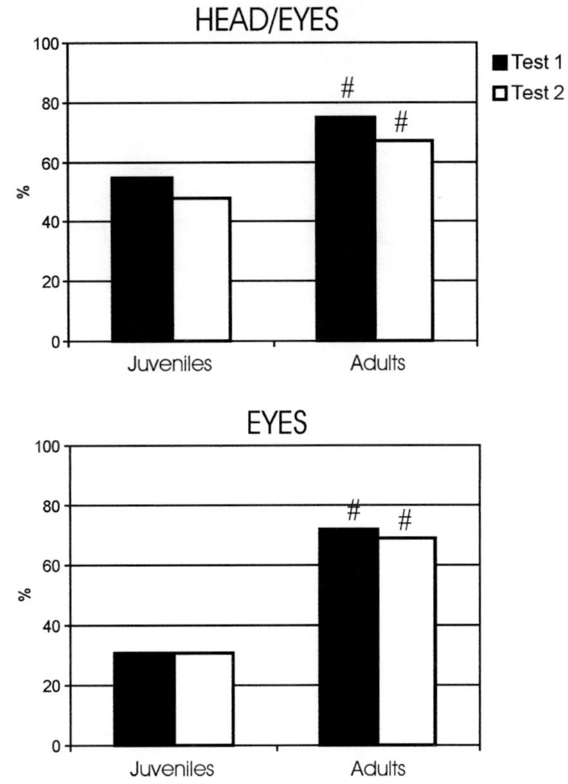

Figure 5. Percent of GFR in juvenile and adult monkeys (Experiment 2). Time interval between Test 1 and Test 2 is two weeks. The data recorded for the juvenile and adult monkeys are averaged and plotted together. # indicates the significance of the comparison between juveniles and adults in Test 1 and Test 2. Top: Head/Eyes condition (see method section). Bottom: eyes condition.

The time of emergence in ontogeny of the GFR (about three years) resulting from our studies is different from that found by Tomasello et al. (2001; about 5 months).

This discrepancy could be attributed to various factors. First, in our study the GFR was defined as

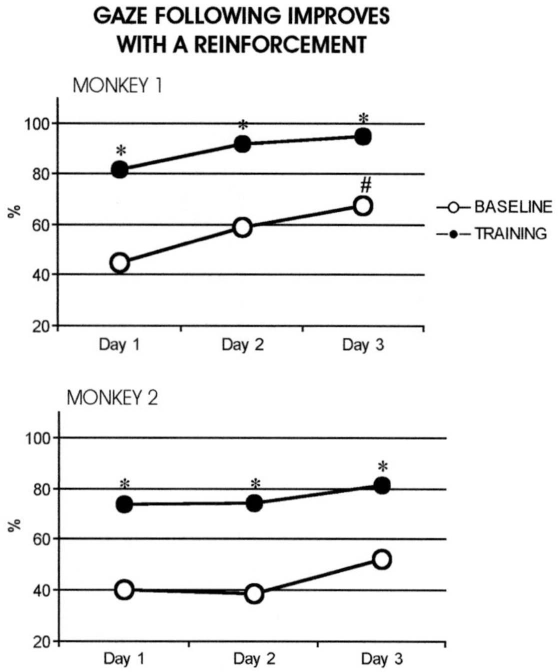

Figure 6. Percent of GFR during baseline and training phase tested in two monkeys on three different days (Experiment 3). Time interval between day 1 and day 2 and between day 2 and day 3 is 1 week. * indicates the significance of the comparison between training and baseline. # indicates the significance of the comparison between day 3 and day 1.

the direction of the first gaze movement after stimulus visual engagement. Thus, we discarded all other orienting gaze responses after the first gaze movement. Since Tomasello et al. (2001) adopted a different procedure, it is possible that they may have overestimated the number of correct gaze responses. In fact they assigned orienting gazes made by observers as correct GFRs, if animals looked (even briefly) in the direction of demonstrator's gaze during a long period (10 s) of exposure. During this period the monkey could also have looked in other directions, thus it is not possible to understand which was the main orienting response. Second, in Tomasello et al.'s study the experimenter always looked in the same direction (i.e., upward). This may have rendered this behavior repetitive and predictable in eliciting the monkeys' orienting responses to the same direction. A third factor could have been a difference in animals' housing and rearing conditions between our and Tomasello et al.'s study. Differences in environmental conditions are known to contribute to differences in behavioral and cognitive development (see also Bastian, Sponberg, Sponberg, Suomi, & Higley, 2003; Suomi & Harlow, 1975).

The study of Tomasello and colleagues on rhesus monkeys (2001) showed that after thirty repetitive exposures to the orienting stimulus (i.e., experimenter looking upward) in adults but not in infants, the GFR habituated. This result shows that learning processes such as habituation could play an important role in modulating GFR in macaques. However, up to now, learning processes underlying the emergence of this behavior in nonhuman primates have not been explored. In this respect, the increased performance of juveniles in GFR in Experiment 1 could be interpreted as the result of learning processes. Although in Experiments 1 and 2 macaques were not employed in an operant task, it is possible that the strong tendency to follow the gaze could have been reinforced by stimuli unnoticed by the experimenter. Monkeys could have increased their performance in GFR in the second test because they associated the experimenter's gaze with interesting stimuli within their environment. However, the results of Experiment 2 clearly ruled out the possibility that further exposure to experimenter's gaze could increase the performance of GFR in juveniles, as we recorded in Experiment 1. In fact, when the monkeys were tested on two different days, separated by a two-week period, their performance on the GFR did not change.

On the other hand, the findings reported here are compatible with the interpretation that in the course of the macaques' life, learning processes affecting GFR ability can take place over a long period of time. Individuals may need several exposures to social stimuli in order to tune their behavioral responses. In Experiment 1, during the two-year interval between Test 1 and Test 2, monkeys had surely the opportunity to practice and orient correctly their gaze based on their group-mates gaze direction. Nevertheless, it is still not clear how developmental and learning factors interact in the emergence of the gaze-following behavior.

The issue of whether gaze-following behavior can be affected by learning processes was addressed more directly in Experiment 3, by using an operant task. To do this, we reinforced this behavior in two monkeys trained to work under restrained and very controlled conditions. The results of this experiment showed that within very few trials the performance of the two juvenile monkeys was dramatically improved to a level that was comparable to that displayed by adults in Experiments 1 and 2. This demonstrated that gaze-following behavior can be strongly and easily influenced by an operant-conditioning methodology. Within three sessions the baseline performance (in which gaze shifts were not directly rewarded) of monkey 1 was already increased when compared to the first session. Also the second monkey displayed a similar trend. Thus, gaze-following behavior associated with positive experiences (i.e., reward) can improve in the course of the ontogeny of the individual.

The possibility of training gaze-following responses has been also tested in 8-month-old infants in a reinforcement paradigm (Corkum & Moore, 1998). During the training an interesting visual stimulus was shown to the infant if he/she followed the adult's gaze. The data showed that it is easier to train infants to look to the same location as the model than to the opposite location. Thus, it is very likely that, during development, similar mechanisms operate in humans and macaques in order to respond appropriately to gaze shift.

If this behavior is so sensitive to learning processes, why, then, does it take such a long time for a young monkey to display a fully established GFR? One possible answer is related to the relatively long time period of adolescence of macaques during which individuals acquire a series of cognitive and social skills including GFR. The timing for the acquisition of a fully developed GFR could be relatively long, probably due to the many factors that may affect this phenomenon, such as proximity to the observed individual, visual engagement with its head and eyes and close co-occurrence of GFR and a reward. Although we have no information on the difference in gaze-following abilities between monkeys in the wild and those reared in captivity, it is possible to postulate that the opportunities to reinforce GFR could be linked to relatively rare events, as all the above-mentioned conditions must be fulfilled.

Furthermore, our study did not explore the nature of the stimuli that can reinforce the GFR. The reward used in our experiment was food. However, other stimuli could have a different value and impact on the learning processes of monkeys, as also demonstrated in humans (Corkum & Moore, 1998). One could speculate that different types of stimuli, either social (e.g., an aggressive conspecific or a receptive female) or non-social (e.g., sources of food), can act as reinforcements of the gaze response although their impact on learning processes responsible for the GFR emergence can be different.

From a neurophysiological perspective, one of the most important perceptual components of GFR consists in the visual processing of others' gaze. Neurophysiological experiments in monkeys demonstrated that a cortical sector corresponding to the anterior part of the superior temporal sulcus contains neurons that respond to faces and eyes. In particular, there are neurons influenced by the specific head profile and others responding to specific eye directions (Perrett, Hietanen, Oram, & Benson, 1992, Perrett et al., 1985). Many cells discharge preferentially when head and eyes are shifted in the same direction. Other cells are sensitive to observation of both arm movement and gaze directed toward an object or a specific space location (Jellema, Baker, Wicker, & Perrett, 2000). This latter finding suggests that the visual information related to eye gaze is often coded together with other biological movements (e.g., reaching an object) relevant for detecting intentions. Noteworthy, this cortical sector has strict connections with the anterior part of inferior parietal lobule, where mirror neurons responding to observation of goal-directed hand actions have been described (Fogassi et al., 2005; Gallese, Ferrari, Kohler & Fogassi, 2002). Most of these neurons are able to code not only the observed motor act, but also the intention of the observed agent (Fogassi et al., 2005). Altogether these findings suggest the possible existence of a circuit able to code others' intentions based on information provided by eye gaze, other biological movements and the context.

Which neurophysiological mechanism determines gaze shift of the observer in response to the demonstrator's gaze is not well known. One could argue that GFR is an automatic/stereotyped reaction that could be completely controlled by subcortical structures, for example the superior colliculus. However, the specific feature of the visual stimulus suggests that its analysis is performed by a cortical structure, such as the temporal cortex (see above) and then the outcome of the analysis is exploited by areas involved in the control of saccadic eye movements (e.g., lateral intraparietal area or frontal eye fields). An alternative hypothesis is that observation of others' gaze can automatically recruit the same circuit involved in the production of gaze shift, that is, a mirror neuron mechanism for gaze behavior (Gallese et al., 2002). The recruitment of this circuit would produce two effects: recognition of the observed gaze and its immediate reproduction. A recent meta-analysis of brain-imaging experiments involving eye movements, shift of attention and gaze perception in humans showed that gaze perception activate the same network of fronto-parietal areas activated by gaze or attentional shifts (Grosbras, Laird, & Paus, 2005).

In the light of our findings, it is very likely that the described neural circuits involved in gaze perception and gaze shift integrate information acquired in the course of life span through learning processes.

The data described in this study corroborate the idea that macaques possess the basic machinery for the evolution of a mind-reading system. GFR in monkeys appears to be an automatic response, that probably gives access to a first level comprehension of the other's intention, paving the way to higher level cognitive phenomena such as joint and shared attention in a reciprocal dyadic relation.

Manuscript received 9 February 2007
Manuscript accepted 30 April 2007
First published online 31 May 2007

REFERENCES

Anderson, J. R., & Mitchell, R. W. (1999). Macaques but not lemurs coorient visually with humans. *Folia Primatolica*, *70*, 17–22.

Baron-Cohen, S. (1994). How to build a baby that read minds: cognitive mechanisms of mindreading. *Current Psychology of Cognition*, *13*, 513–552.

Baron-Cohen, S. (1995). *Mindblindness: an essay on autism and theory of mind*. Cambridge, MA: MIT Press.

Bastian, M. L., Sponberg, A. C., Sponberg, A. C., Suomi, S. J., & Higley, J. D. (2003). Long-term effects of infant rearing condition on the acquisition of dominance rank in juvenile and adult rhesus macaques (*Macaca mulatta*). *Developmental Psychology*, *42*, 44–51.

Butterworth, G., & Cochran, E. (1980). Towards a mechanism of joint visual attention in human infancy. *International Journal of Behavioral Development*, *3*, 253–272.

Butterworth, G., & Jarrett, N. (1991). What minds have in common is space: spatial mechanisms serving joint visual attention in infancy. *British Journal of Developmental Psychology*, *9*, 55–72.

Corkum, V., & Moore, C. (1995). Development of joint visual attention in infants. In C. Moore & P. J. Dunham (Eds.), *Joint attention: its origins and role in development* (pp. 61–83). Hillsdale, NJ: Lawrence Erlbaum Associates, Inc.

Corkum, V., & Moore, C. (1998). Origins of joint visual attention in infants. *Developmental Psychology*, *34*, 28–38.

Emery, N. J. (2000). The eyes have it: the neuroethology, function and evolution of social gaze. *Neuroscience and Biobehavioral Review*, *24*, 581–604.

Fa, J. E., & Lindburg, D. G. (1996). *Evolution and ecology of macaque societies*. Cambridge, UK: Cambridge University Press.

Ferrari, P. F., Kohler, E., Fogassi, L., & Gallese, V. (2000). The ability to follow eye gaze and its emergence during development in macaque monkeys. *Proceedings of the National Academy of Sciences of the USA*, *97*, 13997–14002.

Fogassi, L., Ferrari, P. F., Chersi, F., Gesierich, B., Rozzi, S., & Rizzolatti, G. (2005). Parietal lobe: from action organization to intention understanding. *Science*, *308*, 662–667.

Gallese, V., Ferrari, P. F., Kohler, E., & Fogassi, L. (2002). The eyes, the hand and the mind: behavioral and neurophysiological aspects of social cognition. In M. Bekoff, C. Allen, & M. G. Burghardt (Eds.), *The cognitive animal* (pp. 451–462). Boston: MIT Press.

Grosbras, M.-H., Laird, A. R., & Paus, T. (2005). Cortical regions involved in eye movements, shift of attention and gaze perception. *Human Brain Mapping*, *25*, 140–154.

Heyes, C. M. (1998). Theory of mind in nonhuman primates. *Behavioral and Brain Sciences*, *21*, 101–114.

Itakura, S. (1996). A exploratory study of gaze-monitoring in nonhuman primates. *Japanese Psychological Research*, *38*, 174–180.

Kummer, H. (1967). Tripartite relations in hadadryas baboons. In S. Altmann (Ed.), *Social communication among primates* (pp. 63–71). Chicago: University of Chicago Press.

Jellema, T., Baker, C. I., Wicker, B., & Perrett, D. I. (2000). Neural representation of the perception of the intentionality of actions. *Brain and Cognition*, *44*, 280–302.

Lorincz, E. N., Baker, C. I., & Perrett, D. I. (1999). Visual cues for attention following in rhesus monkeys. *Current Psychology of Cognition*, *18*, 973–1003.

Onishi, K. H., & Baillargeon, R. (2005). Do 15-month-old infants understand false beliefs? *Science*, *308*, 255–258.

Packer, C. (1977). Reciprocal altruism in *Papio anubis*. *Nature*, *265*, 441–443.

Paukner, A., Anderson, J. R., Fogassi, L., & Ferrari, P. F. (in press). Do facial gesture, visibility or speed of movement influence gaze following responses in pigtail macaques? *Primates*.

Perrett, D. I., Hietanen, J. K., Oram, M. W., & Benson, P. J. (1992). Organization and functions of the cells responsive to faces in the temporal cortex. *Philosophical Transactions of the Royal Society of London*, *335*, 23–30.

Perrett, D. I., Smith, P. A., Potter, D. D., Mistlin A. J., Head, A. S., Milner, A. D., et al. (1985). Visual cells in the temporal cortex sensitive to faces and gaze direction. *Proceedings of the Royal Society of London*, *223*, 293–317.

Povinelli, D. J., & Eddy, T. J. (1996). Joint visual attention. *Psychological Science*, *7*, 129–135.

Premack, D., & Woodruff, G. (1978). Does the chimpanzee have a theory of mind? *The Behavioral and Brain Sciences*, *4*, 532–535.

Scaife, M., & Bruner, J. S. (1975). The capacity of joint visual attention in the infant. *Nature*, *253*, 265–266.

Suomi, S. J., & Harlow, H. F. (1975). Effects of differential removal from group on social development of rhesus monkeys. *Journal of Child Psychology and Psychiatry*, *16*, 149–164.

Swindler, D. R. (1998). *Introduction to the primates.* Seattle, WA: University of Washington Press.

Tomasello, M., Call, J., & Hare, B. (1998). Five primate species follow the visual gaze of conspecifics. *Animal Behaviour*, *55*, 1063–1069.

Tomasello, M., Call, J., & Hare, B. (2003). Chimpanzees understand psychological states—the question is which ones and to what extent. *Trends in Cognitive Sciences*, *7*(4), 153–156.

Tomasello, M., Hare, B., & Agnetta, B. (1999). Chimpanzees follow gaze direction geometrically. *Animal Behaviour*, *58*, 769–777.

Tomasello, M., Hare, B., & Fogleman, T. (2001). The ontogeny of gaze following in chimpanzees, *Pan troglodytes*, and rhesus macaques, *Macaca mulatta*. *Animal Behaviour*, *61*, 335–348.

Walters, J. R. (1987). Transition to adulthood. In B. B. Smuts, D. L. Cheney, R. M. Seyfarth, R. W. Wrangham, & T. T. Struhsaker (Eds.), *Primate societies* (pp. 358–369). Chicago: University of Chicago Press.

Walters, J. R., & Seyfarth, R. M. (1987). Conflict and cooperation. In B. B. Smuts, D. L. Cheney, R. M. Seyfarth, R. W. Wrangham, & T. T. Struhsaker (Eds.), *Primate societies* (pp. 306–317). Chicago: University of Chicago Press.

SOCIAL NEUROSCIENCE, 2008, 3 (3–4), 250–260

Social cognition in premotor and parietal cortex

Naotaka Fujii, Sayaka Hihara, and Atsushi Iriki
RIKEN Brain Science Institute, Wako, Saitama, Japan

Socially correct behavior requires constant observation of the social environment. Behavior that was appropriate a few seconds ago is not guaranteed to be appropriate now. The brain keeps the eyes focused on the current social space and constantly updates its internal representation of the environment and social context. Monitoring the behavior of others is essential for this updating. The neural systems involved in perceiving the actions of others have been explored extensively, but the detailed, quantitative character of the system at the single-cell level remains poorly understood. To address this question, we used the new technique of multidimensional recording to record neuronal activity in monkeys simultaneously from ventral premotor cortex (PM) and parietal cortex in the left hemisphere while they performed a food grab task. Motion-related (MR) response was shown by 35% (52/148) of PM neurons and 54% (94/174) of parietal neurons, meaning their activity increased in response to various combinations of arm motions made by self and/or other. Both areas showed robust lateralized preference to Self–Right action. When it came to recognizing the actions of the other monkey, PM-MR neurons showed the same kind of right-arm preference as self-action while parietal-MR neurons, in contrast, did not show arm preference. And while both areas discriminated self-action from other, a significantly larger proportion of PM-MR neurons did so. These results suggest that PM neurons provide information about an action's agent and effector as primitives of action cognition within the mirror neuron network, while parietal neurons represent social space and participate in the recognition of another agent's actions in relation to one's own actions within the parieto-prefrontal network.

INTRODUCTION

The world is full of events, most of which we detect easily and respond to automatically. This suggests that our brains are continuously updating their models of the environment and preparing for likely or expected events. A major unresolved question in neuroscience is how the brain executes such functions. Since the environment changes continuously, this task must impose a heavy cognitive load on our brains. Among the hardest events to predict are the behaviors of others, because others' behaviors are driven by rules different from one's own. But despite the fact that social predictions are difficult, our brains are usually able to make them well enough to behave in a socially safe or advantageous manner.

Social brain function is what allows us to adapt our behavior and understand others' behavior in relation to social context (Adolphs, 2003). Social brain function guides our behaviors according to prevailing social rules in order to maximize the economical benefit as well as minimize the social risk our actions may engender. There are few studies of social brain function at the neural level (Ochsner & Lieberman, 2001). The most important aspect of social brain function is social cognition (Adolphs, 2001; Beer, Mitchell, &

Correspondence should be addressed to: Naotaka Fujii, BSI, RIKEN, 2–1 Hirosawa, WAKO, Saitama 351–0198, Japan. E-mail: na@brain.riken.jp

This research was supported by Grant-in-Aid for Scientific Research on Priority Areas—Integrative Brain Research—from the MEXT of Japan (17021048), Grant-in-Aid for Scientific Research on Priority Areas—Mobiligence—from the MEXT of Japan (18047029) and 2006 Riken Strategic Programs for R&D (President's Discretionary Fund).

We thank Mr T. Notoya for technical assistance.

www.psypress.com/socialneuroscience DOI:10.1080/17470910701434610

Ochsner, 2006; Gallese, Keysers, & Rizzolatti, 2004; Rizzolatti & Craighero, 2004; Saxe, 2006). To perform socially correct behavior we must stay vigilant and update our internal representation of the social environment continuously, because social situations are fluid and behavioral rules are often subtle.

The visual response of mirror neurons is thought to play an essential role in social brain function. Mirror neurons were first described in the primate premotor area in 1992 by di Pellegrino and colleagues (di Pellegrino, Fadiga, Fogassi, Gallese, & Rizzolatti, 1992) and later found in PFG of parietal cortex (Fogassi et al., 2005). Mirror neurons tend to respond both to specific actions by the experimenter and to the same action made by monkey itself (Rizzolatti & Craighero, 2004; Rizzolatti, Fadiga, Gallese, & Fogassi, 1996). Mirror neurons have been discussed in many contexts, including imitation learning (Arbib, 2005; Iacoboni, 2005; Iriki, 2006; Oztop, Kawato, & Arbib, 2006). These studies revealed that the mirror neuron system not only generates a sensorimotor copy of intended actions but also contributes to action learning through imitation. Communication (Ferrari, Gallese, Rizzolatti, & Fogassi, 2003; Lotze et al., 2006) is a process in which the mirror neuron system may be involved in understanding the intentions of others through gestural messages between individuals. This aspect has been discussed in relation to speech communication (Aziz-Zadeh, Koski, Zaidel, Mazziotta, & Iacoboni, 2006), because human imaging studies have demonstrated the contribution of the mirror system in speech (Corballis, 2004; Craighero, Bello, Fadiga, & Rizzolatti, 2002; Gentilucci & Corballis, 2006; Nishitani & Hari, 2002; Tettamanti et al., 2005).

Previous experiments on social brain function were performed in highly controlled and artificial environments that were mostly detached from real social contexts. The social and action stimuli were unidirectional, non-interactive and often rather predictable. Yet the essence of social communication is the bidirectional interaction between individuals and uncertainty in the environment. To study social cognitive brain function, reality, or at least a goodly degree of realism, must be introduced into the experimental environment. Such experiments require careful observation of social activity, which requires a certain amount of behavioral freedom for the animals being studied, which in turn renders conventional electrophysiological methods insufficient. To get around these limitations we developed multi-dimensional recording (MDR), a new technique that combines a motion capture system with a chronic multi-electrode recording system (Fujii, Hihara, & Iriki, 2005). With this technique, we aimed to reveal neural mechanisms of action cognition in the primate premotor and parietal cortices while monkeys were sharing the same social space.

METHODS

Subjects and preparations

Two male Japanese macaques (M1 and M2, 6.0 kg and 5.5 kg, respectively) were used for all recordings. All procedures used in the experiment were pre-approved by the RIKEN animal committee (H18–2B012) preceding the experiment. A recording chamber (30 × 50 mm) was surgically implanted in each monkey's skull over the left hemisphere. Neuronal activity was recorded from multiple tungsten electrodes (FHC, 0.12 mm diameter, impedance 800 k–1.2 MΩ at 1 kHz) that were chronically implanted during the following months (Fujii & Graybiel, 2003). The electrodes were attached to a custom-made micromanipulator that was affixed to the recording grid inside the recording chamber, and were inserted into the brain through a stainless guiding tube that penetrated the dura mater. The depth of each electrode was independently adjusted to obtain the best signal-to-noise (S/N) ratio. A depth adjustment was performed daily for each electrode to compensate for changes in the S/N ratio. Neural activity was recorded using a Digital Lynx system (Neuralynx, Tucson, AZ, USA). Recorded spikes were isolated using offline cluster-cutting software (Offline-Sort: Plexon, Dallas, TX, USA) with manually set parameters. The isolated spikes were then used for further analyses. Neural activity was recorded from both monkeys simultaneously from the ventral premotor cortex (PM) and the parietal cortex as identified by MRI images taken before the experiment (Figure 1B).

The monkeys' behavior was monitored and recorded using a motion capture system (Vicon: Vicon-Peak, Oxford, UK) sampling at 120 Hz and conventional video cameras. Each monkey wore a custom-ordered motion capture suit. Ten reflective markers were attached to each suit at bilateral shoulder, elbow, wrist, and hand, and at

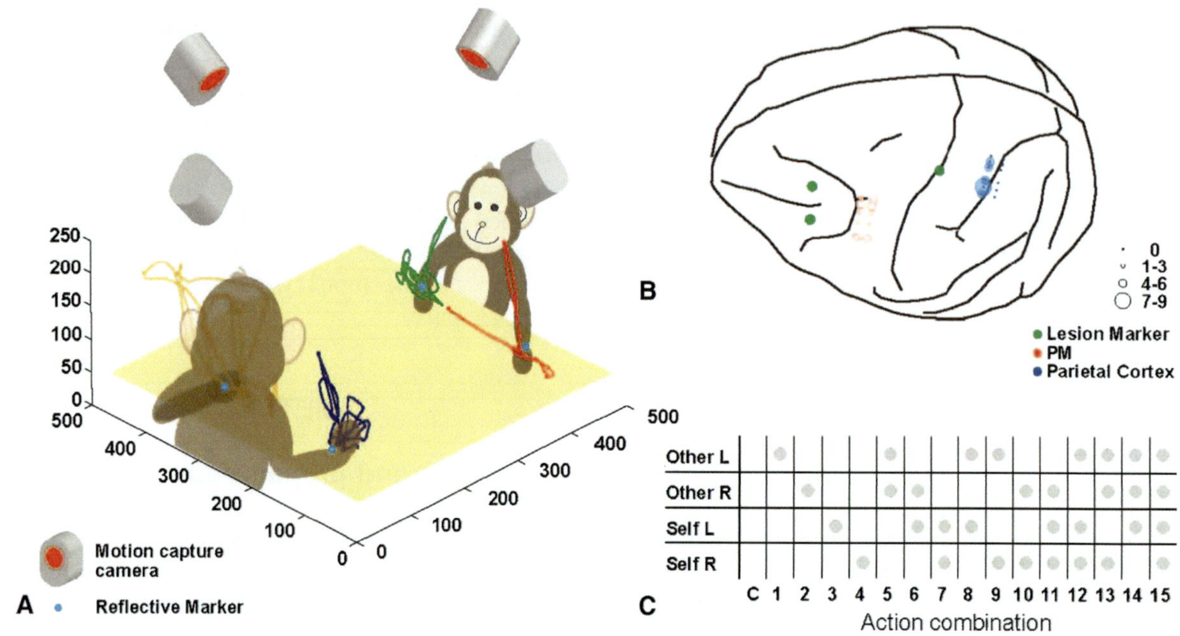

Figure 1. (A) Schematic view of the experimental setup. Two monkeys faced each other from either end of a table. Motion capture cameras were attached to the ceiling. The trajectories of markers attached to the wrists were traced for 1 minute and are plotted here in four colors. XYZ scale is shown in millimeters. (B) Recording map. Electrode tracks in PM and parietal cortex are shown by red and blue dots, respectively. Circles centered on each recording track indicate the number of MR neurons recorded from the track. Green dots represent marker locations used for reconstructions. (C) Table of action combinations (ACs). Sixteen action combinations (one control and 15 ACs) are shown as combinations of four arm movements (Other–Left, Other–Right, Self–Left and Self–Right). Gray dots indicate that the corresponding arm action occurred in the AC.

forehead and back of head. Ten motion capture cameras were placed around the monkeys. Using all motion capture camera views together with calibration data containing the cameras' spatial distribution, the motion capture software reconstructed each marker's location in three-dimensional space (Figure 1A).

Task

During the simultaneous recording of neural activity and motion data, the monkeys faced each other from either end of a square table (50 × 50 cm). They could see each other but could not touch each other. Each monkey sat in a primate chair with his waist, hips and legs restrained by a plastic cover, and his neck restrained by an aluminum collar attached to the chair. Although their waists, legs and necks were restrained, the monkeys could move their arms, torsos, and heads freely. Their task was a simple food grab task—that is, on each trial we placed a piece of food on the table, and the monkeys took the food if it was within reach. Since there was no overlap between their reachable spaces, there was no social conflict between them. No training was required for the performance of this task. However, recordings were not performed until after both monkeys had been exposed to the task situation for more than a month, which included chair training. This period was necessary for the monkeys to become familiar with experimental environment, so that they would feel more relaxed and behave naturally during recording.

Motion analysis

Ten markers were attached to each monkey, but our main interest was in arm movements. To extract arm movements, we used the trajectory data (X, Y, Z positions) of the four wrist markers to calculate their velocities. Motion episodes were separately defined for each wrist marker as epochs during which the marker's velocity exceeded a threshold velocity of 30 mm s^{-1}. Using these motion episodes, the time course of the monkeys' behavior was described by a temporal sequence of action combinations (AC). Four wrist markers, each of which did or did not exceed the threshold during any given epoch, yields a total of sixteen ($2^4 = 16$) ACs, which are shown in Figure 1C. The AC during which no motion episode was observed was defined as the control period. The rest of the 15 ACs consisted of various combinatorial patterns. For instance, AC7 indicates that one monkey's left and right arms moved simultaneously during the episode while the other monkey's arms remained still. By recreating AC sequences from all task periods, we could extract specific epochs in which specific combinations of actions occurred, and use them in subsequent analysis.

Neural analysis

The aim of the experiment was to probe the neural mechanisms of social cognitive function. Since there was no constraint on the monkeys' behavior during the task, conventional neural analysis turned out to be insufficient. In conventional analysis, neural response properties are inferred from histograms created from averaged, task-event-sorted neural activity recordings. This works fine in cases where one can collect a certain number of behavioral epochs during which the identical behavior is made around the same task event. But in our case, even though we could extract repeated behavioral events, such as reaching onset of Self–Right arm motion, there was always the possibility of contamination from other, uncontrollable events, such as simultaneous movements by the other monkey. Such contamination was unavoidable if we were to introduce realistic social interaction into the task environment, and so we found that histograms made by conventional methods were not reliable and could provide misleading results.

To get around this problem, we performed our neural analysis in terms of AC sequences. This allowed us to see how neurons responded to specific combinations of motion by specific body parts of both self and other, and thus freed our motion data of contamination. There were 15 ACs and one control period. For each cell, we generated a single-line histogram along the time course of each task period such that the center of each bin of the histogram was matched in time to a sample point of the AC sequence that was identical to the sample point of the motion capture data. There was no sorting or averaging applied in the histogram. Next, neural activity extracted from the histogram during each AC epoch and during the control period was compared. If a neuron showed a significantly higher firing rate (Wilcoxon test; $p < .05$) in at least one of the 15 AC epochs than in the control period, it was defined as a motion-related (MR) neuron. We also tried to find head-direction-related responses in both cortical areas, intending to use such data as indices of shifts of attention. Neural activity during the control period was compared between two epochs: one when the head was turning toward the right hemifield and the other was when the head was turning toward the left hemifield (Wilcoxon test; $p < .05$).

RESULTS

The MDR technique was used to isolate and identify 148 neurons in premotor cortex and 174 neurons in parietal cortex (Figure 1B). The activity of these neurons was recorded in two monkeys while they performed a food grab task. During the task, the monkeys faced each other from either end of a square table (Figure 1A). In each trial, the experimenter used his right arm to place a piece of food on the table within reach of one of the monkeys. The monkey who could reach the food grabbed it, transferred it to its mouth, and ate it. There was no competition between the monkeys. During the task, monkeys tended to avoid looking at each other and there was no apparent social behavior expressed between them, such as threatening.

First, we manually and subjectively extracted episodes of reaching movements from video images taken from multiple angles. Then neuronal activity was sorted and analyzed in relation to the onset of each of these subjectively identified arm-reaching movements. However, due to the lack of behavioral constraint in the task, there was concern about contamination from responses to other actions or events. We could not control the monkeys' actions to a degree where all movements they made were voluntary or purposeful. In each trial, a piece of food was placed on the table. If the monkeys thought they could reach the food, they attempted to retrieve it. However, until the food placement was final, there was an equal possibility for either monkey to reach the food. During this period, they tended to track the food and tried to grab it if it seemed to be within reach. They often moved both arms when reaching for the food. When we looked over the motion capture data, our concerns were confirmed: We found that less than 25% of the motion periods were free from such contamination. This was especially true during M1's left-hand movement periods, when 90% of the time other movements (mostly of M1's right arm) were also present.

We therefore analyzed our neural data using the action combination (AC) sequences described earlier, which eliminated concern about motion contamination (see methods). A second advantage of this method was that it provided a reliable control period during which no motion occurred. Using the AC sequences and the control period, neural activity was analyzed in response to 15 different combinations of actions made by Self–Left, Self–Right, Other–Left and Other–Right arms. After the analysis, each neuron had 15 statistical results that showed whether it had responded to each of these ACs or not. Ninety-four parietal and 52 PM neurons were identified as motion-related (MR) neurons. Again, MR neurons were defined as cells that showed significantly greater activity (Wilcoxon test; $p < .05$) during at least one AC epoch compared with the control period. MR neurons were found in the anterior wall of IPS but not in the posterior wall. In PM, in contrast, the MR neurons were found evenly throughout most of our recording tracks (Figure 1B). Parietal-MR neurons tended to show somatosensory response to right (but occasionally left) palm, distal arm, proximal arm and shoulder. PM-MR neurons tended to respond to right forearm. The region of parietal cortex where we recorded MR neurons did not include area PFG, where Fogassi and colleagues found mirror neurons (Fogassi et al., 2005). Due to the technical limitations of MDR, we could not define neural properties in relation to the specific actions of reaching, grasping and eating. However, in general, most of the parietal and PM-MR neurons increased their firing rates and peaked during reaching movements or the onset of grasping. Head direction did not modulate the activity of MR neurons in either area.

Figure 2 illustrates data from six sample neurons with averaged neural firing rates during the control period and 15 AC epochs. Red bars

Figure 2. Averaged neural firing rates of six individual neurons during control and AC epochs. Each panel represents the average neural firing rate of a single neuron in parietal cortex (A, B and E) or PM (C, D and F) during the control period (shown as C by green bars in the leftmost columns) and the 15 ACs (shown by numbers). Red bars indicate that the neuron showed MR response during the corresponding AC epoch.

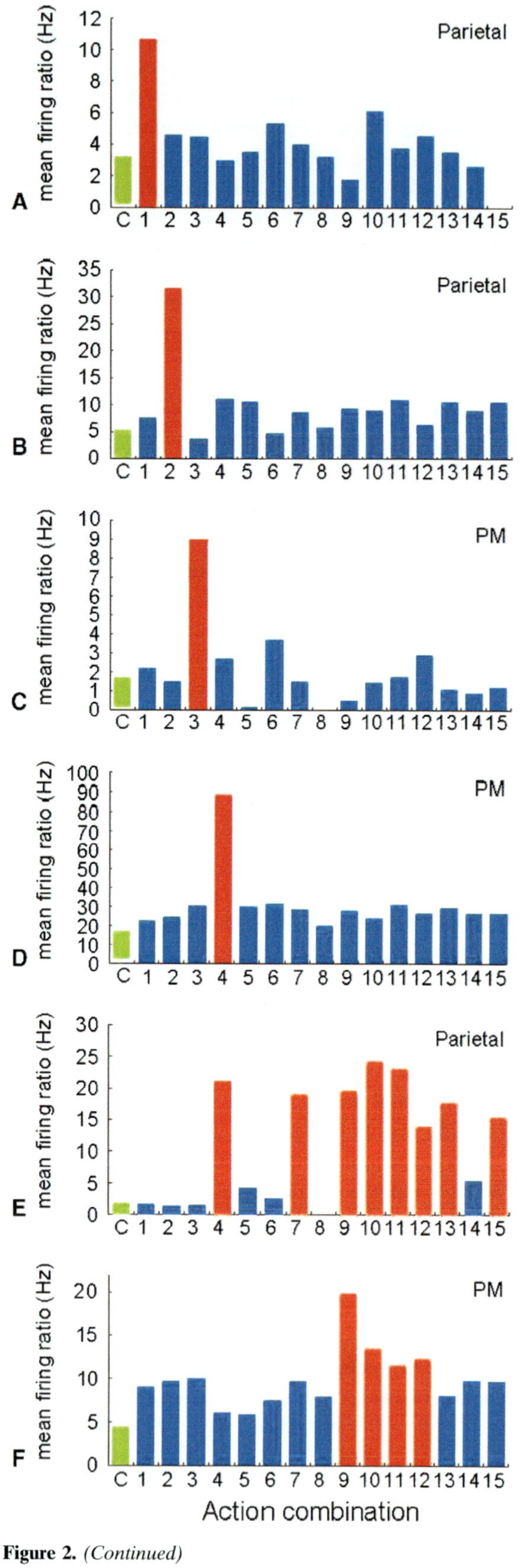

Figure 2. *(Continued)*

indicate that the neuron showed MR response at the corresponding AC epoch. Neurons in Figure 2A–D showed exclusive MR response in ACs 1–4 respectively. In other words these neurons showed MR response exclusively to motion by one particular arm, suggesting that they might be useful in discriminating an action's agent and effector. Figure 2E is typical of the parietal-MR neurons found in our study. The neuron showed MR response in all AC epochs containing Self–Right motion (ACs 4, 7, 9–13 and 15). Parietal neurons often showed such strong Self–Right motion preference and preserved the preference even when other motions occurred simultaneously. Figure 2F is a typical example of a PM-MR neuron, showing MR responses only in AC epochs during which multiple actions occurred but no exclusive MR response to single-arm actions (AC 1–4).

Figure 3A and B show cell counts and proportions of MR neurons in parietal cortex and PM, respectively, that showed positive response in each AC epoch. There was robust representation of Self–Right arm motion in both areas (AC 4). However, the proportion of parietal-MR neurons in eight ACs (indicated by asterisks) was significantly larger than among the PM-MR neurons (Fisher's exact test, $p < .05$). The result suggested that parietal-MR neurons could respond to more ACs than PM-MR neurons. This might be because of parietal-MR neurons' robust preference for Self–Right arm action, which seems to persist even when other actions occur simultaneously. In contrast, PM-MR neurons had weaker Self–Right arm preference and seemed to be more specialized and segregated for the detection of specific ACs as shown in Figure 2C, D and F.

Although Figure 3 shows how parietal and PM neurons discriminated different combinations of actions that occurred in the task, it was not still clear how MR neurons were discriminating between the agents. To address

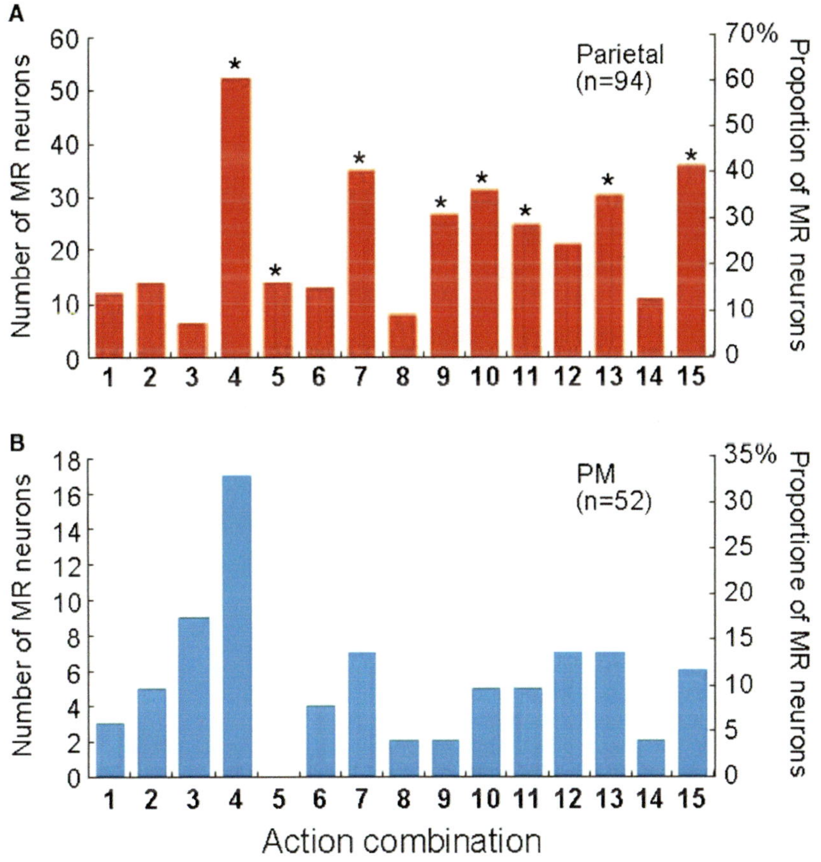

Figure 3. Number and proportion of MR neurons that showed MR response during 15 AC epochs. The MR responses of each neuron during all 15 ACs were tested. The number of MR neurons in parietal cortex (A) and PM (B) showing positive response during each AC was counted and plotted. Ninety-four neurons in parietal cortex and 52 neurons in PM were categorized as MR neurons. Asterisks indicate when there was a significantly larger proportion of parietal MR neurons in the AC compared with PM neurons in the same AC.

the question, we divided ACs into two categories. One was agent-specific ACs (ACs 1–5, 7) in which neurons segregated action of self and other. The other was agent-non-specific ACs (ACs 6, 8–15) in which neurons showed positive responses to actions made by both monkeys and hence did not discriminate between the agents. These two categorical responses did not have to be mutually exclusive, and could be represented in the same neuron. However, only neurons that showed exclusive response to agent-specific ACs (i.e., and no response to agent-non-specific ACs) can identify a specific action agent. Figure 4A and B indicate how MR neurons showed positive responses in these AC categories. Seventy-seven percent of parietal-MR neurons (72/94) and 66% of PM-MR neurons (34/52) had MR response in agent-specific ACs (blue circle). Meanwhile, in parietal cortex, 87% of MR neurons (82/94) showed MR response in agent-non-specific AC and 72% (37/52) in PM-MR (green circle). The most striking difference between the two areas was the cross-representation ratio of agent-specific and agent-non-specific ACs. Parietal-MR neurons showed significantly larger cross-representation than PM neurons (middle column: Chi square test, $p < .05$), indicating that exclusive agent-specific response (left column in Figure 4A and B) in PM was significantly larger than in parietal cortex. Exclusive agent-non-specific response (right column) did not differ between the two areas. (Chi square test, $p < .05$) The results indicated that PM could discriminate action agent better than parietal cortex.

Hence we could find a difference in action agent cognition between the two areas. But one question still remained, which was laterality of response to actions of other. To address the question, two AC categories were selected: "Other–Left" (ACs 1, 8, 9 and 12) and "Other–Right" (ACs 2, 6, 10 and 11). Figure 4C and D indicate the proportion of MR neurons that responded in both categories (middle column), exclusively in the "Other–Left" category (left column) and exclusively in the "Other–Right" category (right column). Response laterality was

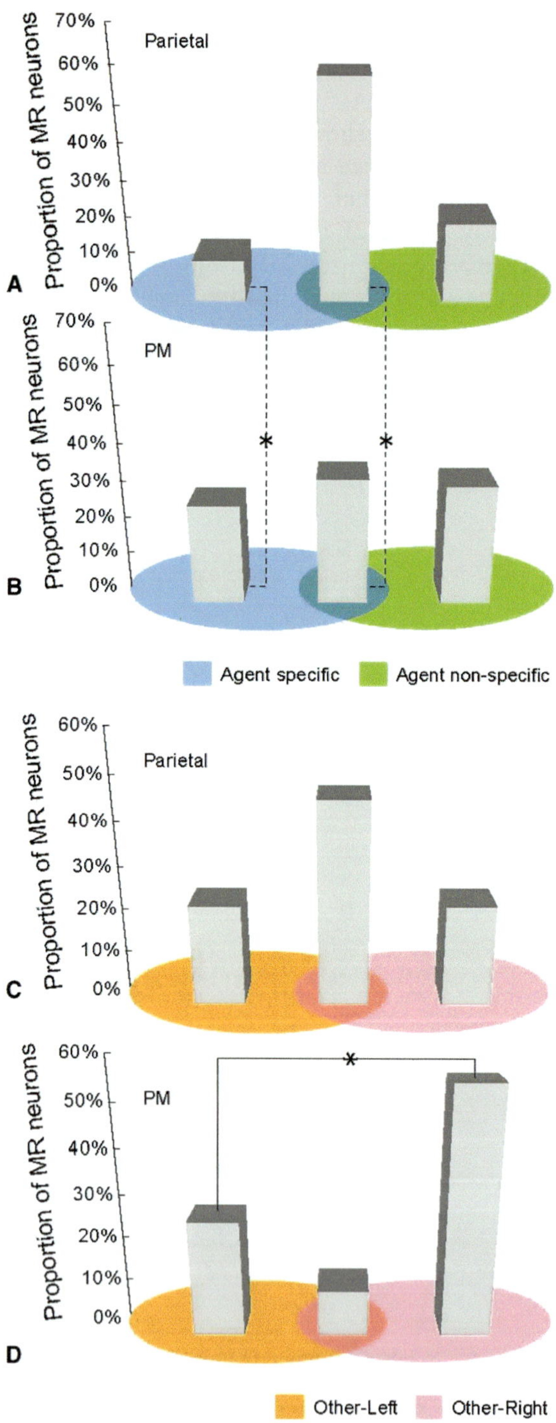

Figure 4. Proportion of MR neurons in parietal cortex (A and C) and PM (B and D) showing agent specificity and arm preference. (A, B) Fifteen ACs were categorized into two groups. One was agent-specific (ACs 1–5, 7; blue circle) and the other was agent-non-specific (ACs 6, 8–15; green circle). Proportion of MR neurons that showed MR response only in agent-specific (left column), only in agent-non-specific (right column), and in both (middle column), were plotted. (C, D) Eight ACs were categorized into two groups. One was "Other–Left" (ACs 1, 8, 9 and 12; orange circle) and the other was "Other–Right" (ACs 2, 6, 10 and 11; pink circle). Proportion of MR neurons that showed MR response only in "Other–Left" (left column), only in "Other–Right" (right column), and in both (middle column), were plotted. Asterisks indicate that there was significant proportional difference between two groups (Chi square test, $p < .05$).

Figure 4. *(Continued)*

not present in parietal-MR neurons, but in PM-MR neurons there was significant right-arm preference associated with cognition about the other monkey's actions.

DISCUSSION

Advantage of MDR

In conventional studies on social cognition, there are two ways of presenting visual stimuli as social cues. One way is for the experimenter to act toward or interact with the subject. The advantage here is that the stimuli are real, which elicits a greater neural response. This method allows the online optimization of action details to obtain maximal neural activity. The other method is to repeatedly present video images taken before the experiment. The advantage of using video stimuli is in the control of the quality and timing of presentation. But there are also disadvantages. The greatest problem is that monkeys tend to ignore or pay less attention to images on a screen compared with the real actions made by the experimenter, because stimuli isolated from true social context are meaningless to monkeys.

We simultaneously recorded neuronal activity from two cortical areas in two monkeys while precisely recording their behavior using a motion capture system. This MDR method (Fujii et al., 2005) has advantages and disadvantages compared with the conventional technique. The largest problem is a set of technical issues concerning the size and complexity of the dataset. Using our current analytical technique, we cannot accurately extract an action's semantics. We can subjectively describe the characteristics of each action, as in the conventional way, but the possibility of motion contamination is a constant concern. Another problem is that we do not have a reliable method of measuring eye positions. Oculomotor information is very important when discussing attention issues. In our current technique, we cannot fully discount potential effects of spatial attention on the neural activity we record. Head direction seems like it should be an indirect index of spatial attention, and in our analysis the PM or parietal neurons did not show head-direction-related modulation.

Nonetheless, MDR has at least two big advantages over other techniques. First, we can use the voluntary movements of real monkeys as visual stimuli that are embedded in real social contexts that matter to each monkey personally. Such stimuli are appropriate for the study of social cognition because the social cognition system in the monkey brain must be tuned to recognize the movements of other monkeys. The motion data allowed us to make quantitative descriptions of the monkeys' behavior that could then be used for neural analysis. In particular, the precise action-combination analysis we applied in the present study cannot be undertaken using other methods. Second, we can record neural activity simultaneously from multiple areas in multiple monkeys while they share the same social environment. These advantages are essential if we are to probe social brain function.

In this study, we aimed to see how PM and parietal neurons discriminate agent and effector in the shared space. For this purpose, MDR worked fine and provided sufficient and reliable results. MDR showed many more advantages than disadvantages.

Motion cognition and laterality

Mirror neurons were first described in 1992 (di Pellegrino et al., 1992). They were found in F5 of PM and were defined as goal-directed neurons (Gallese, Fadiga, Fogassi, & Rizzolatti, 1996). Their response properties were unique in several respects compared with other visually responsive neurons. Mirror neurons responded equally to motions of self and other that appeared to have similar goals. They were most sensitive to a preferred action and did not respond to actions that had different meanings. These properties suggested that mirror neurons may be involved in understanding the meaning of others' actions. This finding had a huge impact because it appeared to have relevance for many higher cognitive functions (Brunet-Gouet & Decety, 2006; Iacoboni & Dapretto, 2006; Saxe, Jamal, & Powell, 2006; Williams, Whiten, Suddendorf, & Perrett, 2001). Subsequently, imaging studies have identified mirror neurons in humans (Buccino et al., 2004; Iacoboni et al., 2005; Molnar-Szakacs, Kaplan, Greenfield, & Iacoboni, 2006). These imaging studies suggested that action recognition is not implemented by a single cortical area alone, but that multiple cortical areas play roles in the mirror system.

Although many aspects of the mirror neuron system have been discussed, some basic questions remain to be addressed. For example, if mirror neurons are important in social cognition, how do they respond to the behavior of another agent in a real social space? A few studies (Rizzolatti et al., 1996) have used the activity of real monkeys as visual stimuli, but none of them could produce the sort of detailed quantitative analysis that we did in this experiment. One little discussed question is preference for action laterality in another agent's motions. Yet this function must be very important in interpreting the meaning of another's actions, since movements of the right and left arms often contain contextually different information. Our study revealed that PM-MR neurons had significant preference for right-arm action by the other monkey, but parietal neurons did not. The information about effector laterality represented in PM-MR neurons might be shared within the mirror neuron system and used for inferring the intentions of others.

Specifying action agent

The sense of agency is one of the largest issues in social neuroscience (Jackson & Decety, 2004). The question of how neurons are discriminating between self and other has been discussed, but the neural mechanism underlying the function has not been fully revealed. Parietal cortex and PM are both thought to be involved in the function (Farrer et al., 2003; Jackson & Decety, 2004; Jeannerod, 2003). In our study, we found that a subpopulation of MR neurons in PM and parietal cortex responded only to the actions of another. To segregate self and other, visual information stemming from another's actions must be integrated with afferent somatosensory and motor information (Cunnington, Windischberger, Robinson, & Moser, 2006). If a visually perceived action does not accompany a simultaneous somatomotor signal of self-action, the observed action is very likely being made by the other. Such integration might be implemented in and between multiple areas in the social brain network, rather than in a single dedicated brain area, with each participating area contributing specific forms or components of social action cognition such as we have described in this study (Farrer et al., 2003; Jackson & Decety, 2004; Jellema & Perrett, 2006).

Role of MR neurons in social cognition

MR neurons responded to multiple ACs in a complex manner. In some neurons, response to self-action was modulated by the co-occurrence of action by the other monkey, as if there was interaction between the responses in different ACs. Similar observations were reported in human imaging studies in inferior frontal cortex and superior temporal cortex (Iacoboni et al., 2001; Nishitani & Hari, 2000). The modulation was observed in both areas and seems to be a result of integration of different action properties. Parietal neurons showed more cross-representation of AC responses than PM neurons. This suggests that parietal neurons have broader response modalities and can integrate action information as well as other environmental parameters that are proposed to be represented in the area (Colby & Goldberg, 1999). If this is indeed the case, parietal cortex is able to represent internal subjective social space by integrating socially important issues (Fujii, Hihara, & Iriki, 2006). In contrast, the population of PM-MR neurons we found could discriminate action agents and action effectors precisely. Such information must be essential in action cognition, and is already proposed to be a function of PM (Rizzolatti et al., 1996; Rizzolatti & Craighero, 2004). The results indicate that PM-MR neurons represent essential primitives of social cognition that might be used in the mirror neuron network for inferring the intentions of others.

PM and parietal MR neurons represent similar information in terms of action cognition at the single-cell level, but at the population level they are involved in different social-cognitive systems—the mirror neuron network and the parieto-frontal network, respectively. These two networks perform different, but parallel and complementary, functions in social cognition (Fuster, 2006; Iriki, 2006).

Manuscript received 8 January 2007
Manuscript accepted 13 April 2007
First published online 1 June 2007

REFERENCES

Adolphs, R. (2001). The neurobiology of social cognition. *Current Opinion in Neurobiology*, *11*(2), 231–239.

Adolphs, R. (2003). Cognitive neuroscience of human social behaviour. *Nature Reviews Neuroscience*, *4*(3), 165–178.

Arbib, M. A. (2005). From monkey-like action recognition to human language: an evolutionary framework for neurolinguistics. *Behavioral Brain Science*, *28*(2), 105–124 [discussion 125–167].

Aziz-Zadeh, L., Koski, L., Zaidel, E., Mazziotta, J., & Iacoboni, M. (2006). Lateralization of the human mirror neuron system. *Journal of Neuroscience*, *26*(11), 2964–2970.

Beer, J. S., Mitchell, J. P., & Ochsner, K. N. (2006). Special issue: Multiple perspectives on the psychological and neural bases of social cognition. *Brain Research*, *1079*(1), 1–3.

Brunet-Gouet, E., & Decety, J. (2006). Social brain dysfunctions in schizophrenia: A review of neuroimaging studies. *Psychiatry Research*, *148*(2–3), 75–92.

Buccino, G., Vogt, S., Ritzl, A., Fink, G. R., Zilles, K., Freund, H. J., et al. (2004). Neural circuits underlying imitation learning of hand actions: an event-related fMRI study. *Neuron*, *42*(2), 323–334.

Colby, C. L., & Goldberg, M. E. (1999). Space and attention in parietal cortex. *Annual Review Neuroscience*, *22*, 319–349.

Corballis, M. C. (2004). FOXP2 and the mirror system. *Trends in Cognitive Science*, *8*(3), 95–96.

Craighero, L., Bello, A., Fadiga, L., & Rizzolatti, G. (2002). Hand action preparation influences the responses to hand pictures. *Neuropsychologia*, *40*(5), 492–502.

Cunnington, R., Windischberger, C., Robinson, S., & Moser, E. (2006). The selection of intended actions and the observation of others' actions: a time-resolved fMRI study. *NeuroImage*, *29*(4), 1294–1302.

di Pellegrino, G., Fadiga, L., Fogassi, L., Gallese, V., & Rizzolatti, G. (1992). Understanding motor events: a neurophysiological study. *Experimental Brain Research*, *91*(1), 176–180.

Farrer, C., Franck, N., Georgieff, N., Frith, C. D., Decety, J., & Jeannerod, M. (2003). Modulating the experience of agency: a positron emission tomography study. *NeuroImage*, *18*(2), 324–333.

Ferrari, P. F., Gallese, V., Rizzolatti, G., & Fogassi, L. (2003). Mirror neurons responding to the observation of ingestive and communicative mouth actions in the monkey ventral premotor cortex. *European Journal of Neuroscience*, *17*(8), 1703–1714.

Fogassi, L., Ferrari, P. F., Gesierich, B., Rozzi, S., Chersi, F., & Rizzolatti, G. (2005). Parietal lobe: from action organization to intention understanding. *Science*, *308*(5722), 662–667.

Fujii, N., & Graybiel, A. M. (2003). Representation of action sequence boundaries by macaque prefrontal cortical neurons. *Science*, *301*(5637), 1246–1249.

Fujii, N., Hihara, S., & Iriki, A. (2005). *Multi-dimensional recording during monkey tool use learning* (2005. 363.2. 2005 Abstract Viewer/Itinerary Planner). Washington, DC: Society for Neuroscience [online].

Fujii, N., Hihara, S., & Iriki, A. (2006). *Conflicting social environment represented in primate parietal cortex* (2006. 63.6 2006 Abstract Viewer/Itinerary Planner). Atlanta, GA: Society for Neuroscience [online].

Fuster, J. M. (2006). The cognit: a network model of cortical representation. *International Journal of Psychophysiology*, *60*(2), 125–132.

Gallese, V., Fadiga, L., Fogassi, L., & Rizzolatti, G. (1996). Action recognition in the premotor cortex. *Brain*, *119*(2), 593–609.

Gallese, V., Keysers, C., & Rizzolatti, G. (2004). A unifying view of the basis of social cognition. *Trends in Cognitive Science*, *8*(9), 396–403.

Gentilucci, M., & Corballis, M. C. (2006). From manual gesture to speech: a gradual transition. *Neuroscience & Biobehavioral Reviews*, *30*(7), 949–960.

Iacoboni, M. (2005). Neural mechanisms of imitation. *Current Opinion in Neurobiology*, *15*(6), 632–637.

Iacoboni, M., & Dapretto, M. (2006). The mirror neuron system and the consequences of its dysfunction. *Nature Reviews Neuroscience*, *7*(12), 942–951.

Iacoboni, M., Koski, L. M., Brass, M., Bekkering, H., Woods, R. P., Dubeau, M. C., et al. (2001). Reafferent copies of imitated actions in the right superior temporal cortex. *Proceedings of the National Academy of Sciences of the USA*, *98*(24), 13995–13999.

Iacoboni, M., Molnar-Szakacs, I., Gallese, V., Buccino, G., Mazziotta, J. C., & Rizzolatti, G. (2005). Grasping the intentions of others with one's own mirror neuron system. *PLoS Biology*, *3*(3), E79.

Iriki, A. (2006). The neural origins and implications of imitation, mirror neurons and tool use. *Current Opinion in Neurobiology*, *16*(6), 660–667.

Jackson, P. L., & Decety, J. (2004). Motor cognition: a new paradigm to study self–other interactions. *Current Opinion in Neurobiology*, *14*(2), 259–263.

Jeannerod, M. (2003). The mechanism of self-recognition in humans. *Behavioral Brain Research*, *142*(1–2), 1–15.

Jellema, T., & Perrett, D. I. (2006). Neural representations of perceived bodily actions using a categorical frame of reference. *Neuropsychologia*, *44*(9), 1535–1546.

Lotze, M., Heymans, U., Birbaumer, N., Veit, R., Erb, M., Flor, H., et al. (2006). Differential cerebral activation during observation of expressive gestures and motor acts. *Neuropsychologia*, *44*(10), 1787–1795.

Molnar-Szakacs, I., Kaplan, J., Greenfield, P. M., & Iacoboni, M. (2006). Observing complex action sequences: The role of the fronto-parietal mirror neuron system. *NeuroImage*, *33*(3), 923–935.

Nishitani, N., & Hari, R. (2000). Temporal dynamics of cortical representation for action. *Proceedings of the National Academy of Sciences of the USA*, *97*(2), 913–918.

Nishitani, N., & Hari, R. (2002). Viewing lip forms: cortical dynamics. *Neuron*, *36*(6), 1211–1220.

Ochsner, K. N., & Lieberman, M. D. (2001). The emergence of social cognitive neuroscience. *American Psychology*, *56*(9), 717–734.

Oztop, E., Kawato, M., & Arbib, M. (2006). Mirror neurons and imitation: a computationally guided review. *Neural Networks*, *19*(3), 254–271.

Rizzolatti, G., & Craighero, L. (2004). The mirror-neuron system. *Annual Review of Neuroscience*, *27*, 169–192.

Rizzolatti, G., Fadiga, L., Gallese, V., & Fogassi, L. (1996). Premotor cortex and the recognition of motor actions. *Brain Research Cognitive Brain Research*, *3*(2), 131–141.

Saxe, R. (2006). Uniquely human social cognition. *Current Opinion in Neurobiology*, *16*(2), 235–239.

Saxe, R., Jamal, N., & Powell, L. (2006). My body or yours? The effect of visual perspective on cortical body representations. *Cerebral Cortex*, *16*(2), 178–182.

Tettamanti, M., Buccino, G., Saccuman, M. C., Gallese, V., Danna, M., Scifo, P., et al. (2005). Listening to action-related sentences activates fronto-parietal motor circuits. *Journal of Cognitive Neuroscience*, *17*(2), 273–281.

Williams, J. H., Whiten, A., Suddendorf, T., & Perrett, D. I. (2001). Imitation, mirror neurons and autism. *Neuroscience & Biobehavioral Reviews*, *25*(4), 287–295.

SOCIAL NEUROSCIENCE, 2008, 3 (3–4), 261–275

Psychology Press
Taylor & Francis Group

Neural substrates for observing and imagining non-object-directed actions

Fausta Lui
Università di Modena e Reggio Emilia, Modena, Italy

Giovanni Buccino
Università di Parma, Parma, Italy

Davide Duzzi and Francesca Benuzzi
Università di Modena e Reggio Emilia, Modena, Italy

Girolamo Crisi
Azienda Ospedaliera di Parma, Parma, Italy

Patrizia Baraldi, Paolo Nichelli, and Carlo Adolfo Porro
Università di Modena e Reggio Emilia, Modena, Italy

Giacomo Rizzolatti
Università di Parma, Parma, Italy

The present fMRI study was aimed at assessing the cortical areas active when individuals observe *non-object-directed* actions (mimed, symbolic, and meaningless), and when they imagine performing those same actions. fMRI signal increases in common between action observation and motor imagery were found in the premotor cortex and in a large region of the inferior parietal lobule. While the premotor cortex activation overlapped that previously found during the observation and imagination of *object-directed* actions, in the parietal lobe the signal increase was not restricted to the intraparietal sulcus region, known to be active during the observation and imagination of object-directed actions, but extended into the supramarginal and angular gyri. When contrasting motor imagery with the observation of non-object-directed actions, signal increases were found in the mesial frontal and cingulate cortices, the supramarginal gyrus, and the inferior frontal gyrus. The opposite contrast showed activation virtually limited to visual areas. In conclusion, the present data define the common circuit for observing and imagining non-object-directed actions. In addition, they show that the representation of non-object-directed actions include parietal regions not found to be involved in coding object-directed actions.

Correspondence should be addressed to: Giacomo Rizzolatti, Dipartimento di Neuroscienze, Università di Parma, Via Volturno 39, I-43100 Parma, Italy. E-mail: giacomo.rizzolatti@unipr.it

This study was supported by MIUR (Ministero Istruzione Università e Ricerca; grants COFIN to GR and FL, and FIRB RBNE018ET9) and EU contract QLG3-CT-2002-00746.

www.psypress.com/socialneuroscience DOI:10.1080/17470910701458551

INTRODUCTION

Non-object-directed actions constitute a large part of the human motor repertoire. They include different types of actions, among which are mimed, symbolic and meaningless actions. Mimed actions are those in which the agent performs a pantomime of an action normally acted upon an object or pretends to use an object. Symbolic actions (sometimes referred to as gestures or emblems) allow the agent to convey a specific *conventional* meaning (such as in the "OK" sign), beyond the motor aspects of the performed actions. This added up, conventional meaning of the action largely depends on the context in which it is executed, and implies a shared cultural background both in the agent and in the observer of the action. Finally, meaningless actions do not express any specific content beyond their motor appearance. They may be done with no specific purposes or even just for fun. Although many animals can perform actions that do not imply the use of an object (they can for example move their heads and/or eyes to look for or indicate danger), even apes are not able to use their forelimbs to mime an action implying the use of an object and only rarely can use their hands to perform symbolic gestures for communicative purposes (see Tomasello & McCall, 1997). Furthermore, non-object-directed actions appear later in the development (see Butterworth & Harris, 1994), thus suggesting the necessity for more sophisticated cognitive abilities compared to object-directed actions.

Despite the great variety of non-object-directed actions, and the large use humans make of them, so far very few studies have been planned to assess brain regions where these actions are represented. As for mimed actions, brain regions active during their observation have only rarely been investigated. In a PET study in which the instruction was either to observe complex hand/arm actions without any purpose, or to observe those actions in order to imitate them later, Grèzes, Costes, and Decety (1998) found increased activity in the inferior parietal lobule (IPL), in the superior parietal lobule and in the premotor cortex. In a more recent fMRI study, Buccino et al. (2001) also found activation in the premotor cortex, but not in the parietal lobe, with different premotor sectors active depending on the effector (hand, mouth, foot) involved in the observed non-object-directed action. Similar results were found by two very recent studies (Sakreida, Schubotz, Wolfensteller, & von Cramon, 2005; Wheaton, Thompson, Syngeniotis, Abbott, & Puce, 2004).

As for symbolic actions, most studies investigated brain areas engaged during the observation of static hand postures conveying a symbolic meaning, rather than symbolic actions themselves (Nakamura et al., 2004; Peigneux et al., 2000; Tanaka, Inui, Iwaki, Konishi, & Nakai, 2001). The results of these studies mainly showed activation of visual areas, but not of the circuit known to be involved in action recognition (mirror neuron system). An exception to this was the study by Nakamura et al. (2004), who showed that the observation of symbolic hand postures, as compared to meaningless ones, activated the inferior parietal lobule, besides visual areas.

To our knowledge, so far no studies have investigated systematically the neural substrates underlying the internal generation of non-object-directed hand actions, be they mimed, symbolic, or meaningless. In fact, most motor imagery studies investigated the cortical circuits involved in imagining simple movements, such as flexion or extension of specific body parts (Binkofski et al., 2000; Gerardin et al., 2000; Hanakawa et al., 2003; Kuhtz-Buschbeck et al., 2003; Porro et al., 1996; Stephan et al., 1995; however, see the recent study by Cross, Hamilton, & Grafton, 2006, for mental representation of complex body movements), while a few studies traced the circuits active during motor imagery of object-directed actions (Decety et al., 1994; Grafton, Arbib, Fadiga, & Rizzolatti, 1996; Johnson et al., 2002; Simon et al., 2004). As a whole, these studies showed that motor imagery recruits a parieto-frontal circuit similar to that active during the execution of object-directed actions (Binkofski et al., 1999; Kuhtz-Buschbeck et al., 2003), including frontal-mesial areas and, at least for some tasks, the primary motor area (e.g., Michelon, Vettel, & Zacks, 2006; Porro et al., 1996). Similarly to action observation, also during motor imagery, different sectors of the premotor cortex have been found active depending on the effector involved in the movement to be imagined (Ehrsson, Geyer, & Naito, 2003).

Given the importance of non-object-directed actions in social interactions and the lack of systematic investigations on how they are coded in the brain, we carried out an event-related fMRI study, with two experimental conditions. In one condition, participants had to observe different video clips showing symbolic, mimed and meaningless hand actions; in the other one they were required to perform "first-person" motor imagery of those same actions, namely the so-called kinesthetic motor imagery (Jeannerod, 1994) in which the subjects imagine themselves actually performing the movements.

The study had two aims. The first one was to assess whether the brain regions that house the motor representations recruited during the observation of non-object-directed actions were also active during the motor imagery of those same actions. The second one was to define whether observing or internally generating non-object-directed actions (and in particular symbolic and mimed actions) causes the activation not only of brain regions housing their motor representations, but also of additional areas possibly conveying the additional information they are endowed with.

MATERIALS AND METHODS

Participants

The experiments were performed on 16 healthy volunteers (5 male and 11 female; mean age 24, range 20–31). They were all right-handed, as assessed by means of the Edinburgh Inventory (Oldfield, 1971), and had normal, or corrected-to-normal, visual acuity. All participants gave their informed consent to the experiment, which had been approved by the Ethics Committee of the University of Modena and Reggio Emilia. Participants received a fee for taking part in the experiment.

Experimental protocol

The participants, while being scanned, were presented with video clips showing purely unimanual movements belonging to three different categories: (1) mimed actions; (2) symbolic actions; and (3) meaningless movements. Each category comprised three movements. Mimed actions: pantomime of turning a large knob, turning a screw, and knocking at a door. Symbolic actions: the "OK" sign, the sign of victory, and the hello gesture. Meaningless actions: three different hand movements devoid of any meaning. All actions were done by the same actress; only her trunk and right arm were visible (Figure 1). The video clips were projected on a screen, placed in front of the gantry, and were viewed by participants through a mirror. The participants were not shown the stimuli before the beginning of the fMRI experiment, but they were warned that some of the actions they were about to see in the video clips were meaningful, and others were meaningless. At the end of the experiment, the participants were debriefed about the observed stimuli (see below) in order to check whether they had paid attention to them.

The experiment consisted of two conditions: (1) action observation; and (2) motor imagery. Instructions given before the experiment emphasized the first-person characteristic of the imagery task (Jeannerod, 1994; Jeannerod & Frak, 1999). Trials in which participants had to observe actions and trials in which they had to imagine actions were intermixed and pseudorandomly presented. For the sake of symmetry, in both conditions the temporal organization of trials was similar. Figure 2 shows the experimental design. All trials started with the presentation of a short video clip lasting 2 s. This clip showed an action, performed only once, belonging to one of the three stimulus categories described above. The participants were instructed to watch it carefully. After the end of the video clip, the participants saw a gray screen that after 10 s turned into either green or red for 2 s. A red screen cued the participants to expect a new video clip (duration 3 s) showing a hand action different from that previously observed, but belonging to the same action category. In this clip, the same action was presented twice. Participants were instructed to carefully watch the new action and to extract its meaning, if present. A green screen cued the participants to imagine themselves performing the previously observed action (first-person motor imagery) starting the motor imagery at the moment when the screen turned blue (duration 3 s). In both action observation and motor imagery trials, an interval of 13 s occurred before the beginning of the next trial, in order to allow the task-related hemodynamic response to return to baseline. Each trial lasted a total of 30 s (Figure 2). Each run consisted of 21 trials performed in a pseudorandom order, with 9 observation trials, 9 imagery trials, plus 3 "null event" trials, where only a short video clip (2 s) was shown at the beginning of the trial, followed by a gray screen. Of all presented actions, one third consisted of symbolic actions, one third of mimed actions and one third of meaningless actions. Each subject underwent 4 runs, for a total of 84 trials.

Figure 1. Frames from the videos showing non-object-directed actions used as stimuli: knocking at a door (mimed action; left column); OK sign (symbolic action; central column); a meaningless hand action (right column).

fMRI data acquisition and analysis

Functional images were acquired from 18 contiguous axial slices (6 mm each) by a GE 1.5 T MR system and an echo-planar BOLD-sensitive sequence (FOV 24×24 cm; matrix 64×64; in-plane voxel size 3.75×3.75 mm; TE = 60 ms; TR = 2000 ms). Structural images were obtained

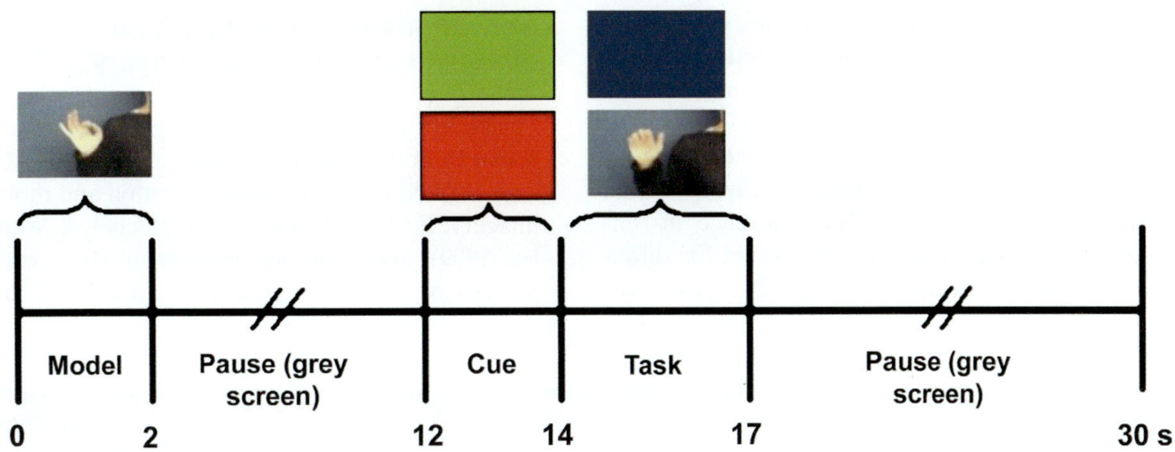

Figure 2. Experimental design. Temporal sequence of events during each trial. The video clip displayed during the first two seconds was the "model" for the imagery task. See methods for other details.

from the same planes using a standard T_1 weighted sequence. In addition, a high-resolution T_1-weighted anatomical image of each subject was acquired to allow precise anatomical localization (voxel size: $0.97 \times 0.97 \times 1.3$ mm; FOV: 24×24 cm; matrix: $256 \times 256 \times 120$).

Image processing and analysis were carried out using MATLAB (Mathworks Inc., Natiek, MA, USA) and the Statistical Parametric Mapping package (SPM99, Wellcome Department of Imaging Neuroscience, London, UK). The functional images were realigned and smoothed, then each subject was analyzed separately; a significance threshold of $p < .05$, corrected for multiple comparisons, was adopted. For each trial, the events that were modeled were either the motor imagery or the action observation task (duration 3 s, occurring at second 14 through 17 of the trial; see Figure 2 for the experimental paradigm). The following contrasts were examined in single subjects and in the group analysis: motor imagery; action observation; the conjunction imagery/observation; and the subtractions imagery vs. observation and observation vs. imagery. Functional images were spatially normalized to allow group analysis. A voxel threshold for statistical significance of $p < .001$ (uncorrected) was adopted in the group random effects analysis (Penny & Holmes, 2004), together with a spatial extent threshold of 20 voxels. Only the results of the group analysis are shown here (same contrasts as mentioned above for the single-subject analysis). Small volume corrections were adopted to test the a priori hypothesis regarding the differential activations between classes of actions in the left parietal cortex, based on the coordinates obtained in previous studies (Buccino et al., 2001; Peigneux et al., 2004).

Participant debriefing

At the end of the experiment, all volunteers recalled the observed movements This is proven by the fact that they could correctly name the meaningful actions and assign them to either mimed or symbolic categories; as to the meaningless movements, they could correctly perform them. All volunteers clearly described having a kinesthetic, "first-person" feeling of the movements they had to imagine to perform. Three of the volunteers attributed a meaning to all meaningless actions; they were therefore discarded from data analysis. The participants were then asked to score their perceived difficulty in performing the first-person motor imagery task for each action, on a 5-point scale from 0 to 4 (0 = *total inability to mentally represent the movement*; 1, 2, 3, 4 = *poor, fair, good, excellent performance*, respectively). Behavioral scores were compared by repeated-measures analysis of variance (ANOVA).

RESULTS

Behavioral data

Mean ($\pm SD$) self-scores of performance in the motor imagery task (on a 0–4 scale) were 3.53 ± 0.61 for symbolic, 3.57 ± 0.44 for mimed, and 2.36 ± 0.82 for meaningless actions, respectively.

Mimed actions and symbolic actions were easier to imagine than meaningless actions, Task: $F(2, 24) = 23.20$, $p < .001$; simple contrasts, $F(1, 12) = 25.45$, $p < .001$ and $F(1, 12) = 28.07$, $p < .001$, respectively. Scores for mimed and symbolic actions were not significantly different from each other ($t = 0.30$, *ns*). No difference in self-scores of imagery difficulty was found for different actions within each class, $F(2, 24) = 1.02$, *ns*.

Activations common to action observation and motor imagery

Figure 3 (top row) shows brain regions commonly active in both conditions (conjunction analysis—logical "AND"—of action observation and motor imagery; Friston, Holmes, Price, Buchel, & Worsley, 1999), after pooling together all three categories of actions (mimed, symbolic, and

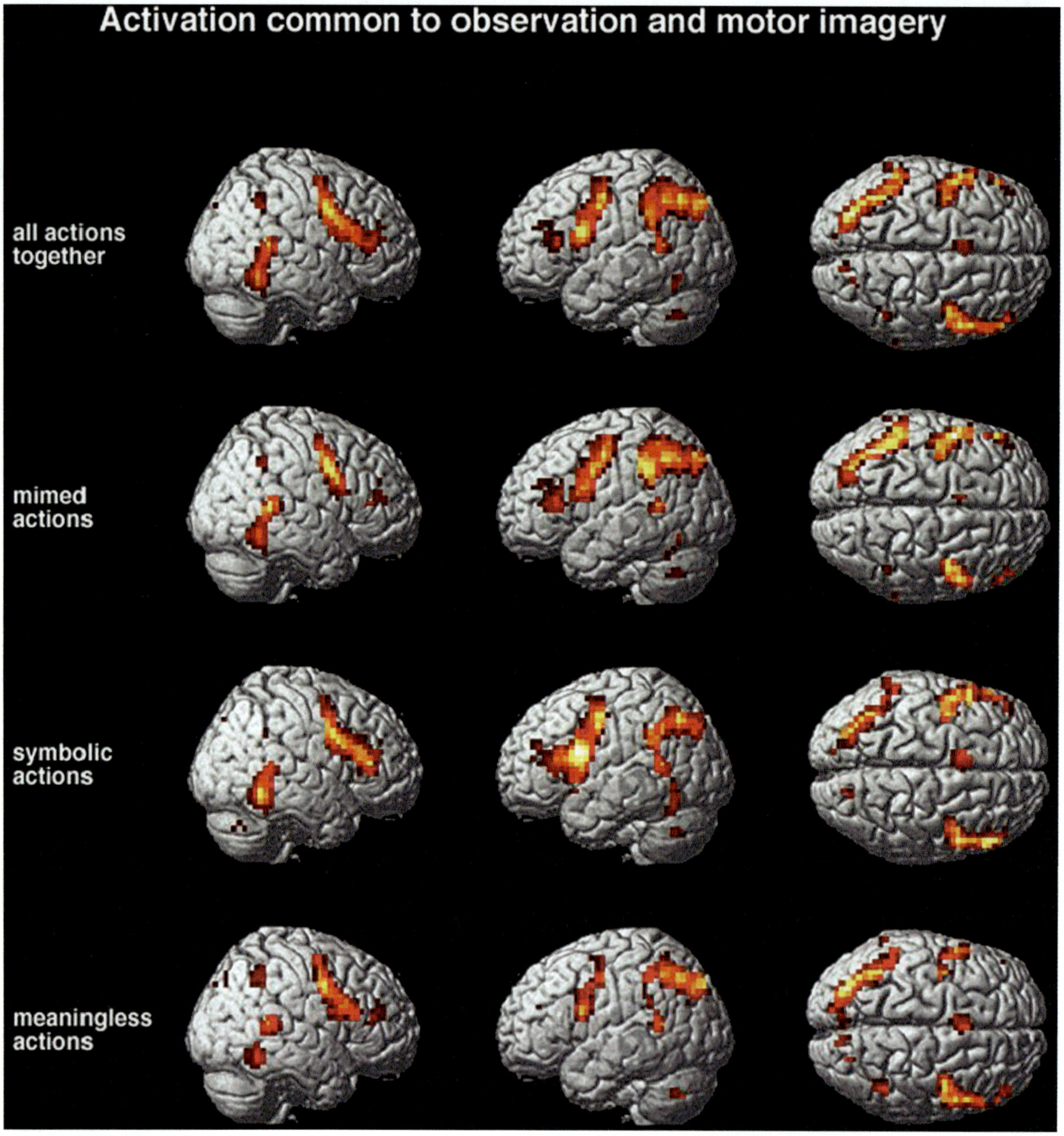

Figure 3. Maps of cortical areas identified from a conjunction analysis of observation and motor imagery (considering all actions), displayed on a 3D surface brain rendering. Random-effect analysis; in this and in the following figures, for illustrative purposes, maps at a threshold of $p < .001$ uncorrected for multiple comparisons are shown.

meaningless). Coordinates of peak activation voxels are shown in Table 1, and histograms of parameter estimates are shown in Figure 4.

Activations were found in the left parietal lobe with a weak activation of the right one, in the frontal lobe bilaterally and in a posterior sector of the temporal lobe, mainly in the right hemisphere. The left parietal activation included a region of IPL corresponding to the posterior part of the supramarginal gyrus (SMG), the cortex adjacent to and inside the intraparietal sulcus (IPS), and the most posterior part of the inferior parietal lobule grossly corresponding to the angular gyrus. The right parietal activation was located in SMG. As for the frontal lobe, activations lay bilaterally in the ventral part of the premotor cortex and included the *pars opercularis* and the *pars triangularis* of the inferior frontal gyrus (IFG). The right temporal lobe activation was located in the most posterior part of the inferior and middle temporal gyri and superior temporal sulcus.

When considering conjunction analyses of action observation and motor imagery for each action category, some differences emerge (Figure 3). In the case of mimed actions, the parietal lobe activation included the cortex adjacent to and inside the intraparietal sulcus; in the case of symbolic and meaningless actions the activation was located more ventrally, centered in the SMG and extending caudally to the angular gyrus. Direct contrast showed higher activity in the intraparietal cortex for mimed than for symbolic actions (Figure 5, top row). A small volume correction (SVC) analysis on a sphere of interest (12 mm radius) based on the coordinates obtained for IPS from a previous study (Buccino et al., 2001) confirmed these results ($p < .01$, corrected). The opposite contrast (symbolic vs. mimed actions) showed an activation located more ventrally in IPL in correspondence of the angular gyrus (Figure 5, bottom row). SVC analysis using a 12 mm radius sphere centered on the coordinates obtained for inferior parietal activation in a previous study (Peigneux et al., 2004) gave a significance level of $p < .05$, corrected.

Differential activations during action observation and motor imagery

Figure 6 (top row) shows the active foci found by contrasting the observation of all types of actions pooled together and the motor imagery of those same actions (see also Table 2). Active foci were present in the visual areas, bilaterally. The activation of visual areas extended, on the right side, to the posterior sector of the inferior parietal lobule. fMRI signal increases were also present in the parietal operculum when contrasting action observation and imagery, but not during action observation per se. This activation is most likely related to the decrease of activity that was found in the same area during motor imagery (data not shown).

Figure 6 (bottom row) shows the activations obtained contrasting the motor imagery of all types of actions pooled together with the observation of those same actions. In the parietal lobe the activation was located in SMG, bilaterally. In the left premotor cortex an active focus was found dorsally and extended to the primary motor cortex. In the frontal lobe an active focus was present in the rostral part of the middle/superior frontal gyrus, and in IFG, bilaterally. In IFG, activations extended to and included the *pars triangularis*, and the *pars orbitalis*. This latter activation extended posteriorly to invade the cortex around the rostral part of the Sylvian fissure. Finally, a strong activation was present on the mesial surface, corresponding to pre-supplementary motor area (pre-SMA), SMA proper, and the anterior cingulate (see Figure 7 for parameter estimates). A bilateral activation was also found in the basal ganglia.

DISCUSSION

This section consists of two parts. In the first one, we will discuss regions of fMRI signal increases common to both observation and motor imagery of non-object-directed actions, be they mimed, symbolic or meaningless. In the second one, we will focus on differential activation between action observation and motor imagery. In this study, we considered the "first-person" type of motor imagery (Jeannerod, 1994; Jeannerod & Frak, 1999; Porro et al., 1996), in which the subjects imagine themselves actually performing the movements, as opposed to the visual imagery of scenes involving motor acts performed by others.

TABLE 1

Local maxima of active foci, expressed in Montreal Neurological Institute (MNI) Standard Brain and Talairach (TAL; Talairach & Tournoux, 1988) coordinates, obtained from a conjunction analysis of observation and imagery after pooling together all three categories of actions (mimed, symbolic, and meaningless)

	Left							*Right*						
	MNI			*TAL*				*MNI*			*TAL*			
Anatomical region	*x*	*y*	*z*	*x*	*y*	*z*	*Z*	*x*	*y*	*Z*	*x*	*y*	*z*	*Z*
Parietal lobe														
Inferior parietal lobule	−28	−72	36	−28	−68	36	5.79	44	−48	44	44	−44	43	3.84
Frontal lobe														
Inferior frontal gyrus	−56	8	20	−55	9	18	5.43	56	32	12	55	32	9	5.17
Inferior frontal gyrus								44	8	20	44	9	18	5.12
Pre-central gyrus	−40	−8	44	−40	−6	41	4.57							
Pre-central gyrus	−8	4	56	−8	6	51	3.99							
Inferior/middle frontal gyrus	−52	36	20	−51	36	17	3.58							
Middle frontal gyrus	−56	4	40	−55	6	37	5.90	52	0	44	51	2	40	4.67
Temporal lobe														
Inferior temporal gyrus								60	−52	−12	59	−51	−8	6.25
Middle temporal gyrus								64	−44	8	63	−42	9	5.45
Superior temporal gyrus	−60	−48	12	−59	−46	13	4.65							

Neural substrates common to observation/motor imagery of non-object-directed actions

There were two main active regions common to both observation and motor imagery of non-object-directed actions: one located in the frontal lobe and the other in the inferior parietal lobule.

The frontal lobe activations included the ventral premotor cortex, the *pars opercularis* and the *pars triangularis* of IFG, bilaterally. Similar frontal activations were found in previous studies in which the task was either the observation of mimed hand actions (Buccino et al., 2001; Grèzes et al., 1998; Grèzes, Armony, Rowe, & Passingham, 2003; Sakreida et al., 2005; Schubotz & von Cramon, 2004; Wheaton et al., 2004) or the motor imagery of simple hand movements (Binkofski et al., 2000; Gerardin et al., 2000; Hanakawa et al., 2003; Kuhtz-Buschbeck et al., 2003; Stephan et al., 1995). The same regions were also found active during the actual execution of object- and non-object-directed hand actions (Binkofski et al., 1999; Ehrsson et al., 2003; Grèzes et al., 2003). The present findings, therefore, strongly support the notion that in the frontal lobe non-object-directed as well as object-directed actions are motorically represented in the same regions. These regions are known to be part of the mirror neuron system in humans (Buccino, Binkofski, & Riggio, 2004a; Rizzolatti & Craighero, 2004).

In the parietal lobe, activation common to motor imagery and action observation was found in a large region of the inferior parietal lobule, including most of the supramarginal gyrus and extending into the angular gyrus.

There is a clear difference between the parietal activation found in the present study and that typically reported in previous experiments in which the participants either observed object-directed actions (Buccino et al., 2001; Grèzes et al., 2003), imagined actions implying the use of an object (Decety et al., 1994; Grafton et al., 1996; Johnson et al., 2002; Simon et al., 2004) or actually executed them (Binkofski et al., 1999; Ehrsson et al., 2003; Grèzes et al., 2003). In all these conditions, the parietal lobe activation was centered on the cortex adjacent to and inside the intraparietal sulcus. This region is considered the parietal sector of the mirror neuron system in humans (Buccino et al., 2004a; Rizzolatti & Craighero, 2004). The results of the present study

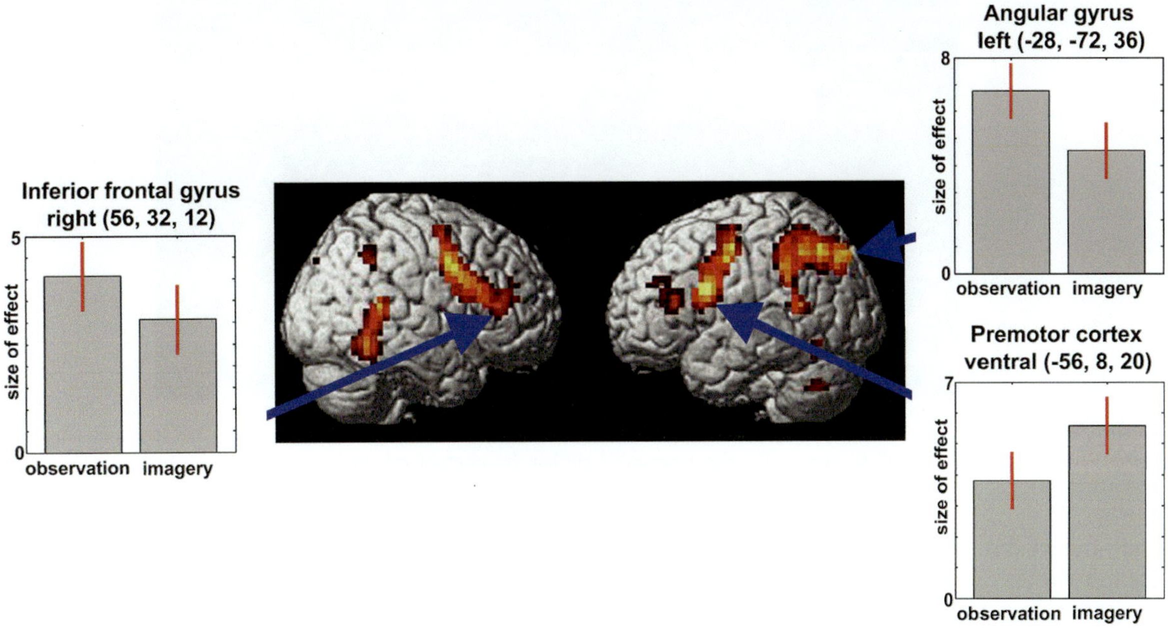

Figure 4. Conjunction analysis of observation and motor imagery (all actions together). Plots of parameter estimates (mean ± *SEM* of 13 subjects) of the effects of observation and imagery, separately, for peak activity voxels in selected fronto-parietal cortical regions.

showed that in the case of non-object-directed actions, only mimed actions led to activation centered in IPS and the adjacent region of the inferior parietal lobule, overlapping that typically active in object-directed actions, whereas symbolic actions and meaningless actions led to activation of SMG and angular gyrus. These findings strongly support the notion that

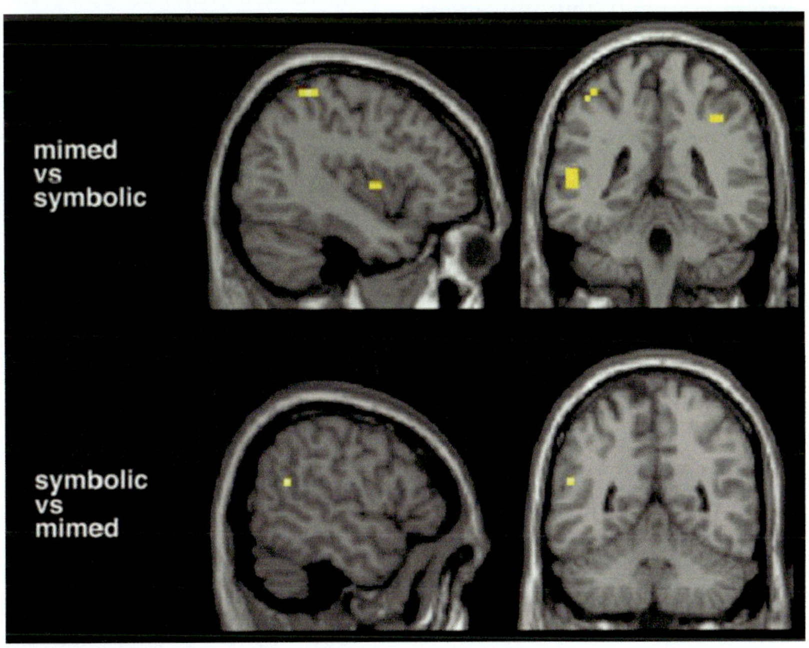

Figure 5. Cortical areas more active when contrasting mimed versus symbolic actions (top row), and symbolic versus mimed actions (bottom row), during both action observation and motor imagery. Small volume correction analyses based on coordinates obtained from previous studies (see text for details); $p < .01$ and $p < .05$, respectively.

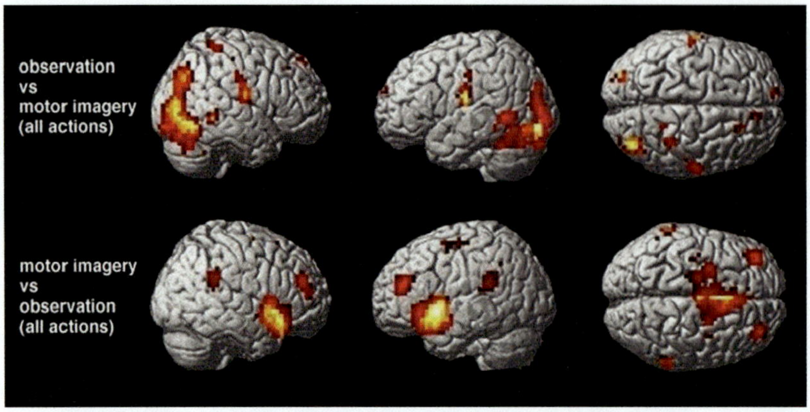

Figure 6. Cortical activations obtained by contrasting action observation versus motor imagery (top row) and motor imagery versus observation (bottom row) of all types of actions pooled together (random-effect analysis, $p < .001$ uncorrected for multiple comparisons).

non-object-directed actions have motor representations in the parietal lobe distinct from those of object-directed actions.

It has been suggested (Rumiati et al., 2005) that meaningless non-object-directed actions and pantomimes could have distinct representations in the brain, so that the imitation of meaningless actions recruits mainly the superior parietal lobule, while pantomimes mainly involve the angular gyrus and inferior temporal gyrus. The present findings lead to different conclusions; however, the experimental protocol and analysis was very different (for instance involving imitation in the Rumiati et al. study), thus preventing direct comparisons.

The functional separation, suggested by the present study, between the parietal region adjacent to IPS and the SMG region is supported by evidence coming from clinical neurology. Lesions centered to the IPL sector, where object-related actions are represented, cause impairment in grasping and manipulating objects (Binkofski et al., 1998; see also Jeannerod, 1986). In contrast, lesions centered to the left supramarginal gyrus typically produce ideomotor apraxia.

The term ideomotor apraxia defines the incapacity to perform an action (mimed, symbolic or meaningless), both on verbal command and/or following a model presentation, in the absence of motor and sensory deficits (De Renzi & Faglioni, 1996; Heilman, 1979). Although in clinical studies, lesions determining ideomotor apraxia include a large sector of the posterior parietal lobe (see Haaland, Harrington, & Knight, 2000), there is consensus that the parietal sector typically damaged in this syndrome is the supramarginal gyrus (see De Renzi & Faglioni, 1996; Heilman, 1979).

The presence of distinct motor representations in IPL for object-directed actions and non-object-directed actions may thus well explain the incapacity of ideomotor apraxic patients to internally rehearse and execute non-object-directed actions, while preserving the capacity to interact with objects.

It should be underlined, however, that in the present study we did not examine brain activation during observation or imagery of actions with objects, nor during execution of these same movements; therefore, we did not directly test the distinction between hand actions with and without objects. Additional studies will be required to further clarify this issue.

Differential activations during motor imagery and observation of non-object-directed actions

When comparing observation of non-object-directed actions with motor imagery of the same actions, activations were found in visual areas, as expected, and in the parietal operculum. Because this last MRI signal increase was not found in the contrast observation versus baseline, this finding will not be discussed further.

In the reverse contrast (motor imagery vs. observation), there were various regions more activated during motor imagery. In the frontal lobe, higher activity was found bilaterally in ventral IFG, extending to the anterior temporal pole. Note that this part of IFG is distinct from the one commonly active during action

TABLE 2

Local maxima of active foci, expressed in Montreal Neurological Institute (MNI) Standard Brain and Talairach (TAL) coordinates, obtained by contrasting the observation versus the motor imagery (A) and the motor imagery versus the observation (B) of all types of actions pooled together (occipital foci not listed)

	Left							*Right*						
	MNI			*TAL*				*MNI*			*TAL*			
Anatomical region	*x*	*y*	*z*	*x*	*y*	*z*	*Z*	*x*	*y*	*z*	*x*	*y*	*z*	*Z*
A. *Observation vs. motor imagery*														
Parietal lobe														
Superior parietal lobule								40	−72	36	40	−68	37	4.23
Post-central gyrus	−64	−16	16	−63	−15	15	3.92	56	−12	20	55	−11	19	4.05
Frontal lobe														
Pre-central gyrus								60	−20	40	59	−18	38	3.24
Temporal lobe														
Middle temporal gyrus	−48	−56	0	−48	−54	3	4.28	48	−40	0	48	−39	2	3.84
Middle temporal gyrus								60	−48	−4	59	−47	−1	4.02
B. *Motor imagery vs. observation*														
Parietal lobe														
Inferior parietal lobule	−68	−36	20	−67	−34	20	3.92	60	−44	28	59	−41	28	3.99
Frontal lobe														
Inferior frontal gyrus	−48	8	4	−48	8	3	4.87							
Inferior frontal gyrus	−44	12	−8	−44	11	−7	5.02	36	28	−8	36	27	−8	5.38
Inferior frontal gyrus								44	20	−20	44	19	−18	4.88
Middle/superior frontal gyrus	−36	40	20	−36	40	16	4.40	28	44	24	28	44	20	4.10
Medial frontal gyrus	−8	4	48	−8	6	44	4.61	8	12	60	8	14	55	5.14
Medial frontal gyrus								4	16	32	4	17	29	4.79
Temporal lobe														
Superior temporal gyrus								64	−44	20	63	−42	21	4.00
Basal ganglia	−12	0	−8	−12	0	−7	4.42	16	−8	4	16	−8	4	5.61

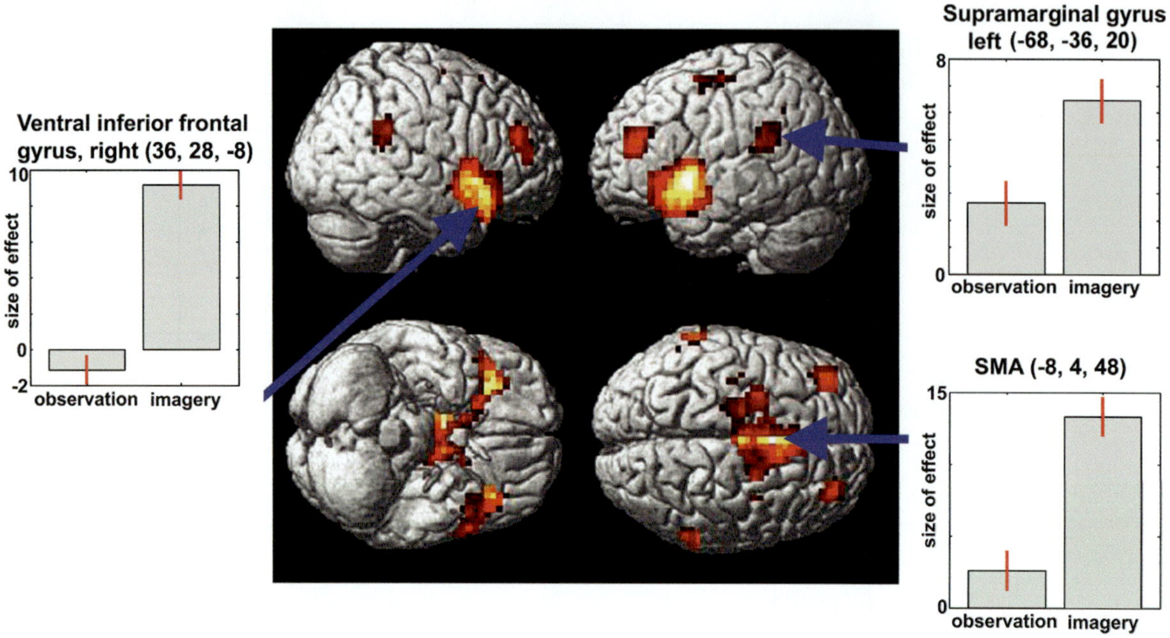

Figure 7. Cortical areas more active during motor imagery than during motor observation. Plots of parameter estimates (mean ± *SEM* of 13 subjects) of the effects of imagery and observation, for peak activity voxels in each of the considered regions of interest.

observation and motor imagery of non-object-directed actions, being more ventrally and caudally located. This region, mainly in the left hemisphere, is known to play an important role in language (see Bookheimer, 2002, for a review on brain imaging studies) and is considered part of a fronto-temporal system involved in semantic processing, possibly devoted to the retrieval of abstract concepts (Noppeney & Price, 2003; Thompson-Schill, Aguirre, D'Esposito, & Farah, 1999; Thompson-Schill, D'Esposito, Aguirre, & Farah, 1997).

In the present experiment, the participants were required to imagine an action after observing it. In principle, therefore, they could simply replicate in their mind the motor aspects of the previously observed action, although it is also possible that, at least for some of the actions to be imagined, the participants retrieved their semantic representations. The active aspect of motor imagery, as compared to the more passive observation task, likely implies a more vivid representation of all aspects of the actions, therefore yielding a greater involvement of the corresponding motor representations in the parietal lobe and in the premotor cortex, bilaterally.

As far as the parietal lobe is concerned, the contrast between motor imagery and action observation showed activation in SMG, in a part near the posterior aspect of the sylvian fissure. The stronger signal increase during motor imagery in this part of SMG may be partly due to the stronger effort that motor imagery requires in comparison to action observation. However, because only a specific sector of SMG appears to be involved, it is likely that this is not the only explanation for this activation. Thus, considering that in the same contrast there was also a large activation of IFG, one may argue that these two regions are functionally related.

A further differential activation in the contrast motor imagery versus observation was found in the fronto-mesial areas including SMA, pre-SMA, and the adjacent cingulate cortex. Activation of mesial cortical areas is a common finding during tasks requiring internal generation of motor representations (Gerardin et al., 2000; Grafton et al., 1996; Solodkin, Hlustik, Chen, & Small, 2004; Stephan et al., 1995; Tyszka, Grafton, Chew, Woods, & Colletti, 1994). Physiological studies in monkeys (Alexander & Crutcher, 1990; Matsuzaka, Aizawa, & Tanjii, 1992; Rizzolatti et al., 1990) showed that these areas exert a control on the activity of sensorimotor circuits. The activation of fronto-mesial areas might be, therefore, a necessary prerequisite for the activation of motor circuits in the absence of external stimuli.

Finally, another difference between motor imagery and action observation was the bilateral activation of the middle frontal gyrus, possibly area 46. This region is considered to be involved in working memory (see Goldman-Rakic, 1995; Levy and Goldman-Rakic, 2000) as well as in selecting the target of the response in free selection tasks (Owen, 2000; Passingham, Toni, & Rushworth, 2000; Rowe, Toni, Josephs, Frackowiak, & Passingham, 2000). Because the action to be imagined was presented to the participants at the beginning of each trial, working memory must have played a significant role in our imagery paradigm. However, the present findings do not allow us to disentangle the weight of working memory with respect to movement selection. Thus, the observed activations, specifically those in prefrontal cortex, could be due both to the memory of the observed action and to retrieval of that action from the motor repertoire of the participants (see also Buccino et al., 2004b, for discussion on this point).

In conclusion, the present data suggest that the observation and imagery of non-object directed actions are subserved by partly shared common areas in the brain. Most interestingly, the present findings show that non-object-directed actions, including mimed, symbolic and meaningless actions, have common motor representations in the frontal lobe, while they are motorically represented in different regions of the IPL. These findings may provide insights in the neurophysiological basis of ideomotor apraxia, a neurological syndrome where the execution of non-object-directed actions on command is impaired. Because non-object-directed actions are a relevant part of the human motor repertoire, especially for their relevance in social interactions, but are poorly developed in monkeys, one may speculate that the region of the parietal lobe where these actions are represented constitutes a specific evolutionary development of the parietal lobe in humans.

Manuscript received 7 February 2007
Manuscript accepted 30 April 2007
First published online 6 September 2007

REFERENCES

Alexander, G. E., & Crutcher, M. D. (1990). Preparation for movement: Neural representations of intended direction in three motor areas of the monkey. *Journal of Neurophysiology*, *64*, 133–178.

Binkofski, F., Amunts, K., Stephan, K. M., Posse, S., Schormann, T., Freund, H.-J., et al. (2000). Broca's region subserves imagery of motion: A combined cytoarchitectonic and fMRI study. *Human Brain Mapping*, *11*, 273–285.

Binkofski, F., Buccino, G., Posse, S., Seitz, R. J., Rizzolatti, G., & Freund, H. J. (1999). A fronto-parietal circuit for object manipulation in man: Evidence from an fMRI-study. *European Journal of Neuroscience*, *11*, 3276–3286.

Binkofski, F., Dohle, C., Posse, S., Stephan, K. M., Hefter, H., Seitz, R. J., et al. (1998). Human anterior intraparietal area subserves prehension: A combined lesion and functional MRI activation study. *Neurology*, *50*, 1253–1259.

Bookheimer, S. (2002). Functional MRI of language: new approaches to understanding the cortical organization of semantic processing. *Annual Review of Neuroscience*, *25*, 151–188.

Buccino, G., Binkofski, F., Fink, G. R., Fadiga, L., Fogassi, L., Gallese, V., et al. (2001). Action observation activates premotor and parietal areas in a somatotopic manner: An fMRI study. *European Journal of Neuroscience*, *13*, 400–404.

Buccino, G., Binkofski, F., & Riggio, L. (2004a). The mirror neuron system and action recognition. *Brain Language*, *89*, 370–376.

Buccino, G., Vogt, S., Ritzl, A., Fink, G. R., Zilles, K., Freund, H. J., et al. (2004b). Neural circuits underlying imitation learning of hand actions: An event-related fMRI study. *Neuron*, *42*, 323–334.

Butterworth, G., & Harris, M. (1994). *Principles of developmental psychology*. Hove, UK: Lawrence Erlbaum Associates, Ltd.

Cross, E. S., Hamilton, A. F., & Grafton, S. T. (2006). Building a motor simulation de novo: Observation of dance by dancers. *NeuroImage*, *31*, 1257–1267.

De Renzi, E., & Faglioni, P. (1996). L'aprassia. In G. Denes & L. Pizzamiglio (Eds.), *Manuale di neuropsicologia* (pp. 557–589). Bologna, Italy: Zanichelli.

Decety, J., Perani, D., Jeannerod, M., Bettinardi, V., Tadary, B., Woods, R., et al. (1994). Mapping motor representations with PET. *Nature*, *371*, 600–602.

Ehrsson, H. H., Geyer, S., & Naito, N. (2003). Imagery of voluntary movement of fingers, toes, and tongue activates corresponding body-part-specific motor representations. *Journal of Neurophysiology*, *90*, 3304–3316.

Friston, K. J., Holmes, A. P., Price, C. J., Buchel, C., & Worsley, K. J. (1999). Multisubject fMRI studies and conjunction analyses. *NeuroImage*, *10*, 385–396.

Gerardin, E., Sirigu, A., Lehericy, S., Poline, J. B., Gaymard, B., Marsault, C., et al. (2000). Partially overlapping neural networks for real and imagined hand movements. *Cerebral Cortex*, *10*, 1093–1104.

Goldman-Rakic, P. S. (1995). Architecture of the prefrontal cortex and the central executive. *Annals New York Academy of Sciences*, *789*, 71–83.

Grafton, S. T., Arbib, M. A., Fadiga, L., & Rizzolatti, G. (1996). Localization of grasp representations in humans by PET: 2. Observation compared with imagination. *Experimental Brain Research*, *112*, 103–111.

Grèzes, J., Armony, J. L., Rowe, J., & Passingham, R. E. (2003). Activations related to "mirror" and "canonical" neurons in the human brain: An fMRI study. *NeuroImage*, *18*, 928–937.

Grèzes, J., Costes, N., & Decety, J. (1998). Top-down effect of strategy on the perception of human biological motion: a PET investigation. *Cognitive Neuropsychology, 15*, 553–582.

Haaland, K. Y., Harrington, D. L., & Knight, R. T. (2000). Neural representations of skilled movement. *Brain, 123*, 2306–2313.

Hanakawa, T., Immisch, I., Toma, K., Dimyan, A. M., van Gelderen, P., & Hallett, M. (2003). Functional properties of brain areas associated with motor execution and imagery. *Journal of Neurophysiology, 89*, 989–1002.

Heilman, K. M. (1979). Apraxia. In K. M. Heilman & E. Valenstein (Eds.), *Clinical neuropsychology* (pp. 159–185). Oxford, UK: Oxford University Press.

Jeannerod, M. (1986). The formation of finger grip during prehension. A cortically mediated visuomotor pattern. *Behavioural Brain Research, 19*, 99–116.

Jeannerod, M. (1994). The representing brain: Neural correlates of motor intention and imagery. *Behavioral and Brain Sciences, 17*, 187–245.

Jeannerod, M., & Frak, V. (1999). Mental imaging of motor activity in humans. *Current Opinion in Neurobiology, 9*, 735–739.

Johnson, S. H., Rotte, M., Grafton, S. T., Hinrichs, H., Gazzaniga, M. S., & Heinze, H. J. (2002). Selective activation of a parietofrontal circuit during implicitly imagined prehension. *NeuroImage, 17*, 1693–1704.

Kuhtz-Buschbeck, J. P., Mahnkopf, C., Holzknecht, C., Siebner, H., Ulmer, S., & Jansen, O. (2003). Effector-independent representations of simplex and complex imagined finger movements: A combined fMRI and TMS study. *European Journal of Neuroscience, 18*, 3375–3387.

Levy, R., & Goldman-Rakic, P. S. (2000). Segregation of working memory functions within the dorsolateral prefrontal cortex. *Experimental Brain Research, 133*, 23–32.

Matsuzaka, Y., Aizawa, H., & Tanjii, J. (1992). A motor area rostral to the supplementary motor area (pre supplementary motor area) in the monkey: Neuronal activity during a learned motor task. *Journal of Neurophysiology, 68*, 653–662.

Michelon, P., Vettel, J. M., & Zacks, J. M. (2006). Lateral somatotopic organization during imagined and prepared movements. *Journal of Neurophysiology, 95*, 811–822.

Nakamura, A., Maess, B., Knoesche, T. R., Gunter, T. C., Bach, P., & Friederici, A. D. (2004). Cooperation of different neuronal systems during hand sign recognition. *NeuroImage, 23*, 25–34.

Noppeney, U., & Price, C. J. (2003). Functional imaging of the semantic system: Retrieval of sensory-experienced and verbally learned knowledge. *Brain Language, 84*, 120–133.

Oldfield, R. C. (1971). The assessment and analysis of handedness: The Edinburgh Inventory. *Neuropsychologia, 9*, 97–113.

Owen, A. M. (2000). The role of the lateral frontal cortex in mnemonic processing: The contribution of functional neuroimaging. *Experimental Brain Research, 133*, 33–43.

Passingham, R. E., Toni, I., & Rushworth, M. F. S. (2000). Specialization within the prefrontal cortex: The ventral prefrontal cortex and associative learning. *Experimental Brain Research, 133*, 103–113.

Peigneux, P., Salmon, E., Van der Linden, M., Garraux, G., Aerts, J., Delfiore, G., et al. (2000). The role of lateral occipitotemporal junction and area MT/V5 in the visual analysis of upper-limb postures. *NeuroImage, 11*, 644–655.

Peigneux, P., Van der Linden, M., Garraux, G., Laureys, S., Degueldre, C., Aerts, J., et al. (2004). Imaging a cognitive model of apraxia: The neural substrate of gesture-specific cognitive processes. *Human Brain Mapping, 21*, 119–142.

Penny, W., & Holmes, A. (2004). Random-effects analysis. In R. S. J. Frackowiack (Ed.), *Human brain function* (2nd ed., pp. 843–850). San Diego, CA: Elsevier Academic Press.

Porro, C. A., Francescato, M. P., Cettolo, V., Diamond, M. E., Baraldi, P., Zuiani, C., et al. (1996). Primary motor and sensory cortex activation during motor performance and motor imagery: A functional magnetic resonance study. *Journal of Neuroscience, 16*, 7688–7698.

Rizzolatti, G., & Craighero, L. (2004). The mirror neuron system. *Annual Review of Neuroscience, 27*, 169–192.

Rizzolatti, G., Gentilucci, M., Camarda, R., Gallese, V., Luppino, G., & Matelli, M. (1990). Neurons related to reaching-grasping arm movements in the rostral part of area 6 (area 6a). *Experimental Brain Research, 82*, 337–350.

Rowe, J. B., Toni, I., Josephs, O., Frackowiak, R. S., & Passingham, R. E. (2000). The prefrontal cortex: response selection or maintenance within working memory? *Science, 288*, 1656–1660.

Rumiati, R. I., Weiss, P. H., Tessari, A., Assmus, A., Zilles, K., Herzog, H., et al. (2005). Common and differential neural mechanisms supporting imitation of meaningful and meaningless actions. *Journal of Cognitive Neuroscience, 17*, 1420–1431.

Sakreida, K., Schubotz, R., Wolfensteller, U., & von Cramon, D. Y. (2005). Motion class dependency in observer's motor areas revealed by functional magnetic resonance imaging. *Journal of Neuroscience, 25*, 1335–1342.

Schubotz, R. I., & von Cramon, D. Y. (2004). Sequences of abstract nonbiological stimuli share ventral premotor cortex with action observation and imagery. *Journal of Neuroscience, 24*, 5467–5474.

Simon, O., Kherif, F., Flandin, G., Poline, J. B., Riviere, D., Mangin, J. F., et al. (2004). Automatized clustering and functional geometry of human parietofrontal networks for language, space, and number. *NeuroImage, 23*, 1192–1202.

Solodkin, A., Hlustik, P., Chen, E. E., & Small, S. L. (2004). Fine modulation in network activation during motor execution and motor imagery. *Cerebral Cortex, 14*, 1246–1255.

Stephan, K. M., Fink, G. R., Passingham, R. E., Silbersweig, D., Ceballos-Baumann, A. O., Frith, C. D., et al. (1995). Functional anatomy of the mental representation of upper extremity movements in healthy subjects. *Journal of Neurophysiology*, *73*, 373–386.

Talairach, J., & Tournoux, P. (1988). *Co-planar stereotactic atlas of the human brain*. Stuttgart, Germany: Thieme.

Tanaka, S., Inui, T., Iwaki, S., Konishi, J., & Nakai, T. (2001). Neural substrates involved in imitating finger configurations: An fMRI study. *Neuroreport*, *12*, 1171–1174.

Thompson-Schill, S. L., Aguirre, G. K., D'Esposito, M., & Farah, M. J. (1999). A neural basis for category and modality specificity of semantic knowledge. *Neuropsychologia*, *7*, 671–676.

Thompson-Schill, S. L., D'Esposito, M., Aguirre, G. K., & Farah, M. J. (1997). Role of left inferior prefrontal cortex in retrieval of semantic knowledge: A re-evaluation. *Proceedings National Academy of Science USA*, *94*, 14792–14797.

Tomasello, M., & McCall, J. (1997). *Primate cognition*. Oxford, UK: Oxford University Press.

Tyszka, J. M., Grafton, S. T., Chew, W., Woods, R. P., & Colletti, P. M. (1994). Parceling of mesial frontal motor areas during ideation and movement using functional magnetic resonance imaging at 1.5 tesla. *Annals of Neurology*, *35*, 746–749.

Wheaton, K. J., Thompson, J. C., Syngeniotis, A., Abbott, D. F., & Puce, A. (2004). Viewing the motion of human body parts activates different regions of premotor, temporal and parietal cortex. *NeuroImage*, *22*, 277–288.

SOCIAL NEUROSCIENCE, 2008, 3 (3–4), 276–288

Psychology Press
Taylor & Francis Group

Activation of motor pathways during observation and execution of hand movements

Paola Borroni and Fausto Baldissera
Università degli Studi di Milano, Milano, Italy

Some neural properties of "motor resonance"—the subliminal activation of the motor system when observing actions performed by others—are investigated in humans. Two actions performed with the right hand are observed by experimental subjects: a finalized (transitive) action (reaching for and grasping a ball) and an intransitive action (cyclic up-and-down oscillation of the hand), while the H-reflex and Transcranial Magnetic Stimulation techniques are utilized to test the excitability of the observer's motor pathways to hand and forearm muscles (first dorsal interosseus, flexor digitorum superficialis, flexor carpi radialis). Results indicate that motor resonance: (1) is mainly mediated by the primary motor cortex; (2) involves the same forearm muscles as used in the execution of the observed movement; (3) is also recorded in the homologous muscles of the arm contralateral to the one observed; and (4) is evoked by both transitive and intransitive movements of the human hand, but not by similar movements of inanimate objects. The similarities and discrepancies between the resonant response in humans and the properties of monkey "mirror neurons" are discussed.

INTRODUCTION

Since the first description of neurons in the ventral premotor cortex of the monkey that fire both when the animal performs a certain action and when it observes the experimenter or another monkey performing the same action ("mirror neurons"; di Pellegrino, Fadiga, Fogassi, Gallese, & Rizzolatti, 1992), a number of investigations in monkeys as well as in humans have been inspired by this discovery. Human research in this field has expanded quickly on the assumption that the "motor resonance" observed in man, i.e., the subliminal activation of the motor system when watching actions performed by others, were mediated by "mirror" neurons. In many of the studies exploring the possible role of this type of neurons in cognitive functions, the label "mirror" was often extended to neural mechanisms underlying any type of motor resonating responses, not only those to vision of body movements but also those to other sensory modalities (e.g., hearing), and even vegetative or emotional reactions (Warren et al., 2006; Wicker et al., 2003). Only a few investigations were focused instead on the mechanisms that supposedly transform the discharge of mirror neurons into the activation of motor pathways. It is our opinion that sharpening the analysis of these mechanisms would improve our understanding of their functional role, both as "motor" and as "mirror" neurons.

An important feature that should be considered when trying to understand the functions of mirror neurons is that, despite being classified as a part of the motor system, their discharge is not always correlated with movement. In fact, they may be strongly activated by their specific sensory

Correspondence should be addressed to: Paola Borroni, Dipartimento di Medicina, Chirurgia e Odontoiatria, Ospedale S. Paolo, Blocco C – 7° piano, Via A. di Rudinì 8, I-20142 Milano, Italy. E-mail: paola.borroni@unimi.it

This study was supported by grants from the "Ministero dell'Università e della Ricerca" and by the "Università degli Studi di Milano".

www.psypress.com/socialneuroscience DOI:10.1080/17470910701515269

stimulus (an action made by others) without generating movement and, conversely, be activated during the execution of that same action in the absence of the sensory input. In view of this double activation mode, can we consider the function of these neurons in their motor mode to be the implementation of the neural tools necessary to perform a voluntary act? If so, we would also have to postulate the existence of a control that can enhance or attenuate transmission through the motor pathway connecting mirror neurons to their effectors, and thus determine whether the activity of these neurons results in movement or not.

Another possibility, perhaps more consistent with the postulated cognitive role of mirror neurons, is that they are placed in a position collateral to both the sensory and the motor streams, so that they are excited when we both see and perform a certain movement and may accomplish such a role without being directly involved in movement execution.

All these considerations underline the importance of investigating how the discharge of mirror neurons is translated into a motor act. In the experimental animal a strict correlation can be searched between firing of the mirror neurons and the activity in other neurons of the motor system and in the pertinent muscles. Accepting the hypothesis that motor resonance is mediated by mirror neurons, less direct but nonetheless valuable evidence may also be collected in human experiments. In the present experiments motor resonance was investigated by recording the subliminal activity of spinal motoneurons driving forearm muscles during observation of two different movements, and compared to the overt activation of the same muscles during the execution of the same movements, by the same subjects. In addition, assuming that human motor resonance originates in the ventral premotor cortex (Buccino et al., 2001; Iacoboni et al., 1999; Perani et al., 2001; Rizzolatti et al., 1996), the involvement of the primary motor cortex in the transmission of motor resonance to spinal circuits was investigated.

METHODS

Informed and consenting subjects participated in these experiments, which were performed according to the Declaration of Helsinki and approved by the local ethics committee. Experimental procedures have been described in detail elsewhere (Montagna, Cerri, Borroni, & Baldissera, 2005, grasping experiments; Borroni, Montagna, Cerri, & Baldissera, 2005, hand oscillation experiments) and are only briefly outlined here.

Grasping experiment

Five right-handed healthy adult subjects (4 females and 1 male, age 22–44) were asked to observe a 5 s video clip showing a human right hand reaching for and grasping a red billiard ball. At the onset of the clip, the hand was prone and resting on a table and the ball was placed 25 cm in front of it. The grasping movement proceeded as follows from the clip onset: 1500 ms hand lift, between 2280 and 3280 ms finger opening, followed by finger closing in the next 1000 ms, contact with the ball at 4200 ms, maintained grasp for about 300 ms and a brief lifting phase of 500 ms, concluding the sequence.

The excitability time-course during the observed action was explored in 3 muscles (flexor digitorum superficialis, FDS; flexor carpi radialis, FCR; and first dorsal interosseus, FDI) by recording motor evoked potentials (MEPs) elicited by supraliminal TMS at 4 relevant delays from the video onset: 2500 ms, i.e., mid hand opening; 3000 ms, i.e., end of hand opening; 3500 ms, i.e., mid hand closing on the ball; and 4300 ms, fingers in contact with the ball. The 8-shaped coil was positioned in order to activate simultaneously the 3 recorded muscles and the stimulator output was set at about 110% the threshold for evoking a MEP response in the less excitable muscle in 5 out of 10 stimuli. Threshold in the latter muscle was never larger than 20% of that of the most excitable muscle. Absolute TMS intensity varied between 40 and 50% of the maximal stimulator output (Magstim 200, maximal power 2.2 T) in the different subjects. To exclude the possibility of voluntary or involuntary activity by the observer, the background EMG of the investigated muscles was monitored throughout the whole video presentation.

For each subject 4 blocks were repeated, and in each block the video was presented 20 consecutive times with 3 s intervals between presentations. During each presentation a MEP was elicited at one of the above delays, collecting a total of 20 responses per delay. Delays were selected in semi-random order, i.e., completing a cluster of all 4 delays (2500 ms, 3000 ms, 3500 ms and 4300 ms) before starting a new random selection of any given delay again. In order to attenuate long-term variability of the MEP responses, independent of timing during action observation, peak-to-peak amplitude of each response was measured and expressed as the deviation (in μV) from the mean of the 4 responses of its own cluster of delays (which are always obtained within a short period of time). This last value was then averaged with those obtained at the same delay in the other clusters. In order to average MEP amplitudes across the different subjects, the mean responses at each delay and for each muscle, were expressed for each subject as a percentage of the grand average of all responses at all delays. One-way analysis of variation (ANOVA) was used to assess whether the MEP responses were significantly modulated during the time course of the observed movement.

Subsequently, subjects were asked to imitate the reaching and grasping movement shown in the video clip, moving as much as possible in synchrony with it, while EMG signals were selectively recorded from their FDI, FCR and FDS muscles. Movement of the hand was monitored by an infrared digital camera (Mac Reflex 3.2) recording the position in space of 5 markers placed on the hand plus 2 markers placed on the supporting surface to identify the horizontal plane. Time-correlation of the EMG signal (sampling rate 1 kHz) with the video signals (sampling rate 60 Hz) was obtained by linearly interpolating the movement signal and subsequently over sampling at 1 kHz.

This procedure allowed the comparison, in each subject, of the time course of the excitability changes recorded during action viewing, with the temporal pattern of activation of those same muscles during execution of the same action.

Hand oscillation experiments

Fourteen right-handed subjects (7 females and 7 males, aged 18 to 48) observed a series of 4–5 flexion–extension cycles of the wrist performed in front of them by one of the experimenters, who followed the 1 Hz tempo of a metronome, heard via headphones. The experimenter's oscillating hand rested on a metal platform that could oscillate around the wrist axis and whose angular position was continuously recorded by a Spectrol 534 1 kΩ potentiometer coaxial with its pivot, and digitized at 250 Hz. The precision of the rhythmic oscillations was checked a posteriori on the movement records.

During the third oscillation cycle, electrical stimulation of the median nerve at the elbow elicited an H-reflex in the FCR muscle. A trigger signal, released when the platform reached a predefined position in the cycle, was used to elicit the median nerve stimulation at one of 5 fixed delays (0, 200, 400, 600 and 800 ms), dividing the cycle period in even parts. Amplitude of the H-reflex at rest was maintained between 5 and 15% of the maximal motor response. Recorded signals (H-reflex and movement traces) were stored for further elaboration. The surface electrodes placed on the FCR muscle to record H-reflexes were also used to confirm the lack of any EMG activity in this muscle during movement observation.

In each subject, the average of all observed hand movements was calculated and fitted by a four-parameter (period, offset, amplitude and phase) sine-wave function; significance of the regression was ascertained with a standard ANOVA test. Since cycle period varied among trials and among subjects by about 5% of its average value, normalization was necessary in order to bring all movement records, from different trials and different subjects, back to unity (1000 ms). Subsequently, to maintain the temporal correlation between the time courses of observed movement and response modulation in observers, the same normalization was performed on the 5 delays at which the H-reflex were recorded. Peak-to-peak amplitude of H-reflexes was measured and (as done for MEP recording in the grasping experiment) expressed as the deviation (in μV) from the mean of the responses belonging to each cluster of 5 delays. In each subject, clusters of 5 delays were repeated 15 times (for a total of 75 movement cycles). All deviations from the mean obtained at the same delay were then averaged and averages fitted with a two parameter (amplitude and phase) sine-wave function (since after normalization period = 1 and offset = 0 for all). Finally, changes in H-reflex amplitude were displayed together with the correspondent average movement trace in a one-cycle diagram.

This protocol was utilized in the following experiments. In Experiment 2a H-reflexes were recorded in the right FCR muscle of subjects observing the oscillating movement of either the experimenter's right hand or the same movement of the empty metal platform. The platform was moved with a long rod by the hand of a person hidden behind a screen and its movement developed about its pivot with a profile indistinguishable from the flexion–extension of the mover's hand (compare Figure 2B and 2F).

In addition, a separate experiment was performed, aimed at establishing the temporal correspondence between the onset of muscular activity, when the movement is actually performed, and the rising phase of reflex modulation, when the same movement is only observed. In this experiment "observers" personally executed 20 cyclic flexion–extensions of the right wrist, while rectified and integrated ($\tau = 20$ ms) EMGs from their FCR and ECR (extensor carpi radialis) muscles were recorded. In this case, recording from both wrist flexors and extensors was necessary since the phase relation between the motoneuron activation and the subsequent hand oscillation can be precisely established only from the EMG onset of both antagonists (Esposti, Cavallari, & Baldissera, 2005). The usual period normalization procedure was applied to the average of hand flexion–extension movements and related EMG records; the onset of EMG bursts was determined by visual inspection of the averaged records. With this procedure, phase relationships between the movement cycle, and both H-reflex modulation cycle and overt muscular activation could be compared directly.

In Experiment 2b the observation-induced modulation of the FCR H-reflex (Experiment 2a) was tested during the cortical depression corresponding to the so-called "silent period" (SP). Should the primary motor cortex be involved in the modulation of motor excitability during movement observation, evoking a cortical SP would depress or remove such modulation. The "silent period", i.e., the silencing of voluntary EMG activity that follows a TM stimulus (Mills, 1999; Reid, Chiappa, & Cros, 2002), is possibly due to after-hyperpolarization refractoriness and postsynaptic inhibition that follow the firing of both cortical neurons and spinal motoneurons. Most studies (Classen & Benecke, 1995; Davey, Romaiguere, Maskill, & Ellaway, 1994; Mills, 1999; Reid et al., 2002) agree that the silent period after TMS is mainly a cortical phenomenon and that the cortical inhibitory process is present even when TMS is kept subthreshold for inducing an MEP (i.e., when no motoneuronal silent period is produced). Thus, we obtained the largest cortical inhibitory effect without any spinal component by using the highest TMS intensity that did not produce any MEP at rest. It was nonetheless verified that a TMS of this same intensity, given during voluntary contraction, produced an EMG SP lasting 60 to 70 ms. Therefore, in the actual experiment, in which the FCR was maintained in resting conditions, the H-reflex excitability was tested during movement observation both within the evoked silent period (i.e., at 50 ms after subliminal TMS) as well as without any TMS conditioning.

Tests were performed at two points of the movement cycle, corresponding to the maximum and minimum of the modulation cycle, as also determined for every subject. In each trial, 20 TMS conditioned and 20 unconditioned H-reflexes were randomly alternated. H-reflex amplitude per se was not influenced by the SP.

Finally, in Experiment 2c FCR H-reflexes were recorded in the right FCR muscle of subjects observing the experimenter's oscillating left hand.

In all experiments mean H-reflex values from all different observers were pooled together. To do this, reflex values were normalized in size to the amplitude of the individual best-fit sine wave of each subject, which equilibrated the weight of different individuals in the estimate of the common phase. Normalized movement cycles from different subjects were all phase-shifted and aligned to the midpoint of their raising phase ($\phi = 0°$). Individual H-reflex records were then shifted accordingly. After this normalization and alignment, all H-reflex data could be plotted together, fitted by a two-parameter sine-wave function and analyzed statistically as above.

RESULTS

Pattern of motor activation during observation vs. execution of a finalized action

These experiments were aimed at establishing the degree of spatial and temporal correspondence between the resonant subliminal modulation evoked by action observation and the overt muscular activation that subjects employ when they execute the same action.

Plots in Figure 1A (means of 5 subjects in A, single subject in B) show that MEP size was modulated in all 3 muscles, though the time course was not identical in each muscle, or in the same muscle of the different subjects. However, amplitude modulation, assessed for

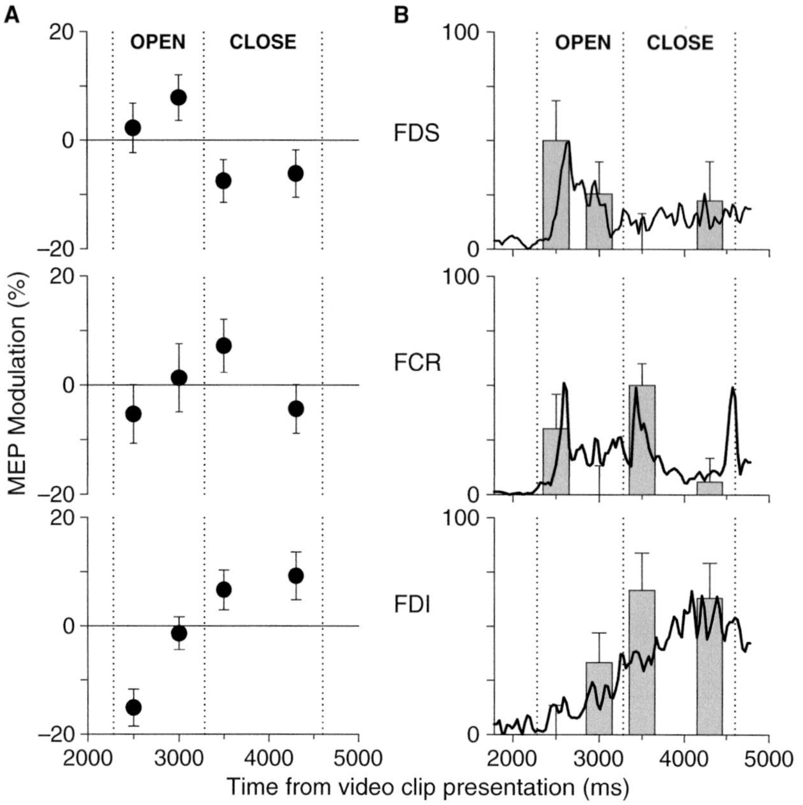

Figure 1. Correspondence between subliminal resonant phenomena during movement observation and overt muscle activation during execution. (A) Average modulation of MEPs in 5 subjects. Each dot represents the mean (± SE) of 75 normalized MEPs (15 for every subject). In each subject, the mean amplitude at each delay was normalized to the mean amplitude of all MEPs of the same subject and then averaged with values obtained in the other subjects. MEP modulation in FDS (top) showed a significant facilitation in the opening phase and a "dis-facilitation" in the closing phase. Changes in MEP amplitude in FCR (middle) were not statistically significant. MEPs in FDI muscle (bottom) were instead significantly facilitated during finger closing. Mean amplitude values for MEPs are respectively 158 ±18 μV for FDS muscle, 154±32 μV for FCR and 263±55 μV for FDI. (B) MEP modulation in one subject (gray columns, error bars = SE), recorded in FDS (top), FCR (middle) and FDI (bottom) during action viewing and matched with the EMG profile recorded in the same muscles during execution of the same action. To visualize the correspondence between the two profiles, in each graph the minimum of the MEP modulation and the baseline of the rectified EMG were both set at ordinate zero and EMG amplitude was stretched to become comparable to the modulation size. Note how in all graphs the trend of EMG changes tracks that of the MEP modulation (Adapted from Montagna et al., 2005).

each muscle by one-way ANOVA, was found to be significant for both FDS, $F(3, 316) = 2.87$, $p < .04$, and FDI, $F(3, 340) = 8.97$, $p < .0001$, while it did not reach significance in FCR. Despite the fact that the three muscles were all flexors, the facilitation time course was not the same for all of them (Figure 1A). In FDS, MEP amplitude was maximal in the opening phase of the observed hand (2500–3000 ms), in FDI it was larger in the closing phase (3500–4300 ms), whereas in FCR (a wrist flexor) its peak was reached at the transition between opening and closing. In conclusion, the motor pathways to three forearm flexors were all excited "in resonance" with the observed action, but only in the FDI did the time-course appear to mirror the mechanical extension–flexion sequence of the movement, whereas the FDS and FCR seemed to escape the "mirror" rule since they were not activated during flexion.

EMG recordings during execution of the observed movement solved this apparent contrast. In separate experiments, each subject was invited to perform the observed action in synchrony with the video, while recording the movement kinetics and the EMGs from the same three muscles. This allowed the comparison, in each individual, of the pattern of "resonant" MEP modulation with the pattern of muscular activation during actual movement. Each muscle was active during both the opening and closing phases of the movement; remarkably, in each muscle the time course of activation and of MEP modulation followed the same pattern, as illustrated in Figure 1B for a representative subject.

Motor resonance in non finalized, cyclic movement

In order to improve the analysis of the correlation between the explicit motor activation during movement and the subliminal excitability modulation during resonance, in this and the following experiments the relatively complex grasping movement was substituted with a mechanically simpler movement, a cyclic oscillation of the wrist. In this movement, forearm flexor and extensor muscles to wrist and fingers are homogeneously co-activated. Moreover, its cyclic nature allows for a better quantitative description of the experimental data: in fact, the same sinusoidal function can be used to fit both the observed wrist oscillation and the resonance effects, to quantify the correspondence between the two events and to determine their precise phase relation. Finally the dynamics of the cyclic wrist oscillation can be easily and precisely reproduced with an inanimate object, thus providing the opportunity to test whether the observer's motor system is engaged into resonance by the specificity of the moving substrate (a body segment) or, more simply, by the physical features of movement (oscillations in space).

Specificity of motor resonance for human movement. The comparison between human and object movement was addressed by recording the excitability changes in the wrist flexor FCR during observation of an oscillating hand resting on a metal platform and, later, during oscillations of the metal platform alone. In this experiment, excitability changes in FCR were tested by the H-reflex technique (see Methods). Figure 2A shows the amplitude changes in the H-reflex of the resting FCR muscle (6 subjects) induced by the observation of cyclic flexion–extension (B) performed at 1 Hz by the prone hand of another subject sitting in front of them. Note the striking correspondence between the movement shape and the modulation time course in this flexor muscle, which consistently showed an excitability peak during flexion of the observed hand. This correspondence was quantified by fitting with the same sine function both the average movement oscillation ($R^2 = .99$, $p < .0001$) and the H-reflex data ($R^2 = .69$, $p < .0001$). In addition, this analysis allowed the calculation of the phase relation ($\Delta\phi$) between the average observed movement and the FCR H-reflex modulation. Interestingly, the resonant response anticipated ($\Delta\phi = 54°$) the observed movement by about the same amount as the contraction in the FCR muscle advanced the oscillation of the prone hand, when the observers actually performed this movement at the same frequency ($\Delta\phi = 65°$, Figure 2C and 2D). Thus, the resonant response may be described as a consistent subliminal reproduction of the FCR motor drive used to produce the observed movement of the human hand.

Next, in a successive experimental session, we tried to verify whether the resonant response was specifically elicited by viewing the movement of a limb or more generally by a rhythmic oscillation. With this aim, subjects were presented with the oscillations (1 Hz) of the metal platform onto which the mover's hand had been placed in the previous experiment, while FCR excitability was tested with the same modality as above. Since kinematic properties appear to be among the key features utilized by observers to identify human movement, the empty platform was moved, through a long rod attached to its pivot, by the hand of a person hidden behind a screen. Despite the kinematic identity with the hand oscillations (compare B and F in Figure 2), the platform movements did not evoke any meaningful modulation of the FCR motoneurons, as show in Figure 2E by the random variability of data points, which could not be fitted by the sine equation describing the observed movement. Thus, in the absence of the human hand, the platform oscillatory movement was not recognized as an effective stimulus in triggering a resonant response.

Involvement of the primary motor cortex in transmission of resonant activation. Assuming that human motor resonance originates in the ventral premotor cortex, it may be argued that it influences the spinal motoneurons either via the corticospinal tract or via premotorspinal connections not passing through M1. Modulation of both the H-reflex and MEP during action observation actually discloses excitability changes occurring at the output of the motor pathways, i.e., spinal motoneurons, and increases of the TMS response might equally well be due to an increase of either cortical or motoneuronal excitability.

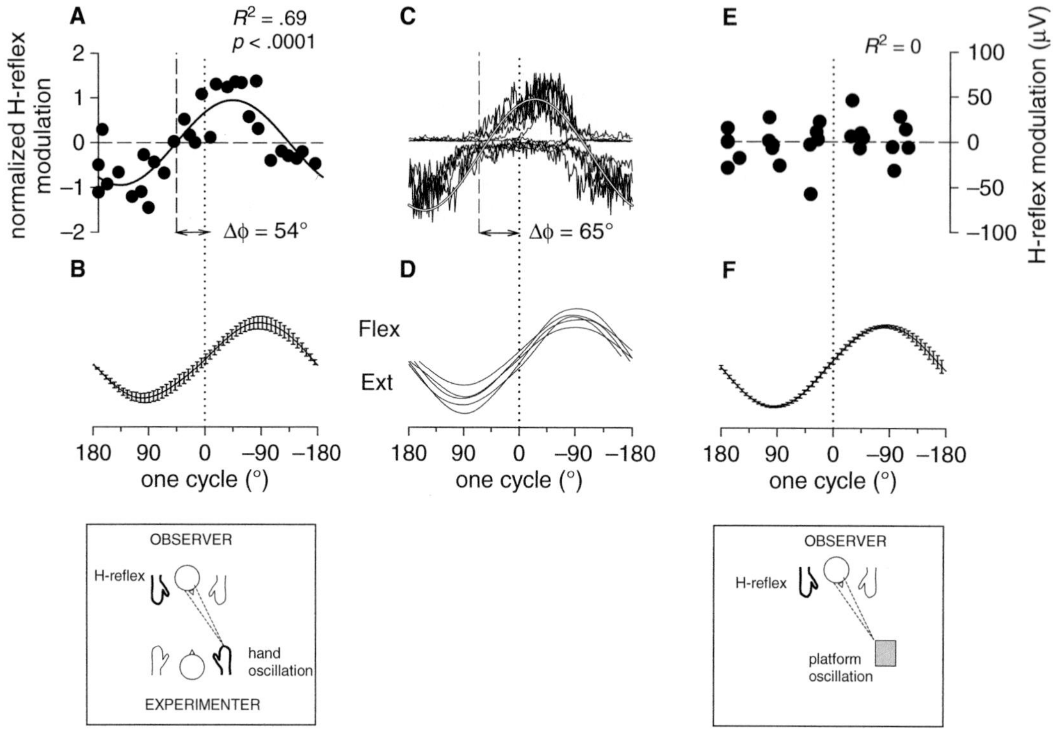

Figure 2. H-reflex modulation occurring during observation of one movement cycle. (A) Cumulative plot for 6 subjects. After time and amplitude normalization (see Methods), average data points from each subject were fitted with a common sinewave function (A, continuous line), with the same period as that of the average movement (B, average movement ± SE). Δϕ = phase difference between reflex modulation in flexor muscle of all observers and wrist oscillation of the experimenter. Flex = downward direction of the hand prone. (C) Single subject records of rectified EMG traces of FCR and ECR (inverted) muscles recorded in 6 subjects during oscillations of the prone hand at 1 Hz. Each record is the average of 20 EMG registrations normalized to the period of that subject's average movement cycle (D). The continuous line overlaid on the EMG traces is the sinewave function fitting the average of the EMG onsets with the same period as the average movement. Here Δϕ = phase difference between the EMG fitting function and movement. Vertical dotted line indicates the zero point of the cycles. (E) H-reflex modulation (5 subjects) recorded at 5 delays during observation of cyclic oscillations at 1 Hz of the empty metal platform upon which the mover's hand rested in previous experiments. Ordinate in μV because the individual data could not be fitted by a sinusoidal function and normalized to its amplitude. The random variability of all data points plotted together could not be fitted with a sinewave function (R^2 = 0). (F) The movement of the empty platform, produced by a human mover hidden behind a screen, was identical to that produced by the mover's hand (B) (Adapted from Borroni et al., 2005). The insets provide a graphic representation of the experiments.

To eliminate one of these possibilities, we reasoned that if the primary motor cortex were the site of transmission for the resonance phenomena, its de-activation would effectively eliminate the resonant response. With this aim, the "resonant" modulation of the FCR H-reflex was tested during the cortical depression ("silent period") following TMS.

Results of this experiment are illustrated in Figure 3, which shows that the amplitude modulation of the FCR H-reflex (empty circles; paired *t*-test, $p < .0001$) is abolished when the reflex was evoked during the silent period (filled circles; paired *t*-test, $p > .2$). TMS alone did not produce any effect on the H-reflex, since in each subject the overall mean amplitude of the reflex at both delays was not different (H-reflex + TMS = 347.7 μV, H-reflex alone = 356.7 μV; paired *t*-test, $p > .6$) in the presence or in the absence of the conditioning cortical stimulation.

The disappearance of the resonant reflex modulation after inhibition of M1 supports the view that influences from visuo-motor areas in ventral premotor cortex reach spinal motoneurons via the primary motor cortex.

Extension of motor resonance to other body segments. The above experiments demonstrated that the close correspondence between subliminal and overt muscle activation during observation and performance of movements, respectively, holds for both ball grasping and wrist oscillations. These movements, though sharing the same effector, the hand, are very different in purpose

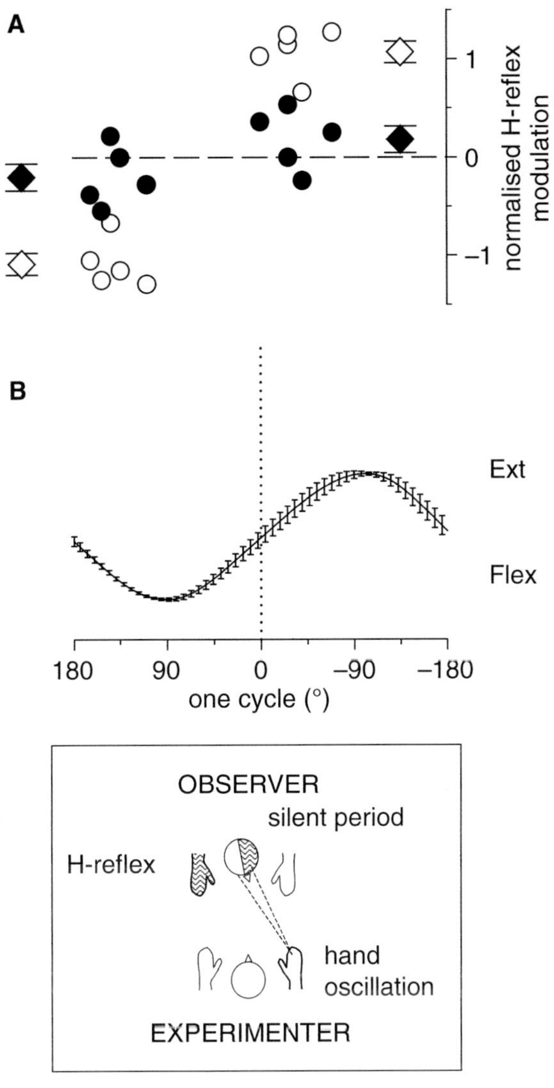

Figure 3. Motor resonance is abolished during the cortical silent period. (A) The H-reflex significant modulation recorded in 5 subjects during observation of the hand oscillation (empty circle: individual data; empty diamonds: average across subjects ± SE) is eliminated during a cortical silent period induced by TMS on the primary motor cortex (filled circles individual and filled diamonds averaged data). In each subject the H-reflex amplitude (both control and conditioned) is normalized to the average reflex amplitude relative to its condition; care was taken to maintain the same amplitude reflexes in both conditions. Data pairs vertically aligned belong to the same subject, and were recorded and plotted at delays corresponding with that subject's maximum and minimum modulation during the movement cycle. In the inset is a graphic representation of the experiment showing that during TMS stimulation of the left primary cortex motor commands to the contra-lateral hand are temporarily silenced.

and complexity. The ball-grasping is a transitive movement and requires the activation of several muscles in a complex sequence, whereas the hand oscillation is an intransitive movement that requires a simple alternation of wrist antagonists. Despite these differences, their observation evoked the same type of response in the motor pathways that we tested: the specific subthreshold reproduction of the motor pattern necessary to produce the observed movement.

Given the profound difference in effectiveness of observing a human limb or an object performing the same movement, it seemed logical to ask if different limbs can engage each other in resonance. Specifically, is the resonant response in a given limb evoked only by observing movement of that limb or it is also elicited by movement of other limbs, suited to perform the observed movement? In the previous experiments both registration and observation involved the right hand: what would happen in the right hand when subjects are observing a movement of the left hand? In the next series of experiments we recorded the H-reflexes of the right FCR muscles, during the observation of a left-hand oscillation at 1 Hz. Results, illustrated in Figure 4A, demonstrate that excitability in the right FCR is cyclically modulated during observation of the (left) hand oscillations (4B) in exactly the same way as during observation of the right hand (Figure 2A). The correlation coefficient R^2, significance level, and $\Delta\phi$ with respect to the observed movement (insets in Figure 4) were virtually identical in the two conditions.

DISCUSSION

The present experiments describe some neural properties of "motor resonance" in humans: (1) motor resonance is mediated by the primary motor cortex; (2) it is evoked by both transitive (finalized) and intransitive movements of human body segments but not movement of inanimate objects; (3) it influences the excitability of those same muscles that are used in the execution of the observed movement; but (4) it can also involve other effectors (different from the one actually observed), which can perform the same movement.

In theory, the cortical influences that produce the subliminal "resonant" excitation of motoneurons may be forwarded by the premotor cortex through its direct projections to the spinal cord (Dum & Strick, 2002) or be mediated via the abundant connections (Cerri, Shimazu, Maier, & Lemon, 2003; Geyer, Matelli, Luppino, & Zilles, 2000; Shimazu, Maier, Cerri, Kirkwood, &

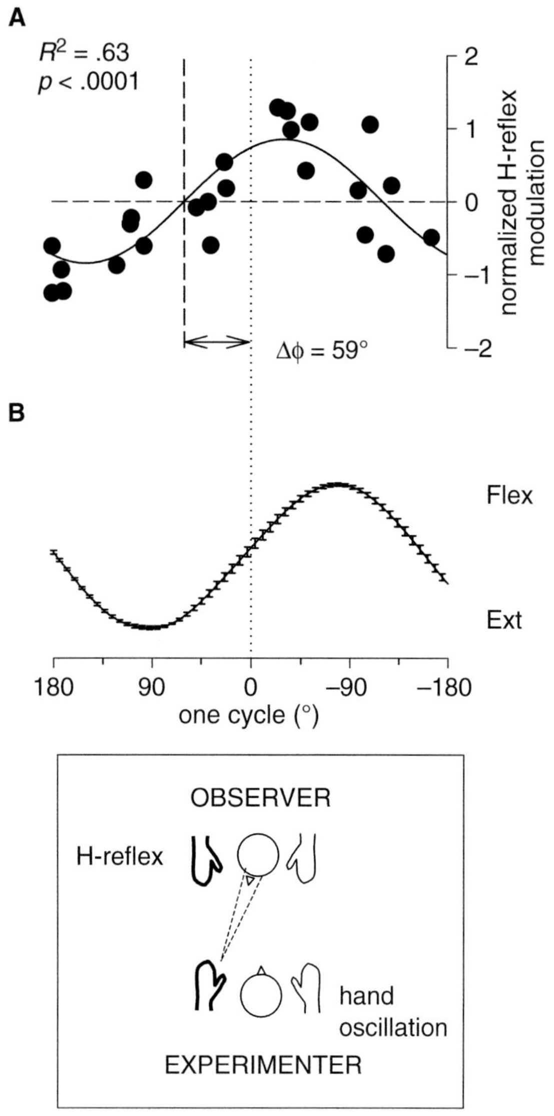

Figure 4. Modulation of the right FCR H-reflex during observation of left-hand oscillations. (A) Cumulative plot (5 subjects) of the H-reflex modulation in the right FCR muscle during observation of a movement cycle performed by the experimenter's left hand. All details as in Figure 2A. (B) average movement traces (± SE) of the experimenter's left hand. The insets provide a graphic representation of the experiments.

Lemon, 2004) between the premotor and the primary motor cortex. Transmission through the primary motor area has been widely accepted, even though no evidence has been specifically gathered to exclude the alternative pathway. PET neuroimaging (Perani et al., 2001; Rizzolatti et al., 1996) or fMRI (Buccino et al., 2001; Iacoboni et al., 1999; Wheaton, Thompson, Syngeniotis, Abbott, & Puce, 2004) revealed consistent activation during action observation of the cortical areas (premotor and parietal) where mirror neurons are located, but failed to detect any activation of the primary motor cortex, probably because such activation is rather weak, as the lack of overt movement suggests. On the other hand, MEG (Hari et al., 1998; Nishitani & Hari, 2002) or EEG (Cochin, Barthelemy, Roux, & Martineau, 1999), as well as TMS (Baldissera, Cavallari, Craighero, & Fadiga, 2001; Borroni et al., 2005; Fadiga, Fogassi, Pavesi, & Rizzolatti, 1995; Montagna et al., 2005) studies provide convincing evidence for M1 activation during both actual and observed movements. Here we tried to obtain further proof of the involvement of M1, with experiments in which this cortical area was temporarily inactivated by a TMS evoked "silent period". Thus the finding that the silent period effectively abolished the "resonant" H-reflex modulation, without producing any effects on the H-reflex itself, strongly suggests that the motoneuronal excitability changes associated with movement observation were produced by M1 descending projections. This would fit well with the common working hypothesis that during action observation M1 is activated from the ventral premotor areas, producing a modulation of its descending output to cervical motoneurons.

The finding that our subjects "resonated" with both complex, finalized, transitive movements (actions), like hand grasping, and simpler, non-finalized, intransitive flexion–extension of the wrist, seems to challenge the accepted notion, derived from experimental observations on the monkey, that mirror neurons encode actions, not movements.

In distinguishing between action and movement, we can agree that a general definition of "action" as a goal-directed movement actually includes its "intention" (Rizzolatti, Fogassi, & Gallese, 2001), i.e., a non-motor property that discriminates between the two terms; we find it difficult, however, to operate the same discrimination based on strictly motor criteria. For instance, the finding that when observing hand grasping some mirror neurons in the monkey F5 area fire during both finger flexion or extension was interpreted (Rizzolatti et al., 1988) as evidence that such activation is not linked to a specific movement but to the whole action, and to its grasping intention. We feel that with this interpretation one risks overlooking important details of motor organization: given the multi-articulated structure of the arm skeleton, practically none of its movements can be performed by synergic muscle groups only. For instance, any finger flexion needs co-activation of wrist extensors, aimed at fixating the wrist, while permitting fingers to move independently. Reciprocally, finger extension requires co-activation of wrist flexors. To support this organization, central neurons are needed to control the reciprocal co-activation of finger and wrist muscles during a flexion–extension sequence of fingers. These "purely motor" neurons would be active during the whole sequence, just as mirror neurons are, whatever the intention. Thus, in the absence of supplementary evidence, their discharge should not be taken as coding for a finalized action.

Another argument in favor of the view that movement intention is the parameter critical to the function of mirror neurons is based on the finding that a given F5 mirror neuron can discriminate between two observed actions (e.g., grasping or scratching), both involving finger flexion but having different intentions, by responding to one but not to the other. This is indeed strong evidence that the different intention of the two actions has been distinguished, but really no proof that the discrimination has taken place in F5. The "sensory specialization" of mirror neurons, which react only to precisely defined visual pattern, suggests instead that the recognition has been done upstream of the premotor cortex.

It seems to us that, when considering mirror neurons, the simpler definition of "action" as a "complex sequence of movements", without implying the goal, would be more suited to focus attention on the important fact that the discharge of these neurons could encode all information necessary to activate the involved muscles in a given and precise spatial and temporal order.

In this light, F5 neurons would be powerful tools in coding a complex movement with a lower number of variables than "if the movements were described in terms of motoneurons or muscles" (Jeannerod, 1995) but would be doing so by selecting organized "time-varying muscle synergies" (d'Avella, Saltiel, & Bizzi, 2003) deriving, for instance, from multiple muscle representations in M1 (Devanne, Cohen, Kouchtir-Devanne, & Capaday, 2002; Holdefer & Miller, 2002; Schneider, Devanne, Lavoie, & Capaday, 2002). Our observation that in each individual there is a strict spatial-temporal correspondence between the subliminal resonant phenomena and the overt activation during execution, seem to support this view for both transitive (goal-oriented) and intransitive movements, and strengthen the assumption that behind motor resonance in man the activation of the mirror system may indeed be engaged. Along the same lines, the connection between resonance and mirror neurons would be further reinforced by analyzing, in the experimental animal, the precise correlation between the discharge of mirror neurons during observation and during action execution and the discharge of other identified neurons of the motor system and, when feasible, with the single muscles involved.

In addition to the strict superimposition found between the distribution of the resonant phenomena and the pattern of muscular activation during movement execution, the present experiments show that the resonant changes may also involve body segments different from the observed one. The finding that the right FCR can be subliminally entrained by observing oscillatory movements of both right or left hands, confirms results of early experiments in the monkey, in which F5 neurons were activated by watching movement of either hand of the experimenter (Gallese, Fadiga, Fogassi, & Rizzolatti, 1996), though with a preference for one of them. Most of these mirror neurons were also active during movement of both hands of the monkey, and indeed neurons in the ventral premotor cortex are thought to be involved in the bilateral control on hand movements (Rizzolatti & Luppino 2001). Should this type of neurons be present in man, one would expect similar results from the complementary experiments, i.e., that motor pathways to both hands can be modulated by motor resonance when watching movements of only one of them. Indeed, preliminary experiments have shown that observing movements of the right hand elicits resonance in both right- and left-hand muscles (Borroni, Cerri, Montagna, & Baldissera, 2006).

In this paper we have chosen to focus on the motor properties of mirror neurons in the effort of fitting the behavior of motor resonance with known properties of the motor system. This seemed particularly important since new interpretative criteria, not linking neural behavior directly to the physical aspect of the environment (as sensory and motor physiology traditionally do) but rather to internal functions as "intention" or "understanding", have been introduced in the description of the function of mirror neurons. It is worth noting that these new criteria have never been, nor are, applied to other less sophisticated motor elements, which are not viewed as supporting cognitive or intentional processes albeit displaying properties per se analogous to those of mirror neurons.

As an example, it seems relevant to this discussion to examine the remarkable descriptive analogies between the mirror neurons and the spinal interneurons that mediate a goal-directed reflex behavior, i.e., the stumbling corrective reaction (studied in the cat; Forssberg, 1979; Quevedo, Stecina, & McCrea, 2005). This oligosynaptic reflex is selectively evoked when the low-threshold cutaneous mechanoceptors of the anterior face of the leg are activated by a light contact with an obstacle. This reflex is present in the newborn and its pathway is located in the lumbar segments of the spinal cord. Briefly, the reflex has a specific and restricted sensory field and two, mutually exclusive, output pathways to flexor or to extensor motoneurons of the stimulated hind limb. Transmission through one or the other pathway is controlled by the spinal central rhythm generator. In resting conditions both pathways are closed, but they open during locomotion, with excitation being forwarded to flexor motoneurons during the swing phase and to extensors during the support phase of the step cycle. Thus, the first order interneurons of these reflex pathways would show many tracts in common with the cortical mirror neurons: (1) they are only activated by a selected sensory input (admittedly much simpler than the visual input to mirror neurons); (2) in certain conditions (at rest) they behave as purely sensory neurons (their activation is not followed by movement; (3) during movement their discharge is causally correlated with a purposeful muscular activation, finalized to assist walking after hitting an obstacle; and (4) this unique aim is pursued by activating one out of two different muscle ensembles (not simply corresponding to the flexors–extensors subdivision), depending on the phase (swing or support) of the step cycle.

Accordingly, these interneurons respond to a specific sensory stimulus and encode a specific action (overcoming an obstacle) that, depending on context, is performed by different muscles; descriptively, the largest difference with respect to the mirror neurons involves the sensory aspects, while on the motor side the similarities are striking.

Is one allowed, on this basis, to conclude that hitting an obstacle would offer the "affordance" of overcoming it and that the above interneurons "understand" or "represent" the meaning of the stimulus? Both the simple tactile information activating the stumbling reaction and the complex visual scenes that excite mirror neurons are effective as such, reasonably just because selective sensory channels reach the respective "motor" target. So why should we say that spinal interneurons "react" to a sensory stimulus while mirror neurons "understand" it?

The supposed understanding capability of the mirror system has originated from widely converging experimental evidence that the motor system is activated during observation of actions performed by others. In the attempt to give a functional role to this activation, it has been suggested that it generates "motor representations" through the same neural circuits in the motor system that are used to perform that action, and that such representation is necessary to understand/recognize actions performed by others and their intentions. This assumption, on the one hand, overlooks the role of the sensory processes in discriminating action and intentions and, on the other hand, postulates that subliminal activation of the motor pathways is able to give rise to cognitive processes concerning a movement, without the need of performing it. While it is quite acceptable that we understand our movements in "motor terms" when we can appreciate their consequences on our body or on the external world, no real evidence is available that we recognize the subliminal activation of motor pathways nor that we need to reproduce an observed movement in order to understand it.

Should this be the case, only piano players should understand the movements of a pianist, because they can activate similar motor patterns. In this context, the term "understanding" seems better applied to the long-lasting learning process that connects each finger movement to the corresponding sound and progressively transforms movement into actions finalized to produce a certain sound; thus, if involved, mirror neurons would be the final result of, not the instrument for, the understanding process. Conversely, having failed to find any resonant phenomena during observation of a moving object, should we conclude that we do not reach "motor understanding" of that movement? In fact, we are able to immediately and automatically reproduce it with different body segments.

Manuscript accepted 1 June 2007
First published online 24 July 2007

REFERENCES

Baldissera, F., Cavallari, P., Craighero, L., & Fadiga, L. (2001). Modulation of spinal excitability during observation of hand actions in humans. *European Journal of Neuroscience, 13*, 190–194.

Borroni, P., Cerri, G., Montagna, M., & Baldissera, F. (2006). The observation of a cyclic movement of one hand induces bimanual motor resonance. *Acta Physiologica, 188*, S652, 157.

Borroni, P., Montagna, M., Cerri, G., & Baldissera, F. (2005). Cyclic time course of motor excitability modulation during the observation of a cyclic hand movement. *Brain Research, 1065*, 115–124.

Buccino, G., Binkofski, F., Fink, G. R., Fadiga, L., Fogassi, L., Gallese, V., et al. (2001). Action observation activates premotor and parietal areas in a somatotopic manner: an fMRI study. *European Journal of Neuroscience, 13*, 400–404.

Cerri, G., Shimazu, H., Maier, M. A., & Lemon, R. N. (2003). Facilitation from ventral premotor cortex of primary motor cortex outputs to macaque hand muscles. *Journal of Neurophysiology, 90*, 832–842.

Classen, J., & Benecke, R. (1995). Inhibitory phenomena in individual motor units induced by transcranial magnetic stimulation. *Electroencephalography and Clinical Neurophysiology, 97*, 264–274.

Cochin, S., Barthelemy, C., Roux, S., & Martineau, J. (1999). Observation and execution of movement: similarities demonstrated by quantified electroencephalography. *European Journal of Neuroscience, 11*, 1839–1842.

d'Avella, A., Saltiel, P., & Bizzi, E. (2003). Combinations of muscle synergies in the construction of a natural motor behaviour. *Nature Neuroscience, 6*, 300–308.

Davey, N. J., Romaiguere, P., Maskill, D. W., & Ellaway, P. H. (1994). Suppression of voluntary motor activity revealed using transcranial magnetic stimulation of the motor cortex in man. *Journal of Physiology, 477*, 223–235.

Devanne, H., Cohen, L. G., Kouchtir-Devanne, N., & Capaday, C. (2002). Integrated motor cortical control of task-related muscles during pointing in humans. *Journal of Neurophysiology, 87*, 3006–3017.

di Pellegrino, G., Fadiga, L., Fogassi, L., Gallese, V., & Rizzolatti, G. (1992). Understanding motor events: A neurophysiological study. *Experimental Brain Research, 91*, 176–180.

Dum, R. P., & Strick, P. L. (2002). Motor areas in the frontal lobe of the primate. *Physiology & Behavior, 77*, 677–682.

Esposti, R., Cavallari, P., & Baldissera, F. (2005). Partition of voluntary command to antagonist muscles during cyclic flexion–extension of the hand. *Experimental Brain Research, 162*, 436–448.

Fadiga, L., Fogassi, L., Pavesi, G., & Rizzolatti, G. (1995). Motor facilitation during action observation: a magnetic stimulation study. *Journal of Neurophysiology, 73*, 2608–2611.

Forssberg, H. (1979). Stumbling corrective reaction: a phase-dependent compensatory reaction during locomotion. *Journal of Neurophysiology, 42*, 936–953.

Gallese, V., Fadiga, L., Fogassi, L., & Rizzolatti, G. (1996). Action recognition in the premotor cortex. *Brain, 119*, 593–609.

Geyer, S., Matelli, M., Luppino, G., & Zilles, K. (2000). Functional neuroanatomy of the primate isocortical motor system. *Anatomy and Embryology, 202*, 443–474.

Hari, R., Forss, N., Avikainen, S., Kirveskari, S., Salenius, S., & Rizzolatti, G. (1998). Activation of human primary motor cortex during action observation: a neuromagnetic study. *Proceedings of the National Academy of Sciences, USA, 95*, 15061–15065.

Holdefer, R. N., & Miller, L. E. (2002). Primary motor cortical neurons encode functional muscle synergies. *Experimental Brain Research, 146*, 233–243.

Iacoboni, M., Woods, R. P., Brass, M. P., Bekkering, H., Mazziotta, J. C., & Rizzolatti, G. (1999). Cortical mechanisms of human imitation. *Science, 286*, 2526–2528.

Jeannerod, M. (1995). Mental imagery in the motor context. *Neuropsychologia, 33*, 1419–1432.

Mills, K. R. (1999). *Magnetic stimulation of the human nervous system*. Oxford, UK: Oxford University Press.

Montagna, M., Cerri, G., Borroni, P., & Baldissera, F. (2005). Excitability changes in human corticospinal projections to muscles moving hand and fingers while viewing a reaching and grasping action. *European Journal of Neuroscience, 22*, 1513–1520.

Nishitani, N., & Hari, R. (2002). Viewing lip forms: cortical dynamics. *Neuron, 36*, 1211–1220.

Perani, D., Fazio, F., Borghese, N. A., Tettamanti, M., Ferrari, S., Decety, J., et al. (2001). Different brain correlates for watching real and virtual hand actions. *NeuroImage, 14*, 749–758.

Quevedo, J., Stecina, K., & McCrea, D. (2005). Intracellular analysis of reflex pathways underlying the stumbling corrective reaction during fictive locomotion in the cat. *Journal of Neurophysiology, 94*, 2053–2062.

Reid, A. E., Chiappa, K. H., & Cros, D. (2002). Motor threshold, facilitation and the silent period in cortical magnetic stimulation. In A. Pascual-Leone, N. J. Davey, J. Rothwell, E. M. Wasswermann, & B. K. Puri (Eds.), *Handbook of transcranial magnetic stimulation* (pp. 97–111). London: Arnold.

Rizzolatti, G., Camarda, R., Fogassi, L., Gentilucci, M., Luppino, G., & Matelli, M. (1988). Functional organization of inferior area 6 in the macaque monkey: II. Area F5 and the control of distal movements. *Experimental Brain Research, 71*, 491–507.

Rizzolatti, G., Fadiga, L., Matelli, M., Bettinardi, V., Paulesu, E., Perani, D., et al. (1996). Localization of grasp representation in humans by PET: 1. Observation versus execution. *Experimental Brain Research, 111*, 246–252.

Rizzolatti, G., Fogassi, L., & Gallese, V. (2001). Neurophysiological mechanisms underlying the understanding and imitation of action. *Nature Reviews Neuroscience, 2*, 661–669.

Rizzolatti, G., & Luppino, G. (2001). The cortical motor system. *Neuron, 31*, 889–901.

Schneider, C., Devanne, H., Lavoie, B. A., & Capaday, C. (2002). Neural mechanisms involved in the functional linking of motor cortical points. *Experimental Brain Research*, *146*, 86–94.

Shimazu, H., Maier, M. A., Cerri, G., Kirkwood, P. A., & Lemon, R. N. (2004). Macaque ventral premotor cortex exerts powerful facilitation of motor cortex outputs to upper limb motoneurons. *Journal of Neurosciences*, *24*, 1200–1211.

Warren, J. E., Sauter, D. A., Eisner, F., Wiland, J., Dresner, M. A., Wise, R. J., et al. (2006). Positive emotions preferentially engage an auditory-motor "mirror" system. *Journal of Neurosciences*, *26*, 13067–13075.

Wheaton, K. J., Thompson, J. C., Syngeniotis, A., Abbott, D. F., & Puce, A. (2004). Viewing the motion of human body parts activates different regions of premotor, temporal, and parietal cortex. *NeuroImage*, *22*, 277–288.

Wicker, B., Keysers, C., Plailly, J., Rovet, J., Gallese, V., & Rizzolatti, G. (2003). Both of us disgusted in my insula: the common neural basis of seeing and feeling disgust. *Neuron*, *40*, 655–664.

SOCIAL NEUROSCIENCE, 2008, 3 (3–4), 289–302

Psychology Press
Taylor & Francis Group

Release of premotor activity after repetitive transcranial magnetic stimulation of prefrontal cortex

Massimo Gangitano
Harvard Medical School, Boston, Massachusetts, USA, and Università degli Studi di Palermo, Palermo, Italy

Felix M. Mottaghy
Harvard Medical School, Boston, Massachusetts, USA, and KU Leuven, Leuven, Belgium

Alvaro Pascual-Leone
Harvard Medical School, Boston, Massachusetts, USA

In the present study we aimed to explore by means of repetitive transcranial magnetic stimulation (rTMS) the reciprocal influences between prefrontal cortex (PFC) and premotor cortex (PMC). Subjects were asked to observe on a computer monitor different pictures representing manipulations of different kind of tools. They had to produce a movement (go condition) or to keep the resting position (no-go condition) at the appearance of different cue signals represented by different colors shown alternatively on the hands manipulating the tools or on the picture background. Motor evoked potentials (MEPs) were collected at the offset of the visual stimuli before and after a 10 minute, 1 Hz rTMS train applied to the dorsolateral PFC (Experiment 1), to the PMC (Experiment 2) or to the primary motor cortex (Experiment 3). Following rTMS to the PFC, MEPs increased in the go condition when the cue for the go command was presented on the hand. In contrast, following rTMS to the PMC, in the same condition, MEPs were decreased. rTMS to the primary motor cortex did not produce any modulation. Results are discussed according to the presence of a visual-motor matching system in the PMC and to the role of the PFC in the attention-related processes. We hypothesize that the perceptual analysis for action selection within the PFC was modulated by rTMS and its temporary functional inactivation in turn influenced the premotor areas for motor programming.

INTRODUCTION

Prefrontal cortex (PFC) can be conceived as a set of cortical areas connected with all sensory and motor systems (Elliott, Dolan, & Frith, 2000; Fuster, 1989; Miller, 2000). This wide network provides the ideal structure for controlling important functions, namely working-memory processes (Goldman-Rakic, 1987), emotion-related behaviors (Bechara, Damasio, & Damasio, 2000) intentional self-generated actions (Jahanshahi & Frith, 1998), planning of high-level processes or simple motor tasks (Miller, 2000). Patients with a PFC impairment could fail to pursue appropriate strategies, be bound to follow wrong rules and be unable to change them when they are required to

Correspondence should be addressed to: Massimo Gangitano, Dipartimento di Neuroscienze Cliniche (DiNeC), Università degli Studi di Palermo, via Gaetano LaLoggia, 1–90129, Palermo, Italy. E-mail: massimo.gangitano@unipa.it

This study was supported in pary by a grant from the National Institutes of Health (K24 RR018875) and grants from Goldberg Family and the National Eye Institute and National Institute of Mental Health to APL and a grant of the Deutsche Forschungsgemeinschaft to FMM (DFG MO 871/3–1)

www.psypress.com/socialneuroscience DOI:10.1080/17470910701516838

plan multiple, complex cognitive processes (Luria, 1966). In the same fashion, PFC patients seem to be unable to select sensory information during the planning and execution of motor tasks because they are captured by useless "sensory cues that reflexively elicit strongly associated actions" (Miller, 2000). During the execution of motor tasks, a PFC elaboration is indeed necessary at multiple levels in order to monitor the ongoing status of both the environment and the action (Petrides & Pandya, 1999). The connections between PFC, visual and sensory cortices make this function possible (Pandya & Yeterian, 1998; Petrides & Pandya, 1999; Rao, Rainer, & Miller, 1997).

In the early 1980s Lhermitte described a group of patients suffering from extensive uni- or bilateral lesions of the PFC, mainly in the basal and lateral areas of the rostral portion of frontal lobe, characterized by the compulsive tendency to interact with every object that was presented to them (Lhermitte, 1983, 1986; Lhermitte, Pillon, & Serdaru, 1986). Lhermitte's patients considered every object falling in their visual field as a potential target for a possible action (utilization behavior) or were compelled to replicate movements executed in front of them without any evident necessity to do it (imitation behavior). Years later, other authors confirmed these observations (Cambier, 1999; Shallice, Burgess, Schon, & Baxter, 1989). However, despite the growing number of new anatomical and neurophysiological evidences on the PFC functions, the mechanism responsible of such behavior has not been yet understood. Lhermitte himself tried to explain this syndrome by attributing the automatic, compulsive tendency to imitate actions or execute movements to an imbalance between the reduced activity of a lesioned PFC and the normal activity of parietal areas functionally related to PFC (Lhermitte, 1983, 1986; Lhermitte et al., 1986).

In recent years, Rizzolatti and his group have shown that mirror neurons localized in the ventral portion of primate PMC automatically fire not only during the actual execution of a movement but also during its passive observation, without the production of an actual movement (DiPellegrino, Fadiga, Fogassi, Gallese, & Rizzolatti, 1992; Gallese, Fadiga, Fogassi, & Rizzolatti, 1996; Rizzolatti & Fadiga, 1998). Several subsequent experimental evidences in humans have shown a comparable activation of motor and PMC areas during observation of actions executed by others. This internal PMC representation is probably used for their understanding (Buccino et al., 2001; Fadiga, Fogassi, Pavesi, & Rizzolatti, 1995; Grafton, Arbib, Fadiga, & Rizzolatti, 1996; Grèzes, Armony, Rowe, & Passingham, 2003; Grèzes, Costes, & Decety, 1999; Hari et al., 1998; Iacoboni et al., 1999; Kohler et al., 2002; Maeda, Kleiner-Fisman, & Pascual-Leone, 2002). This passive automatic activation of PMC-motor circuits, without the production of an actual movement, seems to be the counterpart of the compelling tendency to move of the PFC-lesioned patients.

Moving from these considerations we hypothesize a possible functional relation between PFC and PMC mirror activity. The present study aimed to explore these possible interactions. We model, in healthy subjects, the behavior observed in PFC-lesioned patients by means of repetitive transcranial magnetic stimulation (rTMS). We asked them to execute a go/no-go task on the presentation of pictures reproducing hands manipulating tools. Stimuli were specifically designed to demand both the PFC functions and to evoke the activation of the PMC mirror system by changing the way of analyzing and processing some of their key features (Gentilucci, Benuzzi, Bertolani, Daprati, & Gangitano, 2000; Gentilucci, Daprati, & Gangitano, 1998; Grafton et al., 1996; Kiefer, Marzinzik, Weisbrod, Scherg, & Spietzer, 1998; Konishi et al., 1999; Liddle, Kiehl, & Smith, 2001).

In order to differentiate the single contributions of PFC and PMC in task execution rTMS was employed. rTMS has been shown to be an effective tool in investigating functions of discrete regions of cortex (Hallett, 2000; Pascual-Leone, Batres-Faz, & Keenan, 1999; Pascual-Leone, Walsh, & Rothwell, 2000; Rothwell, 1991; Walsh & Cowey, 2000; Walsh & Rushworth, 1999). In particular, we used a low-frequency (1 Hz) of rTMS, which is thought to depress the excitability of the stimulated cortex for a short period of time after the completion of the train itself (Chen et al., 1997; Hallett, 2000; Pascual-Leone, Valls-Sole, Wassermann, & Hallett, 1994; Walsh & Cowey, 2000). Employing a pre–post paradigm, the effects on behavior and on cortical excitability were observed, along three different experiments, before and after the delivering of rTMS over the PFC, PMC and primary motor cortex, respectively.

MATERIALS AND METHODS

Subjects

A total of 24 subjects were studied in three different experiments. In Experiment 1 we enrolled 8 males and 1 female, mean age 27.2 (±1.4 years). In Experiment 2 we enrolled another 8 males and 1 female, mean age 31.2 (±4.3 years). Finally, in Experiment 3 we enrolled 5 males and 1 female, mean age 33.0 (±3.7 years).

All subjects were right-handed according to the Edinburgh Inventory (Oldfield, 1971) and without any history of neurological diseases or vision impairments. All subjects gave written informed consent to the study, which was conducted according to the declaration of Helsinki and had been approved by the local Institutional Review Board (IRB).

Apparatus and stimuli

Subjects were seated in a dimly illuminated room, 80 cm in front of a computer screen (Macintosh, iMAC, Apple Computers Cuppertino, CA, USA) used for presentation of visual stimuli.

Stimuli consisted of digital images of right hands manipulating different tools (i.e., pliers, scissors, pen, screwdriver, knife, etc.). SuperLab pro, v1.74 (Cedrus Corp., San Pedro, CA, USA) was used for stimuli presentation and reaction time (RT) recording. The images were elaborated using Adobe Photoshop (v5.5).

In different visual stimuli, the hands or the background were painted with one of the following colors (see Figure 1, panel A): (a) red; or (b) one of three colors chromatically close to the red (pink, orange, and purple); or (c) one of three other colors chromatically different from the red and easily distinguishable from it (green, blue, and yellow). Their chromatic properties were assessed according to the RGB scale. The meaning of the colors, regardless of which part of the stimulus (hand or background) was colored, was to convey the instruction for the task that the subjects had to accomplish: red for the go signal, all the other colors for the no-go signal (see procedure below).

Such colors were chosen in order to increase the demands during the perceptual elaboration of the stimuli and thereby, presumably, to modulate the amount of activity within the PFC. We hypothesized that, if the delivering of rTMS can modulate the supposed PFC–PMC functional circuitry, it would be possible to reproduce some features of the unwilling tendency to move of Lhermitte's patients, and that such an effect would be stronger when the stimulus analysis become more difficult (i.e., at presentation of colors chromatically closer to the red) that is when a greater involvement of PFC resources was required. Furthermore, requiring to focus alternatively different part of stimuli, our prediction was likely to induce the subjects to pay more attention to a relevant (at the hand observation) or non-relevant (at the background observation) feature for mirror activation and consequently to change the strength of the mirror effect. In this way, we speculated that we would be able to observe a possible modulation of PFC on the PMC mirror system. Finally, the rationale for the use of static stimuli instead of moving hands was to allow the locking of the evoked activity within the PMC-motor circuit to the time of the TMS pulse.

Procedure

A go/no-go paradigm was employed. Subjects were asked to execute two different tasks: (1) press with the right index finger the space-bar on a computer keyboard every time the red color was presented, either on the hand or on the background (go condition); (2) maintain the resting position every time any color other than red was presented, either on the hand or on the background (no-go condition). The computer keyboard (extended keyboard, Apple Computers, Cuppertino, CA, USA) was used to collect the responses and the RTs in the go condition. Given the employed setup, resolution on RT measures was ±16 ms. The position of the index finger on the keyboard and of the wrist on the table was marked for each subject and kept constant across the experimental sessions.

Each experimental session (before and after rTMS) was composed of 144 trials. For the no-go condition subjects completed 96 trials, 16 for each of the six presented colors, that is 8 trials in which the informative color was presented on the hand (colored-hand condition) and 8 trials in which the color was presented on the background (colored-background condition). For the go condition subjects completed 48 trials, 24 for each one of

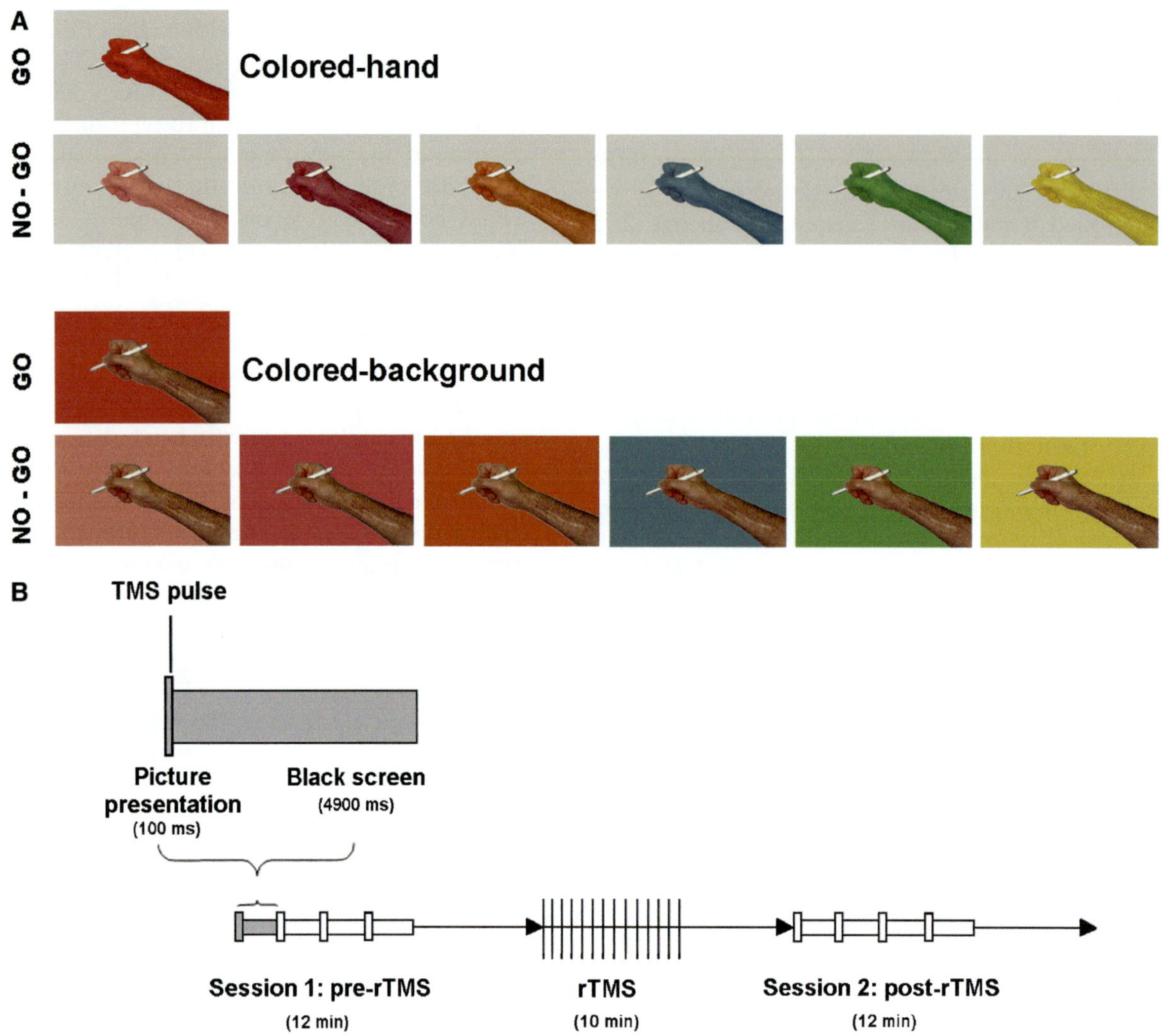

Figure 1. Representative examples of the presented stimuli (panel A) and a schematization of the task design (panel B) are shown. Subjects were requested to press (go) or not to press (no-go) the space-bar of a PC keyboard on the basis of the colors presented on the pictures. Colors were alternatively shown on the hand (first row: "colored-hand" condition) or on the background (second row: "colored-background" condition). Each experiment consisted of two sessions executed before and after rTMS over the dorsolateral PFC (Experiment 1), PMC (Experiment 2) and primary motor cortex (Experiment 3). Stimuli were presented for 100 ms and were followed, for 4900 ms, by a central fixation-cross on a black screen. At the pictures offset a single TMS pulse was delivered on the optimal spot for FDI. One hundred forty-four trials were serially executed in 12 minutes. At the end of this period rTMS was applied for 10 minutes. rTMS was immediately followed by a new execution of the task. For further details see text.

the two kinds of stimuli (colored-hand and colored-background). The order of stimuli was randomized. No-go trials were made more frequent in order to increase the elaboration within the PFC (Jahanshahi & Frith, 1998). The duration of a single trial was 5 s: images were shown for 100 ms and at their offset a central fixation-cross appeared on a black screen for 4900 ms (see Figure 1, panel B). Therefore, each experimental session lasted 12 minutes.

During each trial, when the picture disappeared from the screen, a single magnetic pulse was delivered to the optimal representation of the right first dorsal interosseus (FDI) muscle in the left primary motor cortex (see TMS procedure below). Times for stimuli presentation and TMS were chosen in order to explore the early cortical elaboration before the response generation. Previous EEG (Thut et al., 2000) and TMS single-pulse studies (Hoshiyama et al., 1997; Leocani, Cohen, Wassermann, Ikoma, & Hallett, 2000) employing visuo-motor tasks have shown the activation of the PMC-motor cortices 100–200 ms after stimulus perception. Other studies employing go/no-go paradigms have shown the modulation of MEPs in the interval between

120 and 300 ms after the signal (Yamanaka et al., 2002). In choosing the timing of the TMS we tried to avoid any interference of the single TMS pulses with the impending response movement. Nevertheless, the possible presence of a close muscular activity was checked by recording the EMG trace for a period 50 ms antecedent and 200 ms subsequent to the TMS pulse. The interval between each TMS pulse was at least 5 s in order to avoid any interference between two subsequent stimuli.

Each experiment was divided into two sessions, serially executed. In the first session (pre-rTMS) the basal data were collected. The second session (post-rTMS) was preceded by a 10-minute train of rTMS applied at a frequency of 1 Hz and 90% motor threshold intensity. The cortical area targeted by this rTMS train varied in the three experiments. In Experiment 1 we targeted the left dorsolateral PFC. In Experiment 2, rTMS was applied to the PMC area—Brodmann area (BA) 6. Finally, in Experiment 3, rTMS was applied to the primary motor cortex. These different cortical targets were defined anatomically using each subject's brain MRI to verify the placement of the TMS coil on the scalp (see below for details). In all experiments, the pre-rTMS session was proceeded by a short practice session in which the subjects became familiar with the stimuli and the task.

TMS stimulation

Single-pulse TMS and repetitive TMS were performed using a Magstim Super-Rapid Transcranial Magnetic Stimulator (Magstim Company, Whitland, UK) and a 70 mm figure-of-eight coil. For the purpose of single-pulse TMS and induction of motor-evoked potentials (MEPs) TMS was delivered to the scalp position from which TMS induced MEPs of the maximal amplitude in the contralateral FDI muscle. This position was marked on a tightly fitting Lycra swimming cap placed on the subject's head. The coil was held tangentially to the subject's head, with the handle pointing occipitally, positioned at 45 degrees with respect to the mid-sagittal axis of the subject's head. This coil orientation elicits the maximal response with a predominant, indirect, pyramidal-cells activation (Brasil-Neto, McShane, Fuhr, Hallett, & Cohen, 1992; Mills, Boniface, & Schubert, 1992).

Two surface electrodes were placed on the belly and tendon of the right FDI muscle, the finger used for the response. Electrodes were connected to a Dantec Counterpoint Electromyograph (Dantec, Skovlunde, Denmark) in order to collect the MEPs. The EMG signal was amplified (to 1 mV), filtered (band pass of 20–1000 Hz) and digitized using PowerLab 16S (AD Instruments Limited, Hastings, UK) at the sampling rate of 2 KHz and stored on a computer for subsequent off-line analysis.

Subjects' motor threshold (MT) was initially assessed, before the rTMS application. MT was defined as the minimal intensity of stimulation capable of inducing MEPs greater than 50 μV peak-to-peak in at least five out of ten consecutive trials (Rossini, 1994). MT was used as a reference value to set the single-pulse intensity and rTMS intensity. For the single pulse the intensity was set at 110% of the individual's MT.

Repetitive TMS was delivered at 90% of the individual's MT with a frequency of 1 Hz for 10 minutes, for a total of 600 stimuli. This kind of stimulation conforms to current safety guidelines (Wassermann, 1998). For Experiment 1, the stimulation site for rTMS was established using the optimal spot of FDI motor response and moving the coil 5 cm anterior along a line parallel to the mid-sagittal line in order to target the dorsolateral PFC (BA 9/46). Coil orientation during rTMS was the same as during the assessment of MT. In Experiment 2, rTMS was applied to the caudal PMC (BA 6). This point was defined by moving the coil 2 cm forward from the optimal spot for FDI responses, along a line parallel to the mid-sagittal line. Finally, in Experiment 3 rTMS was delivered to the primary motor cortex itself. This third experiment was conducted because given the anatomical proximity during rTMS of the premotor (Experiment 2) a spread of stimulation to the motor cortex, which could account for the results, cannot be completely excluded (Pascual-Leone et al., 1994). In all three experiments, the anatomical location of the stimulation points was verified by obtaining an anatomical MRI of the brain.

MRI procedure

In order to verify the anatomical correctness of coil placement during rTMS a 3D-MPRAGE MRI scan (160 sagittal slices 1 mm apart with an in-plane resolution of $256 \times 256\ mm^2$) was obtained at the end of the post-rTMS session in four subjects in each of the three experiments. Vitamin E capsules were placed on the scalp to mark the site of rTMS stimulation. Additional markers were placed above Cz of the 10–20 EEG system, on the nasion, on the inion and on the tragus bilaterally. The actual location of the coil position on the scalp with respect to the frontal gyrus was subsequently assessed using MRIcro (Chris Rorden, UK, Version 1.23).

As illustrated in Figure 2, images showed that the targeted TMS scalp positions were indeed above the rostral part of the gyrus frontalis medium (presumed to correspond in most subjects with BA 9/46; Experiment 1) on the rostral part of the precentral gyrus (presumed to correspond with BA 6; Experiment 2) and on the anterior bank of the central sulcus (primary motor cortex, BA 4; Experiment 3). The inter-individual variability of the anatomical targets

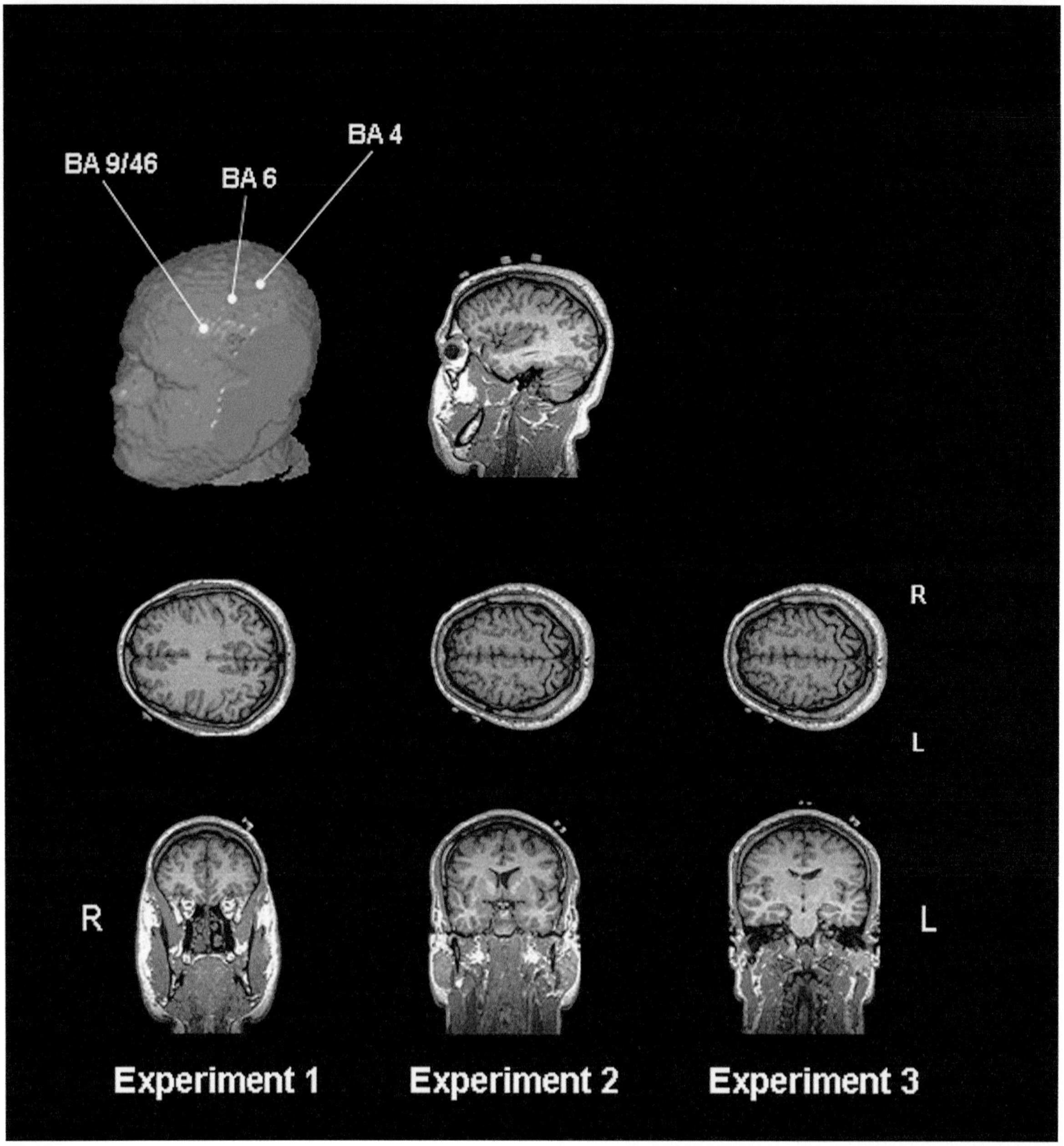

Figure 2. MRI scans obtained from a representative subject who participated in Experiment 1 are shown. Coil placement over the left dorsolateral PFC (BA 9/46), PMC (BA 6) and primary motor cortex (BA 4) was confirmed using a 3D MRI sequence with vitamin E capsules in place. Details are reported in the text.

was well within the presumed spatial resolution of the rTMS with the employed coil (1–1.5 cm).

Data analysis

MEPs, responses in the go condition, and response times (RTs) were collected and analyzed. MEPs were rectified and the area under the curve was calculated. Two different analyses of variance (ANOVA) were executed. In the first analysis the no-go trials were collapsed. Data were averaged across the subjects and submitted to a $2 \times 2 \times 2$ ANOVA, using as within-subjects factors the Stimulation Condition (pre-rTMS vs. post-rTMS), the Colored Section of Stimuli (colored-hand vs. colored-background) and the Response Condition (go vs. no-go). The second ANOVA was carried out contrasting the presented colors separately. A $2 \times 2 \times 7$ design was employed using as factors the Stimulation Condition, the Colored Section of Stimuli and the seven Presented Colors. In all analyses Newman-Keuls test was employed post hoc for the multiple comparisons. Significance level was set at $p < .05$. Errors in the pre- and post-rTMS sessions were compared by means of two-tailed *t*-tests. Errors were considered the space-bar pressure in the no-go condition and the absent response in the go condition. Finally, RTs for each trial in the go condition were submitted to a 2×2 ANOVA using as factors the Stimulation Condition (pre or post-rTMS) and Colored Section of Stimuli (colored-hand or colored-background).

RESULTS

Experiment 1: rTMS applied to the PFC

Colors chromatically close to the red didn't produce any modulation of cortical excitability, neither before nor after rTMS. A $2 \times 2 \times 7$ ANOVA analyzing the influence of single colors on MEP size did not show any effect either when they were presented on the hands or on the background.

After rTMS, a significant increase of the motor excitability was present across all experimental conditions as indexed by the increase in the MEPs size, pre-rTMS: 2.51 mm × mV, post-rTMS: 3.39 mm × mV, $F(1, 8) = 5.92$; $p < .041$. Mean values for each condition are shown in Figure 3A. The post hoc analysis confirmed the overall facilitation of the MEPs after rTMS (all the post-rTMS conditions are significantly different from the pre-rTMS ones; all $ps < .05$). However, after rTMS, the go condition with the cue signal presented on the hands induced a greater activity than alternative conditions (go with cue signal on the background, all no-go conditions), as shown by the significant 3-way interaction between stimulation condition, colored section of stimuli condition and response condition, $F(1, 8) = 6.19$; $p < .038$.

No differences in number of errors and RTs were found across all conditions (see Table 1). The EMG recording didn't show any trial contaminated by any early muscular activity that could have interfered with the MEPs.

Experiment 2: rTMS applied to the PMC

No variation of the overall motor excitability was found after rTMS. As in the Experiment 1, in this experiment the 3-way interaction between stimulation condition, colored section of the stimuli condition and response condition was significant, $F(1,8) = 29.29$; $p < .001$. However, differently from Experiment 1, in which a greater activity after rTMS was observed in the go condition when the hand was painted in red as compared with the other conditions, in this experiment the size of the MEPs was modulated in the opposite fashion becoming smaller (see Figure 3B). A significant effect was observed also in the 2-way interaction between stimulation condition and colored section of stimuli, $F(1, 8) = 5.35$; $p < .05$. The hands were less effective in modulating MEPs size than background. Similar to the findings in Experiment 1, no differences were present among different colors in the no-go condition. No differences in number of errors and RTs before and after rTMS were found (see Table 1).

Experiment 3: rTMS applied to the motor cortex

In this final experiment, rTMS was applied to the motor cortex in order to control for the possible spread of the rTMS effects from the PMC to the motor cortex during Experiment 2. After rTMS an overall, but non-significant trend to MEPs suppression (see Figure 3C) was observed. In contrast to Experiments 1 and 2, no modulation of the MEPs' size across the post-rTMS conditions was present. Interaction

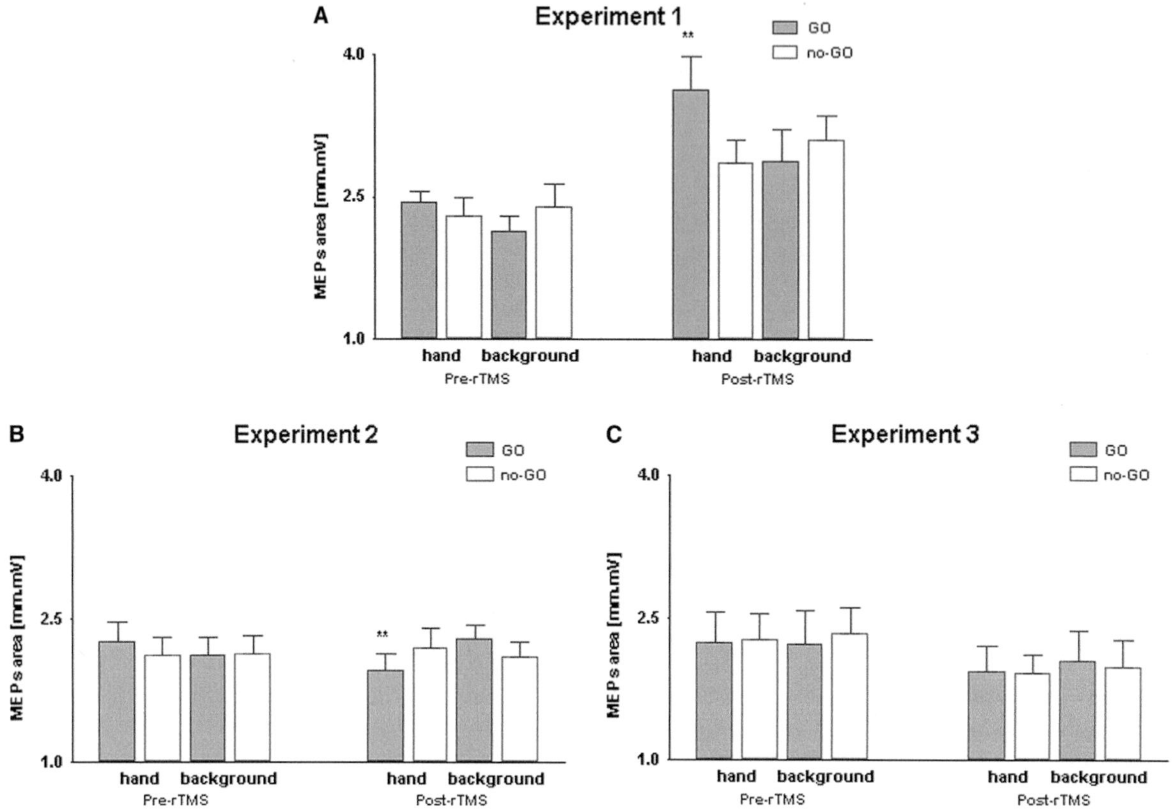

Figure 3. MEPs from FDI collected before and after rTMS for the two conditions of color presentation in the go and no-go tasks during Experiment 1 (rTMS over PFC, panel A), Experiment 2 (rTMS over PMC, panel B) and Experiment 3 (rTMS over primary motor cortex, panel C). Histograms refer to the MEPs area-under-the-curve, averaged across the subjects. Whiskers are standard error of means (*SEM*). $^{**}(p < .05)$ refers to the significant variation in post-rTMS conditions with respect to the pre-rTMS conditions.

between stimulation condition, colored section of the stimuli and response condition was not significant, $F(1, 5) = 1.28$, $p = .31$. RTs collected in the pre-rTMS session were significantly shorter than RTs after rTMS, $F(1, 5) = 6.26$, $p = .05$, but we found no significant effect of rTMS on the number of errors (see Table 1).

DISCUSSION

Effects on cortico-spinal excitability

Several different results of the present study deserve mention and discussion. First, rTMS resulted in differential effects on cortico-spinal

TABLE 1
Mean values of reaction times and number of errors in the go condition

	RTs (ms)				*Errors (n)*	
	Red hand		*Red background*			
	Pre-rTMS	*Post-rTMS*	*Pre-rTMS*	*Post-rTMS*	*Pre-rTMS*	*Post-rTMS*
Experiment 1	439.3 (24.8)	426.6 (36.2)	440.5 (24.1)	435.2 (35.2)	4.0 (1.3)	4.6 (1.8)
Experiment 2	431.2 (42.5)	416.3 (48.0)	437.6 (42.7)	424.7 (53.1)	4.3 (0.7)	3.0 (0.5)
Experiment 3	376.9 (26.7)	390.6 (31.9)	405.6 (44.2)	436.7 (50.1)	4.8 (0.5)	4.2 (0.6)

Notes: RTs = reaction times. Data are collected in the go condition before and after rTMS over the dorsolateral PFC (Experiment 1), PMC (Experiment 2) and primary motor cortex (Experiment 3). For each value the corresponding standard deviation is shown in parentheses.

excitability depending on the targeted cortical region. In Experiment 1, rTMS of the PFC caused an overall increase of MEPs (Figure 3A). Such an effect was not found after rTMS applied over the PMC (Experiment 2, Figure 3B) whereas only a trend toward suppression was found after rTMS over the primary motor cortex (Experiment 3, Figure 3C).

Although the suppression of cortico-spinal excitability following low-rate rTMS of the motor cortex in Experiment 3 is consistent with other observations (Chen et al., 1997; Hallett, 2000; Maeda, Keenan, Tormos, Topka, & Pascual-Leone, 2000b; Pascual-Leone et al., 1999, 2000; Rothwell, 1991; Walsh & Cowey, 2000) the lack of similar effects in Experiment 2 (when the rTMS was applied to the PMC) is surprising in light of findings that have shown the presence of a robust decrease of cortico-spinal excitability after 1 Hz rTMS to the PMC (Gerschlager, Siebner, & Rothwell, 2001) when intensities of 90% of motor threshold has been employed (Rizzo et al., 2003). Other studies employing low intensities of stimulation (80% MT) on the same premotor spot have shown small or no modulatory effects on MEP amplitude (Münchau, Bloem, Trimble, & Rothwell, 2002). It is possible that in our study the relatively short duration of the rTMS train may not have been sufficient to induce a more robust modulation of cortico-spinal excitability. More important is the fact that subjects were engaged in preparing a motor response. This probably may have modified the rTMS effects.

The main finding in our results is the demonstration of a facilitation of cortico-spinal excitability following rTMS to the PFC. Several anatomical studies can support this hypothesis. The PFC is connected to PMC by means of indirect cortico-cortical, i.e., through the parietal lobe (Pandya & Yeterian, 1998; Petrides & Pandya, 1999) or subcortical projections, i.e., through the basal ganglia (Alexander, DeLong, & Strick, 1986; Alexander, Cructher, & DeLong, 1990); other direct connections are between the dorsolateral PFC and rostral part of the PMC. On the basis of these connections, premotor areas can be subdivided into several different subregions endowed with different properties (see Schubotz & von Cramon, 2003, for a review on this argument). In sum, rTMS over the dorsolateral PFC could have influenced the rostral PMC and, from there, the primary motor cortex. Alternatively, rTMS could have primarily exerted an influence on the PFC-connected areas (e.g., the parietal cortex), feeding back to the PMC.

However, we believe that the increase in cortico-spinal excitability following rTMS to the PFC (Experiment 1) could be explained by hypothesizing a suppression of PFC facilitating in turn the activity of the primary motor cortex only when subjects were already engaged by a task that might facilitate the motor cortical outputs. According to this hypothesis, the PFC has a pure modulatory role. This point will be further discussed below. We can exclude that these effects are the consequence of a spread of rTMS from PFC to the nearby premotor and motor cortices. In fact, a different modulation was found after the direct application of rTMS over these sites. The same explanation excludes the presence of a possible "order effect" due to the fixed sequence of sessions.

Interaction between prefrontal and premotor cortices

Against our initial prediction, before rTMS, in all three experiments, we failed to detect any modulation of MEPs when subjects were required to orient their attention toward features capable of evoking (attention toward the hands) or not evoking (attention toward the background) the mirror effect. MEPs collected across the two conditions of color presentation (hand or background colored), were indeed similar. In addition, no significant modulation of the MEPs in the no-go condition for the color group closer to the red was observed. Moreover, our subjects were still able to properly judge the instruction conveyed from the stimuli, and differently from prefrontal-lesioned patients described by Lhermitte no "compulsion to move", revealed by changes in RTs, was ever induced by rTMS when colors close to red were presented.

However, in despite of these apparently negative evidences, a noticeable effect was found. In Experiment 1, after rTMS, MEPs in the go condition increased significantly when the hands conveyed the information for the impending task. We believe that this effect was task specific. This assumption is supported by the following considerations. (i) Although an overall increase of cortical excitability was present after rTMS over dorsolateral PFC, the existence of two opposite modulations in Experiments 1 and 2 (i.e., the

3-way interaction, see Results) indicates that the effect was induced by the visual elaboration of the stimuli. After targeting the premotor areas, we found a decrease of MEPs in the same condition (go with colored hand) that was enhanced in Experiment 1 (see Figure 3A and 3B). The presence of this "reverse-effect" makes a non-specific or artifactual modulation quite improbable. (ii) Methodological biases, like the presentation of non-natural colors that could have surprised the subjects inducing an involuntary muscle contraction can be safely excluded as well. Such a kind of perceptual influence was controlled against by allowing subjects to become familiar with the stimuli before the execution of the task. (iii) A muscle preactivation induced by the preparation of the motor response can be excluded as well because it should have affected all conditions and this was not the case. Furthermore, our on-line EMG recording ruled out any contraction of the target muscles before or after the single TMS pulses.

Our first hypothesis is that such an effect could be attributed to the changes of properties within the circuitry linking the dorsolateral portion of the PFC and the PMC and in turn influencing the mirror system within the PMC. In recent years, a growing number of studies on monkeys have described two different populations of premotor neurons, the canonical and mirror neurons, both of them endowed with similar visuo-motor properties for the programming of goal-directed movements (Fogassi et al., 2001; Rizzolatti & Fadiga, 1998). However, differently from canonical neurons, mirror neurons are activated not only during the execution of actual movements but also when the monkey observes another individual executing an action in front of it (Gallese et al., 1996). It has been proposed that mirror neurons generate the internal representation of the observed action used in movement recognition and imitation processes (Fadiga, Fogassi, Gallese, & Rizzolatti, 2000; Iacoboni et al., 1999; Kohler et al., 2002). TMS and ERP studies have confirmed that analogous properties can be found in humans (Fadiga, Craighero, Buccino, & Rizzolatti, 2002; Fadiga et al., 1995; Gangitano, Mottaghy, & Pascual-Leone, 2001; Hari et al., 1998; Nelissen, Luppino, Vanduffel, Rizzolatti, & Orban, 2005; Strafella & Paus, 2000). In general, a mirror neuron discharges at the observation of "biological" movements (e.g., the movement of an arm or of a hand executed by another animal or by a human being). It has been shown that human mirror system may be more capable than monkey mirror system of processing abstract visual representation of actions (Saygin, Wilson, Hagler, Bates, & Sereno, 2004) and that a mirror effect can also be evoked at the observation of static stimuli suggesting the idea of actions, like pictures of hands holding or manipulating objects (Gentilucci et al., 1998, 2000; Grafton et al., 1996) that is the same kind of stimuli that we used. In our study, it is possible that mirror activity was enhanced by the temporary failure of PFC. The mirror effect (i.e., difference between hand and background condition) was evident only when the activation within the PMC was maximal, that is when it was recruited for the preparation of a motor act (the go response). This explanation can take into account both the overall increase in excitability of the primary motor cortex and the selective modulation in the condition in which the colored hand was analyzed for the go response.

However, we have to consider that mirror recruitment was revealed only by the MEPs modulation in the red-hand condition. Moreover, neither a significant change in the RTs nor in the number of errors was found throughout all experiments. In Experiment 3, the increase in RTs can be explained considering a compromising of motor function induced by an inhibitory frequency of stimulation delivered directly on the primary motor cortex (Pascual-Leone et al., 1994). Consequently, it is possible that the observed effect was caused by the modulation of PFC on the primary motor cortex without the involvement of the PMC mirror system.

PFC plays a key role in the guidance of complex behaviors such as working memory (Elliott et al., 2000; Fuster, 1989; Miller, 2000; Petrides & Pandya, 1999) or decision-making tasks (Frith, 1991; Hyder et al., 1997; Jahanshahi & Frith, 1998). PFC is recruited either when different alternative responses have to be chosen or when an action has to be selected and performed (Miller, 2000). In both cases, signal elaboration within PFC seems to proceed according a common schema. When a non-motor act is required, PFC elaborates and filters information stored elsewhere (Grafman, 1995) making possible the choice between "more than one equally appropriate responses" (Frith, 1991; Jahanshahi et al., 1998; Jahanshahi & Rothwell, 2000). During the execution of motor tasks, PFC helps the analysis, the selection and the focusing of sensorial inputs relevant to the aim of the impending action whether voluntary or automatic

(Norman & Shallice, 2000; Seitz, Stephan, & Binkofski, 2000). Left dorsolateral PFC is engaged in elaborating signals from sensory processing areas during perceptual decision making (Heekeren, Marrett, Ruff, Bandettini, & Ungerleider, 2006; Rorie & Newsome, 2006). Information related to object properties are integrated along pathways linking the parietal the PFC and the PMC (Boussaoud, 2001; Rao et al., 1997). Particularly, the posterior and the dorsal portions of the lateral PFC are involved in the visuospatial and motor processing, whereas the ventral PFC regions seem to be particularly interested in information about visual form and stimulus identity (Pandya & Yeterian, 1998). On the other hand, recent evidence from studies of both humans and monkeys may indicate that the dorsal PMC, besides its traditional function in movement planning and execution plays a role also in attention and working-memory functions. Furthermore, PMC seems to be endowed with pure perceptual functions such as speech perception (Wilson, Saygin, Sereno, & Iacoboni, 2004) or sensory-attentional processes for motor programming such as recognition and prediction of sequential motor patterns (Schubotz & von Cramon, 2002). Attention-related properties seem to be relatively segregated to the more rostral portion of lateral PMC whereas the more caudal portion is endowed with intention-related or motor properties (Boussaoud, 2001; Schubotz & von Cramon, 2003; Simon et al., 2002). The specialization of the rostral PMC subregion derives also from the pattern of connections feeding it, receiving projections from both dorsolateral PFC and the parietal cortex. Differently from the caudal subregion, the rostral PMC does not send noticeable projections to either motor cortex or spinal cord (Boussaoud, 2001; Schubotz & von Cramon, 2003; Simon et al., 2002). For these reasons rostral PMC may be conceived as functionally belonging to the PFC cortex whereas caudal PMC could be seen as a true motor area (Schubotz & von Cramon, 2003).

Moving from these considerations, it is possible to offer an alternative explanation for our results. In our task, subjects had to decide what action (pressing the space bar or keeping the resting position) they had to perform on the basis of the visual analysis of a stimulus. rTMS over the PFC could have interfered with the prefrontal-premotor "attentional switch" for sensory elaboration. It is possible that the perceptual analysis of stimuli was less efficient due to the lack of the PFC sensorial filter, making necessary an over-commitment of the PMC-motor efferent pathway indexed by the increase of MEPs. Hypothetically, the activation in the red-hand condition was more pronounced both because a movement had to be prepared and because hands were more difficult to elaborate. However, this explanation does not take into account the different MEPs modulation in the go condition in Experiment 2 described above. Furthermore, a significant increase in the errors rate after rTMS should be expected and this was not the case.

Lesions of PMC are followed by either deficits in initiation of simple movements or automatic triggering of complex motor acts (Rizzolatti & Luppino, 2001). In the latter case it is possible to observe symptoms like forced grasping, alien-hand syndrome and utilization behavior. It has been proposed that all these neurological signs could be the consequence of a loss of inhibitory afferents to PMC from the PFC and the cingulate control (Rizzolatti & Luppino, 2001). On the other hand, lesions of the mesial cortical areas usually lead to the appearance of negative symptoms like motor inertia. Taken together our results could suggest that rTMS effects on PFC could have produced the release of its inhibitory influence on the premotor activity in turn increasing the excitability of the primary motor cortex. Such modulatory control could be reduced or be absent in patients with PFC lesions hence accounting for their compulsive imitation or utilization behavior. The remarkable behavior of the patients described by Lhermitte (Lhermitte, 1983, 1986; Lhermitte et al., 1986), who depicted their automatic compulsive tendency to imitate actions or execute movements as the direct consequence of an imbalance between parietal and frontal elaboration, could provide clinical support for this hypothesis.

In our study the lack of signs towards a "compulsive tendency to move" stronger than the increase of MEPs could be due to the relative sparing of circuits only partially affected by rTMS capable of "compensating" the transient deficit induced by rTMS on targeted areas. Generally, rTMS was not expected to suppress the function of the targeted brain region, but rather to modulate its activity to a certain degree, by approximately 15 or 20% if consistent with the findings of similar protocols on cortico-spinal excitability (Gangitano et al., 2002; Maeda, Keenan, Tormos, Topka, & Pascual-Leone, 2000a; Romero, Anschel, Sparing, Gangitano, &

Pascual-Leone, 2002). In this sense rTMS effects on PFC can be conceived as the result of the "dynamic" modulation of multiple afferences and efferences in a complex neuronal network (Mottaghy et al., 2000).

Manuscript received 26 March 2007
Manuscript accepted 31 May 2007
First published online 24 July 2007

REFERENCES

Alexander, G. E., DeLong, M. R., & Strick, P. L. (1986). Parallel organization of functionally segregated circuits linking basal ganglia and cortex [Review]. *Annual Review of Neuroscience*, *9*, 357–381.

Alexander, M., Cructher, M. D., & DeLong, M. R. (1990). Basal ganglia-thalamocortical circuits: Parallel substrates for motor, oculomotor, "prefrontal" and "limbic" functions [Review]. *Progress in Brain Research*, *85*, 119–146.

Bechara, A., Damasio, H., & Damasio, A. R. (2000). Emotion, decision making and the orbitofrontal cortex [Review]. *Cerebral Cortex*, *10*, 295–307.

Boussaoud, D. (2001). Attention versus intention in the primate premotor cortex. *NeuroImage*, *14*, S40–S45.

Brasil-Neto, J. P., McShane, L. M., Fuhr, P., Hallett, M., & Cohen, L. G. (1992). Topographic mapping of the human motor cortex with magnetic stimulation: Factors affecting accuracy and reproducibility. *Electroencephalography and Clinical Neurophysiology*, *85*, 9–16.

Buccino, G., Binkofski, F., Fink, G. R., Fadiga, L., Fogassi, L., Gallese, V., et al. (2001). Action observation activates premotor and parietal areas in a somatotopic manner: An fMRI study. *European Journal of Neuroscience*, *13*, 400–404.

Cambier, J. (1999). La perte de l'autonomie de l'homme: Comportament d'utilisation et d'imitation. *Revue Neurologique*, *155*, 879–883.

Chen, R., Classen, J., Gerloff, C., Celnik, P., Wassermann, E. M., Hallett, M., et al. (1997). Depression of motor cortex excitability by low-frequency transcranial magnetic stimulation. *Journal of Neurophysiology*, *80*, 2870–2881.

DiPellegrino, G., Fadiga, L., Fogassi, L., Gallese, V., & Rizzolatti, G. (1992). Understanding motor events: A neurophysiological study. *Experimental Brain Research*, *91*, 176–180.

Elliott, R., Dolan, R. J., & Frith, C. D. (2000). Dissociable functions in the medial and lateral orbitofrontal cortex: Evidence from human neuroimaging studies. *Cerebral Cortex*, *10*, 308–317.

Fadiga, L., Craighero, L., Buccino, G., & Rizzolatti, G. (2002). Speech listening specifically modulates the excitability of tongue muscles: A TMS study. *European Journal of Neuroscience*, *15*, 399–402.

Fadiga, L., Fogassi, L., Gallese, V., & Rizzolatti, G. (2000). Visuomotor neurons: Ambiguity of the discharge or "motor" perception? *International Journal of Psychophysiology*, *35*, 165–177.

Fadiga, L., Fogassi, L., Pavesi, G., & Rizzolatti, G. (1995). Motor facilitation during action observation: A magnetic stimulation study. *Journal of Neurophysiology*, *73*(6), 2608–2611.

Fogassi, L., Gallese, V., Buccino, G., Craighero, L., Fadiga, L., & Rizzolatti, G. (2001). Cortical mechanism for visual guidance of hand grasping movements in the monkey: A reversible inactivation study. *Brain*, *124*, 571–586.

Frith, C. (1991). Willed action and the prefrontal cortex in man: A study with PET. *Proceedings of the Royal Society London*, *244*, 241–246.

Fuster, J. M. (1989). *The prefrontal cortex* (2nd ed.). New York: Raven Press.

Gallese, V., Fadiga, L., Fogassi, L., & Rizzolatti, G. (1996). Action recognition in the premotor cortex. *Brain*, *119*, 593–609.

Gangitano, M., Mottaghy, F. M., & Pascual-Leone, A. (2001). Phase-specific modulation of cortical motor output during movement observation. *Neuroreport*, *12*, 1489–1492.

Gangitano, M., Valero-Cabre', A., Tormos, J. M., Mottaghy, F. M., Romero, J., & Pascual-Leone, A. (2002). Modulation of input–output curves by low and high frequency transcranial magnetic stimulation of the motor cortex. *Clinical Neurophysiology*, *113*, 1249–1257.

Gentilucci, M., Benuzzi, F., Bertolani, L., Daprati, E., & Gangitano, M. (2000). Recognising a hand by grasp. *Cognitive Brain Research*, *9*, 125–135.

Gentilucci, M., Daprati, E., & Gangitano, M. (1998). Implicit visual analysis in handedness recognition. *Consciousness and Cognition*, *7*, 478–493.

Gerschlager, W., Siebner, H. R., & Rothwell, J. C. (2001). Decreased corticospinal excitability after subthreshold 1 Hz rTMS over lateral premotor cortex. *Neurology*, *57*, 449–455.

Goldman-Rakic, P. S. (1987). Circuitry of primate prefrontal cortex and regulation of behavior by representational memory. In F. Plum (Ed.), *Handbook of physiology: The nervous system, higher functions of the brain* (pp. 374–417). Bethesda, MD: American Physiological Society.

Grafman, J. (1995). Similarities and distinctions among current models of prefrontal cortical functions. In J. Grafman, K. J. Holyoak, & F. Boller (Eds.), *Structure and functions of the human prefrontal cortex* (Annals of the New York Academy of Science, Vol. 769, pp. 337–368). New York: Academy of Science.

Grafton, S. T., Arbib, M. A., Fadiga, L., & Rizzolatti, G. (1996). Localization of grasp representations in humans by positron emission tomography: 2. Observation compared with imagination. *Experimental Brain Research*, *112*(1), 103–111.

Grèzes, J., Armony, J. L., Rowe, J., & Passingham, R. E. (2003). Activations related to "mirror" and "canonical" neurones in the human brain: An fMRI study. *NeuroImage*, *18*, 928–937.

Grèzes, J., Costes, N., & Decety, J. (1999). The effects of learning and intention on the neural network involved in the perception of meaningless action. *Brain*, *122*, 1875–1887.

Hallett, M. (2000). Transcranial magnetic stimulation and the human brain [Review]. *Nature*, *406*, 147–150.

Hari, R., Forss, N., Avikainen, S., Kirveskari, E., Salenius, S., & Rizzolatti, G. (1998). Activation of human primary motor cortex during action observation: A neuromagnetic study. *Proceedings of the National Academy of Science USA*, *95*(25), 15061–15065.

Heekeren, H. R., Marrett, S., Ruff, D. A., Bandettini, P. A., & Ungerleider, L. G. (2006). Involvement of human left dorsolateral prefrontal cortex in perceptual decision making is independent of response modality. *Science*, *103*(26), 10023–10028.

Hoshiyama, M., Kakigi, S., Koyama, S., Takeshima, Y., Watanabe, S., & Shimojo, M. (1997). Temporal changes of pyramidal tract activities after decision of movement: A study using transcranial magnetic stimulation of the motor cortex in humans. *Electroencephalography and Clinical Neurophysiology*, *105*, 255–261.

Hyder, F., Phelps, E. A., Wiggins, C. J., Labar, K. S., Blamire, A. M., & Schulman, R. G. (1997). Willed action: A functional MRI study of the human prefrontal cortex during a sensorimotor task. *Proceedings of the National Academy of Science USA*, *94*, 6989–6994.

Iacoboni, M., Woods, R. G., Brass, M., Bekkering, H., Mazziotta, J. C., & Rizzolatti, G. (1999). Cortical mechanism of human imitation. *Science*, *286*, 2526–2528.

Jahanshahi, M., & Frith, C. D. (1998). Willed action and its impairments. *Cognitive Neuropsychology*, *15*, 483–533.

Jahanshahi, M., Profice, P., Bown, R. G., Ridding, M. C., Dirnberger, G., & Rothwell, J. C. (1998). The effects of transcranial magnetic stimulation over the dorsolateral prefrontal cortex on suppression of habitual counting during random number generation. *Brain*, *121*, 1533–1544.

Jahanshahi, M., & Rothwell, J. (2000). Transcranial magnetic stimulation studies in cognition: An emerging field [Review]. *Experimental Brain Research*, *131*, 1–9.

Kiefer, M., Marzinzik, F., Weisbrod, M., Scherg, M., & Spietzer, M. (1998). The time course of brain activations during response inhibition: Evidence from event-related potentials in a go/no go task. *Neuroreport*, *9*, 765–770.

Kohler, E., Keysers, C., Umiltà, M. A., Fogassi, L., Fadiga, L., Gallese, V., et al. (2002). Hearing sounds, understanding actions: Action representation in mirror neurons. *Science*, *297*, 846–848.

Konishi, S., Nakajima, K., Uchida, I., Kikyo, H., Kameyama, M., & Miyashita, Y. (1999). Common inhibitory mechanism in human inferior prefrontal cortex revealed by event-related functional MRI. *Brain*, *122*, 198–991.

Leocani, L., Cohen, L. G., Wassermann, E. M., Ikoma, K., & Hallett, M. (2000). Human corticospinal excitability evaluated with transcranial magnetic stimulation during different reaction times paradigms. *Brain*, *123*, 1161–1173.

Lhermitte, F. (1983). Utilization behaviour and its relation to lesions of the frontal lobes. *Brain*, *106*, 237–255.

Lhermitte, F. (1986). Human autonomy and the frontal lobes: Part II. Patient behavior in complex and social situations: The "environmental dependency syndrome". *Annals of Neurology*, *19*, 335–343.

Lhermitte, F., Pillon, B., & Serdaru, M. (1986). Human autonomy and the frontal lobes: Part I. Imitation and utilization behavior: A neuropsychological study of 75 patients. *Annals of Neurology*, *19*, 326–334.

Liddle, P. F., Kiehl, K. A., & Smith, A. M. (2001). Event-related fMRI study of response inhibition. *Human Brain Mapping*, *12*, 100–109.

Luria, A. R. (1966). *Higher cortical functions in man*. New York: Basic Books.

Maeda, F., Keenan, J. P., Tormos, J. M., Topka, H., & Pascual-Leone, A. (2000a). Interindividual variability of the modulatory effects of repetitive transcranial magnetic stimulation on cortical excitability. *Experimental Brain Research*, *133*, 425–430.

Maeda, F., Keenan, J. P., Tormos, J. M., Topka, H., & Pascual-Leone, A. (2000b). Modulation of corticospinal excitability by repetitive transcranial magnetic stimulation. *Clinical Neurophysiology*, *111*, 800–805.

Maeda, F., Kleiner-Fisman, G., & Pascual-Leone, A. (2002). Motor facilitation while observing hand actions: Specificity of the effect and role of observer's orientation. *Journal of Neurophysiology*, *87*, 1329–1335.

Miller, E. K. (2000). The prefrontal cortex and cognitive control [Review]. *Nature Reviews*, *1*, 59–65.

Mills, K. R., Boniface, S. J., & Schubert, M. (1992). Magnetic brain stimulation with a double coil: The importance of coil orientation. *Electroencephalography Clinical Neurophysiology*, *85*, 17–21.

Mottaghy, F. M., Krause, B., Kemna, L. J., Topper, R., Tellmann, L., Beu, M., et al. (2000). Modulation of the neuronal circuitry subserving working memory in healthy human subjects by repetitive transcranial magnetic stimulation. *Neuroscience Letters*, *280*(3), 167–170.

Münchau, A., Bloem, B. R., Trimble, M. R., & Rothwell, J. C. (2002). Functional connectivity of human premotor and motor cortex explored with repetitive transcranial magnetic stimulation. *Journal of Neuroscience*, *22*, 554–561.

Nelissen, K., Luppino, G., Vanduffel, W., Rizzolatti, G., & Orban, G. A. (2005). Observing others: Multiple action representation in the frontal lobe. *Science*, *310*, 332–336.

Norman, D. A., & Shallice, T. (2000). Attention to action: Willed and automatic control of behavior. In M. S. Gazzaniga (Ed.), *Cognitive neuroscience. A reader* (pp. 376–390). Malden, MA: Blackwell.

Oldfield, R. C. (1971). The assessment and analysis of handedness: The Edinburgh inventory. *Neuropsychologia*, *9*, 97–113.

Pandya, D. N., & Yeterian, E. H. (1998). Comparison of prefrontal architecture and connections. In A. Roberts, T. Robbins, & L. Weiskrantz (Eds.), *The prefrontal cortex. Executive and cognitive functions* (pp. 51–66). Oxford, UK: Oxford University Press.

Pascual-Leone, A., Batres-Faz, D., & Keenan, J. P. (1999). Transcranial magnetic stimulation: Studying the brain–behaviour relationship by induction of "virtual lesions" [Review]. *Philosophical Transactions of the Royal Society of London, Series B: Biological Sciences, 29*(354), 1229–1238.

Pascual-Leone, A., Valls-Sole, J., Wassermann, E. M., & Hallett, M. (1994). Responses to rapid-rate transcranial magnetic stimulation of the human motor cortex. *Brain, 117*, 847–858.

Pascual-Leone, A., Walsh, V., & Rothwell, J. (2000). Transcranial magnetic stimulation in cognitive neuroscience—virtual lesion, chronometry, and functional connectivity [Review]. *Current Opinion in Neurobiology, 10*, 232–237.

Petrides, M., & Pandya, D. N. (1999). Dorsolateral prefrontal cortex: Comparative cytoarchitectonic analysis in the human and macaque brain and cortico-cortical connection patterns. *European Journal of Neuroscience, 11*, 1011–1036.

Rao, S. R., Rainer, G., & Miller, E. K. (1997). Integration of what and where in the primate prefrontal cortex. *Science, 276*, 821–824.

Rizzo, V., Siebner, H. R., Modugno, M., Pesenti, A., Munchau, A., Gerschlager, W., et al. (2003). Shaping the excitability of human motor cortex with premotor rTMS. *Journal of Physiology, 554*, 483–495.

Rizzolatti, G., & Fadiga, L. (1998). Grasping objects and grasping action meanings: The dual role of monkey rostrolateral premotor cortex (area F5). In G. Bock & J. Good (Eds.), *Sensory guidance of movement* (Novartis Foundation Symposium 218, pp. 81–103). Chichester, UK: Wiley.

Rizzolatti, G., & Luppino, G. (2001). The cortical motor system [Review]. *Neuron, 31*, 889–901.

Romero, R., Anschel, D., Sparing, R., Gangitano, M., & Pascual-Leone, A. (2002). Subthreshold low frequency transcranial magnetic stimulation selectively decreases facilitation in the motor cortex. *Clinical Neurophysiology, 113*, 102–107.

Rorie, A. E., & Newsome, W. T. (2006). A general mechanism for decision-making in the human brain? *Trends in Cognitive Science, 9*(2), 41–43.

Rossini, P. M. (1994). Non-invasive electrical and magnetic stimulation of the brain, spinal cord and roots: Basic principles and procedures for routine clinical application. Report of IFCN committee. *Electroencephalography and Clinical Neurophysiology, 91*, 79–92.

Rothwell, J. C. (1991). Stimulation of the human motor cortex through the scalp. *Experimental Physiology, 76*, 159–200.

Saygin, A. P., Wilson, S. M., Hagler, D. J., Bates, E., & Sereno, M. I. (2004). Point-light biological motion perception activates human premotor cortex. *Journal of Neuroscience, 24*, 6181–6188.

Schubotz, R. I., & von Cramon, D. Y. (2002). Predicting perceptual events activates corresponding motor schemes in lateral premotor cortex: An fMRI study. *NeuroImage, 15*, 787–796.

Schubotz, R. I., & von Cramon, D. Y. (2003). Functional-anatomical concepts of human premotor cortex: Evidence from fMRI and PET studies. *NeuroImage, 20*, S120–S131.

Seitz, R. J., Stephan, K. M., & Binkofski, F. (2000). Control of action as mediated by human frontal lobe. *Experimental Brain Research, 133*, 71–80.

Shallice, T., Burgess, P. W., Schon, F., & Baxter, D. M. (1989). The origins of utilization behaviour. *Brain, 112*, 1587–1589.

Simon, S. R., Meunier, M., Piettre, L., Berardi, A. M., Segeberth, C. M., & Boussaoud, D. (2002). Spatial attention and memory versus motor preparation: Premotor cortex involvement as revealed by fMRI. *Journal of Neurophysiology, 88*, 2047–2057.

Strafella, A. P., & Paus, T. (2000). Modulation of cortical excitability during action observation: A transcranial magnetic stimulation study. *Neuroreport, 14*(10), 2289–2292.

Thut, G., Hauert, C. A., Blanke, O., Morand, S., Seeck, M., Gonzalez, S. L., et al. (2000). Visually induced activity in human frontal motor areas during simple visuomotor performance. *Neuroreport, 11*, 2843–2848.

Walsh, V., & Cowey, A. (2000). Transcranial magnetic stimulation and neuroscience [Review]. *Nature Reviews Neuroscience, 1*, 73–79.

Walsh, V., & Rushworth, M. (1999). A primer magnetic stimulation as a tool for neuropsychology [Review]. *Neuropsychologia, 37*, 125–135.

Wassermann, E. M. (1998). Risk and safety of repetitive transcranial magnetic stimulation: Report and suggested guidelines from the International Workshop on the Safety of Repetitive Transcranial Magnetic Stimulation, June 5–7, 1996. *Electroencephalography and Clinical Neurophysiology, 108*, 1–16.

Wilson, S. M., Saygin, A. P., Sereno, M. I., & Iacoboni, M. (2004). Listening to speech activates motor areas involved in speech production. *Nature Neuroscience, 7*(7), 701–702.

Yamanaka, K., Kimura, T., Miyazaki, M., Kawashima, N., Nozaki, D., Nakazawa, K., et al. (2002). Human cortical activities during go/no go tasks with opposite motor control paradigms. *Experimental Brain Research, 142*, 301–307.

SOCIAL NEUROSCIENCE, 2008, 3 (3–4), 303–316

Psychology Press
Taylor & Francis Group

Morphological properties of the action-observation cortical network in adolescents with low and high resistance to peer influence

Tomáš Paus

University of Nottingham, Nottingham, UK, and McGill University, Montreal, Quebec, Canada

Roberto Toro

University of Nottingham, Nottingham, UK

Gabriel Leonard

McGill University, Montreal, Quebec, Canada

Jacqueline V. Lerner

Boston College, Boston, Massachusetts, USA

Richard M. Lerner

Tufts University, Medford, Massachusetts, USA

Michel Perron

CEJEP Jonquiere, Jonquiere, Quebec, Canada

G. Bruce Pike

McGill University, Montreal, Quebec, Canada

Louis Richer

University of Quebec in Chicoutimi, Chicoutimi, Quebec, Canada

Laurence Steinberg

Temple University, Philadelphia, Pennsylvania, USA

(List of authors continued overleaf)

Correspondence should be addressed to: Tomáš Paus, Brain & Body Centre, University of Nottingham, University Park, Nottingham, NG7 2RD, UK. E-mail: tomas.paus@nottingham.ac.uk

The Saguenay Youth Study project is funded by the Canadian Institutes of Health Research (TP, ZP), Heart and Stroke Foundation of Quebec (ZP), and the Canadian Foundation for Innovation (ZP).

We thank the following individuals for their contributions in designing the protocol, acquiring and analyzing the data: MR team (Dr Michel Bérubé, Sylvie Masson, Suzanne Castonguay, Julien Grandisson, Marie-Josée Morin), cardio nurses (Jessica Blackburn, Mélanie Gagné, Jeannine Landry, Catherine Lavoie, Lisa Pageau, Réjean Savard, France Tremblay, Jacynthe Tremblay), psychometricians (Chantale Belleau, Mélanie Drolet, Catherine Harvey, Stéphane Jean, Hélène Simard, Mélanie Tremblay), ÉCOBES team (Nadine Arbour, Julie Auclair, Marie-Ève Blackburn, Marie-Ève Bouchard, Annie Houde, Catherine Lavoie, Dr Luc Laberge), nutritionists (Caroline Benoit and Henriette Langlais), laboratory technicians (Denise Morin and Nadia Mior), Julie Bérubé, Celine Bourdon, Rosanne Aleong, Dr Jennifer Barrett, Candice Cartier, Dale Einarson, Helena Jelicic, Valerie Legge, and Dr Jean Mathieu.

www.psypress.com/socialneuroscience DOI:10.1080/17470910701563558

Suzanne Veillette
CEJEP Jonquiere, Jonquiere, Quebec, Canada

Zdenka Pausova
University of Nottingham, Nottingham, UK, and University of Montreal, Montreal Quebec, Canada

Children with high resistance to peer influences differ from their low-resistance counterparts in the degree of functional connectivity in fronto-parietal and prefrontal cortical networks. Here we explored the possibility that the degree of morphological similarities across the same cortical regions also varies as a function of this behavioral trait. Using structural magnetic-resonance (MR) images, we measured cortical thickness in a total of 295 adolescents (12 to 18 years of age). We found that inter-regional correlations in cortical thickness increased with the resistance to peer influence (RPI); this was especially the case, in female adolescents, in the premotor and prefrontal networks. We also observed significant differences between the adolescents with high and low RPI scores in their general intelligence and the scores of positive youth development. We suggest that these morphological findings might reflect differences, between adolescents with high vs. low resistance to peer influences, in a repeated and concurrent engagement of these networks in social context.

INTRODUCTION

Adolescence represents a major transition taking place over most of the second decade of human life: choice of friends and first sexual partners, vocations and past-time life habits, and the struggle for identity are but a few examples of complex behaviors that the brain must implement at the brink of adulthood. Such choices are often made in a social context dominated by peers (Brown, 2004; Steinberg & Silverberg, 1986). On one hand, peers provide role models that are necessary for the establishment of new social representations during a shift from a caregiver-dependent child to a fully autonomous adult. At the same time, however, the adolescent often strives to distinguish herself/himself from the others in order to establish an individual identity. In a complex social environment, the right balance must be struck between the peer-based influences and the individual's ambitions.

Adolescents differ in their sensitivity to peer pressure, and their ability to resist peer influences; we assess the latter trait with a self-report questionnaire designed to minimize socially desirable responding (Steinberg & Monahan, in press). Scores on the Resistance-to-Peer-Influence (RPI) scale stay low during early adolescence and increase linearly from 14 years of age to reach adult levels at 18 years (Steinberg & Monahan, in press). In a population of serious juvenile offenders, Monahan, Steinberg, and Cauffman (2007) found that the presence of antisocial peers predicts one's own criminal behavior to a greater extent in individuals with low, as compared with high, RPI scores. This observation supports the validity of the RPI scale and highlights the importance of the adolescent's ability to resist peer influences in certain environments.

What are the neural mechanisms underlying resistance to peer influence during adolescence? The following three neural systems may be considered in this context. First, the action-observation (or "bottom-up") network is considered by many to represent the neural substrate of imitation (Brass & Heyes, 2005; Iacoboni, 2005; Rizzolatti & Craighero, 2004); it consists of frontal and parietal regions involved in the preparation and execution of actions. So called "mirror neurons" found within the inferior premotor cortex and/or inferior frontal gyrus, as well as in the anterior inferior parietal lobe, are active both when the subject performs a specific action himself and when he observes another individual performing the same action (Rizzolatti & Craighero, 2004). Second, the biological-motion processing network plays an important role in extracting socially relevant cues, such as those imparted by the movements of eyes or hands; neurons within the superior temporal sulcus (STS) respond selectively to the presentation of dynamic bodies, body parts or faces (Allison, Puce, & McCarthy, 2000; Perrett et al., 1982; Perrett et al., 1985). Third, the executive (or "top-down") network supports a number of cognitive processes underlying decision making, working memory and the suppression of alternative programs interfering with planned actions (Duncan & Owen, 2000; Miller & Cohen, 2001; Paus, 2001; Petrides, 2005); it consists of a set of regions in the lateral and medial prefrontal cortex (PFC). Whether or not an adolescent follows the goals set by peers or those set by himself/herself might depend on the interplay between the above three neural systems, namely the fronto-parietal network (bottom-up imitation of actions), the STS network (social cues) and the PFC network (top-down regulation of actions).

Here we explore the possibility that inter-individual differences in the resistance to peer influences are reflected in the variations of brain morphology in the cortical regions constituting the above three networks. In a previous study, we found that 10-year-old children with high vs. low RPI scores differed in the degree of inter-regional correlations in brain activity, measured with functional magnetic-resonance imaging (fMRI), across the three networks while watching angry hand actions (Grosbras et al., 2007). Based on these results, we have suggested: "that the probability of resisting peer influence depends on neural interactions during observation of emotion-laden actions". If we were to generalize this finding to everyday life, individuals with high RPI scores would be more likely to engage these networks in a coordinated fashion whenever challenged with relatively complex and socially relevant stimuli. We speculate that a repeated and concurrent engagement of the same cortical regions, namely their strong functional connectivity, would induce a strong similarity in their morphological characteristics, such as cortical thickness. Given the observed differences between the children with high and low RPI scores in functional connectivity during action observation, we predict the presence of similar group differences in the degree of morphological similarities across the above three networks.

METHODS

Subjects

All participants were recruited from a geographically isolated population of French Canadian origin living in the Saguenay Lac Saint-Jean (SLSJ) region of Quebec, Canada. At the time of analysis, 408 adolescents (12 to 18 years of age) completed the study protocol. Details of the recruitment and testing procedures are provided in Pausova et al. (2007). Briefly, the subjects were recruited in public schools in the SLSJ region. The recruitment began with the team visiting all classrooms in a given school and presenting the study to the students. At the same time, letters containing an information brochure, a letter from the principal, and a consent form for a telephone interview were sent to the parents. Subsequently, a research nurse conducted a structured telephone interview with interested families (most commonly with the child's mother) to verify their eligibility. Additional information was acquired using a medical questionnaire filled out by the child's biological parent. The main exclusion criteria were: (1) Positive history of alcohol abuse during pregnancy; (2) Positive medical history for meningitis, malignancy and heart disease requiring heart surgery; (3) Severe mental illness (e.g., autism, schizophrenia) or mental retardation (IQ < 70); and (4) MRI contraindications.

Resistance to peer influence

The Resistance to Peer Influence (RPI) questionnaire used in this study has been designed for adolescents and consists of 10 pairs of opposite statements about inter-individual interactions (Steinberg & Monahan, in press). The participant has to indicate which statement is more like her or him and to what degree ("*sort of true of me*" or "*really true of me*") he/she identifies with the statement. The scoring is such that a high score on a 1–4 scale indicates a high resistance to peer influence, whereas a low score indicates a great susceptibility to peer influence.

Positive youth development

In addition to RPI, we assessed a number of external (family, peers) and individual (life habits, personality) determinants of positive youth development using the "5 Cs" model: Competence, Confidence, Character, social Connection, and Caring or compassion (Lerner, Lerner, Almerigi, Theokas, Phelps, et al., 2005). To calculate the score for each of the five scales (i.e., five Cs), all individual items were first rescaled on a 0- to 12-point scale. Overall, the scoring is such that a high score indicates more positive behavior on each of the "5 C" scales. The average of the five scales represents the positive youth development (PYD) score.

Assessment of cognitive abilities

We used the Wechsler Intelligence Scale for Children (WISC-III) to assess general intelligence. This assessment was carried out at the beginning of a six-hour neuropsychological battery. In this report, we also consider three tests of "executive" functions, namely the Stroop test (Stroop, 1935) of color-word interference, the Self-ordered Pointing (Petrides & Milner, 1982) test of the individual's capacity to "work with memory", and the test of word fluency (semantic and phonemic).

Assessment of cortical thickness

Structural MRI data were collected on a Phillips 1.0-T superconducting magnet. High-resolution T1-weighted (T1W) images were acquired using the following parameters: 3D RF-spoiled gradient echo scan with 140–160 sagittal slices, 1 mm isotropic resolution, TR = 25 ms, TE = 5 ms, flip angle = 30°.

We measured cortical thickness using FreeSurfer, a set of automated tools for reconstruction of the brain cortical surface (Fischl & Dale, 2000). For every subject, FreeSurfer segments the cerebral cortex, the white matter and other subcortical structures, and then computes triangular meshes that recover the geometry and the topology of the pial surface and the grey/white interface of the left and right hemispheres. The local cortical thickness is measured based on the difference between the position of equivalent vertices in the pial and grey/white surfaces. A correspondence between the cortical surfaces across the subjects is established using a nonlinear alignment of the principal sulci in each subject's brain with an average brain (Fischl, Sereno, Tootell, & Dale, 1999). Thickness values were determined at each of 163,842 vertices representing the subject's cortical surface. The thickness values were smoothed over the cortical surface with a 30 mm (full width at half maximum) Gaussian kernel.

Inter-regional similarity in cortical thickness

We calculated pair-wise correlations between a set of 22 regions (Table 1) identified in our previous fMRI study, which was carried out on a different set of subjects (Grosbras et al., 2007). This is the set of cortical regions in which children with high RPI scores, as compared with those having low RPI scores, showed a higher degree of inter-regional correlations in brain activity, i.e., stronger functional connectivity, while watching angry hand actions. The details of the fMRI protocol have been described elsewhere (Grosbras & Paus, 2006; Grosbras et al., 2007). Briefly, the stimuli consisted of short (2–5 seconds) black-and-white video clips depicting a hand action. The actions were performed with the right or left hand and involved reaching, grasping and manipulating eight different objects (phone, pencil, spoon, computer mouse, glass, hammer, screwdriver, and cup) in a neutral or angry way. The selected video clips were arranged into 18-second blocks. Each block included 4 to 7 video clips. In each block, 20% and 80% of the total video-clip time contained, respectively, the arm movement alone and the movements involving the interaction between the hand and the object.

For each cortical region identified in the fMRI study (Grosbras et al., 2007), we extracted the value of cortical thickness at the nearest vertex. This was repeated for each subject by matching X, Y and Z coordinates of a given region (as listed in Table 1) with a corresponding vertex on a given subject's cortical surface; the match was based on the sulcus-based registration of the subject's MR image (using FreeSurfer) with the MNI305 stereotaxic space (in which the X, Y, and Z coordinates of each region were reported).

To evaluate the overall strength of inter-regional correlations, we calculated the mean correlation coefficient across all 22 regions (231 pair-wise correlations), as well as within the following three "networks": (1) *Premotor network*, consisting of the dorsal and ventral premotor cortices in both hemispheres (F01 through F04; 6 pair-wise correlations); (2) *Prefrontal network*, consisting of the dorso-lateral and ventro-lateral PFC in both hemispheres (F08 through F11; 6 pair-wise correlations); and (3) *Premotor–prefrontal network*, consisting of the intersection

TABLE 1
Cortical regions identified in the previous functional neuroimaging study of action observation (Grosbras et al., 2007)

Lobe/structure	*Region*	*Label*	*X (mm)*[1]	*Y (mm)*[1]	*Z (mm)*[1]	*Vertex*[2]
Frontal	Premotor dorsal	F01	−32	−12	60	102420
Frontal	Premotor dorsal	F02	36	−4	56	116187
Frontal	Premotor ventral	F03	−54	4	32	47018
Frontal	Premotor ventral	F04	60	10	26	152814
Frontal	Operculum	F05	46	12	0	153299
Frontal	Cingulate motor area (rostral)	F06	−14	12	36	83560
Frontal	Insula (anterior)	F07	−34	14	−4	98147
Frontal	Ventro-lateral prefrontal (posterior)	F08	44	26	10	42476
Frontal	Dorso-lateral prefrontal (mid)	F09	−38	28	20	134530
Frontal	Dorso-lateral prefrontal (mid)	F10	28	34	40	72108
Frontal	Ventro-lateral prefrontal (anterior)	F11	−42	40	6	94169
Frontal	Cingulate anterior	F12	8	40	12	84406
Frontal	Orbitofrontal lateral	F13	−42	46	−10	129739
Frontal	Prefrontal medial	F14	0	52	18	57097
Parietal	Cingulate posterior	P01	0	−28	38	85736
Parietal	Precuneus	P02	−12	−78	50	147388
Parietal	Dorso-lateral	P03	38	−64	44	107018
Parietal	Dorso-medial	P04	2	−50	66	19561
Temporal	STS middle	T01	54	−18	0	107799
Temporal	STS posterior	T02	58	−52	20	158081
Temporal	Hippocampus	T03	30	−34	−10	161424
Occipital	Fusiform	O01	−38	−48	−26	90807

Notes: [1]Coordinates in the MNI305 stereotaxic space (see Grosbras et al., 2007, for details). [2]Vertex on the cortical surface generated by FreeSurfer

of the above two networks (F01 through F04 vs. F08 through F11, 16 pair-wise correlations).

RESULTS

The final sample consisted of 295 adolescents (160 females, 182 ± 23 months of age, range: 145 to 227 months; 135 males, 184 ± 23 months of age, range: 145 to 226 months). Out of the total of 408 subjects, we were able to compute cortical thickness reliably in 314 subjects; RPI scores were missing in 19 out of the 314 subjects. All analyses were carried out in the final sample of 295 subjects.

Resistance to peer influence: Effect of age and sex

The RPI scores increased as a function of age, $F(1, 294) = 11.2$, $p = .001$, and were higher in female vs. male adolescents, $F(1, 294) = 7.4$, $p = .007$; age by sex interaction was not significant, $F(2, 293) = 0.5$, $p = .48$. Given the sex differences in the RPI scores (and other variables), we decided to carry out all subsequent analyses separately in the female ($n = 160$) and male ($n = 135$) groups. In females, RPI scores increased with age significantly, $F(1, 159) = 10.3$, $p = .007$. In males, however, we did not find a significant relation between RPI scores and age, $F(1, 134) = 2.3$, $p = .1$.

Resistance to peer influence: Low, medium and high

In order to evaluate the relationship between resistance to peer influence and the number of dependent variables, we employed the following strategy. First, we adjusted the RPI scores for age using linear regression carried out separately in the female and male groups. Second, in each gender, we created three groups with low (bottom third of the group), medium (middle third) and high (top third) age-adjusted RPI scores (RPIaa), respectively. Table 2A provides the number of subjects in each group, together with the subjects' age and their RPIaa scores. Classifying the adolescents into the low, medium and high groups based on the *age-adjusted* RPI scores guarantees

TABLE 2

Cognitive abilities and score on Positive Youth Development scales in female and male adolescents with Low, Medium and High resistance to peer influence

	Females				*Males*			
	Low	*Medium*	*High*	*Significance (p)*	*Low*	*Medium*	*High*	*Significance (p)*
A								
n	53	53	54	N/A	45	45	45	N/A
RPIaa	2.72 ±0.32 (1.89–3.07)	3.2 ±0.07 (3.08–3.31)	3.5 ±0.16 (3.22–3.97)	N/A	2.5 ±0.3 (1.46–2.89)	3.1 ±0.1 (2.9–3.25)	3.45 ±0.1 (3.28–3.75)	N/A
Age (months)	183 ±25	183 ±25	180 ±22	.8	183 ±25	184 ±23	184 ±21	.95
B								
FIQ	99.6 ±13.8	106.2 ±10.5	108.0 ±9.6	.0005	102.3 ±13.6	106.6 ±12.9	107.1 ±12.2	.17
VIQ	98.1 ±13.6	104.2 ±11.2	105.4 ±10	.004	102 ±13.6	106.6 ±12.8	106.3 ±11.9	.18
PIQ	101.7 ±14.1	107.8 ±11.1	109.7 ±11.1	.003	102 ±13.6	105.9 ±14.97	107.2 ±13.7	.21
C								
Stroop (color words/colors named)	0.57 ±0.1	0.59 ±0.1	0.59 ±0.1	.7	0.59 ±0.1	0.6 ±0.1	0.6 ±0.08	.7
SOP (errors)	6.1 ±3.2	5.6 ±3.2	4.7 ±2.6	.08	6.3 ±3.6	6.6 ±3.9	5.8 ±2.9	.6
Word fluency (semantic)	37.7 ±9	42.2 ±9.8	42.8 ±8.5	.01	35.7 ±9.9	41.1 ±9.4	40.4 ±9.5	.02
Word fluency (phonemic)	23.9 ±9.4	26.1 ±7.8	26.9 ±7.9	.17	22.3 ±8.6	24.9 ±9.6	24.2 ±8.6	.4
D								
Confidence	7.6 ±2.2	8.3 ±2.1	8.7 ±1.9	.03	7.9 ±1.8	9.4 ±1.6	9.3 ±1.3	<.0001
Competence	7.9 ±1.5	8.7 ±1.3	9.3 ±1.1	<.0001	7.5 ±1.3	8.7 ±1.2	8.4 ±1.5	.0001
Character	8.1 ±1.6	8.9 ±1.5	8.9 ±1.5	.005	6.4 ±1.9	7.7 ±1.8	7.7 ±1.7	.001
Connection	8.0 ±1.5	8.4 ±1.1	8.4 ±1.5	.2	7 ±1.8	8 ±1.4	8.1 ±1.5	.003
Caring	9.1 ±2.6	9.5 ±2.2	9.9 ±2.0	.1	6.7 ±3.4	7.7 ±3.2	8.3 ±3.2	.07
Positive youth development	8.1 ±1.2	8.8 ±1.1	9 ±1.1	<.0001	7.1 ±1.6	8.3 ±1.3	8.3 ±1.4	<.0001

Notes: FIQ, Full-scale IQ; VIQ, Verbal IQ; PIQ, Performance IQ; SOP, Self-ordered pointing.

that the different groups do not differ in their age (the mean age being 15 years in all groups). Therefore, any differences in brain structure, cognitive abilities and behavior across the three RPI groups are independent of chronological age.

Low, medium and high RPI: Inter-regional similarity in cortical thickness

Figure 1 provides an overview of the degree of inter-regional similarities in cortical thickness across the 22 regions; in each of the six groups (2 genders × 3 RPI groups), a correlation matrix depicts the magnitude of the 231 pair-wise correlation coefficients. Overall, inter-regional correlation coefficients were high in the frontal cortex, especially across the premotor regions, in all six groups. In females (left panel), the magnitude of the pair-wise correlations appeared to increase linearly as a function of the RPI group. In males (right panel), the magnitude of the correlations increased from the low to medium RPI group but than decreased in the high RPI group.

In order to quantify the above qualitative impressions, we have evaluated the effect of RPI group on the mean pair-wise correlation coefficients using analysis of variance (ANOVA). In females, the mean correlation across all 22 cortical regions varied as a function of the RPI group, $F(2, 692) = 32.8$, $p < .0001$; the mean inter-regional correlation coefficient was the lowest in the low RPI group, intermediate in the medium RPI group and the highest in the high RPI group (Figure 2a). In males, the mean correlation also varied as a function of the RPI group, $F(2, 692) = 29.9$, $p < .0001$, but the highest mean correlation was found in the medium RPI group, with no difference between the low and high RPI groups (Figure 2b). We have confirmed the above statistical significance of the group differences in the magnitude of inter-regional correlations using the sign test, which does not require any assumptions to be met. In females, we can reject the null hypothesis of no difference between the low vs. medium RPI groups ($p = 1.1^{-11}$; medium > low) and between the medium and high RPI groups ($p = 1.7^{-6}$; high > medium). In males, the null hypothesis could be rejected for the difference between low and medium RPI groups ($p = 2.9^{-11}$; medium > low) and between the medium and high RPI groups ($p = 1.7^{-12}$; medium > high). In addition to the overall magnitude of pair-wise correlations in cortical thickness across all 22 regions, we evaluated the effect of the RPI group in three subsets of regions, namely in the premotor (PM) and prefrontal (PFC) networks and their intersection (see methods section). In females (Figure 2c), the effect of the RPI group was significant in the PFC network, $F(2, 17) = 3.96$, $p = .04$, and in the intersection of the PFC and PM networks, $F(2, 47) = 12.0$, $p < .0001$, but not in the PM network, $F(2, 17) = 2.4$, $p = .1$. The direction of these group differences was very similar to that found for the mean correlation across all 22 regions. In males (Figure 2d), the RPI groups did not differ in the magnitude of the correlations in any of the three networks.

Low, medium and high RPI: Cortical thickness

Although our predictions concerned inter-regional *similarity* in cortical thickness, we also evaluated possible group differences in the thickness of the different cortical regions constituting the fMRI-based "RPI" network. The effect of age was highly significant in all but a couple (F14, T02) of regions; as expected, cortical thickness decreased with age. The effect of sex was significant in several regions (F03, F05 through F07, F09, F10, P02, T01, T02, and O01); in all cases, cortex was thicker in the female as compared with male adolescents.

Finally, we evaluated the effect of the RPI group on cortical thickness in each gender. In females, cortical thickness varied as a function of the RPI group only in the right ventro-lateral PFC (F08), $F(2, 159) = 3.7$, $p = .03$, and the precuneus (P02), $F(2, 159) = 3.9$, $p = .02$; the thickness was lower in the medium RPI group as compared with both low and high RPI groups (F08), and lower in the medium RPI group as compared with the high RPI group (P02). In males, the differences in cortical thickness across the three RPI groups were more pronounced. Thus, cortical thickness differed across the three RPI groups in the right dorso-lateral (F10), $F(2, 134) = 3.3$, $p = .04$, and the left ventro-lateral (F11), $F(2, 134) = 4.2$, $p = .02$, PFC, the right anterior cingulate cortex (F12), $F(2, 134) = 4.6$, $p = .01$, the left lateral orbitofrontal cortex (F13), $F(2, 134) = 4.4$, $p = .01$, and in the right dorso-medial parietal cortex (P04), $F(2, 134) = 5.2$, $p = .007$. In most cases, cortical thickness was lower in the high RPI groups, as compared with the low

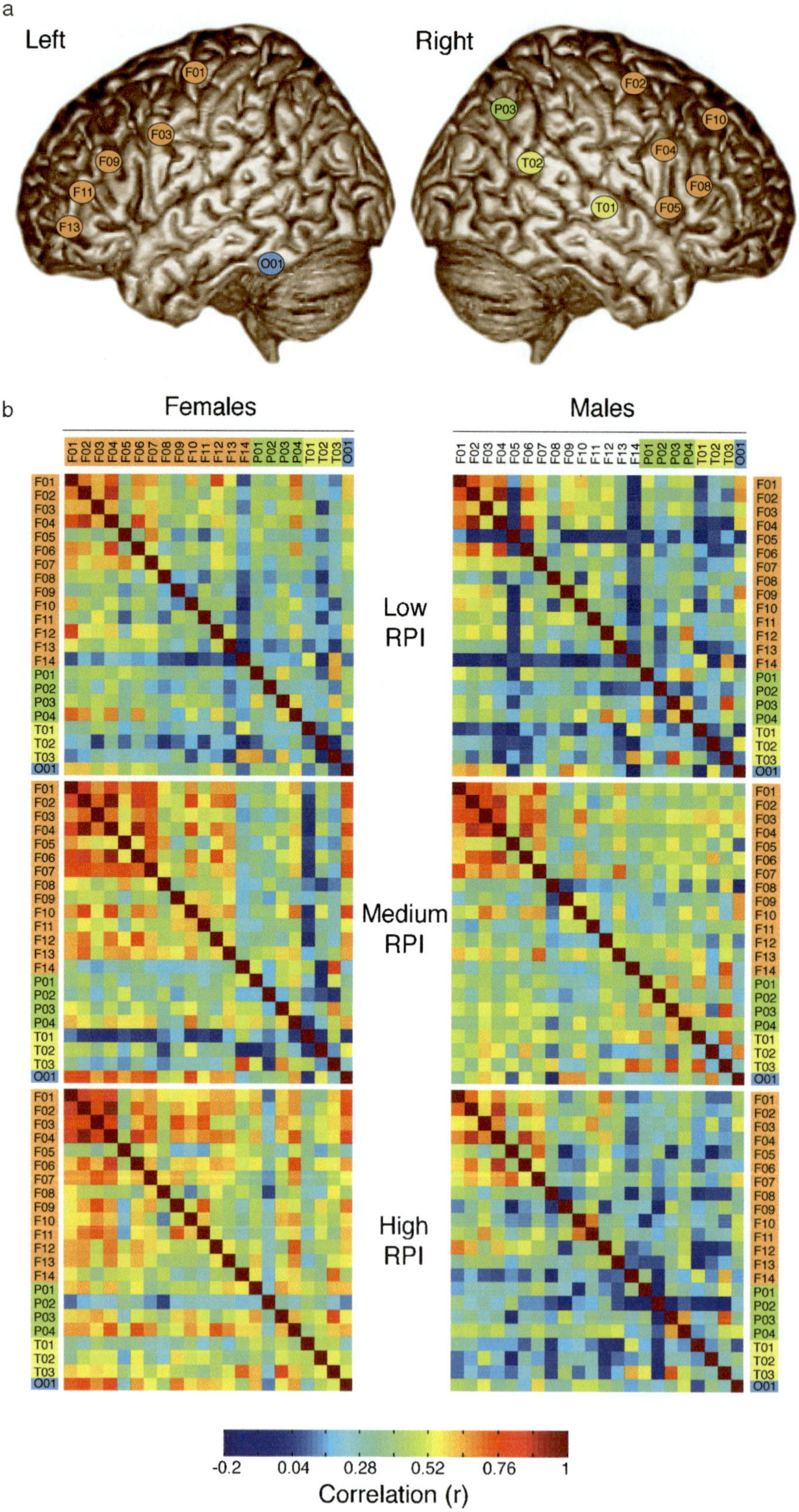

Figure 1 *(Continued)*

RPI group. Note that, in general, cortical thickness decreases with chronological age.

Low, medium and high RPI: Cognitive abilities

Table 2B provides group means and standard deviations of Full Scale Intelligence Quotient (FIQ), Verbal IQ (VIQ) and Performance IQ (PIQ) in each subgroup. In females, IQ varied significantly as a function of the RPI group (FIQ: $F(2, 157) = 7.95$, $p = .0005$; VIQ: $F(2, 157) = 5.8$, $p = .004$; PIQ: $F(2, 157) = 6.1$, $p = .003$). Female adolescents with low RPI had lower IQ, as compared with the medium and high RPI groups. In males, we observed similar trends without reaching statistical significance (FIQ: $F(2, 131) = 1.8$, $p = .17$; VIQ: $F(2, 131) = 1.7$, $p = .18$; PIQ: $F(2, 131) = 1.6$, $p = .21$).

Table 2C provides the summary for the four tests of "executive" functions. In females, the only significant difference across the three RPI groups was observed for the number of words generated in the semantic-fluency task, $F(2, 154) = 4.7$, $p = .01$; the low RPI group generated fewer words that the other two RPI groups. In males, we observed the same group differences in this task, $F(2, 130) = 4.1$, $p = .02$.

Low, medium and high RPI: Positive youth development

The overall PYD score varied significantly as a function of the RPI group in both females, $F(2, 159) = 9.5$, $p < .0001$, and males, $F(2, 134) = 11.1$, $p < .0001$; in both genders, the low RPI groups had lower PYD scores than the other two groups. In females, this pattern of differences between the RPI groups was observed for Confidence, $F(2, 152) = 3.6$, $p = .03$, Competence, $F(2, 159) = 14.7$, $p < .0001$, and Character, $F(2, 159) = 5.4$, $p = .005$. In males, the low RPI group scored lower than the other two groups on Confidence, $F(2, 129) = 11.1$, $p < .0001$, Competence, $F(2, 134) = 9.5$, $p = .0001$, Character, $F(2, 134) = 7.4$, $p = .001$, and Connection, $F(2, 134) = 6.1$, $p = .003$.

DISCUSSION

Adolescents with high and low resistance to peer influence appear to differ in the degree of *morphological similarity* in cortical thickness across a number of regions, including the premotor and prefrontal networks, defined in our previous fMRI study of the relationship between action observation and RPI (Grosbras et al., 2007). This finding confirmed our prediction: adolescents with high vs. low RPI show higher morphological similarity in the same cortical networks in which children with high vs. low RPI scores demonstrated higher *functional connectivity* during the observation of angry hand actions (Grosbras et al., 2007). Conceptually, we assume here that a concurrent functional engagement of a set of cortical regions induces, over time, morphological changes in these regions. We further assume that if a set of regions is engaged repeatedly to a similar extent, the degree of induced morphological change would also be similar. Hence our prediction of high inter-regional correlations in cortical thickness across functionally "connected" cortical regions. In the ensuing discussion, we will first address these two assumptions. We will then discuss the observed sex differences vis-à-vis the relationship between the RPI scores and cortical thickness, as well as the relationship between RPI, general intelligence and positive youth development.

The first assumption, namely that functional engagement of a brain region changes its structure, has been confirmed in a number of studies in

Figure 1. Inter-regional correlations in cortical thickness. (a) Locations of 22 brain regions identified in a previous fMRI study of action observation (Grosbras et al., 2007); only regions visible on the lateral surface of the left and right hemispheres are shown. (b) Correlation matrices depicting inter-regional pair-wise correlations (strength of the correlation indicated by the color code) in cortical thickness across the 22 cortical regions in female (left column) and male (right column) adolescents with low (top row), medium (middle row) and high (bottom row) age-adjusted scores of resistance to peer influence. The region labels match those listed in Table 1. F01, premotor cortex, dorsal, left; F02, premotor cortex, dorsal, right; F03, premotor cortex, ventral, left; F04, premotor cortex, ventral, right; F05, frontal operculum, right; F06, cingulate motor area, left; F07, insula, anterior, left; F08, prefrontal cortex, ventro-lateral, right; F09, prefrontal cortex, dorso-lateral, left; F10, prefrontal cortex, dorso-lateral, right; F11, prefrontal cortex, ventro-lateral, left; F12, anterior cingulate cortex, right; F13, orbitofrontal cortex, lateral, left; F14, prefrontal cortex, medial; P01, posterior cingulate cortex; P02, precuneus, left; P03, parietal cortex, dorso-lateral, right; P04, parietal cortex, dorso-medial, right; T01, superior temporal sulcus, middle, right; T02, superior temporal sulcus, posterior, right; T03, hippocampus, right; O01, fusiform gyrus, left.

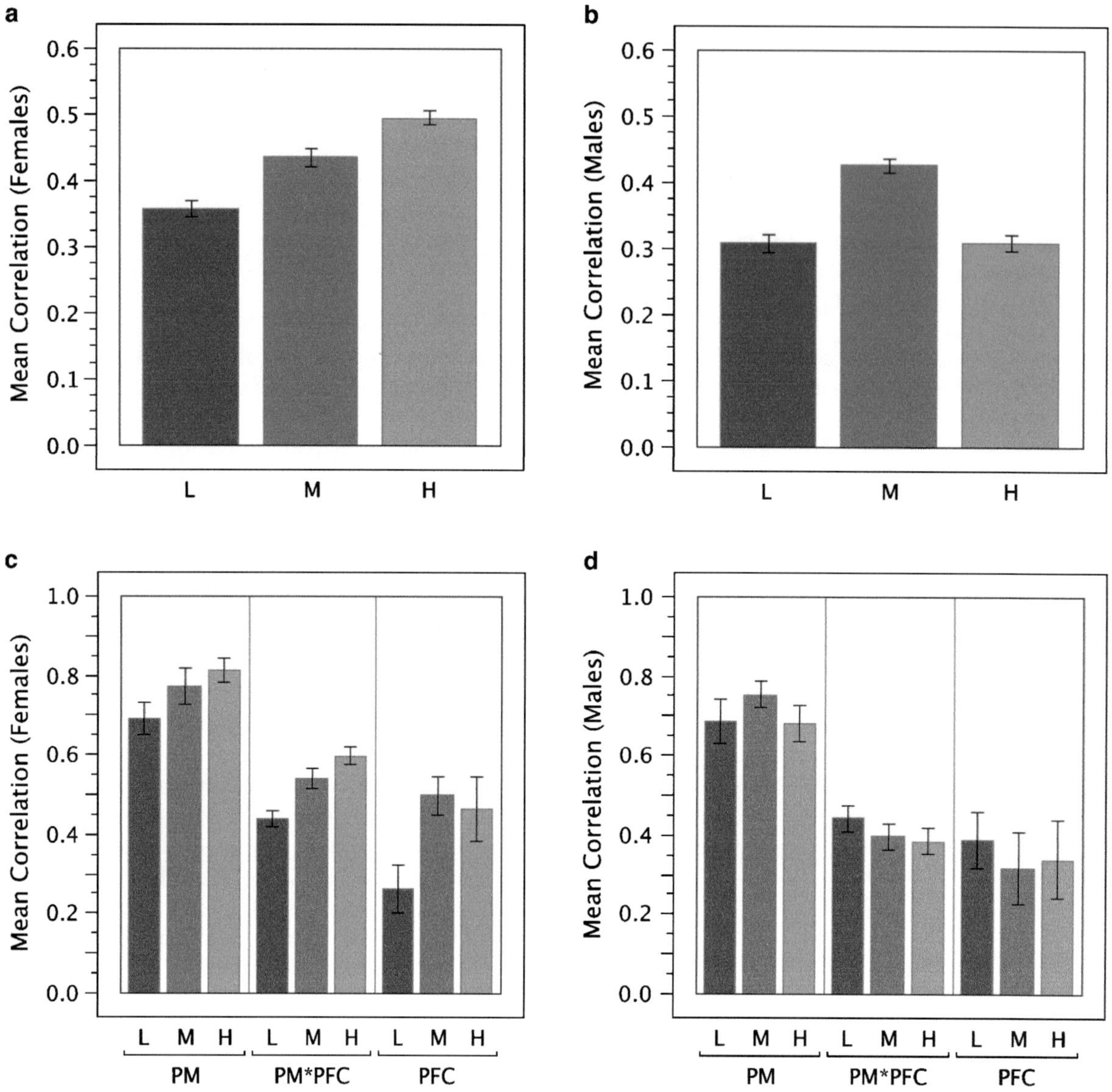

Figure 2. Magnitude of the inter-regional correlations in cortical thickness (Mean ± *SEM*) in female (left column: a, c) and male (right column: b, d) adolescents with low (L), medium (M) and high (H) age-adjusted scores of resistance to peer influence. Graphs on the top row (a, b) depict the mean magnitude of inter-regional correlations in cortical thickness across all 22 regions (see Figure 1 and its legend). Graphs on the bottom row (c, d) depict the mean magnitude of inter-regional correlations in cortical thickness obtained in three different networks: (1) *Premotor network* (PM), consisting of the dorsal and ventral premotor cortices in both hemispheres (F01 through F04; 6 pair-wise correlations); (2) *Prefrontal network* (PFC), consisting of the dorso-lateral and ventro-lateral PFC in both hemispheres (F08 through F11; 6 pair-wise correlations); and (3) *Premotor–prefrontal network* (PM*PFC), consisting of the intersection of the above two networks (F01 through F04 vs. F08 through F11, 16 pair-wise correlations). The region labels (F01 through F11) match those listed in Table 1.

experimental animals and, more recently, in humans. Rats housed in an enriched environment differ from their "standard housing" counterparts in cortical thickness, extent of dendritic branching, spine density, angiogenesis, gliogenesis, and neurogenesis (e.g., Kolb, Gorgie, Gibb, Gorny, & Rowntree, 1998; Lewis, 2004; Sirevaag & Greenough, 1988; van Praag, Kempermann, & Gage, 2000). Humans who have engaged in specific activities for many years show robust differences in brain morphology as revealed by structural MRI (e.g., Gaser & Schlaug, 2003; Maguire et al., 2000). Furthermore, performing a specific behavior for a period as short as three months induces, in a reversible manner, morphological changes in the "stimulated" cortical area, as detected with structural MRI (Draganski et al., 2004). The second assumption, namely that functionally interconnected regions are more alike vis-à-vis their morphology, has less previous support. Some converging evidence comes from a recent study that also investigated inter-regional correlations in cortical thickness in children; high inter-regional correlations were found between functionally related regions, such as Brodmann's area 44 of the frontal cortex and the cortex of the superior temporal gyrus (Lerch et al., 2006). In our dataset, the highest inter-regional correlations were also found across cortical regions that show both high anatomical connectivity and close functional links, namely the dorsal and ventral premotor cortex both within and across hemispheres (see Chouinard & Paus, 2006, for an overview of the structural and functional properties of the motor and premotor cortices). Note that the high similarity in cortical thickness between most of the analyzed cortical regions cannot be simply due to their physical proximity.

At this point, we can only speculate about the cellular events underlying such a hypothesized link between function and structure. It is possible, for example, that increased neural activity within a particular network upregulates molecules, such as brain-derived neurotrophic factor (BDNF), involved in dendritic growth and other morphological changes. Several experiments found that the expression of BDNF and/or its receptors increases as a function of experience/stimulation, including the effects of enriched environment on BDNF in the cerebral cortex, hippocampal formation and the hindbrain (Ickes et al., 2000), visual stimulation on BDNF in the developing visual cortex (Pollock et al., 2001), and whisker stimulation on BDNF in the somatosensory cortex (Rocamora, Welker, Pascual, & Soriano, 1996). Most recently, several studies revealed marked differences between individuals with a substitution of valine (val) to methionine (met) in the promoter region of the human BDNF gene; this polymorphism affects intracellular packaging and the regulated release of BDNF (Chen et al., 2004). Subjects with met/met vs. val/val genotype show poorer performance in episodic memory (Egan et al., 2003), lower fMRI signal in the hippocampus during the performance of a declarative memory task (Hariri et al., 2003), and, most importantly, lower volume of grey matter in the hippocampus and prefrontal cortex (Pezawas et al., 2004).

The above activity-driven explanation of high inter-regional similarity in cortical thickness across regions with strong functional connectivity represents only one potential mechanism, however. We cannot discount other possibilities. For example, morphological features that underlie the observed inter-regional correlations may not be affecting cellular elements located within the cortex but could also stem from subtle changes in the adjacent white matter. As we (Paus, 2005) and others (Gogtay et al., 2004) argued in the context of age-related decreases in cortical grey matter (GM) during childhood and adolescence, such decreases could be driven by increased myelination of intra-cortical axons and/or the adjacent white matter (WM); the increased MR signal of the more myelinated WM adjacent to the cortex would shift the GM/WM boundary and make the cortex appear thinner. It should be noted that myelination can also be activity dependent (Fields, 2005) and, as such, the overall activity-driven explanation of our findings may still hold true. It is also possible that morphological similarities within specific cortical networks are activity independent. It might be that the maturation of cortical regions forming a particular functionally related network progresses at a similar pace, thus making them more similar. But to discern activity-dependent from activity-independent mechanisms of a correlated cortical maturation, an experimental manipulation would be necessary to distinguish between the cause and effect.

In female adolescents, the relationship between the RPI scores and the similarity in cortical thickness was straightforward: the higher the score, the higher the similarity (Figure 2a and 2c). This was not the case for male adolescents; the low and high RPI groups differed from the medium RPI group but did not differ from each other (Figure 2b). Furthermore, no significant differences were observed across the three (male) RPI groups for any of the three networks (Figure 2d). The apparent discrepancy between the lack of significant group differences in the PM, PFC and PM–PFC networks and the presence of the group difference in the mean correlation across all 22 regions could be related to the fact that, in the males with medium RPI scores, relatively high correlations were found between other cortical regions, including the medial prefrontal cortex, orbitofrontal cortex and the parietal cortex (Figure 1). Unlike the female adolescents, the male adolescents with different RPI scores also differed in the actual cortical thickness in a number of regions, including the lateral and medial PFC and the parietal cortex. The direction of these differences suggests that the (thicker) cortex of the male adolescents with low RPI scores is less mature, as compared with the cortex of males with high RPI scores; note that the RPI groups did not differ in their chronological age. It could be that, depending on their sex, different neural processes underlie morphological differences between the low and high RPI adolescents: (1) in males, the RPI groups may differ in the maturational processes reflected in the actual cortical thickness; and (2) in females, the RPI groups may differ in the activity-dependent processes driving the similarity in cortical thickness.

Adolescents with the different resistance to peer influence differed in their general intelligence and in several facets of their positive youth development. Overall, high vs. low RPI subjects had slightly higher intelligence (by about 7 and 5 IQ points in females and males, respectively). They also scored much higher on Competence (females) and Confidence (males) scales, with the other PYD scales showing less pronounced albeit significant differences between the RPI groups. These observations are important in two respects. First, high resistance to peer influences is clearly associated with other cognitive and behavioral characteristics (Brown, Clasen, & Eicher, 1986; Fuligni & Eccles, 1993). At this point, we can only speculate about the directionality of these relationships. Is it, for example, that a slightly higher general intelligence makes an adolescent less likely to follow their peers? Intelligence may also influence the overall scores on the Competence scale, in particular via its relationship with academic competence that is included, together with social and physical competence, in this scale. On the other hand, intelligence is less likely to have a direct effect on the scores in the Confidence scale, which includes positive identity, self-worth and physical appearance. To evaluate the impact of general intelligence on the two scales, we used multiple regressions and tested significance of the differences between the RPI groups in Competence (females) and Confidence (males) after accounting for individual differences in full-scale IQ. In the case of Competence, both FIQ ($p = .003$) and RPI group ($p = .0003$) accounted for a significant amount of unique variance. In the case of Confidence, FIQ had no significant effect on the scores. Second, we need to consider the multifaceted nature of the cognitive and behavioral differences between the adolescents with high and low RPI scores when interpreting our morphological findings. Clearly, it is unlikely that the observed group differences in the inter-regional similarity across the premotor and prefrontal networks are uniquely related to the RPI construct. It is possible, for example, that similar trends in the morphological inter-regional similarities would be found if we were to divide the subjects based on their IQ or on some other characteristics that reflect maturation in ability to coordinate affect and cognition. In fact, Lerch and colleagues (2006) found stronger inter-regional correlations in cortical thickness between Brodmann's area 44 and several cortical regions in children with higher IQ. We have examined the relationship between full-scale IQ and cortical thickness in our set of regions and observed no differences in the magnitude of mean correlation across the 22 cortical regions between subjects with "low" (< 105) and "high" (> 106) full-scale IQ.

Overall, we suggest that individuals with certain personality and cognitive characteristics, compatible with high resistance to peer influences, are more likely to engage relevant neural networks whenever challenged with relatively complex and socially relevant stimuli. These networks include cortical regions activated during action observation and cognitive/executive control. Over time, such a coordinated functional engagement is likely to shape morphological properties of these regions so that they become structurally alike.

Manuscript received 18 April 2007
Manuscript accepted 15 June 2007
First published online 20 September 2007

REFERENCES

Allison, T., Puce, A., & McCarthy, G. (2000). Social perception from visual cues: role of the STS region. *Trends in Cognitive Science*, *4*, 267–278.

Brass, M., & Heyes, C. (2005). Imitation: is cognitive neuroscience solving the correspondence problem? *Trends in Cognitive Science*, *9*, 489–495.

Brown, B., Clasen, D., & Eicher, S. (1986). Perceptions of peer pressure, peer conformity dispositions, and self-reported behavior among adolescents. *Developmental Psychology*, *22*, 521–530.

Brown, B. B. (2004). Adolescents' relationships with peers. In R. M. Lerner & L. Steinberg (Eds.), *Handbook of adolescent psychology* (2nd ed., pp. 363–394). New York: John Wiley & Sons.

Chen, Z. Y., Patel, P. D., Sant, G., Meng, C. X., Teng, K. K., Hempstead, B. L., et al. (2004). Variant brain-derived neurotrophic factor (BDNF) (Met66) alters the intracellular trafficking and activity-dependent secretion of wild-type BDNF in neurosecretory cells and cortical neurons. *Journal of Neuroscience, 24*, 4401–4411.

Chouinard, P. A., & Paus, T. (2006). The primary motor and premotor areas of the human cerebral cortex. *The Neuroscientist, 2*, 143–152.

Draganski, B., Gaser, C., Busch, V., Schuierer, G., Bogdahn, U., & May, A. (2004). Neuroplasticity: changes in grey matter induced by training. *Nature, 427*, 311–312.

Duncan, J., & Owen, A. M. (2000). Common regions of the human frontal lobe recruited by diverse cognitive demands. *Trends in Neuroscience, 23*, 475–483.

Egan, M. F., Kojima, M., Callicott, J. H., Goldberg, T. E., Kolachana, B. S., Bertolino, A., et al. (2003). The BDNF val66met polymorphism affects activity-dependent secretion of BDNF and human memory and hippocampal function. *Cell, 112*, 257–269.

Fields, R. D. (2005). Myelination: an overlooked mechanism of synaptic plasticity? *Neuroscientist, 11*, 528–531.

Fischl, B., & Dale, A. M. (2000). Measuring the thickness of the human cerebral cortex from magnetic resonance images. *Proceedings of the National Academy of Sciences USA, 97*, 11050–11055.

Fischl, B., Sereno, M. I., Tootell, R. B., & Dale, A. M. (1999). High-resolution intersubject averaging and a coordinate system for the cortical surface. *Human Brain Mapping, 8*, 272–284.

Fuligni, A., & Eccles, J. (1993). Perceived parent–child relationships and early adolescents' orientation toward peers. *Developmental Psychology, 29*, 622–632.

Gaser, C., & Schlaug, G. (2003). Brain structures differ between musicians and non-musicians. *Journal of Neuroscience, 23*, 9240–9245.

Gogtay, N., Giedd, J. N., Lusk, L., Hayashi, K. M., Greenstein, D., Vaituzis, A. C., et al. (2004). Dynamic mapping of human cortical development during childhood through early adulthood. *Proceedings of the National Academy of Sciences USA, 101*, 8174–8179.

Grosbras, M. H., Osswald, K., Jansen, M., Toro, R., McIntosh, A. R., Steinberg, L., et al. (2007). Neural mechanisms of resistance to peer pressure in early adolescence. *Journal of Neuroscience, 27*, 8040–8045.

Grosbras, M., & Paus, T. (2006). Brain networks involved in viewing angry hands or faces. *Cerebral Cortex, 16*, 1087–1096.

Hariri, A. R., Goldberg, T. E., Mattay, V. S., Kolachana, B. S., Callicott, J. H., Egan, M. F., et al. (2003). Brain-derived neurotrophic factor val66met polymorphism affects human memory-related hippocampal activity and predicts memory performance. *Journal of Neuroscience, 23*, 6690–6694.

Iacoboni, M. (2005). Neural mechanisms of imitation. *Current Opinion in Neurobiology, 15*, 632–637.

Ickes, B. R., Pham, T. M., Sanders, L. A., Albeck, D. S., Mohammed, A. H., & Granholm, A. C. (2000). Long-term environmental enrichment leads to regional increases in neurotrophin levels in rat brain. *Experimental Neurology, 164*, 45–52.

Kolb, B., Forgie, M., Gibb, R., Gorny, G., & Rowntree, S. (1998). Age, experience, and the changing brain. *Neuroscience and Biobehavioral Reviews, 22*, 143–159.

Lerch, J. P., Worsley, K., Shaw, W. P., Greenstein, D. K., Lenroot, R. K., Giedd, J., et al. (2006). Mapping anatomical correlations across cerebral cortex (MACACC) using cortical thickness from MRI. *NeuroImage, 31*, 993–1003.

Lerner, R. M., Lerner, J. V., Almerigi, J., Theokas, C., Phelps, E., Gestsdottir, S., et al. (2005). Positive youth development, participation in community youth development programs, and community contributions of fifth-grade adolescents: Findings from the first wave of the 4-H study of positive youth development. *Journal of Early Adolescence, 25*, 17–71.

Lewis, M. H. (2004). Environmental complexity and central nervous system development and function. *Ment Retard Dev Disabil Res Rev, 10*, 91–95.

Maguire, E. A., Gadian, D. G., Johnsrude, I. S., Good, C. D., Ashburner, J., Frackowiak, R. S., et al. (2000). Navigation-related structural change in the hippocampi of taxi drivers. *Proceedings of the National Academy of Sciences USA, 97*, 4398–4403.

Miller, E. K., & Cohen, J. D. (2001). An integrative theory of prefrontal cortex function. *Annual Review of Neuroscience, 24*, 167–202.

Monahan, K., Steinberg, L., & Cauffman, E. (2007, March). *Peer groups and deviant behavior: the role of friendship quality and resistance to peer influence.* Boston, MA: Biennial Meetings of the Society for Research in Child Development.

Paus, T. (2001). Primate anterior cingulate cortex: Where motor control, drive and cognition interface. *Nature Reviews Neuroscience, 2*, 417–424.

Paus, T. (2005). Mapping brain maturation and cognitive development during adolescence. *Trends in Cognitive Sciences, 9*, 60–68.

Pausova, Z., Paus, T., Abrahamowicz, M., Almerigi, J., Arbour, N., Bernard, M., et al. (2007). Genes, maternal smoking and the offspring brain and body during adolescence: Design of the Saguenay youth study. *Human Brain Mapping, 28*, 502–518.

Perrett, D. I., Rolls, E. T., & Caan, W. (1982). Visual neurons responsive to faces in the monkey temporal cortex. *Experimental Brain Research, 47*, 329–342.

Perrett, D. I., Smith, P. A., Mistlin, A. J., Chitty, A. J., Head, A. S., Potter, D. D., et al. (1985). Visual analysis of body movements by neurons in the temporal cortex of the macaque monkey: A preliminary report. *Behavioural Brain Research, 16*, 153–170.

Petrides, M. (2005). Lateral prefrontal cortex: architectonic and functional organization. *Philosophical Transactions of the Royal Society of London, Series B: Biological Sciences, 360*, 781–795.

Petrides, M., & Milner, B. (1982). Deficits on subject-ordered tasks after frontal- and temporal-lobe lesions in man. *Neuropsychologia*, *20*, 249–262.

Pezawas, L., Verchinski, B. A., Mattay, V. S., Callicott, J. H., Kolachana, B. S., Straub, R. E., et al. (2004). The brain-derived neurotrophic factor val66met polymorphism and variation in human cortical morphology. *Journal of Neuroscience*, *24*, 10099–10102.

Pollock, G. S., Vernon, E., Forbes, M. E., Yan, Q., Ma, Y. T., Hsieh, T., et al. (2001). Effects of early visual experience and diurnal rhythms on BDNF mRNA and protein levels in the visual system, hippocampus, and cerebellum. *Journal of Neuroscience*, *21*, 3923–3931.

Rizzolatti, G., & Craighero, L. (2004). The mirror-neuron system. *Annual Review of Neuroscience*, *27*, 169–192.

Rocamora, N., Welker, E., Pascual, M., & Soriano, E. (1996). Upregulation of BDNF mRNA expression in the barrel cortex of adult mice after sensory stimulation. *Journal of Neuroscience*, *16*, 4411–4419.

Sirevaag, A. M., & Greenough, W. T. (1988). A multivariate statistical summary of synaptic plasticity measures in rats exposed to complex, social and individual environments. *Brain Research*, *441*, 386–392.

Steinberg, L., & Monahan, K. (in press). Age differences in resistance to peer influence. *Developmental Psychology*.

Steinberg, L., & Silverberg, S. B. (1986). The vicissitudes of autonomy in early adolescence. *Child Development*, *57*, 841–851.

Stroop, J. R. (1935). Studies of interference in serial verbal reactions. *Journal of Experimental Psychology*, *18*, 643–662.

van Praag, H., Kempermann, G., & Gage, F. H. (2000). Neural consequences of environmental enrichment. *Nature Reviews Neuroscience*, *1*, 191–198.

SOCIAL NEUROSCIENCE, 2008, 3 (3–4), 317–333

Psychology Press
Taylor & Francis Group

Mirror neurons and the social nature of language: The neural exploitation hypothesis

Vittorio Gallese
University of Parma, Parma, Italy

This paper discusses the relevance of the discovery of mirror neurons in monkeys and of the mirror neuron system in humans to a neuroscientific account of primates' social cognition and its evolution. It is proposed that mirror neurons and the functional mechanism they underpin, embodied simulation, can ground within a unitary neurophysiological explanatory framework important aspects of human social cognition. In particular, the main focus is on language, here conceived according to a neurophenomenological perspective, grounding meaning on the social experience of action. A neurophysiological hypothesis—the "neural exploitation hypothesis"—is introduced to explain how key aspects of human social cognition are underpinned by brain mechanisms originally evolved for sensorimotor integration. It is proposed that these mechanisms were later on adapted as new neurofunctional architecture for thought and language, while retaining their original functions as well. By neural exploitation, social cognition and language can be linked to the experiential domain of action.

INTRODUCTION

The neuroscientific study of social cognition is opening new perspectives for a better and fuller understanding of what it means to be human. Several aspects of social cognition are nowadays the topic of empirical investigation, particularly after the development of the powerful brain imaging technologies, enabling us to directly look at what happens inside our brains when engaged in a variety of perceptual, executive and cognitive tasks. This ever-growing accumulation of neuroscientific evidence has substantially broadened our knowledge of how the human brain works and suggested new perspectives for the understanding of social cognition. This undoubtedly positive balance, though, should not obscure the risks inherent in a blind reliance upon the epistemic power of this sole approach (see Coltheart, 2006, for a radical criticism of brain imaging in relation to our understanding of the mind). Especially so, if the brain imaging evidence is blindly used to validate a preconceived notion of what the human mind is and how it works.

As recently pointed out by Barrett, Henzi, and Rendall (2007), there are two opposed but equally potentially dangerous biases that may hinder our understanding of social cognition: (1) Anthropocentrism and the related anthropomorphism, by means of which we tend to project onto other species cognitive traits that we consider typical of our species; and (2) the opposite anti-anthropomorphism, according to which human traits are a priori uniquely human. By following the anti-anthropomorphism bias, many scholars in the cognitive sciences exclusively focus on clarifying differences between humans and other primates with respect to the use of propositional attitudes. According to this mainstream

Correspondence should be addressed to: Vittorio Gallese, Department of Neuroscience – Section of Physiology, University of Parma, I-43100 Parma, Italy. E-mail: vittorio.gallese@unipr.it

This work was supported by MIUR (Ministero Italiano dell'Università e della Ricerca) and by the EU grants NESTCOM and DISCOS.

www.psypress.com/socialneuroscience DOI:10.1080/17470910701563608

view, humans have Theory of Mind (ToM), nonhuman primates do not.

This paradigm, still pervasive in contemporary cognitive science, is doomed to failure when trying to establish a direct link between our use of propositional attitudes and their supposed neural correlates. No one can deny that we use what we call "propositional attitudes." However, it is far from clear that this is the sole or even principal character of human social cognition (see Barrett & Henzi, 2005; Barrett et al., 2007; Gallese, 2001, 2006). It must be added that the chances that we will find boxes in our brain containing the neural correlates of beliefs desires and intentions *as such* probably amount to next to zero. I am afraid that such a search might look like an ill-suited form of reductionism leading us nowhere.

The research strategy of social cognitive neuroscience could perhaps benefit by considering the following points: (1) We should adopt a bottom-up approach, by thoroughly investigating the non-metarepresentational aspects of human social cognition, so far unduly minimized or even neglected. (2) The empirical investigation of human social cognition should be informed by an evolutionary perspective, hence complemented by the neurophysiological and psychological investigation of the functional mechanisms underpinning nonhuman primates' social cognition. The only way to go beyond a mere correlative use of brain-imaging data acquired in humans consists in unveiling the neural mechanisms leading to the activation of different brain regions in different tasks. (3) By doing so, it might be established to what extent the apparently different social cognitive abilities and strategies adopted by different species of primates may be underpinned by similar functional mechanisms, which in the course of evolution acquire increasing complexity (see Sommerville & Decety, 2006, for a discussion of similar points).

The empirical data briefly reviewed in this paper on the discovery of mirror neurons and its implications in social cognition are examples of this approach and research strategy. I take these data as strong evidence in support of the crucial role played by action in shaping our cognitive social competence, language included.

By focusing on the experiential and situated aspects of human social cognition, that is, by adopting a neurophenomenological approach to the empirical investigation of social cognition, we may be capable of circumventing the abovementioned biases and getting a more realistic appreciation of what human cognition is and how it relates in evolution with the social cognitive endowments of nonhuman primates. The data on the mirror neuron system (MNS) in monkeys and humans suggest that the ease with which we "mirror" the behavior of others, recognize others as similar to us, and directly comprehend their behavior—in other words, our implicit "intentional attunement" with others (Gallese, 2006)—might rely on a series of neural matching mechanisms that we have just started to uncover.

In the present paper I briefly review the properties of the MNS in monkeys and humans and then specifically focus on the role that the MNS (and the cortical motor system, in general) may play in a crucial aspect of social cognition: language. The recent research on the MNS in humans may shed light on the social nature of language, and provide neuroscientific grounding to aspects of language investigated by psycholinguistics like, among others, situation models and collaborative and interactive accounts of conversation, according to which the perception of shared environment and behaviors helps in maintaining alignment between conversational partners (see Clark & Wilkes-Gibbs, 1986; Pickering & Garrod, 2004).

THE MIRROR NEURON SYSTEM FOR ACTIONS IN MONKEYS AND HUMANS: EMPIRICAL EVIDENCE

About fifteen years ago mirror neurons were discovered in the premotor cortex of the macaque monkey. These neurons discharge not only when the monkey executes goal-related hand and/or mouth actions like grasping objects, but also when observing other individuals (monkeys or humans) executing similar actions (Ferrari, Gallese, Rizzolatti, & Fogassi, 2003; Gallese, Fadiga, Fogassi, & Rizzolatti, 1996; Rizzolatti, Fadiga, Gallese, & Fogassi, 1996). Neurons with similar mirroring properties, matching action observation and execution have also been discovered in a sector of the posterior parietal cortex reciprocally connected with area F5 (PF/PG mirror neurons; see Fogassi et al., 2005; Gallese, Fogassi, Fadiga, & Rizzolatti, 2002; Rizzolatti, Fogassi, & Gallese, 2001). It has been proposed that the MNS may underpin a direct form of action understanding (Gallese, Keysers, & Rizzolatti, 2004; Gallese et al., 1996; Rizzolatti & Craighero, 2004;

Rizzolatti et al., 1996, 2001), by means of embodied simulation, a specific mechanism through which the brain/body system models its interactions with the world (Gallese, 2001, 2003a, 2003b, 2005a, 2005b, 2006). The discovery of mirror neurons has changed our views on the relations among action perception and cognition, and has boosted a renewed interest in the neuroscientific investigation of the social aspects of primate cognition.

Experiments by Umiltà et al. (2001) showed that F5 mirror neurons are also activated during the observation of partially hidden actions, when the monkey can predict the action outcome, even in the absence of the complete visual information about it. Macaque monkeys' mirror neurons therefore respond to acts made by others not exclusively on the basis of their visual description, but on the basis of the anticipation of the final goal-state of the motor act, by means of the activation of its motor neural representation in the observer's premotor cortex.

These data can hardly be reconciled with "minimalist" interpretations of mirror neurons, such as that proposed by Knoblich and Jordan (2002), according to which mirror neurons merely code "the perceived effect the action exerts on the object" (2002, p. 116). Furthermore, these data alone seem to contradict the notion that the functional mechanism at the basis of the activation of mirror neurons qualifies as a form of "direct perception" of the acts of others (see Gallagher, this issue). It is obvious that there must be a system that visually analyzes and describes the acts of others. A "direct perception" of the observed motor acts most likely describes the activation of extrastriate visual neurons sensitive to biological motion. However, the view that such "pictorial" analysis per se is sufficient to provide an understanding of the observed act must be questioned. Without reference to the observer's internal motor knowledge, this description is devoid of experiential meaning for the observing individual. Furthermore, the activation of mirror neurons in the experiment by Umiltà et al. (2001) testifies to something even more different from a "direct perception": it exemplifies a form of simulation-driven "motor inference."

In other experiments it has been shown that a particular class of F5 mirror neurons ("audio-visual mirror neurons") respond not only when the monkey *executes* and *observes* a given hand action, but also when it just *hears* the sound typically produced by the action (Kohler et al., 2002). These neurons respond to the sound of actions and discriminate between the sounds of different actions, but do not respond to other similarly interesting sounds such as arousing noises, or monkeys' and other animals' vocalizations. Events as different as sounds, images, or voluntary acts of the body, are nevertheless mapped by the same network of audio-visual mirror neurons. The presence within a non-linguistic species of such neural matching system can be interpreted as the dawning of an embodied "conceptualization" mechanism, that is a mechanism that grounds meaning in the situated and experience-dependent systematic interactions with the world (see Gallese, 2003b; Gallese & Lakoff, 2005). The world becomes "our world" to the extent that it evokes and is subjected to our actions.

A major step forward in the research on the MNS consisted in the discovery that parietal mirror neurons not only code the goal of an executed/observed motor act, like grasping an object, but they also code the overall action intention (e.g., bringing the grasped object to the mouth or into a container; Fogassi et al., 2005). The MNS maps integrated sequences of goal-related motor acts (grasping, holding, bringing, placing, the different "words" of a "motor vocabulary"; see Rizzolatti et al., 1988) in order to obtain different and parallel intentional "action sentences," that is, temporally chained sequences of motor acts properly assembled to accomplish a more distal goal-state. The "motor vocabulary" of grasping-related neurons, by sequential chaining, reorganizes itself so as to map the fulfillment of an action intention. The overall action intention (to eat, to place the food or object) is the goal state of the ultimate goal-related motor act of the chain. These results seem to suggest—at least at such a basic level—that the "prior intention" of eating or placing the food is also coded by parietal mirror neurons (see de Vignemont & Haggard, this issue, for a different interpretation). Of course, this should not imply that monkeys *explicitly* represent prior intentions as such.

Several studies have also demonstrated in the human brain the existence of a MNS matching action perception and execution (see Gallese, 2003a, 2006; Gallese et al., 2004; Rizzolatti & Craighero, 2004; Rizzolatti et al., 2001, for reviews). During action execution/observation there is strong bilateral activation of ventral premotor (BA 6 and BA 44) and posterior parietal (BA 40) areas, the likely human homologue of the monkey areas in which mirror neurons were originally described. The MNS in humans shows a coarse but consistent somatotopic organization, with distinct cortical regions in the premotor and posterior parietal cortices being activated by the observation/execution of mouth-, hand-, and foot-related acts (Aziz-Zadeh, Wilson, Rizzolatti, & Iacoboni, 2006; Buccino et al., 2001). It has also been shown that the MNS in humans is directly involved in imitation of simple movements (Iacoboni et al., 1999), in imitative learning of novel and complex motor skills (Buccino et al., 2004b), in perception of facial communicative actions (Buccino et al., 2004a), and in understanding the intentions of the actions of others (Iacoboni et al., 2005).

The relevance for social psychology of the discovery of the MNS should be apparent. Social interaction, interpersonal coordination and joint actions require the capacity to understand and anticipate partners' behavior. The MNS seems to provide the right neurofunctional substrate to all these capacities. Furthermore, many interesting phenomena described by social psychologists, like the "chameleon effect"—the unconscious mimicry by the observer of postures, expressions, and behaviors of her/his social partners (Chartrand & Bargh, 1999)—with the MNS can find a neurophysiological explanation.

THE MNS AND ITS RELEVANCE IN THE EVOLUTION OF SOCIAL COGNITION

If the presence of mirror neurons in different species of primates such as macaques and humans seem to favor, on the one hand, a continuist view of the evolution of social cognition, it is also true that, on the other, the very same evidence must be reconciled with the diversity and uniqueness of human (social) cognition. This is a major topic for future research.

It is likely that monkeys use their MNS to optimize their social interactions, by making sense of their conspecifics' behavior. The evidence collected so far suggests that the MNS is sophisticated enough to enable its exploitation for different social purposes. This matching mechanism can indeed support social facilitation in monkeys. The observation and hearing of noisy eating actions facilitates eating behavior in pigtailed macaque monkeys (Ferrari, Maiolini, Addressi, Fogassi, & Visalberghi, 2005). Another study shows that pigtailed macaque monkeys recognize when they are imitated by a human experimenter (Paukner, Anderson, Borelli, Visalberghi, & Ferrari, 2005). Pigtailed macaques look more at an experimenter imitating the monkeys' object-directed acts than at an experimenter manipulating an identical object but not imitating their actions. Since both experimenters acted in synchrony with the monkeys, the monkeys based their looking preference not on temporal contingency, but by tracking the structural components of the experimenters' actions by means of motor simulation.

It has been repeatedly argued that macaque monkeys are not capable of *motor* imitation. Recent evidence by Subiaul, Cantlon, Holloway, and Terrace (2005) suggests that they are capable of *cognitive* imitation. Furthermore, the study by Paukner et al. (2005) shows that when observing the actions of others macaque monkeys do entertain the capacity to discriminate between very similar goal-related acts on the basis of their degree of similarity with the goal-related acts the monkeys themselves have just executed. This capacity seems as cognitively sophisticated as motor imitation, because it implies that monkeys are capable of monitoring their own actions and relating them to the actions of others.

The apparent inability of nonhuman primates (chimps included) to understand others as intentional agents (see Povinelli & Eddy, 1996; see also Povinelli & Vonk, 2003), given the presence of the MNS in nonhuman primates, has led scholars to dispute and argue against a role of the MNS in providing "sufficient basis for agentive understanding" (see Pacherie & Dokic, 2006, p. 106), or as playing—by means of motor simulation—a major role in social cognition (Jacob & Jeannerod, 2004). The chimps' inability to understand others as intentional agents, however, turned out to be only apparent in particular cooperative contexts. In fact, there is evidence that chimps when engaged in a *competitive* setting do indeed deduce what others know on the basis of where they are looking (Hare et al., 2000; Tomasello, Carpenter, Call, Behne, & Moll, 2005).

Even more importantly, it has been recently shown that *rhesus monkeys* can establish a cognitive link between seeing and knowing, by systematically choosing to steal food from the human competitor that could not see the food, while refraining from doing it when the human competitor could see it (Flombaum & Santos,

2006). Similarly, it has been shown that rhesus monkeys choose to obtain food silently only in situations in which silence is crucial to remain undetected by a human competitor (Santos, Nissen, & Ferrugia, 2006).

These results show that nonhuman primates—including macaques—possess the ability to deduce what others know about the world on the basis of ostensive behavioral cues, like the direction of gaze. To what extent this capacity depends on the MNS will require further investigations. However, it is clear that the so far misconceived and underrated social cognitive abilities of nonhuman primates cannot constitute an argument against the relevance of the MNS for social cognition.

Monkeys most likely do not explicitly attribute mental states to others as a causal explanation of others' behavior. Many posit that in order to do that one needs language. To thoroughly understand social cognition we must therefore investigate the neurofunctional mechanisms at the basis of the faculty of language. Before doing that, however, we should clarify what we refer to when we speak of language. Human language for most of its history has just been spoken language. This suggests that language most likely evolved from dialogic speech in order to provide individuals with a more powerful and flexible social cognitive tool to share, communicate and exchange knowledge.

In the next sections I propose to look at the experiential groundings of human linguistic competence and emphasize the tight connection between meaning and action. I then show how the functional mechanism supposedly describing the function of the MNS—embodied simulation—can also ground several aspects of language.

A "NEUROPHENOMENOLOGICAL" LOOK AT LANGUAGE FACULTY: ACTION, EXPERIENCE AND THEIR EXPRESSION

> Speech is comparable to a gesture because what it is charged with expressing will be in the same relation to it as the goal is to the gesture which intends it. (Merleau-Ponty, 1960/1964, p. 89)

The intimate nature of language and the evolutionary process producing it still remain somehow elusive. Such elusiveness is determined by the complexity and multidimensional nature of language. What do we refer to when we investigate the language faculty and its evolution? Barrett et al. (2007) have recently—persuasively, in my opinion—argued that apparent cognitive complexity in the social domain emerges from the interaction of brain, body and world, rather than being a mere outcome of the level of intrinsic cognitive complexity that primate species possess.

Viewing social cognition as an embodied and situated enterprise (see Anderson, 2003; Barsalou, 1999; Barrett & Henzi, 2005; Clark, 1997; Gallese, 2003a, 2003b, 2003c; Lakoff & Johnson, 1980, 1999; Niedenthal, Barsalou, Winkielman, Krauth-Gruber, & Ric, 2005) offers the possibility of a new neuroscientific approach to language. Let us see why and how by first briefly introducing the perspective of phenomenology, which provides stimulating perspectives on the nature and structure of human experience and its connection to language, by putting bodily action at the center of the stage. By following the phenomenological perspective we learn that language is a social enterprise in which action plays a crucial role.

A caveat first. I want to emphasize that neuroscience's goal is not to validate or confute philosophical theories. However, when neuroscience aims at understanding personal-level issues like language and meaning, it cannot escape a serious confrontation with a discipline like philosophy that puts these topics at the core of its investigation. By means of such multidisciplinary dialogue, neuroscience can contribute to the building of a new philosophy of nature.

Probably one of Husserlian phenomenology's greatest merits is to have pointed out that every form of consciousness is intentional, that is, *consciousness of something*, and to have stressed how cognitive forms of intentionality are rooted in the aboutness and relatedness to the world of our bodily actions. The facticity of human experience is even more within the focus of Martin Heidegger, with his notion of being-in-the-world (1927/1962) and his distancing from Husserl's transcendental idealism. According to Heidegger, being and world are to be seen as a unitary phenomenon, intrinsically and ontologically connected. This perspective substantially blurs distinctions between subject and object and between internal and external realms.

In Heidegger's perspective, animals and humans profoundly differ with respect to their relationship with the world. Only humans fully possess a world, because only human existence has a true historical dimension, which, in turn, depends on language (Heidegger, 1929/1995). According to Heidegger, language is meaningful because it reveals and discloses possibilities of contextual actions (1927/1962). Meaning emerges from a peculiar historical world to which humans are connected through their daily interactions with it (Heidegger, 1925/1985). Hence language is ontologically of practical nature. As underlined by Costa (2006), terms like "concepts" and "thoughts," according to Heidegger, are to be understood as originating from our practical experience of the world. This is what Heidegger implies by claiming that meaning has its roots in the ontology of being-in-the-world (1927/1962). Being-in-the-world precedes reflection.

Our understanding of the meaning of a word like "table" does not stem from our use of a linguistic game, which, at best, can specify when to apply a given word as a tag to a given object in the world. The meaning of "table" stems from its use, from what we can do with it, that is, from the multiple and interrelated possibilities for action it evokes.[1]

Neuroscience today shows that the scientific investigation of the "Korper" (the brain–body system) can shed light on the "Leib" (the lived body of experience), as the latter is the lived expression of the former. The neurophysiological aspects of action did not interest philosophers like Husserl and Heidegger, also because of the too mechanistic views purported by neurobiology at the beginning of last century. The phenomenological approach, though, clearly shows that meaning does not inhabit a pre-given Platonic world of ideal and eternal truths to which mental representations connect and conform. Phenomenology thus entertains a perspective partly compatible with many empirical results of contemporary cognitive neuroscience: Meaning is the outcome of our situated interactions with the world.

With the advent of language, and even more with the "discovery" of written language, meaning is amplified as it frees itself from being dependent upon specific instantiations of actual experience. Language connects all possible actions within a network expanding the meaning of individual situated experiences. Language evokes the totality of possibilities for action the world puts upon us, and structures action within a web of related meanings. By endorsing this perspective, it follows that if we confine language to its sole predicative use, we reify a consistent part of language's nature. Our understanding of linguistic expressions is not solely an epistemic attitude; it is a way of being. Our way of being, in turn, depends on what we act, how we do it, and how the world responds to us.

The relationship between language and body is also emphasized by Maurice Merleau-Ponty (1960/1964). According to Merleau-Ponty, signification arouses speech as the world arouses the body. For the speaking subject to express a meaning is to become fully aware of it. In other words, the signifying intention of the speaker can be conceived as a gap to be filled with words. When we speak, by means of the shared neural networks activated by embodied simulation, we experience the presence of others in ourselves and of ourselves in others. This mirroring likely helps in filling the gap.

A further contribution to clarifying the relationship between language, action and experience comes from Paul Ricoeur's hermeneutic phenomenology. According to Ricoeur, language is first and foremost *discourse*, and therefore the "mimetic bond between the act of saying and effective action is never completely severed" (1986/1991, p. XIV). The hermeneutic development of phenomenology in Ricoeur's approach connects intentionality to meaning: the logical sense of language must be grounded in the broader notion of meaning that is coextensive with the notion of intentionality (Ricoeur, 1986/1991, p. 40). In *From Text to Action* (1986/1991) Ricoeur builds upon the historical dichotomy introduced in linguistics by de Saussure (1973/1974) and by Hjelmslev (1959) between *language* and *speech*, or between *schema* and *use*, respectively, and draws an important distinction between the formal language studied by structural linguistics and discourse, and in particular its original form, speech. According to Ricoeur discourse is seen as an event, taking place in time to a speaker who speaks about something. By means of discourse, language acquires a situated world. It is in discourse that all meanings are transferred, hence " . . . discourse not only has a world but has an other, another person, an interlocutor to whom it is addressed" (Ricoeur, 1986/1991, p. 78).

The action-related account of language proposed by phenomenology and its intersubjective

[1] It is worth noting how long it took before a similar perspective emerged in the field of cognitive psychology (see Gibson, 1979; Glenberg, 1997; see also Gallese, 2003c)

framing suggest that the neuroscientific investigation of what language is and how it works should begin from the domain of action. This investigation has already produced remarkable findings. The MNS provides a matching mechanism that seems to play an important role in social cognition, thus it looks like a very good candidate also for grounding the social nature of language. In the next sections I show that when processing language humans, by means of embodied simulation, activate the motor system at the different levels at which traditionally language can be described.[2] The first level, defined as "embodied simulation at the vehicle level," pertains to phono-articulatory aspects of language. The second level, defined as "embodied simulation at the content level," concerns the semantic content of a word, verb, or proposition. Finally, the relationship between action simulation and syntax will be briefly addressed.

EMBODIED SIMULATION AT THE VEHICLE LEVEL

It is now ascertained that Broca's region, formerly considered an exclusive speech-production area, contains neurons activated by the execution/observation/imitation of oro-facial gestures and of hand acts. This region is known to be part of the MNS (Bookheimer, 2002; Nishitani, Schurmann, Amunts, & Hari, 2005; Rizzolatti & Craighero, 2004). In an elegant transcranial magnetic stimulation (TMS) experiment, Fadiga, Craighero, Buccino, and Rizzolatti (2002) showed that listening to phonemes induces an increase of the amplitude of motor-evoked potentials (MEPs) recorded from the tongue muscles involved in their execution. This result was interpreted as a motor resonance mechanism at the phonological level. These findings have been complemented by a TMS study by Watkins, Strafella, and Paus (2003), who showed that listening to and viewing speech gestures enhanced the amplitude of MEPs recorded from lip muscles. A recent fMRI study demonstrated the activation of motor areas devoted to speech production during passive listening to phonemes (Wilson, Saygin, Sereno, & Iacoboni, 2004). Finally, Watkins and Paus (2004) showed that during auditory speech perception, the increased size of the MEPs obtained by TMS over the face area of the primary motor cortex correlated with cerebral blood flow increase in Broca's area. This suggests that the activation of the MNS for facial gestures in the premotor cortex facilitates the primary motor cortex output to facial muscles, as evoked by TMS.

Not only speech perception, but also covert speech production activates the motor system. McGuigan and Dollins (1989) showed with EMG that tongue and lip muscles are activated in covert speech in the same way as during overt speech. An fMRI study by Wildgruber, Ackermann, Klose, Kardatzki, and Grodd (1996) showed primary motor cortex activation during covert speech. Finally, a recent study by Aziz-Zadeh, Cattaneo, Rochat, and Rizzolatti (2005) showed covert speech arrest after transient inactivation with repetitive TMS of the left primary motor cortex and left premotor BA 44.

The presence in Broca's region of both hand and mouth motor representations can not only cast some light on the evolution of language (Arbib, 2005; Corballis, 2002, 2004; Fadiga & Gallese, 1997; Gentilucci & Corballis, 2006; Rizzolatti & Arbib, 1998), but also on its ontogeny in humans. A tight relationship between the development of manual and oral motor skills has been repeatedly documented in children. Goldin-Meadow (1999) proposed that speech production and speech-related hand gestures could be considered as outputs of the same process. Canonical babbling in 6- to 8-month-old children is accompanied by rhythmic hand movements (Masataka, 2001). Hearing babies born to deaf parents display hand actions with a babbling-like rhythm. Manual gestures anticipate early development of speech in children, and reportedly predict later success up to the two-word level (Iverson & Goldin-Meadow, 2005).

The same relationship between manual and oral language-related gestures persists in adulthood. Several works by Gentilucci and colleagues (Gentilucci, 2003; Gentilucci, Benuzzi, Gangitano, & Grimaldi, 2001, Gentilucci, Santunione, Roy, & Stefanini, 2004a; Gentilucci, Stefanini, Roy, & Santunione, 2004b) have shown a close relationship between speech production and the execution/observation of arm and hand gestures. In one of these studies, Gentilucci et al. (2004a) showed that the execution/observation of the action of bringing an object to the mouth activates a mouth articulation posture likely related to food manipulation, which selectively

[2] To what extent these levels can be conceived as distinctly mapped in the brain is not so obvious yet.

influences speech production. This suggests that the system involved in speech production shares (and may derive from) the neural premotor circuit involved in the control of hand/arm actions.

In another related study, Gentilucci et al. (2004b) showed that different observed actions influence lip shaping kinematics and voice formants of the observer. The observation of grasping influences the first formant, which is related to mouth opening, while the observation of bringing to the mouth influences the second formant of the voice spectrum, related to tongue position. All of these effects are greater in children than in adults. When observing hand grasping the observer activates the normally subsequent motor act, that is, mouth grasping. When observing bringing to the mouth, chewing is activated. This in turn affects speech production. As proposed by Gentilucci et al. (2004b), this mechanism may have facilitated the evolutionary shift from a primitive arm gesture communication system to speech. The phono-articulatory aspects of speech production, in principle as remote as possible from meaning, show unexpected connections with the execution/observation of socially meaningful arm motor acts.

In a very recent paper, Bernardis and Gentilucci (2006) showed that word and corresponding-in-meaning communicative arm gestures influence each other when they are simultaneously emitted. The second formant in the voice spectra is higher when the word is pronounced together with the gesture. No modification in the second formant is observed when executing a meaningless arm movement involving the same joints. Conversely, the second formant of a pseudo-word is not affected by the execution of meaningful arm gestures. The same effects occur when gestures are observed. In sum, spoken words and symbolic communicative gestures are coded as a single signal by a unique communication system within the premotor cortex.

The involvement of premotor Broca's area in translating the representations of communicative arm gestures into mouth articulation gestures was recently confirmed by transient inactivation of BA 44 with repetitive TMS (Gentilucci, Bernardis, Crisi, & Volta, 2006). Since BA 44 is part of the MNS, it is likely to posit that through embodied simulation the communicative meaning of gestures is fused with the articulation of sounds required to express it in words. It appears that within premotor BA 44, "vehicle" and "content" of social communication are tightly interconnected. This is consistent with some tenets of "constructionist" approaches to language, according to which *all* levels of linguistic descriptions involve pairing of forms with semantic/discourse functions (Goldberg, 2003).

EMBODIED SIMULATION AT THE CONTENT LEVEL

The meaning of a sentence, regardless of its content, has been classically considered to be understood by relying on symbolic, amodal mental representations (Fodor, 1998; Pylyshyn, 1984). An alternative hypothesis assumes that the understanding of language relies on "embodiment" (Barsalou, 1999; Gallese, 2003c; Gallese & Lakoff, 2005; Glenberg, 1997; Glenberg & Robertson, 2000; Lakoff, 1987; Lakoff & Johnson, 1980, 1999; Pulvermüller, 1999, 2002).

According to the embodiment theory, the neural structures presiding over action execution should also play a role in understanding the semantic content of the same actions when verbally described. Empirical evidence shows this to be the case. Glenberg and Kaschak (2002) asked participants to judge if a read sentence was sensible or nonsense by moving their hand to a button requiring movement away from the body (in one condition) or toward the body (in the other condition). Half of the sensible sentences described action toward the reader and half away from the reader. Readers responded faster to sentences describing actions whose direction was congruent with the required response movement. This clearly shows that action contributes to sentence comprehension.

The most surprising result of this study, though, was that the same interaction between sentence movement direction and response direction was also found with abstract sentences describing transfer of information from one person to another such as, "Liz told you the story" vs. "You told Liz the story." These latter results extend the role of action simulation to the understanding of sentences describing abstract situations. Similar consistent results were recently published by other authors (Borghi, Glenberg, & Kaschak, 2004; Matlock, 2004).

A prediction of the embodiment theory of language understanding is that when individuals listen to action-related sentences, their MNS should be modulated. The effect of this modulation should influence the excitability of the primary motor cortex, henceforth the production of the movements it controls. To test this hypothesis we carried out two experiments (Buccino et al., 2005). In the first experiment, by means of single pulse TMS, either the hand or the foot/leg motor areas in the left hemisphere were stimulated in distinct experimental sessions, while participants were listening to sentences expressing hand and foot actions. Listening to abstract content sentences served as a control. Motor evoked potentials (MEPs) were recorded from hand and foot muscles. Results showed that MEPs recorded from hand muscles were specifically modulated by listening to hand-action-related sentences, as were MEPs recorded from foot muscles by listening to foot-action-related sentences.

In the second behavioral experiment participants had to respond with the hand or the foot while listening to sentences expressing hand and foot actions, as compared to abstract sentences. Coherently with the results obtained with TMS, reaction times of the two effectors were specifically modulated by the effector-congruent heard sentences. These data show that processing sentences describing actions activates different sectors of the motor system, depending on the effector used in the listened action.[3]

Several brain-imaging studies have shown that processing linguistic material in order to retrieve its meaning activates regions of the motor system congruent with the processed semantic content. Hauk, Johnsrude, and Pulvermüller (2004) showed in an event-related fMRI study that silent reading of *words* referring to face, arm or leg actions (e.g., lick, pick, kick) led to the activation of different sectors of the premotor–motor areas controlling motor acts of the body congruent with the referential meaning of the read action words. Tettamanti et al. (2005) showed that listening to *sentences* expressing actions performed with the mouth, the hand and the foot, produces activation of different sectors of the premotor cortex, depending on the effector used in the action-related sentence listened to by participants. These activated premotor sectors correspond, albeit only coarsely, with those active during the observation of hand, mouth and foot actions (Buccino et al., 2001). These results have been recently replicated and expanded by Aziz-Zadeh et al. (2006), who showed in the same group of participants that the same cortical regions activated by action observation were also activated by the understanding of action-related sentences.

The MNS is involved not only in understanding visually presented actions, but also in mapping acoustically or visually presented action-related sentences. It must be added, though, that the precise functional relevance of the MNS and embodied simulation in the process of language understanding remains unclear. Their involvement might simply reflect motor imagery induced by the understanding process, which, in turn, might occur somewhere upstream, within the supposedly "real linguistic part of the brain," whatever it might be. The study of the spatio-temporal dynamic of language processing becomes crucial in settling this issue. ERP experiments on silent reading of face-, arm- and leg-related words showed category-specific differential activations ~200 ms after word onset. Distributed source localization performed on stimulus-triggered ERPs showed different somatotopically arranged activation sources, with a strongest inferior frontal source for face-related words, and a maximal superior central source for leg-related words (Pulvermüller, Härle, & Hummel, 2000). This early differential activation can be hardly reconciled with the "late motor imagery" hypothesis, while it is more consistent with the embodied simulation account of language understanding.

This dissociation in brain activity patterns supports the idea of stimulus-triggered early lexico-semantic processes taking place within the premotor cortex. Pulvermüller, Shtyrov, and Ilmoniemi (2003) used magnetoencephalography (MEG) to investigate the time course of cortical activation underlying the magnetic mismatch negativity elicited by hearing a spoken action-related word. The results showed that auditory areas of the left superior-temporal lobe became active 136 ms after the information in the acoustic input was sufficient for identifying the word, and activation of the left inferior-frontal cortex followed after an additional delay of 22 ms.

In sum, although these results are far from being conclusive on the relevance of embodied simulation of action for language understanding,

[3] A discussion of the facilitatory or inhibitory nature of the specific modulation of the motor system during language processing is beyond the scope of this article, and therefore will not be dealt with here.

they show that simulation is specific, automatic, and has a temporal dynamic compatible with such a function.[4] It should be added that several neuropsychological studies testify that frontal lesions, including those of the premotor cortex, produce deficits in the comprehension of action verbs (Bak & Hodges, 2003; Bak, O'Donovan, Xuereb, Boniface, & Hodges, 2001; Bak et al., 2006; Kemmerer & Tranel, 2000, 2003).

We certainly need more research. More inactivation studies on healthy subjects and the careful neuropsychological study of patients with focal brain lesions will tell us more about the validity of this hypothesis.

EMBODIED SIMULATION AND SYNTAX

In the previous sections I have reviewed evidence showing the involvement of motor cortical circuits in various aspects of social cognition, and in particular in the multi-level processing of language. We should now frame what has been discussed so far about action and language within an evolutionary perspective, and, in so doing, introduce syntax.

Hauser, Chomsky, and Fitch (2002) proposed to differentiate two domains within the language faculty: a "narrow language faculty" (NLF), encompassing aspects that are specific to language, and a "broad language faculty" (BLF), inclusive of more general cognitive functions not unique to humans, but shared with nonhuman animals. According to Hauser et al. (2002), at the core of NLF is "recursion," a specifically human computational mechanism at the basis of language grammar, which, nevertheless, might have evolved for functions other than language. The merit of this proposal consists in its greater evolutionary plausibility when compared with alternative discontinuist views, like those positing a linguistic "big-bang" out of which full-blown human language supposedly emerged (Bickerton, 1995). Pinker and Jackendoff (2005), though critical of the "recursion-only hypothesis," praised the merit of abandoning a monolithic view of language.

If language is the most distinctively human component of social cognition, and if embodied simulation is indeed crucial in social cognition, syntax appears to be an ideal benchmark to test the relevance for human social cognition of this mechanism and of its neural underpinnings, the MNS. Syntax is a basic ingredient of the NLF, as defined by Hauser et al. (2002). According to the modular approach to syntax, syntactic processing is typically operated by a serial parsing encapsulated system, in which the initial phase of processing has only access to information about syntax. According to Fodor (1983, p. 77), " . . . To show that [the syntactic] system is penetrable (hence informationally unencapsulated), you would have to show that its processes have access to information that is not specified at any of the levels of representation that the language input system computes."

Recent studies, *pace* Fodor, show that the syntactic system *is* indeed penetrable. Syntactic ambiguities are evaluated using non-linguistic constraints like real-world properties of referential context (e.g., the actions an object affords). Humans continuously define linguistically relevant referential domains by evaluating sentence information against the situation-specific affordances. These affordances are not encoded as part of the linguistic representation of a word or phrase. Listeners use information like action goals to anticipate upcoming referents. A recent study by Chambers, Tanenhaus, and Magnuson (2004) showed that syntactic decisions about ambiguous sentences are affected by the number of referential candidates that can afford the action evoked by the verb in the unfolding sentence. Even a key component of the supposed NLF is intimately intertwined with action and its embodied simulation.

Is there any evidence about the involvement of the ventral premotor cortex in processing syntax? Several fMRI studies show a clear relationship between the premotor cortex and the mapping of sequential events. Schubotz and von Cramon (2004) contrasted the observation of biological hand actions with that of abstract motion (movements of geometric shapes). In both conditions 50% of the stimuli failed to attain the normally predictable end state. The task of participants was to indicate whether the actions were performed in a goal-directed manner or not, and whether the abstract motions were performed regularly or not. Results showed that both conditions elicited significant activation within the ventral premotor

[4] In the present paper I exclusively focus on action. Other studies, though, also show the involvement of the sensorimotor system in the mapping of other abstract domains, like the case of time mapped onto spatial metaphors (see Boroditsky, 2000; Boroditsky & Ramscar, 2002).

cortex. In addition, the prediction of biological actions also activated BA 44/45, which is part of the MNS. Schubotz and von Cramon (2004) concluded that their findings point to a basic premotor contribution to the representation or processing of sequentially structured events.

The premotor cortex participation to the mapping of sequential events appears to be even more specifically related to language, as fMRI studies have shown selective activation of premotor BA 44 during syntactic processing of natural language, like when detecting grammatical errors (Embick, Marantz, Miyashita, O'Neil, & Sakai, 2000; Newman, Just, Keller, Roth, & Carpenter, 2003), as well as during the acquisition of artificial linguistic grammars characterized by long-distance, non-local syntactic dependencies (Musso et al., 2003; Tettamanti et al., 2002; see also Friederici, 2004).

According to a widely endorsed view in linguistics, the human language faculty is grounded in the unique ability to process hierarchically structured recursive sequences, configured as "phrase structure grammar" (PSG). The human species is capable of mastering PSG, while apparently other nonhuman primate species are confined to the use of much simpler "finite state grammars" (FSG; see Hauser et al., 2002; Hauser & Fitch, 2004). An fMRI study by Friederici, Bahlmann, Heim, Schubotz, and Anwander (2006) showed that the premotor sector of the inferior frontal gyrus is specifically activated during the processing of an artificial grammar bearing the PSG structure.

On the basis of all these results it seems plausible to hypothesize that "PSG" is the output of a cortical premotor network originally evolved to control/represent the hierarchical structure of goal-related action. When in the course of evolution selective pressures led to the emergence of language, the same neural circuits in charge of controlling the hierarchy of goal-related actions might have been "exploited" to serve the newly acquired function of language syntax. A similar functional overlap between action and language acquisition is indeed present during development: Children parallel their capacity to master hierarchical complexity both in the domain of language and goal-related action (Greenfield, 1991).

My hypothesis can be tested with brain-imaging experiments. The prediction is that premotor regions of the inferior frontal gyrus should be activated by tasks involving the processing of complex PSG-like hierarchical structures, both in the domain of action and language.

THE "NEURAL EXPLOITATION HYPOTHESIS"

Let us now turn to the wider implications of the MNS and embodied simulation for social cognition, by formulating the "neural exploitation hypothesis." My main claim is that key aspects of human social cognition are underpinned by neural exploitation, that is, by the adaptation of neural mechanisms originally evolved for sensorimotor integration, later on also employed to contribute to the neurofunctional architecture of thought and language, while retaining their original functions as well (Gallese & Lakoff, 2005; see also Gallese, 2003c, 2007).

The execution of any complex coordinated action makes use of *at least* two cortical sectors—the premotor cortex and the motor cortex, linked by reciprocal neural connections. The motor cortex to a large extent controls individual synergies—relatively simple movements like extending and flexing the fingers, turning the wrist, flexing and extending the elbow, etc. The role of the premotor cortex is more complex: structuring simple motor behaviors into coordinated motor acts. The premotor cortex must thus provide a "phase structure" to actions and specify the right parameter values in the right phases, e.g., by activating the appropriate clusters of cortico-spinal neurons in the appropriate temporal order. This information is conveyed through neural connections by the premotor cortex to specific regions of the primary motor cortex. Similarly, as exemplified by the MNS, the same premotor circuitry controlling action execution instantiates the embodied simulation of the observed actions of others.

There is therefore a "structuring" neurofunctional architecture within the premotor system that can function according to two modes of operation. In the first operation mode, documented by some of the empirical evidence reviewed here, the circuit structures action execution and action perception, imitation, and imagination, with neural connections to motor effectors and/or other sensory cortical areas. When the action is executed or imitated, the cortico-spinal pathway is activated, leading to the excitation of muscles and the ensuing movements. When the action is observed or imagined, its actual execution is inhibited. The cortical motor network is activated (though, not in all of its components), but action is not produced, it is only simulated.

In the second mode of operation, the same system is decoupled from its action execution/perception functions and can offer its structuring output to non-sensorimotor parts of the brain (Gallese & Lakoff, 2005; Lakoff & Johnson, 1999), among which the dorsal prefrontal cortex most likely plays a pivotal role. When engaged in the second mode of operation, the neurofunctional architecture of the premotor system might contribute to the mastering of the hierarchical structure of language and thought.[5] According to the neural exploitation hypothesis, the "words" of the premotor vocabulary (Rizzolatti et al., 1988) are not only assembled and chained to form intentional "action sentences" (see the discussion of the MNS and action intentions); they can also be assembled and chained to structure language sentences and thoughts.

I am fully aware that at present this is pure speculation. It is certainly possible that Broca's region and the ventral premotor cortex are multifunctional, and that the functional overlap testified by the activation of the same premotor cortical sectors during both syntax-related linguistic and action-related non-linguistic tasks is only apparent because of the poor spatial resolution of the currently available brain-imaging technology (see Grodzinsky, 2006, for a critique of the link between syntax and the motor system). However, it must be stressed that the neural exploitation hypothesis has the merit of offering elements for the neurofunctional grounding of the systematic relation observed between syntax and the activation of premotor sectors of the frontal cortex. We certainly cannot be satisfied by merely stating that syntax resides in Broca's region without explaining why, that is, without a clear understanding of what makes Broca's region a "syntax-committed" cortical area.

To make things even more difficult, one should reconcile the hypothesis on the cognitive continuity of social cognition and the role played by the MNS in its evolution in primates, with the apparent *discontinuity* among primate species in their capacity for processing complex recursive structures. My tentative suggestion is that one important difference between humans and non-human primates could be the higher level of recursivity attained in our species—among other neural systems—by the premotor cortex, of which the MNS is part. By considering the evidence reviewed above, the premotor system is likely one of the most important brain regions where this evolutionary process might have taken place. The neural exploitation hypothesis posits that the increased computational power and degree of recursivity attained by the human brain—and in particular by the premotor cortex of which the MNS is part—might have produced a qualitative leap forward in the capacity to process recursive structures.

Is, however, the computational divide between humans and other primates the only explanation? Is the presence/absence of the computational resources enabling PSG the only explanation of the uniqueness of human language and cognition? Probably not. Further elements must be taken into account. The evolution of social cognition is not a monotonic function, strictly correlating the chronological position a species occupies in phylogeny with its level of social cognitive sophistication. For example, it has recently been reported that European starlings (*Sturnus vulgaris*) recognize acoustic patterns defined by a recursive, self-embedding, context-free grammar. They are also able to classify new patterns defined by the grammar while excluding agrammatical patterns. The authors of this study (Gentner, Fenn, Margoliash, & Nusbaum, 2006) concluded that the capacity to classify sequences from recursive, centre-embedded grammars is not uniquely human.

A further example shows that dogs exhibit social communicative skills in tasks in which apes fail, like finding food on the basis of human pointing or gaze cues (Hare & Tomasello, 2005). The specific quality of the social connectedness among individuals of different species, and among different individuals of the same species within particular contexts, bears consequences for the natural selection of specific social cognitive skills,

[5] Establishing a relation between the motor system and the structure of language is by no means a new idea. Lashley (1951) and Marsden (1984), for example, proposed a link between syntax and the action sequencing function of the basal ganglia. A discussion of the role played in syntax by subcortical motor centers like basal ganglia and cerebellum and their thalamo-cortical connections to the premotor cortex is beyond the limited scope of this paper. However, it is perhaps worth noting that the present hypothesis is—at least partly—compatible with the procedural hypothesis of grammar proposed by Ullman (2001) according to which aspects of grammar are subserved by a frontal/basal-ganglia procedural memory system that also underlies cognitive and motor skills.

and for their actual expression. These examples urge great caution when claims about the uniqueness of human social cognition are made. The fact that a given cognitive trait is uniquely expressed by one particular species does not necessarily imply the qualitative uniqueness of the neural mechanisms underpinning its expression.

CONCLUSIONS

The social cognitive endowments of our species are likely the evolutionary outcome of the natural selection of mechanisms that were not mind reading specific. The neural exploitation hypothesis is parsimonious, because it postulates that the quantitative upgrading of pre-existing neurofunctional architecture can produce a qualitative evolution of different cognitive social skills, language included.

The MNS has been invoked to explain many different aspects of social cognition, like imitation (see Rizzolatti et al., 2001), action and intention understanding (see Rizzolatti, Fogassi, & Gallese, 2006), mind reading (see Gallese, 2007; Gallese & Goldman, 1998), empathy (see de Vignemont & Singer, 2006; Gallese, 2003a,b; Sommerville & Decety, 2006) and its relatedness to aesthetic experience (see Freedberg & Gallese, 2007), and language (see Arbib, 2005; Gallese & Lakoff, 2005; Rizzolatti & Arbib, 1998). The posited importance of the discovery of mirror neurons for a better understanding of social cognition, together with a sort of mediatic overexposure and trivialization, have stirred resistance, criticism and even a sense of irritation in some quarters of the cognitive sciences.

I think a clarification is in order. The relevance of the MNS in so many different aspects of social cognition does not stem from a specific endowment of these neural cells, as if mirror neurons were "magical neurons," so to speak. Mirror neurons derive their property from the specific input–output connections they entertain with other populations of neurons in the brain.

The MNS is involved in so many aspects of social cognition because the activation of the multiple and parallel cortico-cortical circuits instantiating mirror properties underpins a fundamental aspect of social cognition, that is, the multilevel connectedness among individuals within a social group. Such connectedness finds its phylogenetic and ontogenetic roots in the social sharing of situated experiences of action and affect. The MNS provides the neural basis of such sharing. Embodied simulation and the MNS certainly cannot provide a full and thorough account of our sophisticated social cognitive skills. However, I believe that the evidence presented here indicates that embodied mechanisms involving the activation of the motor system, of which the MNS is part, do play a major role in social cognition, language included. A second merit of this hypothesis is that it enables the grounding of social cognition into the experiential domain of existence, so heavily dependent on action (Gallese, 2007; Gallese et al., 2004).

To imbue words with meaning requires a fusion between the articulated sound of words and the shared meaning of the experience of action. Embodied simulation does exactly that. Furthermore, and most importantly, the neural exploitation hypothesis holds that embodied simulation and the MNS provide the means to share communicative intentions and meaning, thus granting the parity requirements of social communication.

By attributing to action the crucial role it plays in experientially grounding the meanings we share with others, the neural exploitation hypothesis stresses that the multi-level comparative study of the premotor system of primate brains is a *necessary* starting point for a better understanding of social cognition, and, more generally, for a better understanding of who we are.

Manuscript received 13 February 2007
Manuscript accepted 30 April 2007
First published online 22 October 2007

REFERENCES

Anderson, M. L. (2003). Embodied cognition: A field guide. *Artificial Intelligence*, *149*, 91–130.

Arbib, M. A. (2005). From monkey-like action recognition to human language: an evolutionary framework for neurolinguistics. *Behavioral and Brain Sciences*, *28*, 105–168.

Aziz-Zadeh, L., Cattaneo, L., Rochat, M., & Rizzolatti, G. (2005). Covert speech arrest induced by rTMS over both motor and nonmotor left hemisphere frontal sites. *Journal of Cognitive Neuroscience*, *17*, 928–938.

Aziz-Zadeh, L., Wilson, S. M., Rizzolatti, G., & Iacoboni, M. (2006). Congruent embodied representations for visually presented actions and linguistic phrases describing actions. *Current Biology*, *16*, 1818–1823.

Bak, T. H., & Hodges, J. R. (2003). "Kissing and dancing"—a test to distinguish the lexical and conceptual contributions to noun/verb and object/action dissociations: Preliminary results in patients with frontotemporal dementia. *Journal of Neurolinguistics, 16*, 169–181.

Bak, T. H., O'Donovan, D. G., Xuereb, J. H., Boniface, S., & Hodges, J. R. (2001). Selective impairment of verb processing associated with pathological changes in Brodmann areas 44 and 45 in the motor neurone disease–dementia–aplasia syndrome. *Brain, 124*, 103–130.

Bak, T. H., Yancopoulou, D., Nestor, P. J., Xuereb, J. H., Spillantini, M. G., Pulvermuller, F., et al. (2006). Clinical, imaging and pathological correlates of a hereditary deficit in verb and action processing. *Brain, 129*, 321–332.

Barrett, L., & Henzi, P. (2005). The social nature of primate cognition. *Proceedings of the Royal Society of London. Series B: Biological Sciences, 272*, 1865–1875.

Barrett, L., Henzi, P., & Rendall, D. (2007). Social brains, simple minds: does social complexity really require cognitive complexity? *Proceedings of the Royal Society of London. Series B: Biological Sciences, 362*(1480), 561–575.

Barsalou, L. W. (1999). Perceptual symbol systems. *Behavioral Brain Science, 22*, 577–609.

Bernardis, P., & Gentilucci, M. (2006). Speech and gesture share the same communication system. *Neuropsychologia, 44*, 178–190.

Bickerton, D. (1995). *Language and human behavior*. Seattle, WA: University of Washington Press.

Bookheimer, S. (2002). Functional MRI of language: New approaches to understanding the cortical organization of semantic processing. *Annual Review of Neuroscience, 25*, 151–188.

Borghi, A. M., Glenberg, A. M., & Kaschak, M. P. (2004). Putting words in perspective. *Memory and Cognition, 32*, 863–873.

Boroditsky, L. (2000). Metaphoric structuring: understanding time through spatial metaphors. *Cognition, 75*, 1–28.

Boroditsky, L., & Ramscar, M. (2002). The roles of body and mind in abstract thought. *Psychological Science, 13*, 185–188.

Buccino, G., Binkofski, F., Fink, G. R., Fadiga, L., Fogassi, L., Gallese, V., et al. (2001). Action observation activates premotor and parietal areas in a somatotopic manner: an fMRI study. *European Journal of Neuroscience, 13*, 400–404.

Buccino, G., Lui, F., Canessa, N., Patteri, I., Lagravinese, G., Benuzzi, F., et al. (2004a). Neural circuits involved in the recognition of actions performed by nonconspecifics: An fMRI study. *Journal of Cognitive Neuroscience, 16*, 114–126.

Buccino, G., Riggio, L., Melli, G., Binkofski, F., Gallese, V., & Rizzolatti, G. (2005). Listening to action-related sentences modulates the activity of the motor system: a combined TMS and behavioral study. *Cognitive Brain Research, 24*, 355–363.

Buccino, G., Vogt, S., Ritzl, A., Fink, G. R., Zilles, K., Freund, H.-J., et al. (2004b). Neural circuits underlying imitation learning of hand actions: an event-related fMRI study. *Neuron, 42*, 323–334.

Chambers, C. G., Tanenhaus, M. K., & Magnuson, J. S. (2004). Actions and affordances in syntactic ambiguity resolution. *Journal of Memory and Language, 30*, 687–696.

Chartrand, T. L., & Bargh, J. A. (1999). The chameleon effect: The perception–behavior link and social interaction. *Journal of Personality & Social Psychology, 76*, 893–910.

Clark, A. (1997). *Being there: Bringing brain, body, and world together again*. Cambridge, MA: MIT Press.

Clark, H. H., & Wilkes-Gibbs, D. (1986). Referring as a collaborative process. *Cognition, 22*, 1–39.

Coltheart, M. (2006). What has functional neuroimaging told us about the mind (so far)? *Cortex, 42*, 323–331.

Corballis, M. C. (2002). *From hand to mouth: The origins of language*. Princeton, NJ: Princeton University Press.

Corballis, M. C. (2004). FOXP2 and the mirror system. *Trends in Cognitive Science, 8*, 95–96.

Costa, V. (2006). *Esperire e parlare. Interpretazione di Heidegger*. Milano, Italy: JACA Book.

de Saussure, F. (1973/1974). *Course in general linguistics* (Trans. W. Baskins). London: Fontana/Collins.

de Vignemont, F., & Singer, T. (2006). The emphatic brain: how, when, and why? *Trends in Cognitive Science, 10*, 435–441.

Embick, D., Marantz, A., Miyashita, Y., O'Neil, W., & Sakai, K. L. (2000). A syntactic specialization for Broca's area. *Proceedings of the National Academy of Sciences USA, 97*, 6150–6154.

Fadiga, L., Craighero, L., Buccino, G., & Rizzolatti, G. (2002). Speech listening specifically modulates the excitability of tongue muscles: a TMS study. *European Journal of Neuroscience, 15*, 399–402.

Fadiga, L., & Gallese, V. (1997). Action representation and language in the brain. *Theoretical Linguistics, 23*, 267–280.

Ferrari, P. F., Gallese, V., Rizzolatti, G., & Fogassi, L. (2003). Mirror neurons responding to the observation of ingestive and communicative mouth actions in the monkey ventral premotor cortex. *European Journal of Neuroscience, 17*, 1703–1714.

Ferrari, P. F., Maiolini, C., Addessi, E., Fogassi, L., & Visalberghi, E. (2005). The observation and hearing of eating actions activates motor programs related to eating in macaque monkeys. *Behavioural Brain Research, 161*, 95–101.

Flombaum, J. L., & Santos, L. R. (2006). Rhesus monkeys attribute perceptions to others. *Current Biology, 15*, 447–452.

Fodor, J. (1983). *The modularity of mind*. Cambridge, MA: MIT Press.

Fodor, J. (1998). *Concepts*. Oxford, UK: Oxford University Press.

Fogassi, L., Ferrari, P. F., Gesierich, B., Rozzi, S., Chersi, F., & Rizzolatti, G. (2005). Parietal lobe: From action organization to intention understanding. *Science, 302*, 662–667.

Freedberg, D., & Gallese, V. (2007). Motion, emotion and empathy in aesthetic experience. *Trends in Cognitive Science, 11*, 197–203.

Friederici, A. D. (2004). Processing local transitions versus long-distance syntactic hierarchies. *Trends in Cognitive Science*, *8*, 245–247.

Friederici, A. D., Bahlmann, J., Heim, S., Schubotz, R. I., & Anwander, A. (2006). The brain differentiates human and non-human grammars: functional localization and structural connectivity. *Proceedings of the National Academy of Sciences USA*, *103*, 2458–2463.

Gallese, V. (2001). The "shared manifold" hypothesis: from mirror neurons to empathy. *Journal of Consciousness Studies*, *8*(5–7), 33–50.

Gallese, V. (2003a). The manifold nature of interpersonal relations: The quest for a common mechanism. *Philosophical Transactions of the Royal Society of London. Series B: Biological Sciences*, *358*, 517–528.

Gallese, V. (2003b). The roots of empathy: The shared manifold hypothesis and the neural basis of intersubjectivity. *Psychopathology*, *36*(4), 171–180.

Gallese, V. (2003c). A neuroscientific grasp of concepts: From control to representation. *Philosophical Transactions of the Royal Society of London. Series B: Biological Sciences*, *358*, 1231–1240.

Gallese, V. (2005a). Embodied simulation: from neurons to phenomenal experience. *Phenomenology and the Cognitive Sciences*, *4*, 23–48.

Gallese, V. (2005b). "Being like me": self–other identity, mirror neurons and empathy. In S. Hurley & N. Chater (Eds.), *Perspectives on imitation: From cognitive neuroscience to social science* (Vol. 1, (pp. 101–118). Cambridge, MA: MIT Press.

Gallese, V. (2006). Intentional attunement: A neurophysiological perspective on social cognition and its disruption in autism. *Brain Research. Cognitive Brain Research*, *1079*, 15–24.

Gallese, V. (2007). Before and below theory of mind: Embodied simulation and the neural correlates of social cognition. *Proceedings of the Royal Society of London. Series B: Biological Sciences*, *362*, 659–669.

Gallese, V., Fadiga, L., Fogassi, L., & Rizzolatti, G. (1996). Action recognition in the premotor cortex. *Brain*, *119*, 593–609.

Gallese, V., Fogassi, L., Fadiga, L., & Rizzolatti, G. (2002). Action representation and the inferior parietal lobule. In W. Prinz & B. Hommel (Eds.), *Attention and performance XIX* (pp. 247–266). Oxford, UK: Oxford University Press.

Gallese, V., & Goldman, A. (1998). Mirror neurons and the simulation theory of mind-reading. *Trends in Cognitive Science*, *12*, 493–501.

Gallese, V., Keysers, C., & Rizzolatti, G. (2004). A unifying view of the basis of social cognition. *Trends in Cognitive Science*, *8*, 396–403.

Gallese, V., & Lakoff, G. (2005). The brain's concepts: The role of the sensorimotor system in reason and language. *Cognitive Neuropsychology*, *22*, 455–479.

Gentilucci, M. (2003). Grasp observation influences speech production. *European Journal of Neuroscience*, *17*, 179–184.

Gentilucci, M., Benuzzi, F., Gangitano, M., & Grimaldi, S. (2001). Grasp with hand and mouth: a kinematic study on healthy subjects. *Journal of Neurophysiology*, *86*, 1685–1699.

Gentilucci, M., Bernardis, P., Crisi, G., & Volta, R. D. (2006). Repetitive transcranial magnetic stimulation of Broca's area affects verbal responses to gesture observation. *Journal of Cognitive Neuroscience*, *18*, 1059–1074.

Gentilucci, M., & Corballis, M. C. (2006). From manual gesture to speech: A gradual transition. *Neuroscience and Biobehavioral Reviews*, *30*, 949–960.

Gentilucci, M., Santunione, P., Roy, A. C., & Stefanini, S. (2004a). Execution and observation of bringing a fruit to the mouth affect syllable pronunciation. *European Journal of Neuroscience*, *19*, 190–202.

Gentilucci, M., Stefanini, S., Roy, A. C., & Santunione, P. (2004b). Action observation and speech production: study on children and adults. *Neuropsychologia*, *42*, 1554–1567.

Gentner, T. Q., Fenn, K. M., Margoliash, D., & Nusbaum, H. C. (2006). Recursive syntactic pattern learning by songbirds. *Nature*, *440*, 1204–1207.

Gibson, J. (1979). *The ecological approach to visual perception*. Hillsdale, NJ: Lawrence Erlbaum Associates, Inc.

Glenberg, A. M. (1997). What memory is for. *Behavioral and Brain Sciences*, *20*, 1–55.

Glenberg, A. M., & Kaschak, M. P. (2002). Grounding language in action. *Psychonomic Bulletin & Review*, *9*, 558–565.

Glenberg, A. M., & Robertson, D. A. (2000). Symbol grounding and meaning: A comparison of high-dimensional and embodied theories of meaning. *Journal of Memory and Language*, *43*, 379–401.

Goldberg, A. E. (2003). Constructions: A new theoretical approach to language. *Trends in Cognitive Science*, *7*, 219–224.

Goldin-Meadow, S. (1999). The role of gesture in communication and thinking. *Trends in Cognitive Science*, *3*, 419–429.

Greenfield, P. M. (1991). Language, tools, and brain: The ontogeny and phylogeny of hierarchically organized sequential behavior. *Behavioral and Brain Sciences*, *14*(4), 531–550.

Grodzinsky, Y. (2006). The language faculty, Broca's region, and the mirror system. *Cortex*, *42*, 464–468.

Hare, B., & Tomasello, M. (2005). Human-like social skills in dogs? *Trends in Cognitive Science*, *9*, 439–444.

Hare, B., Call, J., Agnetta, B., & Tomasello, M. (2000). Chimpanzees know what conspecifics do and do not see. *Animal Behavior*, *59*, 771–785.

Hauk, O., Johnsrude, I., & Pulvermüller, F. (2004). Somatotopic representation of action words in human motor and premotor cortex. *Neuron*, *41*(2), 301–307.

Hauser, M. D., Chomsky, N., & Fitch, W. T. (2002). The faculty of language: What is it, who has it, and how did it evolve? *Science*, *298*, 1569–1579.

Hauser, M. D., & Fitch, W. T. (2004). Computational constraints on syntactic processing in a non-human primate. *Science*, *303*, 377–380.

Heidegger, M. (1962). *Being and time* (Trans. J. Macquarrie & E. Robinson). New York: Harper & Row. (Originally published 1927)

Heidegger, M. (1985). *History of the concept of time* (Trans. Theodore Kisiel). Bloomington, IN: Indiana University Press. (Originally published 1925)

Heidegger, M. (1995). *The fundamental concepts of metaphysics. World, finitude, solitude* (Trans. W. McNeill & N. Walker). Bloomington, IN: Indiana University Press. (Originally published 1929)

Hjelmslev, J. (1959). *Essais linguistiques.* Copenhagen, Denmark: Linguistic Circle of Copenhagen.

Iacoboni, M., Molnar-Szakacs, I., Gallese, V., Buccino, G., Mazziotta, J., & Rizzolatti, G. (2005). Grasping the intentions of others with one's owns mirror neuron system. *PLOS Biology, 3*, 529–535.

Iacoboni, M., Woods, R. P., Brass, M., Bekkering, H., Mazziotta, J. C., & Rizzolatti, G. (1999). Cortical mechanisms of human imitation. *Science, 286*, 2526–2528.

Iverson, J. M., & Goldin-Meadow, S. (2005). Gesture paves the way for language development. *Psychological Science, 16*, 367–371.

Jacob, P., & Jeannerod, M. (2004). The motor theory of social cognition: a critique. *Trends in Cognitive Neuroscience, 9*, 21–25.

Kemmerer, D., & Tranel, D. (2000). A double dissociation between linguistic and perceptual representations of spatial relationships. *Cognitive Neuropsychology, 17*, 393–414.

Kemmerer, D., & Tranel, D. (2003). A double dissociation between the meanings of action verbs and locative prepositions. *Neurocase, 9*, 421–435.

Knoblich, G., & Jordan, J. S. (2002). The mirror system and joint action. In M. I. Stamenov & V. Gallese (Eds.), *Mirror neurons and the evolution of brain and language* (pp. 115–124). Amsterdam: John Benjamins.

Kohler, E., Keysers, C., Umiltà, M. A., Fogassi, L., Gallese, V., & Rizzolatti, G. (2002). Hearing sounds, understanding actions: Action representation in mirror neurons. *Science, 297*, 846–848.

Lakoff, G. (1987). *Women, fire, and dangerous things: What categories reveal about the mind.* Chicago: University of Chicago Press.

Lakoff, G., & Johnson, M. (1980). *Metaphors we live by.* Chicago: University of Chicago Press.

Lakoff, G., & Johnson, M. (1999). *Philosophy in the flesh.* New York: Basic Books.

Lashley, K. S. (1951). The problem of serial order in behavior. In L. A. Jeffress (Ed.), *Cerebral mechanisms in behavior* (pp. 112–146). New York: Wiley.

Marsden, C. D. (1984). Which motor disorder in Parkinson's disease indicates the true motor function of the basal ganglia? In *Functions of the basal ganglia* (Ciba Foundation Symposium, 108, pp. 225–241). London: Pittman.

Masataka, N. (2001). Why early linguistic milestones are delayed in children with Williams syndrome: late onset of hand banging as a possible rate-limiting constraint on the emergence of canonical babbling. *Developmental Science, 4*, 158–164.

Matlock, T. (2004). Fictive motion as cognitive simulation. *Memory and Cognition, 32*, 1389–1400.

McGuigan, F. J., & Dollins, A. B. (1989). Patterns of covert speech behavior and phonetic coding. *Pavlovian Journal of Biological Science, 24*, 19–26.

Merleau-Ponty, M. (1964). *Signs.* (R. C. McClearly, Trans.). Evanston, IL: Northwestern University Press. (Original work published 1960).

Musso, M., Moro, A., Glauche, V., Rijntjes, M., Reichenbach, J., Buchel, C., et al. (2003). Broca's area and the language instinct. *Nature Neuroscience, 6*, 774–781.

Newman, S. D., Just, M. A., Keller, T. A., Roth, J., & Carpenter, P. A. (2003). Differential effects of syntactic and semantic processing on the subregions of Broca's area. *Cognitive Brain Research, 16*, 297–307.

Niedenthal, P. M., Barsalou, L. W., Winkielman, P., Krauth-Gruber, S., & Ric, F. (2005). Embodiment in attitudes, social perception, and emotion. *Personality and Social Psychology Review, 9*, 184–211.

Nishitani, N., Schurmann, M., Amunts, K., & Hari, R. (2005). Broca's region: From action to language. *Physiology, 20*, 60–69.

Pacherie, E., & Dokic, J. (2006). From mirror neurons to joint action. *Cognitive Systems Research, 7*, 101–112.

Paukner, A., Anderson, J. R., Borelli, E., Visalberghi, E., & Ferrari, P. F. (2005). Macaques (*Macaca nemestrina*) recognize when they are being imitated. *Biology Letters, 1*, 219–222.

Pickering, M. J., & Garrod, S. (2004). Toward a mechanistic psychology of dialogue. *Behavioral Brain Science, 27*, 169–226.

Pinker, S., & Jackendoff, R. (2005). The faculty of language: what's special about it? *Cognition, 95*, 201–236.

Povinelli, D., & Vonk, J. (2003). Chimpanzee minds: Suspiciously human? *Trends in Cognitive Science, 7*, 157–160.

Povinelli, D. J., & Eddy, T. J. (1996). What young chimpanzees know about seeing. *Monographs of the Society for Research in Child Development, 61*, 1–152.

Pulvermüller, F. (1999). Word in the brain's language. *Behavioral Brain Sciences, 22*, 253–336.

Pulvermüller, F. (2002). *The neuroscience of language.* Cambridge, UK: Cambridge University Press.

Pulvermüller, F., Härle, M., & Hummel, F. (2000). Neurophysiological distinction of verb categories. *Neuroreport, 11*, 2789–2793.

Pulvermüller, F., Shtyrov, Y., & Ilmoniemi, R. J. (2003). Spatio-temporal patterns of neural language processing: an MEG study using minimum-norm current estimates. *NeuroImage, 20*, 1020–1025.

Pylyshyn, Z. W. (1984). *Computation and cognition: Toward a foundation for cognitive science.* Cambridge, MA: MIT Press.

Ricouer, P. (1991). *From text to action. Essays in hermeneutics, II* (Trans. K. Blamey & J. B. Tompson). Evanston, IL: Northwestern University Press. (Originally published 1986)

Rizzolatti, G., & Arbib, M. A. (1998). Language within our grasp. *Trends in Neuroscience, 21*, 188–194.

Rizzolatti, G., Camarda, R., Fogassi, M., Gentilucci, M., Luppino, G., & Matelli, M. (1988). Functional organization of inferior area 6 in the macaque monkey: II. Area F5 and the control of distal movements. *Experimental Brain Research, 71*, 491–507.

Rizzolatti, G., & Craighero, L. (2004). The mirror neuron system. *Annual Review of Neuroscience, 27*, 169–192.

Rizzolatti, G., Fadiga, L., Gallese, V., & Fogassi, L. (1996). Premotor cortex and the recognition of motor actions. *Cognitive Brain Research, 3*, 131–141.

Rizzolatti, G., Fogassi, L., & Gallese, V. (2001). Neurophysiological mechanisms underlying the understanding and imitation of action. *Nature Neuroscience Reviews, 2*, 661–670.

Rizzolatti, G., Fogassi, L., & Gallese, V. (2006). Mirrors in the mind. *Scientific American, 295*(5), 54–61.

Santos, L. R., Nissen, A. G., & Ferrugia, J. A. (2006). Rhesus monkeys, *Macaca mulatta*, know what others can and cannot hear. *Animal Behavior, 71*, 1175–1181.

Schubotz, R. I., & von Cramon, D. Y. (2004). Sequences of abstract nonbiological stimuli share ventral premotor cortex with action observation and imagery. *Journal of Neuroscience, 24*, 5467–5474.

Sommerville, J. A., & Decety, J. (2006). Weaving the fabric of social interaction: articulating developmental psychology and cognitive neuroscience in the domain of motor cognition. *Psychonmic Bulletin and Review, 13*, 179–200.

Subiaul, F., Cantlon, J. F., Holloway, R. L., & Terrace, H. S. (2004). Cognitive imitation in rhesus macaque. *Science, 305*, 407–410.

Tettamanti, M., Alkadhi, H., Moro, A., Perani, D., Kollias, S., & Weniger, D. (2002). Neural correlates for the acquisition of natural language syntax. *NeuroImage, 17*, 700–709.

Tettamanti, M., Buccino, G., Saccuman, M. C., Gallese, V., Danna, M., Scifo, P., et al. (2005). Listening to action-related sentences activates fronto-parietal motor circuits. *Journal of Cognitive Neuroscience, 17*, 273–281.

Tomasello, M., Carpenter, M., Call, J., Behne, T., & Moll, H. (2005). Understanding and sharing intentions: the origins of cultural cognition. *Behavioral and Brain Sciences, 28*, 675–691.

Ullman, M. T. (2001). A neurocognitive perspective on language: The declarative/procedural model. *Nature Reviews Neuroscience, 2*, 717–726.

Umiltà, M. A., Kohler, E., Gallese, V., Fogassi, L., Fadiga, L., Keysers, C., et al. (2001). "I know what you are doing": a neurophysiological study. *Neuron, 32*, 91–101.

Watkins, K. E., & Paus, T. (2004). Modulation of motor excitability during speech perception: the role of Broca's area. *Journal of Cognitive Neuroscience, 16*, 978–987.

Watkins, K. E., Strafella, A. P., & Paus, T. (2003). Seeing and hearing speech excites the motor system involved in speech production. *Neuropsychologia, 41*(8), 989–994.

Wildgruber, D., Ackermann, H., Klose, U., Kardatzki, B., & Grodd, W. (1996). Functional lateralization of speech production at primary motor cortex: An fMRI study. *Neuroreport, 7*, 2791–2795.

Wilson, S. M., Saygin, A. P., Sereno, M. I., & Iacoboni, M. (2004). Listening to speech activates motor areas involved in speech production. *Nature Neuroscience, 7*, 701–702.

SOCIAL NEUROSCIENCE, 2008, 3 (3–4), 334–347

Psychology Press
Taylor & Francis Group

The infant mirror neuron system studied with high density EEG

Pär Nyström
Uppsala University, Uppsala, Sweden

The mirror neuron system has been suggested to play a role in many social capabilities such as action understanding, imitation, language and empathy. These are all capabilities that develop during infancy and childhood, but the human mirror neuron system has been poorly studied using neurophysiological measures. This study measured the brain activity of 6-month-old infants and adults using a high-density EEG net with the aim of identifying mirror neuron activity. The subjects viewed both goal-directed movements and non-goal-directed movements. An independent component analysis was used to extract the sources of cognitive processes. The desynchronization of the mu rhythm in adults has been shown to be a marker for activation of the mirror neuron system and was used as a criterion to categorize independent components between subjects. The results showed significant mu desynchronization in the adult group and significantly higher ERP activation in both adults and 6-month-olds for the goal-directed action observation condition. This study demonstrate that infants as young as 6 months display mirror neuron activity and is the first to present a direct ERP measure of the mirror neuron system in infants.

INTRODUCTION

The discovery of the mirror neuron system in monkeys (Di Pellegrino, Fadiga, Fogassi, Gallese, & Rizzolatti., 1992; Gallese, Fadiga, Fogassi, & Rizzolatti, 1996; Rizzolatti, Fadiga, Fogassi, & Gallese, 1996a) started a search for its human homologue. As the methods differ between human and comparative studies, a range of non-invasive neurophysiological methodologies have been used in the exploration of the human mirror system, such as transcranial magnetic stimulation (TMS), functional magnetic resonance imaging (fMRI), magnetoencephalography (MEG), electroencephalography (EEG) and others (Buccino et al., 2004; Cochin, Barthelemy, Roux, & Martineau, 1999; Decety et al., 1997; Fadiga, Craighero, & Olivier, 2005; Fadiga, Fogassi, Pavesi, & Rizzolatti, 1995; Grafton, Arbib, Fadiga, & Rizzolatti, 1996; Grèzes, Armony, Rowe, & Passingham, 2003; Grèzes, Costes, & Decety, 1998; Hari et al., 1998; Johnson-Frey et al., 2003; Nishitani & Hari, 2000; Rizzolatti et al., 1996b; Strafella & Paus, 2000). Behavioral measures, such as gaze tracking, have also been used (Falck-Ytter, Gredebäck, & von Hofsten, 2006; Flanagan & Johansson, 2003). These studies together form a solid support for the existence of a mirror neuron system in humans.

The characteristics of the mirror neuron system suggest that it plays a role in social functions such as language, gestural communication, imitation learning, action understanding

Correspondence should be addressed to: Pär Nyström, Department of Psychology, Box 1225, Uppsala University, 751 42 Uppsala, Sweden. E-mail: par.nystrom@psyk.uu.se

This study was supported by grants (KR) from the Swedish Research Council (421–2003–1508) and the EU integrated project FP6–004370 (Robotcub).

The author acknowledges the contribution of Robert Oostenveld for making the DIPFIT software available, as well as the whole EEGLAB developer group. Luciano Fadiga and Laila Craighero contributed with valuable discussions and Claes von Hofsten, Kerstin Rosander and Clara Schmitow assisted with important improvements and great support.

www.psypress.com/socialneuroscience DOI:10.1080/17470910701563665

and the understanding of others' emotions (Buccino et al., 2004; Fadiga & Craighero, 2004; Gallese, Keysers, & Rizzolatti, 2004; Kohler et al., 2002; Leslie, Johnson-Frey, & Grafton, 2004; Rizzolatti & Craighero, 2004). These are all functions that are critically important for adults and emerge in infancy and early childhood. This makes it important to investigate the development of the mirror neuron system in infants. For example: when does the mirror system develop in infants, and how is the development of the mirror system related to the development of the infant's own action repertoire? Asking these questions has a twofold purpose: (1) to improve our knowledge of social and motor development, and (2) to learn more about the functioning of the mirror neuron system.

The most direct way of answering these questions would be to investigate normal infants using neurophysiological methods. However, no previous study has directly investigated the maturation of the neural networks involved in the mirror system in infants. One obvious reason is that most neurophysiological methods are unsuitable for infant studies because of ethical problems and/or the physical properties of the equipment (loud noise, restraining of subjects, specific motor responses, etc.). Fortunately, EEG does not suffer from these shortcomings. By using a high-density electrode net it is possible to record brain activity from infants using the same procedure as with adults. Another advantage is that EEG is directly comparable to previous studies done on adults that show responses to mirror neuron system activity.

The first connection between action observation and changes in the EEG was found by Gastaut and Bert (1954). They discovered that a 10–13 Hz rhythm was desynchronized in adults when they observed moving people (a film of boxing). The finding was confirmed and related to the "mu wave" that desynchronizes during motor planning and performance. It has also been shown that the mu rhythm desynchronizes when subjects view object-directed reaching compared to reaches into thin air (Muthukumaraswamy, Johnson, & McNair, 2004), and that this change is related specifically to goal-directed actions (Muthukumaraswamy & Johnson, 2004a). This is important because it associates the mu rhythm with the mirror neuron system, which has been suggested to be tuned to goal-directed actions rather than just movements. A mirror neuron that responds to a grasping movement typically does not respond to the same movement intended for scratching or grooming (Fadiga et al., 2005; Fogassi et al., 2005). Another study showed that mu ($\sim$10 Hz) and beta wave ($\sim$20 Hz) were suppressed in the motor cortex during action observation, but had an increased rebound after approximately 500–800 ms (Muthukumaraswamy & Johnson, 2004b). The same response during performance and observation has been measured and localized to the sensorimotor cortex (mu rhythm) and premotor areas (beta rhythm) by MEG (Hari & Salmelin, 1997; Nishitani & Hari, 2000). As the mirror neuron system is the only network that has been identified to be active in this area of the cortex during both performance and observation of actions, it is suggested that mu and beta wave suppression to observed actions could be used as a selective measure of mirror neuron system functioning (Oberman et al., 2005).

Although debatable, there is evidence that the mu wave is also present in infants, but at lower amplitude and lower frequency (Stroganova, Orekhova, & Posikera, 1999). Stroganova et al. found that the mu rhythm was 7.03 ± 0.47 Hz at 8 months and 7.42 ± 0.46 Hz at 11 months. Another longitudinal study estimated the mu frequency to be 6–7 Hz at 5 months, 7–8 Hz at 10 months, 8 Hz at 14–24 months, and 9 Hz at 4 years of age (Marshall, Bar-Haim, & Fox, 2002). However, in none of theses studies was the functional connection between the mu rhythm and action observation addressed.

The present study investigated infants' functional EEG response of resting mu and beta wave to observed object motion, non-goal-directed actions and goal-directed actions. By unmixing the combined cognitive sources recorded by the EEG with an independent component analysis, this study attempted to extract components that reflect mirror neuron activity. As recommended by Babiloni et al. (1999), both the frequency response and the event-related potential (ERP) were investigated, as these methods may provide complementary information. For the following reasons 6-month-old infants were considered to be a suitable study group. At this age infants have a relatively mature cortical response to visual motion (Braddick, Birtles, Wattam-Bell, & Atkinson, 2005; Rosander, Nyström, Gredebäck, & von Hofsten, 2007). They are also attentive for longer periods, and interested in many kinds of stimuli. But most importantly, at 6 months of age (and not much younger) infants can reach and grasp themselves in a goal-directed manner. As the mirror neurons respond in the same way to observed action as to self-performed actions, it is crucial that the actions shown can be performed by the infants. Following this, the hypothesis is that there will be functional differences in the mu or beta wave response or in the ERP as a result of mirror neuron functioning at 6 months of age.

PROCEDURES AND METHODS

Subjects

A total of 34 infants and 23 adults came to the lab but 13 subjects were excluded due to fussing, imitation of stimuli movements (9 infants) or high impedance (4 adults). After artifact rejection 19 infants and 15 adults passed all exclusion criteria and were fully analyzed. The infants were all born at term and were 24–26 weeks old, and all of them successfully grasped objects that were placed in front of them. The adults were between 20 and 30 years old. All parents except 5 and all adults except 2 were right-handed. Adult subjects and parents of the infants were informed about the experiment upon arrival at the lab and a written consent was signed in accordance with the Helsinki Declaration. The experiment was approved by the Ethics Committee at Uppsala University.

Procedure

An 128-electrode geodesic EEG net (EGI Corp., Eugene, OR, USA) was used and adjusted so that the reference electrode (at vertex) and the ear references were correctly placed. After having attached the net to the infant's head, he or she was immediately positioned in front of a stimulus monitor at a distance of approximately 60 cm. At this distance the display covered 40° visual angle horizontally and 28° vertically. The infants sat in a special baby seat (Bumbo, South Africa) that supported them in an upright sitting position that avoided leaning on the net. The light was switched off during the experiment in order to make the surrounding less distracting. While data was collected the behavior of the infant was recorded by a web camera placed on the top of the display monitor for subsequent removal of inattentive periods. The parent and two experimenters were always in the room. When the adult subjects were measured they sat in front of the monitor, at 60 cm distance, watching the same stimuli as the infant group after an impedance control and adjustment of high impedance channels (>80 kΩ).

Stimuli

The stimuli consisted of 4 short video clips, one for each condition. The video clip also synchronized the stimulus monitor with the EEG measurements by a local white flash sequence that triggered an optic sensor. The optic sensor covered the flashes from the subjects' view, and had a response time of approximately 4 μs, which allowed for accurate timing of visual impression and EEG time-locking. The first condition showed a static colored dot (dot diameter = 2 cm) against a black and white background of artificial clouds. The second condition showed the colored dot moving against the static black and white background. The third condition showed the torso of a person that reached for a colored object in a goal-directed manner. The fourth condition showed the same model with the hand withdrawing from a position near the object. This condition was included as a non-goal-directed action control. The face of the model was hidden to avoid distraction and activation from face recognition. All the fingers of the model's hand were visible (bounding box = 2×2 cm), and stood out against the darker background. A grasping action was chosen in the goal-directed condition for two reasons. First, mirror neurons devoted to grasping are the most common ones in area F5 of the macaque and presumably also quite common in human BAs 6–44 (Fadiga & Craighero, 2004). Second, this is the kind of action that gives the most reliable desynchronization in adult humans (Hari & Salmelin, 1997; Oberman et al., 2005). All video clips had durations between 3 and 3.3 s, and all of them started with the stimulus being stationary. In the static condition the image remained stationary, and in the other conditions the motion started after a random 0.5–0.8 s period to avoid an expectation response. In the reaching condition the hand touched the object exactly 1 s after motion onset. Video clips with dots and hands were interleaved. This was done to make the display more attractive, and to elicit a strong visually evoked potential when the clips changed scenes as a control of signal quality. A whole session took 6.5 minutes, and included 32 trials of each condition.

EEG measurement and analysis

The brain electric potentials were recorded relative to the vertex, at 250 Hz. The analog filter (hardware filter, elliptical) used was 0.1 to 100 Hz (EGI Netstation, Eugene, OR). The recommendations of Picton et al. (2000) and measurement routines suggested by Johnson et al. (2001) were followed as closely as possible. After the experiment the data were transferred to the EEGLAB toolbox (version 5.03; Delorme & Makeig, 2004) in the Matlab environment for off-line analysis. The video of the subject was inspected and longer intervals of inattention (> 10 s) were excluded from further analysis, and shorter periods were rejected in an artifact-rejection routine (described below). Even though the net was properly placed 26 channels at the lowest rows of the net often suffered from high impedance or did not keep in contact with the skin. These channels were removed from all subjects, leaving 101 channels for analysis. The remaining data were segmented into trials (from −0.4 s to 2.0 s after timelock). The data was then band-pass filtered at 0.5 to 30 Hz and the artifact-rejection routine for dense EEG arrays described by Junghöfer, Elbert, Tucker, and Rockstroh (2000) was used. In short, this procedure performs rejection of bad sensors and bad trials based on outliers of max amplitude, max deviation, and max standard deviation before re-referencing to average reference. This minimizes spreading of bad data when re-referencing. The artifact-rejection procedure then rejects bad sensors and bad trials of the average referenced data. In the original procedure remaining bad data from single trials in single channels are spline interpolated, but as the following independent component analysis relies on independent variance between sensors this step was omitted and bad channels and bad trials were simply removed. Subjects with less than 10 trials in any condition or more than 10 rejected channels were removed (6 infants, 4 adults).

A natural-gradient logistic infomax independent component analysis was performed on the data (the runica algorithm; Makeig et al., 1997), which resulted in as many independent components as remaining channels minus one for each subject. Artifacts coming from eye movements and eye blinks were minimized by subtracting eye-related independent components from the raw EEG. Components were automatically identified as eye related if their scalp maps showed a strong far-frontal projection (this was done by normalizing the component weights so that the max absolute weight was 1 and checking if only frontal electrodes had values above 0.5). The pruned raw EEG was then high-pass filtered at 2 Hz in order to prevent the independent component analysis from separating the low frequencies from mu rhythm components. The pruned and filtered data were considered clean from artifacts and trained in a second independent component analysis as recommended by the EEGLAB documentation. The resulting weights were applied to the original dataset pruned from eye component activation. This double training procedure was done to retain low frequencies in independent components with mu rhythm properties.

At the end of the preprocessing the standard deviation of each component's trials max absolute amplitudes was calculated. Trials with max absolute amplitudes greater than 3 standard deviations were excluded from further analysis, as they were considered outliers. The data was also detrended by removing the best straight-line fit linear trend from each trial. Finally a *z*-transform was used to normalize each component's amplitudes using all data points of the component, thereby including all conditions in the same transform.

As mirror neuron activity was expected to be separated into one or a few components in each subject, these components had to be identified and selected from each subject. The fundamental "functional topography" approach (Kuhlman, 1980) infers that identification of rhythmic EEG components should be based on 3 main criteria: (1) frequency characteristics; (2) spatial distribution over the cortex; and (3) functional reactivity to specific conditions. The identification of mu rhythm components was implemented by ordering the components in decreasing order of variance accounted for by their projections onto the scalp, and then selecting the first component with a frequency power peak between 3–8 Hz in infants and 7–15 Hz in adults (determined by a power spectral density estimate via Welch's method, with hamming windows of 256 samples length and 128 samples overlap). A second criterion was that the mu power of the static dot condition should be higher than the mu power of all conditions. Examples of the unmixing of

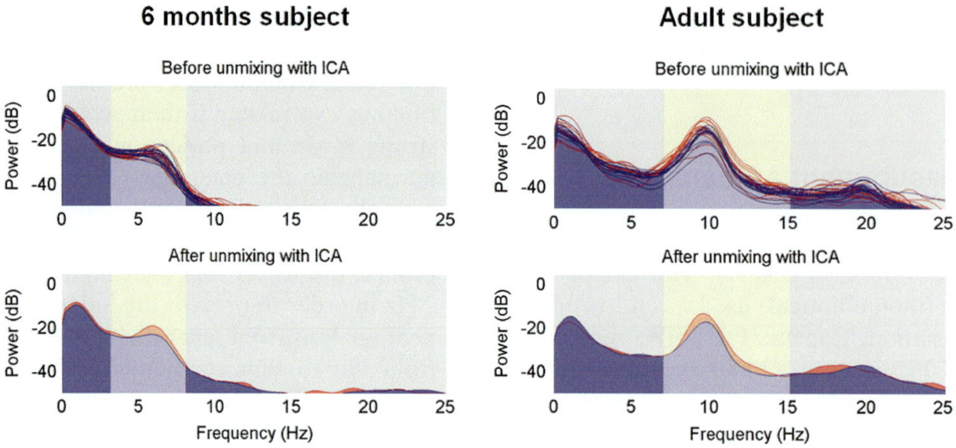

Figure 1. Examples of signal before and after independent component analysis, with logarithmic mean values of the spectral power densities (0 dB means 1 $\mu V^2/Hz$). Blue colors are mean mu rhythm power of all conditions; red colors are mean of the static dot condition. Thin lines in top plots show individual channels of the ROIs used by Muthukumaraswamy and Johnson (2004a) that cover areas around standard C3 and C4 electrode positions. Information as in the bottom plots was used to select the first desynchronizing component from each subject (the critical frequency range is highlighted).

signals using ICA and the resulting information that was used for component selection is found in Figure 1.

By using this strategy it is still valid to compare the moving-dot and action-observation conditions with each other in the selected components. Visual inspection was used to control the quality of the selected components. Components with irregular scalp projections or ERP images were to be identified and discarded, but no such components were identified. The identified mu peaks in the infant group had a mean frequency of 5.4 Hz (standard deviation 0.8 Hz), and the corresponding values for the adult group was 10.4 Hz (standard deviation 1.1 Hz).

To statistically test differences between conditions three measures was used. First, the power of the individual mu frequency was calculated for each subject and condition. The time interval of the frequency analysis was between 0.8 and 1.8 s after motion onset, which covers the time period when the hand reached the object in the goal-directed condition. Since previous time/frequency analyses have shown that mu responses occur mainly after the hand touches the object (Muthukumaraswamy & Johnson, 2004b), the interval included more time after than before completion of the reach. The wide length of 1 s was chosen to capture the responses from both adults and infants with varying response latency. The power values were transformed to decibel values relative to the mean power of all conditions in each component. The goal-directed and non-goal-directed conditions were then compared using paired *t*-tests. Second, time frequency spectrograms were calculated for the goal-directed and non-goal-directed conditions using a short time Fourier transform, with hamming windows of 128 samples length and 124 samples overlap. The frequencies of interest ranged from 0 to 30 Hz, and the time points ranged from 0 to 1.9 s relative timelock, which resulted in power maps with 119×14 time/frequency points for each condition. The power maps were transformed to decibel change from a baseline computed as the mean power from both conditions in each frequency band. The amplitude maps were compared using pixel-wise paired *t*-tests. As multiple significance test inflates the risk of type I errors only groups of 20 or more consecutive tests with $p < .05$ were considered significant. Third, the ERPs from the selected component was mean averaged for each condition, baseline corrected (from $-.4$ s to timelock) and low-pass filtered at 10 Hz to remove high frequencies that added noise variability to the signal. Comparisons between all conditions were performed for each of the 600 time points using paired *t*-tests. Again, only groups of 20 or more consecutive tests with $p < .05$ were considered significant as multiple significance tests inflate the risk of type I errors.

As a final step, the selected components were fitted in a spherical model using the dipole source localization algorithm included in EEGLAB (see Scherg, 1990, for technical details on dipole source localization). The head circumference for adults ranged from 55–60 cm in adults and 40–46 cm in infants. The parameters for scalp

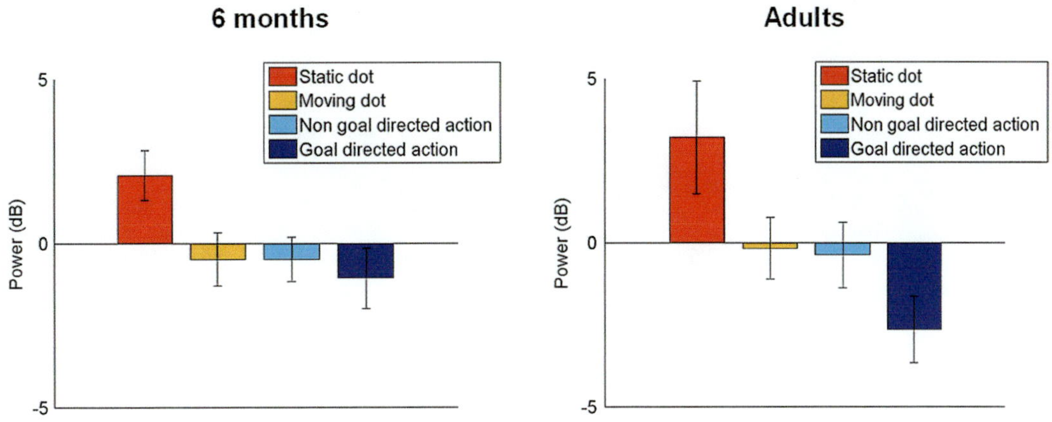

Figure 2. Mu rhythm power in the four conditions in decibel relative all conditions' mean power. Error bars indicate confidence intervals of 95%. In the adult group the goal-directed action condition differs significantly from the non-goal-directed action and moving dot condition ($p < .05$). The static dot condition is significantly higher than the other conditions in both groups.

thickness and conductance were adopted from Grieve, Emerson, Fifer, Isler, and Stark (2003).

RESULTS

Mu power

In the mu power analysis, illustrated in Figure 2, the adult group shows a significant difference between the goal-directed and the non-goal-directed action observation conditions ($p < .05$). There is also a significant difference between the goal-directed condition and the moving-dot condition ($p < .05$). The infants show the same pattern of desynchronization as adults between conditions, but the difference is not significant between non-goal-directed and goal-directed condition ($p = .33$). The mu power differences between the moving dot and the non-goal-directed action is very small in both groups, with values between the static-dot condition and goal-directed condition values.

Time-frequency response

Again, in the more detailed time-frequency analysis, only the adult group show significant desynchronization between the goal-directed and the non-goal-directed condition (paired *t*-tests, $p < .05$). The desynchronization was restricted to the mu frequency band as illustrated in Figure 3, between 4.0 and 13.7 Hz. The onset of desynchronization started approximately when the hand reached the object, but became significant about 0.1 s afterwards (and stayed significant in the time interval 1.1–1.4 s after timelock). No significant desynchronization was found in the beta band, and no significant desynchronization was found in the infant group.

ERPs

The results from the infant group ERPs are illustrated in Figure 4 and the adult group in Figure 5. Both groups showed significant

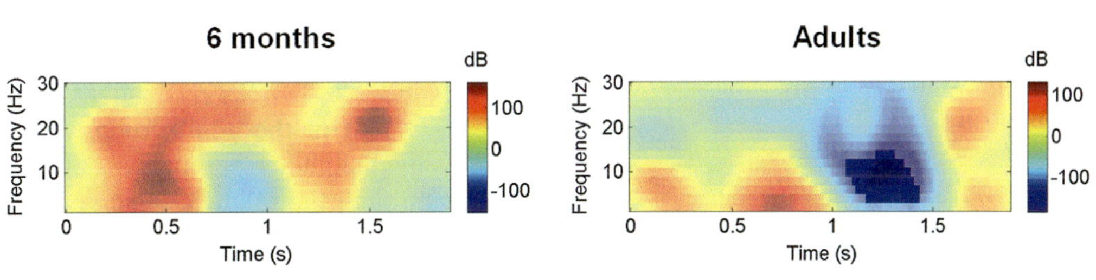

Figure 3. Time frequency spectrogram differences (goal-directed–non-goal-directed conditions) showing desynchronization in blue colors. Pixel-wise statistical probability maps are overlaid and highlight significant areas ($p < .05$). Non-significant values are shown in faint colors. The color scale shows decibel change from baseline (computed as the mean power from both conditions in each frequency band).

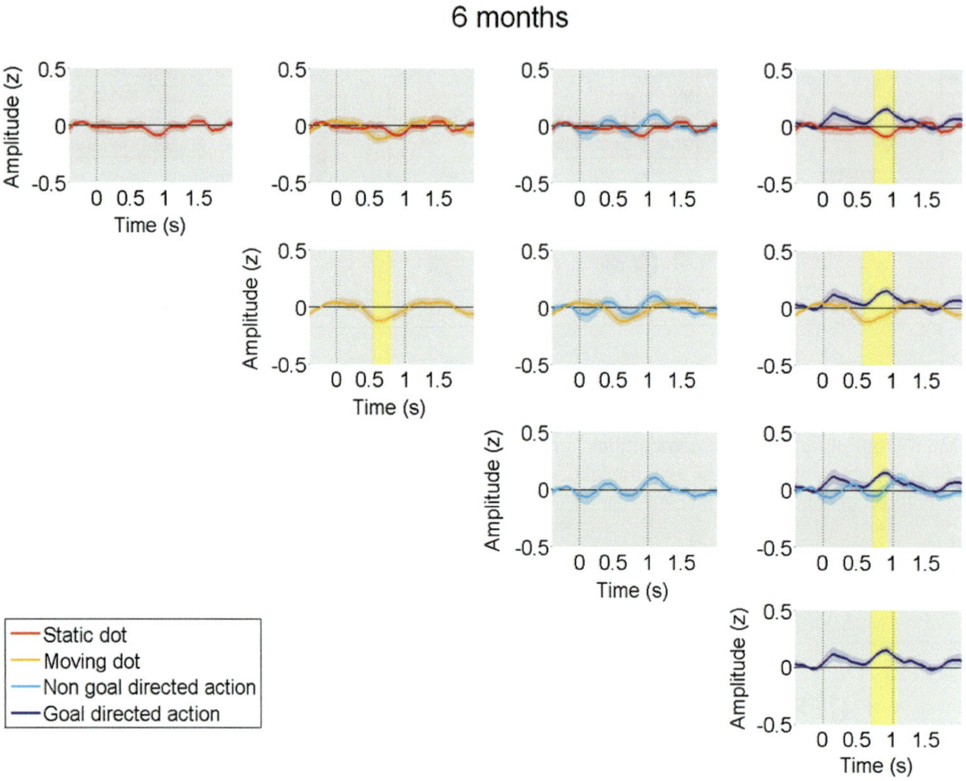

Figure 4. Infant ERPs with z-transformed amplitudes (μV) within subjects. Single ERP traces are tested sample-wise against zero using t-tests, double ERP traces are tested against each other using paired t-tests. Significant intervals ($p < .05$) are highlighted in yellow. Shaded areas are standard error of ERP trace. Dotted lines mark timelock (motion onset, time = 0 s) and time when hand reached object in the goal-directed condition (time = 1 s).

differences between the goal-directed and the other conditions within 0.5 s before the hand reached the object (paired t-tests, $p < .05$). Both groups showed significant differences after the hand touched the object when compared to the static dot condition, and the infant group when compared to a zero mean. The significant intervals in the adult group started marginally earlier (latency differences ranging from 0.1 s to 0.2 s). The adult intervals were also longer (length differences ranging from −0.1 s to 0.2 s) compared to the infant group.

The infant group also showed significant activation in the moving-dot condition compared to a zero mean approximately in the interval 0.6 s to 0.8 s after motion onset.

Source localization

All 16 of the adults' components could be fitted with a residual variance below 20%. The infant skull is thinner than the adults' and gives less distortion of the EEG signal, which allows for easier dipole fitting. However, infants have much more variability in the signal, and only 15 of the 19 infant subjects' components could be fitted with a residual variance below 20%. The mean residual variance of the fitted components was 8.1% in the infant group (standard deviation of 4.1%) and 4.5% in the adult group (standard deviation 2.0%). The localization of dipoles, plotted on the mean component power projections, is illustrated in Figure 6. The mean Talairach coordinates for the infant group were −9, −3, 16 XYZ (standard deviation 23, 12, 11 XYZ) and −6, 1, 7 XYZ (standard deviation 15, 15, 13 XYZ) in the adult group, which locates the individual dipoles roughly along a coronal plane through the rolandic regions. Dipoles were located in both hemispheres, as indicated by the standard deviation, with an inclination to the left hemisphere (8 of 15 dipoles in infants, 10 of 16 dipoles in adults).

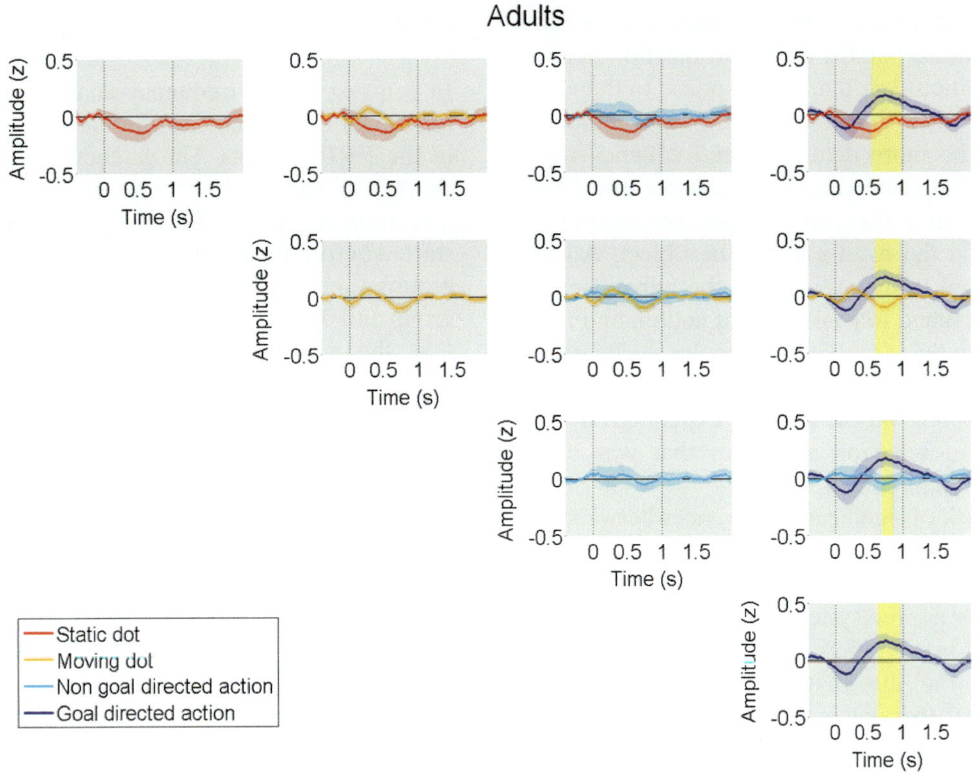

Figure 5. Adult ERPs with z-transformed amplitudes (μV) within subjects. Single ERP traces are tested sample-wise against zero using t-tests, double ERP traces are tested against each other using paired t-tests. Significant intervals ($p < .05$) are highlighted in yellow. Shaded areas are standard error of ERP trace. Dotted lines mark timelock (motion onset, time = 0 s) and time when hand reached object in the goal-directed condition (time = 1 s).

DISCUSSION

Mu and beta responses

The conditional mu power responses in adults were in line with previous studies (Hari & Salmelin, 1997; Muthukumaraswamy & Johnson, 2004a; Nishitani & Hari, 2000). The mean mu power differences were lower in the infant group, a difference that was expected from previous studies on the resting state mu rhythm (Stroganova et al., 1999). The desynchronization in the moving dot condition has also been reported by others (Hari et al., 1998), and it is especially interesting to note that the frequency response between the moving-dot condition and

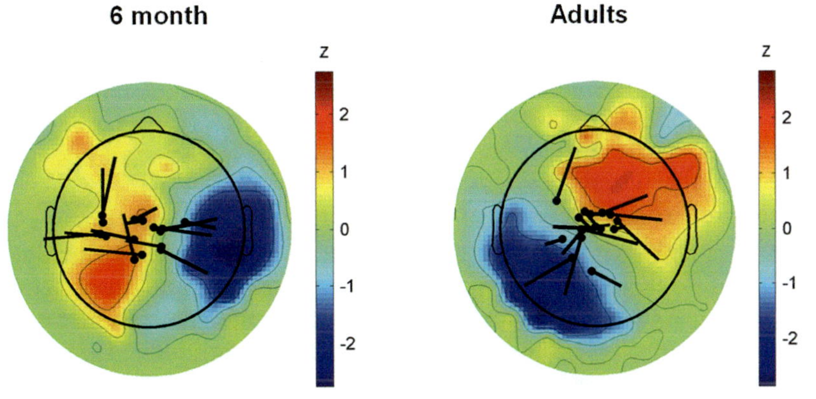

Figure 6. Mean topographic plots of the independent components' power projections (component weights, arbitrary unit). Black circles mark the axial projections of independent components' dipole localization (one per subject). Black lines show the projection of dipoles' directions with normalized length. The color scale show the z-transformed component weights.

non-goal-directed condition is very similar. This could indicate that the desynchronization in these two conditions was due to a response to the visual motion rather than the parsing of the model's action. The more detailed time/frequency result showed that there is an adult mu rhythm desynchronization in the goal-directed condition at the time when the hand reaches the object. All this relates well to the notion that the mirror neuron system is tuned to goal-directed action, and lends support to the idea that the stimulus elicits mirror neuron activity. No beta reactivity was found in either group, which can be explained by the component selection algorithm that was based on mu rhythm detection.

The lack of significant differences between the moving-dot and the reaching-hand conditions in the infant group may lead to the impression that the mirror neuron system is immature at 6 month of age. However, there are many factors that can suppress the mu rhythm beside the stimulus properties, thereby masking the mirror neuron activity. For example, the cortical control of eye movements is known to suppress the mu rhythm, and since the stimuli consist of translational movements, some suppression of the mu rhythm from the smooth pursuit of the targets is expected (which could explain the similarities between the moving-dot and the non-goal-directed conditions mentioned above). This holds for adults and it is reasonable to expect the same from the infant group since 6-month-old infants track objects smoothly in an adult manner (Rosander & von Hofsten, 2002; von Hofsten & Rosander, 1997). Infants also have more motor activity while watching the stimuli due to postural stabilization, which would further mask mirror neuron activity. Finally, infants get quickly tired from being in the experimental environment, and changes in attention, vigilance and fatigue also alter the mu rhythm (Cochin et al., 1999). These factors were considered to be equal across conditions, and expected to reduce the tested differences between conditions. It therefore seems likely that no difference in suppression between the conditions would be observed unless there was a strong conditional response that overcame these factors. In adults this is evidently the case, but the results from the infant group do not quite reach significant mu desynchronization in the goal-directed-action condition compared to the non-goal-directed-action condition.

ERP

In contrast to the frequency analysis there were functional differences for both adults and infants in the ERP analysis. The latency was somewhat shorter in the adult group, but the significant activation from goal-directed action observation started before the hand reached the object in both groups (approximately 0.5 s before in the adult group and 0.3 s in the infant group). This indicates that the subjects anticipated the goal of the action, and that the perception of others' action is predictive even in the infant group. One study by Kilner, Vargas, Duval, Blakemore, and Sirigu (2004) showed predictive ERP activation in an adult group and linked it to the mirror neuron system. Although that study identified the readiness potential of observed actions, the same reasoning applies that activation ahead of time may be used to interpret the intention of others. It is well known that the mirror system is considered to interpret actions on-line (Fadiga et al., 2005) with very short latency of activation, and from the original comparative studies on monkeys (Di Pellegrino et al., 1992; Gallese et al., 1996; Rizzolatti et al., 1996a; Umiltà et al., 2001) it is possible to imagine a weak and slow ERP synchronized to when a hand reaches an object even in humans. The timing of the significant intervals in our study did show a similar time course between the ERP activation and mirror neurons tuned to reaching, but any explicit suggestions on the appearance of an expected mirror neuron ERP were not found in the literature. In this study, the measured ERP traces also varied in appearance. This was especially true in the infant group where the amplitudes of the moving dot and the ERPs in the non-goal-directed conditions had about the same amplitudes as in the goal-directed condition. However, only the goal-directed condition was significantly different from the other conditions and the close resemblance to the adult's significance intervals validates the results.

The infant groups showed a significant negative peak in the moving-dot condition about 0.6 s after motion onset (compared to a zero mean on the goal-directed condition, but not to the other conditions). Effects from moving object observation are also reported by Hari et al. (1998), who found a minor effect in the frequency domain. One possible explanation is that the independent component analysis, which finds spatio-temporally independent sources in the data, decomposed multiple cognitive processes with overlapping brain areas to the same component. This leads to the suggestion that the measured ERP is a result of a combination of different cognitive processes, one of which is the mirror neuron system.

GENERAL DISCUSSION

Many studies have mapped the neural substrates of the adult mirror neuron system. For example, Decety et al. (1997) found increased activation in BA 6 (precentral gyrus) during observation of meaningful compared to meaningless actions. They also report activation in the middle frontal gyrus (BA 8 and BA 9) bilaterally. Grèzes et al. (2003) found similar results, with activation in the precentral gyrus bilaterally together with activation of the intraparietal sulcus and superior temporal sulcus. This network of mirror areas in the human brain suggests that there might be large variation between subjects in both dipole localization and direction, since the signal will be influenced by the sum of different synchronized areas (the more areas the greater the possibilities for differences). Indeed, the result from the dipole analysis shows individual variation. If the dipole moments have different directions then the source signals will be mixed and distributed over different channels in different subjects during raw EEG recording. The resulting mean signal in each channel will then be suppressed or cancelled out in a group analysis, and becomes a problem for simple frequency analyses on channels or groups of channels. As pointed out by Pineda (2005), the sensorimotor cortex also seems to display a variety of mu rhythms with specific topographic and functional properties with the same type of signal suppression within subjects. By applying the independent component analysis it is possible to find a decomposition of sources that minimizes these problems.

The dipole locations of the components in the present study resolve the problem of strong posterior alpha generators: EEG oscillations in the 8–13 Hz frequency over occipital cortex are influenced by states of awareness and overlaps with the mu rhythm (Oberman et al., 2005; Pineda, 2005). One could argue that the independent components might reflect this posterior activity, but the localization of the dipoles suggests that the activity rather originates in the rolandic regions. Although the location of dipoles appears to be somewhat deeper than the cortex, this result can be explained by the orientation of the dipoles. Radially oriented dipoles are typically deeper than the cortical source itself, and the localization is similar to the mu rhythm motor response in Makeig et al. (2004). It is worth mentioning that dipole fitting is approximate, and that groups of dipoles should be considered a statistical sample of the location of activation (Johnson-Frey et al., 2003). Of course, individual differences are included in this consideration, and only a single independent component from each subject was fitted.

One problem with the analysis of independent components is to identify components between subjects that reflect the same cognitive process. One method is to cluster components with regard to parameters such as dipole localization, scalp topography, ERP traces or frequency response. This approach is especially valuable in exploratory studies and differentiation of several cognitive processes. This study aimed at identifying components with mirror properties and investigated the functional response to the stimuli. A component selection algorithm could thus be used with criteria based on a priori knowledge of the frequency response of the mu rhythm. The sensorimotor cortex generates many mu rhythms with specific topographic and functional properties (Pineda, 2005) and if multiple components had been selected from each subject the problem with different numbers of mu rhythms from each subject would have to be considered. Also, if components that do not contain mirror neuron activity are included, it will add noise to the signal. Instead of choosing multiple components from every subject a simplistic approach was used, where the independent mu component that accounts for most variance in the EEG channel data was selected. As the stimuli were designed to maximize grasping mirror activity, which gives the most reliable desynchronization in adult humans (Hari & Salmelin, 1997; Oberman et al., 2005), it is reasonable to believe that this strategy of selecting components extracted the analogous mu rhythm between subjects. Also, the characteristics of the mu desynchronization, ERP appearance and dipole localization is similar to the mu rhythm results of Makeig et al. (2004), who used cluster analysis to classify independent components. In that study, the mu rhythm cluster was derived from manual response, and was convincingly linked to motor performance. There are, of course, other ways of identifying and selecting components, for example by ordering the components on the basis of mu power. However, artifactual components typically have strong power peaks in many frequency bands, including the defined mu rhythm bands, whereas the current ordering tends to bring out cognitive components. The method used in this study is only one of many, and further studies are clearly needed to optimize the detection of mirror neuron system activity with EEG.

The stimuli might be optimized as well, as the different actions may differ in more respects than their goal directedness. A remedy of this question would be to test more conditions, but the short attention span of the infants made this impossible in the current study. Complementary studies are therefore needed to resolve this issue. Another crucial point is that the stimuli are presented as short movie clips on a monitor. A recent article on infant's brain responses to live and televised action (Shimada & Hiraki, 2006) using near-infrared spectroscopy showed increased activation in 6-month-old infants' motor cortex when the stimuli were presented live compared to a TV presentation. (The study was interesting since it showed that infants the same age as in the present study have increased activation in motor areas during action observation. However, goal directedness was not addressed, and the temporal resolution makes it speculative to link the activation directly to mirror neurons.) Many adult studies successfully use video stimuli, but the activation may have been dampened. According to Järveläinen, Schürmann, Avikainen, and Hari (2001) beta wave rebound gets suppressed 15–19% with video presentation, which indicates less activation of the primary motor cortex. In infants, Falck-Ytter et al. (2006) found that 11-month-olds predicted the action goal of a video-presented model, but the effect of video presentation and mirror neuron activity in younger infants is still controversial. To be on the safe side: the influence of monitor presentation could be eliminated by using live actors and actions would follow each other in a more ecological fashion. It is an important empirical question whether this change would further increase the conditional differences in the infant group.

The aim of the present study was to detect mirror neuron activity from action observation in infants by the frequency response and ERP. It is important to emphasis that this is only the first step in the neurophysiological mapping of the developing mirror neuron system, and there is a wealth of important findings in adults that can be investigated in infant groups. Whereas the adult brain resembles a seamlessly integrated patchwork of cortical areas, the developing infant brain may reveal how different areas are interconnected to functional systems. For example, mirror neurons are not only activated by the sight of grasping movements. By investigating audiovisual mirror neurons it might be possible to assess action recognition in infants and study how actions are transformed into abstract, modality-independent representations (see Keysers et al., 2003, for a discussion of modalities and audiovisual mirror neurons). This is in turn related to speech perception (Skipper, Nusbaum, & Small, 2005) and the development of language and mirror neurons. Finally, developmental studies inspired by Keysers and Perret (2004) or Baldissera, Cavallari, Craighero, and Fadiga (2001) can shed some light on how the infant separates (or learns to separate) its own actions from those of others.

In the introduction the question of whether mirror neuron activity emerges together with specific motor acts was raised. This question is still difficult to address, even though the ERP response of the 6-month-old infants suggest a tight coupling between the development of performance and corresponding mirror neurons. A compatible view is provided by Falck-Ytter et al. (2006) who showed that infants predicted the goal of an observed action at 11 months but not at 6 months. The observed action in that study was to place objects in a container, and most 6-month-olds would not be able to perform the same action. Certainly, to test more age groups and to conduct more elaborate studies on different actions (such as with hidden goals as Umiltà et al., 2001; impossible movements as Constantini et al., 2005; or unpredictable movements as Gangitano, Mottaghy, & Pascual-Leone, 2004) could help us understand the separate development or co-development of the mirror system and the motor system in humans.

Over age it might also be possible to measure when the human mirror neuron system diverges from other species. A comparison of the human and monkey mirror systems, for example, reveals a few differences. Whereas monkeys' mirror neurons only fire if an action is geared toward an object, the human mirror neuron system can be activated by an action geared toward an imaginary object (Fadiga & Craighero, 2004). So, another important consideration for future mirror neuron studies in infants is the introduction of both transitive and intransitive actions, as well as mimicking actions and meaningless actions. Without the knowledge of when and how the human mirror neuron system differs from other species it will be speculative to discuss how the human mirror neuron system facilitates the development of theory of mind, imitation learning, language learning and other uniquely human capabilities.

CONCLUSIONS

Taken together, this study investigated mirror neuron system activity in both adults and 6-month-old infants using high-density EEG. The results from the frequency response show that the stimuli causes mirror-related mu rhythm desynchronization in adults and similar patterns in infants. By applying an alternative method of analyzing the data, using the ERP paradigm, functional differences were found in both groups. The ERP results show significantly higher amplitudes in the goal-directed action observation condition compared to non-goal-directed action observation and moving/static dot observation. The time course of the ERP implies that the measured effects reflect mirror neuron activity, and that the mirror neuron system can be detected directly by EEG in both adults and infants as young as 6 months. The possibility of measuring mirror neuron activity in infants using this method opens up a wide range of developmental studies that can help in delineating the maturation of the human mirror neuron system.

Manuscript received 29 January 2007
Manuscript accepted 30 April 2007
First published online 2 April 2008

REFERENCES

Babiloni, C., Carducci, F., Cincotti, F., Rossini, P. M., Neuper, C., Pfurtscheller, G., et al. (1999). Human movement-related potentials vs. desynchronization of EEG alpha rhythm: A high-resolution study. *NeuroImage*, *10*, 658–665.

Baldissera, F., Cavallari, P., Craighero, L., & Fadiga, L. (2001). Modulation of spinal excitability during observation of hand actions in humans. *European Journal of Neuroscience*, *13*, 190–194.

Braddick, O., Birtles, D., Wattam-Bell, J., & Atkinson, J. (2005). Motion-and orientation specific cortical responses in infancy. *Vision Research*, *45*(25–20), 3169–3179.

Buccino, G., Vigt, S., Ritzl, A., Fink, G. R., Zilles, K., Freund, H.-J., et al. (2004). Neural circuits underlying imitation learning of hand actions: An event-related fMRI study. *Journal of Cognitive Neuroscience*, *16*, 114–126.

Cochin, S., Barthelemy, C., Roux, S., & Martineau, J. (1999). Observation and execution of movement: Similarities demonstrated by quantified electroencephalography. *European Journal of Neuroscience*, *11*, 1839–1842.

Constantini, M., Galati, G., Ferretti, A., Caulo, M., Tartaro, A., Romani, G. L., et al. (2005). Neural systems underlying observation of humanly impossible movements: An fMRI study. *Cerebral Cortex*, *15*, 1761–1767.

Decety, J., Grèzes, J., Costes, N., Perani, D., Jeannerod, M., Procyk, E., et al. (1997). Brain activity during observation of actions, influence of action content and subject's strategy. *Brain*, *120*, 1763–1777.

Delorme, A., & Makeig, S. (2004). EEGLAB: An open source toolbox for analysis of single-trial EEG dynamics. *Journal of Neuroscience Methods*, *134*, 9–21.

Di Pellegrino, G., Fadiga, L., Fogassi, L., Gallese, V., & Rizzolatti, G. (1992). Understanding motor events: A neurophysiological study. *Experimental Brain Research*, *91*, 176–180.

Fadiga, L., & Craighero, L. (2004). Electrophysiology of action representation. *Journal of Clinical Neurophysiology*, *21*(3), 157–169.

Fadiga, L., Craighero, L., & Olivier, E. (2005). Human motor cortex excitability during the perception of others' action. *Current Opinion in Neurobiology*, *15*, 213–218.

Fadiga, L., Fogassi, L., Pavesi, G., & Rizzolatti, G. (1995). Motor facilitation during action observation: A magnetic stimulation study. *Journal of Neurophysiology*, *73*, 2608–2611.

Falck-Ytter, T., Gredebäck, G., & von Hofsten, C. (2006). Infants predict other people's action goals. *Nature Neuroscience*, *9*(7), 878–879.

Flanagan, J. R., & Johansson, R. S. (2003). Action plans used in action observation. *Nature*, *424*, 769–777.

Fogassi, L., Ferrari, P. F., Gesierich, B., Rozzi, S., Chersi, F., & Rizzolatti, G. (2005). Parietal lobe: From action understanding to intention understanding. *Science*, *308*, 662–667.

Gallese, V., Fadiga, L., Fogassi, L., & Rizzolatti, G. (1996). Action recognition in the premotor cortex. *Brain*, *119*, 593–609.

Gallese, V., Keysers, C., & Rizzolatti, G. (2004). A unifying view of the basis of social cognition. *Trends in Cognitive Science*, *8*(9), 396–403.

Gangitano, M., Mottaghy, F. M., & Pascual-Leone, A. (2004). Modulation of premotor mirror neuron activity during observation of unpredictable grasping movements. *European Journal of Neuroscience*, *20*, 2193–2202.

Gastaut, H. J., & Bert, J. (1954). EEG changes during cinematographic presentation (moving picture activation of the EEG). *Electroencephalography and Clinical Neurophysiology*, *6*, 433–444.

Grafton, S. T., Arbib, M. A., Fadiga, L., & Rizzolatti, G. (1996). Localization of grasp representations in humans by PET: 2. Observation compared with imagination. *Experimental Brain Research, 112*, 103–111.

Grèzes, J., Armony, J. L., Rowe, J., & Passingham, R. E. (2003). Activations related to "mirror" and "canonical" neurones in the human brain: An fMRI study. *NeuroImage, 18*, 928–937.

Grèzes, J., Costes, N., & Decety, J. (1998). Top-down effect of strategy on the perception of human biological motion: A PET investigation. *Cognitive Neuropsychology, 15*, 552–582.

Grieve, P. G., Emerson, R. G., Fifer, W. P., Isler, J. R., & Stark, R. I. (2003). Spatial correlation of the infant and adult electroencephalogram. *Clinical Neurophysiology, 114*, 1594–1608.

Hari, R., Forss, N., Avikainen, S., Kirveskari, E., Salenius, S., & Rizzolatti, G. (1998). Activation of human primary motor cortex during action observation: A neuromagnetic study. *Proceedings of the National Academy of Sciences USA: Neurobiology, 95*, 15061–15065.

Hari, R., & Salmelin, R. (1997). Human cortical oscillations: A neuromagnetic view through the skull. *Trends in Neuroscience, 20*(1), 44–49.

Järveläinen, J., Schürmann, M., Avikainen, S., & Hari, R. (2001). Stronger reactivity of the human primary motor cortex during observation of live rather than video motor acts. *Neuroreport, 12*(16), 3493–3495.

Johnson, M. H., de Haan, M., Oliver, A., Smith, W., Hatzakis, H., Tucker, L. A., et al. (2001). Recording and analyzing high-density event-related potentials with infants. Using the Geodesic sensor net. *Developmental Neuropsychology, 19*, 295–323.

Johnson-Frey, S. H., Maloof, F. R., Newman-Norlund, R., Farrer, C., Inati, S., & Grafton, S. T. (2003). Actions or hand–object interaction? Human inferior frontal cortex and action observation. *Neuron, 39*, 1053–1058.

Junghöfer, M., Elbert, T., Tucker, D. M., & Rockstroh, B. (2000). Statistical control of artifacts in dense array EEG/MEG studies. *Psychophysiology, 37*, 523–532.

Keysers, C., Kohler, E., Umiltà, M. A., Nanetti, L., Fogassi, L., & Gallese, V. (2003). Audiovisual mirror neurons and action recognition. *Experimental Brain Research, 153*, 628–636.

Keysers, C., & Perret, D. I. (2004). Demystifying social cognition: A Hebbian perspective. *Trends in Cognitive Science, 8*(11), 501–507.

Kilner, J. M., Vargas, C., Duval, S., Blakemore, S.-J., & Sirigu, A. (2004). Motor activation prior to observation of a predicted movement. *Nature Neuroscience, 7*(12), 1299–1301.

Kohler, E., Keysers, C., Umiltà, M. A., Fogassi, L., Gallese, V., & Rizzolatti, G. (2002). Hearing sounds, understanding actions: Action representation in mirror neurons. *Science, 297*, 846–848.

Kuhlman, W. N. (1980). The mu rhythm: functional topography and neural origin. In G. Pfurtsheller (Ed.), *rhythmic EEG activities and cortical functioning* (pp. 105–120). Amsterdam: Elsevier.

Leslie, K. R., Johnson-Frey, S. H., & Grafton, S. (2004). Functional imaging of face and hand imitation: Towards a motor theory of empathy. *NeuroImage, 21*, 601–607.

Makeig, S., Delorme, A., Westerfield, M., Jung, T., Townsend, J., Courchesne, E., et al. (2004). Electroencephalographic brain dynamics following manually responded visual targets. *PLOS Biology, 2*(6), 0747–0762.

Makeig, S., Jung, T.-P., Bell, A. J., Ghahremani, D., & Sejnowsk, T. J. (1997). Blind separation of auditory event-related brain responses into independent components. *Proceedings of the National Academy of Sciences USA, 94*, 10979–10984.

Marshall, P. J., Bar-Haim, Y., & Fox, N. A. (2002). Development of the EEG from 5 months to 4 years of age. *Clinical Neurophysiology, 113*, 1199–1208.

Muthukumaraswamy, S. D., & Johnson, B. W. (2004a). Changes in rolandic mu rhythm during observation of a precision grip. *Psychophysiology, 41*, 152–156.

Muthukumaraswamy, S. D., & Johnson, B. W. (2004b). Primary motor cortex activation during action observation revealed by wavelet analysis of the EEG. *Clinical Neurophysiology, 115*, 1760–1766.

Muthukumaraswamy, S. D., Johnson, B. W., & McNair, N. A. (2004). Mu rhythm modulation during observation of an object-directed grasp. *Cognitive Brain Research, 19*, 195–201.

Nishitani, N., & Hari, R. (2000, January). Temporal dynamics of cortical representation for action. *Proceedings of the National Academy of Sciences USA, 97*(2), 913–918.

Oberman, L. M., Hubbard, E. M., McCleery, J. P., Altschuler, E. L., Ramachandran, V. S., & Pineda, J. A. (2005). EEG evidence for mirror neuron dysfunction in autism spectrum disorders. *Cognitive Brain Research, 24*, 190–198.

Picton, T. W., Bentin, S., Berg, P., Donchin, E., Hillyard, S. A., Johnson, R., et al. (2000). Committee report guidelines for using human event-related potentials to study cognition: Recording standards and publication criteria. *Psychophysiology, 37*, 127–152.

Pineda, J. A. (2005). The functional significance of mu rhythms: Translating "seeing" and "hearing" into "doing". *Brain Research Reviews, 50*(1), 57–68.

Rizzolatti, G., & Craighero, L. (2004). The mirror-neuron system. *Annual Review of Neuroscience, 27*, 169–192.

Rizzolatti, G., Fadiga, L., Fogassi, L., & Gallese, V. (1996a). Premotor cortex and the recognition of motor actions. *Cognitive Brain Research, 3*, 131–141.

Rizzolatti, G., Fadiga, L., Matelli, M., Bettinardi, V., Pauulesu, E., Perani, D., et al. (1996b). Localization of grasp representations in humans by PET: 1. Observation versus execution. *Experimental Brain Research, 111*, 246–252.

Rosander, K., Nyström, P., Gredebäck, G., & von Hofsten, C. (2007). Cortical processing of visual motion in young infants. *Vision Research, 47*(12), 1614–1623.

Rosander, K., & von Hofsten, C. (2002). Development of gaze tracking of small and large objects. *Experimental Brain Research, 146*, 257–264.

Scherg, M. (1990). Fundamentals of dipole source potential analysis. In F. Grandori, M. Hoke, & G. L. Romani (Eds.), *Advances in audiology. Vol. 6: Auditory evoked magnetic fields and electric potentials* (pp. 40–69). Basel, Switzerland: Karger.

Shimada, S., & Hiraki, K. (2006). Infant's brain responses to live and televised action. *NeuroImage, 32*, 930–939.

Skipper, J. I., Nusbaum, H. C., & Small, S. L. (2005). Listening to talking faces: Motor cortical activation during speech perception. *NeuroImage, 25*, 76–89.

Strafella, A. P., & Paus, T. (2000). Modulation of cortical excitability during action observation: A transcranial magnetic stimulation study. *Neuroreport, 11*, 2289–2292.

Stroganova, T. A., Orekhova, E. V., & Posikera, I. N. (1999). EEG alpha rhythm in infants. *Clinical Neurophysiology, 110*, 997–1012.

Umiltà, M. A., Kohler, E., Gallese, V., Fogassi, L., Fadiga, L., Keysers, C., et al. (2001). "I know what you are doing": A neurophysiological study. *Neuron, 31*, 155–165.

von Hofsten, C., & Rosander, K. (1997). Development of smooth pursuit tracking in young infants. *Vision Research, 37*, 1799–1810.

SOCIAL NEUROSCIENCE, 2008, 3 (3–4), 348–355

Psychology Press
Taylor & Francis Group

Preliminary evidence for deficits in multisensory integration in autism spectrum disorders: The mirror neuron hypothesis

Lindsay M. Oberman and Vilayanur S. Ramachandran
University of California at San Diego, La Jolla, California, USA

Autism is a complex disorder, characterized by social, cognitive, communicative, and motor symptoms. One suggestion, proposed in the current study, to explain the spectrum of symptoms is an underlying impairment in multisensory integration (MSI) systems such as a mirror neuron-like system. The mirror neuron system, thought to play a critical role in skills such as imitation, empathy, and language can be thought of as a multisensory system, converting sensory stimuli into motor representations. Consistent with this, we report preliminary evidence for deficits in a task thought to tap into MSI—"the bouba-kiki task" in children with ASD. The bouba-kiki effect is produced when subjects are asked to pair nonsense shapes with nonsense "words". We found that neurotypical children chose the nonsense "word" whose phonemic structure corresponded with the visual shape of the stimuli 88% of the time. This is presumably because of mirror neuron-like multisensory systems that integrate the visual shape with the corresponding motor gestures used to pronounce the nonsense word. Surprisingly, individuals with ASD only chose the corresponding name 56% of the time. The poor performance by the ASD group on this task suggests a deficit in MSI, perhaps related to impaired MSI brain systems. Though this is a behavioral study, it provides a testable hypothesis for the communication impairments in children with ASD that implicates a specific neural system and fits well with the current findings suggesting an impairment in the mirror systems in individuals with ASD.

Individuals with autism spectrum disorders often show both sensorimotor impairments (repetitive, stereotyped behaviors) and cognitive-social impairments (e.g., impairments in pragmatic language, imitation, and empathy; DSM-IV-TR, 2000). Though many theories exist, which attempt to explain one or more of these impairments, the most parsimonious theories are those that are able to link neuroanatomical impairments and functional mechanisms to the multiple behavioral impairments that are unique in ASD. One recent theory, which does exactly this, suggests that a dysfunction in a specific functional system, the mirror neuron system, underlies the behavioral impairments in ASD (Altschuler et al., 2000; Oberman et al., 2005a; Williams, Whiten, Suddendorf, & Perrett, 2001).

The mirror neuron system, originally discovered in area F5 of the macaque premotor cortex (Di Pellegrino, Fadiga, Fogassi, Gallese, & Rizzolatti, 1992) is characterized by its response to both observed and performed actions. Though the original studies were performed in the macaque, there is now strong evidence suggesting that a comparable system exists in the homologous region (Broca's area) of the human premotor cortex (Fadiga, Fogassi, Pavesi, & Rizzolatti, 1995). Mirror neurons are primarily thought to be involved in perception and comprehension of motor actions, but recent studies suggest that they

Correspondence should be addressed to: Lindsay M. Oberman, 9500 Gilman Drive, La Jolla, CA 92093–0109, USA. E-mail: loberman@ucsd.edu

www.psypress.com/socialneuroscience DOI:10.1080/17470910701563681

may also play a critical role in higher-order cognitive processes such as imitation (Ramachandran, 2000; Rizzolatti, Fogassi, & Gallese, 2001), language (Ramachandran, 2000; Rizzolatti & Arbib, 1998), and empathy (Carr, Iacoboni, Dubeau, Mazziotta, & Lenzi, 2003), all of which are characteristically impaired in individuals with autism spectrum disorders (Bacon, Fein, Morris, Waterhouse, & Allen, 1998; Baron-Cohen, 2001; Frith, 1989; Tager-Flusberg, 2000; Rogers, Hepburn, Stackhouse, & Wehner, 2003). The hypothesis that the mirror neuron system is involved in both sensory motor integration as well as cognitive and social skills makes it an ideal candidate mechanism to investigate in autism.

There is now a large amount of evidence for the theory linking a dysfunction in the mirror neuron system to the behavioral deficits in autism in the domains of imitation (Altschuler et al., 2000; Nishitani, Avikainen, & Hari, 2004; Oberman et al., 2005a; Theoret et al., 2005) and empathy (Dapretto et al., 2005). However, it is still a fairly young debate and arguments against these findings have been published as well (Hamilton, Brindley, & Frith, 2007; Jacob & Jeannerod, 2005). Though the link between autism and mirror neurons has been supported through research in multiple laboratories and the link between the mirror neuron system and specific aspects of language that are characteristically impaired in autism, namely metaphor comprehension, has also been investigated (Oberman, Pineda, & Ramachandran, 2005b) a thorough review of the literature failed to produce a single experimental study linking a dysfunction in the mirror neuron system with impairments in language processing in autism. There is, however, evidence for the role of Broca's area, thought to be the human homologue to area F5 in monkeys, in the perception of language in typically developing individuals and evidence for audiovisual mirror neurons in Broca's area (Keysers et al., 2003; Kohler et al., 2002).

The first suggestion that a mirror-like system was involved in language processing came from a theory presented in 1985 (prior to the discovery of the mirror neuron system) called the "motor theory of speech perception" (Liberman & Mattingly, 1985). Liberman and Mattingly proposed that the objects of speech perception are the "phonetic gestures" that are represented in the brain of the observer as motor commands that signal movements of the mouth, lips, and tongue. Thus, as an observer processes spoken language, regions such as Broca's area (which later would be identified as one of the regions thought to contain mirror neurons) that are critical to speech production will respond.

Evidence for the involvement of the motor system in speech perception comes from electroencephalography (EEG), functional magnetic resonance imaging (fMRI) and transcranial magnetic stimulation (TMS) studies. In a series of EEG and fMRI studies, Hauk and colleagues found evidence that reading sentences that related to hand, leg, and head actions activated somatotopically distinct regions of sensorimotor cortex based on the effector that would be used to perform the action (Hauk, Johnsrude, & Pulvermüller, 2004; Hauk & Pulvermüller, 2004). Another study by Wilson and colleagues showed that speech production areas respond while listening to speech sounds (Wilson, Saygin, Sereno, & Iacoboni, 2004). Additionally, fMRI evidence supports activation of the superior temporal sulcus as well as the inferior frontal gyrus (core regions of the mirror neuron system) in response to both the sight and sound of human speech (Calvert & Campbell, 2003). Finally, TMS studies found increased MEP in the lips and tongue while subjects listened to or visually observed speech as compared to non-speech sounds or movements during stimulation of the left motor cortex (Fadiga, Craighero, Buccino, & Rizzolatti, 2002; Watkins, Strafella, & Paus, 2003). Given these findings, researchers are beginning to draw connections from the action-related mirror neuron system to the utilization of this system for communication (see Arbib, 2005, for a review).

Arbib (2005) outlines a theory describing how the MNS evolved from a manual action recognition system in the primate to being involved in verbal language in the human. Though Arbib's theory proposes that proto-language evolved from proto-sign (a primitive gestural language system), it does not explain how specific sounds are mapped onto objects. We suggest that just as the MNS contains neurons with shared observation and execution representations, that similarly there may be systems with shared representations of mouth and larynx movements and visual and auditory sensory perceptions that explains the nonarbitrary associations between objects and their names.

Though the neural structures involved in this proposed system are currently unknown specific multisensory regions of cortex including Broca's area and the superior temporal sulcus are likely involved. The aforementioned studies provided evidence for the activation of Broca's area and the superior temporal sulcus during the perception of human speech. These regions may mediate the shared representation between the auditory perception of the sound and the motor representation of the mouth and larynx movement required to make the sound.

One task that highlights the involvement of sensorimotor processes in language and may support the role of mirror neuron-like processes is the "bouba-kiki task." This task, originally described by German American psychologist Wolfgang Köhler (Köhler, 1929, 1947) requires participants to name nonsense shapes. When this task is performed on neurotypical adults, results suggest that an overwhelming majority of participants match the sound of the name with the visual form of the nonsense shape. For example, if they are shown the top row of shapes in Figure 1 and asked to identify which of the shapes is "bouba" and which is "kiki", 95% of people will pick the jagged shape as kiki and the rounded amoeboid shape as bouba (Ramachandran & Hubbard, 2001). Though typical individuals show this match between the nonsense shape and nonsense name, patients with lesions to the angular gyrus, a region of the inferior parietal lobule located in the temporal–parietal–occipital junction, do not make these associations (Ramachandran, Azoulai, Stone, Srinivasan, & Bijoy, 2005). Given this finding, the angular gyrus may also be involved in multisensory integration of visual/auditory perception and language/motor representations.

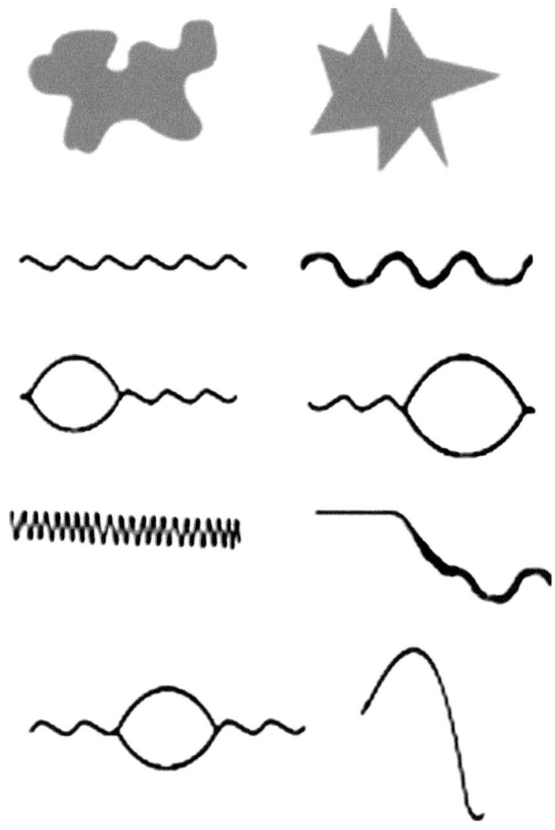

Figure 1. An example of the stimuli used in the experiment. The corresponding names for the figures are (left/right, top to bottom): "Bouba"/"Kiki"; "Mmmm"/"Shhh"; "Ohmmm"/ "Mmmao"; "Rrrr"/"Eeesh"; "Wow"/"Bloop," for the left and right figures respectively.

As the regions of the cortex hypothesized to be involved in the bouba-kiki task (Broca's area, superior temporal gyrus and angular gyrus) overlap with those of the MNS and there is much evidence for an impairment in the MNS in individuals with ASD, the current study sought to investigate whether high-functioning children with autism showed a difference in performance on this task as compared to neurotypical control participants.

METHOD

Subjects

Our sample consisted of 30 children: 20 neurotypical children (age $M = 9.7$ years, $SD = 1.27$) and 10 high-functioning children with autism spectrum disorder (age $M = 9.7$ years, $SD = 1.34$). All participants were male and native English speakers with normal or corrected-to-normal vision and no history of hearing impairments. All of the children with ASD were independently diagnosed by a clinician as well as characterized at the time of testing using the Autism Diagnostic Observation Schedule Revised (ADOS-R; Lord, Rutter, DiLavore, & Risi, 1999) to confirm current symptomatology. They were considered high functioning, defined as having age appropriate receptive language skills as well as an IQ above 80 (within two standard deviations of the population mean) on the Wechsler Abbreviated Scale of Intelligence (WASI; ASD $M = 106.8$, $SD = 15.5$, Control $M = 107.1$, SD 9.8). Children with ASD with known comorbidity with other disorders (including ADD and Specific Language Impairment), an IQ lower than 80, or below age appropriate receptive language skills were excluded from the study. All children were recruited from the community. Control participants were age and gender matched to the ASD group. The project protocol was reviewed and approved by the UCSD Human Research Protections Program and all subjects gave written assent and each subject's parent or guardian gave written consent.

Procedure

Participants were presented with five pairs of nonsense shapes (Figure 1) and five pairs of nonsense "words" created by the research team. Pairs of shapes were designed to have corresponding nonsense words based on similarities between the auditory and visual forms. The experimenter then asked the participant, "In Martian language one of these shapes is a [corresponding or noncorresponding word] while the other is a [corresponding or noncorresponding word], which one is which?" The participant responded by indicating their choice on a response sheet. The order of corresponding and noncorresponding words was counterbalanced. The study was conducted individually with the experimenter sitting across the table from the participant to ensure that the individual understood the instructions and remained on task.

Data analysis

In order to understand the difference in performance on this task, five two-way chi square analyses were conducted on the number of participants in each group who paired the nonsense shape with the predetermined corresponding name and responses where the nonsense shape was paired with the predetermined noncorresponding name for each pair of stimuli. The five resulting chi-square values (with one degree of freedom) were then added together to form a chi square with five degrees of freedom. This analysis was then followed up with two sets of five one-way chi-square analyses to investigate whether each group's proportion of corresponding and noncorresponding responses were significantly different from chance. Again, the five chi-square values from each of these sets of analyses were combined to form one chi-square value with five degrees of freedom.

RESULTS

The two-way chi square revealed a significant difference between the number of participants in the control group who gave corresponding responses and noncorresponding responses as compared to the ASD group, $\chi^2(5) = 21.56$, $p < .001$, (Table 1). Follow-up analyses revealed that while the number of neurotypical individuals giving corresponding and noncorresponding responses was significantly different than chance (50%), $\chi^2(5) = 36.18$, $p < .001$, the ASD group's pattern was not different than chance, $\chi^2(5) = 0.606$, $p > .98$ (Figures 2 and 3).

Additional analyses revealed that proportion of corresponding responses did not significantly correlate with full-scale IQ ($r = .24$, $p > .20$), Matrices subtest of the WASI ($r = .23$, $p > .20$), Verbal IQ subscale of the WASI ($r = .18$, $p > .30$) or age ($r = .33$, $p > .07$) of participants. Additionally, there was not a significant difference in performance between the ASD and control group on the Matrices subtest, $t(28) = -0.739$, $p > .4$, or Verbal IQ subscale, $t(28) = -0.058$, $p > .95$, of the WASI. In fact, the ASD group performed slightly better than the control participants on both the Matrices subtest (ASD $M = 55.2$, $SD = 7.1$; Control $M = 52.9$, $SD = 8.7$) and the Verbal IQ subscale (ASD $M = 107.1$, $SD = 16.3$; Control $M = 106.2$, $SD = 11.9$).

DISCUSSION

The results of the current study support the hypothesis that multisensory integrative brain systems including a mirror-like system in Broca's

TABLE 1

Number of participants in each group who gave corresponding responses for each pair of stimuli

	Bouba/Kiki	*Shhh/Mmmm*	*Ohmmm/Mmmao*	*Eeesh/Rrrr*	*Wow/Bloop*
ASD ($n = 10$)	6	6	5	6	5
Neurotypical ($n = 20$)	19	18	17	19	15

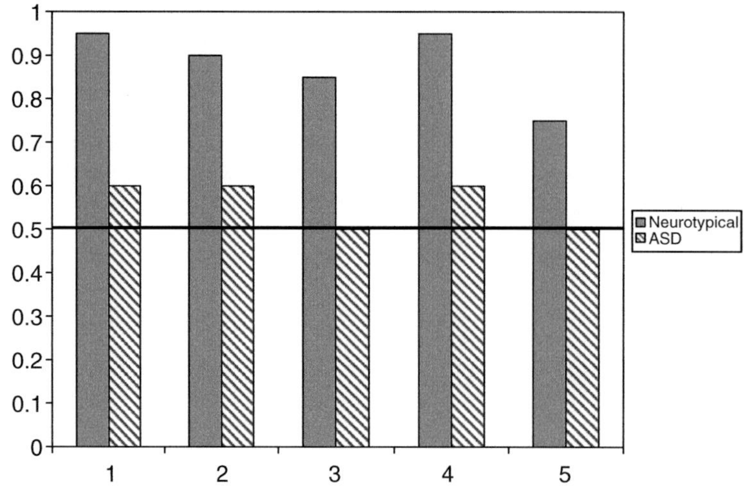

Figure 2. Proportion of participants in each group who chose the corresponding name for each pair of stimuli. The solid gray bars represent the proportion of neurotypical participants while the striped bars represent the proportion of ASD participants. The black line indicates the proportion of participants expected to give the corresponding response assuming no relationship between name and shape (simply by chance) (0.5).

area, angular gyrus or superior temporal sulcus may play a role in the language deficits seen in children with ASD. Not only were children with ASD less likely to choose the name that corresponded with the nonsense shape compared to neurotypical children, but their responses were not significantly above chance. This latter finding indicates that unlike neurotypical children (and adults) there is no evidence that the children with ASD use any type of multisensory integrative process to determine names for nonsense shapes, but rather their responses appeared to be random. This finding is consistent with previous reports indicating deficits in children with ASD in audiovisual speech comprehension tasks (Bebko, Weiss, Denmark, & Gomez, 2006; Smith & Bennetto, 2007).

The additional finding that there was no significant difference in performance between the two groups on the Matrices subtest or the Verbal IQ subscale of the WASI suggests that the poor performance on the bouba-kiki task is not likely to be a result of impaired attention, impaired perception of patterns and shapes, or impaired verbal ability. The Matrices subtest of the WASI requires that the individual provide a missing piece to a pattern composed of shapes. Given that the ASD group performed well on this

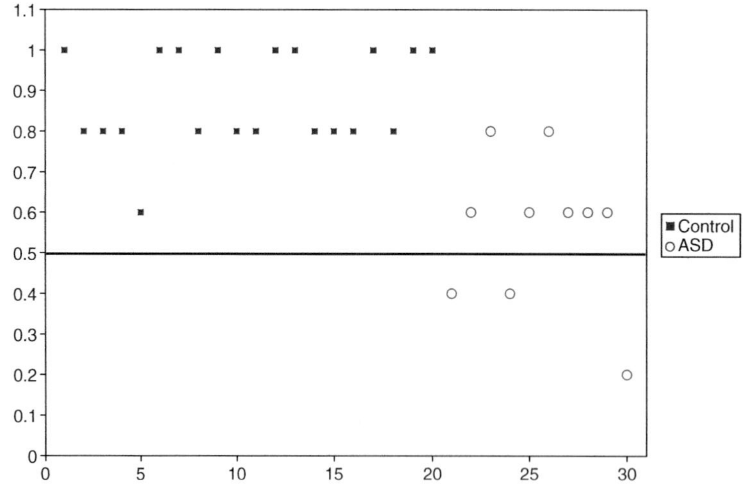

Figure 3. Proportion of corresponding responses given by each participant. Solid squares represent neurotypical participants while open circles represent participants with ASD. The black line indicates the proportion of corresponding responses that would be expected if the child randomly assigned the name to the shape (0.5).

task, which only requires a single modality, provides further evidence that the dysfunction is in cross-modal processing.

We have previously suggested that the reason why neurotypical individuals pick the jagged shape as kiki and the rounded amoeboid shape as bouba is that the sharp changes in visual direction of the lines in the jagged figure mimics the sharp phonemic inflections of the sound kiki, as well as the sharp inflection of the tongue on the palate while the rounded shape of the amoeboid figure mimics the more smooth phonemic inflections of the sound bouba and the motor movements of the lips. This type of multisensory integration may be based on cross-activation between auditory sensory representations and motor representations in Broca's area creating a natural bias toward mapping certain sound contours onto certain vocalizations.

Cross-cultural studies reveal that this is not simply an effect of the shape of the letters in the nonsense name (e.g., bouba is not round because of the round form of the B and kiki is not spiky because of the shape of the K) as the same effect is seen in languages with different alphabets (Davis, 1961).

Anecdotal examples of this natural tendency can be observed in the motor gestures performed when referring to something small or large. Speaking the words such as "little", "petite", or "teeny" results in an unconscious narrowing of the vocal tracts and lips while the words "large" or "enormous" results in the opposite effect. Also, when referring to "you" speakers produce a partial outward pout with their lips (as in English "you", French "tu" or "vous" and Tamil "thoo"), whereas when referring to "me", their lips and tongue move inwards (as in English "me", French "moi" and Tamil "naan").

If it is assumed that this task requires joint activation of auditory representations and motor representations, several neural impairments could be leading to the deficit in this task. An impairment in auditory processing, an impairment in functional connectivity, as well as an impairment in MSI regions including Broca's area or angular gyrus or a combination of all three could lead to the deficits observed in this study. There is evidence supporting impairments in these three functional mechanisms in individuals with ASD. Recent studies have found abnormalities in auditory processing in individuals with ASD (Collet et al., 1993; Gomot, Giard, Adrien, Barthelemy, & Bruneau, 2001; Khalfa et al., 2001; Plaisted, Saksida, Alcantara, & Weisblatt, 2003). Additionally, there appears to be hypoperfusion of the temporal cortex including associative auditory and multimodal regions (Zilbovicius et al., 2000), abnormally low levels of functional connectivity (Just, Cherkassky, Keller, & Minshew, 2004; Villalobos, Mizuno, Dahl, Kemmotsu, & Müller, 2005) as well as hypoplasia and delayed maturation of frontal regions including inferior frontal gyrus regions (Abell et al., 1999; Hadjikhani, Joseph, Snyder, & Tager-Flusberg, 2006; Just et al., 2004; Zilbovicius et al., 1995).

Though previous studies have suggested that multisensory integrative processes are typically used in language processing, the current study suggests that multisensory integration is critical for normal development of language, as children with ASD show a lack of multisensory integration as evidenced by their performance on this task. Though the participants in this study scored in the normal range on measures of verbal IQ, their paradoxically high score is likely a result of compensatory systems as qualitative impairments in language development is a core feature of ASD. Further, it is likely that multisensory processes are involved in the more complex pragmatic aspects of language such as prosody, metaphor, and the use of language for social interaction (not measured with standardized verbal IQ tests), the exact aspects of language processing that are impaired in verbal children with ASD. Finally, it is possible that the participants with ASD categorized these nonsense shapes based on different criteria than the control participants leading to different associations with the words. Results from this study cannot speak to this possibility.

As this study was strictly behavioral, the neural system underlying the observed behavioral deficits can only be speculated. However, the MNS does provide a good candidate to investigate given its location in Broca's area, the presence of multisensory neurons, which integrate auditory and visual sensory information with motor representation, and the previous evidence for its involvement in language perception. Further studies including more stimuli, a larger sample, and neuroimaging will be necessary to corroborate this finding. Based on the deficits we have seen in the bouba-kiki task in ASD, we suggest that such stimuli could be introduced as a valuable experimental probe for exploring intersensory abstraction in a variety of other neurological and psychological syndromes.

Manuscript received 15 December 2006
Manuscript accepted 25 June 2007
First published online 3 October 2007

REFERENCES

Abell, F., Krams, M., Ashburner, J., Passingham, R. E., Friston, K. J., Frackowiak, R. S. J., et al. (1999). The neuroanatomy of autism: A voxel based whole brain analysis of structural scans. *Neuroreport, 10*, 1647–1651.

Altschuler, E. L., Vankov, A., Hubbard, E. M., Roberts, E., Ramachandran, V. S., & Pineda, J. A. (2000, November). *Mu wave blocking by observer of movement and its possible use as a tool to study theory of other minds.* Poster session presented at the 30th Annual Meeting of the Society for Neuroscience, New Orleans, LA.

American Psychiatric Association. (2000). *Diagnostic and statistical manual of mental disorders (DSM-IV-TR)* (4th ed., text revision). Washington, DC: American Psychiatric Press, Inc.

Arbib, M. A. (2005). From monkey-like action recognition to human language: An evolutionary framework for neurolinguistics. *Behavioral and Brain Sciences, 28*(2), 105–124 (discussion 125–167).

Bacon, A. L., Fein, D., Morris, R., Waterhouse, L., & Allen, D. (1998). The responses of autistic children to the distress of others. *Journal of Autism and Developmental Disorders, 2*, 129–142.

Baron-Cohen, S. (2001). Theory of mind and autism: A review. In L. M. Glidden (Ed.), *International review of research in mental retardation: Vol. 23. Autism.* (pp. 169–184). San Diego, CA: Academic Press.

Bebko, J. M., Weiss, J. A., Demark, J. L., & Gomez, P. (2006). Discrimination of temporal synchrony in intermodal events by children with autism and children with developmental disabilities without autism. *Journal of Child Psychology and Psychiatry, 47*, 88–98.

Calvert, G. A., & Campbell, R. (2003). Reading speech from still and moving faces: The neural substrates of visible speech. *Journal of Cognitive Neuroscience, 15*(1), 50–70.

Carr, L., Iacoboni, M., Dubeau, M.-C., Mazziotta, J. C., & Lenzi, G. L. (2003). Neural mechanisms of empathy in humans: A relay from neural systems for imitation to limbic areas. *Proceedings of the National Academy of Sciences USA, 100*, 5497–5502.

Collet, L., Rogé, B., Descouens, D., Moron, P., Duverdy, F., & Urgell, H. (1993). Objective auditory dysfunction in infantile autism. *Lancet, 342*, 923–924.

Dapretto, M., Davies, M., Pfeifer, J., Scott, A., Sigman, M., Bookheimer, S., et al. (2005). Understanding emotions in others: Mirror neuron dysfunction in children with autism spectrum disorders. *Nature Neuroscience, 9*, 28–30.

Davis, R. (1961). The fitness of names to drawings: A cross-cultural study in Tanganyika. *British Journal of Psychology, 52*, 259–268.

Di Pellegrino, G., Fadiga, L., Fogassi, L., Gallese, V., & Rizzolatti, G. (1992). Understanding motor events: A neurophysiological study. *Experimental Brain Research, 91*, 176–180.

Fadiga, L., Craighero, L., Buccino, G., & Rizzolatti, G. (2002). Short communication. Speech listening specifically modulates the excitability of tongue muscles: A TMS study. *European Journal of Neuroscience, 15*, 399–402.

Fadiga, L., Fogassi, L., Pavesi, G., & Rizzolatti, G. (1995). Motor facilitation during action observation: A magnetic stimulation study. *Journal of Neurophysiology, 73*(6), 2608–2611.

Frith, U. (1989). *Autism and Asperger syndrome.* London: MRC Cognitive Development Unit.

Gomot, M., Giard, M. H., Adrien, J. L., Barthelemy, C., & Bruneau, N. (2001). Auditory mismatch process in children with autism: An ERP topographic study. *International Journal of Psychophysiology, 41*, 197–235.

Hadjikhani, N., Joseph, R., Snyder, J., & Tager-Flusberg, H. (2006). Anatomical differences in the mirror neuron system and social cognition network in autism. *Cerebral Cortex, 16*, 1276–1282.

Hamilton, A. F., de, C., Brindley, R. F., & Frith, U. (2007). Imitation and action understanding in autistic spectrum disorders: How valid is the hypothesis of a deficit in the mirror neuron system? *Neuropsychologia, 45*, 1859–1868.

Hauk, O., Johnsrude, I., & Pulvermüller, F. (2004). Somatotopic representation of action words in human motor and premotor cortex. *Neuron, 41*, 301–307.

Hauk, O., & Pulvermüller, F. (2004). Neurophysiological distinction of action words in the fronto-central cortex. *Human Brain Mapping, 21*, 191–201.

Jacob, P., & Jeannerod, M. (2005). The motor theory of social cognition: A critique. *Trends in Cognitive Sciences, 9*, 21–25.

Just, M. A., Cherkassky, V., Keller, T. A., & Minshew, N. J. (2004). Cortical activation and synchronization during sentence comprehension in high-functioning autism: Evidence of underconnectivity. *Brain, 127*, 1811–1821.

Keysers, C., Kohler, E., Umiltà, M. A., Fogassi, L., Nanetti, L., & Gallese, V. (2003). Audiovisual mirror neurons and action recognition. *Experimental Brain Research, 153*, 628–636.

Khalfa, S., Bruneau, N., Roge, B., Georgieff, N., Veuillet, E., Adrien, J. L., et al. (2001). Peripheral auditory asymmetry in infantile autism. *European Journal of Neuroscience, 13*, 628–632.

Kjelgaard, M. M., & Tager-Flusberg, H. (2001). An investigation of language impairment in autism: Implications for genetic subgroups. *Language and Cognitive Processes, 16*, 287–308.

Kohler, E., Keysers, C., Umiltà, M. A., Fogassi, L., Gallese, V., & Rizzolatti, G. (2002). Hearing sounds,

understanding actions: Action representation in mirror neurons. *Science*, *297*, 846–848.
Köhler, W. (1929). *Gestalt psychology.* New York: Liveright.
Köhler, W. (1947). *Gestalt psychology* (2nd. ed). New York: Liveright.
Liberman, A. M., & Mattingly, I. G. (1985). The motor theory of speech perception revised. *Cognition*, *21*, 1–36.
Lord, C., Rutter, M., DiLavore, P. C., & Risi, S. (1999). *Autism Diagnostic Observation Schedule-WPS* (WPS ed.). Los Angeles: Western Psychological Services.
Nishitani, N., Avikainen, S., & Hari, R. (2004). Abnormal imitation-related cortical activation sequences in Asperger's syndrome. *Annals of Neurology*, *55*, 558–562.
Oberman, L. M., Hubbard, E. M., McCleery, J. P., Altschuler, E. L., Ramachandran, V. S., & Pineda, J. A (2005a). EEG evidence for mirror neuron dysfunction in autism spectrum disorders. *Cognitive Brain Research*, *24*, 190–198.
Oberman, L. M., Pineda, J. A., & Ramachandran, V. S. (2005b). EEG evidence for the role of the mirror neuron system in metaphor comprehension. Presented at the 35th Annual Meeting of the Society for Neuroscience, Washington, DC, USA.
Plaisted, K., Saksida, L., Alcantara, J., & Weisblatt, E. (2003). Towards an understanding of the mechanisms of weak central coherence effects: Experiments in visual configural learning and auditory perception. *Philosophical Transactions of the Royal Society of London. Series B: Biological Sciences*, *358*, 375–386.
Ramachandran, V. S. (2000, June). Mirror neurons and imitation learning as the driving force behind the great leap forward in human evolution. *Edge*, *69*. (Available from: http://www.edge.org/3rd_culture/ramachandran/ramachandran_p1.html)
Ramachandran, V. S., Azoulai, S., Stone, L., Srinivasan, A. V., & Bijoy, N. (2005). *Grasping metaphors and thinking with pictures: How brain damage might affect thought and language.* Poster Presented at the 12th Annual Meeting of the Cognitive Neuroscience Society, April 2005, New York, USA.
Ramachandran, V. S., & Hubbard, E. M. (2001). Synaesthesia: A window into perception, thought and language. *Journal of Consciousness Studies*, *8*, 3–34.
Rizzolatti, G., & Arbib, M. A. (1998). Language within our grasp. *Trends in Neuroscience*, *21*, 188–194.
Rizzolatti, G., Fogassi, L., & Gallese, V. (2001). Neurophysiological mechanisms underlying the understanding and imitation of action. *Nature Reviews Neuroscience*, *2*, 661–670.
Rogers, S. J., Hepburn, S. L., Stackhouse, T., & Wehner, E. (2003). Imitation performance in toddlers with autism and those with other developmental disorders. *Journal of Child Psychology and Psychiatry*, *44*, 763–781.
Smith, E. G., & Bennetto, L. (2007). Audiovisual speech integration and lipreading in autism. *Journal of Child Psychology and Psychiatry*, *48*, 813–821.
Tager-Flusberg, H. (2000). Understanding the language and communicative impairments in autism. In L. M. Glidden (Ed.), *Autism* (pp. 185–205). San Diego, CA: Academic Press.
Theoret, H., Halligan, E., Kobayashi, M., Fregni, F., Tager-Flusberg, H., & Pascual-Leone, A. (2005). Impaired motor facilitation during action observation in individuals with autism spectrum disorder. *Current Biology*, *15*, R84–85.
Villalobos, M. E., Mizuno, A., Dahl, B. C., Kemmotsu, N., & Müller, R. A. (2005). Reduced functional connectivity between V1 and inferior frontal cortex associated with visuomotor performance in autism. *NeuroImage*, *25*, 916–925.
Watkins, K. E., Strafella, A. P., & Paus, T. (2003). Seeing and hearing speech excites the motor system involved in speech production. *Neuropsychologia*, *41*, 989–994.
Williams, J. H. G., Whiten, A., Suddendorf, T., & Perrett, D. I. (2001). Imitation, mirror neurons and autism. *Neuroscience and Biobehaviour Review*, *25*, 287–295.
Wilson, S. M., Saygin, A. P., Sereno, M. I., & Iacoboni, M. (2004). Listening to speech activates motor areas involved in speech production. *Nature Neuroscience*, *7*(7), 701–702.
Zilbovicius, M., Boddaert, N., Belin, B. P., Poline, J. B., Remy, P., Mangin, J. F., et al. (2000). Temporal lobe dysfunction in childhood autism: A PET study. *American Journal of Psychiatry*, *157*, 1988–1993.
Zilbovicius, M., Garreau, B., Samson, Y., Remy, P., Barthélémy, C., Syrota, A., et al. (1995). Delayed maturation of the frontal cortex in childhood autism. *American Journal of Psychiatry*, *152*, 248–252.

SOCIAL NEUROSCIENCE, 2008, 3 (3–4), 356–367

Psychology Press
Taylor & Francis Group

Putting oneself in the perspective of the other: A framework for self–other differentiation

Marc Jeannerod and Thierry Anquetil
CNRS-Université Claude Bernard, Lyon, France

Self–other differentiation requires both that one can understand the actions others perform, and that one can attribute these actions to them. Understanding implies that a complete description of the actions of other agents can be available in the brain of the observer. Attributing implies that the agent can be clearly differentiated from the self. The model for the self–other differentiation proposed here can therefore involve two steps: I first displace myself at the location of the person I observe in order to specify her/his location in space. Then, I simulate the action I observe from that person in order to understand what she/he is doing. Assuming that the two operations are more or less synchronous, the action I simulate is automatically attributed to the person I observe, not to myself. The simulation network in the observer's brain overlaps with the execution network in the agent's brain; by contrast, the rotation network is specific to the observer's brain. In a neuroimaging experiment using PET, we compared brain activity during a task where the subjects simulated an action of grasping an object from either first-person or third-person perspectives. This comparison revealed an activation limited to the parieto-occipital junction (area 19), which appeared to be specific to the third-person perspective. The activation of this area is proposed to represent a cue for the self–other differentiation.

INTRODUCTION

The same action as seen from different perspectives

The self–other differentiation implies that one can recognize that others are both agents *like* us, i.e., that they self-generate movements and meaningful actions, and agents *distinct from* us, i.e., that the actions we see them perform are theirs, not ours. In other words, the process of the self–other differentiation requires both that we can understand the actions others perform, and that we can attribute these actions to them. Understanding implies that a complete description of the actions of other agents, from their origin to their end, can be available in the brain of the observer. Attributing implies that the agent can be clearly differentiated from the self.

A given action can be seen from different perspectives. It can be seen from the perspective of the agent who performs it, the first-person perspective, but it can also be seen from the perspective of an observer who watches the agent acting, i.e., from a third-person perspective. The capacity to recognize an action as the same from different perspectives (that of the agent and that of the observer) is far from trivial. Our first task is thus to determine the main parameters that have to be taken into account for identifying an action from different perspectives. To this aim, we will first provide a brief description of a familiar

Correspondence should be addressed to: Marc Jeannerod, Laboratoire sur le Langage, le Cerveau et la Cognition (L2C2), UMR 5230-CNRS-UCB Lyon 1; 67, Boulevard Pinel 69675 BRON Cedex, France. E-mail: jeannerod@isc.cnrs.fr

This work was supported by Université Claude Bernard, Lyon, by a grant from the EU sixth framework programme: "The organization and cognitive role of the mirror system" CEE: QLG3-CT-2002-00746. TA was also supported by fellowships from the FRM (Fondation de la Recherche Médicale) "Action dynamique en Psychiatrie".
We wish to thank N. Costes, F. Lavenne (CERMEP) and J. Redouté for their contribution in processing the PET data.

www.psypress.com/socialneuroscience DOI:10.1080/17470910701563715

visuomotor action, that of reaching toward an object and grasping it. The action of grasping an object can be typically decomposed into two components, the reaching component, which projects the hand at the object location, and the grasping component, which ensures a stable grasp of the object (Jeannerod, 1981). This apparently simple motor coordination involves a number of physiological constraints, which relate to the agent himself (the biomechanical limitations of his arm), to the object (its size, shape and orientation) and to the relative positions of the agent and the object. A successful reach requires that the spatial position of the object has been encoded in a set of coordinates that has its origin on the agent's body (a set of egocentric coordinates), and that the arm movement is planned according to this same set of coordinates. A successful grasp requires that the fingers are placed at the appropriate position on the object surface or, more specifically, that the opposition axis is properly oriented. Things are more complex, however, because it turns out that the orientation of the opposition axis is in fact the controlled parameter, not only of the grasping component itself, but of the reach-and-grasp action as a whole. In other words, the two components have to be coordinated with one another in order to ensure the efficiency of the final grasp (Weiss & Jeannerod, 1998).

Consider for example an object that imposes a specific placement of the fingers on its surface: different orientations of the opposition axis will have to be used for each position of the object relative to the body and, by way of consequence, the configuration of the whole limb will be different for each of these orientations. Different degrees of freedom of the upper limb (e.g., dorsal or ventral flexion of the wrist, abduction or adduction of the shoulder, hyperpronation or supination of the forearm) have to be engaged for different orientations of the object (Stelmach, Castiello, & Jeannerod, 1994). Even with so many degrees of freedom, the number of possible configurations of the arm compatible with a stable grasp is limited by biomechanics. Indeed, there is a tendency of the visuomotor system, whenever possible, to shift to the arm configuration that involves the minimum number of degrees of freedom (Paulignan, Frak, Toni, & Jeannerod, 1997). This spontaneous behavior of spatial adjustment for restoring "natural" or "easy" movements reflects the fact that engaging additional degrees of freedom has a cost (Rosenbaum, Meulenbroek, & Vaughan, 2004). The cost is reflected in an increase in the time taken to prepare more "difficult" movements. As shown by Frak, Paulignan, and Jeannerod (2001), the time to perform reach-and-grasp movements with an easy orientation of the opposition axis is shorter than for movements with a difficult orientation (Figure 1B).

A critical point is that these physiological constraints do not pertain to movement execution per se: they are already taken into account at the planning stage of the movement. This can be demonstrated by using the paradigm of motor mental imagery. In this condition, where the movements are simulated, not executed, the preparation time for simulating the movement also increases with the "difficulty" of the grasp, like it does for overt movements (Figure 1C; Frak et al., 2001; Johnson, 2000; Parsons, 1994). This result is in agreement with the notion of a functional equivalence of overt and covert movements, which assumes that covert movements involve many of the constraints that are met by overtly executed movements (see Jeannerod, 2006, for a review). Thus, the choice of the coordinate system for executing a movement (e.g., in egocentric coordinates or in object-centered coordinates) has to be done prior to execution, at the level of the central representation of the action.

Taking the perspective of the observer: The third-person perspective as a rotated first-person perspective

Using both the reach-and-grasp movement and the motor imagery paradigm, we can now describe what the same action looks like from different perspectives. In a recent experiment (Anquetil & Jeannerod, 2007), we instructed subjects to imagine the same action of reaching and grasping an upright cylinder with different orientations of the opposition axis, as in the experiment by Frak et al. (2001). In addition, the subjects were instructed to adopt different perspectives in simulating the grasping action: they had either to imagine themselves performing the action from their own first-person perspective (the 1P condition) or to imagine another person facing them performing the same action, i.e., from the third-person perspective (the 3P condition). We measured the response time for two orientations of the opposition axis, an easy

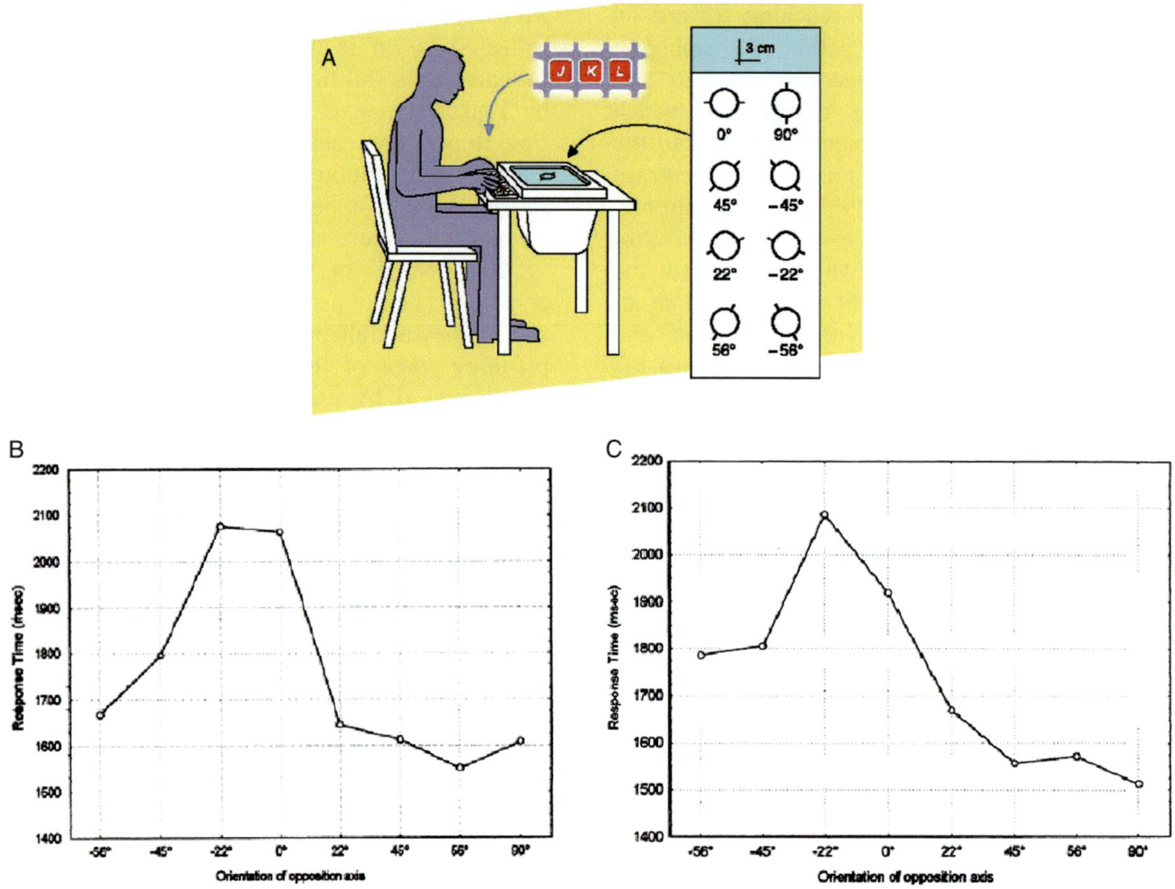

Figure 1. Time to perform and to mentally simulate reach and grasp movements with different degrees of difficulty. (A) Experimental situation for the mental simulation of grasping movements. Subjects press key J, K or L according to whether grasping the object with a given angle of the opposition axis will be easy, difficult or impossible, respectively. (B) Time to reach and grasp a cylinder with different orientations of the opposition axis. Zero degrees represents the orientation of the opposition axis parallel to the subjects frontal plane. Note longer time to perform awkward grasps. (C) Time to give the response in the simulation condition. Note longer response time for awkward orientations of the opposition axis, as for performing the actual movement. Data from Frak et al. (2001).

orientation (45°) and a difficult one (0°) performed from the two different perspectives. As expected, we confirmed that it takes longer to simulate grasping the cylinders with a difficult orientation of the opposition axis than with an easy one. The important finding was that the same constraint on mental movement time equally applied, whether the subject simulated the grasping action as an agent in the first-person perspective, or simulated that same action as performed by another agent facing her/him (Figure 2). No significant difference could be detected between response times in the two conditions of simulation: the mean response times were similar during simulation in the first-person and in the third-person perspective, as was the difference in response time between the two orientations of the grasp.

This result can be better understood if one assumes that the subjects in fact simulated the action in the same way for both first- and third-person perspective conditions. They could do so by mentally rotating themselves so as to superimpose with the virtual subject facing them. In so doing, the spatial relationship between the acting body and the object was preserved: then, they simply had to use the same set of egocentric coordinates from their new perspective to obtain the same movement (see also Sebanz, Knoblich, & Prinz, 2003; Wohlschläger, Haggard, Gesierich, & Prinz, 2003). Note that it is critical that the system of coordinates used by the observer corresponds to that of the agent he/she observes, in order to preserve the laterality of the body parts involved in the observed action. Indeed, this is what distinguishes observing an action made by

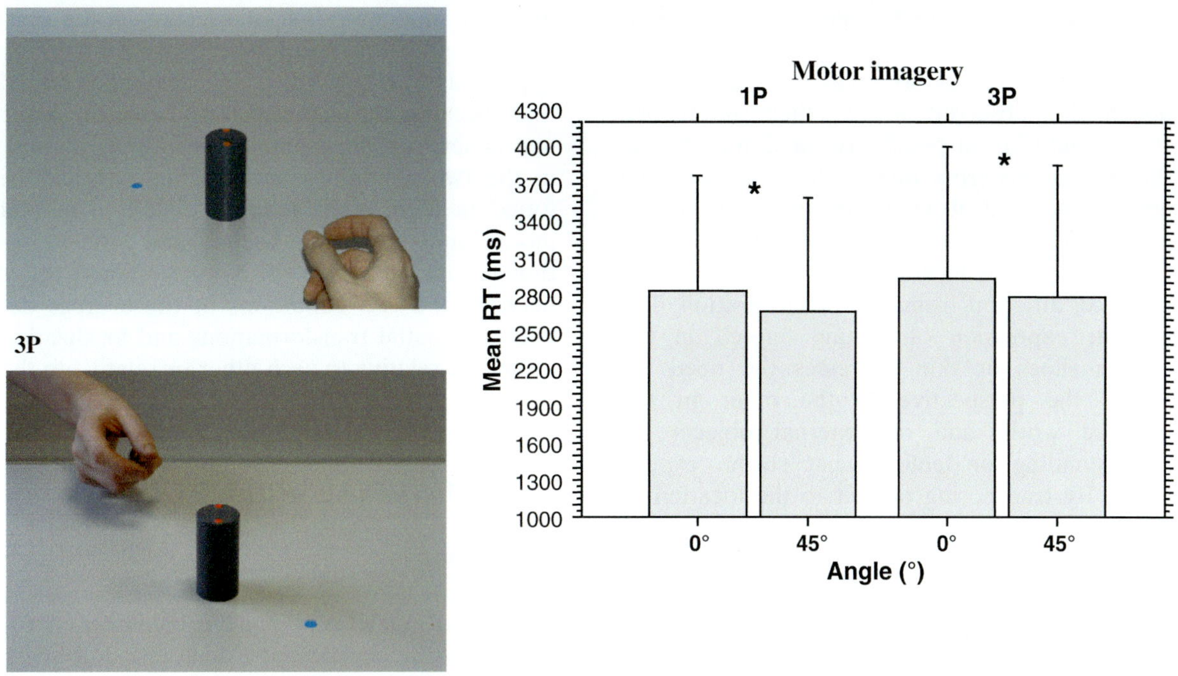

Figure 2. Mental simulation of a reach and grasp movement in the first-person (1P) and in the third-person (3P) perspectives. The left side of the figure depicts the subject's view of the image presented during simulation in the first-person perspective (above) and in the third-person perspective (below). The histograms on the right side of the figure represent response times for mental simulation of the movements with two different orientation of the opposition axis: 0° awkward grasp; 45° easy grasp. 1P: first-person perspective; 3P: third-person perspective. Note similar longer duration of response time for the awkward grasp in the two perspectives. From Anquetil and Jeannerod (2007).

another agent from viewing the mirror image of a self-generated action. This finding has further implications: if the observer simulates the agent's action in the same system of coordinates he/she would use for executing it, so that the action can obey the same constraints in the same reference frame transposed to the agent's spatial position, it follows that the motor simulation network of the observer should match the motor execution network of the agent. The same neural structures should be activated in the brains of the two subjects. Indeed, this hypothesis of a similarity of the neural networks for self-generating an action and for understanding it (e.g., Rizzolatti, Fadiga, Gallese, & Fogassi, 1995; see Jeannerod, 2001) is supported by experimental data obtained in numerous behavioral experiments (Brass, Bekkering, & Prinz, 2001; Kilner, Paulignan, & Blakemore, 2003; Stürmer, Aschersleben, & Prinz, 2000) as well as in experiments involving the measurement of cortical excitability (Clark, Tremblay, & Ste-Marie, 2004; Fadiga, Fogassi, Pavesi, & Rizzolatti, 1995; Maeda, Kleiner-Fisman, & Pascual-Leone, 2002; Strafella & Paus, 2000).

The attribution problem: If we see others as rotated versions of ourselves, why do we attribute the actions we observe to the others and not to ourselves?

The fact that a reach-and-grasp action looks the same from the agent's perspective and from the observer's perspective suggests that the motor simulation mechanism in itself is neutral with respect to where the action is seen and who performs it. The mirror system provides the observer with a copy of the observed action irrespective of the agent's position in space (Rizzolatti et al., 1995). The hard question now is: why does the observer attribute the observed action to the agent and not to him/herself? A tentative answer is that it is the encoding of the spatial transformation made by the observer to match the agent's perspective that provides the cues for the self–other differentiation and for the correct attribution. If the motor simulation is so realistic as to exactly match the observed action, then, in theory, there would be no possibility for differentiating the two agents from one another by using the action cues. Identifying an agent as a self independent from oneself should first require that this agent is localized at a specific position in space, different from one's own position. The popular expression of putting oneself in the other's shoes or skin expresses the need for taking the perspective of the other in the external world and on external objects for understanding or feeling what she/he experiences. By transposing oneself to the location of the other, one sees things as she/he would see them. Thus, the possibility of identifying the other must rely on the mechanism that operates the translation of the egocentric coordinates at a different spatial location. This mechanism, distinct from the motor simulation network, is needed for encoding the spatial transformation and differentiating the spatial positions of the two selves.

Although little is known about the mechanism of this spatial transformation, many data in the literature point to the role of the posterior parietal cortex as the main constituent of a spatial transformation network. In monkeys, posterior parietal areas receive their visual input through the occipitoparietal dorsal visual stream, once called the "space channel" as opposed to the "object" channel in the ventral visual stream (Mishkin & Ungerleider, 1982). Neurons in cortical areas located on the convexity of the parietal lobe, near the occipitoparietal junction, encode spatial relationships between objects, object orientation and spatial transformation of objects (Sakata, Shibutani, Kawano, & Harrington, 1985; Sakata, Tsutsui, & Taira, 2005). In humans, experimental and clinical data fully support this view. These data are discussed below (see discussion).

An investigation of the functional anatomy of the self–other differentiation

We directly investigated this problem of differentiating the spatial positions of two agents in an experiment with a group of normal subjects. We mapped cortical activity during the task of mentally simulating the same action in the first- and in the third-person perspectives. Our working hypothesis was twofold. First, we conjectured that, because the subjects would use the same neural networks for mentally performing the task in the two conditions, no difference should be found in their brain activity related to mental motor simulation per se. Second, and critically, we thought that the level of activity should differ between the two conditions in those areas devoted to spatial transformations and localization of objects relative to each other or relative to the body.

MATERIAL AND METHODS

Participants

Ten normal, male, right-handed volunteers participated in the experiment (Mean age 34.4 years, *SD* 7.88). Right-handedness was assessed using the Edinburgh inventory (Mean score 0.795, *SD* 0.09; Oldfield, 1971). Participants were free from psychiatric antecedents. They all gave their written informed consent for this study, which was approved by the local ethical committee.

Experimental task

During the experiment the participants rested in the scanner with their heads fixed. They looked at a screen placed 35 cm from their gaze plane. The same images as those used in the Anquetil and Jeannerod (2007) behavioral experiment (see Figure 2) were presented on the screen. In their reclining position, their hands were out of their sight and the right one was placed on a response pad. Participants were taught to mentally simulate a grasping action from the visual displays presented on the screen. Two types of simulation trials were randomly run: simulation trials from the first-person perspective (1P trials) and simulation trials in the perspective of another person sitting in front of them (third-person trials, 3P trials).

In the 1P trials, the image of a right hand in the supine posture was presented in the display at a position on the table visually corresponding to the subject's hand position. Subjects were instructed to imagine moving "their" right hand, grasping the dowel with a precision grip with the opposition axis defined by the red marks at the top of the cylinder, lifting it and finally placing it on the blue spot. Finally, they were instructed to press the touch pad with their right hand to indicate the completion of the task on each trial.

In the 3P trials, the only difference was in the visual display presented on the screen. The dowel and the hand appeared in the display in a symmetrical position with respect to the body plane, i.e., as seen by another person facing the subject.

A single trial first involved the presentation of a central fixation point on a blank screen, followed after 500 ms by the presentation of the visual display. The target had an apparent height of 7 cm and an apparent diameter of 3, 4 or 5 cm. Marks were placed on the dowels, indicating where the subject had to place his/her index and thumb fingertips when imagining grasping the dowel. There were two positions for the marks, which determined two orientations for the opposition axis and corresponded to two levels of difficulty of the task. In the 45° orientation, the opposition axis was rotated 45° clockwise, which afforded a comfortable grasp with the right hand. In the 0° orientation, the opposition axis was parallel to the subjects body plane, an orientation which afforded an uncomfortable grasp with an exaggerated dorsiflexion of the wrist. Dowels with different diameters and different mark positions were randomized across trials. In the visual displays, each diameter was presented twice and each mark position 7 times (14 trials). A timer was started at the onset of the visual display and was stopped by the subject pressing the touch pad when he/she had completed the task. At the key press the screen went blank. The time between presentation of the visual display and the subject's signal (the "response time") was measured and used as the dependent variable.

The behavioral data were processed using comparative statistics with a within-subject 2 (Conditions: 1P, 3P) × 3 (Diameter: 3, 4, 5 cm of the cylinders) × 2 (Angle of Orientation of Opposition Axis: 0°, 45°) repeated measures ANOVA, with the response time (RT in ms) as a continuous dependent variable, using the Statview software (Abacus, Inc., London). The significance was set at $p < .05$. Trials where response time exceeded ± two standard deviations from the mean were excluded from analysis. These trials represented 5.12% of the total number and were distributed throughout the blocks.

rCBF Measurements

Positron omission tomography (PET) was preferred to functional magnetic resonance imaging (fMRI) because the results obtained in this experiment with normal subjects would have to be compared with those obtained in the same experiment with a group of schizophrenic subjects (Anquetil, in preparation). For schizophrenic subjects the physical constraints inherent in PET are less stringent than those of fMRI.

Subjects were imaged with H(2)(15)O PET. They were positioned using a thermoplastic facemask that reduced their head movements. Standard procedures were run for measuring rCBF using a Siemens CTI HR+ camera, providing 63 slices with an axial field of view of 15.2 cm, which were acquired during each scan. The effects of radiation self-attenuation were corrected by an initial 10-minute transmission scan of each subject using an external positron-emitting isotope. The rCBF was measured using an i.v. bolus injection of 333 MBq H(2)(15)O, given for each run in the brachial vein of the left forearm through an indwelling catheter. The scan to record rCBF began when the radioactive counts exceeded the background activity by 200% and the acquisition lasted 60 s. Images were attenuation-corrected, reconstructed and analyzed.

Twelve 60-second experimental scans were run for each participant in a random order (3 for the 1P condition, 3 for the 3P condition, and 6 for control conditions). Control blocks comprised one motor control condition (C1, 2 blocks) with the participant repetitively pressing the key in semi darkness; one visual control condition (C2, 2 blocks) where the participant inspected the visual display without specific instruction; one "resting" condition (C3, 2 blocks) with the participant in semi darkness.

Statistical parametric mapping

Image analysis was performed using the SPM2 (Statistical Parametric Mapping; http://www.fil.ion.ucl.ac.uk/spm) software (Friston, Holmes, Poline, Price, & Frith, 1996) implemented on Matlab 7.1. The processing included the following steps for each subject: interscan realignment of images to the first scan, spatial normalization into the standard stereotactic space template defined by the Montreal Neurological Institute's (MNI) reference brain and smoothing of the images using an isotropic 10-mm full-width-half-maximum (FWHM) Gaussian kernel. The statistical parametric maps were thresholded at $p < .001$ uncorrected and activation foci with a minimum cluster size of 10 voxels were reported. The maps were overlaid on the MNI single-subject template and labeled using the atlas of Talairach and Tournoux (1988). Matlab 7.1 was used with the "mni2tal" program (http://imaging.mrc-cbu.cam.ac.uk) to transform MNI into Talairach coordinates and final anatomical identification was done using the above atlas.

Statistical analysis was carried out using fixed effects analysis. At this first level, the 5 following conditions: 3(3P), 3(1P), 2(C1), 2(C2) and 2(C3) were considered for each subject and analyzed for the whole group of 10 subjects. The fixed effects analysis was performed on the whole brain using SPM2, the PET model and the "Multi-subject conditions and covariates model", to average task conditions into a single contrast image.

Contrast images were then analyzed with two-sample *t*-tests to highlight between-condition differences using an uncorrected height threshold ($p < .001$), a cluster of more than 10 adjacent voxels, and a Z-score ≥ 3.40 at the voxel level. The following contrasts were calculated at the fixed effects level:

1. Main effects of 3P versus 1P conditions (3P – 1P) and the reverse (1P – 3P).
2. The contrast [(3P – (C1 + C2 + C3)] – [(1P – (C1 + C2 + C3)]. The activity of [(1P – (C1 + C2 + C3)] was masked (exclusive with an uncorrected mask with $p = .05$) and the threshold set at $p = .001$ in order to reveal the activation that was specific to the 3P condition.
3. Main effects of the contrast [(3P – (C1 + C2 + C3)] in a region limited to the parietal lobes and those of the contrast [(1P – (C1 + C2 + C3)] in the same region. The region of interest (ROI) was limited to the parietal lobes as defined in the software WKU PickAtlas tool version 2.2 (http://www.fmri.wfubmc.edu) in combination with SPM2 (Maldjian, Laurienti, Burdette, & Kraft, 2003). The selection of this region of interest was based on the results obtained in the above contrasts, showing a concentration of activated areas within the parietal lobes on both sides, and also on the basis of previous studies from the literature (see discussion).

RESULTS

1. Behavioral data

Response times followed the same trend as in the behavioral experiment of Anquetil and Jeannerod (2007), namely response times were longer for simulating grasping with a difficult orientation of the opposition axis (0°) than with an easy orientation (45°). This result clearly indicated that the subjects were performing the motor imagery task as requested. However, due to the small number of subjects ($N = 10$) and to the time constraints inherent to the experimental conditions in the scanner (3 seconds per trial and the number of trials limited by the duration of the acquisition time), the difference between the two types of trials did not reach statistical significance.

2. Functional anatomy data

Our main objective in this study was to compare brain activity when the same task of mentally simulating a grasping action was performed from two different perspectives. More specifically, we were interested in visualizing the activity generated by taking the third-person perspective. This was achieved by subtracting the activity generated by performing the mental simulation in the first-person perspective from that generated by performing the same task in the third-person perspective.

Our first analysis aimed to determine which activations were specific to the simulation of grasping from the first-person and the third-person perspectives by calculating the (1P – 3P) and the (3P – 1P) contrasts, respectively. The results obtained with these contrasts are listed in Table 1. The (1P – 3P) analysis revealed activated zones in the right hemisphere: one zone in the paracentral lobule on the mesial surface, and another one corresponding to Brodmann area 22 in the superior temporal gyrus. The (3P – 1P) analysis revealed several activations in the right occipital lobe, corresponding to Brodmann area 19 in the superior occipital gyrus, and in the parietal lobe, corresponding to Brodmann area 7 in the right superior parietal lobule. In addition, areas located in the right lingual gyrus and the left

TABLE 1

Activated areas during the third-person simulation 3P: contrast (3P – 1P) and during the first-person simulation 1P: contrast (1P – 3P)

Condition	Brain region	L/R					
		x	*y*	*z*	*MNI coordinates*	*Cluster size*	*Z-score*
3P – 1P	OL (BA 18)	R	12	−80	−10	1095	5.35
	SPL (BA 7)	R	34	−64	60	92	4.17
	SFG (BA 6)	R	4	16	60	104	3.82
	Cun. (BA 18)	L	−8	−74	12	82	3.73
	SOG (BA 19)	R	26	−88	30	133	3.69
	PLC	L	−46	−50	−46	28	3.45
	PLC	L	−18	−60	−46	11	3.2
1P – 3P	PL (BA31)	R	8	−34	48	24	3.54
	STG (BA 22)	R	60	8	−6	19	3.38

Notes: Contrast height threshold set at $p=.001$; *Z*-score >3.4; L, left hemisphere; R, right hemisphere; BA, Brodmann's area; OL, occipital lobe; SPL, superior parietal lobule; SFG, superior frontal gyrus; Cun., cuneus; SOG, superior occipital gyrus; PLC, posterior lobe of the cerebellum; PL, parietal lobe; STG, superior temporal gyrus. Activated clusters are reported for the extent threshold $k=10$ voxels.

cuneus, corresponding to Brodmann area 18, and an area in the right superior frontal gyrus (Brodmann area 6), were activated. Finally, the posterior lobe of the cerebellum on the left side was activated. The full list of activations with detailed coordinates, cluster sizes and *Z*-scores appears in Table 1.

In the second analysis, we compared the activity in the third-person perspective condition after subtraction of the three control conditions [(3P – (C1+C2+C3)], with the activity in the first person condition minus the control conditions [(1P – (C1+C2+C3)]. An exclusive mask was applied to the [(1P – (C1+C2+C3)] condition. This analysis revealed the existence of several cortical sites with a *Z*-score above 4 (Table 2), which were in global accordance with the results obtained in the first analysis. These clusters were located at the occipito-parietal junction, corresponding to Brodmann area 19, and in the superior parietal lobule (area 7) of the right hemisphere (Figure 3). Another site of activation with a high *Z*-score was detected in the left cuneus. Finally, the posterior lobe of the cerebellum was also found to be activated.

Given the results obtained with the first two analyses, a ROI analysis was performed, limited to the parietal lobes. This third analysis was performed by calculating the [(3P – (C1+C2+C3)] contrast and the [(1P – (C1+C2+C3)] contrast in the defined ROI. In the parietal lobe, the ROI analysis revealed the presence of significantly activated clusters in area 7 on both sides, and for both the first- and the third-person perspective conditions. The right superior occipital gyrus, corresponding to Brodmann area 19 was also found to be activated, but only in the third-person perspective condition (see Table 3).

DISCUSSION

This neuroimaging study revealed that the task of mentally simulating the same action from the two

TABLE 2

Activated areas during third-person simulation, in the contrast: [(3P – (C1+C2+C3)] exclusive masked by [(1P – (C1+C2+C3)]

Brain region	L/R					
	x	*y*	*Z*	*MNI coordinates*	*Cluster size*	*Z-score*
SOG (BA 19)	R	38	−90	22	236	5.25
PLC (BA 18)	R	0	−68	−18	323	4.87
SPL (BA 7)	R	36	−60	52	203	4.62
Cuneus (BA 18)	L	−8	−74	10	128	5.28

Notes: L, left hemisphere; R, right hemisphere; *Z*-score >4.6; Uncorrected mask *p* value $=.05$; Contrast height threshold set at $p=.001$; BA, Brodmann's area; SOG, superior occipital gyrus; PLC, posterior lobe of the cerebellum; SPL, superior parietal lobule. Activated clusters are reported for the extent threshold $k=90$ voxels.

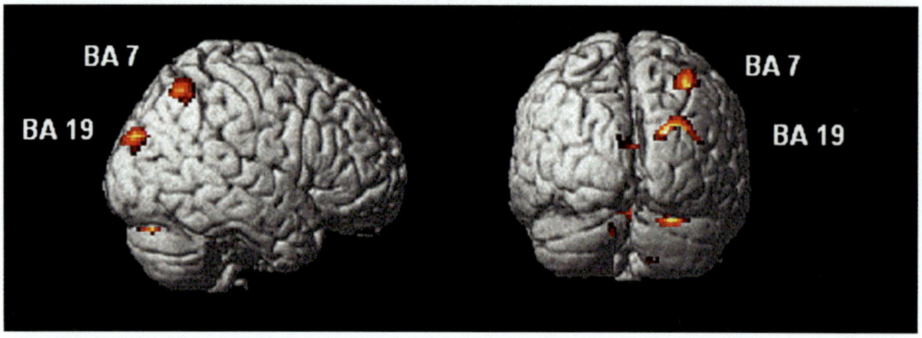

Figure 3. PET data. Cortical rendering of the main activations sites in the 3P condition. Foci of activation ([3P – (C1+C2+C3)] masked by [1P – (C1+C2+C3)]) have been superimposed onto the sagittal (right hemisphere) and posterior view of the single-subject MRI template in SPM2. Some activated clusters are reported for the extent threshold $k = 90$ voxels. Two main areas are shown: in the right superior occipital gyrus (BA 19; x = 38, y = −90, z = 22; *Z*-score 5.25) and in the superior parietal lobule (BA 7; x = 36, y = −60, z = 52; *Z*-score 4.62).

different perspectives activated different neural networks. The main activated zones that survived the comparison between the two conditions were located in the posterior part of the parietal lobe and at the parieto-occipital junction. For this reason, we will focus our discussion on these regions and examine their relevance to the problem of the self–other differentiation.

The localization of the regions activated in our third-person perspective condition correspond to the posterior part of the parietal lobe convexity, predominantly in the right hemisphere. This zone mainly includes Brodmann area 19 at the parieto-occipital junction and area 7 in the superior parietal lobule. Area 7, to begin with, was found to be activated in both the third-person and the first-person perspective conditions, which suggests that this area participates, at different levels of intensity, in aspects of the task that are common to the two conditions. One such aspect is the simulation of grasping an object, i.e., computing the visuomotor transformation for transporting the hand at the object location and shaping it according to the orientation of the grasp. This suggestion is in accordance with previous results from the literature showing the involvement of the superior parietal lobule in visuomotor coordination (Grefkes, Ritzl, Zilles, & Fink, 2004). Another argument in the same direction can be drawn from clinical observation of patients suffering a lesion of the superior parietal lobule: these patients show the typical picture of optic ataxia, with impairment in both reaching and grasping movements (see Rossetti et al., 2005).

Area 19, by contrast, appeared in our experiment to be more specifically related to the third-person perspective. There are two main points to be discussed about this result. First, this region is consistently found to be activated in tasks involving the manipulation of spatial relationships between objects: visual mental imagery with mental rotation of objects (Kosslyn, Digirolomo, Thompson, & Alpert, 1998), processing the relative positions of objects (Haxby et al., 1991), perception of spatial features of objects

TABLE 3

Significantly activated areas during first-person simulation: contrast [(1P – (C1+C2+C3)] and during third person simulation: contrast [(3P – (C1+C2+C3)]; both contrasts limited to parietal lobes ROI

			L/R					
Condition	*Brain region*	*x*	*y*	*z*	*MNI coordinates*	*Cluster size*	*Z-score*	*p corrected*
1P	SPL (BA 7)	R	36	−60	52	365	4.62	.003
	SPL (BA 7)	L	−22	−64	44	431	4.56	.001
3P	SPL (BA 7)	L	−22	−64	44	917	5.81	.0001
	SOG (BA 19)	R	30	−68	30	203	4.54	.019

Notes: $p < .05$ (corrected); *Z*-score >4.5; L, left hemisphere; R, right hemisphere; BA = Brodmann's area; SPL, superior parietal lobule; SOG, superior occipital gyrus; ROI, region of interest, centered on parietal lobes. Activated clusters are reported for the extent threshold $K = 10$ voxels.

(Faillenot, Sunaert, Van Hecke, & Orban, 2001). These data in normal subjects are congruent with clinical data from patients with a lesion in this region of parietal cortex. Patients with bilateral lesions of the parieto-occipital convexity show the typical picture of dorsal simultagnosia, with inability to process spatial relationships (e.g., determine the respective locations of two objects; see Farah, 1990). Right-sided posterior parietal lesions produce various sorts of visuospatial disorders, including right–left disorientation and impairments in spatial exploration (e.g., Colvin, Handy, & Gazzaniga, 2003). The fact that, in our experiment, an area located in this region remains activated when a subject simulates an action from the perspective of another self is therefore in good agreement with our hypothesis of a mechanism, specific to the third-person perspective, for computing the difference in spatial localization between oneself and the other self, and for providing a subject with a critical cue for the self–other differentiation.

The second point to be discussed is the difference between the first-person and the third-person perspectives. The first-person perspective mostly relates to self-identification. A large body of data from the literature dealing with the functional anatomy of self-identification, has pointed to the role of the inferior parietal lobule. The inferior parietal lobule is strongly activated in experimental situations where a discrepancy is created between a self-generated action and its sensory consequences (Farrer et al., 2003; Fink et al., 1999; Leube et al., 2003). These results indicate that the inferior parietal lobule is mostly concerned with the representation of one's own body and actions and their effects on the external world: in other words, this region would provide cues for self-attributing a self-generated action, rather than for disentangling a self-generated action from an action generated by somebody else (Jeannerod, 2006). This argument is congruent with the proposal, made by several authors, that the inferior parietal lobule would be critical for the assignment of the first-person perspective, not the third-person perspective (Decety & Grèzes, 2006; Farrer & Frith, 2002;Vogeley & Fink, 2003; Vogeley et al., 2004). The role of the inferior parietal lobule, particularly on the right side, in the process of self-identification is indeed supported by clinical arguments: lesions in that area frequently produce neglect or misattribution of one's own body parts (asomatagnosia and somatoparaphrenia).

Experiments comparing first-person and third-person perspectives remain difficult and the obtained results may depend on the instructions given to the subjects. Ruby and Decety (2001) found an activation of the inferior parietal lobule on one side (left) in simulating an action in the first-person perspective. They also found an activation of the same structure (on the right side) during simulation in the third-person perspective; however, it is not clear in their experiment what the subject was actually doing when they were verbally instructed to imagine performing an action. In the experiment reported here, we could check the subjects' mental performances by measuring the difference between their response times for easy and difficult actions. Our result of an activation, in the third-person perspective, limited to an area devoted to spatial processing, was obtained in a situation where the subjects did exactly the same task with the same objects in the two conditions: the only difference was the spatial position of the hand from which the subjects simulated the grasping movement. Our result therefore reflects the subtle spatial transformation that was needed for the subjects to change perspective and to displace the origin of the action from their own spatial position to that of the other.

Manuscript received 26 March 2007
Manuscript accepted 15 June 2007
First published online 2 April 2008

REFERENCES

Anquetil, T., & Jeannerod, M. (2007). Simulated actions in the first and the third person perspectives share common representations. *Brain Research*, *1130*, 125–129.

Brass, M., Bekkering, H., & Prinz, W. (2001). Movement observation affects movement execution in a simple response task. *Acta Psychologica*, *106*, 3–22.

Clark, S., Tremblay, F., & Ste-Marie, D. (2004). Differential modulation of corticospinal excitability during observation, mental imagery and imitation of hand actions. *Neuropsychologia*, *42*, 105–112.

Colvin, M. K., Handy, T. C., & Gazzaniga, M. S. (2003). Hemispheric asymmetries in the parietal lobe. In A. M. Siegel et al. (Eds.), *Advances in Neurology: The parietal lobes*, *93*, 321–334.

Decety, J., & Grèzes, J. (2006). The power of simulation. Imagining one's own and other's behavior. *Brain Research*, *1079*, 4–14.

Fadiga, L., Fogassi, L., Pavesi, G., & Rizzolatti, G. (1995). Motor facilitation during action observation. A magnetic stimulation study. *Journal of Neurophysiology*, *73*, 2608–2611.

Faillenot, I., Sunaert, S., Van Hecke, P., & Orban, G. A. (2001). Orientation discrimination of objects and gratings compared: An fMRI study. *European Journal of Neuroscience*, *13*, 585–596.

Farah, M. J. (1990). *Visual agnosia. Disorders of object recognition and what they tell us about normal vision*. Cambridge, MA: MIT Press.

Farrer, C., Franck, N., Georgieff, N., Frith, C. D., Decety, J., & Jeannerod, M. (2003). Modulating the experience of agency: A PET study. *Neuro-Image*, *18*, 324–333.

Farrer, C., & Frith, C. D. (2002). Experiencing oneself vs. another person as being the cause of an action: The neural correlates of the experience of agency. *NeuroImage*, *15*, 596–603.

Fink, G. R., Marshall, J. C., Halligan, P. W., Frith, C. D., Driver, J., Frackowiack, R. S. J., et al. (1999). The neural consequences of conflict between intention and the senses. *Brain*, *122*, 497–512.

Frak, V. G., Paulignan, Y., & Jeannerod, M. (2001). Orientation of the opposition axis in mentally simulated grasping. *Experimental Brain Research*, *136*, 120–127.

Friston, K. J., Holmes, A., Poline, J. B., Price, C. J., & Frith, C. D. (1996). Detecting activations in PET and fMRI: Levels of inference and power. *NeuroImage*, *4*, 223–235.

Grefkes, C., Ritzl, A., Zilles, K., & Fink, G. R. (2004). Human medial intraparietal cortex subserves visuomotor coordinate transformation. *NeuroImage*, *23*, 1494–1506.

Haxby, J. V., Grady, C. L., Horwitz, B., Ungerleider, L. G., Mishkin, M., Herscovitch, P., et al. (1991). Dissociation of object and spatial visual processing pathways in human extrastriate cortex. *Proceedings of the National Academy of Sciences, USA*, *88*, 1621–1625.

Jeannerod, M. (1981). Intersegmental coordination during reaching at natural visual objects. In J. Long & A. Baddeley (Eds.), *Attention and Performance IX* (pp. 153–168). Hillsdale, NJ: Lawrence Erlbaum Associates, Inc.

Jeannerod, M. (2001). Neural simulation of action: A unifying mechanism for motor cognition. *Neuro-Image*, *14*, 103–109.

Jeannerod, M. (2006). *Motor cognition. What actions tell the self.* Oxford, UK: Oxford University Press.

Johnson, S. H. (2000). Thinking ahead: The case for motor imagery in prospective judgements of prehension. *Cognition*, *74*, 33–70.

Kilner, J. M., Paulignan, Y., & Blakemore, S. J. (2003). An interference effect of observed biological movement on action. *Current Biology*, *13*, 522–525.

Kosslyn, S. M., Digirolomo, G. J., Thompson, W. L., & Alpert, N. M. (1998). Mental rotation of objects versus hands: Neural mechanisms revealed by positron emission tomography. *Psychophysiology*, *35*, 151–161.

Leube, D. T., Knoblich, G., Erb, M., Grodd, W., Bartels, M., & Kircher, T. J. (2003). The neural correlates of perceiving one's own movements. *NeuroImage*, *20*, 2084–2090.

Maeda, F., Kleiner-Fisman, G., & Pascual-Leone, A. (2002). Motor facilitation while observing hand actions: Specificity of the effect and role of observer's orientation. *Journal of Neurophysiology*, *87*, 1329–1335.

Maldjian, J. A., Laurienti, P. J., Burdette, J. B., & Kraft, R. A. (2003). An automated method for neuroanatomic and cytoarchitectonic atlas-based interrogation of fMRI data sets. *NeuroImage*, *19*, 1233–1239.

Mishkin, M., & Ungerleider, L. G. (1982). Contribution of striate inputs to the visuospatial functions of parieto-preoccipital cortex in monkeys. *Behavioural Brain Research*, *6*, 57–77.

Oldfield, R. C. (1971). The assessment and analysis of handedness: The Edinburgh Inventory. *Neuropsychologia*, *9*, 97–113.

Parsons, L. M. (1994). Temporal and kinematic properties of motor behavior reflected in mentally simulated action. *Journal of Experimental Psychology: Human Perception and Performance*, *20*, 709–730.

Paulignan, Y., Frak, V. G., Toni, I., & Jeannerod, M. (1997). Influence of object position and size on human prehension movements. *Experimental Brain Research*, *114*, 226–234.

Rizzolatti, G., Fadiga, L., Gallese, V., & Fogassi, L. (1995). Premotor cortex and the recognition of motor actions. *Cognitive Brain Research*, *3*, 131–141.

Rosenbaum, D. A., Meulenbroek, R. G. J., & Vaughan, J. (2004). What is the point of motor planning? *International Journal of Sport and Exercise Psychology*, *2*, 439–469.

Rossetti, Y., Revol, P., McIntosh, R., Pisella, L., Rode, G., Danckert, J., et al. (2005). Visually guided reaching: Bilateral posterior parietal lesions cause a switch from fast visuomotor to slow cognitive control. *Neuropsychologia*, *43*, 162–177.

Ruby, P., & Decety, J. (2001). Effect of subjective perspective taking during simulation of action: A PET investigation of agency. *Nature Neurosciences*, *4*, 546–550.

Sakata, H., Shibutani, H., Kawano, K., & Harrington, T. L. (1985). Neural mechanisms of space vision in the parietal association cortex of the monkey. *Vision Research*, *25*, 453–463.

Sakata, H., Tsutsui, K., & Taira, M. (2005). Toward an understanding of the neural processing for the 3D shape perception. *Neuropsychologia*, *43*, 151–161.

Sebanz, N., Knoblich, G., & Prinz, W. (2003). Representing other's actions: Just like one's own? *Cognition*, *88*, B11–B21.

Stelmach, G. E., Castiello, U., & Jeannerod, M. (1994). Orienting the finger opposition space during prehension movements. *Journal of Motor Behavior*, *26*, 178–186.

Strafella, A. P., & Paus, T. (2000). Modulation of cortical excitability during action observation. A transcranial magnetic stimulation study. *Neuroreport*, *11*, 2289–2292.

Stürmer, B., Aschersleben, G., & Prinz, W. (2000). Correspondence effects with manual gestures and postures: A study of imitation. *Journal of Experimental Psychology: Human Perception and Performance*, *26*, 1746–1759.

Talairach, J., & Tournoux, P. (1988). *Co-planar stereotaxic atlas of the human brain*. Stuttgart, Germany: Thieme Verlag.

Vogeley, K., & Fink, G. R. (2003). Neural correlates of the first person perspective. *Trends in Cognitive Science*, *7*, 38–42.

Vogeley, K., May, M., Ritzl, A., Falkai, P., Zilles, K., & Fink, G. R. (2004). Neural correlates of first person perspective as one constituent of human self-consciousness. *Journal of Cognitive Neuroscience*, *16*, 817–827.

Weiss, P., & Jeannerod, M. (1998). Getting a grasp on coordination. *News in Physiological Science*, *13*, 70–75.

Wohlschläger, A., Haggard, P., Gesierich, B., & Prinz, W. (2003). The perceived onset time of self- and other-generated actions. *Psychological Science*, *14*, 586–591.

SOCIAL NEUROSCIENCE, 2008, 3 (3–4), 368–387

Psychology Press
Taylor & Francis Group

How moving objects become animated: The human mirror neuron system assimilates non-biological movement patterns

Annerose Engel, Michael Burke, Katja Fiehler, Siegfried Bien, and Frank Rösler
Philipps-University Marburg, Marburg, Germany

The so-called mirror neuron system (MNS) responds when humans observe actions performed by a member of their own species. This activity is understood as an internal motor representation of the observed movement pattern. By contrasting meaningless human hand movements with meaningless artificial movements of objects in space, we tested the claim that exclusively movements belonging to the human motor repertoire have direct access to the MNS. Eighteen participants observed video clips of moving hands and objects while the hemodynamic response was recorded with functional magnetic resonance imaging. Second-level analysis of the hemodynamic responses revealed substantially overlapping activation patterns for both types of movements including relevant structures of the MNS (bilateral premotor and parietal areas, occipito-temporal junction, postcentral gyrus and the right superior temporal sulcus). This suggests that perceptual processing of moving hands and objects recruits similar and overlapping cortical networks. Direct comparison of the two movement types revealed stronger activations for hand movements mainly in structures of the MNS suggesting an "expertise effect". Overall, our results provide evidence that observing movements not explicitly belonging to the human motor repertoire can activate the human MNS, most likely because an association with a biological movement is evoked.

INTRODUCTION

The ability to recognize and correctly interpret movements of other living beings is a fundamental prerequisite for survival and successful interactions in a social environment. Therefore, it is plausible to assume that a special mechanism exists dedicated to the processing of biological movements, especially movements of members of one's own species. Results from behavioral (e.g., Brass, Bekkering, Wohlschläger, & Prinz, 2000; Johansson, 1973; Kilner, Paulignan, & Blakemore, 2003; Press, Bird, Flach, & Heyes, 2005), neuropsychological (Schenk & Zihl, 1997; Vaina, Lemay, Bienfang, Choi, & Nakayama, 1990), electrophysiological (Hari et al., 1998; Jokisch, Daum, Suchan, & Troje, 2005; Kessler et al., 2006), and neuroimaging (Grezes et al., 2001; Grossman & Blake, 2002; Pelphrey et al., 2003; Saygin, Wilson, Hagler, Bates, & Sereno, 2004) studies support the idea of a special mechanism in the human central nervous system (CNS) for processing biological motion and, in particular, movements of conspecifics.

The cortical network that is recruited for observing movements and actions is widely

Correspondence should be addressed to: Annerose Engel or Frank Rösler, Experimental and Biological Psychology, Philipps-University Marburg, Gutenbergstrasse 18, D-35032 Marburg, Germany. E-mail: engel@staff.uni-marburg.de or roesler@staff.uni-marburg.de

This research was supported by the research training group "Neural representation and action control" (DFG 885/1), the Max-Planck award for international cooperation assigned to FR, and a grant of the German Research Council (DFG Ro529/18–1).

We thank Valeria Gazzola and Christian Keysers for their support in providing their activation maps of the execution condition of their study and Ferdinand Binkofski and two anonymous reviewers for helpful comments on an earlier version of the manuscript.

www.psypress.com/socialneuroscience DOI:10.1080/17470910701612793

distributed and comprises areas that analyze visual movement cues in general and areas that seem to be highly specialized for biological movement patterns, either when observed or when generated. For general visual movement analysis at least two areas have been identified to be relevant. Electrophysiological studies in monkeys (Maunsell & Van Essen, 1983) and neuroimaging studies in humans (e.g., Watson et al., 1993) revealed that the occipito-temporal junction (i.e., in monkeys MT and MST, in humans MT/V5+) is important for processing visual movement cues. Additionally, the posterior region of the superior temporal sulcus (STS) seems to be important for higher order motion analysis (Noguchi, Kaneoke, Kakigi, Tanabe, & Sadato, 2005), especially for biological motion (Pelphrey, Morris, Michelich, Allison, & McCarthy, 2005) as well as for recognizing animacy induced by motion of simple geometrical shapes (Schultz, Friston, O'Doherty, Wolpert, & Frith, 2005). However, for processing movements and actions of other humans a special action-related processing mechanism seems to be relevant. By extrapolating the ideomotor principle, originally postulated by William James (1890), it has been assumed that a perceived action triggers directly and immediately the equivalent motor representation in the brain of the observer. "Mirror neurons" are suggested to constitute the neural basis for such a matching mechanism. These neurons were first described in monkeys and were found to respond when the animal either observes or when it performs a particular action (di Pellegrino, Fadiga, Fogassi, Gallese, & Rizzolatti, 1992; Gallese, Fadiga, Fogassi, & Rizzolatti, 1996; Rizzolatti, Fadiga, Gallese, & Fogassi, 1996). These visuo-motor neurons were detected in monkeys' ventral premotor area (F5) and the rostral part of the inferior parietal lobe. These areas form a parieto-frontal circuit—the so called "mirror neuron system" (MNS), and are considered as the neural basis for a direct observation–execution matching system (see Rizzolatti & Craighero, 2004, for a review). There is evidence that a homologous system also exists in humans, comprising the ventral premotor area, with parts of the inferior frontal gyrus extending to the precentral gyrus, and the inferior parietal lobe (e.g., Buccino et al., 2001; see Rizzolatti & Craighero, 2004, for a review).

Several findings suggest that the human MNS is exclusively activated by the observation of human movements (Costantini et al., 2005; Kilner et al., 2003; Tai, Scherfler, Brooks, Sawamoto, & Castiello, 2004). In a study by Buccino et al. (2004), participants observed biting and communication behavior of humans and of heterospecific animals (a monkey and a dog). The MNS was activated by visual stimuli showing biting regardless of the species while frontal activation of the MNS was found for observation of communication behavior of humans and lip smacking of monkeys, but not by snout movements of a barking dog. The authors postulated that only actions belonging to an observer's motor repertoire activate the MNS and interpreted this as activation of the corresponding motor representation. In contrast, actions not belonging to an observer's motor repertoire, such as barking, can only be analyzed by their visual properties, i.e., leading to an activation of MT/V5+ and STS only.

However, Press and colleagues (2005) used well-matched movement stimuli of a human and a robotic hand and found that robotic movement was sufficient for visuomotor priming of human movements. The authors argued that stimulus generalization leads to an association of the robotic arm movements with the relevant bodily movement patterns and they concluded that the "action observation-matching system is not tuned exclusively to human input. To varying degrees, we 'simulate' both human and robotic action" (Press et al., 2005, p. 639). The high specificity of MNS activity can also be questioned by the fact that it depends on the familiarity of the observed action, i.e., the more familiar an observed movement pattern the stronger the resonance of the CNS (Calvo-Merino, Glaser, Grezes, Passingham, & Haggard, 2005; Calvo-Merino, Grezes, Glaser, Passingham, & Haggard, 2006; Cross, Hamilton, & Grafton, 2006; Haslinger et al., 2005). In a recent study by Gazzola, Rizzolatti, Wicker, and Keysers (2007) it has been shown that the observation of actions performed by a robot arm and a human arm elicited equally strong activation within the areas of the MNS. The authors suggested that understanding the goal of an action is sufficient to activate the MNS, even when the kinematics of the action do not exactly match the human kinematics.

These results cast some doubt on the claim that exclusively biological movement patterns or, even more restricted, only movements belonging to the human motor repertoire are adequate stimuli to activate the observation–execution matching system. In the present study we used functional magnetic resonance imaging (fMRI) to investigate whether biological hand movements and non-biological object movements evoke different or overlapping activation patterns. If only actions of an observer's motor repertoire are adequate stimuli for the MNS, then only hand movements should activate its core areas, i.e., the ventral premotor area and the inferior parietal lobe, while movements of non-biological objects should activate areas relevant for visual movement analysis only, such as MT/V5+ and STS. We presented biological and non-biological moving stimuli in a delayed matching-to-sample task with different levels of difficulty. Participants encoded and maintained stimulus sets of three movements, with a varying amount of movement repetitions, and later decided whether a test stimulus matched an element of the set or not. In the easiest condition, participants observed the same movement three times, in the intermediate level of difficulty they saw one movement twice and one different movement, and in the highest level of difficulty they were shown three different movements. The variation of difficulty was used to substantiate the impact of an observed activation pattern. Areas showing increased activity to an increasing number of encoded stimuli are specifically involved in processing that stimulus (e.g., Druzgal & D'Esposito, 2001). Furthermore, repetition of a stimulus (as in difficulty level 1 compared to difficulty level 3) leads to an adaptation effect in areas that are specifically involved in processing that stimulus (e.g., Grill-Spector & Malach, 2001; or see Dinstein, Hasson, Rubin, & Heeger, 2007, for a recent study).

METHOD

Participants

Eighteen healthy students of the University of Marburg (nine female, mean age = 23 years, range = 19–26 years) participated in the present study. All were right-handed according to the standard handedness inventory (Oldfield, 1971) and had normal or corrected to normal vision. All participants were naive to the purpose of the study, and they gave their written consent and received monetary compensation.

Stimuli

The experimental stimulus set comprised 120 video clips of meaningless biological movements of two real hands and 120 video clips of meaningless non-biological, artificial movements of two sphere-like objects (see Figure 1 or Movie 1 and Movie 2 in the supplementary material).[1] Each video clip of a single movement lasted for 2 seconds (25 frames per second). The biological stimuli showed two hands and arms moving in front of a male actor's torso. The movements started and ended with the two fists positioned in front of the belly button. Movements over different trials varied in their direction and in the number of stretched fingers. Movement trajectories within one trial were either symmetrical or parallel for the two hands. Video clips of the non-biological movements showed two animated yellow spheres with two cone bulges, produced with the software package Blender 2.36 (http://www.blender3d.org/). These object movements had their common start and end position in the middle of the screen with the two cones facing each other. The sphere-like objects in different trials could move in different directions and could change their cone position by rotation. Movement trajectories for the two sphere-like objects within one trial were also either symmetrical or parallel and had a smooth, sinusoidal characteristic. This was achieved by following a velocity profile with an interpolation of a higher order Bezier curve between defined turning points. This means that the movement trajectories of the object movements were not tracked trajectories of hand movements but were artificial. We matched both movement types in their movement directions: All hand and object movements could follow a movement path of a straight line, a semicircle, a full circle or an ellipse. This means that the movement trajectories of the two hands or the two objects were not identical but highly similar. All movements were artificial, without obvious meaning (i.e., hand movements were not items from sign language, and object movements triggered no obvious associations with familiar objects). As a baseline condition static hands or

[1] The two supplementary movies can be accessed at: http://www.uni-marburg.de/fb04/team-roesler/stimuli/engel_etal_2007/. Movie 1 shows examples of three different hand movements presented during encoding for difficulty level 3. Movie 2 shows examples of three different object movements presented during encoding for difficulty level 3.

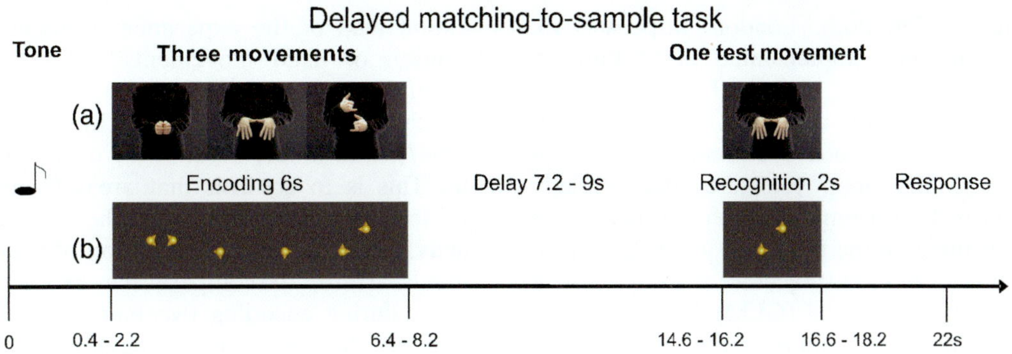

Figure 1. Timing of the working memory task with sample stimuli of the hand movement condition (a) and the object movement condition (b). Shown are selected single frames from the animated videos sequences.

static objects were presented in different positions. None of the movements or static positions were repeated over trials but were always novel.

Procedure

The experiment comprised two parts. In one part participants saw trials with hand movements and trials of the corresponding baseline condition (static hands). In the other part of the experiment trials with object movements and trials with the corresponding baseline (static objects) were presented. Ten of the participants started with the hand movements, the other eight with the object movements. Trial procedure was always the same: We applied a delayed matching-to-sample task (see Figure 1) to ensure that participants paid a comparable amount of attention to all movements and to implement varying levels of difficulty. In each trial participants heard a tone, then they encoded either three hand or three object movements (3×2 s), maintained them over a short delay of about 8 s (depending on the jitter interval), and, finally, saw one test movement (2 s) for which they had to indicate by pushing a button whether it belonged to the memory set or not. In the baseline trials the stimulus sequence was basically the same, but, rather than moving stimuli, only one static image of either two static hands or two static objects were presented during encoding (6 s) and as test stimulus (2 s). For each type of material three experimental conditions with increasing difficulty were constructed by manipulating the memory set size, i.e., the number of different movements presented in the encoding interval. In the easiest condition (level 1), participants saw one movement three times. In the intermediate condition (level 2), two different movements were presented and one was repeated. In the most difficult condition (level 3), participants had to encode three distinct movements. To separate overlapping blood oxygenation level dependent (BOLD) responses in event-related fMRI design and to decorrelate the events, we varied the time interval between the tone and the start of movement presentation (0.4–2.2 s) and between the end of the encoding phase and the start of the test stimulus (7.2–9 s). One trial lasted 22 seconds, and one experimental part comprised 16 trials per difficulty level (3×16 trials) and 16 baseline trials that were completely randomized. Participants practiced two trials of each experimental condition before the fMRI session outside the scanner to become familiar with the procedure and the material. Between the two functional scanning sessions (one with hand and the other one with object conditions) a structural image was acquired.

MRI acquisition and data analysis

All images were collected with a 1.5 T Signa scanner (GE Medical systems) using a standard head coil. To obtain a structural image 124 T1 weighted slices were recorded (slice thickness, 1.4 mm, without gap). Using a gradient echo EPI sequence, 733 functional images for each experimental part were acquired. The first four volumes were discarded to allow steady state equilibrium. Each volume consisted of 19 transversal AC–PC aligned slices (gap 0.5 mm, FOV 240 mm $\times$ 240 mm, matrix 64×64, voxel size 3.75 mm $\times$ 3.75 mm $\times$ 5 mm, TR 2 s, TE 60 ms, flip angle 80°).

The fMRI data were analyzed using SPM2 (Wellcome Department of Cognitive Neurology,

Institute of Neurology, London, http://www.fil.ion.ucl.ac.uk/spm/) implemented in Matlab 6.5 (The mathworks Inc., USA). Images of each subject were motion corrected, slice time corrected, normalized to a Montreal Neurological Institute (MNI) brain template and spatially smoothed with a 6 mm full-width half-maximum Gaussian filter. In the first-level analysis preprocessed images of each subject were analyzed with a General Linear Model (GLM). The predictors of the GLM model comprised the baseline condition, the difficulty level 1, 2, and 3 separately for hand and object movements during the encoding epoch, as well as further predictors of no interest for the delay and recognition epochs. All predictors were modeled as boxcar functions of appropriate length and convolved with the canonical hemodynamic response function, the temporal and the dispersion derivatives. A high-pass filter (time constant 512 seconds—equivalent to twice the duration of the interval between the most infrequently occurring event group) was applied to remove subject-specific low frequency drift that is mostly due to biological rhythms and to magnetic field drift. Statistical parametric maps for the contrast three different movements vs. static images were generated for each of the two movement types of the encoding epoch and for all participants separately. To identify areas that showed increasing amplitudes of the hemodynamic response with increasing level of difficulty during encoding further analyses with contrast weights [3, 1, −1, −3] for the difficulty levels 3, 2, 1, and baseline were calculated for both movement types. All contrasts of each subject were used in a second-level random effects analysis. First, one sample *t*-tests were used to identify regions of significant activation during encoding of three different movements with respect to static images and regions that showed increasing BOLD response with increasing task difficulty during encoding. To visualize the activation for different levels of difficulty the trial averaged voxel time courses were extracted for representative voxels (based on measured grey values compared to averaged signal in this voxel within the whole session). Second, to test whether there were common areas that were significantly activated in both contrasts for hand and object movements (compared to their static baseline) a conjunction analysis was calculated (Nichols, Brett, Andersson, Wager, & Poline, 2005). For Figure A2 in the Appendix the results of the conjunction analysis were masked with the activation map of the experimental condition "execution of hand movements" (thresholded at significance level for $p<.001$, uncorrected), which was recorded in a study by Gazzola et al. (2007), who kindly made these data available to us. This is to confirm that areas found in the present study do overlap with areas that are activated during motor execution of hand movements. Third, to compare the two movement types during encoding two paired *t*-tests of the relative effect movement vs. baseline (to take into account that the data of the two movement types were acquired in two different sessions) were calculated: [(three different hand movements vs. static hands) – (three different object movements vs. static objects)] and [(three different object movements vs. static objects) – (three different hand movements vs. static hands)]. To focus on only those regions that were active in at least one condition, either during hand or object movement encoding, the resulting activation map was masked with the activation map of the contrast [(three different object movements vs. static objects) OR (three different hand movements vs. static hands)]. Results were illustrated by means of software package MRIcro (http://www.sph.sc.edu/comd/rorden/mricro.html) by superimposing SPM{t} maps upon a MNI standard brain. Statistical maps were thresholded for significance at $p<.001$, uncorrected for multiple comparisons and by using a cluster-size criterion > 5 voxels. All reported maxima of a cluster have a significance level of $p<.05$, corrected for multiple comparisons by false discovery rate (FDR).

RESULTS

Behavioral data

Reaction times and response accuracy in the delayed matching-to-sample task were recorded during the scanning session. Response latencies increased with increasing difficulty level (larger memory set size) in both conditions. Mean response latencies in milliseconds (± standard deviation, *SD*) were in the hand condition for baseline: 1486 (±619); level 1: 2082 (±561); level 2: 2225 (±511); and level 3: 2279 (±506), and in the object condition for baseline: 1428 (±599); level 1: 2119 (±545); level 2: 2262 (±513); and level 3: 2371 (±480). Error rates showed equivalent trends for increasing difficulty, mean in percent of incorrect responses ($\pm$SD), for hand movements baseline: 5.2 ($\pm$5.8); level 1: 3.1 ($\pm$5.4); level 2: 17.7 ($\pm$11.0); level 3: 21.5 ($\pm$10.6); and for object movements baseline: 4.5 ($\pm$5.6); level 1: 6.9 ($\pm$10.0); level 2: 11.2 ($\pm$7.4); level 3: 22.6 ($\pm$9.1). Data were analyzed using repeated measures ANOVAs with factors level of difficulty (baseline, 1, 2, and 3) and movement type (hand movements and object movements). ANOVAs revealed a significant main effect of factor difficulty for reaction times, $F(3, 51) = 45.74$, $p < .001$, and for error rates, $F(3, 51) = 34.18$, $p < .001$. Linear contrasts revealed significant differences between all difficulty levels (except for error rates between baseline and difficulty level 1). This result confirms the successful manipulation of difficulty. Main effect movement type was not significant either for reaction times, $F(1, 17) = 0.388$, $p = .541$, or for error rates, $F(1, 17) = 0.191$, $p = .668$, and the same holds for the interactions, reaction times: $F(3, 51) = 1.40$, $p = .281$; error rates: $F(3, 51) = 3.13$, $p = .057$. Thus, the cognitive demands of the working-memory task were comparable for both movement types and differences in the hemodynamic responses between movement types can not be attributed to a variation of difficulty.

fMRI data

Observation of hand movements. The BOLD response pattern during encoding of hand movements (contrast: difficulty level 3 vs. static images of hands) is summarized in Table 1 and in Figure 2, A1. Random effects analysis revealed a widespread activation pattern including the occipito-temporal junction bilaterally, the STS with activation being larger and more prominent in the right hemisphere, the left superior temporal gyrus and the inferior parietal lobe along the intraparietal sulcus. The latter activation extended bilaterally into the superior parietal lobe. Frontal activation was found bilaterally in the ventral premotor area, which partly covered the inferior frontal gyrus, Brodmann area (BA) 44, and extended into the precentral gyrus, and in the dorsal premotor area (PMd) on the crown of the precentral gyrus (PMd proper). At more central sites the supplementary motor area (mainly SMA proper) and the postcentral gyrus were activated bilaterally. The latter activation cluster covers the somatosensory cortex, with the most prominent peak located in BA 2. Apart from the BOLD responses in the occipito-temporal junction and STS, all other activation clusters were more prominent in the left than in the right hemisphere.

Observation of object movements. The observation of object movements (contrast: difficulty level 3 vs. static images of objects) evoked a similar but more circumscribed activation pattern as the observation of hand movements (cf. Table 1 and Figure 2, A2). The random effects analysis for object movements also showed a large activation bilaterally in the occipito-temporal junction, the inferior parietal lobe along the intraparietal sulcus extending towards the superior parietal lobe. Activation in the STS was significant only in the right hemisphere. In the frontal lobe, there was a bilateral activation in the PMd on the precentral gyrus, the left inferior frontal gyrus and the adjacent precentral gyrus (ventral premotor area). Activation of SMA did not reach the significance threshold. Again, the postcentral gyrus was significantly activated with most of its activation located mainly in area BA 2 of the somatosensory cortex.

The separate analysis for the contrast of the results of the eight participants who saw the object condition in the first experimental part, shows a similar activation pattern as the whole group analysis (cf. Figure A1 in the Appendix). In both hemispheres areas of the occipito-temporal junction, the inferior and superior parietal lobe, the ventral and dorsal premotor area, the postcentral gyrus, as well as the right STS were activated.

Activations for levels of difficulty. The contrast (level of difficulty 3 > level of difficulty 2 > level of difficulty 1 > static images) was calculated for hand and object movements separately to identify areas that showed increasing amplitudes of the hemodynamic response with increasing level of difficulty (number of movements to be encoded) and results are reported in Table A1 in the Appendix. The activation cluster for this analysis had almost the same location and distribution as the areas reported for the contrasts (difficulty level 3 vs. static images) for both movement types (cf. Table 1 and Table A1 in the Appendix). To prove and illustrate this result, Figure 2, B, shows the hemodynamic responses for different levels of difficulty for selected, representative voxels of the left ventral premotor area, the left inferior parietal lobe, and the right STS. As can be seen, the amplitude of the BOLD response increased during encoding with increasing level of difficulty.

TABLE 1
Activations for hand and object movements: Contrasts moving vs. static hands and moving vs. static objects

			Hand movements				*Object movements*			
			MNI coordinates				*MNI coordinates*			
Anatomical region	*Hemisphere*	*Brodmann area*	*x*	*y*	*z*	*Z-score*	*x*	*y*	*z*	*Z-score*
Ventral premotor area	L	44/6	−54	6	33	*5.14*	−60	3	33	*3.66*
	R	44/6	48	12	27	*4.26*				
Dorsal premotor area	L	6	−24	−21	66	*4.42*	−30	−12	54	*3.71*
	R	6	30	−12	66	*4.62*	24	−18	57	*3.82*
			51	−9	54	*4.51*	42	−3	60	*3.56*
SMA proper	L/R	6	−6	−12	69	*5.25*				
Postcentral gyrus	L	2	−57	−18	42	*4.66*	−57	−21	42	*3.65*
	R	2	60	−21	39	*4.22*	63	−24	45	*4.32*
Inferior parietal lobe/intraparietal sulcus	L	40	−36	−48	48	*4.09*	−30	−51	48	*3.56*
			−51	−33	33	*4.80*	−54	−30	39	*3.31*
	R	40	33	−42	45	*5.04*	33	−45	51	*4.41*
Superior parietal lobe	L	7	−36	−54	60	*4.69*	−33	−60	63	*4.62*
	R	7	12	−63	51	*3.80*	18	−60	57	*3.36*
			27	−57	54	*4.16*				
Superior temporal gyrus	L	22	−42	−42	18	*3.65*	−51	−39	18	*4.20*
	L	22	−57	−51	3	*3.22*				
Superior temporal sulcus	R	22/21	54	−42	9	*4.97*	57	−42	3	*4.09*
Occipito-temporal junction	L	19/37	−48	−72	−3	*4.72*	−48	−75	−3	*4.36*
	R	19/37	42	−66	−3	*5.41*	45	−66	−6	*4.47*
Body of caudate nucleus	R		12	12	−12	*3.49*				

Notes: Shown are MNI coordinates for significant activation maxima of all clusters of the random effects analyses. Thresholds for whole voxelwise brain analysis: $p < .001$, uncorrected for multiple comparisons. All cluster maxima are significant with $p < .05$, corrected for multiple comparisons with FDR.

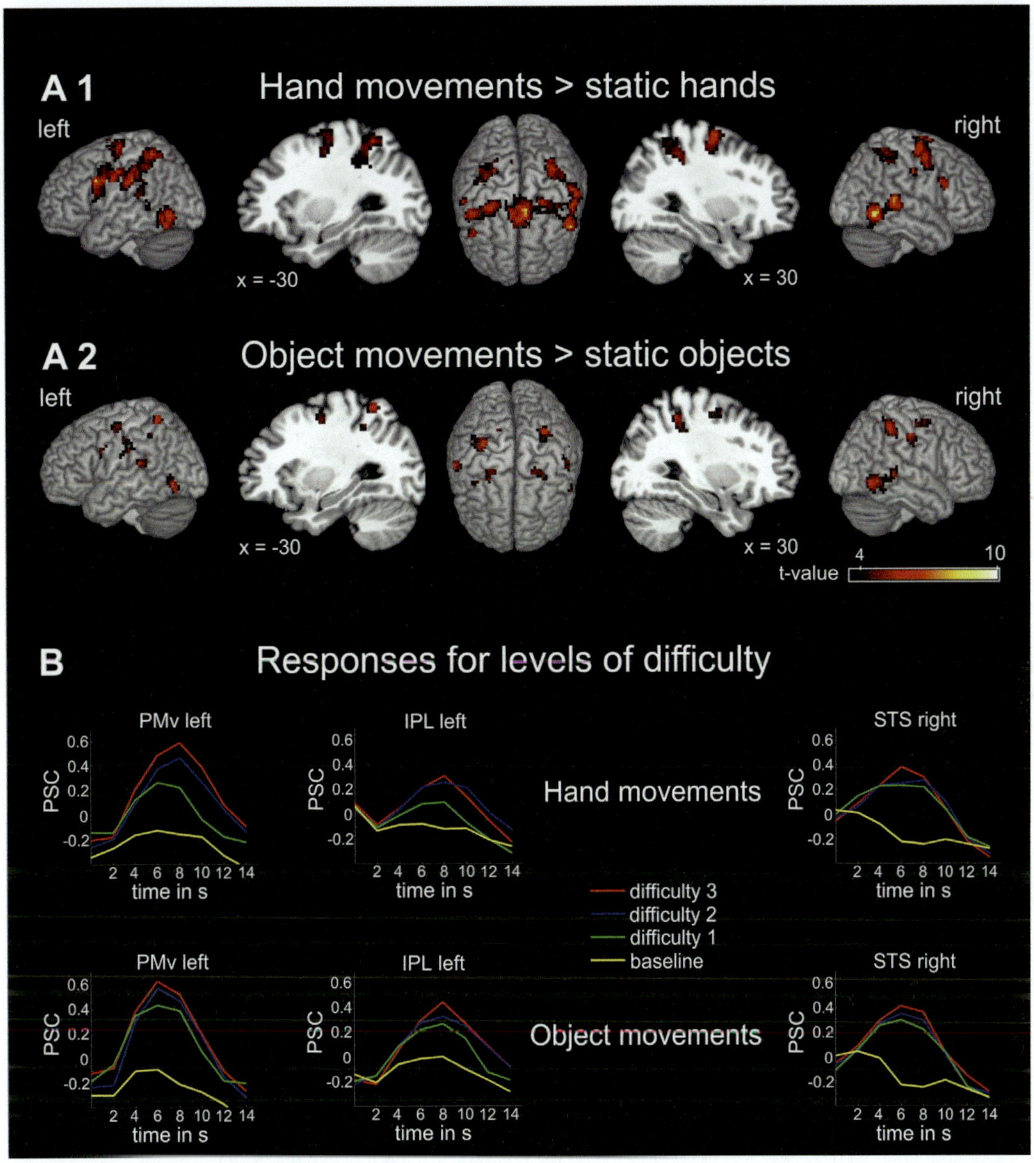

Figure 2. (A) BOLD activation patterns for hand movements vs. static hands (top, A1) and object movements vs. static objects (middle, A2). SPM{t} maps are superimposed on a MNI standard brain. Statistical maps were thresholded for significance with $p < .001$ (uncorrected for multiple comparisons) and a cluster size of >5 voxels. (B) Trial averaged voxel time courses for the difficulty levels of hand (B, upper part) and object movements (B, lower part) for representative voxels of the MNS: ventral premotor area (PMv) for hand [–54, 6, 33] and object [–60, 3, 33] movements, inferior parietal lobe (IPL) for hand [–54, –33, 45] and object [–30, –51, 48] movements; superior temporal sulcus (STS) for hand [54, –42, 9] and object [57, –42, 3] movements. PSC: Percent signal change.

Conjunction analysis. All in all, the two activation patterns obtained while participants observed and stored hand and object movements show substantial overlap, and this similarity increased when the significance threshold for the object movement was lowered. To substantiate this result and to prove which areas are significantly activated during observation of both movement types Figure 3, A, and Table 2 show the result of a conjunction analysis. In both hemispheres the occipito-temporal junction, the inferior and superior parietal lobe, the dorsal and ventral premotor area, the postcentral gyrus, the right STS and the left superior temporal gyrus are significantly activated in both movement observation conditions. To compare whether this activation pattern is overlapping with the activations caused by the execution of real hand movements, we masked the results of the conjunction analysis with an activation map for a condition where

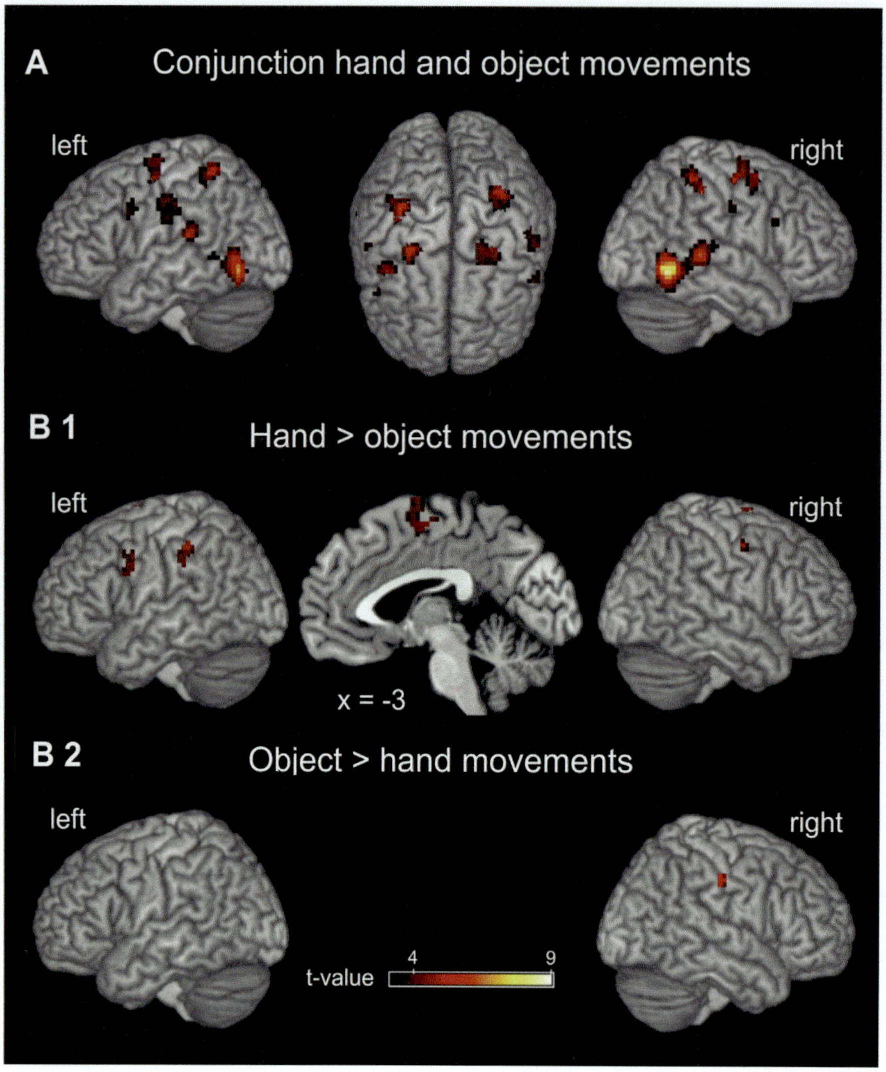

Figure 3. BOLD activation patterns for: (A) a conjunction analysis for hand movements vs. static hands AND object movements vs. static objects; (B) direct contrasts of the two movement types: B1 contrast [(hand movements vs. static hands) > (object movements vs. static objects)]; B2 [(object movements vs. static objects) > (hand movements vs. static hands)]. All SPM{t} maps are superimposed on a MNI standard brain. Statistical maps were thresholded for significance with $p < .001$ (uncorrected for multiple comparisons) and a cluster size of >5 voxels.

participants had to execute hand movements. These data were taken from a study of Gazzola et al. (2007). We used this masking approach to compare activation patterns on cluster level and not only peak coordinates. The masked conjunction (see Appendix, Figure A2) confirms that the activation pattern during observation of hand and object movements found in the present study is strongly overlapping with activations found in the study by Gazzola et al. (2007) for real executed hand movements.

Direct contrast of hand vs. object movements. To further explore congruencies and incongruencies of the BOLD responses evoked by the two movement types we calculated a direct contrast [(hand movements vs. static hands) – (object movements vs. static objects)] and [(object movements vs. static objects) – (hand movements vs. static hand)]. We restricted the results by a mask to the areas that were active either for hand or for object movements. The analysis revealed that the signal strength was stronger for hand movements in the left ventral premotor area, the left inferior parietal lobe (partly in the intraparietal sulcus), the right PMd area, and in SMA proper (see Table 3 and Figure 3, B1). In contrast, stronger activation for object movements was found

TABLE 2
Activations for the conjunction analysis: moving vs. static hands AND moving vs. static objects

			Conjunction analysis			
			MNI coordinates			
Anatomical region	*Hemisphere*	*Brodmann area*	*x*	*y*	*z*	*Z-score*
Ventral premotor area	L	44/6	−57	3	33	*3.74*
	R	44/6	51	9	30	*3.46*
Dorsal premotor area	L	6	−24	−15	54	*4.62*
	R	6	27	−18	57	*5.19*
		6	45	−6	60	4.16
Postcentral gyrus	L	2	−57	−21	42	*3.91*
	R	2	60	−18	39	*3.45*
Inferior parietal lobe/intraparietal sulcus	L	40	−30	−48	51	*3.90*
		40	−51	−30	39	*3.84*
	R	40	33	−45	51	*6.57*
Superior parietal lobe	L	7	−33	−57	63	*4.91*
	R	7	15	−60	51	*3.81*
Superior temporal gyrus	L	22	−42	−42	18	*5.03*
	R	22	63	−39	9	*4.23*
Superior temporal sulcus	R	22/21	51	−42	6	*5.61*
Occipito-temporal junction	L	19/37	−48	−75	−6	*6.01*
	R	19/37	45	−66	−6	*7.06*

Notes: Shown are MNI coordinates for significant activation maxima of all clusters of the random effects analyses. Thresholds for whole voxelwise brain analysis: $p < .001$, uncorrected for multiple comparisons. All cluster maxima are significant with $p < .05$, corrected for multiple comparisons with FDR.

exclusively on the right supramarginal gyrus (see Table 3 and Figure 3, B2).

DISCUSSION

The present study investigated whether the MNS of human observers responds only to movement stimuli belonging to the human motor repertoire or also to non-biological object movements. To this end, we contrasted movements of human hands and of non-biological objects in a delayed matching-to-sample task while the BOLD response was recorded. The results clearly show that both types of moving stimuli do activate a substantially overlapping network of areas, including the relevant structures of the MNS, i.e., ventral premotor areas and the inferior parietal lobe. This means that hand and non-biological object movements, as used in this study, are analyzed similarly by the CNS and that activity in the MNS is not restricted to actions belonging

TABLE 3
Direct contrast of hand vs. object movements, relative dominance of activation level

			MNI coordinates			
Anatomical region	*Hemisphere*	*Brodmann area*	*x*	*y*	*z*	*Z-score*
Hand vs. object movements						
Ventral premotor area	L	6	−51	−3	42	3.51
Dorsal premotor area	R	6	54	−12	51	3.82
SMA proper	L/R	6	−3	−15	60	3.57
Inferior parietal lobe/intraparietal sulcus	L	40	−42	−42	48	3.87
Inferior parietal lobe	R	40	−57	−39	48	3.32
Object vs. hand movements						
Supramarginal gyrus/inferior parietal lobe	R	40	66	−27	42	4.30

Note: Shown are MNI coordinates for significant activation maxima of all clusters of the random effect analyses. Thresholds for whole voxelwise brain analysis: $p < .001$, uncorrected for multiple comparisons. All cluster maxima are significant with $p < .05$, corrected for multiple comparisons with FDR. IPL = inferior parietal lobe. SMA = supplementry motor area.

to the human motor repertoire. Direct contrasts revealed quantitative rather than qualitative differences, i.e., the same neural networks were activated by both types of stimuli, but the relative strength differed. Hand movements evoked stronger BOLD responses than object movements in the left inferior parietal lobe and in the premotor area bilaterally, while objects evoked stronger responses in the right supramarginal gyrus.

In the following, we will relate these findings to evidence available from the literature. We will first discuss the activations of the common network found for both movement types, that is, the areas relevant for the visual analysis of movement patterns as such (MT/V5+ and STS), the activations specifically related to the MNS and relevant for an analysis of actions (ventral premotor area, inferior parietal lobe), and the activations in other areas specialized for somatosensory and motor processing (dorsal premotor area, postcentral gyrus/BA 2). Then we will discuss the differences between the two movement types revealed by direct contrasts. Finally, we will conclude by suggesting that the human MNS dominates processing of complex movement trajectories and, therefore, easily assimilates movements of non-biological objects as biological.

A common network of areas for both movement types

Areas specialized for visual motion analysis: Occipito-temporal junction and STS. Both movement types elicited a pronounced bilateral activation in the occipito-temporal junction and the right STS. The occipito-temporal junction belongs to the human visual extrastriate cortex and is regarded as the homologue to monkeys' area MT/MST, known to play a prominent role in early visual movement analysis (Dukelow et al., 2001; Tootell et al., 1995; Watson et al., 1993). STS is involved in coding movement cues relevant for the perception of biological motion, as suggested by electrophysiology in monkeys (Perrett et al., 1989) and brain-imaging studies in humans (Allison, Puce, & McCarthy, 2000; Bonda, Petrides, Ostry, & Evans, 1996; Grossman & Blake, 2002). However, although the STS has proved to be sensitive to biological motion, it seems not to be tuned exclusively to such stimuli. Several authors have shown that the right STS also responds to non-biological motion, such as movements of dots, although this response was diminished compared to biological motion (e.g., Grossman & Blake, 2002; Noguchi et al., 2005; Peuskens, Vanrie, Verfaillie, & Orban, 2005).

Pelphrey and colleagues (2003) observed a stronger activation in the occipito-temporal junction for non-biological motion (i.e., meaningless movements of cylinders) as compared to biological motion stimuli (i.e., movement of a human), while the reversed pattern was observed in the right STS (stronger activation for biological than non-biological movement stimuli). We could not confirm such differences for the stimuli used in the present study, which suggests similar processing for both movement types in the areas of early movement analysis and STS. At first sight this seems to be contradictory. The major difference between our study and that of Pelphrey et al. (2003) is that our participants had to solve a working memory task, while participants in the Pelphrey study had no specific task and observed all movements passively. During observation without performing a task there is little control over whether participants pay a comparable amount of attention to all conditions and Pelphrey and colleagues (2003) themselves stated that the biological and non-biological stimuli were processed differently. In the following we will consider further arguments in support of the claim that both movement types were processed similarly in the present study.

Areas specialized for action analysis: The mirror neuron system. The inferior parietal lobe (IPL) and the ventral premotor area (PMv) are considered to be core structures of the human MNS (Rizzolatti & Craighero, 2004). These areas are activated when participants observe as well as when they execute an action (see Grezes & Decety, 2001, for a review). In the present experiment these areas were activated by both types of perceptual stimuli—moving hands and moving objects. In our study we had no condition where participants actually performed hand movements, and therefore we cannot prove that the same areas would be activated for execution of the same hand movements. However, the substantial overlap with coordinates of motor execution conditions in other studies (e.g., Bangert et al., 2006; Binkofski et al., 1999; Fiehler, Burke, Engel, Bien, & Rösler, in press; Gazzola et al., 2007) gives strong support to the view that the areas activated in the present study can be interpreted as MNS. To strengthen this claim we checked the overlap of our results with the results from a condition involving motor execution. To this end our results of the conjunction analysis were masked with the activation map for execution of hand movements recorded in the study by Gazzola et al. (2007; cf. Appendix, Figure A2). This analysis confirms the high similarity of the two activation patterns for movement observation and movement execution. This masking approach is more comprehensive and informative than a rough comparison of peak coordinates, because it takes into account the whole cluster of activated voxels. Of course, this masking procedure is subject to possible differences of the functional anatomies between the two groups of participants, and testing motor execution in the same participants would have been a better approach.

The activation pattern elicited by observation of moving hands is highly consistent with previous research (Buccino et al., 2001; Costantini et al., 2005; Grezes, Armony, Rowe, & Passingham, 2003; Grezes, Costes, & Decety, 1998) and confirms that observing hand movements, even if they are meaningless, activates cortical areas that process corresponding motor representations. Thus, the long-standing ideomotor hypothesis, originally proposed by William James (1890) and later thoroughly investigated with electromyographic recordings and in relation to facial expression (see, e.g., Leventhal 1984; McGuigan, 1978), gets strong support now from modern brain imaging measures.

The surprising finding of the present study was that clearly non-biological objects—spheres with two attached cones that followed artificial movement trajectories—also activated the MNS. These activations were in general less pronounced, but they comprised, by and large, the same network as activated by the moving hands. How can this be explained? The object movements in the present study that have more or less similar (but still artificial) trajectories compared to biological movements could be automatically analyzed and "understood" as biological, even if they are in some sense "impossible," or the objects with the two bulging cones could be considered as hands with fingers. If so, this association was not induced by the experimenters, it rather had to be elicited by the stimuli or the task in this study itself. The results of the analysis of the eight participants who saw the object movements first (cf. Appendix, Figure A1), suggest that this association must have been evoked immediately and was not caused by the preceding intensive examination of hand movements. The assumption that object movements are understood as biological is strongly supported by behavioral data, e.g., of Heider and Simmel (1944) and of Michotte (1963), showing that animated objects are interpreted by most people as socially interacting and described with intentional, causal terms (e.g., "The big square is chasing the little circle", if a movie shows two such objects moving across the screen in the same direction, one after another, while the speed of the second is continuously increased). Furthermore, this is confirmed by neuroimaging studies (e.g., Blakemore et al., 2003; Castelli, Frith, Happé, & Frith, 2002; Castelli, Happé, Frith, & Frith, 2000) that used similar stimuli of geometrical shapes as Heider and Simmel (1944). These studies also showed that movements of abstract shapes can activate a cortical network that is known to be involved in mentalizing (Blakemore et al., 2003; Castelli et al., 2000, 2002). It seems very likely that the object stimuli used in the present experiment were also interpreted as biological. Consistent with this hypothesis, Press and colleagues (2005) found that the observation-matching system is not specific for human movements, but that a robotic hand movement can prime a real hand movement, i.e., that both are processed as exemplars of the same category. In a recent study, Amorim, Isableu, and Jarraya (2006) reported for a mental rotation task that abstract Shepard–Metzler cubes can facilitate embodiment when only slight changes are made, e.g., when a head is attached to the otherwise completely abstract figure.

However, the present study does not provide information on why participants interpreted the stimuli as biological. One reason could be that perceptual visual features of the object movements were similar to biological movements, because the objects followed a smooth sinusoidal path (a bottom-up effect). On the other hand, it could also be that the objects were actively interpreted as biological due to task demands (a top-down effect). Participants had to memorize the hand and object movements for a later recognition test, and it might have been a good strategy to encode the object movements also as hand-like or biological to improve task performance. To disentangle these two possible explanations, we conducted another study (Engel, Burke, Fiehler, Bien, & Rösler, 2007) in which we presented objects with different movement trajectories under different task instructions. We observed that activity within the structures of the MNS seemed to depend more on specific task demands rather than on the perceptual properties of the movement trajectories. In accordance with this assumption, Gazzola et al. (2007) found activity in the MNS for the observation of a real hand and a robot hand grasping objects, and stressed the point that understanding the goal of a movement (i.e., a object that is picked up) is more important for activity within the structures of the MNS than the specific kinematics of a movement. Furthermore, the stimuli used in the present study were meaningless per se. Yet due to the fact that the participants had to maintain the movement sequence in memory, it could be that it was helpful to recognize a particular sequence of these meaningless movements. This would be also consistent with Schubotz and von Cramon (2004), who argued that the ventral premotor area may not only be important for encoding goal-directed movements, but also for recognizing particular patterns of sequentially changing object stimuli. They suggested that the ventral premotor area plays a critical role in representing sequential information, and is involved in prediction (Schubotz, 2007). This notion would agree with our finding that the ventral premotor area is active when sequences of either moving objects or moving hands are encoded, because both types of video clips will have been analyzed with respect to sequential transitions of movements.

One may question whether the parieto-frontal network found in the present study might be more closely related to functions of working memory rather than to the MNS and action simulation as such. Basically, many code- and modality-specific theories of memory postulate that areas involved in on-line processing of particular information are also involved in encoding and storing that type of information (Damasio 1989; Martin 2007; McClelland, McNaughton, & O'Reilly 1995; Rösler & Heil, 2003). Therefore, it is assumed that pure observation and encoding of stimuli share common cortical networks. However, a more important question is, if the frontal activation observed in the present study could possibly be better explained by executive functions of working memory demands. The frontal activity is localized mainly on the precentral gyrus (BA 6) and extends only slightly into the inferior frontal gyrus (BA 44). This is consistent with the localization of activation found for the observation of hand movements by others, e.g., Buccino et al., 2001, found activation in the inferior frontal gyrus (IFG)/PMv in a somatotopic manner for mouth, hand and foot movements with peak activations for mouth movements in pars opercularis of the IFG, for hand movements dorsally located mainly in BA 6 and for foot movements even more dorsal than hand movements. In contrast, working memory functions are associated with an activity in the dorsolateral prefrontal cortex with more frontal activation foci (mainly BA 46/9/45; e.g., D'Esposito, Postle, & Rypma, 2000) than observed in the present study. Moreover, even if the activation of the PMv did actually reflect working memory load, there would be no plausible explanation of why hand movements led to a stronger activation than object movements as both were behaviorally equivalent (cf. reaction times and error rates).

Areas specialized for somatosensory and motor processing. Additional activation clusters, besides those seen in areas specialized for visual motion and for action analysis, appeared in the dorsal premotor area (PMd) and in area BA 2 of the postcentral gyrus. These areas are functionally related to sensorimotor information processing, but, in general, are not seen as core elements of the MNS.

The dorsal premotor area has been related to movement programming (Picard & Strick, 2001) as well as to tasks that require spatial attention, spatial coding, mental rotation, and supramodal sequencing of action plans (see Schubotz & von Cramon, 2003, for a review). Moreover, it seems also to be critical for forming associations between visual cues and motor responses (Chouinard, Leonard, & Paus, 2005). In accordance with the reported literature, in our study PMd was activated while participants encoded sequences of three single movements (either hands or objects), i.e., in a task that also needs spatial coding and parsing a movement pattern into its constituting elements.

Activation observed in the postcentral gyrus covered mainly BA 2 of the somatosensory cortex. BA 2 receives information from skin mechanoreceptors and kinesthetic/proprioceptive receptors and is assumed to process higher level somatosensory information (see Grefkes, Geyer, Schormann, Roland, & Zilles, 2001, for an overview). It is also claimed that the sensory motor cortex is involved in mental simulation of actions (Grezes & Decety, 2001). MEG studies (Avikainen, Forss, & Hari, 2002; Mottonen, Jarvelainen, Sams, & Hari, 2005; Rossi et al., 2002), fMRI studies (Haslinger et al., 2005; Schubotz & von

Cramon, 2004) and a study with autoradiographic ^{14}C-deoxyglucose recordings in monkeys (Raos, Evangeliou, & Savaki, 2004) substantiate an involvement of the somatosensory cortex during action observation. Such interplay between motor and somatosensory cortex during action observation seems plausible, because given that perceived actions trigger automatically corresponding motor representations, then these will include also haptic (feedback) information.

The present data supplement previous findings in that not only the core structures of the MNS were activated by moving hands (and objects), but also additional areas that are specialized in visual motion analysis as such and others that are part of a more extended somatosensory motor system (PMd, BA 2). The specific features of the stimulus set and the specific contrasts calculated to accentuate effects will most likely decide about the exact ensemble of areas activated in a particular experiment. Nevertheless, the data accumulated in this study and others provide strong support for the notion that not just narrowly circumscribed brain areas can be functionally related to psychological constructs, but rather that widely extended cortical networks in which many different features are bound together form their basis.

Areas sensitive for the level of difficulty—an argument for the common network. The MNS and most of the other reported areas (e.g., left PMv, left IPL, right STS; cf. Figure 2, B, and Table A1 in the Appendix) revealed increasing hemodynamic responses with increasing difficulty of the task. In particular, the BOLD response increased systematically for observation of both hands and objects when more movements had to be encoded while the response to the static baseline conditions were always rather weak. This effect—as reflected by trial averaged voxel time courses—holds for both conditions and corroborates the specificity of the network for movement analysis. Whether the effect of increasing BOLD responses can by explained by increasing working memory load, or whether it is rather an effect of adaptation in the easiest level of difficulty (presentation of one movement three times), cannot be disentangled in the present study. An explanation in terms of adaptation would be confirmed by the findings of Gazzola, Wicker, Rizzolatti, and Keysers (2004) and Dinstein et al. (2007), who found decreased activity within the MNS for presentation of repeated movements. However, both explanations do substantiate the claim that the areas showing a graded variation of the BOLD response, which is closely related to the variation of difficulty, are specifically involved in processing a particular stimulus type.

Direct contrast of the two types of moving stimuli

By directly comparing the activation patterns of moving vs. static hands with moving vs. static objects we found more activity for the hand stimuli in the left IPL and bilaterally in the premotor area, i.e., in core structures of the MNS. More activity in these areas for biological movements has been related to the degree of expertise (Calvo-Merino et al., 2005, 2006; Cross et al., 2006; Haslinger et al., 2005). For example, Calvo-Merino and colleagues (2005) reported stronger activity in the MNS when experts in classical ballet and experts in capoeira observed dance sequences of their own style compared to dance sequences of the other style for which they had no expertise. Similarly, Cross et al. (2006) found stronger activation in the left IFG/PMv and in the inferior parietal lobe when participants observed dance movements which they had trained before compared to untrained control movements. These studies suggest that the MNS develops through experience with particular movement patterns (see also Heyes, 2001; Keysers & Perrett, 2004). Following this argument, one could say that we also found more activation for the hand condition in these areas, because participants have much more experience with hand movements, both as active performers as well as passive observers. The reduced activity for moving objects in the very same areas would suggest that these movements were interpreted as biological too, or at least that they triggered some associations with biological movements. However, as they had the status of novel, unfamiliar movement patterns the resonance within the matching system was less pronounced.

Confirmed by the direct contrast, only hand movements revealed significant activation of SMA proper with a slight extension into pre-SMA. Functionally, SMA proper has been closely linked to motor planning (Picard & Strick, 2001), although it has also been found to be active when actions were imagined or observed (Grezes & Decety, 2001). Thus, this area seems to be involved in the direct matching process, a hypothesis that is supported by a number of studies: Zentgraf et al. (2005) found activity in SMA proper when complex movements were observed with the aim of imitating them later; Picard and Strick (1996) reported several studies showing that SMA proper is engaged in automatic performance of learned movements; and Cross et al. (2006) showed stronger activation in pre-SMA extending into SMA proper for the observation of trained compared to untrained dance sequences. Therefore, stronger SMA activity for hand movements in our study could indicate that hand movements do automatically trigger motor representations that are well established.

One single area on the right supramarginal gyrus showed stronger activation for objects compared to hand movements. An activation at the same location was also observed when participants watched impossible compared to realistic finger movements (Costantini et al., 2005). The authors argued that the posterior parietal cortex may serve as an interface for transferring somatosensory input and information from joint positions to areas of motor programming and that more activity in this area could reflect an additional effort to map postures to the motor output that are not executable. Something similar might apply to the stimuli in our study. The participants may have encoded the object movements as biological and the bulging cones attached to the spheres may even have triggered an association with fingers. However, the objects performed movements that do not belong to the repertoire of hand movements, e.g., they rotated over larger angles than are possible for hands. Consequently, observing such impossible movements could have imposed extra load on the area of the supramarginal gyrus (cf. Costantini et al., 2005).

CONCLUSIONS

In this study we found that not only hand but also non-biological artificial object movements activate the human MNS. This outcome supports results of other recent studies (e.g., Gazzola et al., 2007; Press et al., 2005). The findings suggest that the human MNS is a highly efficient and, in some sense, dominant structure that assimilates perceived movement patterns whenever this is possible. From both a phylogenetic and an ontogenetic perspective this seems highly plausible. Studies showing that MNS activity is also dependent on experience (e.g., Bangert et al., 2006; Calvo-Merino et al., 2005) provide further support to the notion that this system is tuned by a continuous interaction with the environment. Since biological movement patterns are the first and probably also the most frequently encountered moving stimuli in life, it is not too surprising that movements of non-biological objects are spontaneously analyzed with respect to biological categories that are represented within the neural network of the MNS. The question for future studies, therefore, should not focus so much on whether the MNS is more or less specific for human movements, but rather which visual features, feature combinations and task requirements cause its activation and whether subsets of the system can be delineated that are specialized for an analysis of particular aspects of biological motion, e.g., its intentionality.

Manuscript received 4 April 2007
Manuscript accepted 1 August 2007
First published online 24 October 2007

REFERENCES

Allison, T., Puce, A., & McCarthy, G. (2000). Social perception from visual cues: role of the STS region. *Trends in Cognitive Science*, *4*(7), 267–278.

Amorim, M. A., Isableu, B., & Jarraya, M. (2006). Embodied spatial transformations: "Body analogy" for the mental rotation of objects. *Journal of Experimental Psychology: General*, *135*(3), 327–347.

Avikainen, S., Forss, N., & Hari, R. (2002). Modulated activation of the human SI and SII cortices during observation of hand actions. *NeuroImage*, *15*(3), 640–646.

Bangert, M., Peschel, T., Schlaug, G., Rotte, M., Drescher, D., Hinrichs, H., et al. (2006). Shared networks for auditory and motor processing in professional pianists: Evidence from fMRI conjunction. *NeuroImage*, *30*(3), 917–926.

Binkofski, F., Buccino, G., Posse, S., Seitz, R. J., Rizzolatti, G., & Freund, H. (1999). A fronto-parietal circuit for object manipulation in man: evidence from an fMRI-study. *European Journal of Neuroscience*, *11*(9), 3276–3286.

Blakemore, S. J., Boyer, P., Pachot-Clouard, M., Meltzoff, A., Segebarth, C., & Decety, J. (2003). The detection of contingency and animacy from simple animations in the human brain. *Cerebral Cortex*, *13*(8), 837–844.

Bonda, E., Petrides, M., Ostry, D., & Evans, A. (1996). Specific involvement of human parietal systems and the amygdala in the perception of biological motion. *Journal of Neuroscience*, *16*(11), 3737–3744.

Brass, M., Bekkering, H., Wohlschläger, A., & Prinz, W. (2000). Compatibility between observed and executed finger movements: comparing symbolic, spatial, and imitative cues. *Brain and Cognition*, *44*(2), 124–143.

Buccino, G., Binkofski, F., Fink, G. R., Fadiga, L., Fogassi, L., Gallese, V., et al. (2001). Action observation activates premotor and parietal areas in a somatotopic manner: an fMRI study. *European Journal of Neuroscience*, *13*(2), 400–404.

Buccino, G., Lui, F., Canessa, N., Pastteri, I., Lagravinese, G., Benuzzi, F., et al. (2004). Neural circuits involved in the recognition of actions performed by nonconspecifics: An fMRI study. *Journal of Cognitive Neuroscience*, *16*(1), 114–126.

Calvo-Merino, B., Glaser, D. E., Grezes, J., Passingham, R. E., & Haggard, P. (2005). Action observation and acquired motor skills: An FMRI study with expert dancers. *Cerebral Cortex*, *15*(8), 1243–1249.

Calvo-Merino, B., Grezes, J., Glaser, D. E., Passingham, R. E., & Haggard, P. (2006). Seeing or doing? Influence of visual and motor familiarity in action observation. *Current Biology*, *16*(19), 1905–1910.

Castelli, F., Frith, C., Happé, F., & Frith, U. (2002). Autism, Asperger syndrome and brain mechanisms for the attribution of mental states to animated shapes. *Brain*, *125*(8), 1839–1849.

Castelli, F., Happé, F., Frith, U., & Frith, C. (2000). Movement and mind: a functional imaging study of perception and interpretation of complex intentional movement patterns. *NeuroImage*, *12*(3), 314–325.

Chouinard, P. A., Leonard, G., & Paus, T. (2005). Role of the primary motor and dorsal premotor cortices in the anticipation of forces during object lifting. *Journal of Neuroscience*, *25*(9), 2277–2284.

Costantini, M., Galati, G., Ferretti, A., Caulo, M., Tartaro, A., Romani, G. L., et al. (2005). Neural systems underlying observation of humanly impossible movements: an fMRI study. *Cerebral Cortex*, *15*(11), 1761–1767.

Cross, E. S., Hamilton, A. F., & Grafton, S. T. (2006). Building a motor simulation de novo: observation of dance by dancers. *NeuroImage*, *31*(3), 1257–1267.

Damasio, A. R. (1989). Time-locked multiregional retroactivation: A system-level proposal for the neuronal substrates of recall and recognition. *Cognition*, *33*, 25–62.

D'Esposito, M., Postle, B. R., & Rypma, B. (2000). Prefrontal cortical contributions to working memory: evidence from event-related fMRI studies. *Experimental Brain Research*, *133*(1), 3–11.

Dinstein, I., Hasson, U., Rubin, N., & Heeger, D. J. (2007). Brain areas selective for both observed and executed movements. *Journal of Neurophysiology*, *98*(3), 1415–1427.

di Pellegrino, G., Fadiga, L., Fogassi, L., Gallese, V., & Rizzolatti, G. (1992). Understanding motor events: a neurophysiological study. *Experimental Brain Research*, *91*(1), 176–180.

Druzgal, T. J., & D'Esposito, M. (2001). Activity in fusiform face area modulated as a function of working memory load. *Cognitive Brain Research*, *10*(3), 355–364.

Dukelow, S. P., DeSouza, J. F., Culham, J. C., van den Berg, A. V., Menon, R. S., & Vilis, T. (2001). Distinguishing subregions of the human MT+ complex using visual fields and pursuit eye movements. *Journal of Neurophysiology*, *86*(4), 1991–2000.

Engel, A., Burke, M., Fiehler, K., Bien, S., & Rösler, F. (2007). The perceptual task is crucial for activity in the mirror neuron system—Not the type of movement trajectory. 13th International Conference on Functional Mapping of the Human Brain (HBM 2007), Chicago, USA, June 2007. *NeuroImage*, *36*(Suppl. 1), S40.

Fiehler, K., Burke, M., Engel, A., Bien, S., & Rösler, F. (in press). Kinästhetic working memory and action control within the dorsal stream. *Cerebral Cortex*. Epub June 4, 2007, doi: 10.1093/cercor/bhm071.

Gallese, V., Fadiga, L., Fogassi, L., & Rizzolatti, G. (1996). Action recognition in the premotor cortex. *Brain*, *119*(2), 593–609.

Gazzola, V., Rizzolatti, G., Wicker, B., & Keysers, C. (2007). The anthropomorphic brain: the mirror neuron system responds to human and robotic actions. *NeuroImage*, *35*(4), 1674–1684.

Gazzola, V., Wicker, B., Rizzolatti, G., & Keysers, C. (2004). The anthropomorphic brain: The human mirror system identifies the meaning of an action, and responds both to the sight of humans and robots performing complex actions. *Journal of Cognitive Neuroscience*, Suppl. 1, 50.

Grefkes, C., Geyer, S., Schormann, T., Roland, P., & Zilles, K. (2001). Human somatosensory area 2: observer-independent cytoarchitectonic mapping, interindividual variability, and population map. *NeuroImage*, *14*(3), 617–631.

Grezes, J., Armony, J. L., Rowe, J., & Passingham, R. E. (2003). Activations related to "mirror" and "canonical" neurones in the human brain: An fMRI study. *NeuroImage*, *18*(4), 928–937.

Grezes, J., Costes, N., & Decety, J. (1998). Top-down effect of strategy on the perception of human biological motion: A PET investigation. *Cognitive Neuropsychology*, *15*, 553–582.

Grezes, J., & Decety, J. (2001). Functional anatomy of execution, mental simulation, observation, and verb generation of actions: A meta-analysis. *Human Brain Mapping*, *12*(1), 1–19.

Grezes, J., Fonlupt, P., Bertenthal, B., Delon-Martin, C., Segebarth, C., & Decety, J. (2001). Does perception of biological motion rely on specific brain regions? *NeuroImage*, *13*(5), 775–785.

Grill-Spector, K., & Malach, R. (2001). fMRI-adaptation: A tool for studying the functional properties of human cortical neurons. *Acta Psychologia*, *107*(1–3), 293–321.

Grossman, E. D., & Blake, R. (2002). Brain areas active during visual perception of biological motion. *Neuron*, *35*(6), 1167–1175.

Hari, R., Forss, N., Avikainen, S., Kirveskari, E., Salenius, S., & Rizzolatti, G. (1998). Activation of human primary motor cortex during action observation: a neuromagnetic study. *Proceedings of the National Academy of Sciences, USA*, *95*(25), 15061–15065.

Haslinger, B., Erhard, P., Altenmüller, E., Schroeder, U., Boecker, H., & Ceballos-Baumann, A. O. (2005). Transmodal sensorimotor networks during action

observation in professional pianists. *Journal of Cognitive Neuroscience*, *17*(2), 282–293.
Heider, F., & Simmel, M. (1944). An experimental study of apparent behavior. *American Journal of Psychology*, *57*, 243–259.
Heyes, C. (2001). Causes and consequences of imitation. *Trends in Cognitive Science*, *5*(6), 253–261.
James, W. (1890). *The principles of psychology.* New York: Holt.
Johansson, G. (1973). Visual perception of biological motion and a model for its analysis. *Perception & Psychophysics*, *14*, 201–211.
Jokisch, D., Daum, I., Suchan, B., & Troje, N. F. (2005). Structural encoding and recognition of biological motion: Evidence from event-related potentials and source analysis. *Behavioural Brain Research*, *157*(2), 195–204.
Kessler, K., Biermann-Ruben, K., Jonas, M., Roman Siebner, H., Baumer, T., Munchau, A., et al. (2006). Investigating the human mirror neuron system by means of cortical synchronization during the imitation of biological movements. *NeuroImage*, *33*(1), 227–238.
Keysers, C., & Perrett, D. I. (2004). Demystifying social cognition: a Hebbian perspective. *Trends in Cognitive Science*, *8*(11), 501–507.
Kilner, J. M., Paulignan, Y., & Blakemore, S. J. (2003). An interference effect of observed biological movement on action. *Current Biology*, *13*(6), 522–525.
Leventhal, H. (1984). A perceptual motor theory of emotion. In K. R. Scherer & P. Ekman (Eds.), *Approaches to emotion* (pp. 271–291). Hillsdale, NJ: Lawrence Erlbaum Associates, Inc.
Martin, A. (2007). The representation of object concepts in the brain. *Annual Review of Psychology*, *58*, 25–45.
Maunsell, J. H., & Van Essen, D. C. (1983). Functional properties of neurons in middle temporal visual area of the macaque monkey. I. Selectivity for stimulus direction, speed, and orientation. *Journal of Neurophysiology*, *49*(5), 1127–1147.
McClelland, J. L., McNaughton, B. L., & O'Reilly, R. C. (1995). Why there are complementary learning systems in the hippocampus and neocortex: Insights from the successes and failures of connectionist models of learning and memory. *Psychological Review*, *102*, 419–457.
McGuigan, F. J. (1978). *Cognitive psychophysiology: Principles of covert behavior*. Englewood Cliffs, NJ: Prentice Hall.
Michotte, A. (1963). *The perception of causality.* London: Methuen.
Mottonen, R., Jarvelainen, J., Sams, M., & Hari, R. (2005). Viewing speech modulates activity in the left SI mouth cortex. *NeuroImage*, *24*(3), 731–737.
Nichols, T., Brett, M., Andersson, J., Wager, T., & Poline, J.-B. (2005). Valid conjunction inference with the minimum statistic. *NeuroImage*, *25*(3), 653–660.
Noguchi, Y., Kaneoke, Y., Kakigi, R., Tanabe, H. C., & Sadato, N. (2005). Role of the superior temporal region in human visual motion perception. *Cerebral Cortex*, *15*(10), 1592–1601.
Oldfield, R. C. (1971). The assessment and analysis of handedness: The Edinburgh inventory. *Neuropsychologia*, *9*(1), 97–113.
Pelphrey, K. A., Mitchell, T. V., McKeown, M. J., Goldstein, J., Allison, T., & McCarthy, G. (2003). Brain activity evoked by the perception of human walking: Controlling for meaningful coherent motion. *Journal of Neuroscience*, *23*(17), 6819–6825.
Pelphrey, K. A., Morris, J. P., Michelich, C. R., Allison, T., & McCarthy, G. (2005). Functional anatomy of biological motion perception in posterior temporal cortex: An fMRI study of eye, mouth and hand movements. *Cerebral Cortex*, *15*(12), 1866–1876.
Perrett, D. I., Harries, M. H., Bevan, R., Thomas, S., Benson, P. J., Mistlin, A. J., et al. (1989). Frameworks of analysis for the neural representation of animate objects and actions. *Journal of Experimental Biology*, *146*, 87–113.
Peuskens, H., Vanrie, J., Verfaillie, K., & Orban, G. A. (2005). Specificity of regions processing biological motion. *European Journal of Neuroscience*, *21*(10), 2864–2875.
Picard, N., & Strick, P. L. (1996). Motor areas of the medial wall: A review of their location and functional activation. *Cerebral Cortex*, *6*(3), 342–353.
Picard, N., & Strick, P. L. (2001). Imaging the premotor areas. *Current Opinion in Neurobiology*, *11*(6), 663–672.
Press, C., Bird, G., Flach, R., & Heyes, C. (2005). Robotic movement elicits automatic imitation. *Cognitive Brain Research*, *25*(3), 632–640.
Raos, V., Evangeliou, M. N., & Savaki, H. E. (2004). Observation of action: grasping with the mind's hand. *NeuroImage*, *23*(1), 193–201.
Rizzolatti, G., & Craighero, L. (2004). The mirror-neuron system. *Annual Review of Neuroscience*, *27*, 169–192.
Rizzolatti, G., Fadiga, L., Gallese, V., & Fogassi, L. (1996). Premotor cortex and the recognition of motor actions. *Cognitive Brain Research*, *3*(2), 131–141.
Rösler, F., & Heil, M. (2003). The principle of code-specific memory representations. In R. H. Kluwe, G. Lüer, & F. Rösler (Eds.), *Principles of learning and memory* (pp. 71–92). Basel, Switzerland: Birkhäuser.
Rossi, S., Tecchio, F., Pasqualetti, P., Ulivelli, M., Pizzella, V., Romani, G. L., et al. (2002). Somatosensory processing during movement observation in humans. *Clinical Neurophysiology*, *113*(1), 16–24.
Saygin, A. P., Wilson, S. M., Hagler, D. J. Jr, Bates, E., & Sereno, M. I. (2004). Point-light biological motion perception activates human premotor cortex. *Journal of Neuroscience*, *24*(27), 6181–6188.
Schenk, T., & Zihl, J. (1997). Visual motion perception after brain damage: II. Deficits in form-from-motion perception. *Neuropsychologia*, *35*(9), 1299–1310.
Schubotz, R. I. (2007). Prediction of external events with our motor system: Towards a new framework. *Trends in Cognitive Science*, *11*(5), 211–218.
Schubotz, R. I., & von Cramon, D. Y. (2003). Functional-anatomical concepts of human premotor cortex: Evidence from fMRI and PET studies. *NeuroImage*, *20*(Suppl. 1), S120–S131.

Schubotz, R. I., & von Cramon, D. Y. (2004). Sequences of abstract nonbiological stimuli share ventral premotor cortex with action observation and imagery. *Journal of Neuroscience*, *24*(24), 5467–5474.

Schultz, J., Friston, K. J., O'Doherty, J., Wolpert, D. M., & Frith, C. D. (2005). Activation in posterior superior temporal sulcus parallels parameter inducing the percept of animacy. *Neuron*, *45*(4), 625–635.

Tai, Y. F., Scherfler, C., Brooks, D. J., Sawamoto, N., & Castiello, U. (2004). The human premotor cortex is "mirror" only for biological actions. *Current Biology*, *14*(2), 117–120.

Tootell, R. B., Reppas, J. B., Kwong, K. K., Malach, R., Born, R. T., Brady, T. J., et al. (1995). Functional analysis of human MT and related visual cortical areas using magnetic resonance imaging. *Journal of Neuroscience*, *15*(4), 3215–3230.

Vaina, L. M., Lemay, M., Bienfang, D. C., Choi, A. Y., & Nakayama, K. (1990). Intact "biological motion" and "structure from motion" perception in a patient with impaired motion mechanisms: A case study. *Visual Neuroscience*, *5*(4), 353–369.

Watson, J. D. G., Myers, R., Frackowiak, R. S. J., Hajnal, J. V., Woods, R. P., Mazziotta, J. C., et al. (1993). Area V5 of the human brain: Evidence from a combined study using positron emission tomography and magnetic resonance imaging. *Cerebral Cortex*, *3*(2), 79–94.

Zentgraf, K., Stark, R., Reiser, M., Kunzell, S., Schienle, A., Kirsch, P., et al. (2005). Differential activation of pre-SMA and SMA proper during action observation: Effects of instructions. *NeuroImage*, *26*(3), 662–672.

Appendix

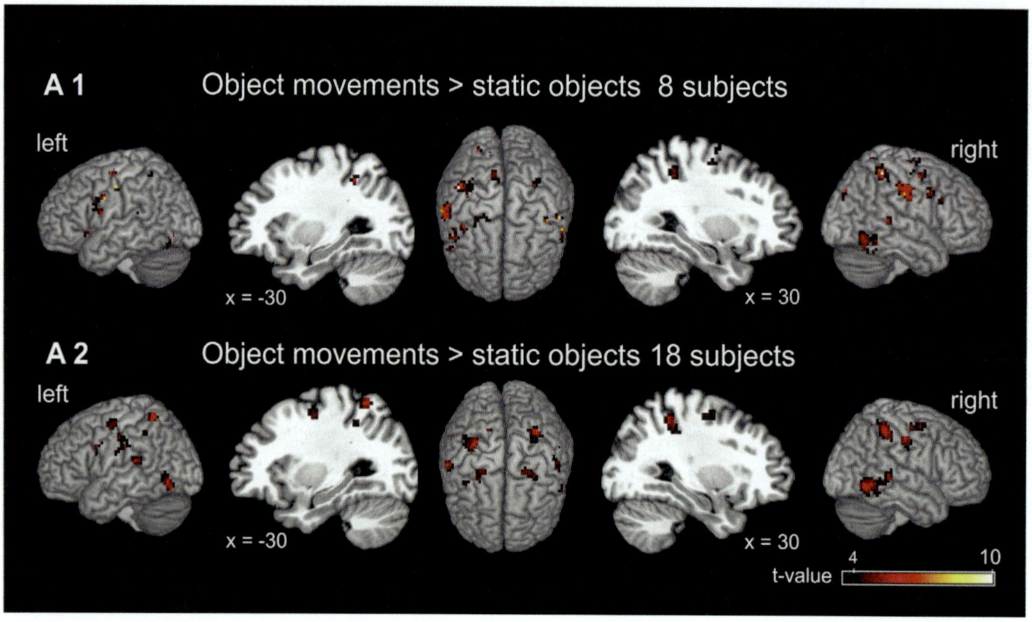

Figure A1. BOLD activation patterns for moving vs. static objects. (A1) Random effects analysis for those participants who saw the object movements in the first experimental part. (A2) Random effects analysis for all 18 participants. SPM{t} maps were thresholded at $t = 3.65$ resulting in a significance level with $p < .004$ (uncorrected for multiple comparisons) for the analysis of the 8 participants and $p < .001$ (uncorrected for multiple comparisons) for the analysis of the 18 participants. Cluster with a minimum size of 5 voxels were superimposed on a MNI standard brain.

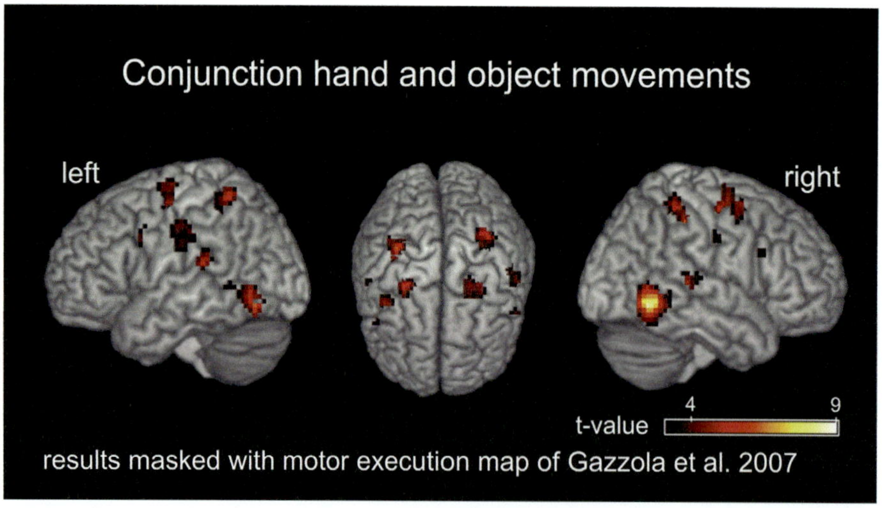

Figure A2. BOLD activation patterns for the conjunction analysis (hand movements vs. static hands AND object movements vs. static objects) masked with the activation map of the experimental condition "execution of hand movements" from Gazzola et al. (2007), who kindly made these data available to us. The SPM{t} map is superimposed on a MNI standard brain and were thresholded for significance with $p < .001$ (uncorrected for multiple comparisons) and a cluster size of >5 voxels.

TABLE A1

Activations for hand and object movements: Contrast for levels of difficulty

			Hand movements				Object movements			
			MNI coordinates				MNI coordinates			
Anatomical region	*Hemisphere*	*Brodmann area*	*x*	*y*	*z*	*Z-score*	*x*	*y*	*z*	*Z-score*
Ventral premotor area	L	44/6	−54	6	33	***5.48***	−60	3	33	***3.97***
	R	44/6	48	12	27	***4.45***	57	12	27	***3.56***
Dorsal premotor	L	6	−24	−21	66	***4.38***	−21	−18	54	***3.66***
	R	6	30	−15	66	***4.85***	27	−9	60	***4.22***
			51	−9	54	***4.20***	39	−6	57	***3.84***
SMA proper	L/R	6	−6	−12	69	**5.28**				
Postcentral gyrus	L	2	−57	−18	42	***4.67***	−57	−21	42	***4.18***
	R	2	60	−21	39	***4.61***	63	−24	45	***4.24***
Inferior parietal lobe/intraparietal sulcus	L	40	−36	−48	48	***4.51***	−30	−51	48	***3.55***
			−51	−33	36	***4.47***	−57	−21	39	***3.49***
	R	40	33	−42	45	***5.00***	33	−45	51	***4.37***
Superior parietal lobe	L	7	−36	−54	60	***4.60***	−33	−60	63	***4.52***
	R	7	42	−54	63	***4.22***	33	−48	57	***4.11***
			12	−63	51	***3.66***				
Superior temporal gyrus	L	22	−54	−39	18	***3.72***	−51	−39	18	***4.21***
Superior temporal sulcus	L	22/21	−60	−48	6	***3.35***				
	R	22/21	51	−42	12	***4.76***	57	−42	3	***3.99***
Occipito-temporal junction	L	19/37	−48	−72	−3	***4.70***	−48	−75	−6	***4.13***
	R	19/37	45	−63	−6	***5.27***	45	−69	−6	***4.51***
Body of caudate nucleus	L		−12	21	−6	***3.49***	−15	21	0	***3.49***
	R		12	12	−12	***3.93***				

Notes: Shown are MNI coordinates for significant activation maxima of all clusters of the random effects analyses. Thresholds for whole voxelwise brain analysis: $p < .001$, uncorrected for multiple comparisons. All cluster maxima are significant with $p < .05$, corrected for multiple comparisons with FDR.

SOCIAL NEUROSCIENCE, 2008, 3 (3–4), 388–400

Psychology Press
Taylor & Francis Group

Virtual lesion of ventral premotor cortex impairs visual perception of biomechanically possible but not impossible actions

Matteo Candidi
Università di Roma "La Sapienza" and IRCCS Fondazione Santa Lucia, Rome, Italy

Cosimo Urgesi
IRCCS "E. Medea", Pordenone, Italy

Silvio Ionta
ITAB, Università di Chieti "G. D'Annunzio", Chieti Scalo, Italy

Salvatore M. Aglioti
Università di Roma "La Sapienza" and IRCCS Fondazione Santa Lucia, Rome, Italy

Single-pulse transcranial magnetic stimulation (TMS) studies show that action observation facilitates the onlooker's cortico-spinal system supporting the notion of motor mirroring. Repetitive transcranial magnetic stimulation (rTMS) over ventral premotor cortex (vPMc) impairs visual discrimination of body actions. Although studies suggest that the action observation–execution matching system may map only actions that belong to the observer's motor repertoire, we demonstrated comparable motor and premotor facilitation during observation of biomechanically possible as well as impossible actions. It has also been shown that seeing impossible body movements activates the extrastriate body area (EBA). Using event-related rTMS, we sought to determine whether vPMc and EBA are actively involved in the visual discrimination of actions performed through biomechanically possible or impossible kinematics and of their biomechanical plausibility. Stimulation of vPMc impaired discrimination of possible actions while leaving intact the discrimination of biomechanically impossible actions and of biomechanical plausibility. No effect of EBA rTMS on any type of action processing was found. Thus, vPMc is crucial for discrimination of the goal of actions that can be actually performed suggesting that this area is involved in the visual processing of goal-directed actions.

INTRODUCTION

Humans are naturally accurate in perceiving and understanding body actions performed by other individuals. Studies report that repetitive transcranial magnetic stimulation (rTMS) of ventral premotor cortex (vPMc) impairs visual discrimination of static (Urgesi, Candidi, Ionta, & Aglioti, 2007) and dynamic displays (Pobric & Hamilton, 2006) of bodily actions. These results supports the notion that action understanding requires motor representations (Rizzolatti & Craighero, 2004).

Correspondence should be addressed to: Matteo Candidi, Department of Psychology, University of Rome "La Sapienza", Via dei Marsi 78, I-00185, Roma, Italy. E-mail: matteo.candidi@uniroma1.it

This research was supported by Ministero Italiano Università e Ricerca (MIUR), University of Rome "La Sapienza" and Fondazione Santa Lucia, Italy.

www.psypress.com/socialneuroscience DOI:10.1080/17470910701676269

vPMc is a crucial node of the fronto-parietal mirror-neuron system that matches action observation and action execution. Behavioral, neurophysiological, and neuropsychological studies suggest that action execution and observation are represented in commensurable formats and share the same neural underpinnings (Brass, Bekkering, Wohlschlager, & Prinz, 2000; Buccino et al., 2001; Craighero, Bello, Fadiga, & Rizzolatti, 2002; Grezes & Decety, 2001; Prinz, 2002; Saygin, Wilson, Dronkers, & Bates, 2004; Wohlschlager & Bekkering, 2002). Importantly, mere action observation influences motor representations and plays an important role in learning new movements (Celnik et al., 2006; Stefan et al., 2005). The motor mapping of visually perceived actions, however, seems to occur only for actions that can be practiced and learned. fMRI studies, for example, compared neural activity during observation of learned and non-learned complex dance movements and found that the former condition induced higher premotor and parietal mirror activation than the latter (Calvo-Merino, Glaser, Grezes, Passingham, & Haggard, 2005, 2006). In a similar vein, observation of human biting actions but not dog barking activates the frontal node of the mirror-neuron system thus indicating that specific motor mapping contingent upon observation occurs only for actions that belong to the observer's behavioral repertoire (Buccino et al., 2004). According to this view, actions that do not belong to the observers' motor repertoire would elicit only visual mapping in posterior areas. However, humans may perceive and understand actions they cannot perform and that therefore are not part of their own motor repertoire. Recent TMS (Romani, Cesari, Urgesi, Facchini, & Aglioti, 2005) and neuroimaging studies (Costantini et al., 2005) reported a comparable motor and premotor activation during observation of biomechanically possible and impossible ab/adduction index finger movements. Based on the notion that one can mirror only actions that can be performed, motor activation during observation of biomechanically impossible movements was not expected. It is worth noting that the biomechanically impossible index finger movements observed in our studies (Costantini et al., 2005; Romani et al., 2005) consisted in an exaggeration of the correspondent possible movements and thus can be conceptually conceived as possible. Therefore, it is plausible that premotor and motor representations of observed actions do not include the mapping of the exact kinematics and the pattern of muscles' activations, but the general meaning of actions. Indeed, the functional significance of finger movements is not changed by the biomechanical extension of joint limits. In this vein, activation of the motor system during observation of biomechanically impossible movements may reflect the representation of the actions' meaning and goal. By contrast, observation of completely new movements that cannot be represented in terms of meaningfulness or goal-directedness, for example non-*species*-specific movements (Buccino et al., 2004) or dance patterns exceedingly complex for naïve observers (Calvo-Merino et al., 2005), do not engage the motor system. In a previous fMRI study we reported that impossible movements engender higher activations of parietal and temporo-occipital cortex than possible movements (Costantini et al., 2005). Thus, premotor and motor responses to impossible movements may reflect modulatory signals from parietal and temporal areas. It is worth noting that the temporo-occipital activity found in this study was close to the location of the so-called extrastriate body area (EBA), a cortical region that is selectively activated by viewing images, silhouettes or even stick drawings of static and moving body or body parts (Downing, Jiang, Shuman, & Kanwisher, 2001). Neural activity in EBA has been proved to be crucial for visual perception of human body parts (Urgesi, Berlucchi, & Aglioti, 2004). Moreover, rTMS of EBA impairs visuo-perceptive discrimination of body morphology but does not affect the discrimination of the action being performed (Urgesi et al., 2007). The role of the EBA in processing body movements, however, is still debated (Astafiev, Stanley, Shulman, & Corbetta, 2004; Peelen & Downing, 2005). The EBA is also activated during perception of point-light displays, which suggests the perception of body actions despite the absence of body-form cues (Downing et al., 2001; Grossman & Blake, 2002), as well as during presentation of static body images both implying and not implying motion (Downing et al., 2001; Peelen, Wigget, & Downing, 2006). It has been reported that observation of distorted hand postures enhances the activation of extrastriate visual areas (Avikainen, Liuhanen, Schürmann, & Hari, 2003). Similarly, the EBA seems to be more activated by incoherent body movements while superior temporal and premotor activations are higher during observation of coherent action sequences (Downing, Peelen, Wigget, & Tew, 2006). These results would suggest that EBA may be involved in the extrapolation of body-form cues even when extrapolating from images unrelated to normal motor functioning. In contrast, temporal and premotor activations may modulate the motor system. Imaging studies, however, cannot establish whether neural activations of cortical areas are crucial for task execution or merely epiphenomenal.

In the present study, we used event-related rTMS to investigate the role played by vPMc and EBA in visual discriminations of biomechanically possible and impossible body actions. In particular, we tested whether neural activations of vPMc and EBA reflect their active involvement in perceiving movements that cannot be performed or are merely epiphenomenal to activations occurring elsewhere in the brain. Rapid rTMS allowed us to transiently disrupt neuronal efficiency by introducing "noise" in the pattern of activity necessary to task execution (Pascual-Leone, Walsh, & Rothwell, 2000). If the targeted area is actively involved in the task being performed, rTMS is expected to impair performance. rTMS was delivered to left and right vPMc and EBA while healthy participants observed snapshots of biomechanically possible or impossible body actions. Participants were asked to match a tachistoscopically presented sample to one of two probes showed in free viewing. The matching and nonmatching stimuli were: (i) two different possible actions (possible action discrimination); (ii) two different impossible actions (impossible action discrimination); or (iii) the same action performed with biomechanically possible and impossible kinematics (biomechanical plausibility discrimination). The biomechanical plausibility action discrimination task allowed us to test whether mapping of observed body actions in vPMc and EBA includes the actions' goal, their motor kinematics, or both. Indeed, while the discrimination between possible and impossible actions may be based on differences in either movement kinematics or goal, the discrimination of the biomechanical plausibility may rely only on kinematic differences (i.e., possible and impossible actions shared the same goal).

EXPERIMENTAL PROCEDURES

Participants

Thirty-two healthy individuals were recruited for the experiment. Based on a random assignment procedure, 16 participants (1 man) underwent left hemisphere stimulations and the other 16 (4 men) right hemisphere stimulations. A standard handedness inventory (Briggs & Nebes, 1975) allowed us to ascertain that all participants were right-handed. Participants were native Italian speakers with normal or corrected-to-normal visual acuity in both eyes. None of the participants had neurological, psychiatric, or other medical problems or had any contraindication to TMS (Wasserman, 1997). Participants were naïve as to the purposes of the experiment, and information about the experimental hypothesis was provided only after the experimental tests were completed. Participants gave their written informed consent and were paid €15 for their participation in the study. The procedures were approved by the ethics committee of Fondazione Santa Lucia (Rome) and they were in accordance with the ethical standards of the 1964 Declaration of Helsinki. No participant complained of any discomfort or presented any adverse effects during rTMS.

Stimuli and tasks

Experimental stimuli were color pictures depicting snapshots of body actions. One male model was videotaped while performing four pairs of different actions. Each pair was composed of two slightly different actions performed with the same limb. Two pairs of actions involved the right upper limb and the other two pairs involved the right lower limb. Pairs of stimuli represented meaningful (precision grip or gross grasping for upper limb and forward or backward walking for lower limb) or meaningless actions (hand approaching the anterior or posterior part of the shoulder for upper limb, and foot moving towards the contralateral knee, either in front of or behind it, for lower limb). To rule out any effect of mere observation of graspable objects (Chao & Martin, 2000) mimicking action stimuli in the absence of any object (i.e., a class of stimuli that has been shown to activate vPMc) were used (Nelissen, Luppino, Vanduffel, Rizzolatti, & Orban, 2005). Furthermore, since our design required fast stimuli presentation, the sense of acting body was elicited selecting snapshots from the middle phase of each action. We have demonstrated that visual perception of static images implying body actions activates the motor system (Urgesi, Moro, Candidi, & Aglioti, 2006b) and that the visual discrimination of static images representing body actions is a task adept to investigate the role of vPMc in action perception (Urgesi et al., 2007). The two stimuli of each pair were matched for the instant at which the snapshot was taken, and for perspective, luminance, and crude contours. For each biomechanically possible action we created a stimulus representing the corresponding action performed with a biomechanically impossible kinematic. The biomechanically impossible action stimuli were created by modifying the original action snapshots using Adobe Photoshop software (Adobe Systems Incorporated, San Jose, CA). In the impossible action stimuli the joints were modified so as to violate the biomechanical constraints of the human body, while the general sense of the corresponding possible action was maintained. For example, in the two impossible grasping movements, the index finger (precision grip) or all fingers (gross grasping) approached the thumb on the dorsum of the hand (Figure 1). To balance the laterality of the stimulus set, the eight right-limb possible- and impossible-action images were mirrored to obtain the corresponding left-limb action images. Therefore, 32 different stimuli were used.

Within the same block, participants performed three types of matching-to-sample tasks. In all tasks, participants had to choose which one of two different probe images matched the target image. The matching and non-matching stimuli could depict: (i) two slightly different biomechanically possible actions (possible actions discrimination); (ii) two slightly different biomechanically impossible actions (impossible actions discrimination); or (iii) a biomechanically possible action and the corresponding biomechanically impossible action with the same general meaning (biomechanical plausibility discrimination). All the discriminations regarded actions made by the same model with the same body part. To investigate any differences between possible and impossible action images that might explain differential rTMS modulation, we collected subjective reports on the stimuli from an independent sample of 10 individuals. They were asked to judge each stimulus by marking a vertical, 10 cm visual analog scale (VAS), with 0 cm indicating "*no effect*" and 10 cm "*maximal effect imaginable*". Subjects rated the following properties of the observed stimuli: (1) quantity of implied motion; (2) unpleasantness; (3) biomechanical plausibility; (4) sense of joint stretch; and (5) painfulness.

Transcranial magnetic stimulation

Participants wore a tightly fitting bathing cap on which scalp stimulation points were marked. Motor-evoked potentials (MEPs) were recorded from first dorsal interossus (FDI) muscle of the dominant hand. Surface Ag/AgCl electrodes were placed in a belly tendon montage with the active electrode placed over the muscle belly and the reference over the interphalangeal joint. Responses were amplified at a gain of 1000 × by a Digitimer D360 amplifier (Digitimer, Hertfordshire, UK), bandpass filtered (20 Hz–2.5 kHz), and digitized (sampling rate: 5 kHz) by means of a CED Power 1401 controlled with Spike 2 software (Cambridge Electronic design, Cambridge, UK). The resting motor threshold (rMT), defined as the lowest intensity able to evoke five out of ten MEPs with an amplitude of at least 50 μV, was determined by holding the stimulation coil over the optimal scalp position (i.e., the motor cortex area contralateral to the dominant hand producing the largest MEPs) for the FDI muscle. Moreover, during the experimental sessions, electromyographic signals were continuously recorded from the FDI and the abductor digiti minimi (ADM) muscles of the responding and non-responding hands to control for MEP that could be evoked by stimulation of vPMc (Uozumi, Tamagawa, Hashimoto, & Tsuji, 2004). Off-line visual inspection of data did not show any MEP or any alteration of the electromyographic signal following stimulation of left or right vPMc or EBA. Stimulation sites were identified on each participant's scalp with SofTaxic Navigator system (EMS, Bologna, Italy). Skull landmarks (nasion, inion, and two preauricular points) and about 60 points providing a uniform representation of the scalp were digitized by means of a Fastrak Polhemus digitizer (Polhemus, Colchester, VT). Coordinates in Talairach space (Talairach & Tournoux, 1988) were automatically estimated by the SofTaxic Navigator from an MRI-constructed stereotaxic template. The scalp locations that corresponded best to left and right EBA and vPMc coordinates (Costantini et al., 2005; Downing et al., 2001; Urgesi et al., 2004) were identified and marked with a pen. Mean coordinates, in Talairach space (Talairach & Tournoux, 1988), of the targeted stimulation sites in the left hemisphere group were $x = -53.7 \pm 0.1$, $y = -71.0 \pm 0.0$, $z = 4.0 \pm 0.0$ for EBA, and $x = -57.1 \pm 0.2$, $y = 11.7 \pm 0.9$,

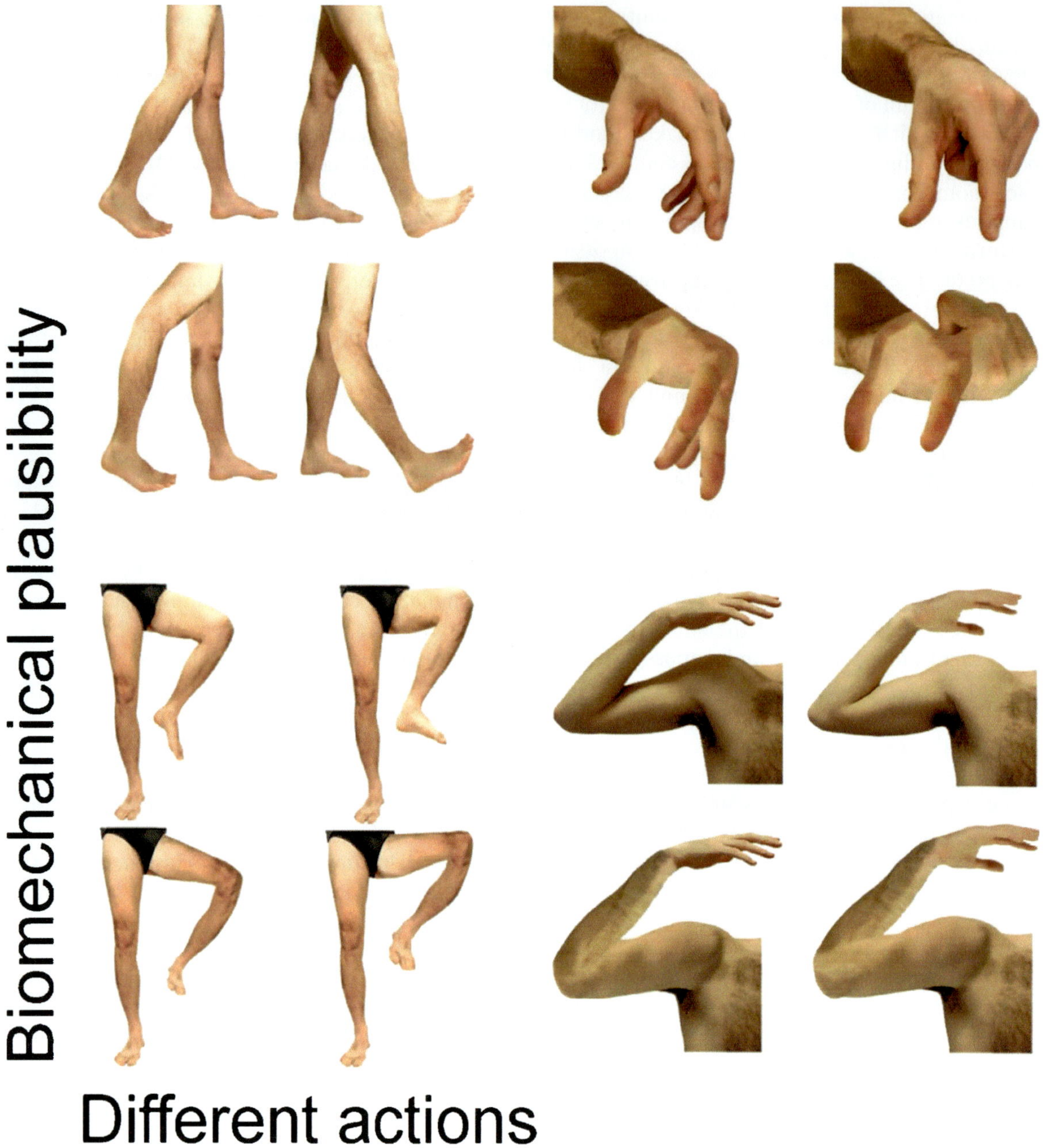

Figure 1. Examples of the experimental stimuli. Images represented upper and lower limbs performing meaningful and meaningless actions. All left images were obtained by mirroring the corresponding right ones.

$z = 24.0 \pm 0.0$ for vPMc; mean coordinates of the targeted sites in the right hemisphere group were $x = 51.7 \pm 0.5$, $y = -72.9 \pm 0.2$, $z = 3.1 \pm 0.6$ for EBA, and $x = 58.1 \pm 0.3$, $y = 12.0 \pm 0.5$, $z = 24.1 \pm 0.3$ for vPMc (Figure 2).

rTMS was performed by connecting two Magstim Mode 200 stimulators with Bistim module (The Magstim Company, Carmarthenshire, UK), producing a maximum output of 1.75 T at the coil surface (stimulus attenuation, 22%; duration, 1 ms; rise time, 110 μs). Two pulses were delivered with an interstimulus interval of 100 ms by means of a 70 mm figure of eight stimulation coil (Magstim polyurethane-coated coil). In keeping with previous studies showing rTMS suppressive effect on EBA (Urgesi et al., 2004) and vPMc (Urgesi et al., 2007), the first TMS pulse was delivered 150 ms after the onset of sample presentation for stimulation of both EBA and vPMc areas. The stimulation timing was consistent with

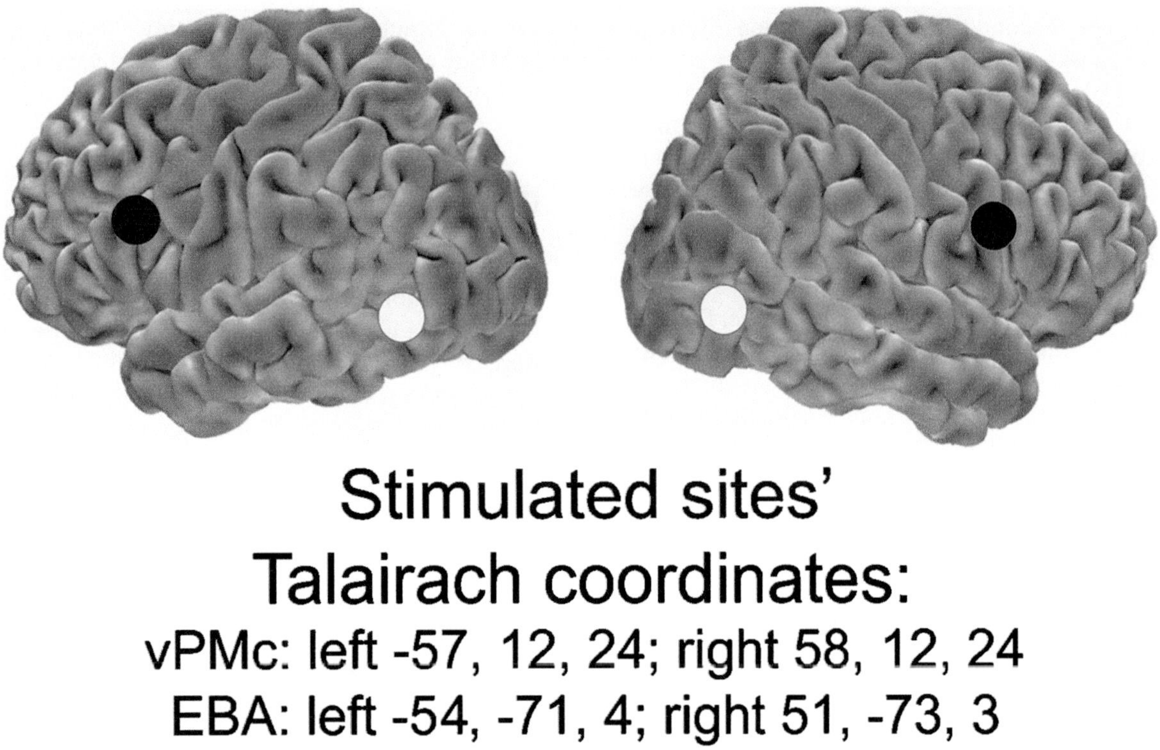

Figure 2. Talairach coordinates of stimulated sites corresponding to left and right vPMc and EBA. For each participant, stereotaxic coordinates corresponding to the target areas were obtained by means of the SofTaxic neuronavigation system.

the time course of vPMc activation during visual presentation of moving body parts as revealed by magnetoencephalography studies (Nishitani & Hari, 2000, 2002). Stimulation intensity was 120% of the rMT for both pulses and ranged from 38% to 63% of the maximum stimulator output (mean = 51.8%) for the group of participants receiving right hemisphere stimulations and from 36% to 64% of the maximum stimulator output (mean = 46.5%) for the left hemisphere group. During magnetic stimulation, the coil was held tangential to the scalp, with the handle pointing backward and laterally at a 45° angle from the middle sagittal axis of the participants' head. For sham stimulation, the coil was held sided-up and tangential to the scalp over the vertex of the participants' head. This ensured that no focal magnetic stimulation reached the brain during the sham stimulation and controlled for noise and sensation of the coil against the head. The same intensity and timing of real magnetic stimulation were used for sham stimulation. The coil was held by hand, and its position with respect to the marks was checked continuously. During sham and real stimulation participants wore commercial earplugs to protect their hearing. None of them reported phosphenes after rTMS of EBA.

Procedure

Each participant was tested in one experimental session lasting approximately 2 hours. Participants completed two practice blocks, followed immediately by the experimental blocks.

Possible- and impossible-actions discrimination as well as biomechanical-plausibility discrimination trials were randomly delivered within the same 24-trials blocks (8 trials per task).

Two blocks of 24 trials (16 trials per task) were performed for each stimulation site (EBA, vPMc, sham), for a total of 144 matching-to-sample trials. Within each block, half of the sample stimuli were images of possible actions and the other half were impossible actions. Given that the different discriminations were randomly requested in the same block, participants could not anticipate the type of discrimination performance required in that particular trial from viewing the sample stimulus. It is worth noting that the same sample stimuli were presented in the biomechanical plausibility as in the possible and the impossible action discrimination tasks. Thus, any differential effect of vPMc and EBA stimulations in the different tasks cannot be due to low-level visual differences in the stimuli, but rather to the type of discrimination implicitly induced by the stimuli. A short rest was allowed before proceeding to a different block. Each individual performed twice all the three stimulation conditions according to an across-participants counterbalanced sequence. Each trial started with the presentation of a central fixation point (lasting 500 ms) aimed at minimizing eye movements. Then the sample stimulus was presented for 150 ms at the center of the monitor. Image persistence was limited by presenting a random-dot mask ($9.1 \times 9.1°$ in size) for 500 ms. This was obtained by scrambling the corresponding sample stimulus by means of a custom-made image segmentation software. Immediately after the disappearance of the mask, the two probe stimuli appeared and remained on the screen until a response was made. Participants were asked to respond as quickly as possible by using their index or middle finger to press the left or the right key of a custom-made response box (Figure 3).

Each key corresponded to one of the two positions on the screen on which the probe stimuli were presented; the positions of the probe stimuli were randomized in each trial. To rule out purely motor effects of rTMS on the speed of response, the responding hand was ipsilateral to the side of stimulation. Thus, the left hand was used in the group receiving left hemisphere stimulations and the right hand in the group receiving right hemisphere stimulation. Reaction times (RTs) and accuracy of response were automatically recorded and stored for analysis.

Data analysis

Individual mean RTs and response accuracy were calculated for each experimental condition (16 trials per cell). Only RTs for correct responses were considered; moreover, RTs that fell below or above three standard deviations from each individual mean were identified for each cell and removed as outliers (0.47% and 0.51% for left and right hemisphere groups, respectively). Mean normalized and raw accuracy and RTs for all EBA, vPMc, and sham stimulation conditions are reported in Table 1 and Table 2. Along with its capability to selectively interfere with neural activity, TMS may introduce some biasing non-specific effects. Touch and noise sensation of the coil over the head may unspecifically influence performance (Blanke et al., 2005; Sawaki, Okita, Fujiwara, & Mizuno, 1999; Terao et al., 1997). Furthermore our experimental design tested two different samples of subjects for the left and right hemisphere, respectively. Thus, to compare the specific effect of rTMS for each task in each individual, RTs and accuracy raw values for left and right EBA and vPMc stimulation conditions were normalized on the sham stimulation condition. This procedure allowed us to test the specific effect of rTMS interference independently from tasks difficulty and interindividual differences in

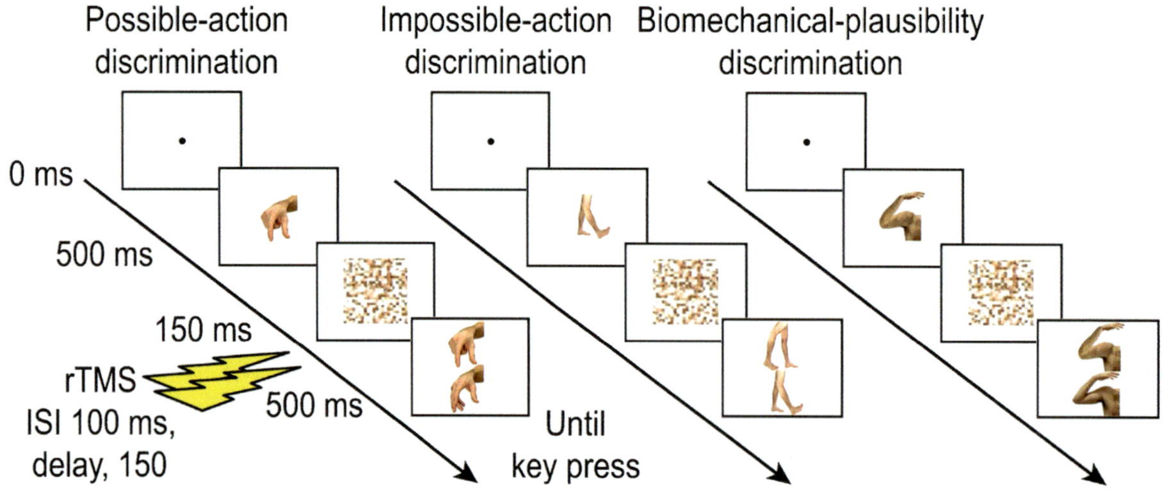

Figure 3. Procedure examples of possible, impossible and biomechanical plausibility discriminations. Repetitive transcranial magnetic stimulation (rTMS) was applied with a delay of 150 ms after sample presentation. On each trial, a 10-Hz dual-pulse train lasting 200 ms was delivered during mask presentation.

TABLE 1
Normalized RTs and accuracy of response means (± *MSE*) of EBA and vPMc stimulation conditions

	Left		*Right*	
	EBA	*vPMc*	*EBA*	*vPMc*
Normalized RTs (sham%)				
Possible action	98.27 (3.25)	101.52 (3.06)	97.30 (2.80)	105.57 (3.55)
Impossible action	100.02 (3.93)	93.44 (3.37)	97.85 (3.04)	104.98 (4.85)
Biomechanical plausibility	100.01 (3.11)	96.96 (2.31)	101.29 (2.16)	101.37 (3.25)
Normalized accuracy of response (sham%)				
Possible action	99.62 (5.22)	101.66 (3.96)	101.60 (3.09)	100.54 (3.21)
Impossible action	105.44 (5.07)	98.42 (4.28)	102.38 (6.07)	96.46 (4.46)
Biomechanical plausibility	99.95 (6.84)	100.15 (5.37)	101.55 (5.52)	100.35 (5.66)

the absolute level of performance. Individual normalized accuracy and RTs were entered in two separate mixed-model ANOVAs, with Group (left, right hemisphere) as between-subjects factor and Task (possible actions, impossible actions, and biomechanical plausibility discriminations) and Stimulated site (EBA, vPMc) as within-subjects variable. Duncan's tests were used for post hoc analysis. The subjective reports of the independent group of individuals for the possible and the impossible body actions stimuli were compared by means of dependent-sample *t*-tests (two tailed).

RESULTS

Analysis on RTs showed that the main effects of Group, $F(1, 30) = 1.21$, $p = .280$, Task, $F(2, 60) = 0.22$, $p = .807$, and Stimulated site, $F(1, 30) = 0.54$, $p = .467$, were nonsignificant, thus ruling out any non-specific effects of rTMS involving group, task, or stimulated site. Crucially, however, the interaction between Task and Stimulated site was significant, $F(2, 60) = 4.62$, $p = .014$ (Figure 4).

Post hoc comparisons revealed that normalized RTs during discrimination of possible actions were increased after stimulation of vPMc (103.55% ± 2.33%) with respect to stimulation of EBA (97.78% ± 2.11%, $p = .004$). In contrast, no significant difference was observed between the effects of vPMc and EBA rTMS for impossible actions discrimination (99.21% ± 3.08% vs. 98.94% ± 2.45%, $p = .886$) and for biomechanical plausibility discrimination (99.16% ± 2.00% vs. 100.65% ± 1.86%, $p = .433$). Furthermore, the interferential effect of vPMc rTMS on discrimination of possible actions was significantly higher than the effect of vPMc rTMS on impossible actions ($p = .022$) and biomechanical plausibility discriminations ($p = .025$), which in turn did not differ from one another ($p = .980$). In contrast, while the effect of EBA rTMS on discrimination of impossible actions was significantly lower than that of vPMc rTMS on discrimination of possible actions ($p = .020$), no differential effect in the three discrimination tasks was obtained after EBA rTMS (all $ps > .153$). No other pairwise comparison was significant. Furthermore no other two-way interactions nor the three-way

TABLE 2
Raw RTs and accuracy of response means (± *MSE*) of all experimental conditions

	Left			*Right*		
	Sham	*EBA*	*vPMc*	*Sham*	*EBA*	*vPMc*
Raw RTs (ms)						
Possible action	796.96 (94.18)	755.26 (70.65)	806.67 (100.41)	799.11 (45.96)	778.60 (51.13)	840.73 (51.46)
Impossible action	890.69 (132.05)	851.87 (96.12)	798.96 (90.97)	843.23 (57.94)	815.50 (51.54)	878.09 (64.47)
Biomechanical plausibility	846.00 (111.65)	814.49 (85.30)	818.86 (110.02)	811.56 (54.51)	817.61 (53.77)	815.27 (54.91)
Raw accuracy of response(% of total)						
Possible action	85.94 (3.05)	83.60 (2.27)	85.94 (2.39)	79.30 (2.53)	79.69 (1.76)	79.30 (2.84)
Impossible action	79.30 (1.78)	82.81 (3.20)	77.34 (2.67)	73.05 (2.72)	73.05 (2.90)	69.14 (2.38)
Biomechanical plausibility	84.77 (3.65)	82.03 (3.27)	82.81 (2.94)	78.91 (2.85)	78.52 (3.12)	77.34 (2.61)

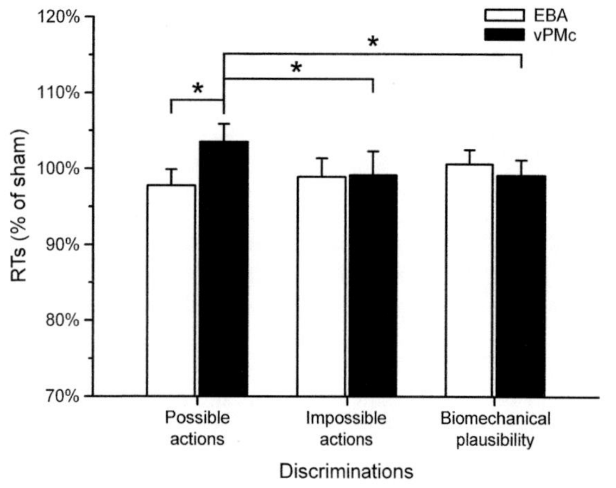

Figure 4. Normalized RTs (mean ± *MSE*) of the interaction Task × Stimulated site. The interferential effect of rTMS was only observed for left and right vPMc (black columns) stimulation during biomechanically possible action discrimination.

interactions reached significance. Given that the interaction Group by Stimulated area failed to reach significance threshold, $F(1, 30) = 3.14$, $p = .087$, stimulation of both left and right vPMc impaired discrimination of possible but not impossible actions. This would suggest that no hemispheric difference exists in processing of body actions. In a similar vein, the nonsignificant effects of the interaction Group by Task, $F(2, 60) = 0.21$, $p = .809$, and of the three-way interaction, $F(2, 60) = 2.58$, $p = .084$, indicate that left and right hemisphere rTMS produced a similar pattern of results in all conditions, thus ruling out any spurious effect due to between-groups differences. The mixed-model ANOVA on normalized accuracy, did not disclose any significant effect. In particular the nonsignificant effect of the interaction Task by Stimulated site, $F(2, 60) = 1.69$, $p = .194$, rules out that rTMS modulations on RTs may be explained by speed–accuracy trade-off effects. Thus, interferential stimulation of vPMc induced slower responses for visuo-perceptive discrimination of possible but not impossible body actions, without affecting response accuracy. No effect of interferential stimulation of EBA was observed (see Tables 1 and 2).

Subjective reports about different properties of the stimuli used in the TMS study showed that the motion implied by the observed stimuli significantly differed from zero for both possible (implied motion, $t(9) = 8.23$, $p = .000$) and impossible actions stimuli (implied motion, $t(9) = 5.79$, $p = .000$). These results suggest that both possible and impossible stimuli induced the perception of implied motion and were perceived as part of an action sequence. More importantly, no differences in the amount of implied motion attributed to possible and impossible action stimuli (5.12 cm ± 0.62 cm vs. 4.08 cm ± 0.70 cm), $t(9) = 1.84$, $p = .099$. Conversely possible and impossible stimuli were differentially rated for unpleasantness (1.38 cm ± 0.29 cm vs. 6.82 cm ± 0.60 cm), $t(9) = -8.03$, $p = .000$, biomechanical plausibility (1.29 cm ± 0.35 cm vs. 7.56 cm ± 0.47 cm), $t(9) = -10.13$, $p = .000$, joint stretching (1.98 cm ± 0.42 cm vs. 6.34 cm ± 0.65 cm), $t(9) = -6.06$, $p = .000$, and painfulness (1.19 cm ± 0.25 cm vs. 6.14 cm ± 0.66 cm), $t(9) = -7.53$, $p = .000$ (Figure 5).

DISCUSSION

The present study sought to determine the role played by left and right vPMc and EBA in the discrimination of biomechanical possible and impossible actions. We asked participants to perform a matching-to-sample task that required the discrimination between two different possible actions, two impossible actions, and between the same action performed with biomechanically possible and impossible kinematics. In different blocks, rapid event-related rTMS trains of two

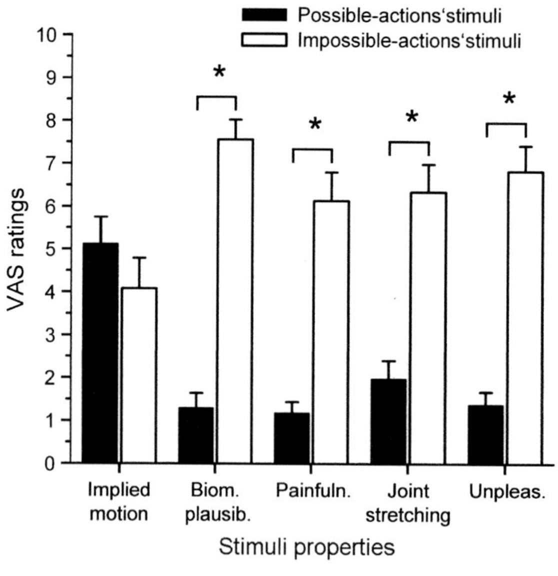

Figure 5. Subjective VAS ratings of the different properties of the experimental stimuli. While biomechanically possible and impossible actions were comparable for implied motion, the latter induced higher sense of biomechanically implausibility, painfulness, joint stretching and unpleasantness with respect to the former.

pulses were applied 150 ms after sample presentation over left and right vPMc and EBA. Magnetic stimulation had no effect on accuracy of response but selectively impaired RTs for possible actions discrimination when applied over both left and right vPMc. No effect of left and right vPMc and EBA rTMS was observed for either discrimination of impossible actions or for discrimination of the biomechanical plausibility of actions.

Visual processing of body actions in premotor cortex

Passive observation of actions activates premotor areas (Keysers & Gazzola, 2006; Rizzolatti & Craighero, 2004), suggesting that action observation triggers the simulative mapping of observed actions onto the observer's motor representations. Recent studies reported that vPMc rTMS impairs discrimination of static (Urgesi et al., 2007) and dynamic (Pobric & Hamilton, 2006) displays of actions. In keeping with previous studies (Pobric & Hamilton, 2006; Urgesi et al., 2007), our results indicate that vPMc neural activity is actively involved in visual perception of biomechanically possible actions. This suggests that motor and premotor areas may be specifically involved in visual processing of action-related features of the visible body parts even when the task does not explicitly require the motor simulation of the observed movements. This may be in keeping with the fact that motor activation during action observation seems to topographically map the moving body part (Buccino et al., 2001; Fadiga, Craighero, & Olivier, 2005; Urgesi, Candidi, Romani, Fabbro, & Aglioti, 2006a). Mapping observed actions onto the onlooker's motor representations may provide the visual system with a fine-grained description of the moving body; motor representations of the acting bodies may thus feed back into visual cortices and refine perception of body forms (Wilson & Knoblich, 2005). Indeed, monitoring our own body postures and actions reinforces the representation of postures and actions of other people's bodies (Reed & Farah, 1995). Furthermore, self-produced limb movements activate EBA (Astafiev et al., 2004), suggesting a functional link between the motor system and the body's visual representations. The interaction between visual and motor body-related areas may subserve the sophisticated human ability to process actions performed by conspecifics.

Neural representations of biomechanically impossible actions

The present study significantly expands previous evidences (Pobric & Hamilton, 2006; Urgesi et al., 2007) by testing whether vPMc is also involved in visual discrimination of movements that cannot be performed. We show that vPMc plays a crucial role only in visuo-perceptive discriminations of biomechanically possible actions, but does not play any causative role in processing pictures of actions that cannot be performed. This suggests that premotor representations of actions only occur for movements that belong to the observer's motor repertoire. This is in keeping with studies showing that activations of mirror neurons system areas are modulated by motor expertise (Calvo-Merino et al., 2005, 2006; Cross, Hamilton, & Grafton, 2006). Similarly, it has been shown that purely motoric learning of specific actions improves their visuo-perceptual discrimination (Casile & Giese, 2006). Furthermore, Buccino et al. (2004) reported that only gestures belonging to the *species*-specific motor repertoire activate the motor system, whereas actions that are typical of other species seem to engender predominantly visual activations. The notion that only doable movements activate observers' motor and premotor cortices has been re-examined by the finding of comparable activations of motor and premotor cortices during observation of impossible movements (Costantini et al., 2005; Romani et al., 2005). Motor activation during observation of biomechanically impossible actions (Costantini et al., 2005; Romani et al., 2005) may reflect the fact that the cortico-spinal motor system does not map the specific kinematics of the observed actions but their general meaning. To test this hypothesis we explored the active involvement of vPMc in a task requiring the discrimination between the meaning of two actions executed with biomechanically impossible kinematics. If vPMc codes the goal of an action regardless of its motor kinematics, this area should play a role independently from the biomechanical plausibility of the observed action. In contrast, our results clearly show that activations of vPMc are not necessary for visual perception of the general meaning of actions that, although conceptually possible, are biomechanically impossible and thus cannot be performed. Thus, motor representation of observed actions does not seem to be constant with respect to kinematics of the movement. Another result of the present study is that vPMc does not seem to play any causative role in the discrimination of actions' biomechanical plausibility. It is worth noting here that this task required the discrimination of two actions that shared the same goal but were performed with either biomechanically possible or impossible kinematics. Interfering with vPMc activity did not affect performance during the biomechanical plausibility discrimination which may suggest that the motor representations of observed actions are not used for the visual perception of action kinematics. Therefore, neural activation of vPMc is not necessary for the discrimination of actions with different kinematics but sharing the same goal. In contrast, vPMc activity is crucial for discriminating the goal of different actions that are performed with biomechanically possible kinematics. This may indicate that the premotor cortex is likely to code a combination of goals and kinematics that allow the representation of actions as goal-directed movements (Rizzolatti et al., 2004). This is in line with imaging and single-unit electrophysiological data showing that premotor cortices may be the neural substrate of actions' goal representation (Johnson-Frey et al., 2003; Rizzolatti et al., 1988).

Processing of body actions in extrastriate body area

The present study shows that, although impossible movements may trigger premotor cortices activations (Costantini et al., 2005), vPMc has no crucial role in perceptual representations of impossible actions. Motor activation during observation of biomechanically impossible movements may reflect modulatory signals from other cortical structures such as temporal and parietal areas (Pavlova, Lutzenberger, Sokolov, & Birbaumer, 2004). Indeed, observation of biomechanically impossible movements engenders higher activations of temporal and parietal areas as compared to observation of possible movements (Costantini et al., 2005). EBA response to acting bodies is enhanced by observation of incoherent sequences of body movements with strong configural changes of the body posture while neural activations of vPMc and of superior temporal sulcus are higher during observation of coherent sequences of body movements (Downing et al., 2006). This suggests that EBA and vPMc play different roles in processing acting bodies: EBA may be involved in the static representation of human bodies' postures and in detecting visual discrepancies in the postural configurations of body images. Enhanced extrastriate activation during observation of impossible movements (Costantini et al., 2005), distorted body postures (Avikainen et al., 2003), and visuo-proprioceptive discrepancies (Dohle, Kleiser, Seitz, & Freund, 2004) may reflect general novelty or emotive salience of the stimuli. Neuroimaging studies, however, cannot establish whether changes of metabolic activity related to a given task is crucial rather than epiphenomenal. In contrast, using rTMS allows the investigation of the active role played by EBA in processing possible and impossible body actions. Previous rTMS studies have shown that interference with neural activity of EBA impairs discrimination performances based on the categorization of morphological details of the human body parts, but does not affect action discrimination (Urgesi et al., 2004, 2007). Here we demonstrate that EBA is not actively involved in discriminating two different possible actions performed by the same person, thus suggesting that the role of EBA in body perception is not causally related to the processing of action-related cues. Furthermore, the present study shows that EBA does not play any crucial role in discriminating impossible body actions as well as their biomechanical plausibility. EBA activity has been proved selective for images of the human body and its single parts (Downing et al., 2001, 2006) and premotor cortices have been demonstrated to be insensitive to observation of actions performed by nonbiological agents like robots (Tai, Scherfler, Brooks, Sawamoto, & Castiello, 2004). In view of this, one may wonder whether the lack of influence of EBA and vPMc on the perception of impossible body postures may be due to the fact that our stimuli were not coded as "body" or "bodily actions". However, the possible and impossible action stimuli used in our study induced the perception of comparable amount of implied motion and were perceived as parts of actions. Subjective ratings indicated that impossible actions stimuli induced higher joint stretching sensations, lower biomechanical plausibility, higher unpleasantness and higher painfulness in comparison with possible actions stimuli. That impossible action stimuli were perceived as body parts in action rules out that the lack of effects of vPMc and EBA rTMS is due to an inappropriate coding of these stimuli. Our data show that EBA is not crucially involved in the visual discrimination of impossible body movements. The suggestion is made that this area may be part of a wide parieto-temporal network related to the multisensorial coding of afferent components of actions (Costantini et al., 2005). Indeed, enhanced neural activity in EBA during observation of impossible body postures may derive from sensorimotor feedback signals that modulate body form perception (Astafiev et al., 2004). Future studies are needed to better understand the functional links between extrastriate visual representation of acting bodies and sensorimotor representations in fronto-parietal areas.

Manuscript accepted 12 September 2007
First published online 16 October 2007

REFERENCES

Astafiev, S. V., Stanley, C. M., Shulman, G. L., & Corbetta, M. (2004). Extrastriate body area in human occipital cortex responds to the performance of motor actions. *Nature Neuroscience*, *7*(5), 542–548.

Avikainen, S., Liuhanen, S., Schürmann, M., & Hari, R. (2003). Enhanced extrastriate activation during observation of distorted finger postures. *Journal of Cognitive Neuroscience*, *15*(5), 658–663.

Blanke, O., Mohr, C., Michel, C. M., Pascual-Leone, A., Brugger, P., Seeck, M., et al. (2005). Linking out-of-body experience and self processing to mental own-body imagery at the temporoparietal junction. *Journal of Neuroscience*, *25*(3), 550–557.

Brass, M., Bekkering, H., Wohlschlager, A., & Prinz, W. (2000). Compatibility between observed and executed finger movements: comparing symbolic, spatial, and imitative cues. *Brain Cognition*, *44*, 124–143.

Briggs, G. G., & Nebes, R. D. (1975). Patterns of hand preference in a student population. *Cortex*, *11*(3), 230–238.

Buccino, G., Binkofski, F., Fink, G. R., Fadiga, L., Fogassi, L., Gallese, V., et al. (2001). Action observation activates premotor and parietal areas in a somatotopic manner: an fMRI study. *European Journal of Neuroscience*, *13*(2), 400–404.

Buccino, G., Canessa, N., Patteri, I., Lagravinese, G., Benuzzi, F., Porro, C. A., et al. (2004). Neural circuits involved in the recognition of actions performed by nonconspecifics: an fMRI study. *Journal of Cognitive Neuroscience*, *16*(1), 114–126.

Calvo-Merino, B., Glaser, D. E., Grezes, J., Passingam, R. E., & Haggard, P. (2005). Action observation and acquired motor skills: an fMRI study with expert dancers. *Cerebral Cortex*, *15*(8), 1243–1249.

Calvo-Merino, B., Grezes, J., Glaser, D. E., Passingham, R. E., & Haggard, P. (2006). Seeing or doing? Influence of visual and motor familiarity in action observation. *Current Biology*, *16*(19), 1905–1910. Erratum in: *Current Biology*, *16*(22), 2277.

Casile, A., & Giese, M. A. (2006). Nonvisual motor training influences biological motion perception. *Current Biology*, *16*(1), 69–74.

Celnik, P., Stefan, K., Hummel, F., Duque, J., Classen, J., & Cohen, L. G. (2006). Encoding a motor memory in the older adult by action observation. *NeuroImage*, *29*(2), 677–684.

Chao, L. L., & Martin, A. (2000). Representation of manipulable man-made objects in the dorsal strema. *NeuroImage*, *12*(4), 478–484.

Costantini, M., Galati, G., Ferretti, A., Caulo, M., Tartaro, A., & Romani, G. L. (2005). Neural systems underlying observation of humanly impossible movements: an fMRI study. *Cerebral Cortex*, *15*(11), 1761–1767.

Craighero, L., Bello, A., Fadiga, L., & Rizzolatti, G. (2002). Hand action preparation influences the responses to hand pictures. *Neuropsychologia*, *40*(5), 492–502.

Cross, E. S., Hamilton, A. F., de, C., & Grafton, S. (2006). Building a motor simulation de novo: Observation of dance by dancers. *NeuroImage*, *31*(3), 1257–1267.

Dohle, C., Kleiser, R., Seitz, R. J., & Freund, H. J. (2004). Body schema gates visual processing. *Journal of Neurophysiology*, *91*(5), 2376–2379.

Downing, P., Jiang, Y., Shuman, M., & Kanwisher, N. (2001). A cortical area selective for visual processing of the human body. *Science*, *293*(5539), 2470–2473.

Downing, P., Peelen, M., Wigget, A. J., & Tew, B. D. (2006). The role of the extrastriate body area in action perception. *Social Neuroscience*, *1*(1), 52–62.

Fadiga, L., Craighero, L., & Olivier, E. (2005). Human motor cortex excitability during the perception of others' action. *Current Opinion in Neurobiology*, *15*(2), 213–218.

Grezes, J., & Decety, J. (2001). Functional anatomy of execution, mental simulation, observation, and verb generation of actions: a meta-analysis. *Human Brain Mapping*, *12*(1), 1–19.

Grossman, E. D., & Blake, R. (2002). Brain areas active during perception of biological motion. *Neuron*, *35*(6), 1167–1175.

Johnson-Frey, S., Maloof, F., Newman-Norlund, R., Farrer, C., Inati, S., & Grafton, S. (2003). Action or hand–object interactions? Human inferior frontal cortex and action observation. *Neuron*, *39*(6), 1053–1058.

Keysers, C., & Gazzola, V. (2006). Towards a unifying neural theory of social cognition. *Progress in Brain Research*, *156*, 383–406.

Nelissen, K., Luppino, G., Vanduffel, W., Rizzolatti, G., & Orban, G. A. (2005). Observing others: Multiple action representation in the frontal lobe. *Science*, *310*(5746), 332–336.

Nishitani, N., & Hari, R. (2000). Temporal dynamics of cortical representation for action. *Neuron*, *36*(6), 1211–1220.

Nishitani, N., & Hari, R. (2002). Viewing lip forms: cortical dynamics. *Proceedings of the National Academy of Sciences, 36*(6), 1211–1220.

Pascual-Leone, A., Walsh, V., & Rothwell, J. (2000). Transcranial magnetic stimulation in cognitive neuroscience—Virtual lesion, chronometry, and functional connectivity. *Current Opinion in Neurobiology, 10*(2), 232–237.

Pavlova, M., Lutzenberger, W., Sokolov, A., & Birbaumer, N. (2004). Dissociable cortical processing of recognizable and non-recognizable biological movements. *Cerebral Cortex, 14*(2), 181–188.

Peelen, M., & Downing, P. (2005). Is the extrastriate body area involved in motor actions? *Nature Neuroscience, 8*(2), 125.

Peelen, M., Wigget, A. J., & Downing, P. (2006). Patterns of fMRI activity dissociate overlapping functional brain areas that respond to biological motion. *Neuron, 49*(6), 815–822.

Pobric, G., & Hamilton, A. F. (2006). Action understanding requires the left inferior frontal cortex. *Current Biology, 16*(5), 524–529.

Prinz, W. (2002). Experimental approaches to imitation. In A. N. Meltzoff & W. Prinz (Eds.), *The imitative mind: Development, evolution and brain bases* (pp. 143–162). Cambridge, UK: Cambridge University Press.

Reed, C. L., & Farah, M. J. (1995). The psychological reality of the body schema: a test with normal participants. *Journal of Experimental Psychology: Human Perception and Performance, 21*(2), 334–343.

Rizzolatti, G., Camarda, R., Fogassi, L., Gentilucci, M., Luppino, G., & Matelli, M. (1988). Functional organization of inferior area 6 in the macaque monkey. II. Area F5 and the control of distal movements. *Experimental Brain Research, 71*(3), 491–507.

Rizzolatti, G., & Craighero, L. (2004). The mirror-neuron system. *Annual Review of Neuroscience, 27*, 169–192.

Romani, M., Cesari, P., Urgesi, C., Facchini, S., & Aglioti, S. M. (2005). Motor facilitation of the human cortico-spinal system during observation of biomechanically impossible movements. *NeuroImage, 23*(9), 2522–2530.

Sawaki, L., Okita, T., Fujiwara, M., & Mizuno, K. (1999). Specific and non-specific effects of transcranial magnetic stimulation on simple and go-no-go reaction time. *Experimental Brain Research, 127*, 402–408.

Saygin, A. P., Wilson, S. M., Dronkers, N. F., & Bates, E. (2004). Action comprehension in aphasia: linguistic and non-linguistic deficits and their lesion correlates. *Neuropsychologia, 42*(13), 1788–1804.

Stefan, K., Cohen, L. G., Duque, J., Mazzocchio, R., Celnik, P., Sawaki, L., et al. (2005). Formation of a motor memory by action observation. *Journal of Neuroscience, 25*(41), 9339–9346.

Tai, Y. F., Scherfler, C., Brooks, D. J., Sawamoto, N., & Castiello, U. (2004). The human premotor cortex is "mirror" only for biological actions. *Current Biology, 14*(2), 117–120.

Talairach, J., & Tournoux, P. (1988). *Co-planar stereotaxic atlas of the human brain: 3-dimensional proportional system. an approach to cerebral imaging*. Stuttgart, Germany: Thieme.

Terao, Y., Ugawa, Y., Suzuki, M., Sakai, K., Hanajima, R., Gemba-Shimizu, K., et al. (1997). Shortening of simple reaction time by peripheral electrical and submotor-threshold magnetic cortical stimulation. *Experimental Brain Research, 115*, 541–545.

Uozumi, T., Tamagawa, A., Hashimoto, T., & Tsuji, S. (2004). Motor hand representation in cortical area 44. *Neurology, 62*(5), 757–761.

Urgesi, C., Berlucchi, G., & Aglioti, S. M. (2004). Magnetic stimulation of extrastriate body area impairs visual processing of nonfacial body parts. *Current Biology, 14*(23), 2130–2134.

Urgesi, C., Candidi, M., Ionta, S., & Aglioti, S. M. (2007). Representation of body identity and body action in extrastriate body area and ventral premotor cortex. *Nature Neuroscience, 10*(1), 30–31.

Urgesi, C., Candidi, M., Romani, M., Fabbro, F., & Aglioti, S. M. (2006a). Motor facilitation during action observation: topographic mapping of the target muscle and influence of the onlooker's posture. *European Journal of Neuroscience, 23*(9), 2522–2530.

Urgesi, C., Moro, V., Candidi, M., & Aglioti, S. M. (2006b). Mapping implied body actions in the human motor system. *Journal of Neuroscience, 26*(30), 7942–7949.

Wasserman, E. M. (1997). Risk and safety of repetitive transcranial magnetic stimulation: report and suggested guidelines from the International Workshop on the Safety of Repetitive Transcranial Magnetic Stimulation, June 5–7, 1996. *Electroencephalography and Clinical Neurophysiology, 108*, 1–16.

Wilson, M., & Knoblich, G. (2005). The case of motor involvement in perceiving conspecifics. *Psychological Bulletin, 131*(3), 460–473.

Wohlschlager, A., & Bekkering, H. (2002). Is human imitation based on a mirror-neurone system? Some behavioural evidence. *Experimental Brain Research, 143*(3), 335–341.

Psychology Press
Taylor & Francis Group

Listening to humans walking together activates the social brain circuitry

Miiamaaria V. Saarela
Helsinki University of Technology, Helsinki, Finland

Riitta Hari
Helsinki University of Technology, Helsinki, Finland, and Helsinki University Central Hospital, Helsinki, Finland

Human footsteps carry a vast amount of social information, which is often unconsciously noted. Using functional magnetic resonance imaging, we analyzed brain networks activated by footstep sounds of one or two persons walking. Listening to two persons walking together activated brain areas previously associated with affective states and social interaction, such as the subcallosal gyrus bilaterally, the right temporal pole, and the right amygdala. These areas seem to be involved in the analysis of persons' identity and complex social stimuli on the basis of auditory cues. Single footsteps activated only the biological motion area in the posterior STS region. Thus, hearing two persons walking together involved a more widespread brain network than did hearing footsteps from a single person.

INTRODUCTION

Human footsteps, even when not consciously attended to, carry a rich pattern of social information. It is often possible to infer the mood, gender, socio-hierarchical status, or even some personality traits of the walking person by only listening to the footsteps in a hallway.

Recently, Bidet-Caulet, Voisin, Bertrand, & Fonlupt (2005) presented, during functional magnetic imaging (fMRI), footstep sounds of two persons who first appeared to walk on separate sides of the subject and subsequently one of them crossed to the opposite side. While the subjects had to detect which of the persons "crossed the street", the biological motion area (Allison, Puce, & McCarthy, 2000) in the posterior superior temporal sulcus (STSp) was activated bilaterally. No other brain area was activated differentially during the footstep task vs. detection of left- or right-sided noise bursts of increasing intensity.

From the walking sounds of human groups, we may deduce the number of walkers and some features of the group dynamics: are the persons walking together, is one escaping or leading another or the others, and so on. Social psychologists have long noted that human groups have a different impact on the individual than the face-to-face interaction between two persons. In this sense, even two persons compared with a single person can be perceived as a group. Here, our goal was to find out whether such a difference can

Correspondence should be addressed to: Miiamaaria V. Saarela, Brain Research Unit, Low Temperature Laboratory, Helsinki University of Technology, P.O. Box 5100, FIN-02015 TKK, Finland. E-mail: miiu@neuro.hut.fi

This study was financially supported by the Academy of Finland (National Centers of Excellence Programme 2006–2011), Finnish Graduate School of Neuroscience, the Sigrid Jusélius Foundation, and the Louis-Jéantet Foundation. We thank Marita Kattelus for help in MRI measurements, Yevhen Hluschuk for advice in data acquisition and analysis, Tiina Parviainen for advice in stimulus preparation, and the Finnish Broadcasting Company (Oy Yleisradio Ab) for providing the professional footstep stimuli. The fMRI recordings were carried out at the Advanced Magnetic Imaging Centre of the Helsinki University of Technology.

www.psypress.com/socialneuroscience DOI:10.1080/17470910801897633

be seen in brain activations when the subjects listen to footsteps of one person walking or two persons walking together. In line with the previous study by Bidet-Caulet et al. (2005), we expected the bilateral STSp to be activated by step sounds of both one person and two persons, when contrasted with control noise sounds. Additionally, we predicted that since the sounds of two persons walking are socially more complex, they could recruit brain areas that are more intensively involved in social cognition.

METHODS

Subjects

Twelve healthy volunteers (six females, six males; ages 22–37 years, mean $\pm$ SD 27 $\pm$ 4) participated in the fMRI experiment. All subjects were right-handed according to the Edinburgh Handedness Inventory (Oldfield, 1971): on the scale from left = –1 to right = +1, the mean score was 0.91. Subjects gave written informed consent before the experiment, and the study had prior approval by the Ethics Committee of the Helsinki and Uusimaa Hospital District.

Stimuli

Footstep sounds and matched noise bursts

Two different types of sound were presented binaurally to the subjects in blocks of 30 s for each: sounds of human footsteps on asphalt and rhythmical bursts of white noise. The human walking sounds were obtained from the Sound Effects Library of the Finnish Broadcasting Company (Oy Yleisradio Ab) and they were either (i) from one human (male) walking ("STEP1") or (ii) from two people (a female with high heels and a man) walking ("STEP2"). The corresponding control stimuli were (iii) rhythmical bursts of white noise of constant amplitude ("NOISE1") or (iv) bursts of white noise with two different amplitudes ("NOISE2").

NOISE1 and NOISE2 were matched to the walking sounds in duration, rhythm, amplitude variation, and sharp acoustic transients. The single noise bursts were 103 $\pm$ 13 ms in duration. Because the STEP1 sound comprised about 2 steps/s and the STEP2 sound about 4 steps/s, NOISE1 contained 1.6 noise bursts/s (mean $\pm$ SEM interburst interval 495 $\pm$ 16 ms) and NOISE2 contained 3.1 noise bursts/s (interburst interval 214 $\pm$ 78 ms).

The footstep sounds and the noise bursts were also matched in the intensity variation so that a noise burst of one amplitude corresponded to one type of step, and a noise burst of another amplitude corresponded to another type of step. Moreover, the step sounds and their respective noise controls were matched in their total root mean square (RMS) power during the 30-s sound blocks.

Stimulus presentation

The STEP1, STEP2, NOISE1, and NOISE2 blocks were presented in a pseudorandom order so that every fifth 30-s block of the session was REST without any stimuli. Subjects participated in two sequential sessions in which the occurrence of STEP1 and STEP2 blocks was counterbalanced. In total, each stimulus block was presented 4 times (twice in each session), and the total recording time was 10 min. The order of sessions was counterbalanced across subjects: for half of the subjects Session 1 was presented first and for the other half Session 2. Subjects were asked to listen carefully to the sounds and to pay equal attention to all of them in order to be able to answer a questionnaire on the sounds after the scanning.

The mean $\pm$ SD intensities of all stimulus sounds were 54 $\pm$ 4 dB HL (hearing level; range 45–63 dB HL across individuals); these sounds were comfortable to listen to, yet well identifiable during the fMRI scan. Before the scan, the maximum loudness of the stimuli was measured in the control room, with ambient noise present.

Post-scan questionnaire

A qualitative questionnaire was aimed to explore the subjects' attention and cognitive evaluation of the stimulus sounds. The questionnaire was filled after the scan to a avoid directing the subjects' attention to any particular features of the sounds during the scanning procedure. On a non-numerical scale, the subjects reported whether they regarded the sounds as (i) not realistic at all, (ii) somewhat realistic, or (iii) very realistic. Moreover, they stated whether they (i) did not guess at all, (ii) mostly did not guess, (iii) mostly guessed, or (iv) always guessed the gender of the walking person.

Experimental setup and data acquisition

During the fMRI scan, the subject was lying in the whole-body General Electric (GE) Signa® 3.0T MRI scanner at the Advanced Magnetic Imaging Centre, Helsinki University of Technology. The sounds were delivered through an ADU2a auditory stimulation system (Unides Design, Helsinki, Finland). Plastic tubes were attached to ER3A earphones (Etymotic Research Inc., USA), and the subjects' hearing was also protected with Silenta Aurora LT hearing protectors (Oy Silenta Ltd, Finland). Stimulus timing was controlled by the Presentation™ software (Neurobehavioral Systems, Inc.).

Functional magnetic resonance (MR) images were acquired in a block design, using a standard head coil and gradient-echo planar imaging (EPI) sequence with field of view = 200×200 mm^2, time of repetition = 2000 ms, time to echo = 32 ms, number of excitations = 1, flip angle = 75°, and acquired matrix size 64×64. Altogether 33 slices (thickness 4.0 mm) were acquired in interleaved order. The resulting functional voxels were $3.125 \times 3.125 \times 4$ mm^3 in size. Structural T1-weighted MR images were acquired using a standard spoiled-gradient echo sequence with a matrix size of 256×256, resulting in $1 \times 1.016 \times 1.016$ mm^3 voxels.

Data analysis

The fMRI data were evaluated with BrainVoyager QX 1.4 software (Brain Innovation B.V., Maastricht, The Netherlands). Preprocessing comprised temporal high-pass filtering at 0.01 Hz, 3D motion correction, and slice scan–time correction. Functional and anatomical data were resampled to $3 \times 3 \times 3$ mm^3 and $1 \times 1 \times 1$ mm^3 voxels, respectively, and they were normalized to the Talairach space (Talairach & Tournoux, 1988). Subsequently, all functional data were resampled to the resolution of anatomical images for the use in statistical maps.

At the group level, brain hemodynamic activations were subjected to random-effects statistical analysis using a general linear model (GLM). The predictors for GLM were obtained by convolving the time courses of the stimulus blocks with a canonical hemodynamic response function to reveal blood oxygenation level dependent (BOLD) activations. Activation threshold was set to $p < .001$ (uncorrected) for statistical maps of STEP1 + STEP2 – REST, NOISE1 + NOISE2 – REST and (STEP2 – NOISE2) – (STEP1 – NOISE1), and to $p < .005$ (uncorrected) for the contrast maps (STEP1 – NOISE1, STEP2 – NOISE2 and STEP2 – STEP1). Cluster size was 70 mm^3.

RESULTS

Behavioral responses

In the post-scan questionnaire, 11/12 subjects rated the sounds as very realistic, and one as somewhat realistic. Five subjects had spontaneously guessed the gender of the walkers in every sound clip (actually, only two different step sound clips, STEP1 and STEP2, were presented although some subjects thought there were more) and seven subjects had spontaneously guessed the gender of the walkers in at least some of the step sound clips.

Brain imaging

Step sounds vs. REST

Figure 1 (left) shows that both types of step sounds compared with the rest state (contrast STEP1 + STEP2 – REST) revealed activations bilaterally in cortical and thalamic auditory areas as well as in the STSp regions. Additional activations occurred in, for example, the left cingulate, the left cerebellum, and the left medial frontal gyrus (Table 1).

Noise sounds vs. REST

Similarly to Step sounds vs. REST, noise bursts compared with the rest state (NOISE1 + NOISE2 – REST) revealed activation bilaterally in cortical and thalamic auditory areas, as well as in the left inferior frontal lobe and the left posterior insula (Figure 1). Additional activation occurred in, for example, the inferior parietal lobules of both hemispheres (Table 1).

STEP1 vs. NOISE1, STEP2 vs. NOISE2, and STEP2 vs. STEP1

Figure 2 combines main activations observed in the group-level analysis of contrasts

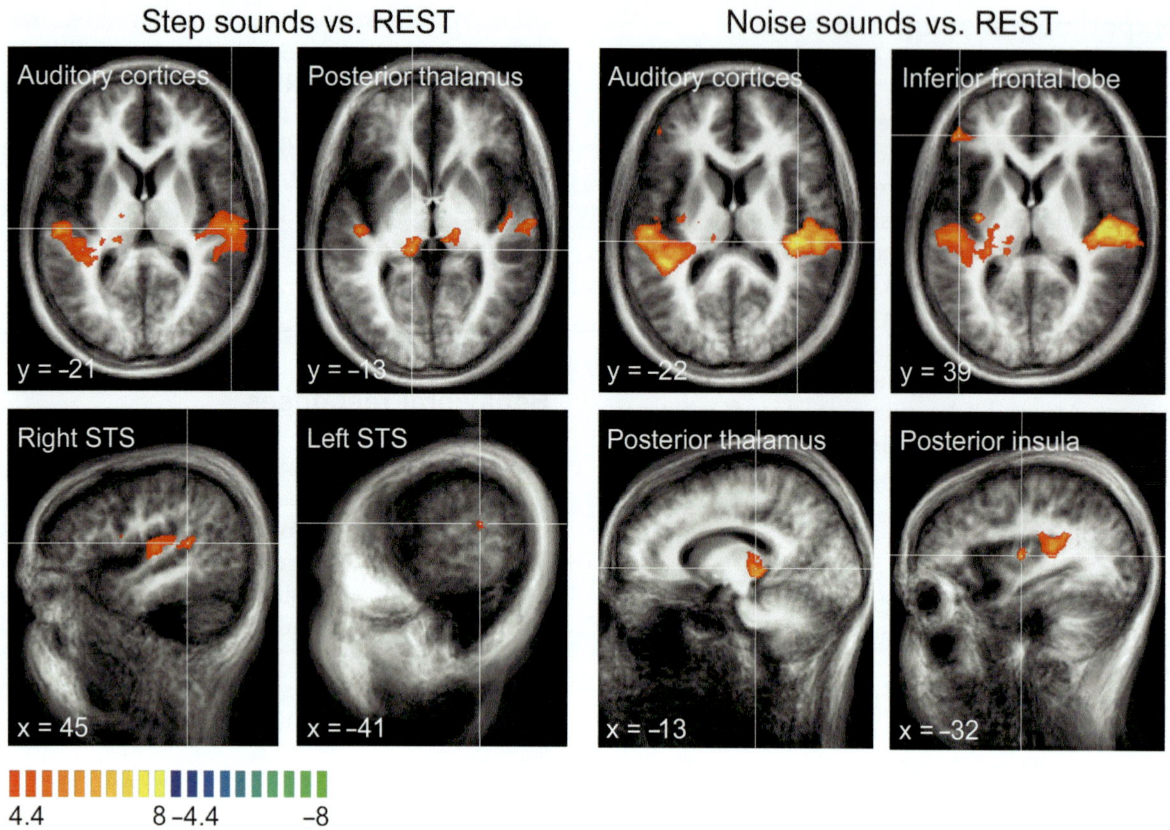

Figure 1. The STEP1+STEP2 – REST contrast on the left shows BOLD activations in the auditory cortices, the posterior thalamus, and the bilateral STSp regions (p uncorrected <.001). On the right, the contrast NOISE1+NOISE2 – REST shows activations in the auditory cortices, the left inferior frontal lobe, the posterior thalamus, and the left posterior insula. All statistical maps are overlaid on the group average anatomical image; T values are presented in the color bar.

STEP1 – NOISE1 and STEP2 – NOISE2 (for exact coordinates of all activations, see Table 2). From top to bottom, the brain images illustrate activations in the left STSp (STEP1 – NOISE1, see also the percentage-of-change histograms on the right), the right temporal pole (STEP2), the bilateral subcallosal gyrus (STEP2), the left amygdala (STEP1) and the right amygdala (STEP2). Additional activation for STEP2 occurred in the anterior cingulate sulcus, the intraparietal sulcus, the anterior insula, the middle frontal gyrus, the pre-supplementary motor area, and the postcentral gyrus of the right hemisphere. Negative BOLD responses were detected bilaterally in the auditory cortices, reflecting stronger auditory-cortex activation by noise than by footsteps.

The percentage-of-signal-change histograms (Figure 2, right) demonstrated that the amygdalar activations in both STEP – NOISE contrasts were strongly contributed by the suppressive effects of the noise bursts on amygdalar activation.

An additional contrast of STEP2 – STEP1 showed differences in cerebellum and inferior parietal lobule; (STEP2 – NOISE2) – (STEP1 – NOISE1) only in cerebellum (Table 2).

DISCUSSION

Walking sounds, STSp, and the mirror-neuron system (MNS)

Hearing other individuals' actions can activate, in both monkeys (Kohler et al., 2002; Barraclough, Xiao, Baker, Oram, & Perrett, 2005) and humans (Gazzola, Aziz-Zadeh, & Keysers, 2006), the MNS that matches executed and observed actions (for review, see Rizzolatti & Craighero, 2004). The core area of the human MNS, the inferior frontal gyrus (IFG), can be activated by STS via inferior parietal lobe (Nishitani & Hari, 2000). In our study, STSp was activated bilaterally in STEP1 + STEP2 – REST and the activation was

TABLE 1

Talairach coordinates of the centers of gravity of the activated brain regions for contrasts (STEP1+STEP2 – REST), (NOISE1+NOISE2 – REST) and (STEP2 – NOISE 2) – (STEP1 – NOISE1)

Brain area	*L/R*	*x*	*y*	*z*	*Area (mm³)*
STEP1+STEP2 – REST					
Auditory cortices	L	−40	−32	14	7470
Auditory cortices and posterior STS	R	50	−24	9	6828
Posterior STS	L	−59	−41	12	88
Posterior cingulate	L	−12	−16	33	348
	L	−18	−22	41	133
	L	−20	−6	38	144
Central sulcus	L	−43	−14	31	102
Medial superior frontal gyrus	L	−7	14	49	101
Inferior precentral sulcus	R	43	7	16	72
Pulvinar and medial geniculate	L	−14	−28	1	720
	R	13	−23	2	192
Lateral posterior thalamic nuclei	L	−14	−13	6	97
Inferior colliculus	L	−6	−28	−8	107
Cerebellum	L	−17	−33	−18	116
NOISE1+NOISE2 – REST					
Auditory cortices*	L	−42	−30	13	7260
	R	48	−22	9	7769
Inferior frontal lobe	L	−45	39	7	434
Posterior cingulate	L	−20	−22	43	412
	L	−8	−2	28	70
Posterior insula	L	−32	−10	9	243
Temporo-occipital fissure	L	−39	−56	−5	230
Parietal lobule	R	22	−26	42	93
	L	−25	−33	42	75
Medial geniculate and pulvinar*	L	−13	−27	1	890
	R	16	−24	1	361
(STEP2 – NOISE2) – (STEP1 – NOISE1)					
Cerebellum	R	19	−70	−36	79

Notes: $p < .001$, cluster size = 70 mm³. STS = superior temporal sulcus. Some large activation clusters marked with * were examined with higher statistical threshold of $p < .0005$ to better discern the local activations.

lateralized to left in STEP1 – NOISE1; however, since the step sounds did not activate the IFG, we cannot attribute this STSp activation to the classical mirror-neuron circuitry. Instead, the observed bilateral STSp activation by the step sounds (STEP1+STEP2 – REST) confirms the findings of Bidet-Caulet et al. (2005) and further supports the involvement of the STS as a "biological motion area" (for review, see Allison, et al., 2000).

The auditory part of the MNS is activated by sounds of object-directed hand or mouth actions, such as typewriting (Aziz-Zadeh, Iacoboni, Zaidel, Wilson & Mazziotta, 2004), hand clapping (Pizzamiglio, Aprile, Spitoni, Pitzalis, Bates, D'Amico & Di Russo 2005), crunching of potato chips (Gazzola, Aziz-Zadeh & Keysers, 2006), and piano playing (Lahav, Saltzman & Schlaug, 2007). Sounds of human footsteps, on the other hand, have failed to activate the premotor/IFG region (Bidet-Caulet et al., 2005), in line with our results. The motor areas forming the core of the MNS have representations mainly for hand and mouth (Luppino & Rizzolatti, 2000), and therefore the lack of IFG activation by sounds of human footsteps could reflect the strong preference of the MNS to hand and mouth actions. This interpretation is also in line with the suggested relationship between the MNS and communicative actions (Rizzolatti & Arbib, 1998).

The direct comparison of activations between STEP2 and STEP1 or the enhanced contrast of (STEP2 – NOISE2) – (STEP1 – NOISE1) did not yield differences in the STS or any other brain region known to be relevant for social interaction; the only small clusters were found in left cerebellum and deep in the left inferior parietal lobe. We interpret the inefficiency of these analyses to be mainly due to the different physical qualities of the stimuli; in addition, the statistical power in contrast (STEP2 – NOISE2) – (STEP1 –

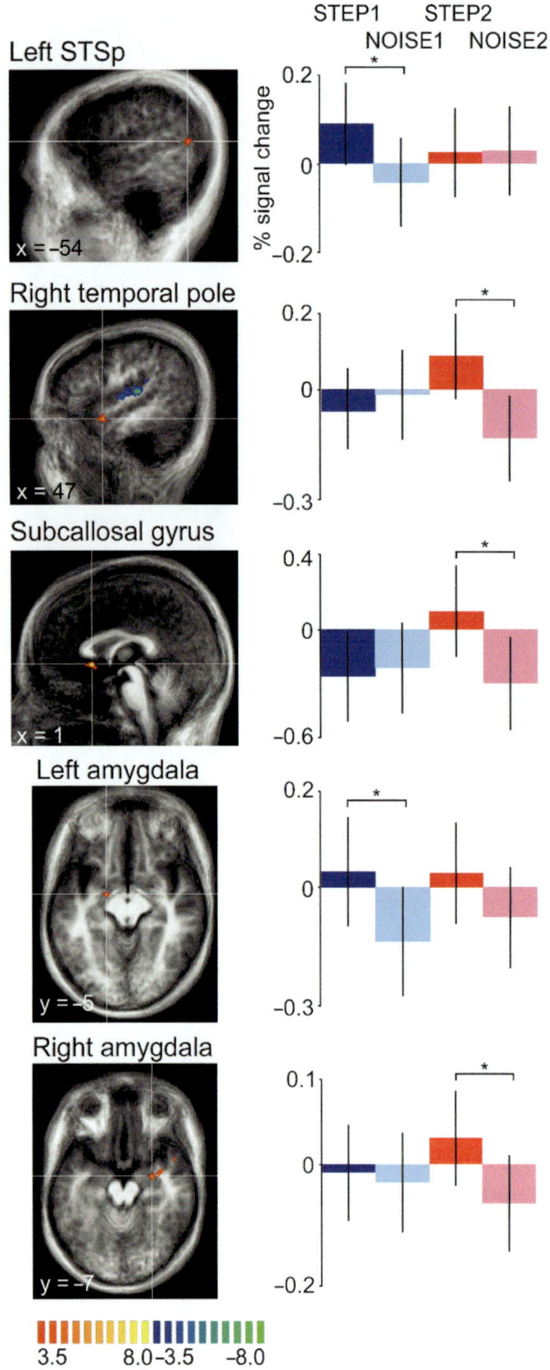

Figure 2. The BOLD activations are shown on the left, superimposed on the group average anatomical image, and the respective percentage-of-signal-change histograms are shown on the right. The respective contrasts, in which the brain region was obtained, are marked * in each histogram (p uncorrected <.005). Blue = STEP1, Light blue = NOISE1, Red = STEP2, Pink = NOISE2. Contrast STEP1 – NOISE1 revealed activations in the left STSp and left amygdala, and contrast STEP2 – NOISE2 in subcallosal gyrus, right temporal pole, and right amygdala. The color bar presents the T values.

NOISE1) was decreased due to multiple subtractions.

The role of temporal poles in listening to humans walking together

The contrast STEP2 – NOISE2 revealed activation in the right temporal pole, where all other stimulus categories except STEP2 induced deactivation, as was evident from the signal change histograms (Figure 2)—which also revealed stronger activation of this brain region during STEP2 than during STEP1.

Temporal poles are considered to belong to the theory-of-mind circuitry (e.g., Siegal & Varley, 2002), and they are connected with, for example, amygdala, superior temporal gyrus, occipitobasal cortex, orbital gyrus and the insula (Chabardes, Kahane, Minotti, Hoffmann, & Benabid, 2002)—areas that also respond to socio-emotional stimuli. The right temporal pole, in particular, responds to viewing fearful faces (Nelson et al., 2003) or video clips of one's own infant (Ranote et al., 2004). These findings emphasize the importance of this region for processing of the social environment, as does the observed decrease of white matter in the right temporal pole of autistic children (Boddaert et al., 2004).

Social and emotional processing are intermingled in a complex manner in any normal social interaction; accordingly, many brain regions—including the temporal poles—are associated with both social and emotional processes (for a review, see Olson, Plotzker, & Ezzyat, 2007). According to our subjects' comments after the scan, the mere presence of two people in the same auditory scene provoked more mentalizing of their intentions (e.g., 'is one following another?') than listening to only one person. Although the footstep sounds are not very emotional stimuli as such, we suggest that in our STEP2 condition the activations of both temporal poles and emotion-related brain regions (see below) were related to mentalizing of the intentions of the walkers.

Socio-emotional processing in subcallosal, insular and amygdalar regions

The contrast STEP2 – NOISE2 indicated activation also in three brain areas associated with socio-emotional processing: the perigenual,

TABLE 2
The Talairach coordinates of activated brain regions in contrasts STEP1 – NOISE1 and STEP2 – NOISE2

Brain region	*L/R*	*x*	*y*	*z*	*Area (mm^3)*
STEP1 – NOISE1					
Activations					
Posterior STS	L	−54	−60	8	143
Amygdala	L	−18	−7	−8	77
Deactivations					
Auditory cortex	R	45	−19	7	1276
	L	−40	−29	8	1631
Middle temporal gyrus	R	20	−69	−38	508
Cerebellum	L	−20	−40	−35	304
	R	27	−47	−30	260
	L	−35	−66	−41	200
	L	−27	−54	−37	176
	R	33	−71	7	129
	R	8	−67	−31	94
	R	3	−39	−25	88
STEP2 – NOISE2					
Activations					
Amygdala	R	31	−5	−14	489
Middle frontal gyrus	R	32	39	15	235
Anterior insula	R	28	23	8	151
Subcallosal gyrus	R/L	1	17	−3	150
Postcentral gyrus	R	24	−37	44	113
Temporal pole	R	47	8	−17	106
Anterior cingulate sulcus	R	15	28	23	102
Intraparietal sulcus	R	20	−44	34	100
Medial frontal gyrus	R	42	−3	49	88
Pre-SMA	R	8	2	57	87
Lateral precentral gyrus	R	62	−13	32	75
Deactivations					
Auditory cortex	L	−45	−25	8	2331
	R	49	−17	6	1836
	R	38	−24	10	250
	R	47	−32	16	77
STEP2 – STEP1					
Cerebellum	L	−20	−41	−34	454
	L	−6	−44	−26	84
	R	18	−43	−25	82
Inferior parietal lobule	L	-35	-30	36	72

Notes: $p < .005$, cluster size = 70 mm^3. SMA = supplementary motor area.

insular and amygdalar areas. The perigenual gyrus (see Figure 2) is in the posterior end of the subcallosal cingulate area (BA 25), anatomically defined as the posterior subgenual prefrontal cortex (Coryell, Nopoulos, Drevets, Wilson, & Andreasen, 2005). The region is involved in affect and emotion: its activity correlates with the increasing pleasantness of the music listened to (Blood, Zatorre, Bermudez, & Evans, 1999) and with differences in negative affect (Zald, Mattson, & Pardo, 2002). The subcallosal region also takes part in self-generated sadness and happiness (Damasio et al., 2000), and the ventromedial frontal cortex as a whole may link the properties of a stimulus to their rewarding or punishment values (Bechara, Tranel, Damasio, & Damasio, 1996). Although our subjects were not explicitly asked to pay attention to the difference between one person vs. two persons walking, the posterior subgenual prefrontal cortex was active during two persons walking only.

The second emotion-related area activated by STEP2 – NOISE2 contrast, the insula, belongs to the interoceptive system. Different parts of the insula have a variety of functions, from pain affect, gustatory sensations, and auditory processing even to awareness of the subject's own internal state (for reviews, see Small et al., 1999; Price, 2000; Bamiou, Musiek, & Luxon, 2003; Craig, 2004). Insulae in both hemispheres are also associated with both self-perceived sensations and these sensations observed in someone else (e.g., Krolak-Salmon et al., 2003; Wicker et al., 2003; Jackson et al., 2005; Saarela et al., 2007). In our study, insular activation was observed during both double footstep sounds and noise sounds: the right anterior insula in our contrast STEP2 – NOISE2 and left posterior insula in our contrast NOISE1 + NOISE2 – REST. These activations support the role of the insular cortex in auditory processing, previously suggested by both anatomical and functional findings (Mesulam & Mufson, 1982; Bamiou et al., 2003).

The third emotion-related brain area associated with our study, amygdala (Figure 2), is involved in social perception, including recognition of emotion from faces and body postures (Adolphs, Tranel, Damasio, & Damasio, 1994; de Gelder, 2006; Fitzgerald, Angstadt, Jelsone, Nathan, & Phan, 2006). In our study, the contrast of STEP1 – NOISE1 showed activation in the left amygdala, whereas the contrast of STEP2 – NOISE2 revealed activation in the right amygdalar region. These activations were, however, confounded by the suppressive effects of the noise stimuli on amygdalar activity. In particular, the activation of the left amygdala in the STEP1 – NOISE1 contrast mainly reflected deactivation by NOISE1 whereas the right amygdala activation seemed more authentic.

Social brain circuitry for detecting complex group stimuli

Our subjects reported that they were able to distinguish the gender of the walkers by only listening to the footsteps. Overall, the present imaging results suggest that the analysis of auditory social scenes involving more than one agent recruits a right-hemisphere dominant social brain circuitry, with core nodes in the subcallosal area, the right temporal pole, and the left STSp. This circuitry seems to treat single and double footsteps differently, implying a separate processing of these two. In particular, the subcallosal area seems to be related to provocation of emotions, the right temporal pole is involved in the analysis of features revealing personal identity within the social auditory scene, and the STSp responds to the auditory biological motion.

Of these nodes, the subcallosal area and the right temporal pole responded to the auditory scenes involving two walkers instead of only one, whereas the left STSp seemed to prefer simpler and more coherent single footsteps. All these areas appear important for the analysis of the complex time-varying features related to group dynamics, perhaps reflecting the difference between the human perception of groups and single persons, and their impact on the behavior of an individual.

Manuscript received 6 March 2007
Manuscript accepted 20 September 2007
First published online 30 January 2008

REFERENCES

Adolphs, R., Tranel, D., Damasio, H., & Damasio, A. (1994). Impaired recognition of emotion in facial expressions following bilateral damage to the human amygdala. *Nature*, *372*, 669–672.

Allison, T., Puce, A., & McCarthy, G. (2000). Social perception from visual cues: Role of the STS region. *Trends in Cognitive Science*, *4*, 267–278.

Aziz-Zadeh, L., Iacoboni, M., Zaidel, E., Wilson, S., & Mazziotta, J. (2004). Left hemisphere motor facilitation in response to manual action sounds. *European Journal of Neuroscience*, *19*, 2609–2612.

Bamiou, D. E., Musiek, F. E., & Luxon, L. M. (2003). The insula (Island of Reil) and its role in auditory processing. Literature review. *Brain Research and Brain Research Reviews*, *42*, 143–154.

Barraclough, N. E., Xiao, D., Baker, C. I., Oram, M. W., & Perrett, D. I. (2005). Integration of visual and auditory information by superior temporal sulcus neurons responsive to the sight of actions. *Journal of Cognitive Neuroscience*, *17*, 377–391.

Bechara, A., Tranel, D., Damasio, H., & Damasio, A. R. (1996). Failure to respond autonomically to anticipated future outcomes following damage to prefrontal cortex. *Cerebral Cortex*, *6*, 215–225.

Bidet-Caulet, A., Voisin, J., Bertrand, O., & Fonlupt, P. (2005). Listening to a walking human activates the temporal biological motion area. *NeuroImage*, *28*, 132–139.

Blood, A. J., Zatorre, R. J., Bermudez, P., & Evans, A. C. (1999). Emotional responses to pleasant and unpleasant music correlate with activity in paralimbic brain regions. *Nature Neuroscience*, *2*, 382–387.

Boddaert, N., Chabane, N., Gervais, H., Good, C. D., Bourgeois, M., Plumet, M. H., et al. (2004). Superior temporal sulcus anatomical abnormalities in childhood autism: A voxel-based morphometry MRI study. *NeuroImage*, *23*, 364–369.

Chabardes, S., Kahane, P., Minotti, L., Hoffmann, D., & Benabid, A. L. (2002). Anatomy of the temporal pole region. *Epileptic Disorders*, *4*(Suppl. 1), S9–S15.

Coryell, W., Nopoulos, P., Drevets, W., Wilson, T., & Andreasen, N. C. (2005). Subgenual prefrontal cortex volumes in major depressive disorder and schizophrenia: Diagnostic specificity and prognostic implications. *American Journal of Psychiatry*, *162*, 1706–1712.

Craig, A. D. (2004). Human feelings: Why are some more aware than others? *Trends in Cognitive Science*, *8*, 239–241.

Damasio, A. R., Grabowski, T. J., Bechara, A., Damasio, H., Ponto, L. L., Parvizi, J., et al. (2000). Subcortical and cortical brain activity during the feeling of self-generated emotions. *Nature Neuroscience*, *3*, 1049–1056.

de Gelder, B. (2006). Towards the neurobiology of emotional body language. *Nature Reviews Neuroscience*, *7*, 242–249.

Fitzgerald, D. A., Angstadt, M., Jelsone, L. M., Nathan, P. J., & Phan, K. L. (2006). Beyond threat: Amygdala reactivity across multiple expressions of facial affect. *NeuroImage*, *30*, 1441–1448.

Gazzola, V., Aziz-Zadeh, L., & Keysers, C. (2006). Empathy and the somatotopic auditory mirror system in humans. *Current Biology*, *16*, 1824–1829.

Jackson, P. L., Meltzoff, A. N., & Decety, J. (2005). How do we perceive the pain of others? A window into the neural processes involved in empathy. *NeuroImage*, *24*, 771–779.

Kohler, E., Keysers, C., Umiltà, M. A., Fogassi, L., Gallese, V., & Rizzolatti, G. (2002). Hearing sounds, understanding actions: Action representation in mirror neurons. *Science*, *297*, 846–848.

Krolak-Salmon, P., Henaff, M. A., Isnard, J., Tallon-Baudry, C., Guenot, M., Vighetto, A., et al. (2003). An attention modulated response to disgust in human ventral anterior insula. *Annals of Neurology*, *53*, 446–453.

Lahav, A., Saltzman, E., & Schlaug, G. (2007). Action representation of sound: Audiomotor recognition network while listening to newly acquired actions. *Journal of Neuroscience*, 27, 308–314.

Luppino, G., & Rizzolatti, G. (2000). The organization of the frontal motor cortex. *Physiology*, *15*, 219–224.

Mesulam, M. M., & Mufson, E. J. (1982). Insula of the old world monkey. III: Efferent cortical output and comments on function. *Journal of Comparative Neurology*, *212*, 38–52.

Nelson, E. E., McClure, E. B., Monk, C. S., Zarahn, E., Leibenluft, E., Pine, D. S., et al. (2003). Develop mental differences in neuronal engagement during implicit encoding of emotional faces: An event-related fMRI study. *Journal of Child Psychology and Psychiatry*, *44*, 1015–1024.

Nishitani, N., & Hari, R. (2000). Temporal dynamics of cortical representation for action. *Proceedings of the National Academy Science of the United States of America*, *97*, 913–918.

Oldfield, R. C. (1971). The assessment and analysis of handedness: The Edinburgh inventory. *Neuropsychologia*, *9*, 97–113.

Olson, I. R., Plotzker, A., & Ezzyat, Y. (2007). The enigmatic temporal pole: A review of findings on social and emotional processing. *Brain*, *130*, 1718–1731.

Pizzamiglio, L., Aprile, T., Spitoni, G., Pitzalis, S., Bates, E., D'Amico, S., & Di Russo, F. (2005). Separate neural systems for processing action- or non-action-related sounds. *Neuroimage*, *24*, 852–861.

Price, D. D. (2000). Psychological and neural mechanisms of the affective dimension of pain. *Science*, *288*, 1769–1772.

Ranote, S., Elliott, R., Abel, K. M., Mitchell, R., Deakin, J. F., & Appleby, L. (2004). The neural basis of maternal responsiveness to infants: An fMRI study. *NeuroReport*, *15*, 1825–1829.

Rizzolatti, G., & Arbib, M. A. (1998). Language within our grasp. *Trends in Neuroscience*, *21*, 188–194.

Rizzolatti, G., & Craighero, L. (2004). The mirror-neuron system. *Annual Review of Neuroscience*, *27*, 169–192.

Saarela, M. V., Hlushchuk, Y., Williams, A. C., Schurmann, M., Kalso, E., & Hari, R. (2007). The compassionate brain: Humans detect intensity of pain from another's face. *Cerebral Cortex*, *17*, 230–237.

Siegal, M., & Varley, R. (2002). Neural systems involved in "theory of mind". *Nature Reviews Neuroscience*, *3*, 463–471.

Small, D. M., Zald, D. H., Jones-Gotman, M., Zatorre, R. J., Pardo, J. V., Frey, S., et al. (1999). Human cortical gustatory areas: A review of functional neuroimaging data. *NeuroReport*, *10*, 7–14.

Talairach, J., & Tournoux, P. (1988). *Co-planar stereotaxic atlas of the human brain: 3-dimensional proportional system—An approach to cerebral imaging*. New York: Thieme Medical Publishers.

Wicker, B., Keysers, C., Plailly, J., Royet, J. P., Gallese, V., & Rizzolatti, G. (2003). Both of us disgusted in my insula: The common neural basis of seeing and feeling disgust. *Neuron*, *40*, 655–664.

Zald, D. H., Mattson, D. L., & Pardo, J. V. (2002). Brain activity in ventromedial prefrontal cortex correlates with individual differences in negative affect. *Proceedings of the National Academy Science of the United States of America*, *99*, 2450–2454.

SOCIAL NEUROSCIENCE, 2008, 3 (3–4), 410–420

Psychology Press
Taylor & Francis Group

Action co-representation: The joint SNARC effect

Silke Atmaca
Rutgers, The New Jersey State University, Newark, NJ, USA

Natalie Sebanz
University of Birmingham, UK

Wolfgang Prinz
Max Planck Institute for Human Cognitive and Brain Sciences, Leipzig, Germany

Günther Knoblich
University of Birmingham, UK

Traditionally, communication has been defined as the intentional exchange of symbolic information between individuals. In contrast, the mirror system provides a basis for nonsymbolic and nonintentional information exchange between individuals. We believe that understanding the role of the mirror system in joint action has the potential to serve as a bridge between these two domains. The present study investigates one crucial component of joint action: the ability to represent others' potential actions in the same way as one's own in the absence of perceptual evidence. In two experiments a joint spatial numerical association of response codes (SNARC) effect is demonstrated, providing further evidence that individuals form functionally equivalent representations of their own and others' potential actions. It is shown that numerical (symbolic) stimuli that are mapped onto a spatially arranged internal representation (a mental number line) can activate a co-represented action in the same way as spatial stimuli. This generalizes previous results on co-representation. We discuss the role of the mirror system in co-representation as a basis for shared intentionality and communication.

INTRODUCTION

At first glance, the idea that the mirror system (Gallese, Keysers, & Rizzolatti, 2004; Rizzolatti & Craighero, 2004) supports communication seems like a long shot. How can a system that resonates with others' actions (Di Pellegrino, Fadiga, Fogassi, Gallese, & Rizzolatti, 1992; Gallese, Fadiga, Fogassi, & Rizzolatti, 1996), perceptions (Keysers et al., 2004), and emotions (Goldman & Sripada, 2005), support the intentional exchange of symbolic information between a sender and a receiver? Obviously, employing this sort of classical engineering definition of communication creates a seemingly unbridgeable divide between action perception and communication.

However, if one accepts a wider definition of communication that allows for nonsymbolic and nonintentional information exchange, the mirror system presents itself as a potentially powerful device in the service of communication and other forms of social interaction. It can be regarded as a basic link between sender and receiver (Rizzolatti

Correspondence should be addressed to: Günther Knoblich, School of Psychology, Behavioural Brain Sciences, University of Birmingham, Edgbaston, Birmingham B15 2TT, UK. E-mail: g.knoblich@bham.ac.uk

We thank Irmgard Hagen, Jana Hiller, and, in particular, Veronika Gärtner for their help in collecting the data. Silke Atmaca would like to thank Stefan Krauss for helpful advice.

www.psypress.com/socialneuroscience DOI:10.1080/17470910801900908

& Arbib, 1998) that provides procedural, perceptual, and emotional common ground between individuals (Sebanz, Bekkering, & Knoblich, 2006). If observing you perform an action is similar to performing it myself (e.g., Grezes, Armony, Rowe, & Passingham, 2003), if seeing you being touched is similar to being touched myself (e.g., Keysers et al., 2004), and if perceiving your pain is similar to being in pain myself (e.g., Singer et al., 2004), there is an interpersonal link between us that requires neither symbols nor the intention to communicate.

How can we build on the mirror system to arrive at more sophisticated (symbolic, intentional) forms of communication that entail common, conventionalized knowledge (Clark, 1996) and shared intentionality (Barresi & Moore, 1996)? One possibility is to claim that the mirroring principle is gradually extended from concrete content to more abstract content. For example, Arbib (2005) proposed a progression from the mirroring of instrumental action to hand gestures and, ultimately, to speech (Galantucci, Fowler, & Turvey, 2006; Liberman & Whalen, 2000). While this proposal focuses on changes in content that can be shared interpersonally, it cannot explain the evolution of shared intentionality (Tomasello, Carpenter, Call, Behne, & Moll, 2005). How is it that people can represent a joint task, represent their role in performing a task together, and coordinate their actions to achieve a shared goal? This seems to be a further critical component boosting social interaction and communication (cf. Galantucci, 2005). In fact, there would not be much use for communication but for the need to successfully engage in joint action (Clark, 1996).

We believe that understanding how the mirror system is recruited in the service of joint action may provide a crucial link between implicit, nonsymbolic, and nonintentional information exchange achieved through mirroring, and explicit, symbolic, and intentional information exchange that characterizes discourse (cf. Garrod & Pickering, 2004). The advantage of calling both "communication" is to leave open the possibility that more sophisticated forms of communication still recruit basic systems for social exchange. However, it is equally important to keep in mind that the functionality of the mirror system alone is not sufficient to support joint action (Knoblich & Jordan, 2002; Pacherie & Dokic, 2006). While the mirror system does allow us to understand and predict others' actions and goals, it does not provide the means to jointly attend to the same objects and events (cf. Tomasello, 2000), to effectively perform different parts of a task (Sebanz, Knoblich, & Prinz, 2005; Sebanz et al., 2006), and to coordinate the timing of actions (Knoblich & Jordan, 2003).

As a first step towards understanding how the mirror system supports joint action, we focus on the question of whether and how individuals represent each other's actions when performing different parts of a task together. If the mirror system gets recruited during joint action, coactors should represent their own and others' actions in a functionally equivalent way. Theoretical frameworks extending ideomotor theory (Greenwald, 1970; James, 1890), in particular common coding theory (Hommel et al., 2001; Jeannerod, 1999; Prinz, 1997), have long postulated such a functional equivalence. The common coding theory postulates that the same representations are involved in action production and action observation. The mirror system can be regarded as the neural implementation of this functional principle.

In line with the common coding principle, prior research has shown that observing somebody else concurrently performing the same action as oneself results in facilitation, whereas observing somebody else concurrently performing the opposite action interferes with performing the action (Brass, Bekkering, & Prinz, 2001; Kilner, Paulignan, & Blakemore, 2003; Stuermer, Aschersleben, & Prinz, 2000). Less is known about how actors influence each other's performance when acting in turns, which is prototypical of many types of joint action. When taking turns, one does not perceive competing (or facilitating) information about the other while acting oneself. Rather, influences of the other's actions are expected only if they are part of one's own task representation. In other words, if facilitation or interference occurs in the absence of action observation, one can conclude that coactors represent not only their own, but also the other's potential actions.

In an earlier study (Sebanz, Knoblich and Prinz, 2003), we demonstrated such effects using a variant of a spatial compatibility (Simon) task (e.g., Simon, 1990; Simon, Hinrichs, & Craft, 1970). We found that two participants—each performing half of the task—showed the same compatibility effects as single participants performing the whole task. In the latter condition, single participants responded to the color of a ring that was placed on the index finger of a pointing hand. One color required a left key press and the other color required a right key press. In addition, the hand was pointing either to the right or to the left. Although the pointing direction was irrelevant for the task, participants responded faster with the left key to stimuli pointing left than to stimuli pointing right and vice versa. This spatial compatibility effect occurs because the spatial stimulus feature automatically activates the corresponding action. If the relevant stimulus feature color demands this action, facilitation occurs. If the relevant stimulus feature color demands the opposite action, there is interference between two competing action representations (e.g., Kornblum, Hasbroucq, & Osman, 1990).

In the critical joint condition, pairs of participants performed the task together. Each individual responded to only one of the two colors using only one key. Although participants performed only half of the task, they showed a similar compatibility effect as individuals performing the whole task. In contrast, no compatibility effect was observed when participants performed their half of the task alone (individual condition). This is surprising because—from the point of view of a single participant—the task was exactly the same in the individual and joint conditions. The irrelevant spatial stimulus affected performance in the joint condition but not in the individual condition.

How can this be explained? In the individual condition, only one action was represented, thus no conflict occurred. In the joint condition, the alternative action under the other's control was (co)represented as if it was part of one's own task. Thus, the results were similar to the two-choice condition where single participants performed the whole task. These effects have been replicated in recent studies (Sebanz, Knoblich & Prinz, 2005; Tsai, Kuo, Jing, Hung, & Tzeng, 2006). Importantly, the joint compatibility effect requires only the belief that the other person performs the other part of the task; it does not require observation of the other's task (Tsai, Kuo, Hung, & Tzeng, in press).

Our interpretation of these results is that a task representation that includes the potential actions of others can be as effective in activating action representations as the observation of somebody else's actions. Constraining the mirror system's functionality by a higher-level task representation allows one to keep one's own and the other's part of the task apart without giving up the basic interpersonal link provided through mirroring.

THE PRESENT STUDY

The aim of the present study was to further investigate how coactors form shared representations when performing complementary tasks. We were particularly interested in the question of whether symbolic information can take on the function of spatial or biological cues, such as the pointing hand in the study described above. Proponents of the embodied cognition approach maintain that many abstract symbols still retain aspects of the physical world they represent. One famous example is numbers (cf. Lakoff & Nunez, 2000). Although they are often regarded as highly abstract entities, Dehaene (1997) contends that our internal representation of numbers takes the form of a mental number line with small numbers on the left and larger numbers to the right. This raises the possibility that even the processing of symbolic information makes use of the close perception-links embodied in the mirror system.

The main empirical finding backing the claim that numbers carry spatial content is the so-called 'SNARC' (spatial numerical association of response codes) effect (Dehaene, Bossini, & Giraux, 1993; Fias, 2001; Iversen, Nuerk, & Willmes, 2004; Nuerk, Wood, & Willmes, 2005). In Dehaene and colleagues' (1993) experiments, participants were asked to perform a two-choice task by pressing one key in response to even numbers, and another key in response to odd numbers. The surprising finding was that participants' left responses were faster than right responses for small numbers and vice versa for large numbers. Thus, number magnitude affected response times (RTs), although it was irrelevant for the task. Further experiments (Dehaene et al., 1993) demonstrated that the SNARC effect occurs relative to the given number range. It is independent of handedness, occurs in different modalities, and for different number notations (Fias, 2001; Nuerk et al., 2005; Iversen et al., 2004). Further studies showed that the SNARC effect seems to have its basis in cultural conventions, mainly the writing direction of words (Dehaene et al., 1993).

According to Dehaene (1997), although numbers do not carry spatial information *per se*, the perception of numbers automatically activates a magnitude representation on a mental number line proceeding from the left to the right. Small numbers are associated with left and large numbers are associated with right. The SNARC effect arises because activation of the left part of the number line automatically activates left actions, and activation of the right part of the number line automatically activates right actions (compare Figure 1(a)). Further support for this explanation was provided by Zorzi, Priftis, & Umiltà's (2002) finding that patients with hemispatial neglect, who show systematic biases to the right in line bisection, showed a similar bias towards large numbers when asked to bisect numerical intervals.

In the present study, we used the SNARC paradigm in a similar experimental design as Sebanz and colleagues (2003) to explore whether action corepresentation also occurs when the stimulus is symbolic rather than carrying direct spatial information. In the joint condition, two participants performed complementary actions. Each participant was assigned to one response key (left or right) and was in charge of one mode of parity (odd or even) (see Figure 1(b), left). In the individual condition, participants performed the same go-nogo task alone (see Figure 1(b), right).

We predicted that a SNARC effect would occur in the joint condition, but that no SNARC effect would occur in the individual condition. The rationale is as follows. If each actor in the joint condition represents both her own *and* the coactor's action alternative, the spatial nature of the numerical stimuli should lead to automatic activation of the corresponding actions. Participants should respond faster to small numbers when they are in charge of the left response than when they are in charge of the right response, and vice versa. In the individual condition, no SNARC effect should occur because there is

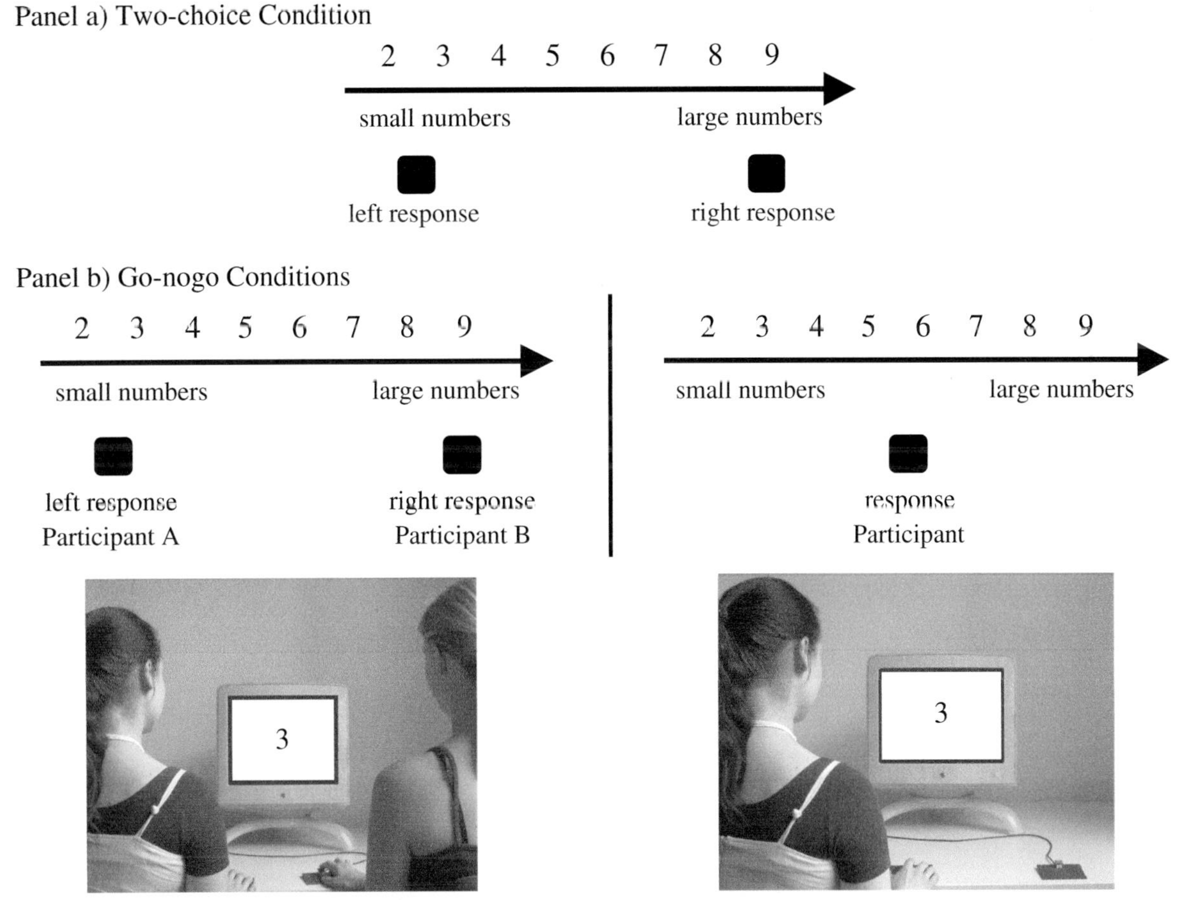

Figure 1. (a) In the two-choice condition, varying degrees of overlap between the spatial number representation and the spatial features of the two actions facilitate left responses to small numbers and right responses to large numbers. (b, left) In the joint condition, the task was distributed between two participants sitting on the left and right. Each participant performed a go-nogo task in response to parity. A SNARC effect in the joint condition would indicate that each participant represents both action alternatives. (b, right) In the individual condition, one participant sitting on the left or right performed the same go-nogo task in response to parity alone. In this condition, no SNARC effect should occur because there is just a single action alternative and thus no conflict.

just a single action alternative at the actor's command and thus no action conflict arises.

EXPERIMENT 1

In this experiment, participants responded to the parity of Arabic digits ranging from 2 to 9. In the joint condition, two participants performed complementary actions, one responding to odd, the other to even (see Figure 2, left). In the individual condition, single participants performed exactly the same task, reacting to only one mode of parity with only one response key (see Figure 2, right). This implies that no response was given on half of the trials (nogo trials). A two-choice condition in which one individual was in charge of both action alternatives, reacting to both even and odd numbers with two different keys, served as a further baseline for the joint condition.

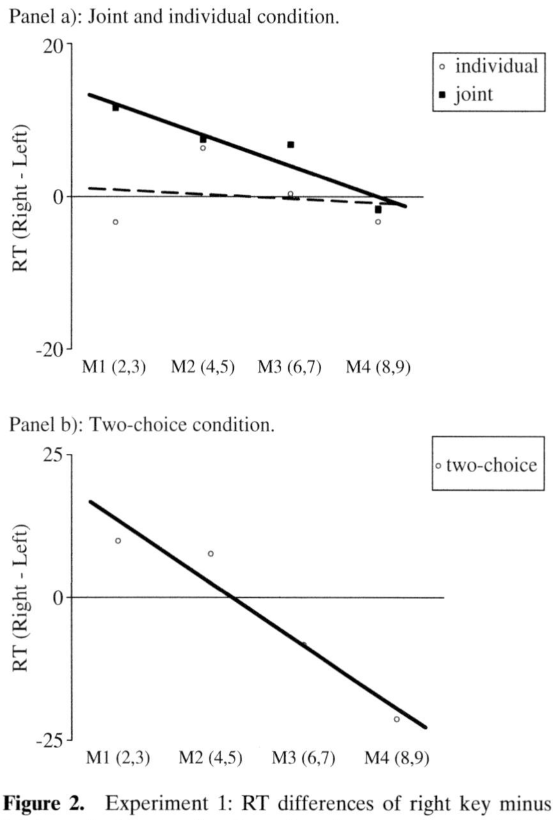

Figure 2. Experiment 1: RT differences of right key minus left key, displayed as function of number magnitude. (a) Joint condition and individual condition (regression line of the joint go-nogo condition: $y = -3.9176x + 15.747$; $R^2 = 0.8633$. Regression line of the individual go-nogo condition: $y = -0.6049x + 1.3982$; $R^2 = 0.0279$). (b) Two-choice condition (regression line: $y = -10.9436x + 24.41$; $R^2 = 0.9334$).

If participants form a representation of each other's actions, a SNARC effect should be observed in the joint condition—resembling performance in a two-choice condition where single participants respond to odd and even numbers—but not in the individual condition.

Method

Of the 56 paid participants (39 female, age range 18–34), 30 performed the individual and joint go-nogo conditions in counterbalanced order. The remaining 26 participants performed only the two-choice task. All participants were right-handed and German native speakers.

Performing exactly the same go-nogo task in the joint and the individual condition, participants gave parity judgments to Arabic digits ranging from 2 to 9, responding with the right index finger (either responding to odd and not even, or vice versa). In the joint condition, two participants were sitting side by side. In the individual condition, there was an empty chair beside the single participant. In the two-choice condition, single participants responded to odd and even numbers with a left and right key press. In each condition, the key assignment varied over the four blocks.

Each trial started with a 500 ms fixation cross (0.57° horizontally and vertically), followed by the number stimulus (0.65° × 1.06°) presented for a maximum of 1500 ms. Once a key was pressed, the stimulus disappeared from the screen and the next trial started after an intertrial interval of 1000 ms. If participants committed an error or took more than 1500 ms to respond, error feedback was provided. Nogo-stimuli in the individual condition were presented for 500 ms, to roughly adjust the presentation time to the joint condition.

In all conditions, participants performed four blocks of 200 trials each. Each block had a different combination of task (respond to odd, respond to even) and response side (left chair, right chair in the individual and joint go-nogo condition, and left and right key in the two-choice condition), and started with eight training trials. Trial order was randomized within blocks.

The experiment was run on an Apple Power PC. The stimulus pictures were presented on an Apple 21 inch monitor (resolution 1024 × 768 pixels). Button presses were recorded with a

PsyScope button box (Cohen, MacWhinney, Flatt, & Provost, 1993).

Results

Results in go-nogo conditions

Incorrect responses did not differ significantly between conditions (joint: 1.4%, individual: 2.1%) and were excluded from further analyses. In order to simplify RT analyses, we averaged over parity, resulting in four levels of number magnitude (2 and 3 constituting Level 1, 4 and 5 constituting Level 2, etc.).

Table 1 gives the mean RTs for each condition. A within-subjects $2 \times 4 \times 2$ analysis of variance (ANOVA) with the factors Condition (joint vs. individual), Magnitude (magnitude level 1–4), and Side (right vs. left key) was computed. There was no significant main effect for Condition ($F(1, 29) = 2.235$, $p = .146$), but there was a significant main effect for Magnitude ($F(3, 87) = 23.876$, $p < .001$). RTs increased over magnitude levels.

Furthermore, there was a significant Magnitude × Side interaction ($F(3, 87) = 3.553$, $p < .05$), and a significant three-way interaction between Condition, Magnitude, and Side ($F(3, 87) = 4.478$, $p < .01$), confirming that there was a significant difference between the joint and the individual conditions regarding the size of the SNARC effect. None of the other interactions was significant.

In a second step, RT differences (right key minus left key) for each level of number magnitude were calculated. The greater the RT difference, the slower the right response compared to the left response to the same number, and vice versa. Thus, a SNARC effect should manifest itself in a negative slope of a regression line, because small numbers should elicit a faster response with the left key, whereas large numbers should lead to faster responses with the right key. Figure 2(a) shows the results. In the joint condition, there was a negative slope that was significantly different from zero ($t(29) = -2.611$, $p < .05$), whereas in the individual condition the slope was not significantly different from zero ($t(29) = -0.515$, $p = .610$). Thus, the SNARC effect was present only in the joint condition.

Results in two-choice condition

There were 3.6% incorrect responses, which were excluded from further analyses. RTs (see Table 1) were entered into a 4×2 within-subjects ANOVA with the factors Magnitude (magnitude levels 1–4) and Side (right vs. left key). There was a significant main effect for Magnitude ($F(3, 75) = 20.565$, $p < .001$) and a significant Magnitude × Side interaction ($F(3, 75) = 13.818$, $p < .001$), confirming that a SNARC effect occurred. There was no significant main effect of Side. Figure 2(b) shows the RT differences between right key and left key. In line with the results of the ANOVA, the regression line had a significant negative slope ($t(25) = -4.458$, $p < .001$).

Discussion

In Experiment 1, the same go-nogo task led to a different RT pattern depending on whether a participant performed the task alone or whether two participants performed complementary tasks. The RT pattern in the joint go-nogo condition more closely resembled the RT pattern in the

TABLE 1

Mean RTs and standard deviations (in parentheses) for Experiments 1 and 2, by condition, magnitude level, and response side

	Magnitude Level 1		*Magnitude Level 2*		*Magnitude Level 3*		*Magnitude Level 4*	
	Left	*Right*	*Left*	*Right*	*Left*	*Right*	*Left*	*Right*
Experiment 1								
Two-Choice	426 (107)	436 (116)	430 (104)	438 (113)	432 (113)	424 (115)	456 (113)	435 (115)
Joint	354 (81)	365 (91)	362 (88)	370 (93)	352 (82)	359 (92)	377 (93)	375 (94)
Individual	347 (77)	343 (73)	351 (76)	357 (80)	346 (75)	346 (76)	363 (77)	359 (76)
Experiment 2								
Joint	513 (117)	522 (121)	559 (126)	570 (135)	592 (144)	585 (146)	623 (146)	611 (147)
Individual	501 (111)	504 (118)	552 (117)	547 (122)	572 (130)	570 (131)	596 (131)	596 (131)

two-choice condition than the RT pattern in the individual go-nogo condition. For the go-nogo task, a SNARC effect was present only in the joint condition (see also Figure 4). These results suggest that participants co-represented each other's actions. Symbolic stimuli can take on the same role as spatial stimuli if they activate representations that carry spatial content.

As can be seen in Figure 2, subjects in the joint condition—and, to a lesser degree, in the individual condition—had an overall tendency to react faster with the left key than with the right key, leading to positive values of RT differences. In contrast, a more symmetrical pattern was observed in the two-choice condition. We do not have a good explanation for the faster left responses in the go-nogo conditions (see discussion of Experiment 2). Importantly, though, this does not affect our interpretation that participants represented the other's action alternative in the joint condition. As predicted, we found a SNARC effect in the joint, but not in the individual condition, the only difference between these two conditions being whether participants performed the task alone or together.

EXPERIMENT 2

The main goal of Experiment 2 was to replicate the joint SNARC effect with a different set of stimuli. We used pictorial representations of numbers formed with the digits of a left and right hand (see bottom of Figure 3). For these stimuli, there are two different types of compatibility. First, there is spatial compatibility: Small numbers involve only digits on the left whereas large numbers increasingly involve digits on the right. Secondly, there is spatial–numerical compatibility, with number magnitude being mapped onto a mental number line proceeding from left to right. Is the activation of the other's action particularly strong when a stimulus refers to the other's action through both a perceptual feature and a spatial feature derived from symbolic information? Although it has been established that the time course of automatic activation is different for perceptual features and spatial features derived from symbolic stimuli (Mapelli et al., 2003), activations from both types of features should converge on the same action. If these two effects add up, the joint compatibility effect should be

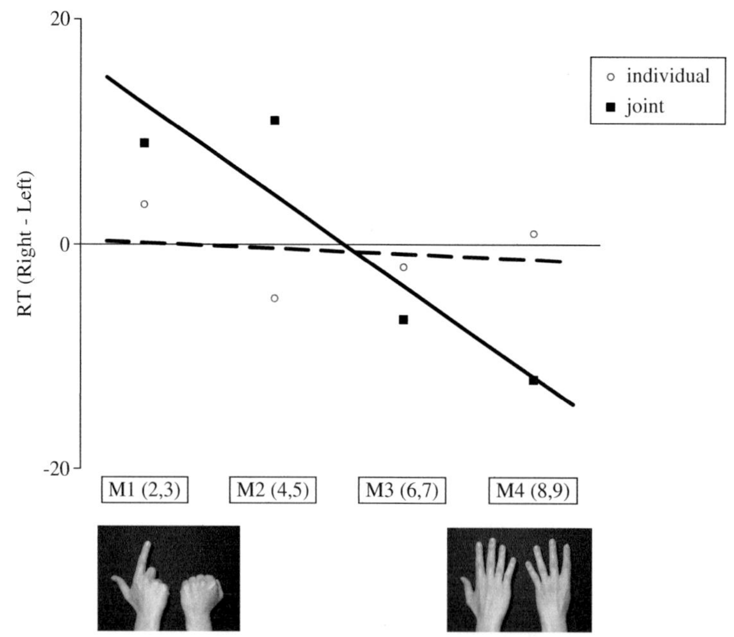

Figure 3. Experiment 2: RT differences of right key minus left key, displayed as a function of number magnitude. Joint condition and individual condition (regression line of the joint condition: $y = -8.0877x + 20.49$; $R^2 = 0.8334$. Regression line of the individual condition: $y = -0.4928x + 0.6131$; $R^2 = 0.0304$). The stimuli were pictures of two hands depicting numbers. The smallest number ("2") was displayed with two fingers extended on the very left. Ascending numbers were formed extending additional fingers from left to right. There was one stimulus picture for each number in the range from 2 to 9 (see numbers "2" and "9" as examples).

even more pronounced in Experiment 2 than in Experiment 1.

Method

Participants

Thirty participants (22 female, age range 20–33) took part in this experiment. All participants were right-handed and German native speakers.

Materials and procedure

The materials and the procedure were the same as in the go-nogo conditions of Experiment 1, except for the stimuli (see bottom of Figure 3). We presented pictures of two hands forming numbers ($16.7° \times 14.04°$ horizontally and vertically). Participants were familiarized with the pictures before the experiment.

Results

Error rates did not differ significantly between the joint (3.8%) and the individual conditions (4.2%). Incorrect responses were excluded from further analyses.

Table 1 gives the mean RTs in each condition. A within-subjects $2 \times 4 \times 2$ ANOVA with the factors Condition (joint vs. individual), Magnitude (magnitude levels 1–4) and Side (right vs. left key) showed no main effect of Condition ($F(1, 29) = 3.723$, $p = .063$), although numerically, RTs in the joint condition tended to be slower. There was a significant main effect for Magnitude ($F(3, 87) = 82.766$, $p < .001$). Furthermore, there was a significant Magnitude × Side interaction ($F(3, 87) = 3.494$, $p < .05$) and a significant three-way interaction between Condition, Magnitude, and Side ($F(3, 87) = 4.767$, $p < .01$), indicating that there was a significant difference between the joint and the individual conditions regarding the size of the compatibility effects. The ANOVA showed no other significant effects.

Figure 3 shows the RT differences of right key minus left key. The negative slope of the regression line significantly differed from zero in the joint condition ($t(29) = -3.476$, $p < .01$), but not in the individual condition ($t(29) = -0.307$, $p = .761$). Thus, there were compatibility effects in the joint condition but not in the individual condition.

COMPARISON BETWEEN EXPERIMENTS

We compared the mean slopes of RT differences of Experiment 2 with those of Experiment 1 (see Figure 4). Whereas the mean slopes were comparable for the individual condition in the two experiments (−0.53 in Experiment 1 and −0.56 in Experiment 2), the mean slope of the joint condition of Experiment 2 (−8.05) was more than twice as large as the mean slope of the joint condition in Experiment 1 (−3.84). Unfortunately, a one-sided *t*-test for independent samples comparing the two slopes of the joint conditions in Experiments 1 and 2 failed to reach significance ($t(58) = 1.536$, $p = .065$).

DISCUSSION

The results of Experiment 2 showed that a joint SNARC effect does not occur only for Arabic digits, but also for frequency depictions using human hands (see, e.g., Nuerk et al. (2005) for similar results with dice patterns). The mean slope of the regression line in the joint condition of Experiment 2 was more than twice as large as the mean slope in the joint condition in Experiment 1 (see Figure 4), supporting the assumption that there were spatial compatibility effects in addition to spatial–numerical compatibility effects. Unfortunately, a statistical comparison between the slopes obtained in the joint conditions of Experiments 1 and 2 failed to reach significance.

However, in support of the additivity assumption, a later follow-up experiment did not show a significant joint compatibility effect for stimuli of

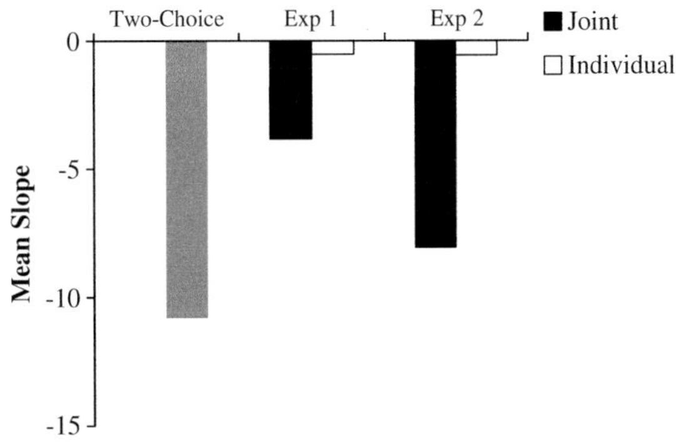

Figure 4. Mean slopes of RT differences of the two-choice condition and of the joint and the individual conditions in Experiments 1 and 2.

human hands where magnitude increased from right to left. These stimuli create a conflict between numerical–spatial compatibility and spatial compatibility. The lack of joint compatibility effects in the follow-up experiment suggests that spatial compatibility and numerical–spatial compatibility cancelled each other out. Thus, the numerically larger negative slope in Experiment 2 likely reflects the combination of two different compatibility effects.

Unlike in Experiment 1, the SNARC effect in the joint condition appeared to be quite symmetrical, indicating that an overt spatial component is possibly necessary for a symmetrical joint SNARC effect to occur. RTs in the joint and the individual conditions in Experiment 2 tended to be about 200 ms slower than in Experiment 1. This could have been due to the inherently more complex nature of the pictures depicting hands compared to the single numbers presented in Experiment 1. Given that previous research has clearly shown that the SNARC effect does not vary as a function of RT (Mapelli, Rusconi, & Umiltà, 2003), we consider it unlikely that this increase alone could explain the increase of the joint SNARC effect compared to Experiment 1.

GENERAL DISCUSSION

The present results suggest that action co-representation is a general phenomenon that occurs whenever complementary actions are distributed across different people. The joint SNARC effect obtained in the present experiments can be explained by the assumption that when two people make complementary parity judgments, each individual forms a representation of both action alternatives. The numerical stimuli automatically activated a representation of the corresponding action, regardless of whether it was at one's own or the other's command. On compatible trials, stimuli activated the action to be performed, facilitating action execution; whereas on incompatible trials, stimuli activated a representation of the action not to be performed, leading to an action selection conflict that slowed down the responses. This was not true for the individual condition, because only one action alternative was represented. Furthermore, the larger co-representation effects in Experiments 2 suggest that perceptual spatial features and spatial features derived from symbolic stimuli can concurrently activate a co-represented action.

More generally, effects of co-representation suggest that when people perform different parts of a task they tend to represent the whole task at hand rather than just their own part in the task. Importantly, action alternatives at another's disposal appear to be represented in a similar way to action alternatives at one's own disposal. Although we have not obtained direct evidence for the neural mechanisms underlying co-representation so far (but see Sebanz, Rebbechi, Knoblich, Prinz, & Frith, 2007), it is likely that the mirror system enables us to represent our own and others' actions in a functionally equivalent way when performing complementary parts of a task together. Note that this does not imply that there is no difference between performing the whole task alone (two-choice condition) and performing the task together with another person. Obviously, response selection conflicts are stronger when both action alternatives really are at one's own disposal (Burle, Possami, Vidal, Bonnet, & Hasbroucq, 2002). However, a conflict also occurs when another action alternative is kept in a state of readiness, be it because one occasionally happens to be in charge of it (Hommel, 1996), or because one knows someone else to be in charge of it, as was the case in our experiments.

The results suggest that the mirror system is not engaged only in action observation, because concurrent perceptual input about a coactor's actions is not required (Kilner, Vargas, Duval, Blakemore, & Sirigu, 2004; Sebanz et al., 2003). Rather, any stimulus that refers to a coactor's action might have the potential to activate action representations in the mirror system. If this assumption is valid, the mirror system could generally support joint task performance because it provides a platform for integrating action alternatives at one's own and others' command (Knoblich & Jordan, 2002).

However, the functionality of the mirror system alone is not sufficient to support joint action. In the present experiments, participants came to represent the other's action alternative in the joint condition because they knew from the start how the respective parts of the whole task would be distributed between the two coactors. In other words, they might have formed a task representation that entailed stimuli they did not need to react to and an action alternative not at their own command (Sebanz et al., 2005; Atmaca, Sebanz, & Knoblich, 2008). Without such a task representation, no mirror system activation can be expected. The claim that higher level planning structures can provide a context within which the mirror system operates (Erlhagen, Mukovskiy, & Bicho, 2006) has the potential to explain how the mirror system supports different (non-imitative) forms of joint action. On one hand, higher-level task representations would ensure flexible links between environmental and social conditions and suitable actions. On the other hand, the task representations would include action representations that are functionally equivalent for self and other and thus ensure that one can interpret (Rizzolatti & Craighero, 2004) and predict (Decety & Grezes, 2006; Wilson & Knoblich, 2005) others' actions even when a joint task requires complementary actions. Clearly, further research is needed to establish how the interplay between higher level task representations and the mirror system enables joint action. We believe that this interplay could be the key to understanding the emergence of shared intentionality that is critical not only for joint action but also for its symbolic counterpart, communication.

Manuscript received 6 March 2007
Manuscript accepted 20 September 2007
First published online 30 January 2008

REFERENCES

Arbib, M. A. (2005). From monkey-like action recognition to human language: an evolutionary framework for neurolinguistics. *Behavioral and Brain Sciences, 28*, 105–124.

Atmaca, S., Sebanz, N., & Knoblich, G. (2008). Co-representation of arbitrary S–R mappings: The joint Flanker effect. *Manuscript scubmitted for publication.*

Barresi, J., & Moore, C. (1996). Intentional relations and social understanding. *Behavioral & Brain Sciences, 19*, 107–154.

Brass, M., Bekkering, H., & Prinz, W. (2001). Movement observation affects movement execution in a simple response task. *Acta Psychologica, 106*, 3–22.

Burle, B., Possami, C.-A., Vidal, F., Bonnet, M., & Hasbroucq, T. (2002). Executive control in the Simon effect: an electromyographic and distributional analysis. *Psychological Research, 66*, 324–336.

Clark, H. H. (1996). *Using language.* Cambridge, UK: Cambridge University Press.

Cohen, J. D., MacWhinney, B., Flatt, M., & Provost, J. (1993). PsyScope: An interactive graphic system for designing and controlling experiments in the psychology laboratory using Macintosh computers. *Behavior Research Methods, Instruments, Computers, 25*, 257–271.

Decety, J., & Grezes, J. (2006). The power of simulation: Imagining one's own and other's behaviour. *Cognitive Brain Research, 1079*, 4–14.

Dehaene, S. (1997). *The number sense – How the mind creates mathematics.* Oxford: Oxford University Press.

Dehaene, S., Bossini, S., & Giraux, P. (1993). The mental representation of parity and number magnitude. *Journal of Experimental Psychology: General, 122*, 371–396.

Di Pellegrino, G., Fadiga, L., Fogassi, L., Gallese, V., & Rizzolatti, G. (1992). Understanding motor events: a neurophysiological study. *Experimental Brain Research, 91*, 176–180.

Erlhagen, W., Mukovskiy, A., & Bicho, E. (2006). A dynamic model for action understanding and goal-directed imitation. *Brain Research, 1083*, 174–188.

Fias, W. (2001). Two routes for the processing of verbal numbers: Evidence from the SNARC effect. *Psychological Research, 65*, 250–259.

Galantucci, B. (2005). An experimental study of the emergence of human communication systems. *Cognitive Science, 29*, 737–767.

Galantucci, B., Fowler, C. A., & Turvey, M. T. (2006). The motor theory of speech perception reviewed. *Psychonomic Bulletin & Review, 13*, 361–377.

Gallese, V., Fadiga, L., Fogassi, L., & Rizzolatti, G. (1996). Action recognition in the premotor cortex. *Brain, 119*, 593–609.

Gallese, V., Keysers, C., & Rizzolatti, G. (2004). A unifying view of the basis of social cognition. *Trends in Cognitive Sciences, 8*, 396–403.

Garrod, S., & Pickering, M. (2004). Why is conversation so easy? *Trends in Cognitive Sciences, 8*, 8–11.

Goldman, A., & Sripada, C. S. (2005). Simulationist models of face-based emotion recognition. *Cognition, 94*, 103–213.

Greenwald, A. G. (1970). Sensory feedback mechanisms in performance control: With special reference to the ideo-motor mechanism. *Psychological Review, 77*, 73–99.

Grezes, J., Armony, J. L., Rowe, J., & Passingham, R. E. (2003). Activations related to "mirror" and "canonical" neurones in the human brain: an fMRI study. *NeuroImage, 18*, 928–937.

Hommel, B. (1996). S–R compatibility effects without response uncertainty. *Quarterly Journal of Experimental Psychology, 49A*, 546–571.

Hommel, B., Muesseler, J., Aschersleben, G., & Prinz, W. (2001). The theory of event coding (TEC). *Behavioral and Brain Sciences, 24*, 849–937.

Iversen, W., Nuerk, H. C., & Willmes, K. (2000). Do signers think differently? The processing of number parity in deaf participants. *Cortex, 40*, 176–178.

James, W. (1890). *The principles of psychology* (Vol. 2). New York: Holt.

Jeannerod, M. (1999). The 25th Bartlett Lecture: To act or not to act: Perspectives on the representation of actions. *Quarterly Journal of Experimental Psychology, 52A*, 1–29.

Keysers, C., Wicker, B., Gazzola, V., Anton, J., Fogassi, L., & Gallese, V. (2004). A touching sight: SII/PV activation during the observation and experience of touch. *Neuron, 42*, 335–346.

Kilner, J. M., Paulignan, Y., & Blakemore, S.J. (2003). An interference effect of observed biological movement on action. *Current Biology, 13*, 522–525.

Kilner, J., Vargas, C., Duval, S., Blakemore, S.-J., & Sirigu, A. (2004). Motor activation prior to observation of a predicted movement. *Nature Neuroscience, 7*, 1299–1301.

Knoblich, G., & Jordan, S. (2002). The mirror system and joint action. In M. I. Stamenov & V. Gallese (Eds.), *Mirror neurons and the evolution of brain and language* (pp. 115–124). Amsterdam: John Benjamins.

Knoblich, G., & Jordan, S. (2003). Action coordination in individuals and groups: Learning anticipatory control. *Journal of Experimental Psychology: Learning, Memory, Cognition, 29*, 1006–1016.

Kornblum, S., Hasbroucq, T., & Osman, A. (1990). Dimensional overlap: Cognitive basis for stimulus–response compatibility – a model and taxonomy. *Psychological Review, 97*, 253–270.

Lakoff, G., & Nunez, R. E. (2000). *Where mathematics comes from*. New York: Basic Books.

Liberman, A. M., & Whalen, D. H. (2000). On the relation of speech to language. *Trends in Cognitive Sciences, 4*, 187–196.

Mapelli, D., Rusconi, E., & Umiltà, C. (2003). The SNARC effect: An instance of the Simon effect? *Cognition, 88*, B1–B10.

Nuerk, H. C., Wood, G., & Willmes, K. (2005). The universal SNARC effect: The association between number magnitude and space is amodal. *Experimental Psychology, 52*, 187–194.

Pacherie, E., & Dokic, J. (2006). From mirror neurons to joint actions. *Cognitive Systems Research, 7*, 101–112.

Prinz, W. (1997). Perception and action planning. *European Journal of Cognitive Psychology, 9*, 129–154.

Rizzolatti, G., & Arbib, M. A. (1998). Language within our grasp. *Trends in Neurosciences, 21*, 188–194.

Rizzolatti, G., & Craighero, L. (2004). The mirror-neuron system. *Annual Review of Neuroscience, 27*, 169–192.

Sebanz, N., Bekkering, H., & Knoblich, G. (2006). Joint action: Bodies and minds moving together. *Trends in Cognitive Science, 10*, 70–76.

Sebanz, N., Knoblich, G., & Prinz, W. (2003). Representing others' actions: just like one's own? *Cognition, 88*, B11–B21.

Sebanz, N., Knoblich, G., & Prinz, W. (2005). How to share a task: Corepresenting stimulus–response mappings. *Journal of Experimental Psychology: Human Perception and Performance, 33*, 1234–1246.

Sebanz, N., Rebbechi, D., Knoblich, G., Prinz, W., & Frith, C. (2007). Is it really my turn? An event-related fMRI study of task sharing. *Social Neuroscience, 2*, 81–95.

Simon, J. R. (1990). The effects of an irrelevant directional cue on human information processing. *Advances in Psychology, 65*, 31–86.

Simon, J. R., Hinrichs, J. V., & Craft, J. L. (1970). Auditory S–R compatibility: Reaction time as a function of ear–hand correspondence and ear–response-location correspondence. *Journal of Experimental Psychology, 86*, 97–102.

Singer, T., Seymour, B., O'Doherty, J. P., Kaube, H., Dolan, R. J., & Frith, C. D. (2004). Empathy for pain involves the affective but not sensory components of pain. *Science, 303*, 1157–1162.

Stuermer, B., Aschersleben, G., & Prinz, W. (2000). Correspondence effects with manual gestures and postures: A study of imitation. *Journal of Experimental Psychology: Human Perception and Performance, 26*, 1746–1759.

Tomasello, M. (2000). Culture and cognitive development. *Current Directions in Psychological Science, 9*, 37–40.

Tomasello, M., Carpenter, M., Call, J., Behne, T., & Moll, H. (2005). Understanding and sharing intentions: The origins of cultural cognition. *Behavioral and Brain Sciences, 28*, 675–735.

Tsai, C.-C., Kuo, W.-J., Hung, D., & Tzeng, O. (in press). Action co-representation is tuned to other humans. *Journal of Cognitive Neuroscience.*

Tsai, C., Kuo, W., Jing, J., Hung, D., & Tzeng, O. (2006). A common coding framework in self–other interaction. Evidence from a joint action task. *Experimental Brain Research, 175*, 353–362.

Wilson, M., & Knoblich, G. (2005). The case for motor involvement in perceiving conspecifics. *Psychological Bulletin, 131*, 460–473.

Zorzi, M., Priftis, K., & Umiltà, C. (2002). Neglect disrupts the mental number line. *Nature, 417*, 138–139.

SOCIAL NEUROSCIENCE, 2008, 3 (3–4), 421–433

Psychology Press
Taylor & Francis Group

Action observation and execution: What is shared?

F. de Vignemont
CNRS-EHESS-ENS, Paris, France

P. Haggard
University College London, London, UK

Performing an action and observing it activate the same internal representations of action. The representations are therefore shared between self and other (shared representations of action, SRA). But what exactly is shared? At what level within the hierarchical structure of the motor system do SRA occur? Understanding the content of SRA is important in order to decide what theoretical work SRA can perform. In this paper, we provide some conceptual clarification by raising three main questions: (i) are SRA semantic or pragmatic representations of action?; (ii) are SRA sensory or motor representations?; (iii) are SRA representations of the action as a global unit or as a set of elementary motor components? After outlining a model of the motor hierarchy, we conclude that the best candidate for SRA is intentions in action, defined as the motor plans of the dynamic sequence of movements. We shed new light on SRA by highlighting the causal efficacy of intentions in action. This in turn explains phenomena such as inhibition of imitation.

INTRODUCTION

In 1992, researchers in Parma reported the existence of neurons that fired both when a monkey was grasping a peanut and when it was watching the experimenter grasping it. They named them "mirror neurons" because they reflect other people's actions (di Pellegrino, Fadiga, Fogassi, Gallese, & Rizzolatti, 1992; Gallese, Fadiga, Fogassi, & Rizzolatti, 1996; Rizzolatti, Fadiga, Gallese, & Fogassi, 1995). In humans, action observation and action execution activate overlapping brain areas including the supplementary motor area, the dorsal premotor cortex, the supramarginal gyrus, the superior parietal lobe and the Broca's area (Grezes & Decety, 2001). It was therefore argued that the same internal representations of action is shared between self and other (shared representations of action, SRA).

By linking self and others within a unique representational framework, SRA have been considered to be at the core of intersubjectivity (Gallese, 2003), potentially playing a role in imitation (Iacoboni et al., 1999), empathy (Preston & de Waal, 2002), mindreading (Gallese & Goldman, 1998), and language (Rizzolatti & Arbib, 1998). According to Ramachandran (2004), mirror neurons had even been a necessary condition for the so-called "big bang" of human evolution 40,000 years ago—a sudden explosion of human mental abilities and culture including even art and mathematics. SRA could indeed parsimoniously solve several problems raised by interpersonal relationships by enabling direct matching between self and others.

However, SRA might not provide such a universal answer, as shown by some recent criticisms both on the empirical and on the conceptual sides (Grèzes & Decety, 2001) about

Correspondence should be addressed to: Frederique de Vignemont, Institut Jean-Nicod, CNRS-EHESS-ENS, 29 rue d'Ulm, 75005 Paris, France. E-mail: fvignemont@isc.cnrs.fr

www.psypress.com/socialneuroscience DOI:10.1080/17470910802045109

the link with language; Saxe (2005) about the link with simulation theory; Jacob & Jeannerod (2005) about the link with mindreading). After the excitement of the discovery of SRA and their possible consequences for social cognition, there is a need for clarifications and conceptual cautiousness. As a preliminary step, it is necessary to understand what is indeed shared between action execution and action observation. Only if we know in detail the content of SRA can we decide what work SRA can perform. In particular, we need to situate SRA within the architecture of action. Both cognitive and neural models identify many representational stages and processes which contribute to action execution (Jeannerod, 1997; Wolpert, Ghahramani, & Jordan, 1995). At what level within the hierarchical structure of the motor system do SRA occur? The aim of this paper is to step back from speculation about the possible roles of SRA and to start at the beginning by asking: what is shared?

DIFFERENT LEVELS OF ACTION REPRESENTATIONS

The hypothesis of SRA can be articulated as follows:

1. Two tokens of the same type of action representation are activated in two individuals' brains.
2. The activation in one individual is triggered by the observation of the other individual acting.

Both claims raise questions, but most recent interest has focused on the latter claim. How is the observation of the performed movement related to the activation of SRA? Is the relationship direct or not (Csibra, 2007)? Does it result from an associative learning mechanism (Heyes and Bird, 2007)? In contrast, we will focus here on the former claim of the SRA hypothesis: what kind of action representation is instantiated both in the agent and in the observer?

SRA are defined relative to their context of activation (execution versus observation), but these two notions are too broad to be useful. According to Anscombe (1957), there is an almost infinite list of possible descriptions of the same action: I turn the tap clockwise, I open the tap, I get some water, I intend to drink. Similarly, at the computational level, the goal of the action is represented at different levels of complexity that are hierarchically organized (i.e. a set of motor commands, a series of intermediary movements, the final outcome) (Wolpert, Doya, & Kowato, 2003). The contextual definition of SRA is not sufficient to define what level of action representation one has access to when observing someone else's movement. Exactly what information is shared? We need to take account of the complexity of the motor system to be able to specify what is common between action execution and action observation.

We begin by considering whether SRA could be localized to the upstream, intentional motor system. There are at least two kinds of intention (Pacherie, 2000; Searle, 1983). *Prior intentions* represent the goal of the action as a global unit (e.g. I intend to drink). They are too rough-grained to specify the movements that have to be performed. There may be several means to realize the same prior intention. The motor system needs to anchor the prior intention in a specific context and to determine the means that will be required to reach the goal, that is, the *intention in action*. Intentions in action represent the action as a dynamic sequence of specific movements (e.g. I intend to reach the tap and to turn it clockwise with the right hand). They initiate the action, guide it and monitor its effects. They correspond to the motor plan, prior to the dispatch of the final motor command to the muscles (Jeannerod, 1995). The intention in action therefore has a level of motor specificity that prior intentions lack. For this reason, intentions in action can be identified with the inverse model in computational frameworks. The inverse model has the role of computing the *motor commands* needed to achieve the desired state given the agent's current body state (Wolpert et al., 1995). The motor system also anticipates both the motor and the sensory consequences of the movement through two kinds of forward model (Frith, 2005; Wolpert et al., 1995). The *forward dynamic model* predicts what an action will be like given the specific body that executes the motor commands (e.g. how far the arm will stretch given its size). The output of the forward dynamic model is encoded in a motor format. It is involved in motor imagery and allows anticipatory control of movements. For example, we need to anticipate the changing gravitational forces when we move a heavy object up and down, and thus to alter the grip force. The *forward output model* predicts the sensory feedback (e.g. where the arm will be at the end of the movement). The output of the forward output model is encoded in a sensory format. The prediction of the sensory consequences of the movements attenuates the actual sensations caused by the movements (Blakemore, Wolpert, & Frith, 1998). This is why one cannot tickle oneself. Finally, there is the actual *sensory feedback* resulting from the execution of the action. Controlling actions requires running the different stages in an open-loop fashion. We may however want to freeze the action system at a moment in time, and ask whether the individual representations one finds might or might not be shareable.

In summary, SRA may happen at different levels: prior intention, intention in action, motor command, predicted motor outcome, predicted sensory outcome, and sensory feedback. These possibilities are not mutually exclusive. However, most of the neuroscience literature about SRA does not distinguish clearly among these levels. The authors sometimes refer to intentions (Iacoboni et al., 2005), but without distinguishing prior intentions and intentions in action. Other authors suggest sharing of the predicted state resulting from the forward output model (Prinz, 2002). Still others include a further level of action representation, the semantic knowledge of what one does (Van Elk, Van Schie, & Bekkering, 2007).

Figure 1 concerns processes and signals, and is based on information engineering. In contrast, most conceptual work on SRA describes representations in terms of their functions (see Figure 2). In order to situate these representations within process models, we suggest that three questions about SRA are essential.

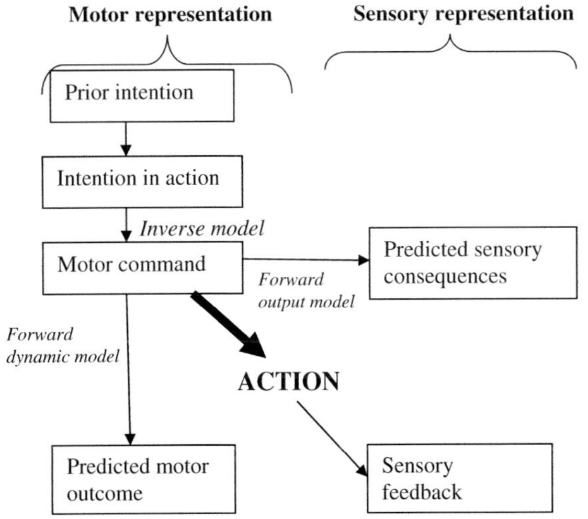

Figure 1. Hierarchical model of motor control.

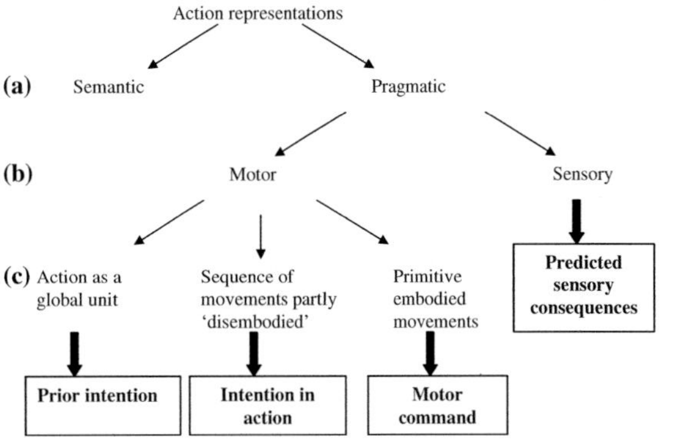

Figure 2. What is the content of SRA?

1. Are SRA semantic or pragmatic representations of action?
2. Are SRA sensory or motor representations?
3. Are SRA representations of the action as a global unit or as a dynamic sequence of elementary motor components?

Basic as they might seem, these questions are not easy to answer, as we will see. The past 15 years have seen an increasing number of studies about the relationship between perception and action, which sometimes provide conflicting results. This paper does not aim to review this vast amount of literature, but rather to suggest some answers based on a few key studies.

SEMANTIC VERSUS PRAGMATIC

According to the generality constraint (Evans, 1983), I master the concept 'to grasp' if I am able to use it to represent both that *I* grasp a peanut/a glass of water and that *John* grasps a peanut/a glass of water ($< x$ grasps $y >$). Such definition of concepts meets the underlying requirement of SRA. And indeed, SRA have been said to encode a "motor vocabulary" shared between self and others (Rizzolatti et al., 1988). In favour of such a view, it was found that Broca's area contributes to action observation and imitation (Iacoboni et al., 1999; Koski et al., 2002). SRA would provide a *conceptual* understanding of action (Rizzolatti, Fogassi, & Gallese, 2000). However, as pointed out by Goldman (2006), the same authors also describe SRA as a kind of "direct *experiential* understanding" of someone else's actions (Gallese, Keysers and Rizzolatti, 2004, p. 396; emphasis added). They emphasize that "Conceptual reasoning is not necessary for this understanding." There is an apparent contradiction here. On the one hand, the relationship between action observation and execution would be mediated by conceptual processes. On the other hand, it would be immediate, leading to a direct experience of someone else's action from a first-person perspective as if one were moving.[1]

The best way to capture the difference between these two views may be to use the distinction between semantic and pragmatic representations of action, as defined by Jeannerod (1994). Semantic representations encode the properties of the observed actions to identify them, and to keep track of them. They are based on visual recognition expertise and they are linked to linguistic representations (e.g. action naming tasks), and to a wider semantic network of other concepts connected with the recognized action. This knowledge is from a *third-person perspective*. The observer does not put herself in the agent's shoes; she remains an external witness. In contrast, pragmatic representations represent actions from the *first-person point of view* of the agent in interaction with the world. They encode the properties of the motor system for optimization of action execution, as well as the properties of the object relevant for the interaction between the agent and the object. They allow the observer to reproduce the same movement through imitation.

This leads us to our first question. Are SRA semantic or pragmatic representations of actions? Like any semantic knowledge, action knowledge can be indifferently applied both to the self and to others. However, if the sharing were limited to conceptual recognition, there would be no particular interest in SRA. I would understand other people's actions in the same way that I understand the movements of the clouds in the sky: in both cases, I apply a semantic knowledge previously acquired. Alternatively, one may argue that what makes SRA special is that they go beyond this mere conceptual sharing. One would not share only the knowledge about the action; one would share the agent's inner perspective. SRA would then allow the observer to internalize someone else's actions as if she were the agent, and not just an external witness.

[1] Gallese & Lakoff (2005) provide an embodied account of concepts, which would erase the contradiction. However, for various reasons, we prefer to maintain a distinction between the experiential nonconceptual level and the conceptual level. Nonetheless, we agree that the nonconceptual level can ground the conceptual level.

Recent behavioral results have shown the influence of semantic representations on action, suggesting that one could have semantically mediated SRA (Gentilucci & Gangitano, 1998; Gentilucci, Benuzzi, Bertolani, Daprati, & Gangitano, 2000; Glover & Dixon, 2002; Glover, Rosenbaum, Graham, & Dixon, 2004). For example, Gentilucci & Gangitano (1998) found a priming effect of action words on movement kinematics. Subjects had to grasp two bars of the same size, one named 'small' and the other named 'large'. The grip aperture was influenced by the tag on the bar. More recently, Van Elk and coworkers have produced several results suggesting a role of conceptual representations of action in mirror phenomena, and thus supporting a semantic view (Van Elk et al., 2007; Lindemann, Stenneken, van Schie, & Bekkering, 2006). Subjects grasped and used one of two objects (cup or magnifying glass) if the word subsequently presented was lexically valid (go) or withheld from moving if a nonword was presented (no-go). Two kinds of words were presented: either congruent or incongruent with the action to perform (e.g. mouth or eye). Subjects responded faster when the word was congruent. The authors showed an interaction effect between action preparation and word reading.

These interesting results underline the importance of our conceptual knowledge for actions. They show that action execution is sensitive not only to action observation, but also to action words. However, they do not show that the pathway between perception and action is *always* mediated by the semantic knowledge of acts. These results do not show that we are sensitive *exclusively* to conceptual representations of actions. Nor do they show that what is shared is *only* semantic knowledge. There might additionally be a direct pathway between observation and action, relying only on shared *pragmatic* representations of action. But how can these two putative representations be untangled?

The distinction between semantic and pragmatic representations of action raises a real difficulty for neuroscience. How can brain imagery studies or cell recording differentiate between pragmatic representations from a first-person perspective and semantic representations from a third-person perspective? A recent study tackles this issue by using motor and visual expertise to differentiate between first-person and third-person perspective (Calvo-Merino, Grezes, Glaser, Passingham, & Haggard, 2006).

Ballet dancers, both male and female, watched short videos of ballet movements. The movements chosen were either performed exclusively by male dancers, performed exclusively by female dancers, or common to male and female. The underlying assumption was that dancers have visual familiarity for all the movements, but only motor familiarity for movements of their own gender. If there was nothing more to SRA than a mere semantic representation of dance, then there should not be any difference between the conditions. However, this was not the case: mirror system activity was greater when subjects watched movements specific to their own gender, for which they had acquired the appropriate motor representations. Questionnaire data and brain activity suggested that semantic knowledge of the different movement types, such as visual recognition and naming, did not differ between the groups. This study provides a conclusive argument in favor of the existence of pragmatic representations of action shared between self and others.

To sum up, although semantic representations can affect action execution, semantic representations do not suffice to account for all the data and pragmatic representations also seem to be involved. It remains however an open question whether semantic representations are necessary or not, although they are not sufficient. It has been proposed recently a dual-route model: the link between sensory and motor can be either direct (through associative learning mechanism for instance) or linguistically mediated (Heyes, 2001; Tessari and Rumiati, 2004). Similarly, the direct matching hypothesis assumes that we do not need semantic mediation (Gallese et al., 2004). On these views, SRA seem to involve sharing of a nonconceptual, nonsemantic, pragmatic form of representation from a first-person perspective based on the representations that agents have of executing actions.

SENSORY VERSUS MOTOR

We have shown that the relationship between action observation and action execution is not always mediated by semantic representations of action. There is, in addition, a direct link between perception and action, which does not require a conceptual translation from one to the other. Such direct matching is possible if and only if some levels in the perceptual process and in the motor process are commensurate. But what code is common to perception and action? Is it sensory: "actions are represented at the common meeting place in terms of their sensory or perceptual consequences" (Prinz, 2002, p. 173)? Or is it motor: "the perception–action mediation relies on motor representations that are already activated (or formed) during observation" (Decety and Grezes, 1999, p. 177)?

The content of SRA is shown in Figure 2; sensory versus motor sharing is depicted in Figure 3.

According to the sensory view, the observation of a kinematic pattern is directly matched with the anticipation of the sensory consequences of the action. The anticipatory image of the sensory feedback of actions is associated in a bidirectional way with the actions that lead to them (effect ⇔ movement). Its activation thus in turn activates the motor representation of the corresponding action. The *mechanism* of SRA is sensory, but the indirect consequence is that two people have common motor representations. The sensory common coding view can explain a number of studies based on interference between execution and action observation. The interference arises because of the similarity between the sensory representations of the movement observed and the movement predicted.

In contrast, according to the motor view, action observation triggers a covert simulation of the motor program (Gallese, 2003; Jeannerod, 1994). A meta-analysis of brain imaging studies has shown an overlap of activations between execution, observation and mental simulation of action (Grèzes & Decety, 2001). To put it another way, motor imagery is the conscious counterpart of SRA (Decety, 2002), and might be considered as

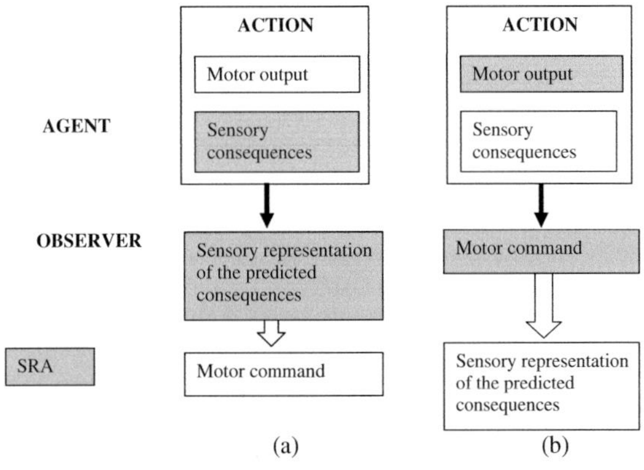

Figure 3. (a) Sensory sharing versus (b) motor sharing.

the key for understanding SRA.[2] However, the activation of the motor program in turn activates also the representation of the sensory consequences.

In addition, there may be several intermediate positions between a purely sensory view and a purely motor view (Hommel et al., 2001; Keysers & Perrett, 2004). How might one dissociate sensory and motor components? Indeed, is it possible to do so? One possibility is to look at the neural network underlying SRA. It includes areas that are classically considered motor (e.g. ventral premotor cortex). This observation formed part of the original interest of SRA: perceptual tasks activate motor areas. However, both the sensory view and the motor view can account for such activation. In both views, both sensory and motor components of action representations are activated by action observation, whether it is directly or indirectly triggered by the representation of the sensory consequences.[3] Consequently, it may be illusory to dissociate the sensory and the motor aspects. They are bound together into united "action files", which group together all the action-related features, both perceptual and motor (Hommel, 2004). What is shared would be the event file itself, and not its perceptual or its motor components.

However, it is possible to dissociate somatosensory and motor components of action mirroring in the cortex (Avenanti, Bolognini, Maravita, & Aglioti, 2007). Those authors investigated observation of possible and impossible movements. Both classes of movement induce activations of mirror system areas thought to contain SRA (Costantini et al., 2005), and motor facilitation effects (Romani, Cesari, Urgesi, Facchini, & Aglioti, 2005). However, Avenanti and coworkers showed that repetitive transcranial magnetic stimulation (rTMS) over ventral premotor cortex abolishes the motor facilitation effect during the observation of biologically possible movements, but not impossible movements. On the other hand, rTMS of primary somatosensory cortex decreases the motor facilitation effect during observation of biologically impossible, but not possible movements. This study thus dissociates two aspects of the motor facilitation effect. Only the first of these, which is specialized for biological action, and housed in ventral premotor cortex, can properly be considered to reflect the functions of the mirror system.

In addition, a few recent results argue in favour of sharing motor representations. Mirror neurons have been shown to fire even if the completion of the action is hidden behind a screen (Umiltà et al., 2001). To put it another way, one does not need to perceive the outcome of the action to activate SRA. This result is not sufficient in itself to argue against the sensory view. One might indeed still be able to make sensory predictions about the action output, although it has not been completed. However, a recent perceptual study has shown the influence of motor expertise on action observation independently of any visual expertise (Casile & Giese, 2006). Blindfolded subjects learned to perform a novel coordinated movement based only on verbal and haptic feedback. The better they were at performing the movement, the better they were at recognizing it on a point-light display. The authors concluded that motor programs might be the dominating factor that explains the influence of motor training on movement recognition.[4]

Even more convincing evidence against the sensory view comes from results showing context dependence of SRA. If SRA represented the sensory consequences of the action, then their activation should be specific to the sensory consequences. They should not be directly affected by the context leading to the movement, since context does not modify the sensory consequences. However, Fogassi et al. (2005) showed that some mirror neurons responded differentially, depending on the kind of action in which the movement was embedded (e.g. grasping for eating versus grasping for placing). Although the sensory consequences were the same, the neural activation was not. The same type of results was found in humans (Iacoboni et al., 2005). The

[2] However, as far as we know, there is no study that directly investigates the relationship between motor imagery and action observation.

[3] In order to untangle these two alternatives, one would need better neuroimaging tools that allow for a better temporal resolution (e.g. EEG and MEG) or an analysis of the effective connectivity (e.g. by dynamical causal modeling). This would permit one, for example, to determine what comes first: the representation of the sensory consequences or the motor representation.

[4] Once again, this study cannot exclude completely a possible role of the anticipation of the sensory consequences of the movement. Although subjects never had any visual feedback on the movement they learned, they might have predicted the visual consequences of their movement. Alternatively, there may be some intermodal translation from haptic to vision (Meltzoff, 1995).

authors found differential activation of the right inferior frontal cortex relative to the context, the physical movement remaining the same. Consequently, the mere representation of the sensory outcome of the action cannot exhaust the content of SRA, as it is identical in both conditions. What matters here is the representation of the surrounding context.

In summary, (i) the lack of visual representation of the outcome does not prevent the activation of SRA (Casile & Giese, 2006; Umiltà et al., 2001), and (ii) the observation of the same outcome can lead to different activation of SRA (Fogassi et al., 2005; Iacoboni et al., 2005). Since SRA are therefore unlikely to be sensory representations, they may instead be motor representations. Of course, motoric SRA might then activate sensory representations of the expected outcome indirectly, but our concern here is with direct sharing. Our suggestion of purely motoric SRA is consistent with Jeannerod's view that "an observer monitoring an action performed by someone else is never far from being also the agent of that action" (Jeannerod, 2003, p. 142).

ACTION AS A GLOBAL UNIT VERSUS ACTION AS A DYNAMIC SEQUENCE OF ELEMENTARY MOTOR COMPONENTS

We have seen that although both sensory and motor representations might be shared, the evidence favours sharing of motor representations over sensory ones. However, there are several possible levels of motor representations. Two factors must be considered to untangle the different levels within the motor system.

First, the *degree of abstraction*. At the computational level, hierarchical models of motor control such as HMOSAIC postulate the existence of at least three layers of motor representations: the goal, the sequence of movements, and the elements of movements (Jeannerod, 1995; Wolpert et al., 2003). The goal is the highest and the most abstract level (e.g. to get a drink of water). It activates the planning of the dynamic sequence of movements to perform in order to achieve the goal (e.g. to pour the water in the glass, to grasp the glass, and to bring it to the mouth). The precise kinematics of the sequence of movements is then computed taking account of the agent's body and the surrounding context (e.g. to stretch the arm for 20 cm, to make a 5 cm grip aperture, to raise the arm with an elbow angle of 45°). We suggest that these three levels correspond to what we call prior intention, intention in action, and motor command (Table 1).

TABLE 1
Three levels of motor representation

	Abstraction	*Embodiment*
Prior intention: the goal	+++	+
Intention in action: dynamic sequence of movements	++	++
Motor command: kinematics of elements of movements	+	+++

In parallel with the motor hierarchy, there is an embodiment hierarchy. Motor representations take account in more or less detail of bodily information necessary to perform the intended action. Bodily information can be either general (e.g. which limbs to move) or specific to the agent (e.g. the size of the limbs, joint angles or hand position) (Wolpert et al., 2003). In the latter case, the body state is not shared between the agent and the observer, who differ in their size and in their posture. SRA experiments can provide evidence about the level of embodiment at which sharing occurs, and this can therefore give empirical data about the level of abstraction.

Do SRA take into account precise bodily parameters? It has been shown that action observation leads to somatotopic activation of the premotor cortex (Buccino et al., 2001). In addition, the motor facilitation effect of action observation is muscle-specific (Fadiga, Fogassi, Pavesi, and Rizzolatti, 1995). Consequently, SRA encode *bodily* movements, and not merely abstract goals. However, SRA cannot represent the precise bodily kinematics in all its details, as shown by several experimental results. Csibra (2007) notes that only 19–41% of mirror neurons are classified as 'strictly congruent' (di Pellegrino et al., 1992; Ferrari, Gallese, Rizzolatti, & Fogassi, 2003; Gallese et al., 1996; Gallese, Fogassi, Fadiga, & Rizzolatti, 2002). Strict means that they fire only for observed actions of exactly the same type (e.g. not just grasping, but grasping with a particular hand configuration). The majority of mirror neurons fire when the observed action is "broadly congruent": they can respond to movements as different as grasping with the mouth and grasping with the hand (Gallese et al. 1996). What matters is the motor repertoire, not the individual body that performs the actions (Calvo-Merino et al., 2006). Somatotopic activation is indeed found even if the movement is performed by nonconspecifics such as monkeys or dogs (Buccino et al., 2004), or robots (Gazzola et al., 2007; Press, Bird, Flach, & Heyes, 2005). What matters is that the observer can perform a functionally equivalent movement.

Furthermore, as we have seen, SRA are activated by the observation of biomechanically impossible movements (Avenanti et al., 2007; Costantini et al., 2005; Romani et al., 2005). It should be noted, however, that these so-called impossible movements are rather the exaggeration of physiologically possible movements, and thus share a number of features with them. Activation of SRA by biomechanically impossible stimuli may thus arise because specific bodily detail is lost when SRA match actions across bodies. Along the same lines, it was shown that two aplasic individuals born without hands activated regions of the mirror system involved in mouth and foot execution when observing hand movements (Gazzola, Rizzolatti, Wicker, & Keysers, 2007). In contrast with Buccino et al. (2001, 2004), the activation was not somatotopic. To put it another way, SRA can and do abstract actions despite intersubjective differences, even when these differences are extreme.

A last argument against fully embodied SRA comes from the mirror neurons literature, and points towards the same conclusion as Gazzola et al. (2007). Some mirror neurons responded to the observation of tool-using actions (e.g. grasping food with a stick), although the monkeys themselves were unable to perform these actions (e.g. they grasped the food with their hand) (Ferrari, Rozzi, & Fogassi, 2005). In this case, the kinematics of the two actions differs in important respects. For example, the direction and speed of motion, the angles between the joints, etc. cannot be shared in such cases.

To sum up, we consider that SRA do not represent movements in all their bodily parameters. SRA match not only the observed action to an executable action, but also someone else's body to one's own body. SRA may (Buccino et al., 2001) or may not (Ferrari et al., 2005; Gazzola et al., 2007) match spatial anatomical detail across bodies. However, they clearly cannot match dynamic information about muscular forces across bodies, since they are activated by observation of nonconspecifics' actions (Buccino et al., 2004). This is not so surprising given the fact that the agent's body almost always differs from the observer's body (e.g. in length and strength of the limbs). We know that children can imitate adults although their bodies differ completely. What they extract from the observed movements is the sequence of movements, not the way this sequence is implemented in the agent's particular body. And what they reproduce is not the precise kinematics, but the sequence of movements (e.g. to reach a target like the adult, they stretch their arm more than the adult). In fact, having access to such a level of bodily details would be useless as they are of no help if one wants to reproduce the movement, overtly or covertly.

Does this mean, however, that SRA represent disembodied abstract goals (Gazzola et al., 2007)? It does not seem so. Mirror activations are somatotopically organized. SRA represent the bodily sequence of movements that best corresponds in the observer's motor repertoire. If the observed effector is not available to the agent (e.g., the hand for the aplasic patients and the stick for the monkeys), then the motor system selects another effector able to perform the observed movement. However, by default, it is the same effector that is activated. One may even speculate that if the aplasic patients had phantom hands, one would find mirror activation in the region involved in hand movements. It was shown indeed that there are differences in action observation in aplasic patients with and without phantom limbs (Funk, Shiffrar, & Brugger, 2005). They found that an aplasic individual with a phantom hand showed kinesthetically modulated perceptions of apparent hand motion, similar to controls, while an aplasic without a phantom did not. Thus, when the hand representation is present in the cortex, it appears to mediate action observation.

Let us now consider the level of abstraction of SRA. The classical view of mirror neurons has emphasized the congruence between the perceptual and the motor properties of the action: a neuron that is tuned for execution of a specific motor action shows visual selectivity for observing the same action (Gallese, 2003). Action understanding through SRA would be based on a one-to-one matching. Mirror neurons were said to be a replicative mechanism, which directly duplicates in a motor code the perceptual properties of actions. Recent evidence, however, has argued against such replicative mechanisms (for review, see Csibra (2007) and Jacob (2008)). On this view, SRA are far from being a faithful reproduction of what is observed. There is no one-to-one matching. But how far up should we go in the level of abstraction?

Rizzolatti, Fadiga, Fogassi, & Gallese (2002) make the distinction between low-level and high-level resonance mechanisms. The former encodes the specific movements; the latter encodes the global goal-directed action itself. The authors suggest that mirror neurons involve high-level intentional resonance, as suggested by Fogassi et al. (2005) and Iacoboni et al. (2005).[5] This would seem to exclude the possibility of SRA operating at the most specific motor level, but it does not disentangle between intention in action and prior intention. Prior intentions differ from intentions in action in that they can be achieved by different means, whereas intentions in action specify in more detail the selected mean. To argue that SRA detect prior intentions, one would need to show similar brain activations when the displayed movements are completely different, although the global goal remains the same. As far as we know, this is not the case. In addition, access to the prior intention based on the observation of the movements only is difficult or impossible (Jacob & Jeannerod, 2005).

We described at the beginning of this section three levels of action representations: the prior intention, the intention in action, and the motor command. These levels should not viewed as a conceptual tree-like structure where one can derive the most abstract level from the most concrete level (e.g. a human is a mammal). In the case of action, this sort of derivation (e.g. grasping is for eating) is not possible, because many possible prior intentions can correspond to a single specific movement (Jacob & Jeannerod, 2005). A movement may be made for any of a number of purposes (Anscombe, 1957). It is thus difficult to directly "read" the prior intention from someone else's behavior, which remains ambiguous without further information.

SRA, by definition, begin with the observation of an action. The raw information is therefore a dynamic sequence of specific movements. We suggest that the motor system can abstract from the specific bodily parameters of the agent's movement to represent the underlying intention in action. But to go as far as the prior intention, one would need to abstract beyond the intention in action to a global goal. We agree with Jacob and Jeannerod that such abstraction is not possible based only on motor information. Therefore, one cannot have access to the prior intention based on the observation of the movements only.

We will illustrate our point here by using the key example of imitation. We define imitation as the reproduction of the goal of someone else's action. We assume that SRA contribute to imitation, not least because of their role in understanding action goals. There is currently considerable debate about the true nature and cognitive significance of imitation, but we will remain neutral within this debate (Rizzolatti et al., 2002; Wohlschläger & Bekkering, 2002; Brass & Heyes, 2005). We claim that sharing intentions in action is a minimal prerequisite of imitation. Imitation thus requires being sensitive to the dynamic sequence of movements that constitutes the action. In the absence of a common intention in action, imitation would be merely a kind of emulation or mimicry, a reproduction of the motor outcome by the observer's own means. Does imitation also require the understanding of prior intentions? In some cases, there might be no prior intention, as for meaningless gestures, yet one is still able to imitate them. However, when there is a prior intention, is it also shared?

Meltzoff (1995) claims that children as young as 18 months are able to "read" the underlying prior intention (i.e. grasping the stick) from the observation of the attempted but failed version of the action (the demonstrator's hand slipping several times). They did perform the target action correctly, even though they had only observed the failed movement. Interestingly, Meltzoff's study was conducted in a way that made the goal meaningful (grasping a stick by the two ends), while the failed movement observed by the children was meaningless (clumsy slipping movements). Melzoff claimed that they understood the demonstrator's prior intention. However, one could also suggest that they detected the affordances provided by the stick (e.g. meaningful actions that one can perform with a stick) and reproduced the action most similar to the observed movement, independently of the demonstrator's prior intention. It would be easy to check this interpretation experimentally. If the children

[5] For instance, Fogassi et al. (2005) assumed that the content of the intention detected by the monkey is something like "to eat", while it could be as well described as "to place in the mouth". It would be interesting to know what would happen if the monkey had to place either something eatable or something non-eatable in the mouth (hoping that everything is not eatable by monkeys). Then there would really be a similarity of intention in action with a difference of prior intentions.

read the prior intention from the movements observed, then they should be able to do so whether the act is meaningful or meaningless. For instance, they should be able to detect the demonstrator's prior intention to have his hand slipping and missing the stick end. But one would be very surprised if they could do so based on the observed movements. The problem with this study is that it confuses two different notions: meaningful and intentional.

We suggest that intentions in action already represent a dynamic sequence of movements as meaningful or meaningless and that we do not need to go as far as the prior intention to grasp this dimension. However, it is important to understand here that the fact that imitation requires a shared intention in action does not imply that imitation has to be to a perfect slavish copy of a set of movements independently of the global intention. The intention in action should not be confused with the motor command. It is more articulated, linking the set of movements into meaningful sequences when possible.

A further characteristic of imitation sheds new light on SRA. Imitation is a prepotent response tendency, which needs to be inhibited. Subjects make more errors and are slower to perform a movement when they watch an incongruent movement (Brass, Bekkering, Wohlschäger, & Prinz, 2000). For instance, subjects move their index finger while they see the little finger moving. The observation of the little finger movement induces the subjects to do the same and they need to inhibit this tendency in order to perform the task. However, some patients with frontal lesions are no longer able to inhibit and compulsively imitate others (Lhermitte, 1983; Brass, Derrfuss, Matthes-von Cramon, & von Cramon, 2003). Consequently, unless inhibited, the activation of the SRA during observation automatically leads to the execution of the corresponding action. It needs to be inhibited if the agent intends to perform another movement, or no movement at all.

In contrast with the inhibition mechanisms involved in non-imitative situations such as the Stroop task, the inhibition of imitation activates the anterior fronto-median cortex and the temporal-parietal junction (Brass, Derrfuss, & von Cramon, 2005). Both areas are known to be involved in the sense of agency and in perspective-taking. Brass and colleagues (2005) claim that the distinction between internally generated and externally triggered motor representations plays a key role to prevent us from imitating someone else's movements. To put it another way, my brain incorporates a specific process to ensure that I do not imitate your movements. This process is adaptive and appropriate because your movements are yours, and do not match my own prior intentions.

One consequence of the phenomenon of inhibition of imitation is that SRA are *causally efficient*: they can play a significant role in action generation. We have argued that the main causal role of SRA is in supporting imitation of goal-directed action. Indeed, according to Searle (1983), both kinds of intention play a causal role: the prior intention causes the intention in action, which in turn causes bodily movements. Neuroscience has challenged the view that conscious prior intentions do actually play a causal role (Libet, 1985), but these results have no relevance for unconscious intentions in action. Causal efficacy would even be part of the content of intentions in action, which are "causally self-referential" (Searle, 1983, p. 93). It is part of the content of an intention in action that this intention in action causes certain bodily movements (see Pacherie (2000) for discussion). If SRA do represent intentions in action, then, they include causal efficacy as well as the causally self-referential component.

SRA do indeed contribute to the observers themselves generating the action they observe, at least in imitation contexts. They correspond to the level in the motor hierarchy where action observation interacts with action execution, as shown for instance by interference effects and imitation inhibition effects. Observing someone else moving automatically activates the intention in action associated with this movement. This in turn automatically induces the fulfillment of this intention by virtue of the causal efficacy of the intention, unless it is inhibited. Such inhibition would in fact be the default state, and might be released only when the agent has the corresponding prior intention. Thus, an important part of higher motor cognition would be a tonic inhibition to keep SRA at bay, and to prevent our behavior being captured by others during social interaction. This inhibition is imposed by top-down influence outside the SRA system itself. Simulating an observed action is so close to doing it that a level of inhibition is required. However, it is interesting to note that in Brass's studies, subjects had the prior intention to move. What was affected by the observation of the incongruent movement was the selection of the performed movement (e.g. which index finger I move), not the decision to perform an action.

To sum up, SRA must represent (i) bodily movements, independently of the agent's or the observer's specific bodily parameters to allow transfer across individuals in imitation, (ii) the intermediate level of the planning of the dynamic sequence of movements. We consider therefore that intentions in action are a good candidate for SRA. Although the mirror neuron community has always considered SRA to be more about action understanding than about imitation, we think that this is not incompatible with our view. We are defining imitation not as slavish mimicry, but as reproducing a movement with some representation of the immediate goal, and that requires understanding what the observed sequence of movement is.

CONCLUSION

We have seen that SRA are causally efficient, in the sense that they tend to make me imitate. Consequently, they must be representations within the motor system, rather than just a conceptual label that I apply to your action in the same way I think about all other moving objects in the world. SRA must therefore involve intentional representations of action prior to the dispatch of a motor command. One should not, however, go too far up in the motor hierarchy. SRA must occur at a level indeterminate enough to apply to movements performed by different bodies, but also determinate enough to be extracted from the mere observation of movements. Intentions in action, defined as the planning of the dynamic sequence of elementary movements that causally triggers the motor command, appear then to be the best candidate for SRA.

Manuscript accepted 11 March 2008
First published online 23 May 2008

REFERENCES

Anscombe, G. E. M. (1957). *Intention*. London: Harvard University Press.

Avenanti, A., Bolognini, N., Maravita, A., & Aglioti, S. M. (2007). Somatic and motor components of action simulation. *Current Biology*, *17*(24), 2129–2135.

Blakemore, S. J., Wolpert, D. M., & Frith, C. D. (1998). Central cancellation of self-produced tickle sensation. *Nature Neuroscience*, *1*, 635–640.

Brass, M., Bekkering, H., Wohlschläger, A., & Prinz, W. (2000). Compatibility between observed and executed finger movements: Comparing symbolic, spatial, and imitative cues. *Brain and Cognition*, *44*(2), 124–143.

Brass, M., Derrfuss, J., Matthes-von Cramon, G., & von Cramon, D. Y. (2003). Imitative response tendencies in patients with frontal brain lesions. *Neuropsychology*, *17*(2), 265–271.

Brass, M., Derrfuss, J., & von Cramon, D. Y. (2005). The inhibition of imitative and overlearned responses: A functional double dissociation. *Neuropsychologia*, *43*(1), 89–98.

Brass, M., & Heyes, C. (2005). Imitation: Is cognitive neuroscience solving the correspondence problem? *Trends in Cognitive Sciences*, *9*, 489–495.

Buccino, G., Binkofski, F., Fink, G. R., Fadiga, L., Fogassi, L., Gallese, V., Seitz, R. J., Zilles, K., Rizzolatti, G. and Freund, H.-J. (2001). Action observation activates premotor and parietal areas in a somatotopic manner: An fMRI study. *European Journal of Neuroscience*, *13*, 400–404.

Buccino, G., Lui, F., Canessa, N., Patteri, I., Lagravinese, G., Benuzzi, F., Porro, C. A., & Rizzolatti, G. (2004). Neural circuits involved in the recognition of actions performed by nonconspecifics: An FMRI study. *Journal of Cognitive Neuroscience*, *16*(1), 114–126.

Calvo-Merino, B., Grezes, J., Glaser, D. E., Passingham, R. E., & Haggard, P. (2006). Seeing or doing? Influence of visual and motor familiarity in action observation. *Current Biology*, *16*(19), 1905–1910.

Casile, A., & Giese, M. A. (2006). Nonvisual motor training influences biological motion perception. *Current Biology*, *16*(1), 69–74.

Costantini, M., Galati, G., Ferretti, A., Caulo, M., Tartaro, A., Romani, G. L., & Aglioti, S. M. (2005). Neural systems underlying observation of humanly impossible movements: An fMRI study. *Cerebral Cortex*, *15*, 1761–1767.

Csibra, G. (2007). Action mirroring and action interpretation: An alternative account. In P. Haggard, Y. Rosetti, & M. Kawato (Eds.), *Sensorimotor foundations of higher cognition. Attention and performance XXII*. Oxford, UK: Oxford University Press.

Decety, J. (2002). Is there such a thing as functional equivalence between imagined, observed and executed action? In A. N Meltzoff and W. Prinz (Eds.), *The imitative mind*. Cambridge, UK: Cambridge University Press.

Decety, J., & Grezes, J. (1999). Neural mechanisms subserving the perception of human actions. *Trends in Cognitive Science*, *3*(5), 172–178.

Di Pellegrino, G., Fadiga, L., Fogassi, L., Gallese, V., & Rizzolatti, G. (1992). Understanding motor events: a neurophysiological study. *Experimental Brain Research*, *91*, 176–180.

Evans, G. (1983). *The Varieties of Reference*. Oxford, UK: Oxford University Press.

Fadiga, L., Fogassi, L., Pavesi, G., & Rizzolatti, G. (1995). Motor facilitation during action observation:

A magnetic stimulation study. *Journal of Neurophysiology, 73*, 2608–2611.

Ferrari, P. F., Gallese, V., Rizzolatti, G., & Fogassi, L. (2003). Mirror neurons responding to the observation of ingestive and communicative mouth actions in the monkey ventral premotor cortex. *European Journal of Neuroscience, 17*, 1703–1714.

Ferrari, P. F., Rozzi, S., & Fogassi, L. (2005). Mirror neurons responding to observation of actions made with tools in monkey ventral premotor cortex. *Journal of Cognitive Neuroscience, 17*, 212–226.

Fogassi, L., Ferrari, P. F., Gesierich, B., Rozzi, S., Chersi, F., & Rizzolatti, G. (2005). Parietal lobe: From action organisation to intention understanding. *Science*, 308, 662–667.

Frith, C. D. (2005). The self in action: Lessons from delusions of control. *Consciousness and Cognition, 14*(4), 752–770.

Funk, M., Shiffrar, M., & Brugger, P. (2005). Hand movement observation by individuals born without hands: Phantom limb experience constrains visual limb perception. *Experimental Brain Research, 164*(3), 341–346.

Gallese, V. (2003). The manifold nature of interpersonal relations: The quest for a common mechanism. In C. Frith & D. Wolpert (Eds.), *The neuroscience of social interaction*. Oxford, UK: Oxford University Press.

Gallese, V., & Lakoll, G. (2005). The brain's concepts: The role of the sensory-motor system in reason and language. *Cognitive Neuropsychology, 22*, 455–479.

Gallese, V., Fadiga, L., Fogassi, L., & Rizzolatti, G. (1996). Action recognition in the premotor cortex. *Brain, 119*, 593–609.

Gallese, V., Fogassi, L., Fadiga, L., and Rizzolatti, G. (2002). Action representation and the inferior parietal lobule. In W. Prinz and B. Hommel (Eds.), *Attention and performance XIX. Common mechanisms in perception and action*. Oxford, UK: Oxford University Press.

Gallese, V. and Goldman, A.I. (1998). Mirror neurons and the simulation theory of mindreading. *Trends in Cognitive Sciences, 2*(12), 493–501.

Gallese, V., Keysers, C., and Rizzolatti, G. (2004). A unifying view of the basis of social cognition. *Trends in Cognitive Sciences, 8*(9), 396–403.

Gazzola, V., Rizzolatti, G., Wicker, B., & Keysers, C. (2007). The anthropomorphic brain: The mirror neuron system responds to human and robotic actions. *NeuroImage, 35*(4), 1674–1684.

Gazzola, V., van der Worp, H., Mulder, T., Wicker, B., Rizzolatti, G., & Keysers, C. (2007). Aplasics born without hands mirror the goal of hand actions with their feet. *Current Biology, 17*(14), 1235–1240.

Gentilucci, M., & Gangitano, M. (1998). Influence of automatic word reading on motor control. *European Journal of Neuroscience, 10*(2), 752–756.

Gentilucci, M., Benuzzi, F., Bertolani, L., Daprati, E., & Gangitano, M. (2000). Language and motor control. *Experimental Brain Research, 133*(4), 468–490.

Glover, S., & Dixon, P. (2002). Semantics affect the planning but not control of grasping. *Experimental Brain Research, 146*(3), 383–387.

Glover, S., Rosenbaum, D. A., Graham, J., & Dixon, P. (2004). Grasping the meaning of words. *Experimental Brain Research, 154*(1),103–108.

Goldman, A. I. (2006). Simulating Minds: The Philosophy, Psychology and Neuroscience of Mindreading. Oxford, UK: Oxford University Press.

Grèzes, J., & Decety, J. (2001). Functional anatomy of execution, mental simulation, observation, and verb generation of actions: A meta-analysis. *Human Brain Mapping, 12*(1), 1–19.

Heyes, C. (2001). Causes and consequences of imitation. *Trends in Cognitive Science, 5*, 253–261.

Heyes, C. M., & Bird, G. (2007) Mirroring, association and the correspondence problem. In P. Haggard, Y. Rossetti, & M. Kawato (Eds.), *Sensorimotor foundations of higher cognition, attention & performance XX*. Oxford, UK: Oxford University Press.

Hommel, B. (2004). Event files: Feature binding in and across perception and action. *Trends in Cognitive Science 8*(11), 494–500.

Hommel, B., Musseler, J., Aschersleben, G., & Prinz, W. (2001). The Theory of Event Coding (TEC): A framework for perception and action planning. *Behavioral and Brain Sciences, 24*(5), 849–878.

Iacoboni, M., Molnar-Szakacs, I., Gallese, V., Buccino, G., Mazziotta, J.C., and Rizzolatti, G. (2005). Grasping the intentions of others with one's own mirror neuron system. *PLoS Biology, 3*(3), 529–535.

Iacoboni, M., Woods, R. P., Brass, M., Bekkering, H., Mazziotta, J. C., & Rizzolatti, G. (1999). Cortical mechanisms of human imitation. *Science, 286*, 2526–2528.

Jacob, P. (2008). What do mirror neurons contribute to human social cognition? *Mind & Language, 23*(2), 190–223.

Jacob, P. and Jeannerod, M. (2005). The motor theory of social cognition: A critique. *Trends in Cognitive Sciences, 9*(1), 21–25.

Jeannerod, M. (1994). The representing brain. Neural correlates of motor intention and imagery. *Behavioral and Brain Sciences, 17*, 187–245.

Jeannerod, M. (1995). Mental imagery in the motor context. *Neuropsychologia, 33*(11), 1419–1432.

Jeannerod, M. (1997). *The cognitive neuroscience of action*. Oxford, UK: Blackwell.

Jeannerod, M. (1999). The 25th Bartlett Lecture. To act or not to act: perspectives on the representation of actions. *Quarterly Journal of Experimental Psychology, 52*(1), 1–29.

Jeannerod, M. (2003). Consciousness of action and self-consciousness: A cognitive neuroscience approach. In J. Roessler & N. Eilan (Eds.), *Agency and self-awareness: Issues in philosophy and psychology*. Oxford, UK: Oxford University Press.

Keysers, C., & Perrett, D. I. (2004). Demystifying social cognition: A Hebbian perspective. *Trends in Cognitive Science*, 8(11), 501–507.

Koski, L., Wohlschlager, A., Bekkering, H., Woods, R. P., Dubeau, M. C., Mazziotta, J. C., & Iacoboni, M. (2002). Modulation of motor and premotor activity during imitation of target-directed actions. *Cerebral Cortex, 12*(8), 847–855.

Lhermitte, F. (1983). Utilization behaviour and its relation to the lesion of the frontal lobe. *Brain, 106*, 237–255.

Libet, B. (1985). Unconscious cerebral initiative and the role of conscious will in voluntary action. *Behavioral and Brain Sciences, 8*, 529–566.

Lindemann, O., Stenneken, P., van Schie, H. T., Bekkering, H. (2006). Semantic activation in action planning. *Journal of Experimental Psychology: Human Perception and Performance, 32*(3), 633–643.

Meltzoff, A. N. (1995). Understanding intentions of others: Reenactment of intended acts by 18 months-old children. *Developmental Psychology, 31*, 838–850.

Pacherie, E. (2000). The content of intentions. *Mind and Language, 15*(4), 400–432.

Press, C., Bird, G., Flach, R., & Heyes, C. (2005). Robotic movement elicits automatic imitation. *Cognitive Brain Research, 25*(3), 632–640.

Preston, S. D. and de Waal, F. B. M. (2002). Empathy: Its ultimate and proximate bases. *Behavioral and Brain Sciences, 25*, 1–20.

Prinz, W. (2002). Experimental approaches to imitation. In A. N Meltzoff & W. Prinz (Eds.), *The imitative mind*. Cambridge, UK: Cambridge University Press.

Ramachandran, V. S. (2004). *Mirror neurons and imitation learning as the driving force behind "the great leap forward" in human evolution*. Edge Foundation. Retrieved March 18, 2008 from www.edge.org/3rd_culture/ramachandran/ramachandran_p1.html

Rizzolatti, G., & Arbib, M. A. (1998). Language within our grasp. *Trends in Neuroscience, 21*(5),188–194.

Rizzolatti, G., Camarda, R., Fogassi, M., Gentilucci, M., Luppino, G., & Matelli, M. (1988). Functional organization of inferior area 6 in the macaque monkey: II. Area F5 and the control of distal movements. *Experimental Brain Research, 71*, 491–507.

Rizzolatti, G., Fadiga, L., Fogassi, L., & Gallese, V. (2002). From mirror neurons to imitation: Facts and speculations. In A. N Meltzoff and W. Prinz (Eds.), *The imitative mind*. Cambridge, UK: Cambridge University Press.

Rizzolatti, G., Fadiga, L., Gallese, V., & Fogassi, L. (1995). Premotor cortex and the recognition of motor actions. *Cognitive Brain Research, 3*, 131–141.

Rizzolatti, G., Fogassi, L., & Gallese, V. (2000). Cortical mechanisms subserving object grasping and action recognition: A new view of the cortical motor functions. In M. Gazzaniga (Ed.), *The new cognitive neuroscience*. Cambridge, MA: MIT Press.

Romani, M., Cesari, P., Urgesi, C., Facchini, S., & Aglioti, S. M. (2005). Motor facilitation of the human cortico-spinal system during observation of bio-mechanically impossible movements. *NeuroImage, 26*(3), 755–763.

Saxe, R. (2005). Against simulation: The argument from error. *Trends in Cognitive Sciences, 9*(4), 174–179.

Searle, J. (1983). *Intentionality: An essay in the philosophy of mind*. Cambridge, UK: Cambridge University Press.

Tessari, A., & Rumiati, R. I. (2004). The strategic control of multiple routes in imitation of actions. *Journal of Experimental Psychology: Human Perception and Performance, 30*, 1107–1116.

Umiltà, M. A., Kohler, E., Gallese, V., Fogassi, L., Fadiga, L., Keysers, C. & Rizzolatti, G. (2001). 'I know what you are doing': a neurophysiological study. *Neuron, 32*, 91–101.

Van Elk, M., van Schie, H. T., & Bekkering, H. (2007). Using conceptual knowledge in action and language. In P. Haggard, Y. Rossetti, & M. Kawato (Eds.), *Sensorimotor foundations of higher cognition, attention & performance XX*. Oxford, UK: Oxford University Press.

Wolpert, D. M., Doya, K., & Kowato, M. (2003). A unifying computational framework for motor control and social interaction. In C. Frith & D. Wolpert (Eds.), *The neuroscience of social interaction*. Oxford, UK: Oxford University Press.

Wolpert, D. M., Ghahramani, Z., & Jordan, M. I. (1995). An internal model for sensorimotor integration. *Science, 269*(5232), 1880–1882.

Wohlschläger, A. and Bekkering, H. (2002). Is human imitation based on a mirror-neuron system? Some behavioural evidence. *Experimental Brain Research, 143*(3), 335–341.

SOCIAL NEUROSCIENCE, 2008, 3 (3–4), 434–442

Psychology Press
Taylor & Francis Group

Emotional states influence the neural processing of affective language

Nikki L. Pratt
Colgate University, Hamilton, New York, USA, and University of Louisville, Louisville, Kentucky, USA

Spencer D. Kelly
Colgate University, Hamilton, New York, USA

The present study investigated whether emotional states influence the neural processing of language. Event-related potentials recorded the brain's response to positively and negatively valenced words (e.g., love vs. death) while participants were directly induced into positive and negative moods. ERP electrodes in frontal scalp regions of the brain distinguished positive and negative words around 400 ms poststimulus. The amplitude of this negative waveform showed a larger negativity for positive words compared to negative words in the frontal electrode region when participants were in a positive, but not negative, mood. These findings build on previous research by demonstrating that people process affective language differently when in positive and negative moods, and lend support to recent views that emotion and cognition interact during language comprehension.

INTRODUCTION

Recent studies in emotion and cognition suggest that changes in emotion may subsequently alter the neurocognitive processing (Atchley, Ilardi & Enloe, 2003; Chung et al., 1996; Compton, 2003; Lang et al., 1998; Schupp et al., 2006; Vuilleumier, Armony, & Dolan, 2003). Positive and negative stimuli mediate cognition through subjective evaluation of the motivational relevance of incoming stimuli (Compton, 2003). Assessing the significance of stimuli, therefore, rests on current mood states as associated with motivation and goals. The current study investigates how mood may modify the neural processing involved in viewing positive or negative words.

Recent theories of embodied cognition claim that high-level cognitive processes are deeply rooted in the body (Barsalou, 1999; Damasio, 1999; Decety & Grezes, 2006; Dolan, 2002; Glenberg & Kaschak, 2002; Tucker, 2001). These theories view cognition not as a detached processor of abstract and arbitrary symbols, but rather as an embedded process grounded in meaningful physical experiences gathered through perception and action. Previous research supports an embodied-cognition view of mood and language processing (Atchley et al., 2003; Barsalou, 1999; Glenberg & Kaschak, 2002; Glenberg, Havas, Becker, & Rinck, 2005). Behavioral evidence suggests that subjective emotional states influence language comprehension. For example, Glenberg and colleagues induced positive or negative moods in participants and then asked them to respond to positive and negative sentences (Glenberg et al., 2005). Participants

Correspondence should be addressed to: Nikki Pratt, Department of Psychological & Brain Sciences, Belknap Campus, Louisville, KY 40292, USA. E-mail: nikki.pratt@louisville.edu

We thank Harry Whitaker, Dennis Molfese and Phan Luu for feedback on ideas presented in this paper. In addition, we thank Kevin Carlsmith and Regina Conti for their suggestions to make our mood induction more effective.

www.psypress.com/socialneuroscience DOI:10.1080/17470910802188339

were faster to comprehend the sentences when their mood was congruent versus incongruent with the meaning of the sentences.

Previously, researchers indicated that lexical representations are mediated by current motivations and underlying mood (Kissler, Assadollahi & Herbert, 2006). Emotional states enhance certain cortical connections representing lexical knowledge (Kissler et al., 2006). Insight from neuroscience reveals the prefrontal cortex (PFC) assesses stimuli with regard to subjective appraisal and motivation (Bechara, Tranel, Damasio & Damasio, 1996; Luu, Collins, & Tucker, 2000). The incoming information is assessed by current drives and motivation. Top-down processing, initiated in the PFC, mediates attention and cognition by evaluating emotional relevance (Mayberg, 1997; Taylor & Fragopanagos, 2005).

Evidence from event-related potentials (ERPs) suggests that positive and negative linguistic stimuli are differentiated around 400 ms (Dietrich et al., 2001; Dillon, Cooper, Grent-'t-Jong, Woldorff, & LaBar, 2006; Schupp, Junghofer, Weike, & Hamm, 2003). In assessing the significance of emotional words, Schapkin, Gusev, & Kuhl (2000) found that positive words compared to negative words produced a larger component at approximately 400 ms. Other researchers note changes in the brain response in a similar time window when emotional words are encoded (Dietrich et al., 2001; Dillon et al., 2006). Around 450 to 700 ms, emotional words (both positive and negative) produced larger effects in the frontal region compared to encoding neutral words (Dietrich et al., 2001; Dillon et al., 2006). These findings suggest that forming decisions about the affective valence of emotional words engages rather slow-developing (late ERP components) cognitive processes in the frontal region.

Because language is a pervasive and effective tool for expressing and comprehending emotional meaning, it is possible that the comprehension of emotionally valenced language recruits or activates brain areas involved in the actual physical experience of emotion. Electrophysiological research on the interaction of mood and language has demonstrated that certain ERP components reflect the processing of emotional information while in an emotional state (Chung et al., 1996; Dietrich et al., 2001; Federmeier, Kirson, Moreno & Kutas, 2001). In one study, Chung et al. (1996) placed participants in a positive or negative mood and then presented emotional passages of real-life events. ERPs recorded brain responses to the final word of the text revealing the emotional meaning of the passage. The relevant result in that study was that participants in a negative mood showed larger amplitude changes in the N400 to passages with a mood-incongruent—in this case, positive—ending. This suggests that current mood states influence high-level language processing and provides preliminary evidence supporting Glenberg et al.'s (2005) embodiment view for the interaction of mood and language processing.

Building on previous research in emotion and language processing (Chung et al., 1996; Schapkin et al., 2000), the present study investigates how a more *direct* mood induction affects emotional word processing. Specifically, whereas previous research required participants to "imagine" being in a specific mood state (Chung et al., 1996; Damasio et al., 2000; Esslen et al., 2004), the present study used feedback based on an appraisal of the participants' mental ability and psychological state, to directly induce changes in current mood state. Providing participants with positive and negative feedback has previously been shown to alter mood and interfere with performance (Anshel, 1988), and previous research indicates that using feedback to alter an emotional state is a more effective and ecologically valid way to induce mood than indirect methods (Nummenmaa & Niemi, 2004).

The current study examined the neural underpinnings of emotionally valenced language while participants were induced in different mood states. The hypotheses were structured around examining differential processing of positive or negative words in congruent or incongruent mood states. Based on previous findings with emotional language, we predicted that mood-congruent stimuli will produce an enhanced effect around 400 ms in the frontal regions (Chung et al., 1996; Dietrich et al., 2001; Federmeier et al., 2001). Specifically, we predicted that a positive mood will enhance the processing of positive words, and a negative mood will enhance the processing of negative words.

METHODS

Participants

Thirteen right-handed, Caucasian college undergraduates (5 males, 8 females; mean age: 20) participated for course credit. All participants had normal or corrected-to-normal vision. Prior to testing, each participant signed an informed consent approved by the university's Institutional Review Board.

Materials

The word stimuli were selected from a list of emotionally valenced nouns used in previous research (Rubin & Friendly, 1984). In a stimulus norming session, a small group of undergraduates ($n = 8$), not included in the ERP testing session, rescaled the selected words by ranking them according to how positive and negative they were. In addition, they rated the words on a 7-point scale (1 being the least emotionally charged, 7 the most). From this norming session, we selected the 20 words with the most extreme emotional valance (10 positive and 10 negative words). The words were then placed into the MRC Psycholinguistic Database: Machine Usable Dictionary: Version 2.00 (Wilson, 1987). Independent samples t-tests found that there were no differences between the two groups of words for concreteness, $t(18) = -0.662$, *ns*; familiarity, $t(18) = 1.148$, *ns*; number of syllables, $t(18) = -1.282$, *ns*; Kucera-Francis written frequency, $t(18) = 0.784$, *ns*; and meaningfulness: pavio norms, $t(18) = -1.005$, *ns*. See Table 1 for a list of 10 positive and 10 negative words.

Procedure

ERP specifications and stimulus presentation

Participants were fitted with a 128-electrode Geodesic ERP net. The EEG was sampled at 250 Hz using a band pass filter of $0.1 - 30$ Hz.

TABLE 1
Word stimuli: 10 positive and 10 negative words

Positive words	*Negative words*
Love	Anxiety
Passion	Tragedy
Joy	Panic
Happiness	Agony
Friend	Anger
Hope	Hatred
Miracle	Grief
Kindness	Murder
Freedom	Misery
Pleasure	Death

Impedances were kept below 50 kΩ using high-impedance amplifiers. Previous research indicates that using high-impedance amplifiers allows for accurate detection of signal (Ferree, Luu, Russel, & Tucker, 2001). Eye artifacts were monitored with four electro-oculography (EOG) electrodes. Trials with artifacts were removed offline. Individual ERPs were segmented starting 100 ms before, and continuing 900 ms following stimulus onset.

Participants sat 3 feet (0.914 m) from a 13 inch (0.33 m) LCD screen. The words were visually presented for 500 ms in 36pt Arial Black font on a white background. The ten positive and ten negative words were each presented five times in random order for a total of 100 trials per mood condition. The variable interstimulus interval ratio varied between 1.5 s to 2.5 s. Participants were instructed to press one key on a button box if the stimulus was a positive word and another key if the stimulus was a negative word. Reaction times and ERPs were measured at the presentation of the word.

Mood induction

Prior to stimulus presentation, the experimenter induced either a positive or negative mood in the participants. The mood induction was based on an appraisal of the participants' mental ability and psychological state—a procedure that is a successful and ecologically valid mood induction technique (Nummenmaa & Niemi, 2004). Participants were randomly assigned to begin with one of the two mood conditions, the order of which was counterbalanced across subjects. All subjects received both mood inductions and received the same instructions and comments. The only difference was the order in which the mood conditions occurred.

To induce mood, the experimenter explained that a printout of the participant's brainwaves would be used to "verify" whether he or she was suitable for data collection. After the experimenter returned, she brought the printout to the participant and had a conversation with the second experimenter and the participant regarding the brainwaves. Unknown to the participants, the printouts were fabricated and the same for everyone.

In the positive mood condition, the first experimenter explained to the second that the brainwaves were very impressive and, in fact, the best so far in this experiment. The experimenter also commented that the brainwaves would make excellent data and add to the results of the study. Finally, the experimenter presented to the participant the fabricated printout of brainwaves that were very clean and clear (see Figure 1 (top)).

In the negative mood condition, participants saw a different printout and heard different comments, but the procedure remained the same as the positive mood induction. The first experimenter explained that there was a concern about the participant's "unusual" brainwaves and that the professor was wary about proceeding with the experiment. This was followed by comments concerning the participant's stress or anxiety level. The experimenter then showed the participant a printout with erratic and incoherent brainwaves (see Figure 1 (bottom)).

Following the mood induction, the experimenter asked a series of questions about the participant's mood. The cover story was that these questions were standard procedure to ensure that results across different participants were comparable. Participants were asked to rate current emotional states on four emotional levels (happy, sad, positive, negative) on a scale of 1 through 7 (1 = do not feel this way at all to 7 = feeling this way to a great degree).

After participants viewed the positive and negative words following the first mood induction (approximately 8–10 min), the experimenter

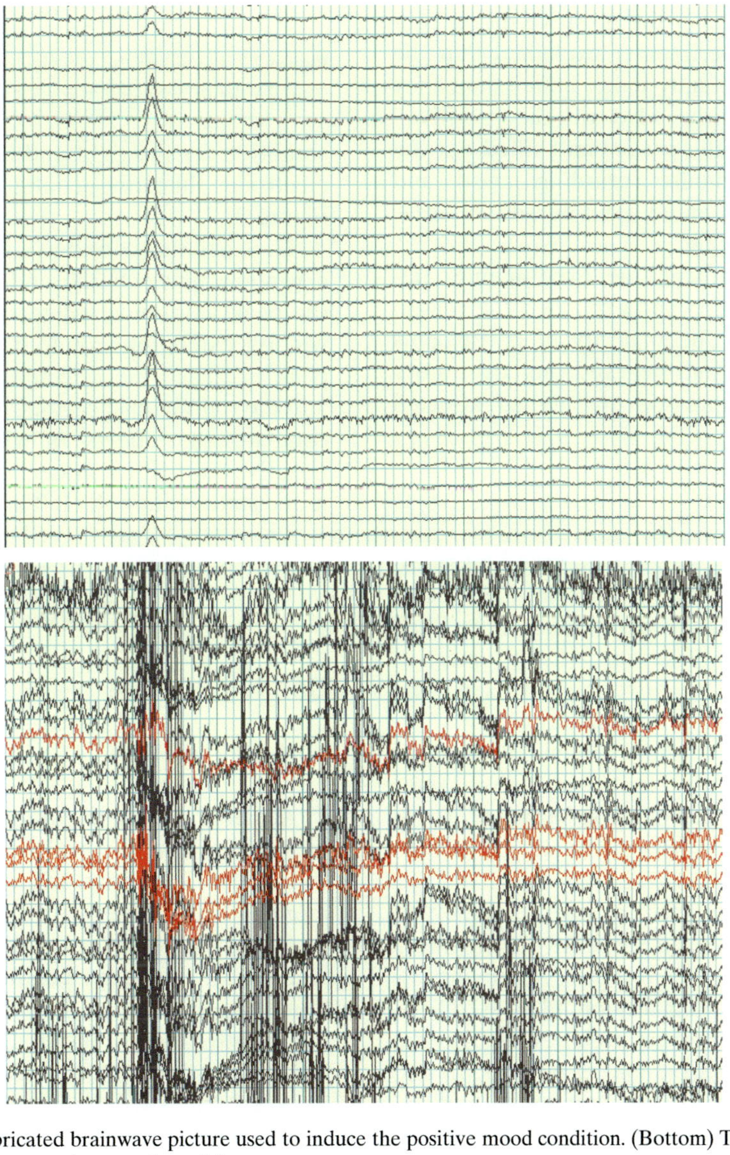

Figure 1. (Top) The fabricated brainwave picture used to induce the positive mood condition. (Bottom) The fabricated brainwave picture used to induce the negative mood condition.

induced the second mood. To do this, the experimenter entered the testing room and explained that there had been a problem with the software collecting the brainwaves. Therefore, the computer system was rechecked and the brainwave data was reassessed. After correcting the problems, another brainwave printout—this time, "correct"—would be checked before proceeding. At this point, participants received the *opposite* mood induction. To account for the switch in the cover story, the experimenter explained that the faulty software misrepresented the participant's brainwaves in the first session. If the participant had been in the positive mood condition first, the experimenter explained that the brainwaves were actually much worse than they first appeared, and proceeded with the "negative" cover story. If the participant had been in the negative mood condition first, the experimenter explained that the brainwaves were actually much better than they first appeared, and proceeded with the "positive" cover story. Again, the participants filled out the behavioral questionnaire regarding mood, and the stimuli were presented again in random order for a total of 100 trials.

After the experiment, the experimenter debriefed all participants and explained the reason for the deception. The majority of participants indicated that they had believed the cover story and anecdotally expressed that it had affected their mood.

Design and analysis

Behavioral analyses examined mood by assessing the ratings from the questionnaire. Emotion ratings were averaged before and after each brainwave recording session. Each question (happy, sad, positive, negative) was assessed using paired *t*-tests between mood conditions.

In addition, the other behavioral analysis examined the reaction times and error rates during the ERP portion of the experiment. These data were analyzed using a 2 (Mood) × 2 (Word) repeated-measures ANOVA.

Because we had such a small number of participants, we analyzed the ERP data using a small number of *a priori* contrasts (planned *t*-tests) rather than a four-way omnibus ANOVA. Specifically, we focused on a cluster of bilateral frontal electrodes (Schapkin et al., 2000) and compared ERP responses (amplitude and latency) within the time window of 350 to 600 ms to positive and negative words within each mood

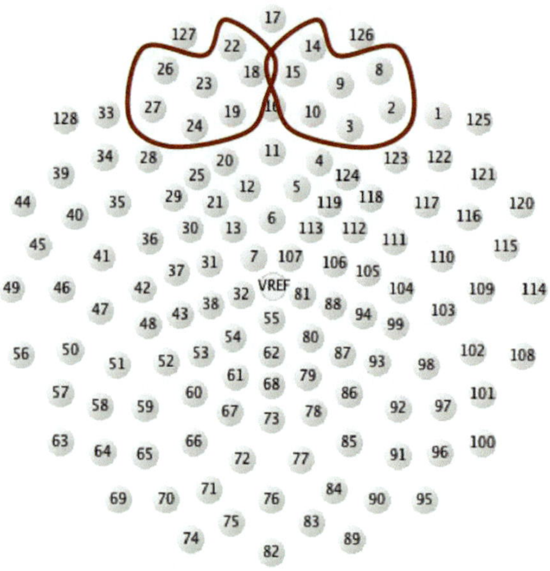

Figure 2. Layout of the 128-electrode net and the cluster of frontally distributed channels used for the ERP analysis.

condition for the right and left hemispheres. The electrode clustering configuration is shown in Figure 2.

The analysis quantified a negative waveform in a window between 350 and 600 ms. Analysis of the peak amplitude included an 8 ms (inclusive) window extending around the negative peak. The peak averaged the selected channels in the left and the right hemispheres. Contrasts were used to compare the effects of viewing positive and negative words in either positive or negative mood states within the left and right hemispheres.

RESULTS

Behavioral data

Mood manipulation

A paired *t*-test compared the subjective mood measures across the positive and negative mood conditions. Subjective ratings were significantly more sad in the negative mood condition compared to the positive, $t(12) = -2.132$, $p = .05$). Ratings for the happy condition were marginally more happy in the positive mood condition than the negative mood condition, $t(12) = -2.007$, $p =$ .068. No other rating values were significant between the two mood states: positive mood rating, $t(12) = -0.64$, *ns*; negative mood rating, $t(12) = -1.148$, *ns*.

Reaction time data

The reaction time data were submitted to a two-way repeated-measures ANOVA with Mood (2) × Word (2) as the conditions. No significant effects were found for Mood, $F(1, 12) = 0.48$, *ns*; Word, $F(1, 12) = 1.65$, *ns*; or Mood × Word, $F(1, 12) = 0.01$, *ns*, interaction. Thus, no changes occurred in response time due to mood or word manipulations.

ERP data

Peak amplitude

The ERP analysis used planned contrasts to compare the difference between positive and negative words in the positive and negative mood conditions between 350 and 600 ms in the frontal leads. Positive words were more negative in amplitude than negative words when participants were in the positive mood state in both the left hemisphere, $t(12) = 2.162$, $p = .05$, the right hemisphere region, $t(12) = 3.918$, $p = .002$. In contrast, there were no significant differences between positive and negative words in the negative mood condition in either the left, $t(12) = -0.115$, *ns*, or right hemisphere, $t(12) = -0.265$, *ns* (see Figure 3).

DISCUSSION

The results indicated that pleasant and unpleasant feedback influenced the neural processing of affective language. Participants' subjective ratings of their emotional states suggested that they did feel a change in their mood based on our induction technique. The electrophysiological changes indicated that when participants were placed in the positive mood state, positive words generated a larger negative response compared to negative words. The results in the positive mood condition are consistent with the hypothesis that one's emotional state differentially influences the neural processing of positive and negative words.

Previous research suggests that contextual analysis of emotional words influences the brain response at approximately 400 ms (Kissler et al., 2006). In the Kissler et al. (2006) study, participants in a positive mood state produced more negative peaks to positive words compared to negative words. This result suggests that the positive mood induction influenced the neural activity associated with evaluating positive and negative words. The present study extended this work by using a more direct and ecologically valid mood induction procedure. Together, this body of work fits well with research on neural mechanisms for subjective experience of emotions interacting with cognition (De Pascalis & Morelli, 1990; Federmeier et al., 2001). Federmeier et al. (2001) found that positive mood facilitated processing the last word of a sentence, which was either an expected or unexpected ending, as revealed by a negative waveform around 400 ms. Indeed, other researchers conclude that positive moods tend to improve our ability to form semantic connections (Bolte, Goschke, & Kuhl, 2003). As with the current study, positive and negative words were processed differently while subjects were in the positive mood state. Findings from Bolte et al. (2003) and Federmeier et al. (2001) suggest that positive mood may facilitate semantic processing. This lends support to the fact that the differential processing of positive and negative words occurred only in the positive mood state. The current study suggests that even with slight changes in subjective ratings of feeling "happy", the neural response generated an increase to the presentation of positive words, compared to negative words, while in a positive mood state.

The present effect of mood and language is interesting because of the simplicity and directness of our induction technique. A meta-analysis by Nummenmaa and Niemi (2004) suggested that mood inductions that are direct, ecologically valid and based on performance appraisals may be highly effective in inducing mood in participants. Indeed, our mood induction technique was very direct in that it did not require participants to imagine being in a mood state—rather, it put them in that state directly. It was ecologically valid because it avoided demand characteristics by inducing mood without artificially drawing attention to the goals of the experiment. The mood was also a powerful type of performance appraisal because it highlighted an aspect of neurocognitive functioning (quality of one's brain functioning) that is certainly a sensitive topic for college students.

Although there were no significant findings for differentiating positive and negative words in the negative mood state, the plotted waveforms suggest that negative words produce a more negative wave in the left hemisphere while participants were in the negative mood

Figure 3. ERP waveforms to positive and negative words within frontal left and right hemisphere regions and different mood conditions. The top panels display the negative-going peak to positive and negative words within the negative mood condition; the bottom panels display the negative-going peak to positive and negative words within the positive mood condition The boxes indicate the significant results found between positive and negative word processing from 350 to 600 ms. The *y*-axes show µV.

state (see Figure 3). The lack of a significant effect suggests that the negative mood may not have been as effective as the positive mood manipulation across all of the subjects. In the future, further research is needed to investigate the effect of transient negative mood changes using a direct mood manipulation.

A notable limitation of the study concerns the lack of a neutral mood condition. Although this condition would have established a baseline for participants, the mood induction procedure was meant to determine that *any change* in mood would influence the neural comprehension of words. Because our mood induction was exploratory, future research is needed to understand the full effects of a direct mood manipulation. Moreover, additional studies should incorporate a neutral mood condition to further clarify the specific influences of different moods on language processing.

CONCLUSION

The current results extend the behavioral research of Glenberg et al. (2005) and provide preliminary electrophysiological support for an embodied view of emotion and language processing. One interpretation of our findings is that directly eliciting a positive mood enhances the meaning of congruent emotional words over the frontal region. These results suggest that just as we recruit neural areas associated with producing actions when comprehending action words (Pulvermuller, 1999), neural regions associated with emotional experience may be activated when one is comprehending emotionally valenced language. The novelty of the present study is that it is one of the first to use a direct mood induction technique (see Nummenmaa & Niemi, 2004) to explore how the brain processes emotionally valenced language differently in varying emotional mental/

physical states. Building on this work, future research should continue to explore how underlying emotions and mental states serve as ubiquitous contexts for how people comprehend language in everyday, naturalistic and situated face-to-face interactions.

Manuscript received 6 March 2007
Manuscript accepted 20 September 2007
First published online 16 June 2008

REFERENCES

Anderson, A. K., & Phelps, E. A. (2001). Lesions of the human amygdala impair enhanced perception of emotionally salient events. *Nature*, *411*(6835), 305–309.

Anshel, M. H. (1988). The effect of mood and pleasant versus unpleasant information feedback on performing a motor skill. *Journal of General Psychology*, *115*, 117–129.

Atchley, R. U., Ilardi, S. S., & Enloe, A. (2003). Hemispheric asymmetry in the processing of emotional content in word meanings: The effect of current and past depression. *Brain & Language*, *84*(1), 105–118.

Barsalou, L. (1999). Perceptual symbol systems. *Behavioral and Brain Sciences*, *22*, 577–660.

Beauducel, A., & Debener, S. (2003). Misallocation of variance in event-related potentials: Simulation studies on the effects of test power, topography, and baseline-to-peak versus principal component quantifications. *Journal of Neuroscience Methods*, *124*, 103–112.

Bechara, A., Tranel, D., Damasio, H., & Damasio, A. (1996). Failure to respond autonomically to anticipated future outcomes following damage to prefrontal cortex. *Cerebral Cortex*, *6*(2), 215–225.

Beck, A. T., Ward, C. H., Mendelson, M., Mock, J., & Erbaugh, J. (1961). An inventory for measuring depression. *Archives of General Psychiatry*, *4*, 561–571.

Bolte, A., Goschke, T., & Kuhl, J. (2003). Emotion and intuition: Effects of positive and negative mood on implicit judgments of semantic coherence. *Psychological Science*, *14*(5), 416–421.

Borod, J., Cicero, B., Olber, L., Welkowitz, J., Erhan, H. M., Santschi, C., Grunwald, I. S., Agosti, R. M., & Whalen, J. R. (1998). Right hemisphere emotional perception: Evidence across multiple channels. *Neuropsychology*, *12*, 446–458.

Chung, G., Tucker, D. M., West, P., Potts, G., Liotti, M., Luu, P., & Hartry, A. L. (1996). Emotional expectancy: Brain electrical activation associated with an emotional bias in interpreting life events. *Psychophysiology*, *33*, 218–233.

Cicero, B. A., Borod, J. C., Santschi, C., Erhan, H. M., Obler, L. K., Agosti, R. M., Welkowitz, J., & Grunwald, I. S. (1999). Emotional versus nonemotional lexical perception in patients with right and left brain damage. *Neuropsychiatry, Neuropsychoogy, and Behavioral Neurology*, *12*(4), 255–264.

Compton, R. (2003). The interface between emotion and attention: A review of evidence from psychology and neuroscience. *Behavioral and Cognitive Neuroscience Reviews*, *2*(2), 115–129.

Damasio, A. R. (1999). *The feeling of what happens*. San Diego, CA: Harcourt.

Damasio, A. R., Grabowski, T. J., Bechara, A., Damasio, H., Ponto, L. L. B., Parvizi, J., & Hichwa, R. D. (2000). Subcortical and cortical brain activity during the feeling of self-generated emotions. *Nature Neuroscience*, *3*(10), 1049–1056.

De Pascalis, V., & Morelli, A. (1990). Anxiety and individual differences in event-related potentials during the recognition of sense and nonsense words. *Personality & Individual Differences*, *11*(7), 741–749.

Decety, J., & Grezes, J. (2006). The power of simulation: Imagining one's own and other's behavior. *Brain Research*, *1079*(1), 4–14.

Dietrich, D. E., Waller, C., Johannes, S., Wieringa, B. M., Emrich, H. M., & Munte, T. F. (2001). Differential effects of emotional content on event-related potentials in word recognition memory. *Neuropsychobiology*, *43*, 96–101.

Dillon, D. G., Cooper, J. J., Grent-'t-Jong, T., Woldorff, M. G., & LaBar, K. S. (2006). Dissociation of event-related potentials indexing arousal and semantic cohesion during emotional word encoding. *Brain & Cognition*, *62*(1), 43–57.

Dolan, R. J. (2002). Emotion, cognition, and behavior. *Science*, *298*, 1191–1194.

Esslen, M., Pascual-Marqui, R. D., Hell, D., Kochi, K., & Lehmann, D. (2004). Brain areas and time course of emotional processing. *NeuroImage*, *21*(4), 1189–1203.

Federmeier, K. D., Kirson, D. A., Moreno, E. M., & Kutas, M. (2001). Effects of transient, mild mood states on semantic memory organization and use: An event-related potential investigation in humans. *Neuroscience Letters*, *305*, 149–152.

Ferree, T., Luu, P., Russel, J. S., & Tucker, D. M. (2001). Scalp electrode impedance, infection risk, and EEG data quality. *Clinical Neurophysiology*, *112*, 536–544.

Glenberg, A. M., Havas, D., Becker, R., & Rinck, M. (2005). Grounding language in bodily states: The case for emotion. In R. Zwaan & D. Pecher (Eds.), *The grounding of cognition: The role of perception and action in memory, language, and thinking*. Cambridge: Cambridge University Press.

Glenberg, A. M., & Kaschak, M. P. (2002). Grounding language in action. *Psychonomic Bulletin & Review*, *9*, 558–565.

Kissler, J., Assadollahi, R., & Herbert, C. (2006). Emotional and semantic networks in visual word processing—insights from ERP studies. *Progress in Brain Research*, *156*, 147–184.

Lang, P. J., Bradley, M. M., Fitzsimmons, J. R., Cuthbert, B. N., Scott, J. D., Moulder, B., & Nangia, V. (1998). Emotional arousal and activation of the visual cortex: An fMRI analysis. *Psychophysiology*, *35*, 199–210.

Luu, P., Collins, P., & Tucker, D. (2000). Mood, personality, and self-monitoring: Negative affect and emotionality in relation to frontal lobe mechanisms of error monitoring. *Journal of Experimental Psychology: General, 129*(1), 43–60.

Mayberg, H. S. (1997). Limbic-cortical dysregulation: A proposed model of depression. *Journal of Neuropsychiatry and Clinical Neurosciences, 9*(3), 471–481.

Nummenmaa, L., & Niemi, P. (2004). Inducing affective states with success–failure manipulations: A meta-analysis. *Emotion, 4*(2), 207–214.

Ortigue, S., Michel, C. M., Murray, M. M., Mohr, C., Carbonnel, S., & Landis, T. (2004). Electrical neuroimaging reveals early generator modulation to emotional words. *NeuroImage, 21*, 1242–1251.

Pulvermuller, F. (1999). Words in the brain's language. *Behavioral and Brain Sciences, 22*(2), 253–279; discussion 280–336.

Rubin, D. C., & Friendly, M. (1984). Predicting which words get recalled: Measures of free recall, availability, goodness, emotionality, and pronunciability for 925 nouns. *Memory & Cognition, 14*(1), 79–94.

Schapkin, S. A., Gusev, A. N., & Kuhl, J. (2000). Categorization of unilaterally presented emotional words: An ERP analysis. *Acta Neurobiologiae Experimentalis, 60*, 17–28.

Schupp, H. T., Junghofer, M., Weike, A. I., & Hamm, A. O. (2003). Emotional facilitation of sensory processing in the visual cortex. *Psychological Science, 14*(1), 7–13.

Schupp, H. T., Stockburger, J., Codispoti, M., Junghofer, M., Weike, A. I., & Hamm, A. O. (2006). Stimulus novelty and emotion perception: The near absence of habituation in the visual cortex. *NeuroReport, 17*(4), 365–369.

Taylor, J. G., & Fragopanagos, N. F. (2005). The interaction of attention and emotion. *Neural Networks, 18*, 353–369.

Tucker, D. M. (2001). Motivated anatomy: A core-and-shell model of corticolimbic architecture. In G. Gainotti (Ed.), *Handbook of neuropsychology*. Amsterdam: Elsevier.

Vuilleumier, P., Armony, J. L., & Dolan, J. (2003). Reciprocal links between emotion and attention. In R. S. J. Frackowiak, et al. (Eds.), *Human Brain Function* (2nd ed., pp. 419–444). San Diego, CA: Academic Press.

Vuilleumier, P., Armony, J. L., Driver, J., & Dolan, R. J. (2003). Distinct spatial frequency sensitivities for processing faces and emotional expressions. *Nature Neuroscience, 6*(6), 624–631.

Wilson, M. (1987). *MRC psycholinguistic database: Machine USABLE DICtionary*. Version 2.00. Retrieved May 12, 2008, from http://www.psy.uwa.edu.au/mrcdatabase/uwa_mrc.htm

For Product Safety Concerns and Information please contact our EU representative GPSR@taylorandfrancis.com Taylor & Francis Verlag GmbH, Kaufingerstraße 24, 80331 München, Germany